HENRY M. TRC

THE LIFE

OF

MOLIÈRE

THE LIFE OF MOLIÈRE

MOLIÈRE

From the Picture attributed to Pierre Mignard
By permission of Messrs Hachette & Co

THE LIFE

OF

MOLIÈRE

BY

HENRY M. TROLLOPE

"Molière, c'est la morale des honnêtes gens."
SAINTE-BEUVE, *Port-Royal*,
Book III. ch. xv.

LONDON
ARCHIBALD CONSTABLE AND COMPANY
LIMITED
1905

Edinburgh: T. and A. CONSTABLE, Printers to His Majesty

PREFACE

I ought at once to express my acknowledgments and my thanks to the many French authors who within the last two generations or more· have done so much to elucidate the story of Molière's life. Of these writers Taschereau was the first who collected and put together in a biographical form the facts and the doings in the career of the great comic dramatist. His *Histoire de la Vie et des Ouvrages de Molière,* the first edition of which appeared in 1825 and the fifth in 1863, has served as a sure foundation for many subsequent labours. The third edition of this book, published in 1844, is the one I have generally used; and in my footnotes I have, though perhaps wrongly, given *Vie de Molière* as its title. In 1863 Eudoxe Soulié published his invaluable *Recherches sur Molière et sur sa Famille.* The greater part of Soulié's book is devoted to the publication, for the first time, of legal documents relating to Molière and his affairs; and I have referred to these documents chiefly in my earlier chapters. Also in the year 1863, M. Louis Moland published the first edition of his *Œuvres Complètes de Molière,* in which he gave the biography of the poet at different periods of his life. This biography was given in a more connected form some twenty years later, when M. Moland brought out a second and much enlarged edition of his book. The edition of Molière which I have used habitually, and to which I generally refer, forms part of the Collection des Grands Écrivains de la France, published by MM. Hachette. It is unfortunate for the purpose of reference that in the various editions of Molière's comedies the Scenes in the different Acts should not begin and end in the same place.

All my references to the numbers of the scenes in Molière's plays apply to the edition last mentioned—unless, of course, any other edition is specified. I have, however, tried to simplify the references. The first volume of the Molière in the Collection des Grands Écrivains de la France appeared in 1873, the last two, vols. xii. and xiii., containing a *Lexique de la Langue de Molière*, in 1900. Eugène Despois was its first editor, but he lived to finish only the first three volumes and part of the fourth. After his death M. Paul Mesnard continued and completed the work—except the *Notice bibliographique* (vol. xi.), which was compiled by M. Arthur Desfeuilles, and the *Lexique* by MM. Arthur and Paul Desfeuilles. I should say that M. Mesnard's *Notice biographique sur Molière*, which forms the tenth volume in this edition, has been of very great assistance to me in unravelling the facts in the story of Molière's life.

Thus, all my authorities are French. I know that within the last twenty years some English writers have made a study of Molière, and have brought out editions with notes of the chief of his plays. But as the greater part of my work was done out of England, where I had not access to these books, it is not altogether my fault that I have not been able to apply to them for assistance.

I acknowledge very gladly my obligations to many French authors, for they have taught me much; and it is only natural to suppose that to some extent my thoughts have followed theirs. But I wish to say that I have not knowingly stolen their ideas and given them as my own. It is generally easy to quote the source of authority when dealing with facts, and I believe I have done so sufficiently. I trust I shall not be trespassing too far on the goodwill of French writers on Molière if I assume that literary courtesy is willing to allow fair borrowing of facts and details when due acknowledgment is made of the loan. But literary courtesy does not extend its hospitality to robbery of ideas with silence about the theft. I hope I have not sinned in that respect.

Besides the authors already mentioned I have made use of the labours of others. Their names will be found in my footnotes with references to their pages. Some of them, however, should be mentioned here. MM. Victor Fournel; A. Jal; Jules Bonnassies; Édouard Fournier; Paul Lacroix; Jules Loiseleur; Georges Monval; again Eugène Despois, my earliest instructor in his book *Le Théâtre Français sous Louis XIV.*; and also again, Louis Moland, another instructor at about the same time in his *Molière et la Comédie Italienne,* and later in the two editions of his *Œuvres Complètes de Molière.* And though I have spoken of it at the beginning of Chapter VI., I should not omit to mention here the publication in 1876 by the Comédie Française of La Grange's Register; for that book gives a knowledge of events in connection with Molière's troop, and of the successes or the failures of his plays when they first appeared on the stage, which no one can hope to obtain who has not carefully studied its pages.

I have mentioned by name the registers of La Thorillière and of Hubert. Both of these men were members of Molière's troop. A small book, *Le premier registre de La Thorillière,* has been published; it deals only with the year 1663-64, and it tells nothing of importance that is not to be found in La Grange. I do not know if Hubert's Register has been printed; it is not in the British Museum Catalogue. My one quotation from it was taken from a volume already published. There is a source of contemporary authority from which I have not quoted—the doggerel verses by Loret and by Robinet. These men were weekly chroniclers of events, and they were bound to describe everything that they related in glowing colours. Their lines may have their charms, but terseness of expression is not one of them. I could not repeat their verses because of their long-windedness, which often ceases to be amusing. When their verses refer to Molière's plays they have already been quoted sufficiently by Despois, by M. Paul Mesnard, and by M. Louis Moland.

It will be seen that in speaking of a theatrical company of

actors I have used the word "troop" very frequently. To some persons this word will have a peculiar or an ugly look. A short word, however, was necessary, and I soon found that "company" would not do. Early in the first scene of his *Critic*, Sheridan uses the word "troop" in the sense of a theatrical company of actors; also Malone, in his edition of Shakspeare published in 1821 (vol. iii. p. 175), uses the word "troop" in the same sense. I must quote them as my authority. Perhaps I may be wrong, but I prefer "troop" to "troupe."

Both of the portraits of Molière in this volume are from paintings by Mignard. The frontispiece is the same as one of the portraits in the Album to the edition of Molière in the Collection des Grands Écrivains de la France, and has been reproduced here by the kindness of MM. Hachette. The original is in the Condé Museum at Chantilly, and is the finest of all the four portraits of Molière by Mignard. It was painted in 1668. The artist preserved it until his death in 1695. Then it became the property of his daughter, the Comtesse de Feuquières. After her death all traces of it were lost, until it was purchased by the Duc d'Aumale in 1876. The other portrait, facing page 410, was painted probably in 1666. Paul Lacroix describes this picture in his *Iconographie Moliéresque*, No. 46, and says that there are engravings from it in five different states. The one reproduced here corresponds with the fifth state, and is the same as that seen in vol. i. of Charles Perrault's *Hommes Illustres*, published in 1696. The best known portrait of Molière was painted by Mignard at Avignon in 1658. Molière is there represented as Cæsar in Corneille's tragedy *Pompée*. This picture was bought by the Comédie Française in 1869.

Hardly more than two qualifications are necessary for an enjoyment of Molière: a liking for and an appreciation of comedy and of comic personal characterisation, and a fair and easy reading knowledge of French. The first of these qualifications must be possessed by everybody who wishes to understand how Molière thought, how he wrote, and how he mixed together earnestness and mockery, farce and comedy, and how he used his ridicule to show a serious purpose. The second qualification, which goes with the first, is not so difficult to English readers as it may seem to be, for Molière's humour is large, true, and sympathetic, and it will appeal to all who have an open sense of fun, and also to those who are heartily pleased when they see the usually dangerous gift of satire turned to good and noble uses.

H. M. T.

CONTENTS

INTRODUCTION

GENERAL VIEW OF FRENCH COMEDY BEFORE MOLIÈRE

CHAPTER I

MOLIÈRE'S BIRTH AND PARENTAGE

CHAPTER II

YEARS OF SCHOOLING

CHAPTER III

MINOR THEATRES

CHAPTER IV

THE ILLUSTRE THÉÂTRE

CHAPTER V

STROLLING IN THE PROVINCES

CHAPTER VI

RETURN TO PARIS

CHAPTER VII

SOCIETY IN PARIS BETWEEN 1620 AND 1660—*LES PRÉCIEUSES RIDICULES—SGANARELLE*

CHAPTER VIII

MOLIÈRE'S IDEAS OF COMEDY—SHAKESPEARE AND MOLIÈRE

CHAPTER IX

STAGE CUSTOMS

CHAPTER X

DIFFERENT ASPECTS OF THE HÔTEL DE BOURGOGNE AND PALAIS ROYAL THEATRES—MOLIÈRE AS AN ACTOR

CHAPTER XI

THE FORTUNES OF MOLIÈRE'S COMEDIES WHEN NEW

CHAPTER XII

CHAPTER XIII

CHAPTER XIV

CHAPTER XV

L'AMOUR MÉDECIN—LE MISANTHROPE

CHAPTER XVI

LE MÉDECIN MALGRÉ LUI—LE BALLET DES MUSES—OTHER EVENTS— AMPHITRYON—L'AVARE—GEORGE DANDIN

CHAPTER XVII

MONSIEUR DE POURCEAUGNAC—LES AMANTS MAGNIFIQUES—CHANGES IN THE TROOP—LE BOURGEOIS GENTILHOMME—LES FOURBERIES DE SCAPIN—PSYCHÉ.

CHAPTER XVIII

LES FEMMES SAVANTES—LA COMTESSE D'ESCARBAGNAS—LE MALADE IMAGINAIRE—POÉSIES DIVERSES

CHAPTER XIX

BIOGRAPHICAL DETAILS AND CONCLUSION

PORTRAITS

[For details of the portraits, see p. viii.]

INTRODUCTION

GENERAL VIEW OF FRENCH COMEDY
BEFORE MOLIÈRE

AT the time of Molière's birth, in 1622, the Hôtel de Bourgogne was the only permanently established French theatre in Paris. Another theatre, whether then known or not by the name of the Théâtre du Marais, had probably had an interrupted existence for some years; but it is likely enough that it had not then acquired sufficient renown to keep its doors open with constant regularity, and that it did not become established permanently until some years later. The Hôtel de Bourgogne, however, was always regarded as the chief theatre, and the majority of French actors who did not belong to it hoped, often vainly enough, to be enrolled among its members upon some future happy occasion. Before speaking of early French comedy a few words may be said showing how these two theatres arose; for their members and those of Molière's troop, after his death, were the ancestors of the Comédie Française of the present day.

The playhouse known as the Hôtel de Bourgogne carries us back historically to the ancient brotherhood, Les Confrères de la Passion. They were the earliest representatives of dramatic art in Paris, and they formed a society made up from the artisans of the capital for the purpose of representing *Les Mystères de la Passion de Jésus Christ*. They used to act at first at Saint Maur, near Vincennes. In 1398 their performance was forbidden, but in 1402 Charles VI. allowed them to form themselves into a dramatic corporati The brotherhood then began to play at the hospital de a Trinité, outside the Porte Saint Denis; and there they founded the first known Parisian theatre at which a money payment was demanded for entrance. They continued their performances there until 1539, when they migrated to the Hôtel de Flandre, inside the gates of the town. A little later, François I. ordered that house, and the old Hôtel de Bourgogne—which was not a theatre—and other houses to be pulled down. In 1548 the Confrères bought part of the land on which the Hôtel de Bourgogne stood, and on that site they built for themselves, in the Rue Mauconseil, a theatre which they called the Hôtel de Bourgogne, after the old house. But in the same year the Parliament, while confirming their ancient privilege and giving them a monopoly for theatrical representations in and near to Paris, said that they might act secular plays, but forbade for the future performance of the "mysteries." The mysteries therefore died out in Paris, but in the provinces they were acted for some years.[1] From this Act of Parliament, in 1548, dates the opening of the Hôtel de Bourgogne theatre. The Act probably expressed the feeling of the better-minded persons, for the reverential feeling which for many years had accompanied the performance of the mysteries was lost; what had been looked upon as a holy office came to be a pastime, and at length fell into unseemly buffooneries. The Confrères continued to play in the Hôtel de Bourgogne, but the new law took from them their chief means of attraction. Dramatic performances had always been popular in Paris, but the brotherhood could not act worldly plays in a way that the people liked. Their position was unfortunate, and it would seem that they did not take the best means to improve it. The people had always supported them, and they set themselves resolutely against the popular will. They still had their monopoly, allowing them to play where they liked in or near Paris, but they were unable to use it; and they prevented at different times troops of provincial actors from trying to gain a living in the capital. A roving company would now and then surreptitiously give one or two perform-ances, but as soon as the Confrères heard of what was going on they quoted their privilege in a law court, and the interlopers were ordered to shift.[2] The ancient brotherhood found that their theatre was no longer a paying concern, so in 1578 they

[1] Victor Fournel, *Les Contemporains de Molière*, vol. i. pp. xvii-xix; Soulié, *Recherches sur Molière et sa famille*, 27 and 152, under dates 30th August and 17th November 1548.

[2] Suard, *Histoire du Théâtre Français*, in vol. i. of his *Mélanges de Littérature*, p. 110.

hired a theatrical company.[1] But ten years later, in 1588,
forty years after they had been forbidden to act the mysteries,
they let the Hôtel de Bourgogne to a troop of actors who
wished to amuse the public and to make some money by it.
From 1588, therefore, the troop known afterwards as "la
troupe de l'Hôtel de Bourgogne" began to play at the Hôtel de
Bourgogne theatre, and they continued to play there until the
year 1680. Molière had then been dead seven years.

Though the Confrères de la Passion had let their theatre,
they were always stoutly determined to maintain their privilege forbidding any other playhouse in or near to Paris. Other
actors made their appearance at various times, and the Confrères went to law to have them ousted, or to claim from
them penalties for acting elsewhere than at the Hôtel de
Bourgogne. Sixty sous, or three francs, was the fine imposed
for each irregular performance; and there are several instances
proving that this penalty was judicially awarded to the
members of the brotherhood.[2] These sentences, though con-
demnatory, show a certain toleration. Other troops of actors
were to be allowed to play in or near Paris if they paid a fine
of three francs for each performance. The fine went to the
Confrères,[3] not to the actors at the Hôtel de Bourgogne,
though they must have lost patronage by the temporary
rival playhouse. The theatre-loving Parisians liked the actors
who amused them, and they cared nothing for the super-
annuated religious brotherhood whose only interest in the
theatre was that of a money-making investment. The old
guild existed until 1677, when Louis XIV. suppressed the
Corporation of Les Confrères de la Passion, and ordered that
their property should be sold for the benefit of the general
hospital; the actors who were tenants of the Hôtel de
Bourgogne were to pay their rent to the same hospital.[4]

The Théâtre du Marais had but an uncertain existence
during the first three decades or more of the 17th century.
The origin of this theatre is doubtful even now. Some writers
have said that it was founded in 1598, some in 1635, others

---

[1] Soulié, *Recherches sur Molière*, 27 ; 152-3.
[2] *Ibid.* 155, under dates 10th and 13th March 1610; 157-8, under date
16th February 1622; and 162-3, under date 25th February 1631.
[3] Parfaict, *Histoire du Théâtre François*, iii. 244, and note c.
[4] Eugène Despois, *Le Théâtre Français sous Louis XIV.*, 5 and 241.

at various dates in the interval. M. Victor Fournel, who may be taken as a sure guide in matters relating to the dramatic history of his country, says that during this interval "there was not one Théâtre du Marais, there were several, and even after a settled resting-place had been found different troops succeeded each other."[1] The word "theatre" is here taken to be synonymous with the company of actors who played inside it.

In the 17th century in France the theatre virtually belonged for the time to the troop of actors who paid rent for the use of it, and all the members of the company had equal rights. Those who think that the Marais troop was first formed when Alexandre Hardy—a terribly prolific playwright, but who is not known to have acted upon the stage—came to Paris from the provinces with a strolling company, and tried with them to found a new theatre in the Marais quarter of the town about the year 1600, have at any rate rational grounds on which to establish their belief. Perhaps that was the earliest determined attempt to found the Théâtre du Marais, though there is no authority for saying that it was then called by that name. A company was playing at the Hôtel d'Argent, near the Place de Grève, in 1610, but most probably they did not stop there very long. Owing to the precarious livelihood to be obtained, there were frequent changes in the troop. At times it was broken up and had no existence; at other times a "scratch" team was formed and played in Paris for a while; then, if its members would hold together, they left Paris to go strolling in the provinces. Rouen was the town to which they would be most likely to go; and there, under the direction of Mondory, their leader, Corneille's first play, *Mélite*, a comedy, was acted in 1629. This play was afterwards brought out by Mondory at a theatre in the Marais quarter of Paris in the same year. Corneille says that his play set on foot a new troop of actors in the capital. It may be doubted, however, if this establishment of a new troop was more permanent than the others had been. In 1632 or 1633 a company, bearing the title of "Le Théâtre du Marais," used to play in a tennis-court known as La Fontaine, in the Rue Michel le Comte. But the

---

[1] M. Fournel gives the best and fullest account of this theatre in his book *Les Contemporains de Molière*, iii. 7, etc. Despois in his *Le Théâtre Français sous Louis XIV.*, 10-18, has also a chapter on the subject.

inhabitants of the neighbourhood addressed a complaint to the Parliament of Paris, saying that the theatre caused great obstruction by the number of horses and carriages that went to its doors. The theatre was then closed. At last, in 1635, the Marais troop found a home in the Rue Vieille du Temple. There they stayed, and quite at the end of the year 1636 they brought out Corneille's tragedy, *Le Cid*. They had their red-letter days before and afterwards, but their theatre was probably never so well filled as during the few weeks after the first performance of the *Cid*. Before a month had passed young Poquelin, whom we are to know later as Molière, had his fifteenth birthday; and there are fair grounds for thinking that, standing or seated by his grandfather's side, he joined in the general admiration of the new play. Corneille gave most of his tragedies to the Hôtel de Bourgogne, for tragedy was better acted at that theatre. He returned, however, to the Marais in 1642 with his comedy *Le Menteur*, and his *Suite du Menteur* was also performed there in the following year. To the first of these plays the town gave a very warm welcome.

It is intended in this introductory chapter to say in what spirit the French comic dramatists before Molière wished to make comedy show her face and features, and that when they were not successful, their failure was largely due to imitation. I take it that comedy means an amusing dramatic representation of the humours of men in a broad sense, and comic what is fit for such representation or having the attributes of comedy. What passed for comedy in France before the renaissance of the drama—say before 1560—gave on the whole a truer and more lively picture of the essential office of comedy, satirising or playing with general faults and foibles, and thus creating amusement, than in 1660, a few years after Molière began to write. Farce has always been the mother of comedy, and before 1552, the date of Jodelle's *Eugène*, the word comedy was hardly used in France; the old term "farce" was employed, and authors tried to make their plays amusing, and people liked to laugh in the theatre. Gradually the word comedy was adopted. And later, by degrees, those who were considered the best judges of plays thought that farce was low. It was banished from the Hôtel de Bourgogne about the middle of the 17th century, and comedies acted

there were written more to be admired intellectually than
to afford hearty amusement. Indeed there is generally very
little cause for laughter to be found in them. They were
called comedies, but they were sadly wanting in animation.
This severance of inanimate or pretended comedy from farce
was due to pedantic officialism rather than to the wishes of
the playgoers. The change was, so to say, administrative; it
was not natural. It was made, however, partly with good
intentions, to show a greater refinement of manners. But it
came too quickly to mark a step really accomplished in the
right direction. As years went on dramatists grew more used
to their work, and thanks very largely to the efforts of Pierre
Corneille, high comedy began to try to show itself.

Such theatrical performances as were given before the
mysteries were prohibited in 1548 were of a popular kind
Mysteries, moralities, soties, and farces had been acted, and it
was to the people that they owed their success. There were
connecting links, more or less strong, between all these plays;
but as the mysteries, acted by the Confrères de la Passion, and
the moralities, acted by the Clercs de la Bazoche, had only a
very distant influence upon French comedy, it is not necessary
to speak of them here. The soties and farces, however, though
crude and coarse as we should look at them now, were lively
and amusing; they represented the manners of many who saw
them, and they were, in fact, comedies of the time. Consequently they were understood and enjoyed by the people.
Much of the sotie was improvised. It was at first a kind of
satirical allegory in the form of a dialogue, with little or no
action; by degrees the spoken words were accompanied by
gestures, and action was introduced. The actors loved to
attack what they thought were public abuses, and, to make
their satire more telling, they indulged freely in personal
allusions.

"It is chiefly in these small pieces," says Sainte-Beuve,[1] "that we
should look for the satirical wit and raillery of our grandfathers and
their inborn love of making fun of ridiculous things and of criticising
authority. . . . The sotie was lighter-handed and more delicate than
the farce, and its satire was more direct. From the first it was full

---

[1] *Tableau de la Poésie Française au XVIᵉ Siècle*, ed. 1843, 201 and 203.

of the sharp, biting wit which showed itself in philosophical tales and in political pamphlets. It showed almost at the same moment the banter of Marot and the audacity of Aristophanes."

The spirit of Molière's comedies is partly reflected here. He had plenty of satirical wit, though it was good-natured, and he certainly loved making fun of ridiculous things. His personalities, as far as they existed, were those of comedy, and they were never offensive in the sense of being unjustifiable. He did not directly criticise authority, for in his day authority was stronger than it was a hundred and fifty years before his time. The latter part of Sainte-Beuve's sentence shows a likeness, which he has mentioned elsewhere, between the spirit in men in the 16th and in the 18th centuries. This was a taste in some for scepticism, in others for mere unbelief, and a love of quizzing mockery or of persiflage. Molière also was sceptical, but his love of ridicule was shown in another and a better way. Both he and Rabelais had a much better idea of reverence than Voltaire.

Quite early in the second half of the 16th century a new school of French dramatists arose who tried to improve the condition of the stage. This has been called the Renaissance of the French drama. Greek tragedies were imitated in French, and the new plays were perhaps admired in the colleges before picked audiences, but they lacked the spark that would kindle enthusiasm in a popular assembly. But it would be hazardous to say if any of their performances took place at the Hôtel de Bourgogne while the theatre remained in the hands of the Confrères de la Passion. Very likely, of the tragedies there was no performance there at all. Most of these plays were written by young men about the time they had finished their college education. The author often acted a part in his own play, the other parts were filled by his colleagues or by his friends. The lads were proud of their skill, and they were ambitious to show off their learning before a well-selected audience.

These were the days when the seven authors, known as La Pléiade—Ronsard, du Bellay, Dorat, Remi Belleau, Jodelle, Baïf, and Pontus du Thyard—wrote poetry far sweeter than anything of its kind that was produced in the 17th or 18th centuries, and which is still read with pleasure. But the men who formed the Pléiade were not distinctively playwrights. Three of them did not write plays at all. Nevertheless, the four who did, and others who are not known as belonging to this circle of friends, formed a school, as it were, and their example was followed. Besides the tragedies, taken from the Greek, comedies, which were far less numerous, were written, and they were for the most part borrowed from Latin and afterwards from Italian authors. In both kinds of plays imitation was the groundwork. This revival of what was thought to be the Greek and Latin form of play is worth noticing, because it shows in what way the earliest definite attempt was made to put tragedy and comedy on to the French stage; and we shall see presently that the French dramatists of two generations later thought they were doing right in discarding their own observations, and instead taking Aristotle and Horace for their guides when they were writing plays for the amusement of the people.

One member of the Pléiade—Jodelle—wrote a single comedy, *Eugène*, acted at the College of Reims in 1552. It would have been well if other comic dramatists had followed the lead given to them by Jodelle in trying to form their comedies on the manners of people round about them. *Eugène* is a satire on the self-indulgences of the clergy. It is thoroughly good-natured, and may easily have provoked laughter; and it spoke to the people about their own affairs in a style and language which was their own. Setting aside the plays commonly known as farces, this was the earliest instance of a French comedy intending to show the manners of contemporary life. A claim, therefore, has been made on behalf of Jodelle that he was the founder of French comedy. But he left no school, for succeeding dramatists did not follow his good example. He chose for his play a subject that was French, and wrote about it in a French manner; those who came after him, instead of trying to do the same, imitated dramatists from a foreign land. He gave them a line to follow, but they chose another and a worse direction, and made a detestable track of their own. In his prologue to *Les Corrivaux* (1562) Jean de la Taille takes credit to himself that his play is a comedy, not a morality nor a farce—idle follies which corrupt the language and which should be banished from the kingdom. Written comedy of a very dull kind, and borrowed directly from the Latin, had existed in Italy before it came into France, and the new school of French playwrights—of which it would be unjust to Jodelle to call him the founder—wished to put on to their stage comedies that might not be despised by other nations, and which their own countrymen would regard with satisfaction. But as the feathers were not fine they did not make fine birds. The plays at first were almost farces put into the guise of comedies, and Jean de la Taille's play, in spite of his boast, was no better than others of his time. The chief evil, however, did not lie there. Not until many years later did the French playwrights free themselves from Italian influences, and before this was accomplished they began to take Spanish dramatists for their models.

Among the comic playwrights that are known to have written about this time, the most fertile was Larivey. He was a scholar and a canon of Troyes. Six of his comedies were printed in 1579, three others in 1611. It is not known where or when his plays were acted, but it has been said, on the authority of one who was conversant in such matters, that it is doubtful if they were acted publicly in the theatre.[1] Perhaps Larivey's connection with the church prevented this. But they may have been played in some of the colleges, and so have had a semi-public performance; or they may have been acted under the patronage of a nobleman in his own house. Larivey translated Italian plays, or borrowed scenes from them or from Latin comedies, and manufactured his comedies to suit French tastes. He was therefore more of a playwright than a dramatist. It seems to me that he worked quickly and carelessly, and that his habit of borrowing his plots or bits of stories where he could find them made him think more of joining his threads together than of working out the idea of a story which would lend itself to dramatic action. At rare intervals there is a bit of strong natural characterisation; it is shown in a few lines, or in a few words; it was a happy inspiration at the moment of writing, but he does not make it lead to anything. If he got a good scene here and there he was satisfied; he was either incapable of doing more

---

[1] Charles Magnin, *Journal des Savants* for 1858, p. 202, and note 1.

or he did not attempt it. And yet, with a dramatic instinct keen in some respects, Larivey thought that a humorous representation of events would please upon the stage. He did more than any other writer before Molière to put the dialogue of comedy upon easy-rolling wheels. His dialogue is his chief recommendation to merit. It is lively, and shows that he knew how to make his actors move and speak as though they had life in them, not as talking machines. He insisted upon using homely and familiar language, and all his comedies are in prose. He formed his personages upon the types in vogue in Italian comedy. These are constantly reproduced, and though the outward events in each play may vary, the same sort of incidents are to be found in them all. *Les Esprits* is one of the best of Larivey's comedies. The chief circumstance there is a valet persuading an old man that there are devils in his house in order to rob him.

There is much sameness in the comedies written in the latter half of the 16th century. They do not differ essentially in manner from those of Larivey, except that they have not his sparkle; but it is probable that the writers learned something from him. The plots are mainly Italian; the interest was meant to lie in the schemes laid to bring the lovers together, and sometimes in the consequent troubles that arise. Besides the lovers, there are the valets; they play the principal parts, and always gain the upper hand over their masters. Sometimes a professional intriguer is introduced. There is generally an old man to be cheated, or there may be two; there is often an old woman, a nurse or a servant, and perhaps a neighbour. One of the old men may have a wife; if so, not much is seen of her. As a rule the heroines in the play have not an actively arduous part to perform; they are made to remain on the stage saying very little. As their parts were taken by boys or young men, their chief task was to make themselves look pretty. Not unfrequently an old man is made to be in love with a young girl. She naturally hates him, for he is " old, rotten, and toothless "; and she is of course won by his son or by his nephew. The old man is ridiculous in his love for the girl, and the schemes laid to prevent his designs are so trivial or base that little commendation is due to the intriguing valet who succeeds in entrapping him. One sees easily from all this how Molière was affected by Italian influences, especially in his first two comedies, the *Étourdi* and the *Dépit Amoureux*. But Molière's plays very rarely show anything objectionable; and besides, he had the gifts of strong characterisation and liveliness of manner. His valet in the *Étourdi*, though a rascal of romance, is an honest-minded fellow at bottom; if he found a £5 note of his master's, he would give it to him. In most of the 16th century comedies stock types of men and women are reproduced with certain variations, but the predominating point in them all is a display of roguery and cheating, of one man trying to outwit another. The groundwork of most of the plots was Italian. And they showed, one would say, a less bright intelligence than the wit, doubtless often rough and coarse enough, displayed in the older soties and farces which had been written before the French playwrights thought of giving a smart appearance to their comedies by clothing their own people in an Italian dress. Crudeness of manner is excusable, for it may amuse by its simplicity. We often see, especially in the plays in verse, that while two of the personages are on the stage together, they are both made to deliver at considerable length speeches that the other is not intended to hear. Long monologues spoken in this way are frequent, reminding one curiously of the pictures of the early Egyptians. These ancient people did not know how to make a picture of a group of men, so they drew them in profile, one standing behind the other. Nevertheless, the plays should be classed perhaps as comedy, not as farce, for the events described are made to follow each other with a tolerable sequence of ideas.

From such lists as the historians of the drama have been able to compile, it would appear that from 1552, the date of Jodelle's *Eugène*, to 1629, when Corneille wrote his first comedy, the number of tragedies, tragi-comedies, and pastorals, exceeded the comedies in the proportion of about ten to one. At first the plays were tragedies, or they were comedies or farces; and the tragedies were very greatly in excess. The taste of the people in favour of tragedy may be partly seen from the fact that the tragedies were generally printed; while the comedies, more often than not called farces, were acted a few or more times, and then very many of them were lost and disappeared from memory. It should be said that more light comedies or farces were printed before the renaissance of the drama than after it. Before dull tragedy and comedy had appeared, people were contented with such simple farces as they could get. These plays had a show of life and fun in them, and the audiences were amused at the homely wit displayed. Consequently the farces were printed and were read. The newer comedies might be more elegant, but there was very little wit or fun in them. Tragi-comedies and pastorals were not introduced until near the close of the 16th century, and they did not become common until some years after the beginning of the 17th. The difference between tragedy and tragicomedy was more nominal than real: it was thought that tragedy should be taken from ancient history; if the story came from a more modern source, the play fell from tragedy to tragi-comedy. When the French dramatists began to borrow romantic incidents from Spain, what was called the romantic drama crept in and was recognised. Tragi-comedies and pastorals became common about the same time, and in 1629 about the same number of each had been represented. A few years before this a more hybrid kind of play was introduced, called tragi-comedy-pastoral. Thus in France, as in England, and at about the same period, plays were of almost all kinds—"tragical-comical-historical-pastoral." The actors thought, too, that "Seneca was not too heavy for them, nor Plautus too light." For after the performance of the important piece a farce nearly always followed, so that those who liked laughing should be sent home in a good humour. Farce died out at the Hôtel de Bourgogne perhaps between 1640 and 1650; at the Marais it was probably played for some time longer. After Corneille began to write his comedies other comedies appeared with greater frequency. But before this the style and the outward form of comedy had changed. Fewer comedies were written in prose, and in those in verse the short eight-syllabled line had given way generally to the long Alexandrine line of twelve syllables. There is no instance of a French play in blank verse. The "genre noble," too, was introduced, and in the best interests of comedy too much was thought of stateliness of manner.

Some notice should be taken of Alexandre Hardy, and of his

position as a dramatist, though he is not known to have written a single comedy. He was born about 1560 and died about 1632, and is said to have wandered about the country with a troop of strolling players who succeeded for a time in establishing a new theatre in Paris in the Marais quarter of the town. Hardy's pen was fabulously fertile. He speaks himself of having written six hundred plays; the brothers Parfaict ascribe to him seven hundred;[1] while Scudéry, his contemporary, charges him with eight hundred. A few years before his death he printed forty-one of his tragedies and tragi-comedies, each in five acts and in the long Alexandrine verse, and it should be presumed that to many more he gave the same full measure. Like many of the dramatists in England and in France at this period, Hardy appears to have been a scholar; but wiser in his generation than his compatriots, he was willing to throw his scholarship to the winds. He knew instinctively that if a dramatist wants to please the public he must write plays that they like. He was a wonderful improviser at second-hand, for he could make the most of what he had read. He drew a great deal from ancient history and from the writings, then new, of Cervantes and of Lope de Vega. The idea of plagiarism in those days was not much considered. And the French dramatists had not yet invented for their own torture and self-destruction the so-called laws of the unities. Like Lope, Hardy allowed himself to be very slightly bound by rules: the only law which he made for himself was to please. Tradition, which generally magnifies when it wants to admire, says that his plays charmed the public because of the impossible adventures related. It is probable enough that his plays were rough and ready, and that they did please those who saw them. Classical and romantic ideas were huddled together and were enjoyed by a non-critical audience. For some thirty years Hardy was lord and master of the Paris stage, and he, more than any one else, introduced the romantic drama. I was not surprised to see the opinion of a well-known critic of our day, M. Ferdinand Brunetière, who says it is evident enough that though Hardy has been written about a good deal, he has been little read.[2] Speaking of Hardy's work generally, M. Brune-

---

[1] *Histoire du Théâtre François*, iv., preface, p. 1.
[2] *Revue des deux Mondes*, 1st October 1890, p. 706.

tière says:—"Jamais peut-être on n'a pas plus mal écrit en vers, d'un style à la fois plus emphatique et plus plat. Jamais non plus on n'a dépensé plus de mots pour dire moins de choses, ou entassé plus d'invraisemblances pour produire un total avec moins d'effet." I had read three of Hardy's plays, *Mariamne* and two others, and found it impossible to read more. Page after page caused a still, painful dulness, relieved only by the harshness of the verses, which grated on my ear like the noise made by the sawing of a stone. In many French tragedies, especially at this early period, the idea of the writers was to produce a play in which the action should be simple, but in *Mariamne* the simplicity is appalling. There is but one point of interest, and everything is made to centre upon it. There is no under-plot and no by-play. And though we are told that Hardy liked to put some appearance of gaiety into his plays, there is none of it in this tragedy. There are few personages, and all they have to say relates to one incident. Consequently there arises the necessity for long speeches to make up the prescribed five acts. The result is monotonous and very dreary. Any dramatic interest the play may have is terribly maimed when the narrative is spun out to a great length. The story is over-weighted with words, the action becomes stifled and is virtually lost.

If there is fair ground for believing in the traditional idea that Hardy occupied a high eminence above his fellows, I cannot help thinking, though there is no direct evidence of his having written a single comedy, that he did write or sketch the outlines of many light comedies or farces which were not thought worth printing and of which nothing now remains. His reputation is said to have declined quickly after his death; but if we accept his own estimation of the number of his plays—which was the lowest of the three that have been given—it is certain that he must have worked with startling rapidity, and that most of his work has perished.

The laws of the unities, which were held to govern all plays that were seriously meant, were observed for the first time in France in a tragedy by Mairet called *Sophonisbe*, acted in 1629. The laws were that in every drama there should be a unity of time, a unity of place, and a unity

of action or of interest; in other words, all the incidents
described in a play should be supposed to happen within
twenty-four hours, the place of the scene should remain
unchanged, and the action or the interest in the play
should be confined to one event. The French dramatists
in the early part of the 17th century imagined, not very
correctly, that these laws had been laid down by Aristotle;
and they adopted them, or were made to follow them by the
pedants of the day, not knowing quite what they were doing.
They were actuated by some preconceived idea that rules
defining the purpose and aim of the drama would be valuable;
they thought that laws of restraint preventing an author
from incongruities or from absurd complications in his story
would have a salutary effect on his play.

If human actions were regulated by logic these laws might
perhaps be rational; but in tragedy we have to consider
men's deeper passions, and how they are drawn, and comedy
endeavours to give a picture of men's humours, and to show
how contradictory they often are. If a play is to be at all
true to nature, hard and fast or cut and dried rules limiting
or defining human conduct are manifestly out of place. The
best of all rules to guide an author in writing his play will be
found in Voltaire's preface to his comedy *L'Enfant Prodigue*:
"Tous les genres sont bons hors le genre ennuyeux." For,
short of flagrant iniquity, dulness is the worst fault a play
can have. Had the French dramatists of nearly three hundred
years ago made the action of their plays extend over ten or
twenty years, and had they crowded their plots with incidents,
or had they placed a scene on the sea-coast of Bohemia (as
Shakespeare did in Act III. sc. 3 of his *Winter's Tale*), they
might have written plays that appealed to the imagination,
instead of making a listener or a reader feel the constraint of
their self-imposed mechanical contrivances. Suard relates[1]
amusingly the outline of an old French play, which, in spite
of its absurdities, inclines one to a belief that the author
may have interested his audience. The scene is laid at the
North Pole. Nevertheless, two lovers walk about together in
a wood. During their interview, the gentleman, a Frenchman
by birth, is warned that his ship is waiting for him in the

[1] *Histoire du Théâtre Français*, i. 113 of his *Mélanges de Littérature*.

harbour. As he leaves his mistress to go to his ship he meets his rival. They fight and kill each other. Then the young lady kills herself. In the meanwhile her father has died. Suard adds naïvely: "It is very clear that this play was a tragedy." Whether the unities were preserved here or not, it is certain that abstract notions and strict ideas of propriety, formed with the belief that they would have been sanctioned by Aristotle, find no place in this play. The system of the laws of the unities was inaugurated by Mairet in his tragedy, *Sophonisbe*, but it did not begin with him. The ideas which he promulgated had been for some time in the air, and in a preface to an earlier play he had pleaded the same cause. The actors at the Hôtel de Bourgogne knew what was being said among the dramatists and their friends, and they declined at first to have anything to do with a play conducted on the new principles. Perhaps they were strengthened in their opinion by advice given to them by Hardy. But either through persuasion or compulsion they consented to what was proposed to them. *Sophonisbe* appeared on the stage : unfortunately it was very successful, and the pedants were triumphant. They formed themselves into a sort of literary administration ; some writers followed implicitly the instructions that were given to them, others—the minority—obeyed against their will ; and so a new doctrine was set up against those who wanted to work with a free hand. The new-fangled creed with its dogmas applied of course to comedy as well as to tragedy. It makes one think that it would have been better for the French stage if its writers, instead of considering the ancient drama which had been formed on ideas long dead and gone, had chosen, and especially in comedy, to look at their own daily lives and record as best they might what was passing in them. Their work would, at any rate, have left upon it the impress of the feelings of the age, and thus have shown one of the essential features of comedy. At a time when the stage was becoming popular in Europe it is curious that a lively, sensitive people, in whom the gift of perception was quick, and who enjoyed the love of ridicule, should not have given dramatic expression to their own thoughts, that they should not have shown better comedy of their own. They would have done so if they had left old books alone, if they had used their wits in their own way, and had not tried to imitate the comedies seen on the Italian and the Spanish stages. There is necessarily some imitation in every art, but an author will generally show whether he is working out his own thoughts or trying to reproduce those of others because they have been considered fine. La Fontaine, who knew what the early dramatic literature of his country was like, says at the end of his fable, *Le Singe* :—

> " N'attendez rien de bon du peuple imitateur,
> Qu'il soit singe, ou qu'il fasse un livre :
> La pire espèce c'est l'auteur."

Besides his *Sophonisbe* Mairet is known as the author of one comedy and some pastorals. These latter gave him a great reputation at the time, but as pastoral plays with their love-sick shepherds and shepherdesses are hardly included in the denomination of comedy, I need not say much about them. People then liked the conceits of language that were common in pastoral plays : what we now think is ridiculous they considered as ornament. The taste for pastorals came from Italy, and they became popular in France after the publication of the first part of d'Urfé's novel *Astrée*, in 1610. In 1627 Mairet's comedy, *Les Galanteries du duc d'Ossonne*, was acted at the Hôtel de Bourgogne. The scene is laid at Naples, but the events betray a conception partly Italian and partly Spanish clothed in a French garb. Like nearly every other comedy at the time, it seems wooden as one reads it now, for the lines spoken by the different personages do not show their real characters. Yet those·people who saw the play when it was new were pleased at what they thought were its beauties. This was Mairet's only comedy, but it sealed his reputation, and he became the fashionable author. His glory was not undeserved. *Les Galanteries du duc d'Ossonne* was a step in advance of the comedies which preceded it. The language, too, was better chosen, and shows that the writer knew how to hold his pen. What he wanted most was a knowledge of men and women and how they should show themselves on the stage.

A few pages must be given to the comedies of Pierre Corneille, for he was one of the fathers of comedy in France, as he was, in a fuller sense, the father of French tragedy.

It was to his tragedies that he owed his greatest triumphs; his comedies have always been considered much less highly. Though they are not now widely read, they should not be passed over as plays of no account, for they show an important step in the progress of comedy in France. One cannot expect as much enjoyment from them now as was felt by those who first saw them acted, or even as much as was felt in a quieter way by those who first read his lines. Then the comedies were new, and of a new kind. They had a freshness of their own that had not been seen before, and for truthfulness of portraiture they were the best that had been written.

Pierre Corneille was born at Rouen in 1606. He was called to the bar when he was eighteen, but got little practice. It may be that, apart from his dislike to the profession, his timidity or his shyness prevented him from setting about in the right way to get work. His first play, *Mélite*, a comedy, was performed at Rouen in 1629. Apparently it was successful in the provincial capital, for when Mondory's troop returned to Paris they acted the comedy before a metropolitan audience, who were surprised and charmed with its new style and natural manner. In the Examen of his play, published in 1660, Corneille says:—

"This was my trial piece, and it was far from being written according to the rules, for at that time I did not know that there were any. I had only a little common-sense to guide me, and the plays of the late Hardy, whose pen was more fertile than polished, and a few modern writers who were not more correct than he was. . . . The novelty of this kind of comedy, of which there is no example in any language, and its *naïf* style, which gave a picture of the conversation of well-bred people, were no doubt the reason for this surprising good fortune which then made so much noise. Up to that time there had been nothing laughable in comedies except the ludicrous personages, such as the jesting valets, the Spanish Captains, the doctors, and so forth. This play gained approbation by the lively good humour of people in a rank above those that are seen in the comedies of Plautus and Terence, for they are only tradesmen. With all that, I confess that the audience were very simple-minded to applaud a play in which there was no sort of regularity in the plot."

Instead of a boasting air, which these lines convey if they are read too literally, we should understand rather the expressions of an honest, open-minded man, justly proud of his own success, and who wished to tell his readers the satisfaction that he himself had felt. Corneille was a proud man, but he was not a braggart.

Corneille was the first French dramatist who strove to write comedies which should represent in a natural manner the way in which people of the upper middle classes met each other in the world. He tried to show how those of his own rank talked and bore themselves among their equals. He explains himself in the " Avis au lecteur " to his second comedy, *La Veuve* :—

" Unless you are a man who is pleased with a simple style and with the subtlety of the plot, I will not ask you to read this play; its excellence is not in the brilliancy of the verses. It is a fine thing to make lines powerful and majestic. This display usually delights the mind, or at least dazzles it; but the subject should give rise to the occasion, otherwise you are making a show out of place, and though you gain the name of a poet you lose that of a judicious man. Comedy is only a picture of our actions and of our speech, and the perfection of the picture consists in the resemblance. On this principle I try to make my actors say nothing which those whom they are intended to represent might not reasonably say in their place, and to make them talk as well-bred persons, not as authors."

There is much here that is admirable, and thirty years later a better reading of the same ideas was given by Molière in his *Critique de l'École des Femmes*. But Molière knew intuitively what was wanted on the stage, and he carried out the lesson given by Corneille more fully and with stronger effect than he who had first tried to teach it.

When Corneille began to write he set to work gallantly, and in his early plays he did something to improve the tone of comedies. He set his face resolutely against indecencies and coarse laughter, and his example was noticed. Other instances besides Corneille's might be mentioned of dramatists between 1630 and 1660 who glorified the improved condition of the stage, especially in comedies;[1] but as we are now

---

[1] See Quinault's play *La Comédie sans Comédie*, Act I. sc. 5, given by M. Victor Fournel in the third volume of his *Contemporains de Molière*, and M. Fournel's note on page 85. There were of course exceptions to the general tone of improvement.

speaking of Corneille, some often-quoted lines from the last scene of his comedy, *L'Illusion Comique*, may be cited here :—

" A présent le théâtre,
Est en un point si haut que chacun l'idolâtre,
Et ce que votre temps voyoit avec mépris
Est aujourd'hui l'amour de tous les bons esprits.
.   .   .   .   .   .
D'ailleurs si par les biens on prise les personnes,
Le théâtre est un fief dont les rentes sont bonnes."

At that time the remuneration given to dramatic authors was very small, and it may be that the successes of Corneille's early plays helped to make the condition of the dramatist more lucrative. The practice of an author sharing in the profits made by his play had not been introduced. The actors as a body rented the theatre, they generally paid the author so much for each performance of his play, and they divided the profits amongst themselves. Mlle. Beaupré, an actress at the Hôtel de Bourgogne, is supposed to have expressed the feelings of the troop to which she belonged when she said : " Monsieur Corneille has done us great harm. We bought our plays formerly for three écus " [the écu was three francs] " a night ; everybody was accustomed to it, and we used to make money. Now Monsieur Corneille's plays cost us a great deal, and we make very little." It is impossible to say now how much money Corneille received for his plays ; he appears, however, to have been satisfied with what he got, and he expressed his delight at receiving his honorarium. That he, a provincial, who lived at Rouen, and only came up to Paris when his plays or other business demanded his presence, should have made men in the capital talk about him as one who, by his honest labour, had helped to clear away many of the disadvantages with which a career otherwise honourable was surrounded, was to him a source of much natural gratification. He was a man of high spirit, with a full idea of his own worth, but he deserves all the praise he gave to himself a few years later in his own proud line :—

" Je ne dois qu'à moi seul toute ma renommée."

When Corneille began to write, character-painting, as a distinctive feature in comedy, did not exist in France. He was the first dramatist, or one of the first, who really attempted it; he was perhaps the first who wrote comedies that were honestly French in thought and in manner. Some of his plots—those in the *Illusion Comique* and in the *Menteur*— were borrowed from Spain, but even there he discarded imitation and trusted to his own powers. He wished to portray men and women as he saw them, or as he imagined they might appear; and this endeavour was an innovation, for the idea of revealing the natural comedy of life in a well-bred manner had not been shown. So far Corneille was an originator. He had admirable intentions, but he followed the lessons that he set before himself too closely. When he said that "comedy is only a picture of our actions and of our speech," he spoke truly enough in a limited sense, but he omitted to say that other qualities are necessary to make the picture of comedy amusing or instructive; while of the higher purposes of satire, so well exemplified by Molière, as a means of showing men's foibles and condemning their faults, Corneille had apparently little idea. And a natural manner of talking will not suffice to make a natural comedy, though alone it will make a very dull one. But what is naturalness? Conversation which is natural in a room will not appear to be natural on the stage, and *vice versâ*. The naturalness of time, place, and manner must be taken into account, even though the same subject be related. Most of Corneille's scenes are embellishments of the actions of daily life, given in polished language and with some poetry; but usually they want mirth and merriment, and those light but pointed touches that really paint and which are so necessary for defining and showing clearly a character or a situation on the stage. Some of the traits in the character of Dorante in the *Menteur* are well told, and also in a different sense those of the braggadocio in the *Illusion*; but it would seem generally that Corneille feared to draw an original character in comedy lest he should give an exaggerated picture:—

> "Poets, like lovers, should be bold and dare,
> They spoil their business with an over care;
> And he, who servilely creeps after sense,
> Is safe, but ne'er will reach an excellence." [1]

---

[1] Prologue to Dryden's tragedy, *Tyrannic Love*.

In tragedy Corneille was as bold as the laws of the French
stage allowed him to be, but in comedy, which we are only
considering here, he never attained his highest level. His tone
is always delicate and refined, he has shown that he remarked
the verses of other playwrights, and he almost said when he
was a young man that he took pains with his own; but
as a rule his style wants playfulness and varied humour.
His comedies betray too often a want of fun or sparkle, and
they rarely make one laugh. So at least they appear to us
now. Instead of seeing the comedy of life through the
natural humours of the personages portrayed, we see formal
representations of people who meet each other with the
intention of being friendly, but who are prevented from
showing themselves for what they are by the etiquette of
conventionality. And yet Corneille was far from meaning
this. He wished to be gently amusing, and there is evidence
to show that he did amuse those who saw his plays when they
were first acted. Unfortunately or not, our more modern
tastes have become more exacting. One feels now that
Corneille's scenes in which men and women are brought
together and made to converse are wooden, and give a doll-
like resemblance. There is plenty of love-making of an
insipid kind, or rather it seems to be playing at making
love; but even then it shows no comfortableness or jollity.
Ladies are introduced for this purpose, and they generally
prove themselves to be masters of the situation. There is a
pleasant notion of gallantry about it all, in irreproachably
good taste, but shown with monotonous effect. The lovers in
one play are of the same type as the lovers in another play.
The men have no individuality, no distinctive features by which
Philiste may be recognised from Florame, or Léandre from
Alcidor. The heroines appear to be captivating at first sight,
they are amiable and willing to accept the attentions paid to
them; but when known they are either strong-minded, a
quality which no man likes in a wife, or they love only by
duty, which no man looks for in a mistress :—

> " His gallants are all faultless, his women divine,
> And comedy wonders at being so fine."

The stateliness or the magnificence of the manners shown does
much to kill the life and soul of the play.

Yet there must have been something in Corneille's comedies which pleased the people of those days; there must have been the expression of some sentiment which found an echo in the hearts, or at least in the minds, of those who heard his lines spoken and saw them acted by men and women who were the representatives of ladies and gentlemen in good society. The age of chivalry had passed away. Cervantes' novel had helped to kill it in France as elsewhere; but noble feelings in man die hard, they rarely pass away altogether. Chivalry had given way to gallantry—a watered form of chivalry, but which was practised more easily and on the whole was more agreeable. At that time gallantry was not only an amusement, it was a school through which every young man of birth had to pass who wished to be well considered or who hoped to gain soft smiles. Every fine gentleman paid his court to some lady, if only to show his breeding and to establish his claim as an *honnête homme*. In the 17th century an *honnête homme* meant a man of good address and polished manners, who could talk well and take his part agreeably in society, say pleasant things to ladies, knew what was being said and done in the world, was intelligent, considerate liberal-minded, obliging, and who on occasion could use his sword either for himself or for his friend. This was the type of hero Corneille wished to portray in his comedies, and the best instance of the type is Dorante in the *Menteur*. His lies are so charmingly told that they are among his qualifications.

In the Examen of his *Galerie du Palais* there are a few lines referring to a matter that is worth noticing. Corneille says that the personage of the nurse belonged to old comedy; it was preserved because few actresses appeared on the stage, and men used to play these parts wearing a mask; but he changed the nurse into the "suivante," and made a woman represent a woman. The suivante usually agreed with her mistress in everything; if the young lady had a lover, the waiting-woman was her confidante. In the fourth scene of a comedy by La Tuilerie, called *Crispin Bel Esprit*,[1] of a much later date (1681), there are a few bright lines that may be quoted.

[1] Reprinted by M. Victor Fournel in the first volume of his *Petites Comédies Rares et Curieuses du XVIIᵉ Siècle*.

Lise says to her young mistress :—

"Comment ? Vous étiez l'un de l'autre amoureux,
Et vous m'avez pu faire un secret de vos feux !
Allez, vous avez tort : l'emploi d'une suivante,
Madame, de tout temps, fut d'être confidente ;
Et c'est faire l'amour irrégulièrement,
Que d'avoir pu manquer en ce point seulement."

The part of the suivante was not often interesting or amusing. For this reason, perhaps, Molière did not make much use of her; or he altered the character, giving her a more active part to perform. She is seen with a brightness of her own as Dorine in the *Tartuffe*. After Molière's time the character of these women changed : they were always self-interested, and they were made to lend their hands to ignoble trickeries.

It is said that Corneille was one of the five authors whom Richelieu employed to write the verses of plays that the autocratic minister wished to have acted on the stage. But whatever the total labours of his colleagues may have been, Corneille's part in this singular joint undertaking appears to have been small. Richelieu arranged in his own mind the plan of a play, *La Comédie des Tuileries*, and set his five pensioners to work upon it after having told each of them what he was to do. Corneille was entrusted with the third act, and he deviated from the instructions he had received. The Cardinal got angry, and told him " qu'il fallait avoir un esprit de suite "; that is, bring himself into line with the others and obey orders. The play, however, was acted before the queen in the year 1635. Little else is known of the work done by Corneille under Richelieu's command. The poet was evidently hurt by the treatment he had received, for he withdrew from Paris to Rouen, where he then lived, saying that he was called there by his private affairs.[1]

In the *Illusion Comique* Corneille introduced a personage known as " Le Matamore." He is well shown, after his kind ; he is the best French example of a poor type. This was a stock character well known on the older French stage, but hitherto it had been confined to farce, and with one exception it had not appeared in a play in verse until Corneille showed it in

[1] *Œuvres de P. Corneille*, Édition des Grands Écrivains de la France, ii. 305-308.

the *Illusion*.[1] The Matamore was a descendant of the Miles
Gloriosus in Latin comedy, like Bobadil and Bessus on our
English stage; he was put on to the stage in France to make
people laugh, but after the middle of the 17th century
the character was not seen. A few quotations will be given
to show that Corneille put the rhodomontades of his Matamore into full sounding lines. His valet advises him to wait
until he has collected his army before beginning fresh con-
quests, but he is indignant at the idea that his own arm
should not be thought sufficient :—

> " Le seul bruit de mon nom renverse les murailles,
> Défait les escadrons et gagne les batailles.
> Mon courage invaincu contre les empereurs
> N'arme que la moitié de ses moindres fureurs ;
> D'un seul commandement que je fais aux trois Parques
> Je dépeuple l'État des plus heureux monarques ;
> Le foudre est mon canon et les Destins mes soldats :
> Je couche d'un revers mille ennemis à bas.
> D'un souffle je réduis leurs projets en fumée,
> Et tu m'oses parler cependant d'une armée ! "

There is a good bow-wow noise here which serves admirably to show the ridicule that the dramatist wished to cast
upon his personage; and Corneille was always at his best
when moved by some inward passion of indignation or of
tenderness. The Matamore is made to affect gallantry because
other men did the same. As he is a warrior some lady must
be dear to him, and when he recollects his mistress, his
thoughts fly instantly from deeds of glory to acts of love :—

> " Et pensant au bel œil qui tient ma liberté
> Je ne suis plus qu'amour, que grâce, que beauté."

The man is of course an arrant coward. Hit him hard and
he is like an air-ball exploded by a pin prick. At one time
he is alone, he thinks he sees his enemies coming towards him,
and he prepares to run away :—

> " J'ai le pied pour le moins aussi bon que l'épée.
> Tout de bon je les vois : c'est fait, il faut mourir ;
> J'ai le corps si glacé que je ne puis courir."

Corneille's lines do much to put an appearance of life into
an absurd character; but, except as an example of what used
to amuse people long ago, these " Spanish Captains " do not
offer much interest now.

[1] *Œuvres de P. Corneille*, ii. 424.

Corneille's best comedy, *Le Menteur*, acted in 1642, six years after the *Illusion*, contains some scenes which, when well played, produce a capital effect on the stage. Dorante lies splendidly, and he is always a gentleman. His narrative to his father (Act II. sc. 5, 7), telling him how he had been compelled to marry a girl who did not exist, is amusing and graphic, but it is too long to quote. In the next scene Dorante says to his valet, Cliton :—

"Oh ! l'utile secret que mentir à propos !

Cliton.

Quoi ? ce que vous disiez n'est pas vrai ?

Dorante.

Pas deux mots ;
Et tu ne viens d'ouïr qu'un trait de gentillesse
Pour conserver mon âme et mon cœur à Lucresse.

Cliton.

Quoi ? la montre, l'épée, avec le pistolet . . .

Dorante.

Industrie ! "

In Act IV. sc. 1 Dorante tells Cliton that he has just had a duel with Alcippe :—

"Je le mets hors d'état d'être jamais malade.
Il tombe dans son sang.

Cliton.

A ce compte il est mort ?

Dorante.

Je le laissai pour tel.

Cliton.

Certes, je le plains son sort.
Il était honnête homme."

Immediately these words are spoken Alcippe appears, and Cliton whispers to Dorante :—

"Cette place pour vous est commode à rêver."

And a few lines later:—

"Les gens que vous tuez se portent assez bien."

In the next scene :—

"*Dorante.*

Quoi, mon combat te semble un conte imaginaire ?

Cliton.

Je croirai tout, Monsieur, pour ne vous pas déplaire ;
Mais vous en contez tant à toute heure, en tous lieux,
Qu'il faut bien de l'esprit avec vous, et bons yeux.
More, juif, ou chrétien, vous n'épargnez personne."

Cliton asks his master to tell him his secret of being able
to lie so well, and he will serve him without wages. The
secret consists in knowing a few words of Hebrew, but these
are difficult to pronounce :—

" *Cliton.*

Vous savez donc l'hébreu ?

Dorante.

L'hébreu ? parfaitement.
J'ai dix langues, Cliton, à mon commandement.

Cliton.

Vous auriez besoin de dix des mieux nourries
Pour fournir tour à tour à tant de menteries ;
Vous les hâchez menu comme chair à pâtés.
Vous avez tout le corps bien plein de vérités,
Il n'en sort jamais une."

There is some humour in these lines, but mirth was not
Corneille's strongest characteristic. Had he shown it oftener,
his comedies would hold a higher place.

In 1637 Desmarets brought out his comedy *Les Visionnaires*, and it was very successful. This is one of those plays
that please the town for a few years while the crazes it laughs
at are followed, and then is forgotten when people no longer
take an interest in the follies they have ceased to admire.
It would be unfair, however, to belittle Desmarets because
he had not the strong or playful humour which makes the
satire in a comedy appreciated by people who live long after
the play was written. Though the *Visionnaires* was commonly spoken of as "l'inimitable comédie," the characters
are so forced that many who saw it must have regarded the
play as a piece of elegant fooling. When that is well done
it may give very good amusement. The play was meant to
be a caricature, but it certainly gives an indication of good
comedy. It is pleasantly satirical, though the raillery is a
little heavy. The plot is slight, and the scenes are linked
together only just enough to give an idea of a story. The

comedy laughs at some of the absurdities that were current among fashionable men and women in Paris in the latter part of the reign of Louis XIII. The visionary ideas are ridiculed in a way that pleased those who saw the play, and they enjoyed the satire all the more because it was thoroughly French, and because it was handled in a French spirit without the aid of foreign imitation.

After Corneille, Rotrou was the most popular dramatist in the second quarter of the 17th century; and he enjoyed the position, enviable or not, of poet to the troop at the Hôtel de Bourgogne theatre. I must speak of him shortly, for though he wrote a great many plays of all sorts between 1628 and 1650, his comedies have been less highly thought of than his tragedies. *La Sœur* is perhaps the best of his comedies, and it contains some bright lines which for the moment are pleasant reading. The valet in the comedy, who has concocted the story which forms the subject of the play, says to his master's father :—

" Nous venons de Turquie, et dans cette contrée
Des plus religieux l'église est ignorée ;
C'est un climat de maux, dépourvu de tous biens,
Car les Turcs, comme on sait, sont fort mauvais chrétiens."

If any one after reading Molière's *Étourdi* had been told that these lines were to be found there, and that they had been spoken by Mascarille, he would not probably be much surprised. Rotrou's plays showed an improvement in style and in language, but they were for the most part substantially borrowed from Latin, from Italian, or from Spanish authors. In this way, in his comedies, he was an imitator like other playwrights of his age. A romantic plot, if well handled, will always be popular on the stage, and it was in romantic plots and incidents that the Spanish dramatists were strong, though they show no careful delineation of character. Their plays and their novels were used freely ; their plays were put on the French stage often with no more alteration than was necessary to suit French requirements. The marriage of Louis XIII. to the daughter of Philip III. of Spain gave greater vogue to the French taste for Spanish subjects. This marriage took place in 1615. The year following, the first part of *Don Quixote* was translated into French ; the second part appeared two years later. The translation of the immortal novel naturally confirmed the liking for Spanish incidents of romance.

Scarron's comedies, like others of the time, are now dull reading, but he had a certain vivacity and strength of style which was his own; and Molière seems to have thought well of them, for he put them on to his stage oftener than the comedies of any other playwright before his day. Scarron's plays (1645-1655) may all be ranked as comedies. Two are called tragi-comedies, because somebody is killed in them or dies; but Scarron was essentially a comic writer. His tone was often burlesque; had he attempted a high style he would, in spite of himself, have botched his lines with absurdities. All his plays were borrowed from Spanish authors, the plots are Spanish clothed in a French dress. Scarron took the incidents as he wanted them, and attempted to introduce character by grafting his own wit on to a Spanish story. The result is not splendid, but it has a show of brightness and gaiety, in comparison with other comedies of the time, due rather to his sense of fun than to his imagery or powers of observation. He held his pen easily; and even in his long speeches he endeavoured to give the idea of a man speaking because he had something to say, and not of a person making a soliloquy with the principal object of talking. The audiences in those days expected at least one long speech from each of the principal personages. They liked listening to an actor who could speak well the lines that were set down for him; and the actors liked having to speak thirty or forty consecutive lines, for they could thus show their powers of elocution.

In the dedication of *Le Marquis Ridicule* Scarron says that "in his opinion this is the best written play he has given to the public." The story told is not especially good, but there is a certain pleasure in following it out, because some of the scenes are well described and the situations clearly shown. Perhaps Scarron's best character appears in this play in the person of the fantastic Marquis.

Don Japhet d'Arménie has been considered the best of his plays, and here, as in all his other comedies, the merit lies chiefly in the humour of the scenes described. Don Japhet wishes to say who he is. He begins:—

" Du bon père Noé j'ai l'honneur de descendre ;
Noé, qui sur les eaux fit flotter sa maison
Quand tout le genre humain but plus que de raison."

At that time there was a rage for burlesque; it suited
Scarron's humour, and of burlesque writers he was the chief.
His fun is not generally refined, and it may descend into
buffoonery. But he is bold and straightforward; he says
what he wants to say and has done with it. Nearly all of
his plays were acted at the Marais. He was one of the principal writers for that theatre; his plays were welcomed by the
troop, for they found favour with those who went to see them.
When speaking of Scarron something should be said of the
position of the valets in old French comedy. They are the
best part of Scarron's work. But the best instance by far of
these characters is Mascarille, in Molière's *Étourdi*. The
motive for the valet in comedies was to plan schemes for his
master, to amuse the audience, and to make them laugh. The
man was a thief, a rogue, a liar, one who, if he got his deserts,
would be in his proper place chained to a galley; yet following
the idea given in the play he enlists our sympathies, we pity
him and wish him success in his undertakings. He knew
right from wrong, and did wrong, not because he was vicious
and liked evil things, but because he could not help himself.
He had an idea of honour among thieves. He served his master
faithfully, thought of nobody else, was eager and willing in his
service, though for his pains he often got blows and no wages.
His lot was cast, and the poor fellow had to make the best of it
and be contented with fine promises. He lived on terms of
great intimacy with his master; that was the bright spot in his
existence. He compensated himself by his freedom of speech,
and by telling his master in plain words what he thought of him.
He was free with his tongue in giving good counsel. The master
did not want a lecture, but he did want assistance in his love
affairs. The servant's head was the best for planning schemes,
hence in many comedies his was the most important part. In
Scarron's play *Jodelet ou le Maître Valet*, Don Juan asks his
valet to change clothes with him, and Jodelet answers:—

" Et ne pourrai-je pas, pour mieux représenter
Le seigneur Don Juan, quelquefois charpenter
Sur votre noble dos ? Bien souvent, ce me semble,
Vous en usez ainsi."

Don Juan replies :—

"Quand nous sommes ensemble,
Tous seuls et sans témoins, oui, je te le permets."

Recognising the position of the valet on the stage, there is a note of comedy in these lines, and they probably amused the young men among the audience who heard them spoken.

It is in these little touches that Scarron is seen at his best; unfortunately they are not very frequent. He sought for his materials among Spanish novels and plays, and so long as he produced a comedy that was liked, he was easy in his mind how he had done it. His narratives, of which there is an ample share, and his dialogues, show a freshness of speech which was all his own. Freshness of speech is a great element in a comedy. But little of it is seen in the early French comedies that have been printed, though in the unprinted farces it was probably abundant. It will hardly be found, I think, to a fair extent before Scarron's time in any dramatist who wrote more than one comedy except Larivey. All of Larivey's comedies, however, were in prose. Corneille is no doubt superior as a writer to Scarron, but Scarron's comedies show more raciness of language, and his style is more truly comic than that of any dramatist who wrote in verse before Molière. Corneille had not Scarron's sense of humour, he had rather the feeling of a man of letters; but poor Scarron sought relief from his bodily infirmities by indulging in his fun. M. Louis Moland says :[1] "The burlesque poet has generally been treated with some contempt. Molière did not feel this. Perhaps he borrowed from Scarron more than from any of his contemporaries. He did not forget how popular had been *Jodelet Maître Valet*, or *Don Japhet d'Arménie*, and he did justice to their author on many occasions."

In the middle of the 17th century, and about the time that Scarron's comedies were being acted at the Théâtre du Marais, Boisrobert's comedies were for the most part played at the Hôtel de Bourgogne. The abbé Boisrobert was nominally a churchman, but he seems to have liked the stage better than ecclesiastical work, and was nicknamed the abbé Mondory. It is doubtful whether Mondory, the late chief of the troop at the Marais, would have felt that a compliment was paid to him.

[1] *Œuvres de Molière*, 1st ed. ii. 316.

Boisrobert was a sort of gentleman-jester to the Cardinal de Richelieu. It was from Boisrobert that Richelieu heard of the meetings of a small circle of men who came together once a week to talk about books; and from these meetings, against the wish of the nine or twelve friends, Richelieu founded the French Academy in 1635. Boisrobert wrote five tragedies and one tragi-comedy before his first comedy was acted. Then other comedies followed, of which *La Folle Gageure, Les Trois Orontes,* and *La Belle Plaideuse* are the best. At a time when comedy was bound by fetters of different kinds Boisrobert tried to make a step towards freedom. He borrowed from various sources, but did not take Spanish plays as the groundwork for his comedies so completely as did Rotrou, Scarron, and Thomas Corneille, and he wished to give a French tone of thought to his characters and to the incidents that he related. His comedies had their day, and more should not be expected of them than a feeble picture of people when they chose to indulge in romantic ideas. Boisrobert tried to show the feeling of romance, but fell short in his attempt. It would seem that he liked writing for the stage, though he could not, from want of imagination, succeed as well as he wished. He knew partly what was required, and his dialogue runs quickly and is easily read. There is a note of comedy in his plays, but he was not big enough to make it strongly felt. His scenes are washy. They give the notion of wanting a firmer hand than his to knit them together. While for real characterisation and for the lessons to be taught by honest satire, they will not be found in any comic dramatist before Molière.

Thomas Corneille — the brother of Pierre, "le grand Corneille," and nineteen years his junior — wrote eight comedies before the time at which this sketch is brought to a close. They were all borrowed from Spanish authors, and do not otherwise deserve remark. They have an appearance of forced brightness, but as comedies have little interest. They are not unlike the comedies of Scarron, though higher in tone, but have not his vivacity or sense of humour. Thomas Corneille was a facile and a very successful playwright; and some of his plays, either those composed by himself or in collaboration with another, in which he probably did the lion's share, had the good fortune of being acted oftener than any other plays in the 17th century. But these successes came while Molière was at the Palais Royal theatre or after his death, and came perhaps more from tragedy than from comedy, though among his comedies *Le Baron Albikrac* and *La Devineresse* were very popular. It is singular that among the dramatists and other French writers in the first half of the 17th century a large proportion were born in the province of Normandy. Boileau said of Thomas Corneille: " Pauvre Thomas ! Tes vers, comparés avec ceux de ton aîné, font bien voir que tu n'es qu'un cadet de Normandie." In fact, the greater reputation of Pierre Corneille has damaged Thomas in the world's esteem. In tragedy he was far from his brother's equal, and was much inferior to Racine; and in comedy he was a very long way indeed below Molière. These men were his contemporaries, consequently he has been overshadowed by them.

I have not been lavish of praise in speaking of French comedies before Molière's day, but as a matter of fact very few Frenchmen who know what their early comic drama was like have extolled it highly. According to an anecdote, which need not be repeated for the sake of a bon mot, Boileau said to Louis XIV. that until Molière wrote there was no good comedy in France;[1] and I believe that his verdict has not been substantially set aside.

There is some difficulty in speaking of the pleasure to be found in these old comedies. I have tried to like them and to interest myself for the time in the characterisation of the personages and of the incidents described, but on the whole with small success. I imagine comedy to be a mirthful dramatic representation of the humours of a people, and if their humours are shown fairly they will tell what the people are like better than any other kind of description. In comedy we look for a mirthful picture, with some satire or raillery, of men's likes and dislikes, their thoughts, their actions, their aspirations, their amusements, their hopes and their fears, their foibles and their faults. It is only partially true to say that human nature is everywhere the same. Manners are not

[1] *Œuvres de Jean Racine*, Édition des Grands Écrivains de la France, 1st ed. i. 290 note—continuation of note from previous page : and 2nd ed. i. 297 note 2.

C

everywhere the same; and as time progresses they change gradually, especially in the better classes of society. It is, of course, difficult to see in old comedies the humours of a people of nearly three hundred years ago with the same eyes as did those who were alive when the comedies were written. Still, one may look at the plays broadly and try to learn from them how far they exhibited the tastes and the pleasures of the age intended to be represented, and try to see how the men and women who took their parts in them were made to show themselves and what they were like. Much is left to the imagination; yet if the idea just given of comedy be accepted, I think that comedy will not often be found except in a dead-alive way in French plays before the second half of the 17th century.

When we consider what a delicate thing is the comedy of manners, how slow was its birth in England, and how long it took to grow and flourish amongst ourselves, we cannot be surprised that its birth should have been slow also in France. Before Molière's day their comic writers were apprentices. Many of them set bravely to work to learn their art, but instead of trusting to their own brains they used too much those of others. Consequently they fell into the vice of imitation. As in other countries in the youthful days of the drama they wrote much in verse, and this created a wish to exhibit fine ideas. Their ambitions had their good sides, for it is certainly well that a drama should seek to elevate by inspiring wholesome sentiments; and high ideas are perhaps seen to more advantage in verse than in plain-running prose. The desire to appear fine prompted also the English dramatists in the latter part of the reign of Elizabeth and under James I. That was a proud age in England, and the writers for the stage who courted popular favour expressed themselves proudly. The great dramatists had something more to show than their pride, but·the lines of many of the others are often hollow enough and have little meaning. The glories of the drama came later in France than with us, and were not won by so many competitors. But when their comic dramatists tried to show what were the thoughts and ways of living of the people described, one feels that they were hampered by the laws of the unities and by the laws of versification, and that they thought too much of exhibiting a grand behaviour and nice deportment in their personages. Their plays are neither imaginative nor poetical; they are so stilted and stiff that comedy is crushed out of them. The comic stage, instead of giving hearty amusement, became too largely a school for mental exercises. This did not arise so much from a wish on the part of the public, or of the actors, as from advice given to authors by pretended critics. Pedantry got the upper hand of popular sentiment; and formal comedy, without sap, without freshness, without strength, was admired and thought to be fine. A hundred years earlier, when farce was current, people enjoyed it; but farce with its laughter was now thought to be coarse. And it would seem that at the Hôtel de Bourgogne theatre pedantry thought that laughter was irregular in comedies, because it was loudest when farces were being played. It was therefore degraded and put out of court. This was a pity, for, like charity, laughter covers a multitude of sins. Something good would have come from it, and by degrees the coarseness would have diminished. In the 15th century and the first half of the 16th, when farces were common in the theatres, they were printed and presumably read; but few of the early 17th century farces were printed, and of those only a small number have been preserved. Yet in our day editions have been made of the *Chansons de Gaι 'tier Garguille* and of the *Œuvres de Tabarin*!

The following paragraph, written by George Henry Lewes, may be quoted here with advantage :—

"It is worthy of remark that in each country, when the separation of the profane from the sacred element took place in the representations originally founded by the priests—when, in short, the first step was taken towards the first formation of a drama—there was a struggle between the scholars and the popular writers. As soon as the drama became an art the scholars naturally looked to the ancient models. They could conceive no other form of excellence. What the ancients had done the moderns strove to imitate ; otherwise they would never rise above the vulgar. In Italy and in Germany the scholars were triumphant. A lifeless abortion was the result. Italy had to wait for Alfieri and Goldoni before it had a drama ; Germany had to wait for Lessing. But in England and Spain the scholars were beaten." [1]

---

[1] *The Spanish Drama. Lope de Vega and Calderon*, p. 18—a small volume published by Charles Knight in 1846.

Though Lewes omitted to take into account the popular improvised drama in Italy, known as "La Commedia dell' arte," what he says shows a large part of the foundation of the history of modern dramatic literature in Europe. In France for many years the scholars had the upper hand, and their influence was visible long after the popular writers had arisen. What the ancients had done Frenchmen strove to imitate, because they could not imagine anything better. After the renaissance of the drama they tried to form their tragedies on Greek models; and the most highly accredited writers for the comic stage, wishing to discard farce, took their comedies from Italy and from Spain—Italy having borrowed in the first instance from Greece and from Rome.

The chief drawbacks to the enjoyment of French comedy before Molière's time are, in my opinion, that the plays were imitations; that the dramatists were content to follow each other too much in the same groove, taking existing comedies for their models, instead of working from the world as they saw it and trying to imagine for themselves how men and women speak and act when they are together. As regards imitation and routine, Pierre Corneille should be honourably excepted, for he did try to carve out a way of his own, and so far he was original. On the whole, some show of comedy was doubtless produced in the long run by the mechanical methods in vogue, and the plays were gradually becoming more French and a little more inspiriting; but the writers would have done better if they had trusted more to their own observation and less to books. The plays and the composition of the plays were borrowed, first from Latin, afterwards from Italian, and later from Spanish models; long speeches form a large part of the dialogue; characterisation in any animate sense was unknown; therefore to us who live more than two hundred and fifty years after the plays were written they appear lifeless, barren of almost everything that is human except long-winded talk. There is a great deal too much talking and far too little done; the action is drowned in a sea of words. You want to interest yourself in the personages before you, whether you like them or not, and in their concerns, in the way they tell their story and show themselves to be what they are; but this is set forth in such a heavy-handed manner that you are awfully bored by the dulness of the picture. As plays, these comedies are essentially undramatic; for the sense of quick movement, of touch and go, of sparkle, of raciness of thought or of expression, is not in them. In the great majority of comedies the language spoken by one man is like that spoken by another of the same rank, that of one woman is like that of another of the same condition; consequently it is half colourless in portraying the features of the various personages. And one is tempted to think that not unfrequently a leading part or two might be taken out of the middle of one comedy and put into the middle of another, without showing much difference in the mental attitude of the speaker. At the same time, it is only fair to add that vitality in characterisation has always been a difficult matter, and that within the last three hundred years the power of showing people's characters clearly by the way they talk to each other has not been given to many writers.

Running abreast with the spirit of imitation, the obedience to authority, which became almost compulsory with those authors who wished to have their plays accepted and to stand well with the critics, exercised a baneful influence on French comedy. The restraints which limited the scope of the action in a play compelled the dramatists to plan their comedies after some imaginary model of excellence which existed nowhere. The writers did not try to show the humours of life, taking human characteristics as their guide, but rather strove to interest their audiences in intended romantic or heroic scenes and incidents. These, however, were painted coldly and in a pompous manner. The Spanish drama was romantic. The French playwrights tried to be romantic also; but the French fettered themselves by rules which the Spaniards disregarded, and which, instead of guiding them, prevented a natural use of their powers. The rules were too strict, and bound those who used them too severely. Comedy is like a free horse that should be ridden with a firm but light hand and a close but easy seat; and the writer of a comedy, as he is planning his incidents and forming his characters, should feel that he is free to dispose of them as he will, governed only by the laws of composition and by the habits and fancies that guide men and women in their different walks of life. But the "genre noble" was a feature a great deal thought of in French comedy, and all the personages were made to behave according to the customs of a strictly conventional etiquette. And they were not allowed to do anything contrary to the administrative laws of the unities. As we look now at the comedies that were acted at the Hôtel de Bourgogne theatre for a generation after Molière's birth, it would seem that there was no comic dramatist strong enough and lively enough with natural fun, or wit, or humour, to take the matter into his own hands, overthrow bad custom, and write a play that was really good comedy and which would heartily amuse an audience and send them to their homes rejoicing. The critics held that farce was low; they tabooed it, and put it outside the pale. Farce is not high art, but perhaps it is better than pretended comedy so dull that there is no comedy in it.

The comic ideal sought after was a high one, but its principles were too abstract and too authoritative. The playwrights were young at their work, they were often conscientiously ambitious; but they had not learned that the play of life must be shown mirthfully, often irregularly, and without absoluteness. They aimed at conceiving a drama which should be at once romantic and formally decorous. The romance was maimed because it was not allowed to be carried out fairly; and in plays that should amuse, ceremonious decorum, unrelieved by laughter or by poetical or imaginative pictures, is worthless. In the course of one play a reader thinks to himself ten times :—

> "J'aime mieux un vice commode
> Qu'une fatigante vertu."

The Parisians of one or two hundred years earlier were bright-witted, and they had their current topics of conversation as well as those who live now. These found their place in the soties and other impromptu plays, satirical personal allusions were introduced and were put into words which were either spoken or sung; and so the Vaudeville—song of the town—was created. This is the meaning that should be given to Boileau's line :—

> "Le Français né malin forma le Vaudeville."

These light plays were really the comedies of the time. From the farces which had been popular before the middle of the 16th century, if they had not been too hardly and unfairly judged, comedy would have come to life gradually; but according to ideas that were ruling in the second quarter of the 17th century, farce bore much the same relation to comedy as the slang of young men in Paris of the present day does to an academical discourse.

Of the dramatists who wrote between 1550 and 1650 a few names stand out of men who tried to originate; but though changes took place gradually, they came perhaps rather from a slow and general awakening to better ideas than because good examples were followed. Jodelle, in 1552, in his single comedy *Eugène*, drew a picture of contemporary life; nearly a generation later, Larivey, a manufacturer of plays, but a semi-originator, frenchified in a way of his own Italian comedies, and gave to his plays a good deal of vivacity and quick movement; (a generation afterwards, Hardy was working at his tragedies and tragi-comedies like a young horse in a plough to break away from the older classical school—and if report speaks truly he did more than any one else to initiate a new system—but if he wrote any comedies, they have not come down to us;) shortly before Hardy's death Pierre Corneille appeared, and he strove to conceive comedy that should represent a natural and a decent way of living, and he tried to introduce characterisation into his plays, though he succeeded but feebly in this attempt. I have mentioned the names of a few who wrote comedies after Pierre Corneille; but for the most part, though their style may be a little easier, they worked on the well-beaten lines and showed little originality. They did as their fathers had done before them, and in this way tradition was maintained and inanimate types kept their place on the stage. The chief change that took place, was working from Spanish instead of from Italian models, and this brought with it a change of manner. Italian impromptu comedy was light; their written comedy, born later, was heavy: at first the former prevailed in France, afterwards the latter. Spanish comedy, though romantic and dignified and lacking in real characterisation, was light-handed, but it was not suited to the tastes of the French people; yet French writers adopted it, less fully than they had previously adopted Italian comedy, but still working from it because it furnished them with incidents.

And though French comedies were written in carefully prepared verse, their language does not often command attention by the expression of poetical ideas. It is prosaic in sound and in feeling, it was meant to be stately, and it is usually devoid of humour or wit. Most French playwrights until about 1640 or 1645 did not show a style suitable to comedy when they were exhibiting their personages before their audience. They wished to avoid a conversational manner, they meant to create a show of magnificence, often out of place, and they were dull. They were formal instead of being refined, and they do not seem to have understood that comedies in verse as well as in prose should be mirthful, and that the audience should be made merry over them.

Any sort of fun to be seen in the regular Paris theatres in the first half of the 17th century, was reserved for the farce which was played as an after-piece. Before farce was allowed to die out at the Hôtel de Bourgogne, perhaps in the fourth or fifth decade, the actors had quite enough vitality and mother-wit of their own to amuse their audiences without borrowing a show of gaiety which did not belong to them. But not much opportunity was given to them to exercise their powers. Good-humoured farce full of satirical banter—"malice," though not in its natural sense,—has always been essentially a French quality, and from this, if authors and actors, unconstrained by laws which they were told had come from Aristotle, had been allowed to have their way, comedy would have sprung. The light plays, or farces, acted when Molière was a boy, were crude, silly, and coarse, but they often had vitality ; they sprang from the thoughts of the people, they showed roughly in a ludicrous manner the lives of those who acted them, and of those who enjoyed them. They were their own offspring, their own flesh and blood, not adopted bastards borrowed from a foreign land. Farce has always been the mother of comedy, and from it comedy would have at length emerged, at first nearly invisible, but it would have come to light after a slow birth. Decently behaved farce might have been allowed to exist by the side of comedy as its humble rival; but the theatrical critics, who did not know what comedy was because they had hardly seen it, gave themselves pretentious airs, and wished to send farce ruthlessly into banishment. We are told, however,

that farce was played at the Théâtre du Marais for some years
after it was driven from the Hôtel de Bourgogne, the older and
more important theatre. By farce I fancy we should understand here small light comedies or trifles, written only with
the intention of affording amusement, and which were often
thought to be not worth printing.

Molière knew the tastes of his countrymen, and he knew
how absurd were the laws which tried to govern those tastes.
It would seem that he wished to learn his lesson gradually, for
he foresaw that it was difficult. But he set about it in his own
way. He began by writing farces, two of which only have
been preserved. Then he wrote two plays taken straight from
Italy, but into which he introduced vivacity and his own
characterisation. Then came the *Précieuses Ridicules*, his first
purely French comedy, though it was at the same time a caricature. In his next play the plot was mainly Italian, but the
style was altogether French. The comedies seen on the Italian
stage often influenced him in his later work, but the tendency
of his mind was always to make characterisation the most important feature in his plays. Such a lesson has never been
learned all at once. Molière's predecessors, if they attempted
it, succeeded but a little way. They began their work at the
wrong end. They wrote their five-act comedies in verse before
they had learned how important are the details and smaller
incidents in a play, that these should be told graphically; and
they did not see how essential it is that comedy should show
the features of characterisation, both of the personages and of the
incidents, in a true and lively manner. One should remember,
however, that the special requirements of the stage were little
understood then, and that audiences were more easily contented than they are now with what was given to them.
Before the days of gas people used candles or small lamps
after dark, and were contented with the dim light because they
knew of none brighter. As they stand, the comedies in verse
that were acted in the French theatres in the first half of the
17th century appear to us now to be more like dramatic
poems—sadly deficient in poetry and in the thoughts that
poetry should inspire—than plays intended to amuse an
audience. The presence of long speeches does much to give this
appearance. Yet Molière, who ranks much higher as a drama-

tist than as a poet, even in most of his early comedies in verse gave long speeches that were instinct with life in marking the features of his personages or in describing the incidents in his story. A show of quickness of thought, a more or less rapid exchange of opinions upon the event of the moment, and a brightness of expression, are very necessary in comedy ; and Molière's first plays in verse—*Don Garcie de Navarre* excepted —show that he understood the business of a dramatist very much better than his predecessors. Their plays gave far too often pictures of men making speeches while others had to stand by and listen to them until it was their turn to talk. However fine the lines may be, work of that kind shows self-importance and egotism rather than comedy; and reading plays which leave such an impression is not exhilarating.

It is difficult to determine how far any one dramatist was the founder of comedy in his own country. For comedy did not arise suddenly; it was not created all at once by the strength of one man's genius, any more than was Greek sculpture or the art of painting in Italy. Its birth, like that of other arts, was gradual, formed by successive attempts until a picture, idealistic or real, or, better still, one that shows a mixture of both, of what might be supposed to happen in the play of life had been drawn. And the comedy of manners will hardly be found in any state of excellence until society had so far progressed that a cultivated and familiar intercourse between men and women took place with tolerable frequency. It cannot be said, of course, that the art of comedy has always been progressive. As in other arts, there have been times when it flourished; then for a generation or more it has been decadent; and it has afterwards acquired a fresh and generally a different kind of strength. But as regards the early French comic drama, when all is urged about the claims of Jodelle, of Larivey, of Pierre Corneille, as founders of comedy in France, Molière was in truth the first French comic dramatist who gave a true, amusing, and lively representation of the humours and actions of men and women in his own country. Molière was the first who knew how to form his characters so well that their personations are still studied with care, and whose scenes or whose lines are remembered for their pleasantry or their wit. He, too, was the first who taught that strong satire in comedy may be put to noble uses, and who knew at the same time how to show it with good comic effect. There had been earlier comic dramatists—Mairet, Desmarets, Scarron, Boisrobert—who deserved the distinctions they had won, but neither their grasp of human life nor their sympathies were shown broadly or vividly enough to attract much notice after Molière's more spirited representations had appeared. They had created no pictures, showing the features of comedy, which could stand the test of comparison with his. Corneille's *Menteur* was the last but one of his comedies, and it has been thought to be the best; the *Étourdi* was the first of Molière's—after his farces—and it is certainly not his best. These are the only plays of these two writers that can be spoken of together; and I think it is felt that Molière's comedy is the brighter of the two and more natural in the improbabilities related, because they are better told and shown with greater fun.

THE LIFE OF MOLIÈRE

CHAPTER I

BIRTH AND PARENTAGE

OF all the writers commonly included in the term "le siècle de Louis XIV.," there are none so widely popular as La Fontaine and Molière. They were the two most original authors of their time, and of French classics they are among the most frequently quoted. In France La Fontaine is the prince of fabulists, among dramatists Molière is the greatest; and perhaps they will both be studied when their contemporaries are forgotten. Sympathy and humanity, a fellow-feeling with and for others, were their strongest characteristics. For these writers speak from the heart to the heart, they appeal to the intelligence and become favourites with everybody. They knew so well the feelings of the men and animals they wished to portray, that in making them talk to each other they could counterfeit their words, imitate their tones of voice, and so characterise them by their speech and personate them. Without the touch peculiar to familiarity, which comes generally from sympathy, no man can be a dramatist or a novelist in the sense of representing the thoughts or manners of his fellow-creatures, and of making others interested in his pictures. Brain-power alone is not sufficient. We may all be sure that without the instinctive chord of sympathy, Scott could not have created the strong interest in his scenes and characters which these undoubtedly possess; Dickens's fanciful or idealistic pictures would not have their clearness; Shakespeare could not have given us Coriolanus, Rosalind, or Falstaff; nor Molière Alceste, Agnès, or his different Sganarelles. La Fontaine's name will only be mentioned incidentally in these pages, but it will be part of my endeavour to show in what spirit Molière looked at the men and women among whom he lived and in what tone he satirised them.

To feel the seriousness of Molière's comedies a reader must first learn for himself what his laughter was like and what it meant. The tone of mirth or of laughter in any comedy is one of its most important features. Racine's *Plaideurs*, his only comedy, is bright and amusing, but his fun is not so open as that of Molière; and the sparkle in Molière is more spontaneous than in Beaumarchais, whose effort to appear gay is a little too evident. And both Racine and Beaumarchais lacked Molière's earnestness and his power of making us laugh at people's oddities, while he sympathises with them in their troubles. Some of us Englishmen who enjoy the hearty laughter in Shakespeare's comedies can hardly force a smile from the wit of Congreve. If the smile does come there it is painful. The comedy in his plays is real enough, though the manners exhibited are artificial. Actual men and women are shown, and they are reprobates against honest living. With no comfortableness or jollity, they make sport with vice and are as cold-blooded as fishes. They were wicked, not because they liked it, but because it was fashionable to be so. The pictures are true of their kind, but no sorrow, no anger is shown in painting them. That was not the case with Molière, and his plays are singularly free from objectionable scenes. Sheridan comes nearer to Molière in thought, and is more like him. He has something of his playfulness, of his kindliness, though none of his grimness; and several of Sheridan's scenes recall to mind those of Molière as though he had been prompted by them. But Molière wrote many more plays than Sheridan, and he had greater powers of personal characterisation; his "vis comica" was stronger, and his pictures of comedy are fuller and leave a more lasting impression. The way in which Molière mixed together earnestness and ridicule, comedy and farce, sadness and laughter, and showed his purpose in a light-handed manner and with true comic effect, is very wonderful indeed. To learn this you should read his big comedies and his lighter ones together, conciliate them and see how the different pictures came from the pen of one writer. A strong characteristic in Molière's satire is that it is honest and pleasant; it leaves a clean taste in the mouth. Though he taught by laughter, he was never ill-natured; neither was he a scoffer, for his mind was too reverential. As satire was his humour, he portrayed men's natures by means of ridicule, in which there is always some worldly cynicism, emphasising and colouring their features more or less, and necessarily with some caricature. A humorist may well use caricature without exceeding the lawful province of comedy; indeed he must often use it if he wishes to give force, truth, delicacy or the effect of naturalness to his picture.

In 1821, Louis François Beffara found among the registers of the church of Saint Eustache, in Paris, the certificate of baptism of Jean Poquelin, better known by his assumed name, Molière; and the certificate shows that he was christened on the 15th of January 1622. Nothing is said about the boy's birth in this document. It was then customary in France to have a child baptised the day it was born; if the baptism was delayed, the certificate stated the day of the birth.[1] It has therefore been generally supposed that the 15th of January was the poet's birthday. Though he had only one Christian name, Jean, given to him at his baptism, he had a second Christian name, Baptiste, given to him early in life, perhaps to distinguish him from a younger brother also christened Jean, and who is spoken of as "l'autre Jean" in the inventory made after their mother's death.

Not much is known of Molière's ancestors, but something may be shortly told. His father's father, Jean Poquelin, left Beauvais, probably towards the end of the 16th century, and established himself as an upholsterer in Paris, in the Rue de la Lingerie, then in the centre of the commercial part of the town. He carried on an apparently prosperous business; he married in 1594, had eight or ten children, and died in 1626. His eldest son, also a Jean Poquelin, father of the poet, was born probably in 1595. He began his work in the world as an upholsterer and was enabled to marry young. His marriage settlement,[2] dated 22nd of February 1621, shows that his father was still living in the Rue de la Lingerie, in the parish of Saint Eustache, and that he (the son) then qualified as a

---

[1] Taschereau, *Vie de Molière*, 3rd ed. 205; *Œuvres de Molière*, x. 9. As I said in the preface, this last quoted volume is altogether devoted to the *Notice biographique sur Molière* by M. Paul Mesnard.

[2] Soulié, *Recherches sur Molière et sur sa famille*, 127.

marchand tapissier, lived in the Rue Saint Honoré in the same parish. He was betrothed to Marie Cressé on the 25th of April 1621, and they were married on the 27th of that month.[1] They each contributed to their marriage settlement 2200 livres in money or in kind, of which each was to keep one half as his or her share, and the other half was to go to them jointly.[2] Nothing is known of the commercial relations between this Jean Poquelin and his father, whether the son was admitted into partnership with his father, or whether he began his business life in partnership with anybody else or on his own account. The son, however, must have prospered, for ten years after his marriage he became one of the privileged tapissiers du roi, and some few years later one of the still more privileged tapissiers valets de chambre du roi.—Molière's mother's father was Louis de Cressé, another upholsterer. There had been le sire Simon de Cressé, échevin of Paris in 1570, possibly his father;[3] so that Louis de Cressé, who liked to see the particle before his name, thought he had a right to use it. He had a son Louis Cressé, an upholsterer in Paris, at least in the year 1656,[4] but little or nothing more is known about him. This maternal grandfather of Molière's, of whom we are to hear a little and who may have been responsible for a great deal, lived and carried on his business in the Marché aux Poirées in Paris.[5] He was a rich man, he had a house of his own at St. Ouen,[6] a northern suburb of the capital, and he died in 1638.

Molière was descended therefore on both sides from a line of upholsterers; and when as a lad his father wished to make an upholsterer of him, after much anxious thought on his part and probable unpleasantness between them, he said No, and stuck to it. In its descent the members of his family belonged to one class, they had one interest, and they would be likely to have hereditary ideas and to cling to them tenaciously. Such people often participate each other's thoughts; and if this creates narrow-mindedness, it also often creates a peculiar strength of instinct in family affairs not easily acquired by those whose male ancestors have successively followed different

---

[1] Jal, *Dictionnaire critique de biographie et d'histoire*, 989, col. i.
[2] Soulié, *Recherches sur Molière*, 12, 128, 129.
[3] E. Révérend du Mesnil, *La Famille de Molière*, 28 and note 2.
[4] Soulié, *Recherches sur Molière*, 197.
[5] E. Révérend du Mesnil, *La Famille de Molière*, 28.
[6] Soulié, *Recherches sur Molière*, 16, 142.

callings. Molière was certainly not narrow-minded, and he did not get his skill in writing from his grandfathers; but perhaps his deep and thorough nature and the consistency of his opinions came in some measure from his unmixed or undivided ancestry. Every old family has a breeding and a training of its own, and in social intercourse this will generally show itself. No one can see Molière now. As with other authors, the best way to try to learn what he was like is to read his own words. From them I think it will be gathered that the tone of his remarks about men and women of the world affords good evidence that he possessed both a strength and a delicacy of feeling which may be seen in the expression of his thoughts. In his quarrel with the actors at the rival theatre, in his satire against men well known at the time, he showed his wit, but he was not charged with unfairness or coarseness. He ridiculed the ladies of fashion with so much good grace that he has always had honest laughter on his side. And when young women and girls of our day laugh at his comedies, they feel that his fun is pleasant and wholesome. That alone is a lesson in morality. Molière was a large-natured man, and he did not write idly. When his satire is strong it is healthy and compassionate; you feel that he is angry, but he gives you also his play. He taught by laughter that often shows a vein of sadness, but he was able to throw aside his bad blood and show with ridicule the harm produced by evil ways.

The house now generally believed to have been Molière's birthplace was pulled down in 1802 on the score of old age. This was the Maison des Singes—so called because of its signboard, or because at the outside left-hand corner there was a wooden post fastened into the wall with some monkeys climbing up a tree carved upon it.[1] The old house was numbered 16 Rue Saint Honoré, and stood at the angle of that street and the Rue des Vieilles Étuves, now the Rue Sauval. The house now standing on its site bears the number 96 Rue Saint Honoré; and upon it in 1876 was placed a marble tablet saying that Molière was born there on the 15th of January 1622.[2] The tradition that Molière was born in the

---

[1] There is an illustration of this corner post, or "poteau cornier," in the album forming part of the *Œuvres de Molière*.
[2] Taschereau, *Vie de Molière*, 3rd ed. 206, 207; also two articles by M. Romain Boulenger in the *Moliériste* for July and October 1879 (i. 108,

Maison des Singes is not quite free from doubt.[1] But it appears to be better established than the idea current at the end of the 18th century that the house then known as No. 3 Rue de la Tonnellerie, where now stands No. 31 Rue du Pont Neuf, was the birthplace of the future dramatist. And there is now on this house a bust of the poet by Coysevox, with an inscription, wrongly dated, saying that he was born there. The idea set on foot in 1705 by Grimarest, Molière's first biographer, that he was born in the market-place "sous les piliers des halles," may be dismissed.

It should be said that the Maison des Singes had been sold in 1638 to one Le Camus; but he was bound to continue to Molière's father the lease already made to him of the front portion of the house facing the Rue Saint Honoré. There was also a back portion, divided from the front by a courtyard, that looked into a side street, the Rue des Vieilles Étuves: this portion had been let to a tenant, and the lease of it had expired. Then Le Camus, who became Poquelin's landlord, occupied the back part of the house, facing the Rue des Vieilles Étuves, at a right angle with the Rue Saint Honoré. This Le Camus was an apothecary, so that Molière's acquaintance with the Faculty began at an early period of his life.

Some idea of the interior of the Maison des Singes may be formed from the description given of it by Soulié, aided by enumeration of the various articles found in each room of the house after Marie Cressé's death.[2] I may state here, in parenthesis, that it will be most convenient to follow the usual practice of calling Molière's mother by her maiden name: French writers nearly always speak of her as Marie Cressé, rarely as Marie Poquelin, and in law documents this was the common custom. On the ground-floor of her husband's house there was a shop, and behind it a kitchen, probably used also as a dining-room; over this room there was a loft or garret. Between the ground-floor and the first story there was a sort of entresol, in which there was a bedroom and a cabinet. The first story was turned into a room for business purposes.

197); and an article by Auguste Vitu in the same periodical for September 1879 (i. 166).
[1] Œuvres de Molière, x. 6, 7.
[2] Recherches sur Molière, 14-16, 132-147.

Apparently the house did not go higher.[1] Marie Cressé's bedroom was in the entresol, and there Molière was born. In the 17th century the bedroom of the mistress of the house was a room of importance. It was her room, in which she used to receive her friends, and much of her social life, apart from her duties in the kitchen, was passed there. Molière's mother had many beautiful articles of furniture and other things betokening the wife of a man in easy circumstances, showing also that she had been nicely brought up and liked to have pretty things about her.

Jean Poquelin was evidently thriving in his profession, for on the 2nd of April 1631 he bought from his elder brother Nicolas his appointment of tapissier ordinaire du roi;[2] the title of valet de chambre does not appear to have been included.

In spite of the smallness of his premises in the Maison des Singes, it would seem that Molière's father had the capacity for doing business on a large scale. For on the 29th of May 1631 Jean Poquelin alone signed a contract binding himself and one Étienne Lhoste to deliver to the War Office within twenty days 300 mattresses, 300 palliasses, 300 bolster-covers, 300 counterpanes, and 600 pairs of sheets.[3] Nothing, I believe, is known about Lhoste; the document which records this transaction says little more than that he and Poquelin were to be joint providers in the affair.

In the meantime Poquelin's family was growing, and our little Jean was allowed some years of play with his younger brothers and sisters. How they romped together may be known from the games of other children, though their playground must have been a scanty one. But death took away some of them at an early age, and of those that grew up it would only be a surmise to say that there was much opportunity for pleasant intercourse between them. They probably received some early rudimentary instruction at home; and perhaps their father engaged the services of George Pinel, "maître écrivain à Paris," to teach them how to write. Their mother is said to have been of delicate constitution and to

[1] See the etching of the outside of the house in vol. i. of the *Moliériste*, facing p. 108.
[2] Soulié, *Recherches sur Molière*, 13, 146-147.
[3] *Le Moliériste*, January 1888 (vol. ix. 313).

have transmitted her weakness to her children. She died at the early age of thirty-one, in May 1632.[1] In January 1633 an inventory [2] was made of the effects in her house at the time of her death, and from this it may be seen that her husband was a man well-to-do in the world. Among his customers some were bourgeois like himself; others were of noble birth, showing that he sent his wares into good houses.

Marie Cressé's inventory tells the names of the four of her children who were alive at her death; two others had died previously. Beffara thought that she had given birth to eight children, but subsequent and better knowledge makes it evident that he mistook two of Molière's uncles for his brothers. Here are the names of Marie Cressé's six children; the date following their names is that of their baptism:—

(1) JEAN (Baptiste), 15th January 1622.
This was Molière.

(2) LOYS, 6th January 1623.
Died before his mother.

(3) JEAN, 1st October 1624.
Called "l'autre Jean" in his mother's inventory. In documents of after years this second Jean was called "Jean le jeune," to distinguish him from his father. Became tapissier valet de chambre du roi. Married Marie Maillard, 15th January 1656. Had one son, and died in 1660.

(4) MARIE, 10th August 1625.
Died before her mother.

(5) NICOLAS, 13th July 1627.
Alive at his mother's death; died, Soulié thinks, a few years later.

(6) MARIE, 13th June 1628.
So christened, but always called Madeleine or Marie

---

[1] The register in the parish of Saint Eustache says that Marie Cressé was buried on the 11th of May (Taschereau, *Vie de Molière*, 3rd ed. 208, note 6); but the inventory taken after her death (Soulié, *Recherches sur Molière*, 131) says that she died on the 15th of May. This was not a wilful attempt to put the cart before the horse; it is rather an instance showing how careless people used to be in recording the dates of important matters in their family affairs. I mention the circumstance because other examples will be brought forward later showing probable inaccuracies in the dates of burial certificates.

[2] Soulié, *Recherches sur Molière*, 13-17; 130-147.

Madeleine. Married, 14th January 1651, André Boudet, marchand tapissier in Paris. Had two children. Died, Soulié says, in 1665.

Of the four children that survived their mother none were long-lived. Molière, the eldest born, died last. Their father did not long remain a widower. On the 30th of May 1633 he married Catherine Fleurette, the daughter of a Paris tradesman. She had two daughters: Catherine, christened 15th March 1634, who took the veil in 1655; and Marguerite, born 1st November 1636, but who did not live long. On the 15th of that month Poquelin's second wife died; he did not marry a third time.

French writers may possibly be correct in saying that Marie Cressé was a pattern of motherly goodness, and that Catherine Fleurette was a harsh stepmother; but in fact little is known about Poquelin's first wife, and nothing about his second. To suppose that Molière intended to portray his stepmother in the character of Béline in the *Malade Imaginaire* is ungenerous towards himself and towards the woman who had been dead close upon forty years. Béline was a stepmother, but so also was Elmire in the *Tartuffe*, a woman whom we should all be glad to reckon amongst our friends. Yet perhaps it may be said that the poet recollected his own loss, and that he wished to show how strongly girls might be made to feel the want of motherly affection at a time when they were most likely to be guided by its influence. Léonor and Isabelle, the two sisters in the *École des Maris*, are orphans brought up very differently by two brothers, friends only of their late father; Agnès in the *École des Femmes* is left to the care of a selfish, silly man who is also no relation; and Cléante and Élise in the *Avare* have good reason to regret the loss of their mother, for no sense of duty can make either of them respect their father Harpagon. Molière's father has been represented as a man close in his money affairs, and who, as he advanced in life and saw his business diminishing, became difficult to deal with and miserly. Part of this accusation may perhaps be not untrue; yet if Jean Poquelin had really possessed the characteristics of a miser, I doubt very much if his son would have written the *Avare* and painted his Harpagon even in the spirit of excellent comedy. Everything that is known of Molière's personality would preclude the idea of his drawing a picture of his own father.

Grimarest's *Vie de Molière*, printed in 1705, was the earliest biography of the poet written and published as such in book form.[1] Other biographical documents had appeared earlier, but they were short, or they relate only to particular events. Speaking of Grimarest's work, Boileau wrote to Brossette on the 12th of March 1706: "As regards the *Vie de Molière*, it is really not a book worth talking about. It is done by a man who knew nothing of the life of Molière. He is perpetually falling into error, for he does not even know the things which everybody else knows." It is admitted now that this judgment is too harsh. Grimarest's book is still readable, though it contains many errors. Some of the anecdotes he relates are on the face of them absurd, but others show the character of the dramatist more or less truly; and in an account of an author's life, biographical details were not then always examined very scrupulously. Jal says that Grimarest was born in 1659. As a small boy therefore he may have seen Molière, but he could have had no other personal recollection. He knew Baron, however, who as a lad was Molière's pupil, and he says that from Baron he got many details and some stories about Molière. But though Baron may have endeavoured to give facts that did not concern himself as well as he knew them, there were other matters as to which his word would be worthless. For the rest, Grimarest picked up information from those who could give him any. On the whole, we may be thankful to him. He tried a generation after Molière was dead to tell his readers in an easy manner what the great man was like, and with all his faults of inaccuracy and of omission he did not fail altogether in his object. Had Boileau been the biographer his style would have been more severe; he would have said what were the chief elements in Molière's nature, and he would have tried to describe his comedy. Boileau respected Molière as a man and admired him as an author, ranking him above Corneille and Racine; and in those days that was high praise. He was

---

[1] All references made here to Grimarest's *Vie de Molière* apply to the modern edition of 1877.

honest-thinking himself, with strong common-sense, and he tried to do right for right's sake. His chief strength lay there. He often criticised severely, but he had the power of looking into things and seeing their meaning. His opinions of the verse writers of the time are still of value; but we should prize more highly his judgments of Molière, who from his double calling was honoured and made much of by some because they felt his power, and was condemned ignorantly by others because they thought that he laughed at God's ministers and made virtue appear ridiculous. Boileau has often been called " le législateur du Parnasse "—a title which now raises a smile —but in spite of the taunt at being thought dull which is sometimes made against him, it should be remembered that as a critic he did most valuable service to the writers of the time, that he tried to defend Molière when unjust attacks were made upon him, and that he was very loyal to Racine. The year after the king's prohibition of the *Tartuffe*, Boileau, in his *Discours au Roi* (1665), writing of the eagerness shown by bigots to crush any attempt to decry their hollow piety, says :—

" Leur cœur, qui se connoît, et qui fuit la lumière,
S'il se moque de Dieu, craint *Tartuffe* et Molière."

One of the first things related of young Jean Poquelin is that he was often taken to the theatre by his mother's father, Louis de Cressé. No dates can be given to these visits, except that they cannot have taken place after 1638, for the old man died in that year. The boy and his grandfather were fond of each other, and the lad naturally enjoyed the excitement and the fun of the plays. His fancy was pleased, his imagination was kindled, and doubtless he described to his younger brothers and sisters the fine or the droll things that he had seen. But Papa Poquelin did not think that so much theatre-going was good for little boys, and he told his father-in-law that he took his son to the theatre too often. " Do you want to make an actor of the boy ? " he asked. The old man answered warmly : " Would to God he was as good an actor as Bellerose ! " Grimarest, who relates this story,[1] adds that the lad was so much struck by his grandfather's answer, that though he had shown no predilection he began to conceive a distaste for his father's profession, and seeing that his grandfather wished him

[1] *Vie de Molière*, 4, 5.

to go on the stage, he thought he might aspire to something better than his father's business. There may be some fable here, yet the story is not in all points incredible. Very likely Grimarest had it from Baron, to whom the dramatist may have told something of the sort as he was teaching him how to become an actor. That young Poquelin, then or a few years later, did dislike very much the idea of being brought up as an upholsterer may be taken for granted, but it is doubtful if his grandfather, who died when the lad was sixteen, persuaded him to become an actor. Louis de Cressé's exclamation in praise of Bellerose was in all probability merely an outburst at the moment, and meant nothing more.

It was said in the introductory chapter that the Hôtel de Bourgogne was the only theatre in Paris where, perhaps as late as Molière's birth, dramatic representations were allowed without payment of a fine to its owners; and that these owners, known as Les Confrères de la Passion, let their theatre to a company of actors in the year 1588. But it was not said that in the lease there was a clause by which the Confrères reserved to themselves a box in the theatre called "la loge des anciens maîtres," and also a space above this box called "le Paradis." These two places still belonged to the brotherhood, and they were allowed to give a seat to their friends, but not to take money for it. The Confrères were all men belonging to the bourgeoisie of Paris; and in the days of Molière's boyhood their doyen or oldest member was one Pierre Dubout, a tapissier du roi, and therefore a colleague of Jean Poquelin. Dubout, we may be sure, was applied to with tolerable frequency for an order into the Hôtel de Bourgogne.

The Paris tradesmen of those days enjoyed going to the theatre quite as much as they do now. The honest shopkeepers of the Rue Saint Denis, one of the most actively commercial streets in the town, were specially eager to see the first performance of all new plays.[1] Louis de Cressé appears to have been no exception to the rule. He seems to have liked going to the theatre and having his grandson by his side. The Hôtel de Bourgogne was only a short walk from the Maison des Singes in the Rue Saint Honoré. It lay not half a mile off to the north-east in the Rue Mauconseil, which

[1] Œuvres de Molière, x. 16 and note 1 to p. 17.

small street still runs from east to west between the Rue Saint Denis and the Rue Montorgueil. Louis de Cressé's house in the Marché aux Poirées was about a quarter of a mile to the east of the Poquelins. So that a family party may now and then have been made up for an afternoon's enjoyment.

Taking young Molière to the play was like preparing a soil which would in return yield an abundance of the rarest fruit. We know now that the comic instinct was born in him, and we can fancy that as he watched a play that he liked he must have felt himself all ablaze, like a well-laid fire recently kindled. Inside the theatre his young imagination was stirred, and while he was observing with keen delight much that he saw, he was learning the most important lesson of his life—how to please others. If any part of his early self-instruction can be traced, I should say that he soon became convinced that movement of some kind is the life and soul of a play intended for representation on the stage, and that a play must appeal to the feelings and enlist human sympathies before the audience can be interested in it. So much, at least, he understood before the beard began to grow upon his face. But even with Molière this did not come all at once. At the time of his early visits to the theatre, farce had not been quite banished from the Hôtel de Bourgogne, and after the performance of the set piece there was a lively entertainment by Gaultier Garguille and his companions, or their successors. These the lad could laugh at and enjoy, though it is difficult to imagine how he could enjoy the heavy tragedies, the tragi-comedies and the pastorals, which were then the mainstay of the chief theatres. It is probable that the Théâtre du Marais attracted him more than the Hôtel de Bourgogne. Comedies were given there more frequently than heretofore, yet they were largely exceeded by plays of a more exalted kind. But it is impossible to say what may not have pleased a very quick-witted boy nearly three hundred years ago.

Tastes have been so much altered by circumstances, that one is tempted for a moment to think that our natures have altered also. Education, or bringing-up, has changed our habits and ways of thought, and this is more observable among the young than among their elders. It is certain, however, that many of us, whether young or of more mature age, can enjoy an amusing play without understanding the spoken words. The actor may so perform his part that his movements and gestures speak to us. We then learn what is going on upon the stage, and may become intensely interested. Many persons with a small knowledge of French have felt a very lively sense of pleasure from a representation of Molière's lighter comedies, such as the *Médecin Malgré Lui* or the *Bourgeois Gentilhomme*, but their excitement has been less keen during a performance of the *Tartuffe*.

CHAPTER II

YEARS OF SCHOOLING

THAT Molière when he was a boy should have made evident his delight at being taken to the theatre is not wonderful, but it may be that he showed a keener pleasure and a more appreciative enjoyment of the plays he saw than other boys of his age would have done. The delights of the play-house, however, did not satisfy all the requirements of his mind. Apparently he was unhappy and wanted something. One evening after he had come back from the theatre, his father asked him why he had lately been so melancholy. The lad made a clean breast of the thoughts that were oppressing him, and said that he disliked very much the idea of being an upholsterer. His father had a good business and wished his son to enter it. The boy was brought up with this idea, but it was extremely distasteful to him. Selling stuffs and keeping accounts of what he sold did not appeal to his imagination. He wished for a different life. He asked to be sent to school to be educated. At that time he was about fourteen years old, and had only been taught reading, writing, and some arithmetic. But he wanted more than that. He felt that knowledge is the first step to any sort of success that migh come in after life. And his young human instincts told him that he wanted to be with other boys, to mix with them and learn from them how they thought and talked and how they acted their parts in their daily lives. Louis de Cressé was present at this interview between the father and son, and supported the boy in his demand. The father consented to do what was asked of him, and sent his son to the Collège de Clermont, which was directed by the Jesuits, and was the best school in Paris.[1] Grimarest's story is engaging, and traditionally it has been accepted, for there is no other. But

[1] Grimarest, *Vie de Molière*, 5, 6.

it need not be supposed that things passed quite in that way. Jean Poquelin must have been a very dull man indeed if he had not seen for himself that his son did not like being in his shop, and it is not probable that after a first intimation of his son's wishes he should suddenly have abandoned his own long-cherished desires.

M. Jules Loiseleur has shown that young Poquelin first went to the Collège de Clermont at the beginning of the October term in 1636, and that he finished his education there at the same time that the Prince de Conti (the brother of Condé and of Madame de Longueville) had finished his rhetoric at the same school in 1641. The prince took his degree of maître ès arts in 1644, when he was fifteen years old.[1] La Bruyère might well write: " Les enfants des dieux naissent instruits." The preface to the first complete edition of Molière's plays, published in 1682, nine years after his death, says, in speaking of the school career of the future dramatist :—

" As he had the advantage of going through all the classes at the same time as the late Prince de Conti, his quick intelligence, which distinguished him from all the others, won for him the esteem and the favour of that prince, who always honoured him with his goodwill and his protection." [2]

Perhaps there was some double flattery here, though the eulogistical tone about the prince may have had its purpose when the sentence was written. But it is not to be supposed that young Poquelin was a school friend of the Prince de Conti. If they met in a class-room, they were strangers there ; outside it they did not see each other. The Jesuits who directed the Collège de Clermont were admirable masters in the art of teaching, and they knew also how to divide their pupils. Fathers of the best families in France used to send their sons to this school, but it was understood that young noblemen should not mix familiarly with boys of inferior rank. The preface goes on to say :—

" The result of his [Molière's] studies was what might be expected from a mind so well constituted as his. If he was an excellent

---

[1] *Les Points Obscurs de la vie de Molière,* 40-43.
[2] *Œuvres de Molière,* vol. i. pp. xii and xiii.

classic, in philosophy he became stronger still. His inclination for poetry made him study the poets with very great care. He knew them well, and especially Terence, whom he chose as the best model he could put before himself ; and nobody has imitated him so well as he has done."

Five years was the term prescribed for education at the Collège de Clermont, and it may be believed that Poquelin made rapid progress in his studies. The teaching was good, and that, joined to a quick intelligence, would naturally produce a happy result. Latin was, of course, one of the subjects to which much attention was paid. And the Jesuits, wishing to cultivate a literary taste in their pupils, allowed them now and then to act a Latin play—sometimes composed by one of themselves.[1] Similar performances took place in the colleges in the provinces as well as in Paris,[2] and as entrance money was demanded a certain publicity was given to the representations. Perhaps young Poquelin was one of the actors in the performances given at his school, and perhaps his admiration for Terence came from his having to study a part he had to play. Admitting so much in the way of supposition, we may easily go a step further and imagine that these school theatricals may have helped to strengthen an idea, already not improbably floating in his mind, that he would like to become an actor and make the stage his profession. One thing is certain, that when he had made up his mind, he was not to be turned from his purpose.

Too much has been said as to the illiterate condition in which Jean Poquelin wished to keep his son. To my mind there is very little evidence to show that the father wished to keep his boy ignorant, thinking that too much learning was a bad thing and that it would distract his thoughts from the work he had to do. The father had become settled in business early in life, he had married early, and his affairs were prosperous. It may be urged rather that Jean Poquelin wished to see his son better educated than was usually the case with lads of his rank of life. There was then a feeling among the upper middle classes in Paris that knowledge—one sign of which was the ability to read Latin—

[1] Œuvres de Molière, x. 23.
[2] E. Despois, Le Théâtre Français sous Louis XIV., 96-98.

gave a young man an advantage over the nobility, who piqued themselves upon not being obliged to learn. The boy was sent to a school where the instruction was as good as could be obtained, and the next year the father took active steps to procure for his son the right to succeed him in the office of court upholsterer. These two facts may be taken as showing that Jean Poquelin wished to see his son "better himself" in the world.

The offices of tapissier du roi and valet de chambre du roi were distinct, though they were sometimes joined together. We have seen that Nicolas Poquelin held the first of these two offices, and that on the 2nd of April 1631 he sold it to his brother Jean, Molière's father. There were some restrictions in the sale, but in March 1637 the transaction was completed, and Jean Poquelin was then at liberty to ask that his son might have the reversion of his appointment. In December of that year, Molière, when he was not quite sixteen, went through the formalities which would enable him at a future date to succeed or replace his father in the office. The warrant which gave him this power conferred upon him also the office of valet de chambre du roi.[1] His father had probably bought this last-named office from somebody who had the power to sell it. Jean Poquelin, therefore, had not abandoned the thought of putting his son into his own business. He had shown himself willing to give up his position as court upholsterer and chamber valet to the king in favour of his son, so that his boy might be well established early in life and rise a step in the social scale.

There were eight tapissiers valets de chambre du roi; the office might be bought and sold, though usually it passed from father to son. The holders of this appointment formed part of the domestic officers and messmates of the royal table. Two served together at one time for a period of three months. Jean Poquelin's quarter of service was from the first day of April to the last day of June, and he performed his service in 1631, the year that he bought his office from his brother Nicolas.[2] His duty was to help the valet de chambre, strictly

[1] Œuvres de Molière, x. 14, referring to Soulié's Recherches sur Molière, 288 cote dix.

[2] Ibid. x. 64, note 4, referring to Soulié's Recherches sur Molière, 146 cote vingt-huit.

called, to make the king's bed; and during the royal progresses he had to watch over the king's effects. The appointment was worth three hundred livres a year, besides thirty-seven livres given as honorarium, and eating and drinking during the period of service. The tapissiers valets de chambre du roi had also to make the royal furniture, hang the tapestry, and prepare the king's apartments when the court was travelling. The post was an honourable one, the holders bore the title of écuyer, and during their term of service each one had his valet. Except for a period of about six years, to be spoken of at the end of the next chapter, Molière bore the title of tapissier valet de chambre du roi until his death. Fortunately or not, little is told of his duties in connection with the office.

Besides the Prince de Conti there were three of Molière's schoolfellows whose names are more or less remembered: François Bernier, Jean Hesnaut, and Chapelle. For any good they did in the world, Bernier was worth the other three three times over. He lived twelve years in India, was physician to Aurungzebe, the Emperor of Hindostan; and the value of his account of the conquest of Cashmere and his description of the country has been well recognised. Later he wrote several books on philosophical subjects which gave him reputation. The Prince de Conti was a friend to Molière when the future dramatist was strolling with his troop in the provinces; later he became a bigot and wrote a treatise abusing the stage which he had so much admired. Hesnaut was one of the small Epicurean poets of the 17th century. He composed a satire against the minister Colbert; then, fearing the consequences, he destroyed all the copies he could find. He wrote his verses easily, and lived on the reputation they gave him. Chapelle is the only one of Molière's schoolfellows who is known to have kept up his friendship with the dramatist in after life, and if a certain well-known conversation between them at Auteuil took place as is reported, their intimacy must have been close. Chapelle was one of those clever, idle ne'er-do-wells who, if they could only give themselves a chance, might succeed now and then by a brilliant flash. In fact, Chapelle did make one happy hit, but his glory ended there. He is credited with having written the greater part of a short account in prose and in verse of a journey he made with Bachaumont in the south of France in or about the year 1656. The book is entitled *Le Voyage de Chapelle et de Bachaumont.* Though much of this narrative relates to gastronomic pleasures, the style is easy and agreeable. It was intended as a jeu d'esprit and nothing more. Other men have tried their hand at the same kind of thing, but have not succeeded so happily. Chapelle could talk well at times, and his brightness made him known to most of the literary men in Paris. They enjoyed his conversation and his wit, and they envied his brilliancy, but they lamented that steadiness was beyond his power; and some of them endeavoured to make him overcome his habit of drinking too much wine. Louis Racine, the son of the poet, tells a story that Boileau met Chapelle one day in town and began to admonish him. "You are quite right," Chapelle said, "and I feel the truth of all you say. Let us go in here where you can talk more easily." Chapelle led the way into a wine-shop and called for a bottle. This was followed by another. Boileau got so animated with the advice he was giving to his friend that he continued preaching and drinking until both he and the intended convert got tipsy.[1]

We come now to a short period of Molière's education after he left school, and it appears that two of his school friends were associated with him in it. As a boy Chapelle had shown himself to be apt at his books, and when he left the Collège de Clermont, his father engaged Gassendi to give him further instruction at home. At this time Bernier, though young, was Gassendi's secretary, and he was allowed to join in the lessons. Then, at Chapelle's request, Molière and Cyrano de Bergerac were also admitted.[2] Cyrano was clever, and it was said of him that he was greedy of learning, but not in after life that he was remarkable for quiet behaviour. He had imagination which he allowed to run riot, and he became notorious for lawlessness and wild buffoonery. He spent a good deal of his time in fighting duels. He had a violent quarrel with Montfleury, an actor at the Hôtel de Bourgogne, a man who was very fat; and Bergerac said of him : "Because

---

[1] *Mémoires sur la Vie de Jean Racine,* in the *Œuvres de J. Racine,* by Paul Mesnard, 1st ed. i. 227 ; 2nd ed. i. 235.
[2] *Œuvres de Molière,* x. 43, 44.

this rascal is so big that one cannot beat him all round in one day, he gives himself grand airs." Molière was about nineteen when he was reading philosophy with Gassendi, and at that age an eager, intelligent lad would welcome anything that stimulated his thoughts. Grimarest says that Gassendi was struck with his ready understanding and that he took pleasure in teaching him. Of the four pupils, Cyrano de Bergerac, the eldest, was about twenty-two; Molière, nineteen; Bernier, sixteen; Chapelle, fifteen. Is it to be supposed that the master gave the same lessons to lads of such different ages? One of the points of Gassendi's teaching was freedom and independence of thought, and it is likely that this doctrine would find a ready acceptance among his four pupils. The ultimate advantage that each might derive from the lessons would depend on many circumstances. Neither Bergerac nor Chapelle showed that they did benefit materially from the teaching. Bernier was a thinking man, and he retained a grateful recollection of the professor's lessons; and in 1678 he published his *Abrégé de la philosophie de Gassendi*.

The soberness of judgment and the well-balanced mind which were characteristic of Molière in his mature years leads one to think that the same faculties were at work when he was young. Gassendi's teaching doubtless strengthened those faculties; had they been non-existent no Gassendi could have created them. From such knowledge of Molière's disposition as may be gathered from his comedies, it is not difficult to imagine that lessons on the value of self-dependence and freedom of thought would be grateful to him at a time when his boyish strength was budding into manhood. Free thought is our highest liberty, but those who have made the best use of it have shown that besides enthusiasm they possessed also modesty and common-sense as balancing qualities. Speaking generally, the man who deliberately tries to think differently from others runs great risk of being led away into strange vagaries by wrong-headedness and self-conceit. In after years the dramatist gave an immortal picture of this form of egotism, among other features, in Alceste in the *Misanthrope*. As a young man, Molière wished, I imagine, to be allowed to think of men and things as he found them, and to form his opinions from what he saw and heard. His written words

E

do not show that he was theoretical or that he tried to be a reformer. He knew that censure alone was not his proper function, and he did not believe that mere strictures on the world's conduct would do much good. He was a satirist, of course, but in making ridicule his weapon of attack he used it without coarseness or petulancy. He thought much of his teaching, but in his earnestness he always showed the spirit of comedy. His irony, his raillery, shows a strong and open nature, and it provokes healthy laughter. Constituted as Molière's mind was, always thoughtful, never transcendental, observing closely the ways of men, prone to melancholy but not morbid or dreamy, it is not wonderful that he should have trusted to his own senses where others were ready to believe blindly what was told to them. If unorthodoxy means thinking differently from accepted authority, Molière was content to remain unorthodox and form for himself his own views. Probably enough, even when young, he was not ruled by dogmas, for his mind was naturally sceptical. Scepticism of course means want of belief, but it is not synonymous with disbelief or incredulity. It has, I imagine, a further and a higher signification, and means, in secular as well as in religious matters, looking or searching through doubt for some truth, some belief, some end. If Molière's mind was sceptical, his heart was not until distrust had been forced upon him. He was not what many persons would have called religious; yet unless he had been actuated by the spirit of religion he would not have written the *Tartuffe*, nor afterwards *Don Juan*. In his conduct he was earnest, hearty, and considerate; and his sympathetic style shows that he held naturalness of expression to be the best way to make his ideas understood easily.

Gassendi taught Molière to admire Lucretius, and at the master's request the pupil translated the poem *De Rerum Natura* partly into verse and partly into prose.[1] He kept the manuscript until he died; how it disappeared afterwards is not known. It is most probable that his translation of Lucretius, and seven of his still unprinted comedies, were sold after his death by his widow for 1500 livres to Thierry,

---

[1] Taschereau, *Vie de Molière*, 5th ed., 108, 109; *Œuvres de Molière*, x. 53, 54; and for some corrections see pp. 481, 482.

the bookseller, who in 1682 published the first complete edition of his works. Thierry had wished to publish the different passages of Molière's translation, but did not do so, because he thought they were too strong in their bearing against the immortality of the soul. So much may be seen from an extract from the MSS. of Nicolas de Tralage, first printed by Édouard Fournier in his *La Valise de Molière.*[1] All that remains of Molière's translation of Lucretius is a paraphrase of certain lines on the blindness of love in a speech by Éliante, in Act II. sc. 4 of the *Misanthrope*, commencing by :—

> " L'amour pour l'ordinaire est peu fait à ces lois,
> Et l'on voit les amants vanter toujours leur choix." [2]

The chief value that these lines have for us now is that the dramatist thought they were suitable to the character of the girl who spoke them.

In the last paragraph of his book Grimarest assures his readers, as though there were doubt in the matter, that Molière went through his law studies and was admitted as an advocate. And there is an earlier authority to the same effect in a comedy, *Élomire Hypocondre ou les Médecins Vengés,* published in 1670, by Le Boulanger de Chalussay. Little is known of this author, perhaps the name he wrote under was not his own. His play was not acted and was suppressed, perhaps at Molière's request, the year after it was printed.[3] As a comedy it is wretched stuff, but it contains certain passages which, in spite of the writer's hostility to Molière and certain mistakes made, show that Le Boulanger de Chalussay was not ill informed on the early part of the poet's dramatic career. His lines have been quoted constantly, and I must refer to them as occasion demands. Élomire is an anagram of Molière, and had been used some years earlier. De Chalussay was clearly of opinion that Molière had been called to the bar. He makes Molière say of himself, that after he left school he went to Orleans to take his law degree, and that during the vacation he was made an

---

[1] Introduction, p. xvii ; *Œuvres de Molière*, x. 53, 54. There is a short article on Nicolas de Tralage (or Trallage) in the *Moliériste* for October 1880 (vol. ii. 216).

[2] *Œuvres de Molière*, v. 559, 560.

[3] Paul Lacroix, *Bibliographie Moliéresque*, No. 1159 ; *Œuvres de Molière*, xi. 124, par. 3, and 182, 183 ; also Paul Lacroix's notice to his edition of the comedy, published at Geneva in 1867, forming part of the Collection Moliéresque.

advocate [in Paris]; that he followed the bar for five or six months, but as he got no practice he left it, shaking the law's dust off his feet.[1] Later in the same play de Chalussay repeats, through Angélique, who is very bitter against Molière, much of what he had said before, and then he tells with rough satire that Jean Poquelin had made his son become an advocate. Soulié seemed inclined to cast a doubt on Molière's lessons from Gassendi; but he says that in all probability, after Molière had finished his course of philosophy, he read theology and canon law.[2] On the next page Soulié says that young men "used to go to Orleans, not to read law, as they went there generally during the vacation, but to take their degrees in civil and canon law, and that they returned immediately to Paris to be called to the bar."

We all know that men of genius have a quickness of their own in adapting unfamiliar phraseology to their own uses. Nevertheless, in *Monsieur de Pourceaugnac* (Act II. sc. 10) and *Les Fourberies de Scapin* (Act II. sc. 5), there are instances of complicated legal terms shown with exactness and apparent ease; and it is quite possible that in both of these instances the dramatist was using, with the good comic effect that was natural to him, some of his early legal training.

It is uncertain whether Molière, in the capacity of tapissier valet de chambre du roi, formed part of the king's suite in a journey to the south of France in the spring of the year 1642. There are some who favour this idea, but I cannot help thinking that the wish to believe it to be a fact forms part of the ground for their belief.

---

[1] *Élomire Hypocondre* (p. 77 in the edition of 1867), Act IV. sc. 2 of the *Divorce Comique*. This last is an intercalated play, given after the first scene in the fourth act of the longer comedy.

[2] *Recherches sur Molière*, 19.

CHAPTER III

THOUGH Louis de Cressé took his grandson to the Hôtel de Bourgogne and Marais theatres, it is probable that the future dramatist's keenest early recollections of histrionic display were the performances of mountebanks and buffoons close to the Foire de Saint Germain, then just outside Paris. Also he was probably taken, or went later of his own accord, to see entertainments of various kinds given by charlatans on the Pont Neuf and in the Place Dauphine. When he was older he certainly learned much from Italian actors in Paris, and their influence may be seen in an altered and better form in many of his lighter comedies. Something, therefore, should be said shortly of the minor or irregular theatres in Paris during the first half of the 17th century.

The Foire de Saint Germain, the chief of the Parisian fairs, was established by Louis XI. in 1482, and was meant for the benefit of the abbey of Saint Germain des Prés, and also for the advantage of the Parisians. Merchants placed their stalls there, and paid annual rent for them to the abbots. At the time which now concerns us the fair lasted from the 3rd of February until Easter Sunday, or often later. It was held upon the site at present occupied by the Marché de Saint Germain. Good articles of almost every description were to be bought there, and Molière's father was one of the traders. Our little Jean had sometimes to watch his father's stall, or was sent to deliver messages; and when he could escape he would run off to look at the fun going on in front of one of the theatres. But the fair was a noisy place; card-playing and cheating went on there, and Jean Poquelin could not have allowed his son to wander about in it as he pleased.

The first appearance of a theatre in the Foire de Saint Germain was in 1595, when Jean Courtin and Nicolas

Poteau pitched their tent just outside the fair; and they prospered so well that the actors at the Hôtel de Bourgogne, who, as we have seen, enjoyed a monopoly for theatrical performances in or near Paris, brought an action to restrain the irregular exhibitions. But the case went against them. Courtin and Poteau were allowed to play as long as the fair lasted on payment of a fine of three francs for each performance; and they became the pioneers of the théâtre de la foire for which Le Sage afterwards wrote so much, and which in the latter half of the 18th century developed into the Opéra Comique.[1]

When the Foire de Saint Germain was closed, open-air entertainments were frequent elsewhere. The Pont Neuf became, what it long remained, in a popular sense, the centre of Paris. The people used to assemble on the newly built bridge, and there Orviétan and other charlatans used to amuse the people, sell them their drugs and draw their teeth. Not far from the Pont Neuf was the Place Dauphine, then also new. Mondor and Tabarin used to put up their booths there, and recite their jests and play their antics before an admiring populace.

Perhaps there was a better show of acting in a small tennis-court in the Faubourg Saint Jacques at the southern extremity of the town, where Gros Guillaume, Turlupin, and Gaultier Garguille were often seen playing together. They were three clever buffoons, and after some migrations they all appeared at the Hôtel de Bourgogne, where they were acting in 1634. Report says that when one of them died the two others were so inconsolable that they both died within a week. But in the Hôtel they had other employment besides farce-acting. They were called upon to play the king's parts or those of his councillors. Then they dropped their popular names and took others more befitting their positions. Buffoonery, however, was their speciality; much of it was more or less impromptu, and sallies of Jackpudding wit were abundant. Each of the three men had his own line, each had a distinctive part assigned to him which never altered very materially.

[1] Émile Campardon, *Les Spectacles de la Foire*, Introduction; V. Fournel, *Les Spectacles Populaires et les Artistes des Rues*; and Jal, *Dictionnaire critique de biographie et d'histoire.*

Turlupin was a comical rogue; he was a valet who at the same time was a bit of a sharper, and his natural quick wit enabled him to play the part admirably. Gros Guillaume was a very fat man, and he appears to have been a sort of Sancho Panza. He used to appear with his face thickly covered with flour, and sometimes he blew a great volume of flour out of his mouth. Gaultier Garguille played the parts of old men, of doctors, or pedants, and he astonished the spectators by his extraordinary agility. Such were the three most popular farceurs at the Hôtel de Bourgogne. They were succeeded by Bruscambille, Guillot Gorju, and probably others. These five names, by their appearance and by their sound, almost tell what kind of wit was then enjoyed. But outside or inside the theatre men of this stamp were much alike. A friendly rivalry existed among them. They stole from each other and quizzed one another as they pleased. The jesters who acted at the Hôtel de Bourgogne and made part of "la troupe royale" were not more highly considered than those who played before the crowd in the open air. Farce is not a high form of art, but good comedy had not been born when Molière first went to the theatre. I mention farce here to say that it was then common in Paris, and that people liked laughing at a farce after the heavy set piece for the day had been performed. Had good comedies been written in those days, French actors would have been found to play them well. Instead, playwrights manufactured tragedies, tragi-comedies, and pastorals, all terribly ponderous and lifeless, which were no doubt acted in the same spirit.

Italian comedy seems to have been popular in Paris, judging from the number of companies of Italian actors who came there in the 16th and 17th centuries; and the successes gained by these foreign troops aroused the susceptibilities of the men at the Hôtel de Bourgogne. In 1599 matters were arranged; and then the Italians were to play in that theatre on alternate days with the French actors, though later they generally played in a large room, lent to them by the king, in the Hôtel du Petit Bourbon. Long before this time there had been in Italy two kinds of comedy which, in spite of mutual borrowings, showed such broad distinguishing features that one could not be mistaken for the other. There was the written and the unwritten comedy. Written comedy began in Italy in the 15th century, but the names of authors and of their plays were not known until early in the 16th. J. Addington Symonds said there were very many comedies and comedy writers in Italy in the 16th century; thousands of plays are supposed to have been written. But, "in spite of this extraordinary richness in comic literature, Italy cannot boast of a great comedy."[1] This was because of its hybrid nature. Plautus and Terence were taken as a necessary basis, and on this the writers tried to graft Italian manners. And on p. 141 of the same volume: "The Pegasus of the Italian drama, if I may venture on a burlesque metaphor, was a mule begotten by the sturdy ass of the Latin on the fleet mare of the Italian spirit; and it had the hard sterility of the mule." To a great extent French comedy was sterile from the same cause until Molière gave it a life and a spirit of its own. But I am glad to quote Symonds' opinion that one of the causes of the poverty in Italian comedy was because its writers discarded their own natural instincts in favour of an imitation of a Latin model.

The unwritten or impromptu comedy in Italy, the "commedia dell' arte," was famous before her more pretentious sister was born, and remained famous long after the younger sister had died from inanition. Impromptu comedy in Italy began first at the fairs and with the amusements during the weeks of Carnival.[2] Rude theatres were put up in the open air or inside booths. They were to be seen in every country town and on the commonest stages. Play-acting was a national amusement, and the people liked it. By degrees types were created which were followed. Different provinces furnished their own peculiar personage, each characteristic of itself. The idea of the pedant or the doctor who interlarded his talk with Latin arose in one of the university towns, such as Padua or Bologna; Venice gave the merchant and the pantaloon; from Naples came the cheat; and from Spain,

---

[1] *Renaissance in Italy: Italian Literature*, part ii. 181; ed. 1881.
[2] My chief authority on this matter is M. Louis Moland's interesting volume, *Molière et la Comédie Italienne*. See also *Masques et Bouffons* by Maurice Sand. And J. A. Symonds has written at length on the same subject in the Introduction to his translation of the *Memoirs of Count Carlo Gozzi*.

whose influence was then strong in Italy, came the braggart captain, though no doubt the idea of the Miles Gloriosus of Plautus had not died out in Italy. To these the lovers were added, and the valets and the intriguing waiting-women to deceive the old men. These were the chief parts; they were the stock characters who had to play stock parts. The whole thing was arranged to go in a machine-like way as much as possible. The subject and a sketch of the play was written down and posted up in what passed for the greenroom. This the actors had to learn. They got by heart a number of sententious sayings, conceits, and funny phrases, suitable to the occasion and to the parts they had to play. Each actor knew his own line, and the public knew what to expect from him when he first came on the stage. They knew also from his dress the part he had to play. There was much improvisation, but the constant repetition of the same parts by each actor made the improvisation easy to those who had a talent for it. The pieces were short, and gesture largely supplied the place of words. Action was the life and soul of every piece that was played. To make a dramatic show lively and amusing was the only end kept in view. Clown wit was given in large doses. And much of the roaring fun that is, or used to be, seen in English pantomimes is of Italian origin, though it has been considerably modified. But buffoonery was not the only element on the Italian stage. There were plays in which sentiment and passion had their place. There was generally a love story showing the wrongs on the part of the husband or of the wife, and the situations were often of a doubtful character. Whether they were moral or not, they represented the lives of the people who saw them acted, and in that sense the plays were comedies. The plays were very like each other, and no attempt at individual character-painting was attempted. The spectators were interested to see how the piece would end, and they enjoyed still more the acting of the play. They were intensely pleased with any dramatic representation of events which might be likely to happen amongst themselves. Burlesque was added, for it was popular; but serious plays would have been foreign to the nature and the understanding of the people. The audiences knew what they wanted, and the amusement they liked was given to then. Among a people who loved acting for its own sake the art or knack of acting simple pieces would come easily; therefore in a simple way it was likely to be well done. In their "commedia dell' arte" the Italians thought very much more of outward show, of a lively personification of the thing to be represented, than of the language used or of the elegance with which the actor spoke what he had to say. They were in no sense literary, but they had simple critical tastes which came to them easily and without fastidiousness.

Molière learned his lessons willingly from Italian impromptu comedy, and he never wished to forget them altogether. They taught him that action of some kind should be the principal feature in the representation of a play; and there is no doubt that before his day French plays were sadly deficient in this quality. M. Louis Moland, after fully recognising that Molière's tastes and the traditions that were floating in his mind were those of his own country, says: "Molière owed the animation in his plays chiefly to the Italians. Dramatic action does not seem to have come very naturally to the French mind, which has always shown itself much in favour of talking."[1] This does not mean that we should not remember what Molière owed to himself, nor that the Italian actors changed the bent of his nature. They could not have given him his strong powers of personal characterisation nor his rare faculty of teaching by satire, for in their comedies these features did not exist. Incidents were characterised plainly enough on the Italian stage, but they were shown with buffoonery, as were also their personages; and both personages and incidents were of a stock kind, and were repeated very constantly. Molière soon became master of his thoughts and of his style; what he had learned from Italian comedy he altered and improved by his love of healthy satire, even in his smaller plays which betray Italian influences most clearly. There he gave types of real personages, and showed by broad and pointed touches that he knew how to form a character and make a man talk with the feelings of a man, not like a puppet.

Though Italian companies attracted large numbers of French theatre-loving people, the troop of Spanish actors, brought to Paris by Queen Maria Theresa in 1660 shortly after her

[1] *Molière et la Comédie Italienne*, 5.

marriage with Louis XIV., and maintained by her there until 1674, fared indifferently. When they played at court they appear to have been tolerably fortunate, but people would not go to see them in the public theatre. In a show of the humours of life intelligence and sympathy must precede success, and as the French could not understand the Spaniards they naturally did not like them. Men in the pit of the theatre may have been as ignorant of Italian as of Spanish, but the conventional types among the Italian actors prepared the audience for what was going to happen; and the very large part that expressive pantomimic gesture had among the Italians, and which they knew so well how to use, supplied in a great measure the meaning of the spoken words. Though after the French translation of the first part of *Don Quixote* in 1613 French playwrights began to borrow the plots of many of their comedies from Spain, and continued to do so for a hundred years or longer, it cannot be said that the acting of the Spaniards in Paris had the slightest influence on the French stage. There is certainly no trace of it in Molière. If the Spanish acting was good it did not appeal to French tastes.[1]

[1] Despois, in his *Le Théâtre Français sous Louis XIV.*, has a short chapter on this subject, pp. 70-76.

CHAPTER IV

THE ILLUSTRE THÉÂTRE

IT is time to dismiss Tallemant des Réaux's story that Molière became an actor because he fell in love with Madeleine Béjart. She was the daughter of Joseph Béjart, huissier des eaux et forêts, and of Marie Hervé, his wife—I follow the usual practice of calling Béjart's wife by her maiden name—and was born in January 1618; consequently she was four years older than Molière. She was a good-looking young woman of fair complexion, with reddish hair, was clever, and supposed to be capable of managing her own affairs. She had been the mistress of a Comte de Modène and had borne him a child, christened Françoise on the 11th of July 1638. Though Madeleine had never played at the Hôtel de Bourgogne, nor probably at the Théâtre du Marais, she had gained some experience at the small and temporary playhouses in Paris, and very likely also by strolling in the provinces. Tallemant des Réaux mentions her when speaking of the actors of his day :—

"I must conclude with the Béjart. I have never seen her play, but I am told she is the best actress of them all. She belongs to a strolling company. She has played in Paris, but that was in a third troop which was only there for a short time. . . . A fellow called Molière—un garçon nommé Molière—left his studies at the Sorbonne to go after her. He was in love with her for a long time, and at last he made up his mind to marry her. He writes plays in which there is some wit. He is not a wonderful actor, except in ludicrous parts. It is only his company that play his comedies ; they are amusing." [1]

There is a mixture of truth and fable here such as Tallemant loved. What he said of Madeleine Béjart was written while Molière was travelling with his troop in the provinces ; the rest of the paragraph was added after Molière returned to

---

[1] *Les Historiettes*, by Tallemant des Réaux, 3rd ed. (1854-1860), vii. 177 and note 2.

Paris. But it is tolerably certain that Molière was never a student at the Sorbonne. And it is quite certain that he did not marry Madeleine Béjart, for she signed the certificate of his marriage with another woman. It may be taken for granted that Molière had an affection for Madeleine Béjart, and that he told her so; they were both young and intelligent, and both were interested in the same cause. But his fondness for her did not give him his earlier love for the stage, it did not create in him his love of satire and irony and the desire for dramatic characterisation. These faculties must have existed, if hazily, before he first saw her. Had he not been born with comic insight he could not as an actor have so constantly amused the public in his theatre, nor could he have written so many comedies which still delight readers and spectators even in our day.

I think that Molière would have gone on the stage if he had never seen Madeleine Béjart, though possibly she strengthened his determination. De Visé, in his *Nouvelles Nouvelles*, a sort of novel, published in 1663, says:—

"The famous author of the *École des Maris*, having in his youth a strong passion for the theatre, took to the stage, though he might have done without this occupation, as he had money enough to live honourably in the world." [1]

And La Grange says in his preface in 1682 :—

"When he [Molière] had finished his legal studies he chose the profession of an actor because he had a liking for the stage he could not overcome. All his study, all his thoughts, were bent towards acting." [2]

And Charles Perrault, also a contemporary, says :—

"Molière was born with such a strong inclination for the stage that he could not help becoming an actor. He had hardly finished his course of study, in which he acquitted himself admirably, when he allied himself with other young persons of his own age and way of thinking; and he determined to form a troop of actors and go and play with them in the provinces." [3]

Molière had made up his mind not to go into his father's business, and in all probability his father felt himself bound to give up his long-cherished desire that his eldest son should work beside him in his well-established house. Nevertheless,

---

[1] *Œuvres de Molière*, x. 464, 465. [2] *Ibid.* vol. i. p. xiii.
[3] *Les Hommes Illustres*, ed. 1696, vol. i. art. *Molière*.

Jean Poquelin was much annoyed when he heard that his son meant to forego the advantages of stepping into a good business for the sake of joining a band of actors of no reputation and whose calling was thought by many to be disreputable. Molière did not make his choice so much from love of gain as from love of liberty. I think that his natural inclinations prompted him, and that an ambition equally natural did the rest. He loved the art of acting. He admired it so much in others that he wished to perform the same parts himself. Dramatic personation of character stirred his fancy, and he wished to be in a position to indulge his tastes. Of course he had ambition—"that last infirmity of noble minds." It was ambition that spurred him on, but throughout his life he showed great perseverance and soberness of judgment. It is easy for us who are wise after the event, and had no personal care whether he made his fortune or was ruined, to think that he was impelled by laudable desires; but we may recollect that his father, who saw only the disobedience of a wayward boy and who felt that his son was dishonouring himself, would not look upon this ambition with favourable eyes. In vain did Jean Poquelin try to dissuade his son. He sent his friends to him, offering through their mediation to buy for him any situation that he could afford. Charles Perrault relates, in his article on Molière already mentioned, that Jean Poquelin sent as a special ambassador one who had been his son's master, hoping that by his influence his son might be brought to reason. But this embassy fared worse than the others, for the young enthusiast got the better of his would-be converter and persuaded him to give up his teaching, and made him promise that he would join his (Molière's) friends and play the part of the pedant in their comedies. There are two charming lines in the *Étourdi* in which Mascarille ironically tells his master what he ought to think of his father's counsels :—

> " Moquez-vous des sermons d'un vieux barbon de père,
> Poussez votre bidet, vous dis-je, et laissez faire."

When Molière wrote these lines he had not forgotten the disagreeable interviews with his father. He did not scorn his father's advice because he could not accept it; but in writing his play he turned what had been his own heavy thoughts into a piece of drollery. And this was not the only time that he did so.

The legal documents which form the greater part of Soulié's volume *Recherches sur Molière et sur sa Famille* are the chief authorities for showing the fortunes of Molière and his comrades when he first went on the stage. Here many facts are found which before their publication in 1863 were unknown, and these must now engage our attention. I shall be as sparing as possible on these matters; but facts are stepping-stones to the biographer on which he tries to found his opinion how the man he is writing about acted under certain conditions, and from them attempts at characterisation are made. I do not wish to weigh the knowledge of details in the story of an author's life against an intelligent understanding of what he has written. If all the books printed about Molière were put into a room together they would not be worth the *Misanthrope*. What one wants most to know about an author is what he has to say and how he expresses himself; and with an imaginative writer the last point is important. Nevertheless, it is part of the province of biography to try to get at and explain the facts in a man's life—those which show him in his boyhood, in his youth, in his struggles to gain for himself a place in the world; which show later how he persevered and where he failed; what were the causes of his failures and how he met his disappointments; what were his successes, to what they were owing, and how he bore his triumphs. All these circumstances, when they can be discovered, belong to biography, and they may perchance be made interesting if they are handled judiciously and without ill-nature. Facts may then possibly bring a great man closer to our eyes and help to show us what he was like.

The inventory taken after Jean Poquelin's death in 1669 says, among other things, that on the 6th of January 1643 Molière gave his father a receipt stating that he had received from him 630 livres for the purpose mentioned therein—"pour l'employer à l'effet y mentionné."[1] If this receipt had been preserved the words "pour l'employer à l'effet y mentionné" might have been made clear. The most natural supposition is that Molière asked for the money to prepare himself for his new

[1] Soulié, *Recherches sur Molière*, 28 ; 227, par. 2.

career. The year of majority then in France was twenty-five, and the lad was not actually twenty-one. Jean Poquelin was a close man with his money, and it is not likely that he would have given his son 630 livres, equal in value to £125 now, except under pressure. But in giving his son this money the father became, against his will, a consenting party to his son's desires.

Le Boulanger de Chalussay makes Molière say in the presence of the charlatans Orviétan and Bary, that he had taken lessons from both of them,[1] also from a celebrated Italian actor Tiberio Fiorilli, popularly known as Scaramouche. Part of the passage relating to Molière's lessons from this man deserves to be quoted:—

> ". . . Par exemple, Élomire
> Veut se rendre parfait dans l'art de faire rire ;
> Que fait-il, le matois, dans ce hardi dessein ?
> Chez le grand Scaramouche il va soir et matin.
> Là, le miroir en main, et ce grand homme en face,
> Il n'est contorsion, posture ni grimace,
> Que ce grand écolier du plus grand des bouffons
> Ne fasse et ne refasse en cent et cent façons." [2]

Then follows a description of the characters he was learning to represent. I have spoken of these lessons from Orviétan, from Bary, and from Scaramouche, after the 6th of January 1643, because I imagine that Molière felt he wanted tuition before going formally on the stage, and that these men would not teach him without payment. But before beginning the story of his public life it is necessary to speak of the Béjart family.

Joseph Béjart died most likely early in 1643.[3] He was the father of Joseph and Louis, of Madeleine and Geneviève, and nearly certainly of Armande,—all of whom were connected with Molière's history until the end of their joint lives. When Joseph Béjart died he left large debts which his widow Marie Hervé had no means of paying; and soon after his death, she, acting under the advice of her friends, renounced by deed, on the 10th of March 1643, both in her own name and in that of her five children, all share in her late husband's inheritance, as it was more likely to bring them loss than profit.[4] All of

---

[1] *Élomire Hypocondre*, Act I. scs. 1 and 3.
[2] *Ibid*. Act I. sc. 3.
[3] Soulié, *Recherches sur Molière*, 31 ; Jal, *Dictionnaire*, 185, col. 1.
[4] Soulié, *Recherches sur Molière*, 31 ; 172, 3 ; *Œuvres de Molière*, x. 471. (In quoting the text of this deed M. Mesnard has printed "Georges" Béjart; Soulié also printed Georges, but showed in note 2 that the name should be "Joseph." In his text, M. Mesnard always speaks of Joseph Béjart.)

the five children were mentioned in the deed. Both Soulié[1] and Jal[2] thought that Joseph, known later as "Béjart aîné," was the eldest because he was mentioned first, though the date of his birth is not known; Madeleine, already spoken of, was christened on the 8th of January 1618;[3] Louis, known later as "Béjart cadet," was christened on the 4th of December 1630;[4] Geneviève, known later, until her marriage in 1664, as Mlle. Hervé, was born probably in 1631;[5] and a "petite non baptisée," that is at the time of the deed of renunciation, was born probably at the end of 1642 or early in 1643, shortly before her father's death.[6] This last child, though her baptismal certificate has not been found, was almost certainly Armande.[7] I will say here in parenthesis that, though I am strongly inclined to agree with those who hold that Armande was the legitimate daughter of Joseph Béjart and of Marie Hervé, her parentage has not been proved absolutely; and that this question will be dealt with when speaking of her marriage with Molière, at the end of chapter xii. In the deed of 10th March 1643, five of Marie Hervé's children were named, but many others were dead; Soulié[8] and Jal[9] thought there had been eleven or twelve.

Joseph Béjart, the father of these five children, had been huissier des eaux et forêts, but Soulié thought that in the latter years of his life he gave up his office to join a strolling company of actors in the provinces.[10] In the marriage settlement between Molière and Armande Béjart, he is spoken of as the late "Sieur de Belleville." His widow, Marie Hervé, owned some small properties producing altogether only a small

[1] *Recherches sur Molière*, 32.   [2] *Dictionnaire*, 185, col. 1.
[3] *Ibid.* 177, cols. 1 and 2.   [4] *Ibid.* 177, col. 2.
[5] Jal says that Marie Hervé had two children called Geneviève: the eldest christened 2nd July 1624, but she died before March 1643 (*Dictionnaire*, 177, col. 2, and 185, col. 1); the younger Geneviève, the one mentioned above, whom he presumes to have been born about 1631 (*Dictionnaire*, 177, col. 2, and pp. 182, 183).—As I read Soulié's text, he seems not to have known that there were two Genevièves, and to have taken the elder one for the younger (*Recherches sur Molière*, 33 and 75). As the elder one died before March 1643 it is only the younger one that can concern us. She married, first, Léonard de Loménie, in 1664; in 1672, Jean Baptiste Aubry. And see *Œuvres de Molière*, ix. 48, note 2.
[6] Soulié, *Recherches sur Molière*, 33, 34.
[7] Besides Soulié (p. 33), Jal (pp. 184, 185), M. Mesnard is also strongly of this opinion, *Notice biographique sur Molière*, 251.
[8] *Recherches sur Molière*, 30, 31.   [9] *Dictionnaire*, 177, 178.
[10] *La Correspondance Littéraire* for 25th January 1865, p. 80, col. 1.

income; she appears to have done the best she could for her children, and one hears of her chiefly as assisting them in becoming a guarantor in their undertakings. The names of these children have been given; what more there is to be said about them will appear by degrees as their names come forward.

In the first half of the year 1643 Molière saw a good deal of Madeleine Béjart. He had left his father's house and was living close to where she lived with her mother in the Marais quarter of the town. An enterprise was on foot; and on the 30th of June, Joseph, Madeleine and Geneviève Béjart, with Molière and four other men and two women—ten in all—bound themselves to act together, and their troop was to be known as the Illustre Théâtre. In those days the word "illustre" was often used in rather a smart sense; socially it was synonymous with "précieux." "Une précieuse" meant a lady of distinction, though the title was a little affected, and the ladies at the Hôtel de Rambouillet called themselves "précieuses" or "illustres." The name Illustre Théâtre was intended to tell the public that the new troop of actors wished to attract all the intelligent playgoers in Paris. The existence of this troop has long been known, but the "Contrat de Société entre les comédiens de l'Illustre Théâtre" was first published by Soulié, though not in full, in *La Correspondance Littéraire* for 25th January 1865 (pp. 80-81), two years after the publication of his volume, *Recherches sur Molière*. The deed, with the names of those concerned in it, is given at length by M. Mesnard in vol. x. p. 462 of the *Œuvres de Molière*. It shows when Molière definitely undertook to begin his career as an actor, though not that he had then changed his name.

Besides Molière and the Béjarts, there is not much interest attaching to any of these actors. But one of them, George Pinel, was perhaps the "maître écrivain" whom Jean Poquelin had engaged to teach his young children how to read and write; also perhaps he was the ambassador whom Poquelin had sent to his son to try to dissuade him from choosing the stage as a profession. Besides the actors there were three other signatories to the deed: A. Maréchal, then known as a dramatic author; Françoise Lesguillon, the mother of Catherine des Urlis, a young actress; and Marie Hervé, whose name we know already.

The deed of agreement of the 30th of June 1643 stipulates that when a new play is brought to the troop the author shall have the undisputed right to distribute the parts as he pleases; that in cases of printed plays, if the author has not previously distributed the parts, they shall be determined by the majority of votes among the troop, unless the agreement is followed which already exists between Clérin, Poquelin, and Joseph Béjart, that they shall be allowed alternately to play the hero. Madeleine Béjart was to be allowed to choose what part she pleased. In other respects the document was drawn up in the spirit of republicanism common in the French theatres in the 17th century. Informal acting associations were not uncommon in those days, and it is likely that before the date of this document, most of those who signed it had played together for amusement, or with the intention of learning how to act, giving their performances gratis; and the clause between Clérin, Poquelin, and Béjart points that way. But when the new troop had bound themselves by a formal deed to play together, they would demand the payment of entrance money.

The young actors had to determine where to pitch their tent. They decided to cross the Seine, and on the 12th of September 1643 they hired a tennis-court known as Le Jeu de Paume des Mestayers, situated on the rampart and near to the Porte de Nesle. Tennis-courts were very frequently used for theatres in olden days in France, and they were sometimes built upon the trenches or ramparts surrounding a town. The theatre where Molière first tried to earn fame, and, if might be, a little money, stood at the angle of what is now the Rue de Seine and the Rue Mazarine, immediately behind the present Institut de France, which was not then built. Auguste Vitu gave an elaborate description of the tennis-court transformed into the Illustre Théâtre.[1] The inside of the building was a rectangular oblong, and as a theatre was exceedingly primitive. Besides some curtains which had to be drawn aside to let the actors pass, there was no other stage decoration. The lighting was of course by candles. Of musical instru-

---

[1] *Le Jeu de Paume des Mestayers*, 36 *et seq.*

ments there was a flute, a drum, and one or two violins. There was a gallery running along each side of the room and along the wall facing the stage. Here were placed the boxes, the price of each seat being ten sous; the groundlings stood during the performance, and paid five sous. The doors were open at one o'clock, the performance began at two; and by six the visitors were on their way home.

There was delay in getting the theatre put into order. In the meanwhile the troop went to Rouen, and played there during the fête known as "la foire du pardon," or "la fête de Saint Romain," which began on the 23rd of October and lasted for some days. Of the large towns in France, Rouen was the nearest to Paris, it was the capital of the province of Normandy, and it was customary with strolling companies when they left the capital to begin their performances there. It was at Rouen that Mondory, the head of his troop, brought out Corneille's first play *Mélite*, in 1629; and it is probable that in the same city Jean Baptiste Poquelin, afterwards Molière, first appeared on the stage as a professional actor. Apparently the young enthusiasts were kept at Rouen longer than they liked, for on the 3rd of November, Molière and his comrades signed a power of attorney there, urging Noël Gallois, from whom they had hired the Jeu de Paume des Métayers in Paris, to bestir himself and get the theatre ready for them. This document was discovered by E. Gosselin, and was published by him in the *Revue de la Normandie* for April 1870,[1] and with it may be seen a facsimile of the signatures of all the members of the troop. They had found a new recruit in the person of Catherine Bourgeois.

On the 28th of December they were back in Paris, and it has been thought that the Illustre Théâtre was first opened on the 31st of December 1643.[2] On the front of the house now numbered 12 Rue Mazarine there is a tablet bearing the following inscription:—

"Ici s'élevait le Jeu de Paume des Métayers, où la troupe de Molière ouvrit en Décembre 1643 l'Illustre Théâtre."

But it is not known what was the play chosen wherewith to charm the public. Le Boulanger de Chalussay seems to say

[1] Vol. x. pp. 239, 240.   [2] A. Vitu, *Le Jeu de Paume des Mestayers*, 6.

that the theatre was opened on a jour de fête, when the applause was continually given at the wrong moment; and he adds that on the following days nobody entered the house except a few watermen and the friends of the actors to whom orders had been given.[1] A few lines previously he had made some very uncomplimentary remarks upon the members of the troop. His evidence is altogether hostile, but much of what he says cannot be contradicted.

Yet the troop had done their best to make a bid for the public favour. They bought and paid for plays by authors of reputation. One play was *Scévole*, a tragedy by Du Ryer ; Tristan l'Hermite furnished two others, *La Mort de Crispe* and *La Mort de Sénèque*. Both of these writers were Academicians. If any of Maréchal's plays were acted in the Jeu de Paume des Mestayers they passed into oblivion, like so many plays acted elsewhere after the few days on which they were performed. And the troop had lately admitted into their membership Nicolas Desfontaines, who was not a novice in stage matters. He had written several tragedies or tragicomedies, some of which appear to have been acted by Molière and his friends.[2] It would seem that he was an actor as well as an author, for his name appears at the foot of five documents relating to the Illustre Théâtre.

Some friend of the actors—the Comte de Modène, according to Soulié,[3] Tristan l'Hermite, according to M. Mesnard[4]—introduced them to Gaston, Duke of Orleans, brother of Louis XIII., and this prince became their patron. Perhaps because of their new honour the troop hired on the 28th of June 1644 Daniel Mallet, a dancer—not to be one of themselves, but to be at their service both for acting and for ballets—at the rate of thirty-five sous every day there was a performance, and five sous more each day that he took a part in a play.[5] The engagement of Mallet points to an employment outside the ordinary business, for dancing was not then customary in the Paris theatres. Ballets, however, were a favourite court amusement, and M. Fournel thinks that the troop hired Mallet with a view to his dancing before their new protector

---

[1] *Élomire Hypocondre*, Act IV. sc. 2 of the *Divorce Comique*.
[2] *Recherches sur Molière*, 38. [3] *Ibid.* 39.
[4] *Œuvres de Molière*, x. 89-95.
[5] Soulié, *Recherches sur Molière*, 38, 175.

at the Luxembourg Palace, where they sometimes went "en visite" when the duke wished to entertain his guests.[1] Perhaps Molière and his comrades, with Daniel Mallet as a dancer, appeared in an entertainment at the Luxembourg in August 1644.[2] It is not known when the patronage of the Duke of Orleans was first accorded to the members of the Illustre Théâtre, but it had certainly been given before the 9th of September 1644.[3]

The agreement concerning Daniel Mallet shows the first instance of young Poquelin having changed his name. He is there described as " Jean Baptiste Poquelin, dit Molière," and at the end he signed himself boldly DE MOLIÈRE.[4] In later documents he signed himself occasionally by his family name, though generally as Molière; but after the 28th of June 1644 he never omitted to give also the name Poquelin, or its initial letter. As for the particle de, that was not always intended or accepted as a sign of nobility; actors often used it, and nobody thought of depriving them of the privilege. I do not know that Molière of his own accord ever used the particle again, though it was afterwards given to him on the title-pages to his plays, and La Grange constantly wrote of him as M. de Molière. It is to be remarked, in this and later documents concerning all the members of the Illustre Théâtre, that the name Jean Baptiste Poquelin is the first mentioned, as though, says Soulié, he were the leading man in the troop.

It will probably never be known why he chose the name Molière. He was often asked the reason for his choice, but always refused to answer. Édouard Fournier said that the pseudonym was perhaps taken from the name of a small property owned by a distant relative which was called Molière or La Molière.[5] It was common for actors to give themselves well-sounding names, and if Molière when he was quite a young man chose a territorial title as his nom de guerre, he was wise in not saying that he had done so. This reason for the choice of his name is of course doubtful, but it is not altogether fanciful. In the École des Femmes (Act I. sc. 1, near

---

[1] Les Contemporains de Molière, ii. 185.
[2] Soulié, Recherches sur Molière, 39.
[3] Loiseleur, Les Points obscurs de la Vie de Molière, 379.
[4] Soulié, Recherches sur Molière, 176.
[5] Le Roman de Molière, 38, note 2.

the end), Chrysale rallies Arnolphe for wishing, because he owns a tumble-down farmhouse, to be called by the seigneurial title, M. de la Souche; and I should not be surprised if in fact Molière was here laughing at himself for having been actuated by the same idea. A little later in the same scene are the lines :—

> "Je sais un gros paysan qu'on appeloit Gros-Pierre,
> Qui n'ayant pour tout bien qu'un seul quartier de terre,
> Y fit tout à l'entour faire un fossé bourbeux,
> Et de Monsieur de l'Isle en prit le nom pompeux."

The ridicule here is manifest, and perhaps there was an allusion to Thomas Corneille, who called himself Corneille de l'Isle.

This place will do as well as another to say that besides the comic dramatist, whose name everybody knows, there was a Louis de Mollier, a musician and a dancer at the court ballets in the middle of the 17th century. His name was pronounced Molière, and was sometimes so written. And there was also a writer of novels, François de Molière, the author of *La Semaine Amoureuse, Le Mépris de la Cour*, and *La Polixène*; he was assassinated, perhaps in 1632.

The protection of the Duke of Orleans does not appear to have enriched the troop materially, and money was what they most wanted. On the 9th of September 1644 they borrowed 1100 livres from Louis Baulot to pay for the plays already mentioned and for expenses connected with the theatre.[1] And on the 17th of December following they borrowed from François Pommier 2000 livres in two bonds—300 livres in one bond, and 1700 livres in the other.[2] And in both they declared that the lender might seize the profits taken at the theatre until his debt was paid. From the second bond to Pommier it may be seen that they had paid off 500 livres of their debt to Baulot, so that they then owed 2600 livres, or about £520 of our money now. They passed a deed of agreement amongst themselves not to divide any profits until their debts were cleared.[3] Most of the members found a guarantor for their share of liability. But it is curious to learn that Marie Hervé became guarantor for Molière, as well as for her two daughters; and from this one may infer that Molière had

---

[1] J. Loiseleur, *Les Points obscurs de la Vie de Molière*, 379.
[2] Soulié, *Recherches sur Molière*, 177, 178.
[3] *Ibid.* 181.

not asked his father to help him, or that his father had refused to give assistance.

In these last documents Joseph Béjart's name is not seen. He had probably left his companions for a while; for on the 14th of April 1644 his mother promised to pay to Alexandre Sorin, "médecin de la faculté d'Angers," 200 livres to cure him of an impediment in his speech.[1] His name is next seen with those of his comrades on the 13th of August 1645. De Chalussay twice alludes to the stammering of Joseph Béjart, and out of spite he mentions the lameness of his brother Louis. But Louis Béjart did not become lame until many years later, and his name does not appear in any of the documents connected with the Illustre Théâtre.

In the lease of the Jeu de Paume des Mestayers there was a clause saying that the actors might terminate the tenancy by giving three months notice to quit in writing. On the 19th of December 1644 the lease was cancelled, and the surrender was signed by Molière alone in the name of the company.[2] Undismayed by failure, they went to a different part of Paris and hired another tennis-court, known as La Croix Noire, in the Rue des Barrés at the Port Saint Paul. It was near the river, on the north side, a little higher up than the Ile Saint Louis. Here, too, on the present Quai des Célestins, No. 32, may be seen a marble tablet which tells its own tale :—

"A cette place s'élevait le Jeu de Paume de la Croix Noire, où Molière et la troupe de l'Illustre Théâtre jouèrent en 1645."

The actors engaged a master carpenter to take away the boxes and other woodwork from their old theatre and put them up in the new one, and everything was to be ready for them on the 8th of January 1645.[3] The troop still retained the privilege of belonging to Son Altesse Royale Gaston, Duke of Orleans; and on the 7th of February the duke gave a ball at the Luxembourg Palace and engaged his actors to entertain his guests.[4] It is not unlikely that on this occasion the ballet L'Oracle de Sybile et de Pansoust was danced, and that some members of Molière's troop took a part in it.[5] The only play

---

[1] Soulié's article in the Correspondance Littéraire for 25th January 1865, pp. 83, 84.
[2] Le Moliériste for July 1885 (vii. 123).
[3] Soulié, Recherches sur Molière, 41 ; 183-185.   [4] Ibid. 41, 42.
[5] V. Fournel, Les Contemporains de Molière, ii. 263.

known to have been acted by the members of the Illustre Théâtre at the Port Saint Paul, was a tragedy by Magnon called *Artaxerce*. It was printed in 1645, and bears on the title-page the words, "Représentée par l'Illustre Théâtre." Magnon was the author of seven other tragedies or tragi-comedies. Desfontaines was perhaps still in the troop when they went to the Jeu de Paume de la Croix Noire; if so, probably some of his tragi-comedies were acted there, for two of his plays were printed in 1645.

As the troop was not in a position to buy new plays, it must be supposed that they acted old ones, that is plays that had been printed and in which there was no dramatic copyright. It appears, however, plainly enough, that the members of the Illustre Théâtre could not make their business a paying concern. The Hôtel de Bourgogne was the old-established theatre, and most plays of importance were brought out there; sometimes the Théâtre du Marais was well filled, though ordinarily it was less fortunate. Playgoing was becoming a fashionable amusement among the Parisians, but the town was not large enough to support three theatres with profit to them all. And if it was the custom for people to go to the Hôtel de Bourgogne, the less lucky members of the Illustre Théâtre could only recognise the fact as disadvantageous to them. They were in debt when they began their new venture at the Port Saint Paul, and while they were there their troubles increased upon them.

On the 31st of March 1645 Molière signed a bond acknowledging that he had borrowed 291 livres from Jeanne Levé, a "marchande publique,"[1] and he was careful that his title tapissier valet de chambre du Roi should be given to him. As there is no mention in this bond of anything connected with the theatre, it is probable that Molière had borrowed the money for his own personal needs. The debt was not finally extinguished until the 13th of May 1659, and then he was described as "ci-devant valet de chambre du Roi."[2] It will be seen presently that he had allowed the title to be given to his younger brother.

It is sufficiently evident that the affairs of the members of the Illustre Théâtre were in a bad way; and it would seem

[1] Soulié, *Recherches sur Molière*, 42; 185.   [2] *Ibid.* 42; 201.

that for money owing by the troop Molière, as their leading
man, was put into prison at the Grand Châtelet two or three
times in quick succession. The first term of imprisonment
is not known, but probably it was quite short. Antoine
Fausser had obtained two sentences against him, amounting
to 142 livres, for candles; and when on the 2nd of August
1645 Molière presented a petition praying that he might be
let out of prison, saying that the claim made against him was
very small, and that he did not owe anything, he was discharged on parole, unless he were confined for more than 142
livres.[1] Later in the same day François Pommier, who had
lent 2000 livres to the troop, brought a claim against Molière
for that amount; and the same judge who had heard Molière's
petition against Fausser, liberated him from prison and from
the claim made by Pommier, on the condition that a substantial
person would pay for him 40 livres a week for eight weeks.[2]
A guarantor was found at once in the person of Léonard Aubry,
and Molière was set free.[3] And on the 4th of August Molière
obtained a third release from the Châtelet, again by the same
judge, on the same conditions as were given in the first discharge, against a claim made by one Dubourg, a linendraper,
for 150 livres.[4] These details are taken from the documents
published by Soulié and from his text in the earlier part of
his volume; but Soulié acknowledged that all the facts have
not come to light with perfect clearness. If a man has been
imprisoned for such causes as these, and five-and-twenty years
later he writes the *Tartuffe* and the *Avare*, posterity will look
upon the fact of his having been sent to jail as a bright feather
in his cap. The Léonard Aubry who came to Molière's rescue
was a man of good repute; he was a "paveur ordinaire des
bâtiments du Roi," and it was he who had paved the ground
in front of the Jeu de Paume des Métayers in December
1643.

On the 13th of August 1645 the members of the Illustre
Théâtre, including Joseph Béjart, gave a bond to Léonard
Aubry that they would refund to him the 320 livres he was
about to pay for Molière's release from prison.[5] They were

---

[1] *Recherches sur Molière*, 43, 44 ; 186.   [2] *Ibid*. 44, 45 ; 187, 188.
[3] *Ibid*. 45 ; 188.   [4] *Ibid*. 45, 46 ; 189.
[5] *Ibid*. 46 ; 189, 190.

no longer styled "comédiens de Son Altesse Royale"; but apparently they meant to continue their acting, for among the signatures to the bond is that of Germain Rabel, a new recruit. And in this bond there was another self-denying ordinance, that they would divide no profits among themselves until Aubry was paid. The profits from the theatre, we may be sure, were very small, and money must have been scarce with the young actors. No one can tell if Pommier ever got all the 2000 livres owing to him; the only known instance of repayment, except that made by Aubry on behalf of Molière, was made by one Prieur, who paid 120 livres on behalf of Catherine Bourgeois.[1] But how did Léonard Aubry get back the 320 livres he had so generously advanced? Jean Poquelin did pay his son's debts later, and he seems to have done so with a very bad grace. The inventory taken after his death, made in 1670, shows that sixteen months after Molière and his comrades had given their bond to Aubry, Poquelin gave Aubry a written promise (on the 24th of December 1646) that he would refund to him what he had spent on his son's behalf—"unless his son himself paid the money." The promise was kept, but not until two years and a half later. Poquelin also paid 125 livres to Pommier's wife (or to his widow) on his son's behalf, on some 4th of August before the year 1651.[2]

If the members of the Illustre Théâtre meant to continue their acting after their meeting on the 13th of August 1645, there is no evidence of their performances in any part of Paris. Their numbers were reduced from eleven to seven, and after Molière had been imprisoned the Duke of Orleans withdrew his protection from the troop. They had met with great reverses in the two theatres where they tried to gain the public favour, they had no money in their pockets, they were in debt, and could not show that their credit was good. It is, therefore, most unlikely they should have thought that by a third venture they could gain their once coveted glory.

I will say something now of the money accounts and other business transactions between Jean Poquelin and his children. When Molière gave his father a receipt for 630 livres on the 6th of January 1643, he promised to surrender his claim to the office of tapissier du Roi in favour of "such other of his

---

[1] *Recherches sur Molière*, 47; 191.   [2] *Ibid.* 47, 48; 227, 228.

father's children as his father should please to name."[1]   Jean
Poquelin had then only one other son. This boy was also
named Jean, and was born in 1624. He was described in the
inventory taken after his mother's death as "l'autre Jean," to
distinguish him from his elder brother Jean, afterwards
Molière; and in a document to be mentioned presently he is
spoken of as "Jean le jeune," to distinguish him from his
father.   M. Loiseleur thinks[2] that Molière's surrender of the
title to his brother was only a private family arrangement
demanded by the father, and that while Jean Poquelin the
father was alive, it would have been both useless and
dangerous to have troubled the Gentlemen of the King's
Chamber, who had granted the letters patent for the office,
with the family disagreements. It would seem also that the
surrender of the title by Molière was not voluntary on his
part, but that his father exacted from him the promise when
he gave him the 630 livres in January 1643. But Molière
did not cease to use the title for some years after 1643. We
have seen that when he borrowed money from Jeanne Levé in
March 1645, he qualified himself as "tapissier et valet de
chambre du Roi"; and later, when he was travelling with his
troop in the provinces, on two occasions when he stood godfather to a child, he was described as "valet de chambre du
Roi"—the first time was at Narbonne, on the 10th of January
1650,[3] the second at Montpellier on the 6th of January 1654.[4]
Some time later in 1654 the title was taken from him and
given to his younger brother Jean.

Molière's maternal grandfather, Louis de Cressé, was a rich
man when he died in 1638. His daughter, Marie Cressé, Jean
Poquelin's wife, was then dead; but three of her children—
Molière, "l'autre Jean" or "Jean le jeune," and Marie Madeleine—were due to receive, as from her, 5000 livres. It is
nowhere stated at what times Marie Cressé's children were to
get their money, but their father kept their portions in his own
hand as long as he could do so. On the 14th of September

---

[1] Soulié, *Recherches sur Molière*, 28; 227.—In the analysis of the receipt
given in the inventory taken after Jean Poquelin's death, the court title is
styled "tapissier du Roi." I do not gather that the omission of the words
"valet de chambre" had any bearing on the matter.
[2] *Les Points obscurs de la vie de Molière*, 112.
[3] *Le Moliériste* for April 1881 (iii. 20); *Œuvres de Molière*, x. 120.
[4] *Le Moliériste* for May 1879 (i. 45).

1654 Jean Poquelin sold his business in Paris to his younger son Jean, then close upon thirty years of age, who in the deed of sale was called "Jean le jeune" and was qualified, like his father, as "tapissier et valet de chambre ordinaire du Roi," for 5218 livres, at which sum Poquelin's stock had been valued. The father took his son's 5000 livres, which were due to him from his mother, and so paid himself the greater part of the purchase money; the remaining 218 livres the son paid his father in the following November.[1] Also on the 14th of September 1654, Jean Poquelin leased to this son Jean his house "sous les piliers des halles" for five years at a rent of 600 livres, stipulating that he should have for himself, or might use, certain parts of the house.[2] Poquelin had bought this house in 1633, but he did not live in it until nearly ten years later;[3] and these two last facts refute the idea set on foot by Grimarest that Molière was born there. On page 257 of the article referred to in the last note, Vitu remarked that Molière's father seems to have relinquished his business at one time and to have taken to it again later. It has been supposed by more than one writer that Jean Poquelin was much less prosperous in the latter part of his life than he had been formerly. He was probably a hard man of business, and as he got older and as his affairs declined, he became close-fisted in money matters. Before he went to live in his house sous les piliers des halles, he had let it to an old-clothes man; he was nearly fifty years of age when he did go to live there, and old-clothes men were common in the immediate neighbourhood. He married his second son Jean in 1656 to Marie Maillard, who could neither read nor write, but who brought her husband 11,500 livres in money and effects. This Jean died in 1660, leaving a son, christened Jean Baptiste after his godfather, Molière.[4] At some date after his brother's death Molière again took up the title of tapissier valet de chambre du Roi, and kept it until he died.

There was still left, besides Molière, one child of Marie

[1] Soulié, *Recherches sur Molière*, 51 ; 192, 193.
[2] *Ibid.* 51, 52 ; 193, 194.
[3] *Œuvres de Molière*, x. 8, 9 ; and a long article by A. Vitu, referred to by M. Mesnard, on the *Maison des Poquelins aux Piliers des Halles* in the *Mémoires de la Société de l'Histoire de Paris et de l'Ile de France*, vol. xi. p. 256.
[4] Jal, *Dictionnaire*, 989, col. 1.

Cressé, Madeleine (who had been christened Marie). She married André Boudet, an upholsterer, in 1651, and died in 1655, leaving two sons. She also was due to receive 5000 livres as from her mother, but her father did not pay the whole of this money until after her death.[1]

There is a certain interest in learning what were the sums of money Molière received out of the 5000 livres owing to him from his mother, for it will be seen either that he was not greedy of money, or that his father could not or would not give him his due. The original accounts between father and son have not been preserved; the reckoning is to be found in the inventory taken after Jean Poquelin's death in 1669. Before Molière left Paris for the provinces, his father had paid for him 630 livres, 320 livres, and 125 livres—making so far 1075 livres. During the next few years' Molière got from his father, in addition, 890 livres; for on the 19th of April 1651 he gave his father a written acknowledgment that he had received from him altogether 1965 livres.[2] That sum, when Poquelin's estate came to be divided among his heirs, Molière declared he had paid back to his father, with the knowledge of his brother-in-law André Boudet, and of his brother's widow, though neither of these two persons accepted his statement.[3] Also between 1660 and 1664, Poquelin had paid to his son various sums amounting to 1512 livres, 7 sous. These sums, too, Molière declared he did not owe to his father's estate, and this declaration his brother-in-law and sister-in-law were willing to accept.[4] Nothing is known of André Boudet or of the widow of Molière's brother; but I think that the fact of Molière having lent his father—unknown to him, through the intermediation of a third person—10,000 livres the year before his death,[5] may be taken as a sign that he would not have made a false declaration about a much smaller sum. Except to the intermediator Molière said nothing about this loan to his father, he asked for no interest for the money, and the circumstance was not discovered until after his own death. Is it likely, therefore, that he would have wished to cheat his co-

[1] Soulié, *Recherches sur Molière*, 63 ; 215.
[2] *Ibid.* 48 ; 227.
[3] *Ibid.* 64, 228, 1st paragraph signed by Molière, and 2nd paragraph signed by Boudet.
[4] *Ibid.* 64, 65 ; 234, 235.   [5] *Ibid.* 65, with references in notes 2, 3, and 4.

heirs about 2000 livres ? Taking his declaration as true, Soulié
has shown that Molière received from his father no more than
3477 livres, thus leaving in his favour at his father's death an
unpaid balance of over 1500 livres.

It is evident that Jean Poquelin gave his children the
money due to them from their mother with a sparing hand.
He did not give his son Jean le jeune his money until he was
close upon thirty years of age, when the father sold his business to his son; he did not pay his daughter during her lifetime all that was owing to her; and as to Molière's share of
the inheritance, the facts which have come to light show that
the father was loth or unable to give money, or that his son
was unwilling to ask for it. Some French writers have
assumed that Jean Poquelin's once prosperous business had
declined very considerably. It is not known when Molière
got the 890 livres for which he gave his father a receipt on the
14th of April 1651. Molière had then been absent from Paris
for some years; for after the members of the Illustre Théâtre
had failed so signally, the future dramatist and some of his
comrades left Paris and went strolling in the provinces.

CHAPTER V

STROLLING IN THE PROVINCES

SCARRON'S novel, *Le Roman Comique*, published in 1651, may serve nominally as an introduction to this chapter. The idea present to the author's mind was that of a romance which should tell of the doings of a company of strolling players in a humorous manner. The term "la comédie" was used in France in a wide sense, and meant a play of any kind acted in a theatre; "aller à la comédie" meant going to the play. And if the tastes of the Parisians can be taken as a guide, provincial audiences expected that the company which came to their town should be able to play tragedy as well as comedy. But Scarron does not say much about the concerns of a troop of strolling actors that would be most interesting to us now. If he speaks of the performances given or of the successes and failures of the troop, if he tells how the plays were put on the stage, how the troop travelled from place to place, and what were the usages and customs observed, he only does so incidentally. He does describe in a way of his own some of the adventures which he supposed might happen to a band of provincial actors, the shifts they were put to, and how they lived together among themselves. But he narrated the events as they arose in his mind, without other wish than to say what happened in the form of a novel. A tone of burlesque, of buffoonery, runs through all his tale. Buffoonery was Scarron's humour. The picture he has drawn is not flattering, and perhaps it was his intention to paint in dark colours rather than with a show of gay magnificence. If so, it is probable that his novel gained in truth what it may have lost in outward brightness. In spite of what is considered to be the dulness common to most old novels, the *Roman Comique* is written in a clear and rapid style; but a modern reader who refers to it with the idea of learning what were the theatrical customs in France two hundred and fifty years ago may find himself disappointed. The footnotes to M. Victor Fournel's edition of this book, published in 1857, tell us much that Scarron's first readers knew without explanation. It must not of course be assumed that Scarron intended to depict Molière and his comrades during the first years of their travels in the provinces. M. Louis Moland may be believed when he says that "*Le Roman Comique* was not intended to show any one special troop. What Scarron . . . had seen of provincial actors furnished him with a colouring. His fancy led him to imagine a troop of actors, and he introduced various incidents which he had seen at various times."[1] The characteristics of the personages in Scarron's novel are not so like what is known of the principal actors in Molière's troop as to lead one to suppose that his imaginary persons were intended to show actual men and women ; and the events which the novelist related are not known to have happened in Molière's troop. Scarron's novel is fiction, as a novel of the present day is fiction ; two hundred years hence people will refer to Mr. Vincent Crummles and his company as we refer nowadays to the *Roman Comique.*

Nearly everything that is known about Molière and his comrades during the thirteen years between 1645 and 1658 has been obtained from scraps of information collected here and there, telling that they were at a certain place at a more or less certain time. Certificates of baptism and registers of marriages, witnessed by one or more members of the troop, form one large source of authority ; or their presence has been sometimes revealed by a request to the magistrates of a town asking permission to allow theatrical representations. Occasionally these were given in a large room or hall ; but tennis-courts, where they existed, were preferred. It must always be remembered that Molière's company gave performances in other places than those of which any record has been preserved. They probably played at the fairs, or they may now and then have been invited by some nobleman to give a performance at his château, though the instances have not been related. Extremely little is known, however, of instances of their successes and failures. It is hardly doubtful that the greater number of plays they acted had already been

---

[1] *Œuvres de Molière,* 2nd ed. i. 63.

printed; in these there was no dramatic copyright. For
tragedy Corneille was more under requisition than any other
author, and some of his comedies may have been played. Also
the comedies of Scarron, Boisrobert, Desmarets and others;
and Rotrou, who wrote plays of all sorts, must have been seen
upon their boards. And Molière's own two comedies, the
Étourdi and the *Dépit Amoureux*, were probably acted pretty
constantly during the last years of their strolling. It is
believed that Molière wrote several farces while he was in the
provinces, and that these were acted to the great delight of
the country people; other farces, too, now quite unknown,
were probably acted and enjoyed. I shall be as brief as I can
with the dry bones of dates and names of places; but in connection with the subject other matter is sometimes introduced
which may perhaps lend a little interest to the narrative.

Soulié thought that Molière and his friends who had been
so unlucky at the Illustre Théâtre were preparing to leave
Paris at the end of the year 1646,[1] though later writers say,
probably with reason, that they must have left fully twelve
months earlier.[2] The actors had no cause to love Paris, and
they could do themselves no good by remaining there idle.
Madeleine Béjart had played in the provinces before; to do
so again was her only hope. She was still under thirty years
of age, and what is known of her does not show her to be a
feckless woman. Molière, too, was eager in his wish to
succeed. He had chosen his own career against his father's
wish, and he felt that he must go on with it. It was not love
for Madeleine Béjart that prompted him. He was driven on
by the earnestness and by the persistency of his own nature.
If he had had his youthful ambition, that had well-nigh disappeared; if there had been romance, that also had vanished.
The gilt had been taken off his gingerbread, but he would eat
his dry cake even though it choked him. It is probable that
the actors who volunteered to join in the new campaign were
few in number. That Molière was accompanied by the four
Béjarts—Joseph, Madeleine, Geneviève and Louis—may be
conceded. And Marie Hervé, the mother of the Béjarts, was

[1] *Recherches sur Molière*, 47.
[2] Louis Moland, *Œuvres de Molière*, 2nd ed. i. 60; *Œuvres de Molière*,
x. 102, 103. (*Notice biographique*, by M. P. Mesnard.)

with them for a few years. She was then an elderly woman, and in the printed plays of the time elderly women did not often have parts given to them. Not improbably she gave her services as cook. As to the other members of the troop, no one can guess who they were. Some of the old friends may have clung together, or there may have been new recruits. But it appears that the high-sounding title of the Illustre Théâtre was dropped.[1] All French acting companies were strongly imbued with a spirit of republicanism, owning no master to govern their actions ; still, there must have been one or more ruling head to direct the affairs of the troop. As far as can be judged, this responsibility was shared quite at first by Molière and Madeleine Béjart. If they were agreed in their counsels most of their comrades would wish to follow their advice. The one or two leaders would probably say in what towns the troop should play, though all the actors had a voice in the matter. There is a clause to this effect in a minute of agreement between the actors of a strolling company passed in Paris in the year 1664: "Et les voyages se feront dans les villes et lieux qui seront accordés entre eux à la pluralité des voix, pour y représenter la comédie."[2] Even at the Hôtel de Bourgogne in Paris matters were arranged on social principles, no one being allowed to dictate his will or to expect obedience except on the stage. This system had long been in force, and it continued for many years. All strolling companies governed themselves by the same laws, as far as circumstances would permit, that prevailed at the two theatres in Paris.

It was customary in those days for strolling companies to put themselves under the protection of some nobleman of importance. He was their patron, and besides lending to them the support of his name he gave them material assistance. Molière's name is now so well known that the actors who played with him in the provinces are commonly spoken of as belonging to "la troupe de Molière," but for the first few years of their strolling they were known as belonging to "la troupe du duc d'Épernon." This duke was then governor of the province of Guienne ; and he was already the patron of a troop of actors, headed by Charles Dufresne, when Molière

---

[1] Louis Moland, *Œuvres de Molière*, 2nd ed. i. 61.
[2] Soulié, *Recherches sur Molière*, 211, first par.

and his friends became their allies—the two companies joining their forces together. The duke's protection, thus given to Molière, was first accorded probably late in 1645 or early in 1646. There is a tradition that Bordeaux was the first town where Molière acted in the provinces; and though it seems most likely now that, because the plague was strong there in 1646, he did not play at all in Bordeaux, he may nevertheless have acted in a small neighbouring town or in some château belonging to the Duc d'Épernon, the governor of the province.[1]

Dufresne was some years older than Molière, and had a longer theatrical experience. He saw that in Molière's troop there were at least two persons of more than ordinary intelligence. Overtures were made, the companies were united, and the post of captain, so far as it existed, was given to Dufresne. It was then a less difficult matter to collect a company of strolling players than to keep them together for a length of time. When an engagement was made it might have lasted from one Easter to another, the beginning and the close of the theatrical year. For the while the actor belonged to the troop, had his vote in its concerns and shared its fortunes; and he, like the older members, wished to maintain his feelings of independence. Some actors, known as "gagistes," were hired temporarily and were paid for their services, but they did not belong to the troop. If the troop, known afterwards as Molière's, held together better than most others, it was, perhaps, because they made more money. In later years Molière knew very well what he was saying when he cried in a fit of vexation: "Ah! les étranges animaux à conduire que des comédiens."[2] After the union between Dufresne and Molière, Dufresne became, nominally at least, the director of the troop; he was now and again the spokesman of the company in petitioning the authorities of a town to be allowed to give theatrical representations. In this way Dufresne's presence argues Molière's presence also. By degrees Molière came to the front; his name stands forward while that of Dufresne falls into the shade. But they continued to be allies until the troop went to Paris in 1658.

---

[1] Louis Moland, *Œuvres de Molière*, 2nd ed. i. 66, 67 ; *Œuvres de Molière*, x. 103-109 (*Notice biographique*, by Paul Mesnard) ; Arnaud Detcheverry, *Histoire des théâtres de Bordeaux*, 12-16.

[2] Early in sc. 1 of the *Impromptu de Versailles*.

In the autumn of 1647 Molière was at Albi, now the capital of the Tarn, in the south of France. In October of that year the town of Albi gave 500 livres to the troop of actors belonging to the Duc d'Épernon, and the receipt for the money was signed by Charles Dufresne, René Berthelot, and Pierre Revelhon.[1] The name of this last man should read Réveillon, but no great interest is attached to him. René Berthelot is better known by his stage name du Parc; he was the Gros René in the *Dépit Amoureux*, and he was the husband of a handsome wife. When the patron of a strolling company did not desire the presence of his actors, they were free to go where they pleased, and it would seem that in 1647 Dufresne, with Molière and the Béjarts, played at Toulouse, Albi, and Carcassonne, towns in the province of Languedoc.[2]

From the south the troop went as far north as Brittany. The registers of the Hôtel de Ville at Nantes show that on the 23rd of April 1648, "le sieur Morlierre [*sic*] l'un des comédiens de la troupe du sieur Dufresne," went to the office and humbly asked to be allowed to play their comedies. After a delay caused by the illness of the governor of the province, Dufresne was sent for on the 17th of May, and was told that he might give a performance the next day for the benefit of the hospital of the town, according to the custom which other troops of actors had observed. Dufresne complied with the stipulation demanded, and the money taken at the door of the tennis-court on the first day's performance was given to the hospital.[3] This hospital money, or means of taxing the theatre for the benefit of the poor of the town, was an old institution. The fine was levied, I believe, only on the first day; on subsequent days the actors were allowed to keep what they had earned.

After leaving Nantes, Dufresne went to Fontenay le Comte in La Vendée; and there on the 9th of June a petition was granted to him in a court of law that one Benesteau should let to him a tennis-court for twenty-one days, at the rate of seven livres a day.[4]

Nearly a year later Dufresne was at Toulouse; and there on

[1] L. Moland, *Œuvres de Molière*, 2nd ed. i. 69, 70; P. Mesnard, *Notice biographique sur Molière*, 107, 108.
[2] P. Mesnard, *Notice biographique sur Molière*, 113-115.
[3] Benjamin Fillon, *Recherches sur le séjour de Molière dans l'Ouest de la France en 1648*, pp. 3, 4.   [4] *Ibid.* 1.

the 16th of May 1649 Messieurs les Capitouls ordered that his troop should be paid seventy-five livres for having "joué et fait une comédie" in honour of the arrival of the king's lieutenant, the Comte de Roure.[1]

It would be difficult to say what effect the Civil War in France, known as La Fronde, had upon Molière's troop during their travels. The Fronde broke out in Paris in 1648, and for some months the theatres there were closed, and the actors were under arms.[2] Skirmishing went on for some four years. The number of new plays acted in Paris from 1648 to 1653 was rather less than half of those that had been acted from 1642 to 1647; and comparatively few new plays were acted in Paris until the year 1659.[3] While the Fronde lasted the people were in distress in many parts of the country; and for this reason, when Molière made a request to the civic authorities at Poitiers, on the 8th of November 1649, to be allowed to come there "avec ses compagnons pour y passer un couple de mois," the maire and his colleagues refused to give their consent.[4]

In the introductory chapter I mentioned Rotrou's name. He wrote very many plays between 1628 and 1650; and for an account of what a French provincial theatre was like in his day, perhaps I may be allowed to quote part of a speech made by Édouard Thierry, at one time administrator of the Comédie Française, on the occasion of the unveiling of a statue of Rotrou at Dreux, in Normandy, in the year 1869.   The extract is from pages 120, 121, of a pamphlet called *Rotrou le Grand*, published at Dreux in 1869:—

"There were at that time more troops of strolling companies than those which were permanently stationed in one place. The same customs governed them all. Performances were given when they were possible. On each occasion they were announced by a drum played in the street. A harlequin used to follow the drum, and all the little children came out to see the fun. If the call was not re-

---

[1] *Œuvres de Molière*, x. 118, 119 (*Notice biographique*, by M. P. Mesnard).
[2] *Œuvres de P. Corneille*, by Ch. Marty-Laveaux, v. 248-251. (Édition des Grands Écrivains de la France.)
[3] See the chronological table of plays at the end of the *Histoire philosophique et littéraire du théâtre français*, by Hippolyte Lucas (1843).
[4] Bricauld de Verneuil, *Molière à Poitiers en* 1648 *et les comédiens dans cette ville de* 1646 *à* 1658; 26, 27, and 55; *Le Moliériste* for January 1886 (vol. vii. 300, 301).

sponded to with sufficient liberality, somebody said a polite 'Thank you' to those who had been willing to disturb themselves, and the thing was put off till the next day or that day week. But if it happened that there might be a tolerable audience, the candles were lighted and the performance began. The actors got their supper that night; for after each performance, the money taken at the doors was put upon the table and the house-porter gave to each actor his share of the receipts. To find a theatre was not difficult, though it might not be so good as the Hôtel de Bourgogne nor as the Théâtre du Marais. A tennis-court was hired; at one end a raised platform was erected with two primitive ladders by which the actors could descend into the pit before the performance began and show themselves in their fine clothes. The pourtour and the galleries formed part of the tennis-court, and the rope network put up to prevent the balls from hitting the spectators were not taken down. The remembrance of this is still preserved by the network in front of the pourtour in some of our present theatres. The fine gentlemen had the privilege of being allowed to sit on the stage. They pushed their chairs about as they pleased, and they hid what was going on from the small people in the pit. They used to get up during the performance, gossip with the actresses behind the stage, talk in a noisy manner, and oblige the actor who was playing to halt in the middle of his wail of despair or of his cry of passion, so that silence might be observed."

This is a lively description of a provincial theatre in France about the time that Molière and his troop were strolling in the country towns. It will be said in a later chapter how men used to sit upon the stage and often behave themselves badly. I have seen somewhere, though I cannot put my finger on the authority, that in some provincial theatre a player was so constrained in his movements that he uttered a loud aside: "Allow me, my lord; I must pass to kill Orestes." Things may have been done a little better in the capital than in the provinces, but a countryman going from Rouen to Paris would not have found many material differences.

Two certificates of baptism witnessed by some members of Molière's comrades show that the troop was at Narbonne, in the province of Languedoc, in the winter of 1649-50.[1] At one of these ceremonies Molière was godfather to the child, and was described as "Jean Baptiste Poquelin, valet de chambre du Roy." The godmother signed herself Catherine du Rosé. This was then the stage name of Catherine Leclerc.[2]

---

[1] Le Moliériste for April 1881 (vol. iii. 20, 21); L. Moland, Œuvres de Molière, 2nd ed. i. 75, 76; Œuvres de Molière, x. 120, 121 (Notice biographique, by M. P. Mesnard).   [2] Jal, Dictionnaire, 282, col. 1.

Mention is first made of her this winter at Narbonne. It is most likely that she joined Molière's troop at Lyons in 1653. She was then married to an actor named de Brie, and as Mlle. de Brie—for actresses were never called Madame—she gave most valuable service to Molière's troop when she played in Paris in after years.

From Narbonne the actors returned to the province of Guienne, and on the 13th of February 1650 Dufresne appeared before the municipal authorities at Agen to pay his respects and to say that he had come there by the order of the governor, the Duc d'Épernon.[1]

The duke remained at Agen until the 25th of July, when he gave up the governorship of the province of Guienne, and probably his patronage or "protection" of Molière and his friends ceased at the same time. At first his support had doubtless been useful to the actors, but as they found that they were at the beck and call of a nobleman who was everywhere very unpopular in his province, it is easy to suppose that they were glad to be released from serving a master who made himself generally disliked.[2]

It was an object with strolling companies of importance to go to the town where the Provincial States were holding their session. The Provincial States—Les États Provinciaux—were something like our English County Councils, but with larger powers. These assemblies, dating from the middle of the 13th century, used to take place periodically. They were held under the king's authority, and were presided over by a nobleman appointed for that purpose. But every province did not have the honour of holding a separate assembly of its own. This was originally confined to the *pays des états*, a name given in the ancient French monarchy to those provinces which, by virtue of treaties with the crown, had maintained the right to govern themselves. The Provincial States were in fact local parliaments, in which the church, the nobility, and the tiers état were represented. In the province of Languedoc, which concerns us now, the clergy and the nobles each sent twenty-three deputies; the tiers état sent sixty-eight. But lest the tiers état should outvote the more

---

[1] Adolphe Magen, *La Troupe de Molière à Agen*, 2nd ed. 21.
[2] *Œuvres de Molière*, x. 121, 122 (*Notice biographique*).

noble orders, their sixty-eight votes were counted as forty-six, and these men were considerably under the influence of the clergy and the nobility.[1]   At all events, the number of deputies was one hundred and fourteen, so that the town where they met was often full while the session lasted. There is a letter from an Archbishop of Toulouse, saying that Montpellier was not suitable for the purpose, for it was a town of pleasure; that small towns such as Béziers or Pézenas were more convenient, for there the deputies would soon get tired, and be likely to do their business with greater despatch.[2] Rightly or wrongly, some of the deputies liked to amuse themselves in the afternoon, and for this purpose an order was often sent to a troop of actors commanding their presence. There is some evidence to show that when strolling companies were engaged in the service of the States, their travelling expenses were defrayed by the province,[3] though it might be hazardous to say this was always the case.   From 1648 to 1658 sessions were held by the States annually in different towns in the province of Languedoc.   When, as was frequent, the session began in the latter part of one year and finished in the next, that session was said to belong to the year in which it terminated.[4]

An autograph receipt by Molière for 4000 livres shows that he and his friends were at Pézenas in December 1650, and that they played there before the States.   This session lasted from the 24th of October 1650 to the 14th of January 1651. The receipt was discovered by M. de la Pijardière among the departmental archives of the Hérault, and was published by him with a facsimile of the original in the *Moliériste* for November 1885.[5]   From the records of moneys spent by the States during this session, M. de la Pijardière gave the following extract:—"To the actors who have served for three months while the States were on foot, the sum of four

[1] Emmanuel Raymond, *Histoire des pérégrinations de Molière dans le Languedoc*, 121.
[2] *Correspondance administrative sous le règne de Louis XIV.*, par G. B. Depping (in the Collection des documents inédits sur l'histoire de France), vol. i. introduction, pp. xx, xxi.
[3] *Le Moliériste* for August 1879 (vol. i. 142, 143).
[4] There is an article by M. de la Pijardière in the *Moliériste* for December 1880 (vol. ii. 264), where the places and dates of these sessions are given.
[5] Vol. vii. 233.   Another facsimile is given in the album to the *Œuvres de Molière* in the Collection des Grands Écrivains de la France.

thousand livres which has been paid to them after deliberation of the States, and by their receipt—4000 livres." Then follows the receipt written and signed by Molière :—

> "*J'ay receu de Monsieur de Penautier* [1] *la somme de quatre mille livres ordonnees aux comediens par Messieurs les Etats. Faict à Pezenas ce 17ᵉ decembre mil six cent cinquante.*
> "*Pour* 4000 *liv.*   MOLIÈRE ·/."

It may be seen that though the actors were paid for three months' service, they had not served quite eight weeks when they got their money. M. Mesnard thinks that as soon as they were paid they were released from their engagement.[2] This facsimile of Molière's handwriting, though it is only a short receipt for money, is of interest. The writing is almost as legible as print, in something of. a running hand, but the character of it is singularly bold and firm. Besides the mere signature of his name, I think there is only one other known instance of Molière's handwriting. It will be spoken of presently. Examples of Molière's signature are not very uncommon. Jal reproduced two,[3] written in 1667 and in 1668; in the album of Molière's works lately referred to there are facsimiles of the poet's signature, written in 1662, 1668, and 1672. Three of these are written "J. B. P. Molière," and two "J. B. Poquelin Molière." And there is in the Manuscript Room at the British Museum, among the Foreign Literary Autographs, in Case VIII., an instance of Molière's signature attached to a Notarial Certificate, dated 25th January 1664. The character of all of these signatures is strongly the same, and Molière seems to have used the mark or sign following his name consistently.

From what has been said and from what follows, I should be inclined to date the pecuniary success of Molière's strolling in the provinces from about the latter part of the year 1650, when mention is first made of his troop playing before the States. Success may have come before this time, but perhaps it will be seen upon the whole that for the remaining seven or eight years that his troop were in the provinces they were in easy circumstances as regards money. Henceforward Molière's name comes to the front, he is spoken of as though

---

[1] Trésorier de la Bourse de Languedoc.
[2] *Œuvres de Molière*, x. 122.   [3] *Dictionnaire*, 874.

he were the virtual head of the troop. Dufresne, on the other hand, is not mentioned; he was one of the company, but is not now distinguishable from the other members.

In the spring of 1651 Molière was in Paris. All that is known of his visit there is that on the 14th of April in that year he gave an acknowledgment that he had received 1965 livres from his father.[1] But there is no evidence to show that he was accompanied by his friends. Samuel Chappuzeau, the author of a volume called *Le Théâtre François*, published at Lyons in 1674, from which I shall make a good many extracts in a later chapter, says that few people in the provinces went to the theatre during Lent, but that at that time strolling companies often went to Paris to learn good lessons from the masters in the art of acting as well as to make new engagements. Chappuzeau thought there might have been some twelve or fifteen strolling companies in the provinces, that the art of acting was first learned there, and that from these strolling troops the best actors and actresses were taken as they were wanted to fill the theatres in the capital.[2] The theatrical customs in Chappuzeau's day had been doubtless the same twenty years earlier. But there is nothing to show that Molière's comrades made any visit to Paris while they were strolling in the provinces. In the year 1651 his troop was pretty well filled; there is reason to think that the actors were learning their business satisfactorily in the country towns, and one would say that they would not have undertaken a journey to the capital without a definite object before them.

In endeavouring to follow the traces of Molière's wanderings through the provinces, when there is any fair indication of his having been at a given place it is well to mention the circumstance, though the interest in these bare details is not of a lively kind. There are towns to which he is believed to have gone, but at what period cannot be easily determined. Among these places is Vienne in the Dauphiné, some twenty miles south of Lyons. M. Mesnard thinks that Molière was at Vienne in 1651, other writers say in 1653 or 1654.[3] And

[1] Soulié, *Recherches sur Molière*, 48 ; 227, 228.
[2] Page 134 of the modern edition of this book published in 1875.
[3] *Œuvres de Molière*, x. 124-26 ; *Le Moliériste* for June 1882 (vol. iv. 72).

it is likely that he played at Carcassonne while the States of Languedoc held their session there from the 31st of July 1651 to the 10th of January 1652.[1]

From 1652 to 1655, both years more or less inclusive, Molière was a good deal at Lyons. It is not known when he came or when he went, but during these years he probably made Lyons his headquarters. On the 19th of December 1652, Pierre Réveillon, one of his troop, was godfather to a child christened in that town.[2] And at Lyons, on the 19th of February 1653, J. B. Poquelin and Joseph Béjart signed the marriage contract between René Berthelot, otherwise du Parc, and Marquise Thérèse de Gorla.[3] The marriage itself was solemnised at Lyons four days later, and was witnessed by Dufresne and Réveillon.[4] Du Parc and his wife were then members of Molière's troop. Mlle. du Parc is said to have possessed beauty of an elevated kind, and perhaps for this reason some writers have thought that Marquise was a nickname given to her in a friendly way; but it is more probable that she was so christened. Jal[5] gives the year 1633, doubtfully, as the date of her birth; and her burial certificate, also given by Jal, states that she died on the 11th of December 1668, "aged about twenty-five years." Perhaps thirty-five years was meant. Before she saw Molière she had played in a troop of clowns and mountebanks, of which her father was the head; and doubtless she was glad to find herself promoted into a troop of actors who endeavoured to amuse in a more intelligent manner. She and her husband were comrades with Molière for many years.

Mention was made a few pages back of Mlle. de Brie, and now Mlle. du Parc is heard of for the first time. Both of these actresses belonged to Molière's troop in 1653, but it is not certain that either of them was a member of it before that date. Mlle. de Brie was then perhaps thirty-three years of age, her figure was thin and graceful, and she continued to act at least one young part until she retired from the stage in 1685.

---

[1] *Le Moliériste* for September 1884 (vol. vi. 174-180) ; L. Moland, *Œuvres de Molière*, 2nd. ed. i. 81 ; P. Mesnard, *Notice biographique sur Molière*, 128.

[2] C. Brouchoud, *Les Origines du théâtre à Lyon*, 51.

[3] *Ibid.* 31, 32 (the facsimile of this contract is given facing p. 56 of *Œuvres de Molière*, x. 129).

[4] Brouchoud, work just cited, pp. 45, 46.   [5] *Dictionnaire*, 936.

We are told that Molière loved both of these women, and tradition has said that Madeleine Béjart had been his mistress.   If all these reports are true, he must have had some embarrassing moments.   In the fourth paragraph of a libellous little book, *La Fameuse Comédienne ou Histoire de la Guérin auparavant femme et veuve de Molière*,[1] probably first published at Frankfort in 1688, and of which the authorship is not known, we read that when Molière and his friends arrived at Lyons they found another troop of actors there in which were Mlle. du Parc and Mlle. de Brie.   Molière, we are told, was charmed with the good looks of Mlle. du Parc, but she, hoping for a more glorious conquest, treated him with disdain; he therefore turned his thoughts to Mlle. de Brie, who received him more favourably. Madeleine Béjart, the writer goes on to say, bore this attachment with much pain, but as she saw she could not prevent it, she consoled herself by exercising over Molière an authority which she had always maintained, and obliged him to conceal his intercourse with Mlle. de Brie; and they remained for some years on this understanding.   It is impossible to prove or refute these assertions now.   Some of them may be more or less true, though a good deal depends on the way one looks at them. It is easy to say that in those days among a troop of actors a husband's presence did not count for much, and that he allowed his wife to go her own way so long as she did not interfere with him.   That does not mean that Molière made love openly to another man's wife.   It may mean, however, that there was a friendship, Platonic or not, between Molière and Mlle. de Brie which her husband had neither the power nor the inclination to prevent.   But before accusing Mlle. de Brie of faithlessness to her husband, there should be some grounds for the accusation better worthy of belief than the pages of *La Fameuse Comédienne.*

The authorship of that book has been ascribed to Chapelle, to La Fontaine, to Racine, and to an actress named Boudin, of whom nothing is known except her name.   On first thoughts suspicion might easily fall upon Chapelle.   M. Jules Bonnassies, however, published an edition of the book in 1870, and at the end of a preliminary notice he refused to believe

[1] Four years after Molière's death his widow married an actor named Guérin.

that Chapelle was its author.   He thought that on the whole the least unlikely theory is that it should be attributed to Mlle. Guyot, an actress, and that she was perhaps assisted by a woman named Chasteauneuf, who was or had been the wife of the portier at the Palais Royal theatre.   M. Bonnassies is well versed in the details of the French stage in the 17th century, but I cannot think that either of the women just named had much to do with the actual writing of the story told.   Their tongues may have been nimble enough, but I doubt altogether that either knew how to write two lines without showing an entire absence of any sort of literary education.   Possibly these women may have related the story verbally, but the printed narrative shows that it was written by some one who could say what he thought with a pen in his hand.   The responsibility was put upon Chapelle because of his old friendship with Molière, and because of an often told tale, to be given in a later chapter, of a scene in the poet's garden at Auteuil, for which Chapelle may, consciously or not, have furnished the substance.   Even assuming so much, it would be unfair to Chapelle to say that, for all the rest of the book, he had compiled or written at anybody's instruction a pamphlet of spiteful garbage, showing a certain small intimacy in Molière's affairs and with the doings of his wife and later of his widow.   Paul Lacroix hinted that La Fontaine was the author, but there is no evidence to justify the insinuation.   As to Racine, he had for at least ten years before this book appeared totally disconnected himself from the stage and from persons belonging to it, and the charge against him is unwarrantable.   Like other books of its kind, *La Fameuse Comédienne* should be received with caution. It was dictated by ill-will chiefly against Molière's widow, and was not published until some thirteen years after the poet's death.

While Molière was at Lyons two important performances took place there, but to neither of them can a certain date be assigned.   One of these was Corneille's tragedy *Andromède*, played some time before the autumn of 1653.[1]   This play was first acted in Paris in January 1650, and was printed in March in the following year.   The fact of the performance of

[1] *Œuvres de Molière*, x. 138 (*Notice biographique*).

Corneille's tragedy by Molière's troop at Lyons has been revealed in a curious way. In a copy of the first edition of the play which had belonged to the Comte de Pont de Veyle, by the side of the names of each of the personages represented was written the name of the actor who took that part at Lyons.[1] If this list is trustworthy it shows with fair probability a pet name, "Mlle. Menou," given to a little girl who afterwards became Molière's wife. She played the part of Éphyre and had to recite only four lines. The list also shows that many of the actors had to take more than one part; and there are some whose names are found for the first time in connection with Molière, though one cannot say whether they were members of his troop or whether their engagements were merely temporary. One name must be mentioned, that of Mlle. de Brie. She had three parts given to her to play in the tragedy. Her husband also appeared as an actor, and it is most likely that both of them had been enrolled in the troop.

The other performance at Lyons about this time, and more important for us now, was that of Molière's first comedy, *L'Étourdi*. This was the earliest of his plays—if we except the farces he wrote while in the provinces, but as to none of which can a date be given—and it was certainly produced for the first time at Lyons. It is generally believed that the *Étourdi* first appeared on the stage in 1653; but from the evidence it may be urged with at least equal reason that the play was not acted until 1655. On the fourth page of his Register,[2] La Grange, speaking of the *Étourdi*, says: "Cette pièce de théâtre a été représentée pour la première fois à Lyon, l'an *1655*." The language of that sentence cannot be misconstrued. But in the preface to the first complete edition of Molière's plays, published in 1682, which is usually credited to La Grange, and of which he must have shared the responsibility if he did not write it—for La Grange and Vivot were the joint editors of the whole work—are the words: "Il [Molière] vint à Lyon en 1653, et ce fut là qu'il exposa au public sa première comédie: c'est celle de l'*Étourdi*." There should be

---

[1] *Œuvres de P. Corneille* (ed. Marty Laveaux), v. 255; *Œuvres de Molière*, x. 136 (*Notice biographique*).

[2] I shall speak of La Grange's Register at the beginning of the next chapter.

no reasonable doubt what these words mean, though Despois criticised them,[1] as they do not agree with what La Grange had written in his Register twenty-three years earlier. La Grange's testimony is the only authority on the matter. The manuscript of his Register is still in existence, but not that of the preface. Probably there has been a mistake between the figures 3 and 5. French writers have generally followed the date given in the preface, and have said that the *Étourdi* was first performed in 1653. They have, very naturally, thought that La Grange would have taken pains to be careful in his last words about his late intimate friend whose plays he was editing. On the other hand, I am disposed to think that after La Grange had joined Molière's company in Paris at Easter, 1659, and many of those who had taken part in the performance at Lyons still belonged to the troop, human memory would be fresher and more trustworthy than twenty-three years later when the preface was written. At that time both Molière and most of his old comrades were dead, and Mlle. de Brie is the only one of those who played with him at Lyons who is now known to have been alive and in Paris in the year 1682. Both the editors of Molière's plays in the edition to which I usually refer—Eugène Despois, and after his death M. Paul Mesnard—refuse to pronounce affirmatively in favour of either year, though M. Mesnard evidently inclines to the later one.[2] M. Louis Moland holds to the earlier date.[3] No direct record appears to have been left expressing approbation of the new play. But it will be seen presently that Molière stayed all the summer of 1655 at Lyons, and that fact may lead one to think that the *Étourdi* was well enjoyed by the Lyons public. It will be better to defer speaking of the comedy in this play until the next chapter.

Some time in 1653, perhaps early in September,[4] Molière saw again the Prince de Conti, his former schoolfellow. Conti

---

[1] *Œuvres de Molière*, i. 80.—"This sentence means only one thing: that the first performance of the *Étourdi* took place at Lyons after 1652, but it does not specify the date."

[2] *Œuvres de Molière*, vol. i., Notice on the *Étourdi*, by E. Despois, specially pp. 84, 86 ; and M. Mesnard's *Notice biographique sur Molière*, pp. 133, 154, 161, 162.

[3] *Œuvres de Molière*, by Louis Moland, 1st ed. vol. i. p. lxiii ; and 2nd ed. vol. i. 82 ; 95.

[4] P. Mesnard, *Notice biographique sur Molière*, 150.

had left Bordeaux in August, and he sent his mistress, Madame de Calvimont, whom Sainte-Beuve describes as being as "silly as she was handsome," to his château, La Grange, near Pézenas. Among the prince's household were Sarrasin his secretary, and the abbé de Cosnac, the first gentleman of his chamber, later Bishop of Valence and afterwards Archbishop of Aix. Cosnac has left a curious account of how Molière was summoned to appear before the prince :—

"As soon as she [Madame de Calvimont] came to live at La Grange, she wished that a troop of actors should be summoned. As I was entrusted with the prince's private purse I had to negotiate the matter. I had heard that Molière's company was in Languedoc, and I sent word to them to come to La Grange. While this troop was preparing to obey my orders, another troop headed by one Cormier arrived at Pézenas. The prince's natural impatience and the presents made to Madame de Calvimont by Cormier's troop prevailed, and their services were bespoken. When I told the prince that by his order I had engaged Molière, he answered that he had engaged Cormier, and that it was more fitting that I should break my word than that he should break his. In the meantime Molière arrived, and when he asked that his travelling expenses at least should be paid, I could not satisfy him, though there was much justice in his demand. M. le prince de Conti thought well to hold to his own opinion in such a trifling matter. This unfair dealing annoyed me so much that I determined that Molière and his friends should show themselves on the stage at Pézenas, and I gave them a thousand écus of my money rather than break my word to them. When they were ready to open their theatre in the town, the prince, importuned by Sarrasin, whom I had enlisted on my side, found that his honour was in question after what I had done. He allowed them, therefore, to give one performance at La Grange. This did not please Madame de Calvimont, consequently the prince did not like it, though everybody else thought them infinitely superior to Cormier's troop, both in their acting and in the magnificence of their costumes. A few days afterwards they played again, and Sarrasin, by dint of extolling their praises, made the prince see that he must employ Molière in place of Cormier. Sarrasin had watched them and had upheld them from the first on my account; but later, becoming smitten with Mlle. du Parc, he thought of furthering his own ends. He brought Madame de Calvimont to his way of thinking, and not only did he get Cormier's troop sent away, but he obtained a pension for Molière's."[1]

In this affair the narrator of the story, then a young man of twenty-three, appears to the best advantage; but one would like to know if he told quite the truth when he said that "he

[1] *Mémoires de Daniel de Cosnac*, published by the Société de l'histoire de France, i. 126-128.

gave Molière's troop a thousand écus [three thousand francs] of his money." It would seem, however, that Molière was fortunate in having in his company a handsome woman to engage the attentions of Sarrasin. M. Mesnard may well be right in thinking that, as Cosnac does not mention the title of any play acted before the Prince de Conti in the autumn of 1653, it is probable that the *Étourdi* was not acted then. A clever-witted man like Cosnac would have noticed the brightness of the verses in Molière's play, he would have seen that the sparkle of fun in that comedy was much stronger than in other comedies of the time.

Both Soulié[1] and M. Mesnard[2] think that it was about the end of 1653 that Molière's troop obtained a pension from the prince, and that they first became known by the title of "les comédiens du Prince de Conti."

From Pézenas, Molière probably went to Montpellier.[3] He was godfather to a child christened there on the 6th of January 1654, and in the certificate of baptism he was described as "valet de chambre du Roy."[4] It is likely that he stayed there for some weeks, as the States held their session that year at Montpellier. Two baptismal certificates seem to show that his troop was at Lyons on the 8th of March.[5] Authorities differ as to whether he remained at Lyons during the summer of 1654, but two of his comrades, Réveillon and Mlle. du Parc, were there on the 3rd of November in that year.[6]

It is tolerably certain that the troop played before the States at Montpellier during the session of 1655; and it was probably in the carnival of that year[7] that there was a gala performance of a ballet, known in its printed form as "*Le Ballet des Incompatibles,* dansé à Montpellier devant Mgr. le prince et Mme. la princesse de Conty." Twelve months, more or less, previously, the prince had married in Paris, Anne Martinozzi, niece of Cardinal Mazarin; and very likely the ballet had been composed in her honour. Those who took part in it were chosen from the gentlemen of the prince's household,

---

[1] *Revue du Lyonnais,* 3rd series, vol. i. 291.
[2] *Notice biographique sur Molière,* 154.   [3] *Ibid.* 155.
[4] *Le Moliériste* for May 1879 (vol. i. 45).
[5] Brouchoud, *Les Origines du théâtre à Lyon,* documents ii., iii.
[6] *Ibid.,* document iv.
[7] *Œuvres de Molière,* i. 524; *Le Moliériste* for April 1887 (vol. ix. 24).

from those who had been called to serve in the States, and certain parts were given to some of the actors in Molière's troop—but they were not required to dance. At that time it was not thought right that any woman should take a part in the performance of court ballets; a generation later they did so, and the custom was introduced among the nobility.[1] Ballets were always considered as aristocratic amusements. The title "Le Ballet des Incompatibles" meant that the different personages forming part of it were of a very heterogeneous character. A printed copy of the pamphlet—the programme or "livre," as it was then called—was found by Paul Lacroix, who reprinted it twice in the conviction that it was written by Molière.[2] Despois also printed this ballet in the appendix to the first volume of the Œuvres de Molière, but he did not think that the future dramatist was its author, though perhaps he may have written a small part of it. His opinion, I believe, is general.

As a mark of respect to the prince, Joseph Béjart dedicated to him a book on the heraldry of the nobility of Languedoc. The book was published at Lyons in 1655, and it will be said presently that the States gave him 1500 livres for it.

Molière's troop were now known as "les comédiens de son Altesse le Prince de Conti." They were in receipt of a pension from their patron, and they were bound in a measure to be under his orders. Grimarest says that during this session at Montpellier, the prince had entrusted to Molière the management of all the entertainments; and he adds a story which has the merit of being engaging.[3] Conti wanted to make Molière his secretary, but Molière begged leave to be excused:—

"Ah! gentlemen," he said to those who urged him to accept the offer, "we ought not to misplace ourselves. If I can believe public opinion, I am a tolerable author, but I might make a very bad secretary. I amuse the prince by the pieces I play before him, but I should annoy him by serious work badly done. Do you think, too,

---

[1] The best and fullest account of the ballets de cour has been given by M. Victor Fournel in the second volume of his Contemporains de Molière.
[2] At the end of his little book, La Jeunesse de Molière; and the same subject forms one of the small volumes of the Collection Moliéresque, to which there is an Introduction.
[3] Vie de Molière, 13, 14.

that a misanthrope, such as I am, capricious even, if you like, can be of any use to a great man? My ways are not flexible enough for such domesticity. And more than all that, what would become of those people who have come with me from so far? Who would lead them? They count upon me, and I should reproach myself if I were to abandon them."

There is a lifelike character about this story that makes it interesting, though, unfortunately, no date can be given to the circumstance related. Whether Molière had then written the *Étourdi* or not is uncertain; if not, he had composed some of his farces. But he had seen enough of the ways of the grands seigneurs to know that he of all men was not fitted for the post offered to him. And he did not wish to surrender his liberty and jeopardise the fate of those who were dependent upon him, in order to become the factotum of a royal prince. He felt, too—

> "The wish—which ages have not yet subdued
> In man—to have no master save his mood."

From Montpellier the troop went again to Lyons, passing by Montélimart. There, on the 18th of February 1655, Madeleine Béjart lent to one Antoine Baratier 3200 livres. She never saw her money again. After her death some of it may have been recovered, though there was endless cheating on the part of Baratier and of his widow.[1] And on the 1st of April in that year Madeleine Béjart is said to have lent 10,000 livres to the province of Languedoc,[2] but this circumstance has not been fully verified.

Molière was at Lyons on the 29th of April, for on that day he and four of his friends signed the marriage certificate of two of their comrades;[3] and the troop remained there until October.[4]

At Lyons Molière met Charles Coypeau d'Assouci, a poor burlesque writer. M. Mesnard says of him happily enough that he was "much further from being a fool than a madman." Though d'Assouci has left behind him an unfortunate reputation, and in after years he fell under Boileau's lash, he sang

---

[1] Soulié, *Recherches sur Molière*, 48, 49; E. Campardon, *Nouvelles pièces sur Molière*, 113, 128.
[2] Louis Lacour, *Le Tartuffe par ordre de Louis XIV.*, 99-111.
[3] P. Mesnard, *Notice biographique sur Molière*, 161.
[4] *Ibid.* 164.

the praises of Molière and his friends in prose and in verse.[1] But whenever a man does not stand well in the world's esteem, people generally do not believe all that he says. D'Assouci meant that when he was in trouble Molière and the Béjarts comforted him and gave him food to eat. Probably on his side he made himself an amusing table companion. But he remembered the hospitality shown to him and was grateful.

D'Assouci said that he went with Molière down the Rhone as far as Avignon. There the troop received an order to go to Pézenas, where the States met on the 4th of November.[2]

I said a few pages back that M. de la Pijardière had found a receipt for money from the States of Languedoc, written and signed by Molière at Pézenas in December 1650. But M. de la Pijardière had made a previous similar discovery— also a receipt for money, written and signed by Molière at Pézenas under similar circumstances, dated 24th of February 1656. This he published in a pamphlet in 1873, with a facsimile of Molière's handwriting.[3] The latter written acknowledgment runs :—

"*J'ay recu de Monsieur le Secq thrésorier de la bource des Estats du languedoc la somme de six mille liures à nous accordez par messieurs du Bureau des comptes de laquelle somme ie le quitte. Faict a Pezenas ce vingt quatriesme iour de feburier* 1656.

MOLIÈRE ·/.

quittance de six mille liures."

The character in both of these instances of Molière's handwriting is what might be called old style, when men wrote less quickly than they do now and took more pains to form their letters; but both specimens present the same features in a clear and firm hand. They show, as M. de la Pijardière says, "a man sure of himself."[4] These two receipts are, I believe, the only instances of Molière's handwriting that have been preserved, with the exception of some bare signatures of

---

[1] *Aventures burlesques de Dassouci*, ed. Colombey, chap. ix.

[2] P. Mesnard, *Notice biographique de Molière*, 169.

[3] *Rapport sur la découverte d'un autographe de Molière*, présenté à M. le Préfet de l'Hérault, par M. de la Pijardière, archiviste du département. Montpellier, 1873. Another facsimile of this receipt is given in the album of the *Œuvres de Molière* to which I usually refer.

[4] In the *Moliériste* for July 1886 (vol. viii. 110) there is an article, *Molière jugé par son écriture*, by the Abbé Michon, who had previously written a volume on the handwritings of Frenchmen since the Merovingian era !

his name. Other examples have been put forward, but they
have been found to be spurious.

M. de la Pijardière was very strongly of opinion that
this sum of 6000 livres was given to the troop under
pressure from the Prince de Conti; and he says that although
all smaller sums granted by the States are duly recorded in
the official minutes, there is no mention in these reports of
the large amount given to Molière and his comrades.[1] This
was not the case in December 1650, when Molière gave the
States an acknowledgment for 4000 livres. And there is
also no official record of 1500 livres which the States granted
this session to Joseph Béjart for his book on heraldry which
he dedicated to the Prince de Conti and presented to the
States. Béjart, however, got his money and gave his receipt
for it on the 24th of February 1656.[2]

The author of a volume already mentioned tells a story
with some diffuseness, to the effect that after the close of the
session of the States at Pézenas on the 26th of February 1656,
the Prince de Conti gave Molière an order for payment of 5000
livres to be charged on the taxes of the province.[3] It would
seem that the prince had no right to do this, and that the
order was not signed by the treasurer. Raymond was the
first writer who mentioned this matter. Apparently he took
his story from the proceedings in a court of law, but he related
them two hundred years after they took place without giving
any authority by which his statements can be controlled.
The whole affair has not yet come to light, though it may be
that the prince's order for 5000 livres was for an arrear of
pension due from him to the troop which bore his name.[4]

From Pézenas Molière and his comrades went to Narbonne,
and there on the 26th of February 1656 leave was given to
them to play in the hall belonging to the consuls of the town.[5]
The use of the hall had been granted to them for a fortnight,

---

[1] *Rapport sur la découverte d'un autographe de Molière*, 13.
[2] *Ibid.* 8 and note.
[3] Emmanuel Raymond, *Histoire des pérégrinations de Molière dans le Languedoc*, 103-153.
[4] Jules Loiseleur, *Points obscurs de la vie de Molière*, 179-182 ; *Le Moliériste* for August 1885 (vol. vii. 149, 150); P. Mesnard, *Notice biographique sur Molière*, 177, 178.
[5] *Le Moliériste* for April 1881 (vol. iii. 22, 23) ; P. Mesnard, *Notice biographique sur Molière*, 176, 177.

but it is impossible to say how long Molière remained at Narbonne. A troop of actors, whether his or not is uncertain, was there on the 12th of June;[1] but he cannot be traced with sureness until the November or December following, when he was certainly at Béziers.

We have seen that the Prince de Conti was for a while Molière's friend, and that the troop bore his highness's name, but now we must take our leave of him. Some time in the year 1656 Conti had been admonished by Nicolas Pavillon, Bishop of Aleth, and he had gone to Paris intending to lead a new and a better life. Sainte-Beuve says that after his conversion "he changed his conduct, but his character remained unaltered. He went to extremes both before and afterwards."[2] From a weak-minded man of uncertain temper no real change for the good was to be expected. At one time he was the friend and protector of a troop of actors, and some years after his conversion he wrote a treatise against the stage, denouncing it with all the fury of a fanatic. His *Traité de la Comédie et des Spectacles*, etc., published at the end of 1666, was a posthumous work, for he died early in that year. By nature Conti was cruel and a bully, and his newly found religion did not teach him charity.[3]

I will now tell a few stories that have been related of Molière as happening about this time. The future dramatist on one of his journeys is said to have lost his wallet with some of his early farces. As he was going from Gignac to Montagnac his pack became unfastened and dropped from the saddle of his horse. Molière, as soon as he perceived his loss, turned back to make inquiries for his wallet, but to no purpose. It was gone. Some time afterwards he related the event and said: "How could I have helped losing it? I had left Gignac, I was at Brignac, I was going to pass Lavagnac on the way to Montagnac;—among all the *gnacs* I lost my wallet."[4]

A drinking-fountain had been erected at Gignac, and the

[1] *Le Moliériste* for April 1886 (vol. viii. 19, 20).
[2] *Port-Royal*, 3rd ed. v. 33.
[3] See a letter written by Racine to Vitart, 25th July 1662, given by M. Paul Mesnard in the *Œuvres de Racine*, vi. 497. An extract of this letter is given by Sainte-Beuve, *Port-Royal*, v. 34, 35.
[4] Altered from the story given by Taschereau, *Vie de Molière*, 3rd ed. 17, 18.

magistrate of the town caused an inscription to be engraved upon it:—

"Quæ fuit ante fugax, arte perennis erit."

Molière passed by one day and saw an admiring crowd collected wondering what these words meant. He gave as his translation:—

"Avide observateur, qui voulez tout savoir,
Des ânes de Gignac c'est ici l'abreuvoir."

Then the magistrate caused this inscription also to be engraved upon the fountain.[1] "Abreuvoir" means a watering-place for cattle, so Molière revenged himself for the loss of his wallet.

Molière's armchair at Pézenas is one of his few relics that have been preserved, though at one time it was thought that it had perished in the fire at the Odéon theatre in Paris in 1799. The Odéon was then the home of the Comédie Française. A few words may be said about the chair. Before cafés were introduced into France, the barber's shop was one of the places where loungers used to meet to see their friends and talk over the news of the day. We have seen that Molière's troop was a good deal at Pézenas, and at that time there was in the town a barber named Gély, whose shop was well known, and there every market-day Molière used to go to hear what the world of Pézenas was talking about, and observe the manners of the people. He would note the words of the speakers and watch their faces. This was a natural habit with him; it was his way of learning how thoughts passed in men's minds. He was a very close observer, and would see more in five minutes, and see it better—whether in a barber's shop or elsewhere—than another would see in an afternoon. The power of keen, quick, and accurate observation is given only to a few, and it is one of the most distinctive and important features in those who have it. Tradition says that Molière, when he went into barber Gély's shop, used to sit in a large armchair with a very high, straight back. He was liked and respected in the place, and when it became known in Pézenas many years later that he had been a great man in Paris, the chair was prized all the more highly. This

---

[1] *Vie de Molière*, 3rd ed. 17.

chair, made of walnut, bears now the honourable name of "le fauteuil de Molière." It stands 6 ft. 4 in. high, the seat is 20 in. high by 22 wide and 16 deep. A picture and description of it are given in the *Magasin Pittoresque*, quatrième année (1836), pp. 247, 248. The first written notice of it was in a letter dated "Pézenas, 7 Ventôse an 7" (19 January 1800), addressed by Poitevin de Saint Cristol to Cailhava, and published by the latter in his volume *Études sur Molière*.[1] Édouard Fournier traced the history of the chair,[2] and said that it had been brought to Paris early in the 18th century. The owner tried in vain to sell it, so it was taken back to Pézenas. But in 1873 it was brought again to Paris for the Musée Molière, and in Paris it has since remained.

We come now to Molière's second comedy, *Le Dépit Amoureux*. Speaking of this play, La Grange says on the fourth page of his Register:—"Cette pièce de théâtre a été représentée pour la première fois à Béziers, l'an 1656"; and this testimony has been nowhere contradicted. The first performance is believed to have taken place on the 19th of November.[3] But the Prince de Conti was not there; he did not enforce his wishes upon the deputies of the province. When the prince ceased to preside over the States the deputies were less friendly to Molière's troop, and at an official meeting on the 16th of December the majority of them complained that the actors were giving to the members of the States free passes into the theatre with the hope of getting some reward, and it was determined to tell the actors to withdraw these orders, and that no recompense should be given.[4] Probably enough there had been some cause for friction which has not been explained. At the same time, the deputies did not decline very graciously the offer of free seats from the troop, who, as they had received past favours, desired, not unnaturally, to show that they were grateful.

The *Dépit Amoureux* will be spoken of in the next chapter, after the *Étourdi*.

---

[1] P. 305. See also the *Moliériste* for November 1881 (vol. iii. 238).
[2] *Roman de Molière*, 175 *et seq.*
[3] P. Mesnard, *Notice biographique sur Molière*, 485, showing a correction in his text on p. 183.
[4] De la Pijardière, *Rapport sur la découverte d'un autographe de Molière*, 15, 16.

Joseph Béjart wrote a second book on heraldry, which he presented to the States this session. But the deputies did not want the book, or they disliked having to pay for it. They had given him 1500 livres for his first volume, and he was now petitioning again. The States voted him 500 livres, but declared they would pay nothing more for any other book unless it was written by their order.[1]

The session of 1657 at Béziers lasted until the 1st of June. There is no reason for thinking that the deputies made any payment to Molière's troop that winter, nor can it be said how long the actors remained at Béziers. Very likely they went from there to Lyons, for the registers of the Hôtel Dieu at Lyons show that on the 19th of February 1657 there was a theatrical performance in the town for the benefit of the poor, which brought 234 livres to the hospital after 14 louis d'or (154 livres) had been deducted for the actors.[2] Some writers have thought that Madeleine Béjart was at Nîmes on the 2nd of April.[3] The troop appears to have been at Lyons on the 15th of May, for on that day the Prince de Conti wrote to his confessor, the abbé Ciron: "Il y a des comédiens ici qui portoient autrefois mon nom; je leur ai fait dire de le quitter, et vous croyez bien que je n'ai eu garde de les aller voir."[4]

From Lyons Molière went to Dijon.[5] Though Conti had told the actors that they were no longer to bear his name, the order was not obeyed immediately, for the municipal registers of Dijon show that on the 15th of June in this year permission was granted to "les comédiens de M. le prince de Conti" to give performances in the tennis-court known as La Poissonnière. But the actors were to pay 90 livres to the hospital for the poor; and they were not allowed to charge more than 20 sous when the pieces played were new, and when they were old not more than 10 sous.[6]

I will copy here "Une affiche de comédiens en 1662," as given by M. Monval in the periodical under his management.[7]

[1] De la Pijardière, *Rapport sur la découverte d'un autographe de Molière,* 16 note.
[2] J. Loiseleur, *Points obscurs de la vie de Molière,* 211 and note.
[3] P. Mesnard, *Notice biographique sur Molière,* 188 ; Émile Campardon, *Nouvelles Pièces sur Molière,* 118.
[4] Sainte-Beuve, *Port-Royal,* 3rd ed. v. 33.
[5] P. Mesnard, *Notice biographique sur Molière,* 189.
[6] Henri Chandon, *La Troupe du Roman Comique,* 72.
[7] *Le Moliériste* for May 1886 (vol. viii. 33-35).

It will be seen that this affiche or playbill was issued by the troop belonging to the Prince de Condé—Conti's brother—but in all probability the playbills of different strolling companies were not much unlike. It would have been more interesting if a playbill issued by Molière had been found, but these relics of the 17th century are scarce. The affiche published by M. Monval runs as follows :—

"LES COMÉDIENS

DE SON ALTESSE SÉRÉNISSIME

MONSEIGNEUR LE PRINCE

"Nous ne pouvons pas faire mieux connoitre l'envie que nous avons de plaire à tout le beau Monde, dont tous les jours nous sommes honorez de la presence, qu'en leur donnant aujourd'huy 16 Novembre Vne magnifique Représentation de l'incomparabe EUDOXE de M.ʳ DE SCUDÉRY. La vertu de cette grande Princesse est si approuvée qu'elle dort seruir d'exemple à toutes les dames de venir à sa représentation, dont sans doute Elles n'emporteront vne satisfaction entière. Ensuite vous aurez la comédie du COCU IMAGINAIRE qui vaudra seul la pièce de vingt sols. En attendant le Grand SERTORIUS.
"C'est au lieu ordinaire à trois heures précises."

This playbill does not mention the name of any place, but the absence of such indication, and the fact that the only date given is the 16th of November, made M. Monval think that Condé's troop of actors were staying for the time in some large town. And the words at the end, "C'est au lieu ordinaire," tend perhaps towards this supposition. The suggested date, 1662, is at any rate approximate. Scudéry's *Eudoxe* gives no clue, for that play had been printed in 1642; the *Cocu Imaginaire* was a one-act comedy by Molière, first played in Paris in May 1660; and the promise that Corneille's *Sertorius* was to be acted a day or two hence shows that the playbill could not have been issued before 1662, for that play was first brought out in Paris in February in the same year. M. Monval thinks that the provincial audience was to be treated to an early representation of the tragedy of the great dramatist. The remark near the end of the playbill that the performance of the *Cocu Imaginaire* was alone worth twenty sous, seems to show that the comédiens de M. le Prince charged the public at a higher rate than was allowed to Molière's troop when they were at Dijon in 1657. I cannot say if strolling companies ever doubled the prices in the greater part of the theatre, as was sometimes the case in Paris when a new play was performed; but Molière's comedy was not then a new play. It would perhaps be unsafe to make a conjecture as to how much was the entrance money into the pit of a provincial theatre at this time. If Le Boulanger de Chalussay can be trusted, it was only five sous.[1] But he was speaking quite generally, as though in all towns the price was the same; or as he was sneering at Molière's early attempts on the stage, perhaps he wished to give a low estimate of what Molière thought he could ask from the public. It may be, however, that in large towns the charge made was generally higher than in smaller places.

We have seen that Molière was at Dijon in June 1657. From there he probably returned to the south. The States of Languedoc opened their session on the 8th of October at Pézenas, and if Molière then went to play before the deputies, he found himself in the presence of a rival troop belonging to the Duke of Orleans, which had been called officially. The fact that such an order was given to a company of actors under the patronage of the Duke of Orleans, seems to show that they were preferred to Molière and his comrades. M. Mesnard says that a meeting of two rival troops in the town where the States were sitting was a very ordinary occurrence.[2] He is of opinion that Molière was at Pézenas in the latter part of 1657, and quotes a story from Grimarest showing that Molière, some years later, said that he had acted with one Mondorge who, at the time of which we are now speaking, was an actor in the troop belonging to the Duke of Orleans.

Probably at the end of 1657 Molière made the acquaintance of Mignard, the artist, at Avignon; and perhaps it was here that Mignard painted the portrait of Molière as Cæsar in Corneille's tragedy *Pompée*. At that time Molière was nearly thirty-six, and the portrait shows a man of about that age. Mignard was apparently on terms of close friendship with the Béjarts; for in 1664 he signed the marriage contract of Geneviève

---

[1] *Élomire Hypocondre*, Act iv. sc. 2 of the *Divorce Comique* (p. 80, ed. 1867). [2] *Notice biographique sur Molière*, 190.

Béjart, and later Madeleine Béjart by her will made him
trustee of all the money she possessed at the time of her death.
It appears that Mignard's friendship was, in the first instance,
with the Béjarts rather than with Molière.[1] However this
may be, Molière in 1669 addressed to Mignard his poem *La
Gloire du Val de Grâce*, in honour of the painter's fresco in the
cupola of the church of the Val de Grâce in Paris. By " La
Gloire " we are to understand a painting of heaven and the
angels.

From Avignon it is most likely that Molière's troop went
to Grenoble. They appear to have incurred a reprimand
from the civil authorities there on the 2nd of February 1658,
for having put up their playbills without permission. It was
ordered that these should be taken down until they were
allowed by the Consuls.[2] Molière must have made his peace
with the Consuls, for he stayed at Grenoble until after Easter.
It would seem that on the 1st of May following, Mlle. du
Parc was at Lyons, for on that day a son of hers was christened
there,[3] but nothing is heard of the other members of the troop
being at Lyons at that time.

From Grenoble they went to Rouen and remained there for
some months. And at Rouen Mlle. du Parc won compliments
from the two Corneilles—Pierre and his younger but less
illustrious brother Thomas. Pierre Corneille was then fifty-
two years of age. It was long since he had written the plays
that had made him famous, but he still had the heart to appre-
ciate the charms of a pretty woman. And one would like to
think that there had been some friendly intercourse between
Corneille and Molière. There is nothing known, however, of
the relations between them to justify a belief that they saw
much of each other at Rouen during the summer of 1658.
Nevertheless, one would willingly lend an ear to the thought
that they had met, and that the acquaintance did not stop after

[1] *Notice biographique sur Molière*, 191-193 ; Soulié, *Recherches sur Molière*,
62, 71, 214. (I may say, perhaps, that at the end of the last line but one,
on page 192 of M. Mesnard's *Notice biographique sur Molière*, there is a misprint. The date 1662 should be 1664. The reference to Soulié's volume,
given in note 1 on p. 193 of M. Mesnard's *Notice*, shows that the date was
1664.)
[2] P. Mesnard, *Notice biographique sur Molière*, 195.
[3] Brouchoud, *Les Origines du théâtre à Lyon*, 48 ; Soulié, article in the
Revue du Lyonnais, 3rd series, vol. i. 292.

the first civilities had been exchanged. With such knowledge as we have got of their characters it would seem that the advances, if they were made, came from Molière. He was the younger man, and he would naturally be ambitious to know the great dramatist whose plays he must have seen and admired when he was a boy, and which, without doubt, he had since often placed on his own stage and in which he had played one of the principal parts. Molière would surely have been glad to be allowed to pay his respects to him whose name stood highest among the dramatists of his country. Corneille, on the other hand, was timid, his great glory had gone from him; he was then an elderly man of a retiring disposition, and perhaps not eager to make new friends. Yet it was to the chief of a strolling company, Mondory, that Corneille owed the success of his first play in 1629 ; and it might be supposed that he would have welcomed Molière who was now the chief of a strolling company, and also one of the interpreters of his own plays in the tennis-court known as the Jeu de Paume des Braques at Rouen, his own native town.

For some time past Molière and his friends had been longing to get to Paris. They thought themselves strong enough to satisfy the tastes of the theatre-goers in the metropolis, and they wished to make a fair bid against the actors at the Hôtel de Bourgogne. For thirteen years the troop had been strolling in the provinces, where they had won success ; and their purses were fuller than when they had started upon their travels. And they knew their business better than when they had been driven out of Paris by their repeated failures. Le Boulanger de Chalussay, alluding to their former attempts at the Jeu de Paume des Mestayers and at the Port Saint Paul, puts some words into Molière's mouth which may be quoted here :—

> "Piqué de cet affront, dont s'échauffa ma bile,
> Nous prîmes la campagne, où la petite ville,
> Admirant les talents de mon petit troupeau,
> Protesta mille fois que rien n'était plus beau.
>
> . . . .
>
> Enfin dix [1] ans entiers coulèrent de la sorte,
> Mais au bout de ce temps la troupe fut si forte,
> Qu'avec raison je crus pouvoir dedans Paris
> Me venger hautement de ses sanglants mépris." [2]

---

[1] *Dix* here should be *douze* or *treize*.
[2] *Élomire Hypocondre*, Act iv. sc. 2 of the *Divorce Comique*, pp. 79, 80, edition 1867.

While the troop were at Rouen in the summer of 1658 they were making preparations for their return to the capital. On the 12th of July Madeleine Béjart signed an agreement with the Comte Louis de Talhouet to take from him the remainder of his lease, of eighteen months, of the Théâtre du Marais at Paris, from the 1st of October 1658 to the 1st of April 1660, at a yearly rent of 3000 livres.[1] Though this agreement fell through from some cause unexplained, it offers a point of interest. Madeleine Béjart gave as her address in Paris : " La maison de Monsieur Poquelin, tapissier valet de chambre du roi, demeurant sous les halles, paroisse Saint Eustache." If, as is most likely, this Monsieur Poquelin was Molière's father, it may be gathered that the old man had become reconciled to his eldest son's profession.

During that summer Molière was more than once in Paris. The preface to the edition of his plays published in 1682 says :—

" In 1658 his [Molière's] friends advised him to come near to Paris and bring his troop to some town not far distant. That would be the best way to take advantage of the favour his reputation had won for him among many persons of importance ; for those who were interested in his future prospects had promised to introduce him to the court. He had passed the carnival at Grenoble, he left there after Easter and went to Rouen. He remained at Rouen during the summer, and after some private journeys to Paris he was fortunate enough to have his services and those of his comrades accepted by Monsieur, the king's only brother,[2] who promised him his protection and said that the title of the troop should bear his name. Monsieur also presented him in this capacity to the king and to the queen-mother." [3]

After Molière and his comrades were entitled to say that they belonged to Monsieur they all, with the exception of Pierre Réveillon,[4] went to Paris. What is first heard of them there happened on the 24th of October 1658.

[1] P. Mesnard, *Notice biographique sur Molière*, 199, 200 ; *Le Moliériste* for January 1886 (vol. vii. 202, 203).
[2] In France the title of Monsieur was always given to the king's brother next after himself in age.
[3] *Œuvres de Molière*, i. pp. xiii, xiv.
[4] *Revue du Lyonnais*, 3rd series, i. 294.

CHAPTER VI

BEFORE relating how Molière's troop became established in Paris after their strolling in the provinces, I must speak of La Grange, whose name is so well known as the author of a Register of the future performances of the company. La Grange was also one of the editors of the first complete edition of Molière's works, published in 1682, nine years after the poet's death; and he was the reputed author of the preface to that edition, to which allusion has already been made.

La Grange joined Molière's troop at Easter 1659, six months after they had begun to play at the Hôtel du Petit Bourbon, and he described himself as an "acteur nouveau à Paris." He was then not more than twenty years old. His real name was Charles Varlet, but when he went on the stage he took his mother's name. He used to play the lovers in Molière's comedies, not the most important parts, but they had to be acted carefully and with nice taste. If, as is most likely, he played Don Juan, that certainly was his most important rôle. He was a man on whose good sense and tact Molière could depend, and in November 1664 he replaced his chief as "orateur" in the troop. The functions of the orateur will be described later.

As soon as La Grange became a member of Molière's company he began to keep a diary or daily register, merely for his own use or gratification. He recorded every day the play that was acted, and in the case of new plays he said when they were new; and he noted daily the amount of money taken at the box-office of the theatre, and the share due to each actor out of this receipt after the expenses had been deducted. Every now and then he stated shortly particulars connected with the affairs of the troop. Sometimes, too, in his pages one sees a coloured disk or lozenge—blue being

128

meant to show joy and black sorrow. To anybody looking at the Register for the first time it will seem little more than an account-book with annotations; but when its pages are studied they prove to be the key to much valuable knowledge. Édouard Thierry called it "le livre d'or de la Comédie Française." The best way for Englishmen to realise the value of La Grange's Register is to suppose that either Heming or Condell had given similar information about Shakespeare's plays when they were new. Had such a book appeared in England it would doubtless have been studied very closely. Though we have had no such luck, we may congratulate Frenchmen on their good fortune. But it should be remembered that the Register was La Grange's own property, which he might have burned without doing legal injury to anybody. There is nothing to show that its existence was known to Molière or to any of his comrades. La Grange went on with his diary until the end of August 1685. Why he stopped it then is not known. He was at that time the foremost man in the Comédie Française. He remained on the stage until the day of his death, which happened suddenly on the 1st of March 1692. He was then fifty-three years old.

It would seem that after his death the manuscript of his Register went into his brother's family: that it descended to a Madame Varlet, the widow of the grandson of La Grange's elder brother, Achille Varlet, who at the time of Molière's death was an actor at the Théâtre du Marais, and whose stage-name was Verneuil. This Madame Varlet gave the manuscript to the Comédie Française in 1785; and in return for the gift, in September of that year, the sociétaires issued an order "de payer à Mad. Varlet pour un registre la somme de 250 liv." M. Monval has shown that for a good many years the actors did not know the value of their treasure.[1] Little notice was taken of the Register, and it was not quoted by any writer on the French stage before the year 1825.[2] Some ten

---

[1] Le Moliériste for April 1885 (vol. vii. 3-9).
[2] Édouard Thierry's biographical notice on La Grange prefacing the printed publication of the Register, pp. xliii. and xliv. (In the numbering of these pages there is a misprint: the first of the two is numbered lxiii. instead of xliii.) See also an article by Despois in the Revue Politique et Littéraire for 18th March 1876, pp. 265-271.

or twelve years later Régnier, then a sociétaire of the Théâtre Français, was one of the first who recognised its value, and it was used occasionally by him and by a few writers of articles in periodicals. Taschereau also used it in his accurate history of the dramatist's life and works. At last, on the 15th of January 1876, the anniversary of Molière's birthday, La Grange's Register was published by the Comédie Française, with a long biographical notice of its author by Édouard Thierry, a late administrator of that institution. Since that time it. has become public property, and frequent reference will be made to it here.

La Grange's co-editor in the first complete edition of Molière, published in 1682, was one Vivot, whose name until lately has been written Vinot.[1] The earliest mention made of the authorship of the preface to this edition was in a manuscript note written some time late in the 17th century by Nicolas de Tralage. He ascribed it to Vivot and La Grange: "La préface qui est au commencement de ce livre est de leur composition."[2] Thierry upholds very strongly the general belief in crediting La Grange with the work; and he rejects altogether the claim to its authorship made on behalf of one Marcel by Bruzen de la Martinière, editor of an edition of Molière, published at Amsterdam in 1725.[3] And it is surely very much more likely that La Grange would have chosen to say a few words himself in honour of his late friend than that he should have left the duty to another. The preface errs only in saying too little about one of whom the world would willingly have learnt more from so safe a hand.

La Grange married Marie Ragueneau de l'Estang on the 25th of April 1672. Before her marriage she had been engaged in some employment in connection with the theatre, and quite occasionally she acted a small part, and was paid for her day's service; after her marriage she was admitted into the troop with half a share. When La Grange died he left one daughter; his widow survived him fifty-five years, but little is heard of her.

It was stated at the end of the last chapter that Monsieur

---

[1] Œuvres de Molière, xi. 72, end of first paragraph.

[2] Paul Lacroix, Iconographie Moliéresque, No. 557; Œuvres de Molière, xi. 72.

[3] As to Marcel, see Œuvres de Molière, t. i. p. xxii. note 3.

—the king's brother—promised his "protection" to the troop which was henceforward to bear his name. He promised also 300 livres a year to each actor; but after recording this fact in his Register, La Grange added in a marginal note: "*Nota*, que les 300 l. n'ont point été payées." Nevertheless, Monsieur's protection may have been of service to his actors; for on the 24th of October 1658 they played before their Majesties and all the court in the Salle des Gardes (now the Salle des Cariatides) in the old Louvre. La Grange tells in his preface that the play chosen was Corneille's tragedy *Nicomède*, that the acting of the women gave especial pleasure, and that "the famous actors who made the reputation of the Hôtel de Bourgogne stand so high were also present." After this performance Molière addressed the king from the stage in a tone of apology on behalf of his comrades, and said at the end:—

"But since the king had been kind enough to tolerate their country manners, he very humbly begged his Majesty to be pleased to allow him to show one of the trifles which had won for him some reputation, and with which he had entertained the people in the provinces."

Then Molière gave one of his own now long-lost farces, the *Docteur Amoureux*. La Grange goes on:—

"As many years had passed since small comedies were in vogue, the invention appeared to be new, and the little play which was acted that day amused everybody as much as it surprised them. M. de Molière acted the part of the Docteur, and the manner in which he acquitted himself placed him in such high esteem that his Majesty permitted him to establish his troop in Paris. He was allowed to play in the large room in the Petit Bourbon alternately with the Italian actors. They [Molière's troop] began to play in public on the 3rd of November 1658, and they gave as new plays the *Étourdi* and the *Dépit Amoureux*, which had never been acted in Paris."

The Hôtel du Petit Bourbon was royal property. It contained a large room which had been used for court ballets, and here the different troops of Italian actors played when they came to Paris. It was situated near the Seine, and stood between the old Louvre and the church Saint Germain l'Auxerrois.[1]

Though Molière and his company began to act there on the

[1] Despois, *Le Théâtre Français sous Louis XIV.*, 23 *et seq.* ; 407 *et seq.*

3rd of November, neither the *Étourdi* nor the *Dépit Amoureux* was put on the stage quite at first. Both de Visé in his *Nouvelles Nouvelles*,[1] published in 1663, and Le Boulanger de Chalussay in his *Élomire Hypocondre*, printed in 1670, agree as to this. De Visé says: "After he [Molière] had brought out old plays for some time, and when he had in a manner established himself in Paris, he gave his own *Étourdi* and the *Dépit Amoureux.*" According to de Chalussay the first play that Molière produced in public was Corneille's tragedy *Héraclius*, and this was followed by four other plays by the same author. There may have been more than one performance of each; in any case, all were damned. After de Chalussay had made Molière relate his failures at the Petit Bourbon, he goes on to make him tell of the great successes of his own two comedies, the *Étourdi* and the *Dépit Amoureux.*[2] Before beginning his daily Register La Grange says that each of these plays gave to every actor in the troop seventy pistoles. The pistole was then worth eleven livres or francs. Despois thinks that in all probability neither of these plays was acted until about the middle of November;[3] and this, taken with de Chalussay's statement that they ran for three months, shows that they remained on the stage almost until Easter 1659.

At the theatres in Paris the theatrical year always began after the Easter holidays, which lasted for about three weeks; and at Easter 1659 there were important changes in Molière's troop. Du Parc and his wife left their old friends and went to the Théâtre du Marais. From a letter written by Chapelle to Molière in the early spring of 1659 it would seem that there were bickerings among the actresses at the Petit Bourbon as to the parts that each was to play, causing Molière much annoyance, and that Mlle. du Parc and her husband left the troop in consequence.[4] Dufresne caused another vacancy, for he retired from the stage; and Croisac, the gagiste, was discharged from his temporary services. On the other hand,

---

[1] M. P. Mesnard has given extracts from this book in the *Œuvres de Molière*, x. 464-68.

[2] *Élomire Hypocondre*, Act IV. sc. 2 of the *Divorce Comique* (pp. 80, 81, ed. 1867).

[3] *Œuvres de Molière*, i. 86-88.

[4] P. Mesnard, *Notice biographique sur Molière*, 146-48.

L'Espy and his brother Jodelet left the Marais for the Petit
Bourbon.   Du Croisy and his wife joined Molière, as also did
La Grange.[1]   The troop was then made up of twelve " parts,"
each actor having one share in its concerns.   Their names
were :—

Molière.	Mlles. Béjart.
Béjart aîné.	„ De Brie.
Béjart cadet.	„ Hervé.
De Brie.	„ Du Croisy.
L'Espy.	
Jodelet.	
Du Croisy.	
La Grange.	

The four Béjarts, we know, were with Molière during his
thirteen years of strolling in the provinces.   Mlle. Hervé
was Geneviève Béjart; she took her mother's name on the
stage to distinguish her from her elder sister Madeleine, but
she was not a good actress.   De Brie and his wife, it may
be remembered, joined Molière's troop, probably at Lyons, in
1653.   The husband was an indifferent actor; he was said to
be a bully, and Molière did not like him.   His wife gave very
valuable service to the troop, and her greatest triumph was
as Agnès in the *École des Femmes*.   Of the new recruits L'Espy
and his brother Jodelet were old stage hands, for they were
both at the Hôtel de Bourgogne in 1634.[2]   Not much is known
of L'Espy, but Jodelet had gained a reputation at the Marais
in the part of Cliton in Corneille's *Menteur* in 1642.   Scarron
had named many of his valets after him; and there are other
instances of characters in French plays being named after the
actor entrusted with the part.   Jodelet was an amusing actor,
though he spoke strongly through his nose.   He died, unfortunately, in March 1660.   Du Croisy always remained staunch
to Molière, and did not leave the stage till many years after the
dramatist's death.   It was he who was first entrusted with the
part of Tartuffe.   His wife, however, was a poor actress.   We
shall hear again of Du Parc and his wife, for they returned to
the troop at Easter 1660.

Unfortunately Molière soon lost Béjart aîné, one of his
oldest friends.   La Grange says on page 6 of his Register:

[1] La Grange's Register, 4 and 5.
[2] *Œuvres de Molière*, ii. 39, note 2.

"Le Samedi, 11 Mai, joué au Louvre *L'Étourdi* pour le Roi. M. Béjard acheva son rôle de *l'Étourdi* avec peine." A little later, after mentioning the performance on the 20th of May, La Grange wrote: "Interruption à cause de la mort de Monsieur Béjard." If, as is believed, he took originally the parts of Lélie in the *Étourdi*, and of Éraste in the *Dépit Amoureux*, he must have been accounted one of the best actors in the troop. The story that Joseph Béjart left 24,000 écus in gold when he died is pure fable.[1]

Something may be gained in considering for a moment Molière's earliest attempts at authorship. Of the farces he is said to have written while strolling in the provinces only two remain. They are *La Jalousie du Barbouillé* and *Le Médecin Volant*.[2] They were printed for the first time in a pamphlet entitled *Deux pièces inédites de J. B. P. Molière,* published by Viollet le Duc in 1819; and they are now generally included in good editions of Molière's comedies. The text of these plays was taken from a manuscript which belonged to Jean Baptiste Rousseau in 1731. It is not known where this manuscript came from, nor how Rousseau acquired it. Rousseau did not think that Molière was the author of these plays in the present sense of authorship, and he did not wish to see them printed. What he says may be quoted as showing how light comedies were then put upon the stage:—

"Touching the small pieces which our author played in the provinces, it is true that two of them have fallen into my hands, but it is easy to see that it was not he who wrote them. They are outlines which he gave to his actors, who filled them up on the spot, as the Italians do, each one according to his ability. But it is certain that he did not finish either play upon paper, and what I have got is written in the style of a clownish country actor, and is worthy neither of Molière nor of the public."[3]

Again:—

"The gist of the farce may be Molière's. At that time nothing higher had been seen; but as all these farces were played in an impromptu manner, as was the custom with the Italian actors, it is easy to see that it was not he who put the dialogue upon paper; and these

---

[1] *Le Moliériste* for July 1885 (vol. vii. 115-122).
[2] *Œuvres de Molière*, i. 3-14; 17-19; 47-51; and xi. 49-51. Also M. L. Moland's 2nd edition of Molière's plays, vol. ii. p. 3 *et seq.*
[3] Letter of J. B. Rousseau to Chauvelin de Beauséjour, quoted by Despois, *Œuvres de Molière*, i. 10, 11.

sort of things, even when they are better done, ought never to be counted among the works of a celebrated author." [1]

Despois took his text of the two comedies from a manuscript in the Bibliothèque Mazarine. He thought it likely that the manuscript he copied was the same as that owned by Rousseau, and he had no doubt it was the same as that used by Viollet le Duc. In *La Jalousie du Barbouillé*, which in part seems to have been an early sketch of *George Dandin*, Molière ridiculed the pedants or the so-called scholars. This was a groundwork which had been common in the French theatres for many years, both at the Hôtel de Bourgogne and on the open-air stages where Tabarin and other buffoons used to hold forth for the amusement of the crowd. And though Molière put into the dialogue of his farce a better idea of comedy than Tabarin had done, he was working upon an idea that had long been popular. *Le Médecin Volant* shows his first attack upon the doctors of medicine whom he afterwards satirised so frequently; and in the early farce may be found sentences which occur again in his later comedies. The chief fun in this play is in Sganarelle's representing himself to be a doctor and the doctor's brother at the same time. Part of the groundwork of this comedy is seen again in *Le Médecin Malgré Lui*. And Boursault, of whom something will be said later, brought out a play in 1661 called *Le Médecin Volant*, taken from the same source as Molière's. Boursault said in his "Avis au lecteur" (1665): "The subject is Italian, it has been translated into our language and has often appeared on our stage."

It would be idle now to criticise J. B. Rousseau's opinion that the *Jalousie du Barbouillé* and the *Médecin Volant* were not written by Molière. At the same time it may be remarked that the author of these little sketches knew how to form a character; and that in these sketches one sees the easy language and the direct form of expression which was always characteristic of Molière's prose. Perhaps these latter qualities are more necessary to a comic dramatist than to any other class of writer.

Names have been given to other farces which Molière is said to have written, but the names give rise to some uncertainty. Those who are curious may refer to the authorities

[1] Letter of J. B. Rousseau to Brossette, quoted by Despois, *ibid.* p. 12.

given above. It may be assumed that the farces which have been lost were not unlike the two which are extant. Whatever Molière may have thought himself of his first attempts at dramatic composition, he was endeavouring to please the public with what he knew would amuse them if the work were done in an amusing way. I imagine that he wished to write plays, and that perhaps he looked forward to a day when he should write a comedy in accordance with the prescribed rules; but that he kept his ambition in check and set about his task in what he thought was the surest way to please his audience. He saw that the small Italian plays were full of vitality, and this he tried to give in his own attempts. Comedy of a better kind, if he could achieve it, would come later. In the meantime he would do what was nearest to his hand, and not strive after what might be beyond his reach. He partly followed some of the types well known on the Italian and French stages before his day—the doctor or the pedant, the jealous lover and the more urbane lover, the rustic and perhaps the bragging soldier—and though most of these personages were meant to be grotesque, Molière's sense of fitness would not allow him to go beyond the limits of fair caricature. He tried to characterise in a fanciful manner the ridiculous personages, and to show that, however much they were buffeted about, they were men who had thoughts and wills of their own. This was not a feature in the stock personages on the Italian stages. It was customary that the actor who performed one of these parts considered that on his theatre the character should belong to him and be his stage property. The frequent repetition of the name Gros René in the titles of the plays makes one feel tolerably sure that the fat René Berthelot, whose stage name was du Parc, must have been popular with the audience. None of Molière's farces had more than one act, they were all in prose, and they were performed after the set piece of the day to send the people home in a good humour. One cannot tell how often they were acted before La Grange joined the troop, but it may be noticed that Molière put them on the stage occasionally, and that the *Médecin Volant* was played oftener than any of the others. The last time that La Grange records a performance of one of Molière's early farces was on the 7th of September

1664, when *Gros René* was acted after Corneille's *Sertorius*. Almost the only word of mention of these unprinted farces is the testimony of Monchesnay, given in the middle of the 18th century, to the effect that Boileau " regretted very much that Molière's little comedy, *Le Docteur Amoureux*, had been lost, because there was always something bright and instructive even in his lightest works." Boileau was quite a young man when he saw this play, for there is no mention of a performance of the piece after Easter 1659, when he was twenty-two years old; and if we are to trust the opinion he is reported to have expressed, the play must have left a lively impression upon his memory.

It has been said already that the *Étourdi* was first played at Lyons in 1653 or 1655, and the *Dépit Amoureux* at Béziers in 1656; and mention has been made of the welcome given to both comedies in Paris when they were first acted there. I must now speak of the two plays and try to show what kind of comedies they were.

In writing his first comedy in verse, Molière followed ideas that were prevalent at the time on the French stage. Plays with stirring adventures and striking incidents were liked best, and these the dramatists tried to give, throwing over them, if they were able to do so, an air of romance to make them engaging. The *Étourdi* was meant to be a "comedy of intrigue"; that is, a comedy in which the intrigue or the plot of the play lies chiefly in the schemes laid to entrap some one or more persons for the benefit of another. A comedy of intrigue is not necessarily the same therefore as a comedy of incident. But besides the scheming, the *Étourdi* shows an interest of a higher kind for those who read it with the idea of seeing how Molière made his personages talk, and how much life he threw into their characters. He wrote better plays afterwards of a different kind, showing true comedy, but every one must feel that this play has a freshness and a vigour of spirit that for the while are very amusing.

The style of the *Étourdi*, or the manner in which it is written, resembles the agility shown by an athlete in winning a hurdle race; or it is like the boldness of a bright young orator in a dull assembly who astonishes his hearers by his wit, by his hard-hitting, and by his eloquence. He is persuasive, if nothing more, and great expectations are formed of his future. The promise thus held out Molière kept afterwards, but in a better way. The events told in this play are improbable as are many of those in Lever's delightful Irish novels, they are described in something of the same joyous and racy manner and are made to appear veracious—thus fulfilling legitimately the purposes of fiction. In imitating Italian comedy, Molière has given in Lélie and Mascarille, the master and valet, excellent pictures of the type each is meant to represent, and he has sketched their manners in such a lively way—very different from the play from which he is said to have borrowed most—that his work shows all the charm of originality.

I think that in writing the *Étourdi*, Molière had two objects in view: to please his audience by the lawless adventures related, and to satisfy himself by the way he told them. The superiority of treatment over the subject already shows itself in his mind, and in this play, which may be called his first comedy, he was aiming at dramatic exposition and dramatic characterisation. These were two objects which he always kept steadily before him, and he showed the characterisation of his personages as clearly as the style of his comedies would permit. He was not imaginative in creating strong plots; but if he had been forced to describe the thoughts of three men as they broke stones on the roadside, he would have given a picture of the feelings of each, and would have made an acting comedy out of their dialogue.

The *Étourdi* betrays an Italian origin throughout. It was borrowed mainly from *L'Inavvertito*, a comedy by Niccolò Barbieri, called Beltrame, though some of the amusing incidents in it are not found in that play. Molière makes Mascarille, the valet, play the principal part; nearly all the interest of the comedy is thrown upon him. He is a son of the valets who were common upon the Italian stage, but he is represented here with so much natural feeling that he might be anybody's countryman of three hundred years ago, of to-day, or of three hundred years hence. He has no self-interest, his wish is to serve his master by any means that he can imagine. His master profits by his cunning, lauds his skill when he is successful, and beats him when he is unlucky. This master,

Lélie, is the "étourdi"; and the word describes him exactly, for a more inattentive, giddy-pated fellow never was seen. He has found out that Léandre is his rival for Célie, a beautiful slave, and if he had not Mascarille at his elbow to assist him his chance of success would be small. Célie is the slave of Trufaldin, and there is another girl, Hippolyte, but neither comes much on to the stage. In the older French comedies beautiful girls were a good deal talked about, but they were not often seen. This arose from the fact that it was not customary to allow unmarried daughters to come prominently forward in private life, and from the objectionable situations in which they would have to appear before an audience. The *Étourdi* is free from this drawback, but one feels now that the comedy is deficient in female interest. The nurse, too, was a feature in old comedies; she was put in more from necessity than from choice, but she was never interesting, and here she is not seen. But there are three old men, and they are all fair game to the valet for displaying his mischief.

I can only allude indirectly to Mascarille's schemes for assisting his master to obtain possession of Célie, the beautiful slave. These schemes might go on for ever if Lélie was not made to tumble on his feet at last in spite of himself. At the end of the first act he has already by this thoughtlessness thwarted three plans devised by his valet; and Mascarille goes out in a towering rage, vowing that any evil may happen to himself, and that the devil may twist his master's neck, before he will give him more assistance. But in the second act they are again together. Mascarille's anger has disappeared, and he has been persuaded to make another effort. He is again good-humoured and ready for another frolic. He says of himself :—

> "Je suis ainsi facile, et si de Mascarille
> Madame la Nature avait fait une fille,
> Je vous laisse à penser ce que ç'auroit été."

At the end of the second act there is a capital speech by Mascarille. Lélie had been boasting of his imaginative powers; he thought he had invented a plan which could not fail to win Célie. Of course his plan was only another blunder. Mascarille turns upon him with a look of contemptuous anger, but still showing comedy, and asks :—

> "Vous avez fait ce coup sans vous donner au diable ?"

Then he rallies his master, at first with cool and elevated irony; afterwards he heaps up invective against him until he can no longer find terms in which to express himself.

Eleven times at least Lélie has by his blundering frustrated Mascarille's devices to obtain possession of Célie. Hence, no doubt, the comedy. In one sense the interest in the play flags when it is seen that Lélie cannot keep what he has got, and that he is little better than a greenhorn. But the character is admirably drawn. The young man is impulsive, full of vitality, self-confident, and he blurts out his love affairs almost to the first friend he meets when reticence is especially needed. He is a type of an irrepressible blunderer whom no experience can cure, or teach not to be giddy-headed when running after a sweetheart. But Mascarille is the chief feature in the comedy. He is a perfectly honest rogue. He is a rascal of romance without one atom of meanness in him. He is full of stratagems, one half of which would at that time have sent a man to the gallows. Yet you can fully trust him, knowing him to be noble-hearted. His freshness and vigour throughout are amazing. His plans are perpetually baffled by his master's folly, but he perseveres in spite of many resolutions that he will do nothing more. The quick-witted valet is like a good hound when he comes upon the scent of a fox. He cannot help himself. If his game is before him he must follow it. Mascarille re-enlists himself in Lélie's favour, not from a wish to forgive his master, but from his own love of devilry and a determination not to be beaten. We all give him our good wishes and subscribe heartily to the inscription he would like to see written of himself:—

"Vivat Mascarillus fourbum imperator!"

Aimé-Martin published his first edition of Molière in 1824-26, and gave for the first time the names of the actors who played originally most of the characters in the poet's comedies, assigning each rôle to a particular actor. His information was doubtless valuable, though in a good many cases no certain attribution could be made; and later knowledge has shown that some of his surmises were not correct. It is fairly certain, however, that in the *Étourdi* Molière played Mascarille, and Béjart aîné, until he died, Lélie.

From an engraving in the British Museum.

But as there were only six men in the troop, and there were eight male characters in the comedy, some of these parts were doubled or were taken by actors hired for the occasion. For the women, Mlle. de Brie most likely played Célie, and Mlle. du Parc Hippolyte, while she remained in the troop.[1]

It is supposed generally that Molière was the first who used the name Mascarille on the stage in France, though in 1620 there was a book published at Lyons entitled *Les Œuvres du Marquis Mascarille*. In any case Mascarille is the French form of mascarilla, a Spanish word signifying a small mask which covered the upper part of the face. As may be seen from old prints, Italian actors of those days often wore masks; and as Molière formed his valet upon the types of valets common on the Italian stages he may have worn a mask while acting this part.[2] There is a Marquis de Mascarille in his *Précieuses Ridicules*, a comedy of a very different kind from the *Étourdi*; but to suppose that the actor wore a mask in that part would be absurd.

Le Dépit Amoureux is another comedy of intrigue, and in writing it Molière copied again from an Italian model. His play was an imitation of *L'Interesse* by Niccolò Secchi, printed at Venice in 1581. Practically it may be divided into two parts. There is the imbroglio of romantic and startling incidents, told more in the form of a consecutive story than in the *Étourdi*, of which I shall say nothing; and there are two scenes of lovers' quarrels which have caused the comedy to be remembered. It has long since been found that on the stage this play is too long; therefore abridgments into two acts— not differing materially one from the other—have been made. The version followed is that made in 1773 by Valville, an actor then belonging to the Comédie Française.[3]

One perceives, even in the first part of the *Dépit Amoureux*, a better note of actual comedy than in the *Étourdi*, though otherwise the play is less brilliant. Éraste is in love with Lucile; and Gros René, Éraste's valet, is in love with Marinette, Lucile's waiting-woman. Éraste is jealous. Molière here touched upon a subject which he afterwards described with better

---

[1] *Œuvres de Molière*, i. 93-95.   [2] *Ibid.* 90 ; 536.
[3] See M. Moland's 2nd edition of Molière's plays, iii. 3 *et seq.*, where the present acting version is given. Also *Œuvres de Molière*, xi. 124, 125.

success when experience had taught him to rely more fully upon his own powers. He has often described jealousy because he thought that a man's jealous feeling of anger towards his mistress was a good subject for comedy.

The lovers' quarrels are in the third and fourth scenes of the fourth act. Éraste and Lucile give back presents they have received from each other, they tear up each other's verses and letters; while their servants, who also have quarrelled, stand by abetting them. A Latin poet has said that the quarrels of lovers mean only a renewal of love; for if lovers are in earnest in their affection they do not enjoy being thoroughly angry with each other. At length, after beating about the bush, Éraste asks Lucile if she will forgive him.

> " Je le demande enfin ; me l'accorderez-vous,
> Ce pardon obligeant ? "

She answers him :—

> " Remenez-moi chez-nous."

These last words, "take me home," are charming in their subtlety; they are worth all the rest. Lucile keeps the upper hand all through the dispute, and at the end she gives way, maintaining her supremacy but telling Éraste that she loves him. Gros René and Marinette, the valet and the waiting-woman, are both angry at this reconciliation. They now wrangle as their betters had done, but more fiercely. The same tune is played over again, but with more noise. They are both determined to separate, though they know they are two fools for their pains. And this scene ends as the other did, but with heartier expressions of love.

> " *Gros René.*
> "Mon Dieu, qu' à tes appas je suis acoquiné !
>
> " *Marinette.*
> " Que Marinette est sotte après son Gros René."

Despois has shown[1] that among the men in the troop Molière played the part of Albert, Lucile's father : Béjart aîné Éraste, and du Parc Gros René. There is no evidence to show how the four female characters were distributed among the four actresses; the most likely guess would be Mlle. de Brie as Lucile.

[1] *Œuvres de Molière*, i. 395, 396.

This is the place to say shortly in what way Molière's borrowings in his two first comedies differed from those of French playwrights who preceded him. In all probability he borrowed more than they had done, but he made a much better use of his loan. The result was as if he had borrowed money which he could spend in any market, and as if his predecessors had bought "reach-me-down" clothes which would not fit them. In his two first comedies there was a good deal that Molière did not invent: the outlines of the plots and of the characters were not his. But because he knew how men thought, how they spoke to each other, what they did, how they ought to be made to appear before an audience;—and because he could invest these attributes of comedy in lively and appropriate language, he made his plays seem natural in spite of the improbabilities related, and he gave to his work a freshness and a vigour which had not existed in French comedy before his time. Hitherto French comedies had been sadly deficient in characterisation. This Molière was able to give, even in his two first plays, where he borrowed most. The presence or the absence of characterisation was the chief distinguishing feature between his comedies and those of his predecessors. He portrayed human beings instead of personages which hardly showed the signs of humanity. Hitherto in French comedies characterisation had been at best of a dummy kind. In reading them now, one has to force oneself to imagine that a man is behind the words he is supposed to speak. The effect is not inspiriting. But Molière did make his personages move and talk with all the appearance of people acting their parts on the stage. His pretended pictures appear to be so natural, that without effort you think you see his men and women, hear them, and feel their pulses beat. Unless these signs of outward life are present, characterisation cannot have real vitality.

In the middle of the 17th century the sense of plagiarism, unless it was very barefaced, did not exist. Molière borrowed other men's plots, but he used them in his own way, and not in a spirit of imitation. Our English dramatists before his day had done the same. It might be more difficult to say now what is plagiarism than it was two hundred and fifty years ago. About that time Pascal wrote: " Let it not be urged that

I have not said anything new. The disposition of the matter is new. When men play at tennis, they both hit the same ball, but one places it better than another." Molière had the inventiveness of a command of easy language always suitable to the occasion. He makes each of his characters say what might be expected from them at the moment. Even in his earliest attempts he has shown that he knew how to form a character and bring forward the features he wished to represent. This was not borrowed art; still less was it imitation. His borrowings either relate to external incidents, or they may be defended in the way so wittily explained by Pascal. What was dull he brightened; to men and women who were hardly more than speaking automatons he gave a flesh and blood movement that transformed them into actual living creatures. Anybody making their acquaintance perceives at once their humanity.

Even in his two first plays, where Molière was most actuated by Italian influences, he dominated them and made them his own. Later he wrote comedies that were purely French, and some that had a wider application, though he constantly reverted in his lighter plays to the idea of outward show and quick movement and of fun which formed the chief elements in the plays acted on the Italian stages. What I mean by purely French comedies is plays that in thought and characteristics were in no way dependent upon a foreign origin. The *Précieuses Ridicules*, the *Fâcheux*, the *Tartuffe*, the *Femmes Savantes*, are purely French comedies; but *Monsieur de Pourceaugnac* is partly foreign, and the *Fourberies de Scapin* is still more so. The main ideas and the tone of the *Critique de l'École des Femmes*, *Don Juan*, the *Misanthrope*, and the *Avare*, are general, and might be seen in any country, though the skill shown in writing is another matter. It is of little consequence whether the legend on which one of Molière's plays was founded was his own invention, or whether it came from Italy or from the Andaman Islands; but it is important to see what use he made of his story, and if his play betrayed a foreign style of thought. Like Shakespeare, he did not care much where he found his plot, but he was very particular as to the way he used it so as to show the characteristics of the personages he wished to introduce, and to make his scenes animated and amusing. It is not of prime importance to know from what source an author has taken the plot of his play, but his comedy can hardly be a good one unless it is bright with his own work. And the play is not really his own unless it bears the stamp of his own individuality.

There was another particular in which Molière differed from the playwrights a little before his time. They borrowed more from Spanish tales and plays than he did. Italian influences are seen in some of his comedies plainly enough, but Spanish plays were never sympathetic to him. In the early part of the 17th century a taste for Spanish plays had arisen in Paris, and this was fostered by the marriage of Louis XIII. with the daughter of Philip III. of Spain. Then the French translation of *Don Quixote*, which followed very shortly, helped to confirm the liking for romantic incidents. But romance on the French stage had no real sense or being. It existed outwardly in a formal way; it did not exist in fact and deed, because the French are not a romantic people, and because the rules which then governed their drama prevented the scope of its action. When a man is told that he must woo and win a lady in twenty-four hours on a given spot, he feels that he has a difficult task to perform, and he has to ask for adventitious aid. His valet assists him by stratagem, and the young lady is won. If there be romance in courtship of this kind, you only get the skin of it. Ingenuity is required, and when that is successful it is generally applauded. Though Molière saw that all this artifice was hollow he generally complied with it in point of form, and he tried to draw advantage from it in other ways. His love-scenes, as such, are more often than not indifferent. He was not romantic by nature, but he took what show of romance he could find and used it as a peg whereon to hang his satire and the play of his scenes. If a romantic scene had been well handled by another he would have applauded it, but he could look through his own thoughts and see that he was not well fitted for work of that kind. Occasionally he borrowed bits of Spanish plots, but he discarded Spanish ideas as though he did not like them. He found that he could not adapt them to his own thoughts, and therefore did not use them. The Spanish dramatists wished to interest their audiences by exciting stories told in a dramatic

K

form.   Molière cared little for tales of wonder; his endeavour was even from the first to show personal characterisation in a comic manner and with comic effects.   The movement on the Italian stages was quick, and that attracted his fancy.   The scenes played by the actors of the commedia della bella arte were crude and often coarse, but they contained the germs of comedy in that they showed the manners of the people intended to be portrayed and gave signs of personal characterisation.   In that way they appealed to Molière, and by degrees his genius substituted real characterisation and comic raillery for masks and clever buffooneries.

CHAPTER VII

THE *Précieuses Ridicules,* more than most of Molière's comedies, demands some explanation in order to understand its fun and who were the people against whom its satire was directed. A glance at the drawing-room society of those days will enable us to see the environment of the scene, and will show Molière's object in writing his comedy. Its date was 1659.[1]

La Marquise de Rambouillet was a lady of high birth and gentle manners who, disliking the tone of the court, formed for herself her own circle of acquaintance. For some years past a want had been felt among the more refined ladies of the aristocracy in Paris that they had no society of their own that was independent of the court. Marie de Medici had been appointed regent of the kingdom, and she was governed by confidants and favourites whose main ambitions were greed and love of place. Factions therefore arose, and the general tone of court life was noisy and vulgar. Partly with the idea of creating a circle of social intercourse among her own friends, Madame de Rambouillet, while yet a young woman, built for herself a house in the Rue Saint Thomas du Louvre—a short street which ran between the Louvre and the Tuileries. The house was built early in the reign of Louis XIII., between 1610 and 1617. Her receptions began soon afterwards, certainly in or before 1620; they gained celebrity and maintained their high reputation for nearly thirty years. No exact date can be given to the dissolution of the Hôtel de Rambouillet, but it is not likely that the hostess, who was once so well known, continued to receive her friends after the Civil War in

---

[1] I am indebted for much of the matter in the first part of this chapter to Roederer's *Mémoire pour servir à l'histoire de la société polie en France*; to Cousin's volumes on French society in the 17th century; to M. Ch. Livet's edition of Somaize's *Dictionnaire des Précieuses*; and to M. Livet's volume *Précieux et Précieuses.*

Paris, known as La Fronde, which broke out in 1648. Probably, too, in 1645 the receptions were discontinued for some time, for in that year Madame de Rambouillet lost her son, the Marquis de Pisani, at the battle of Nordlingen. Three years later Voiture died, and his absence deprived the ladies of much of the sparkle and pleasantry of conversation. Then came social disturbances caused by the Civil War, so that probably enough until that was over, in 1652 or 1653, afternoon visiting was discontinued. When the streets became quiet after the Fronde receptions multiplied, and then the late éclat of the meetings at the Hôtel de Rambouillet became somewhat lessened by other meetings in other places. Though these newer assemblies never gained the same distinction, "at homes" became popular and were therefore common. Society in Paris may have benefited by the larger number of receptions, but the glory of the pioneer which had for so long maintained its unrivalled supremacy faded away until it was revived by the afterglow of tradition.

Who were the guests invited to the Hôtel de Rambouillet? Perhaps it may be said shortly that many of the "best people" in Paris might have got an introduction. But Madame de Rambouillet was particular in the choice of her friends, and would not have agreed with everybody as to who the "best people" were. "Best" in this sense means those whose minds and manners were the best trained through hereditary descent and by custom in the general ways of good breeding and politeness. Ladies must be known to the hostess, or known well by her intimate friends, and they must be of good birth, before the invitation would be given. If a gentleman had pleasant manners and could talk well, and especially if he was in any way distinguished, he might gain admittance inside her doors. Doubtless at a time when society was divided by the line of nobility, it was not so easy for a bourgeois to find himself among his social superiors as it might be now when such differences are less clearly marked. But Madame de Rambouillet did not wish to make her distinctions appear invidious. Her house was not of easy access, and she wished it to be a little difficult; yet if a gentleman was well spoken of, and came to her with pleasant recommendations, she would have smiled and bid him welcome.

Men of letters were generally well received at the Hôtel de Rambouillet, if they were of good repute. Some went rarely, some went often and became more or less intimate in the house, according to circumstances. Among the earliest visitors were Malherbe, Gombauld, Gomberville, and the Marquis de Racan; later might be seen there Voiture, Balzac, Descartes, Pierre Corneille, Georges de Scudéry, Benserade, Sarrasin, Costar, Bussy-Rabutin, Vaugelas, Segrais, Ménage, Cotin, and quite in its latter days the gossip chronicler Tallemant des Réaux. And when the French Academy was established, in 1635, most of its first members went at least once a year to pay their court to the lady who had first set the fashion for social gatherings. Among them, besides those mentioned already, were Chapelain, Conrart, Desmarets, Faret, Boisrobert. We may be sure that churchmen also were present, though most of their names are not remembered now. Of those who are known, we read that Richelieu, Retz, Bossuet, Fléchier, were guests at different times in the salon bleu at the Hôtel de Rambouillet; though even in its last days Bossuet was a very young man and Fléchier a mere boy. There was also Godeau, afterwards a bishop, a very little man, who became popular and was liked by the ladies. On account of his diminutive stature, and because he was made much of by Mlle. de Rambouillet, he was called "Julia's dwarf." Among the nobility fewer names have been recorded; many probably found no pleasure in going into a drawing-room in the afternoon, and of the others there was often little to be said. Yet there were Condé, who at that time was the Duc d'Enghien; La Rochefoucauld, who later was the author of the *Maximes*; the Duc de Longueville, who married Condé's sister; the Marquis de Montausier, who married Madame de Rambouillet's eldest daughter, Julie d'Angennes; and Madame de Rambouillet's son, the Marquis de Pisani.

Amongst the ladies, besides the hostess and her two daughters (she had indeed three other daughters, but they went into convents probably before they were of an age to appear in the world), there were Condé's mother, known as Madame la Princesse; later her daughter, Mlle. de Bourbon, afterwards Madame de Longueville; Madame de Sévigné, for she married when she was eighteen; Madame de Motteville, lady of honour to Anne of Austria, and about whom she wrote her *Mémoires*;

Mlle. de Montpensier, la Grande Mademoiselle, the daughter of Gaston, Duke of Orleans, and niece of Louis XIII., also a writer of memoirs; Mlle. de Gournay, another writer, but earlier in date; Mlle. de Scudéry, whose novels, in spite of their absurdities, are valuable in giving pictures of the time; Madame de La Fayette, another writer of novels, but at a later time; Madame de Sablé, about whom Cousin wrote one of his pleasantest volumes; her friend Madame de Maure; Madame de Hautefort, also written about by Cousin; Mlle. de Vigean, whom Condé wished to marry; Madame Cornuel, celebrated for her bons mots; Mlle. Paulet, called "la lionne"; and the Vicomtesse d'Auchy and Madame des Loges. These two last-mentioned ladies "held academies," that is, had receptions of their own. I have given these names because they are all known, and they may recall to some readers ideas or facts in connection with the time.

It has been thought that the Hôtel de Rambouillet was a hotbed of affectation and of literary purists, but some modern French writers repel the charge as a gross exaggeration. Probably enough there was affectation of a skin-deep sort. This was shown chiefly in the use of words; and Madame de Rambouillet, who was sensitive in these matters, liked her friends while they were in her house to be nice in the expressions they used. In such things ladies would naturally set the example, at least indirectly; and it is more probable that there should have been affectation in words or in language than false pretensions in manners among people who belonged to the best families in France. Affectation in language was then a plaything among the better classes in other countries besides France. In England there had been Euphuism at the end of the 16th century; in Spain, Gongorism at the beginning of the 17th; and an Italian, Marini, wrote his *Adonis*, which was read everywhere by educated persons at the time when the Hôtel de Rambouillet was gaining its reputation as a fashionable assembly. These causes had their influence upon Madame de Rambouillet's friends, who took what they thought were the good things provided for them, and played with them as children play with their toys. There was an endeavour made to say things nicely and with good taste, and when good taste is put forward too prominently it defeats its own object, and affectation naturally follows. At the same time, the intentions of these ladies were not altogether ridiculous, and in the end they bore good fruit, though it is difficult to trace the steps in the progress that was made. Madame de Rambouillet was spoken of by all her contemporaries, with a singular unanimity of opinion, as being a very charming woman. She was constant to her friends, kind, considerate, and agreeable. And yet we are told that this lady, whose position was unrivalled in having the best company in Paris, among whom good breeding and politeness of thought and of manners were essential, lent her countenance to unnatural and forced behaviour on the part of her guests. In point of fact, the salon [1] at the Hôtel de Rambouillet has been confounded with others of a later date, and it has been largely credited with the faults of its imitators. About these imitators something will be said presently.

Probably, also, too much has been written about the literary aspirations of the Hôtel de Rambouillet. Bookwriters doubtless did go there, but these men were often poor and ill-dressed or had not the charm of polished manners. In comparison with our own time few books were printed then, and literary ideas did not often exist except amongst the learned. In 1629 a knot of nine men used to meet once a week at Conrart's house to talk about books, and their meetings were kept secret for some years. When through the indiscretion of one of the nine they became known to Richelieu, he approved of them, and he determined against the wish of the small circle of friends to make the members form themselves into a company. This was the origin of the French Academy, established in 1635. But the Hôtel de Rambouillet was not a literary society; as a body it was not ambitious of literary honours, though a good number of the ladies who went there were or were about to become authors. Still, the tastes of most of the guests did not run that way. Even with the best will in the world people do not suddenly acquire a taste for literature. A love of reading for its own sake must come first, and this was only in its childhood. Madame de Rambouillet did not ask her friends to her house to discuss literature, though perhaps in later years there was some hero-worship for the

[1] I use the word "salon" because it has been generally adopted, but two hundred and fifty years ago it was not in use: "cabinet" was the word then generally heard.

literary oracles. She would gladly have left the talking about books to the members of the newly formed Academy; that was their business, and she did not want to meddle with it. Because Corneille read his *Polyeucte* in her drawing-room, it is not to be supposed that other authors were commonly invited to read aloud what they had written. In 1640 Corneille was at the apogee of his reputation, and his name stood very high in France at that time. But the ladies did not like his play; they said that the Christianity shown in it was too strong. This may have been only another way of saying that they had been intensely bored by the reading, for it is well known that Corneille read badly. Literature was played with by some of the frequenters of the Hôtel de Rambouillet as a thing of fashion, but the greater number did not care much about it; they thought it rather tiresome than otherwise. It is rational to suppose that ladies and gentlemen went to the famous salon with the intention of seeing their friends, being seen in return, and of amusing themselves by rubbing their wits together. In that way the art of conversation was acquired by those who had a natural aptitude for learning it. In such an assembly the vein of affectation was not likely to run very deep. Doubtless it existed, but it was shown with heartiness and enthusiasm, as though it were a plaything; and probably it was stronger in the last eight or ten years than it had been in the twenty years previous. People talked on all manner of subjects as they do in a modern drawing-room, and those who were accustomed to the place spoke with the same ease of manner. If a dozen ladies and a dozen gentlemen were to meet each other frequently in society now, one cannot suppose that their conversation should constantly be about books. If they spoke of them they would mention them as novelties, without attaching an over-importance to what they said. So it was generally at the Hôtel de Rambouillet. The opinions of two or three who liked to express themselves sententiously were listened to by some other two or three who liked sententious sayings—for this was a fashion that was just then beginning—but on the whole these opinions were not more noticed than those uttered on the spur of the moment, and in most cases were less worth hearing. A few very successful novels had been written, and plays also were printed and sold; but most of the ladies who read these things interested themselves in the adventures related and spoke of them with the enthusiasm of children. D'Urfé's novel *Astrée* was a source of much delight; also in a lesser degree the novels of Gombauld, Gomberville, and La Calprenède. Among the plays, Racan's *Arténice ou Les Bergeries*, Corneille's tragedies, Rotrou's tragedies and tragi-comedies, Tristan l'Hermite's tragedy *Mariamne*, and Desmarets' comedy *Les Visionnaires*, were very popular on the stage, and were talked about by those who went to see them. I imagine, however, that many ladies did not go to the theatre then. And people had not learned to read then as they read now; they would read more slowly and less often. They liked talking better, and found more amusement in it. They talked a good deal about themselves, and that was surely less tiresome than reading. They were persons of understanding like ourselves, but very few of the women, and not very many of the men, had read so much as people read in our time. They came together for social purposes, and though some perhaps wished to show their cleverness and rather overshot the mark, there was probably not more fastidiousness than might be expected from a new society of friends who were aware that in belonging to that society they were envied, and that their position was more fortunate than that of others who wished to belong to it but had not been admitted.

Among their amusements verse-making was considered as an elegant accomplishment for a gentleman; and enigmas, epigrams, portraits, and madrigals were read aloud to be laughed over and talked about. This society literature was largely created by Voiture, and in his and similar productions by other men there was an air of gallantry that pleased the ladies. It was all meant and taken as pleasant frivolity, and the man who could pay the most neatly turned compliment was the most applauded. Discussions arose sometimes as to the preference to be given to one set of verses over another. The most famous dispute was the great battle, waged with all the heat that good-humoured raillery and fun will allow, between the "Jobelins" and the "Uranistes." Benserade had composed a *Sonnet de Job* and Voiture a *Sonnet d'Uranie*. Opinions were divided as to the merits of each, and when

Corneille was drawn into the contest he wrote a sonnet expressing his opinion. He said in effect: "This one is the best done, but I would sooner have written the other." We might, in England, imagine that while these games were being played some flirtation went on among the younger members of the party. But, then as now, the young people in a French drawing-room were not permitted to separate themselves from the others and sit apart in a corner where no ear could hear what was being said. Platonic love-making was allowed and admired at the Hôtel de Rambouillet, but any warmer expressions of enthusiasm were not considered respectful either towards the lady of the house or her guests. The gallantry of a gentleman who had an easy habit of saying nice things to half a dozen ladies in turn, and in the presence of them all, was highly esteemed, but love-making was not allowed to go further. The conversation was open, and everybody was supposed to take part in it. The man who could talk well on the subject of the moment was sure to be listened to and made welcome.

An extract from Fléchier's Oraison Funèbre on the abbesse d'Hières, one of Madame de Rambouillet's daughters, has often been quoted. It shows that the Hôtel de Rambouillet was not free from affectation, but it shows also that nice manners and good taste were its predominating features. Fléchier said:—

"Recollect, my brethren, those cabinets which men still look back upon with so much veneration, where the mind was purified, where virtue was worshipped under the name of 'the incomparable Arthénice';[1] where were brought together so many persons of high birth and distinction, who formed a select court, numerous without confusion, modest without constraint, learned without pride, polite without affectation."

All this may seem to be farther off than it really is from Molière's comedy. One thing is certain: that if Molière's comedy had not been written, we should have heard much less about the "précieuses." In a novel by the abbé de Pure, *La Précieuse ou Le Mystère de la Ruelle*, published in 1656, the word "précieuse" is thus explained:—"C'est un mot du temps, c'est un mot à la mode, qui a cours aujourd'hui . . . ainsi on

---

[1] Arthénice was an anagram of Catherine, Madame de Rambouillet's Christian name. Such anagrams were then in fashion.

appelle aujourd'hui les précieuses certaines personnes du beau sexe qui ont su se tirer du prix commun des autres et qui ont acquis un espèce et un rang tout particulier."[1] In fewer words Cousin said that une précieuse meant simply "une femme distinguée." And Ninon de l'Enclos wittily described the précieuses as "les jansénistes de l'amour," meaning that they were severe in love matters. But the abbé de Pure must not be understood to say that the word was new when he wrote. For at that time there were précieuses in the provinces. Chapelle and Bachaumont were travelling in 1656, and they spoke of the précieuses of Montpellier, whom they did not like. "Elles ne paraissaient que des précieuses de campagne et n'imitaient que faiblement les nôtres de Paris." Walckenaer says that the word was in use at the Hôtel de Rambouillet, and that there the ladies were proud of the title; they were known as "les précieuses," or as "les illustres." The word "illustre" was in vogue in 1643, for Molière and his first comrades opened the Illustre Théâtre in that year,[2] and it is likely that "précieuse" dated from before that time. Preciosity was taken up as a thing of fashion by the ladies at the Hôtel de Rambouillet. It was played with and laughed over by those who adopted it for no other reason than because they liked the fun of the thing.

A few years after the dispersion of the Hôtel de Rambouillet—say between 1645 and 1648—the number of précieuses increased. The Fronde broke out in 1648, and for a time Paris was in a disordered state. When the town had become quiet after the Civil War, in 1652 or 1653, a good many societies arose which took the late Hôtel de Rambouillet as their model; but they were of a more bourgeois character, and the general tone was not so good. It was less refined, and in some cases there was a "shoddiness" of manner that was in truth ridiculous.

Of the "assemblées" after the Fronde, the best and most famous was the salon of Mlle. de Scudéry. This lady had a reception every Saturday, and her "at homes" were well attended. Some of the old frequenters of the Hôtel de Rambouillet went to her house, but people's thoughts were not quite the same in the two places, or they were shown in rather

---

[1] Vol. i. 24, 25.　　　　　[2] *Ante*, p. 84.

a different way. What had been a good set in the Rue Saint Thomas du Louvre before the Fronde, degenerated afterwards into a clique in the Marais quarter of the town, not quite so far eastward as the Bastille, where Mlle. de Scudéry lived. No doubt there was merriment in the Marais, as there had been at the Hôtel de Rambouillet, which most of the visitors enjoyed; but beside the playfulness there was a greater pedantry in the conversation which tasted of intellect, and by degrees much of the talk acquired a pseudo-literary tendency. This was fostered by the dryasdusts Chapelain and Ménage, while Conrart and Pellisson, men of better understanding though of less learning, who would willingly have "dropped the shop," were led into discussing matters which they felt were out of place in a lady's drawing-room. The titles "académie" or "bureau d'esprit" that were given to some of these weekly assemblies show sufficiently that their conversation was high-flown. Ladies who went to Mlle. de Scudéry's and to other receptions wrote verses and maxims, they corrected each other's productions, and they liked it to be known that the authors were their friends.

Mlle. de Scudéry was a very clever woman, with creative faculties, though not of the best kind nor shown in the best way. She was not at all pretty, and she disliked pretentiousness. But she liked to see and hear the quick movement of opinions on the topic of the moment, and as she was in the middle of the stream, she could not swim against it. She published her novel *Le Grand Cyrus* under her brother's name, but when her secret became known she had to admit the authorship. That book appeared at intervals between 1649 and 1653. It was an allegorical novel containing written portraits of people well known at the time; it spoke under assumed names about persons in high society, their love-affairs, real or imaginary, and how they amused themselves; and naturally everybody who wished not to be thought behind-hand in social matters read it, or pretended that he had done so. D'Urfé was the first who had written what were called "portraits" of his contemporaries. This he did in his famous novel *Astrée*, the first part of which appeared in 1610, others at succeeding long intervals. Mlle. de Scudéry followed D'Urfé in describing her contemporaries, and it was chiefly her portraits that gave to her book its great popularity. Cousin made long and copious extracts from it in his *Société Française au 17ᵉ siècle*, with a key to the personages described. These extracts have their value, but reading many of them seems to fill one's mouth with cotton wool. Yet the style is clear and graphic, though often terribly long-winded. To modern limited ideas the portraits are hyperbolically flattering to an extent almost beyond belief. This was the fashion of the day. If the authoress described the people who came to her drawing-room, she was bound to speak well of them; but because she wrote in very exaggerated terms her own feelings need not be measured by the same standard, any more than we should think now that ladies in the early sixties of the last century were all pompous because they wore enormously wide crinolines. These monstrosities were one of the fashionable oddities of the age, and they also passed away. I feel as if I should like to have known Mlle. de Scudéry. She was a sensible woman who could see into things, and did not like being bespattered with clap-trap by her admirers. She would willingly not have spoken of her book in her own house, though she was glad to listen to what was said of the productions of others in the *Recueils* which were then popular. She enjoyed the verse-making, the portraits, the enigmas, and the imaginary conversations, all of which were written and sometimes printed, and then handed round amongst her friends. She liked society, but she was not a woman vain of her own work. Her novels had their vogue because they were written according to the taste of the time, and described its pleasures. But as pleasures are largely artificial, people in every age are generally intolerant against those which do not appeal to their sympathies. Every one who went to Mlle. de Scudéry's house recognised her portraits and liked talking about them. Forty years later, when all these persons were dead, the new generation did not know them and did not care about them.

Besides Mlle. de Scudéry there were, between 1650 and 1660, a good many ladies who kept a certain day of the week for seeing their friends; and apparently those who went to these receptions thought they liked them. All the ladies— the hostesses and their guests—took up the ball that had been set rolling by the Hôtel de Rambouillet, and made it roll farther. An air of distinction was aimed at by those who wished to be considered as superior people. They affected elegance of manner, and they ascribed to themselves a tone of thought that was beyond the reach of those who were not initiated in their mysteries.

"Nul n'aura de l'esprit hors nous et nos amis"[1]

might have been their motto.

At first the précieuses had tried to speak nicely; later they tried to speak differently from anybody else. Their language became as full of technicalities as the pleadings in a Court of Chancery, or as the slang of thieves. It was, in fact, a jargon of their own. They delighted in superlative adverbs, such as "furieusement," "terriblement," "effroyablement"; and they used symbolical expressions for common words and common things. For *les dents* they said "*l'ameublement de la bouche*"; for *les yeux*, "*les miroirs de l'âme*"; for *le miroir*, "*le conseiller des grâces*"; for *un éventail*, "*un Zéphir*"; for *le secret*, "*le sceau de l'amitié*"; for *les sièges*, "*les commodités de conversation*"; for *une laide*, "*une belle à faire peur*"; for *un nouvel amant*, "*un novice en chaleur*"; for *le mariage*, "*l'amour fini*," or "*l'abîme de la liberté*." These expressions help to show what was the preciosity then in vogue; they are verbal instances of the "air précieux," and ladies who followed this fashion were the précieuses. Molière laughed at these women and called them "précieuses ridicules," and with the fair licence of comedy he caricatured some of their absurdities.

La Bruyère, a moralist and a satirist, who wrote at the end of the 17th century, said in his volume *Les Caractères*, in the latter part of the chapter "De la société et de la conversation":—

"It may be remembered that there were, not long ago, a company of persons of both sexes who came together to talk and to show their wit. They left to the vulgar the art of speaking intelligibly. One obscure utterance was followed by another still more obscure; thereupon they vied with one another in their enigmas. In everything that they called delicacy, sentiment, turn and nicety of expression, they went to such a pitch that no one could understand them and they could not understand each other. For conversation of this kind neither common sense, reason, memory, nor the smallest ability were

---

[1] End of sc. 2 in Act III. of Molière's *Femmes Savantes*

required ; wit was wanted, not of the best sort, but make-believe wit, in which imagination has too large a share." [1]

And three paragraphs later :—

"For some years there was a craze for insipid and childish conversation, turning altogether upon idle questions of sentiment, and what one calls love or tenderness. Some novels read by the best-bred people of the court and of the town brought on this fashion. They shook it off, and it was taken up by the bourgeoisie who added to it their silly phrases and their puns." [2]

As the name of the Hôtel de Rambouillet is better known than that of other and later societies, La Bruyère's words have been taken to apply to the people who met in the salon bleu in the Rue Saint Thomas du Louvre. There ladies and gentlemen had their affectations, no doubt, and some were proud of them, especially during the last ten or twelve years before the receptions were discontinued—say from 1635 to 1645 or 1648. But I do not think that the cause for La Bruyère's satire existed so fully while Madame de Rambouillet's house was open as it did afterwards. It should be borne in mind that there were two epochs in the reign of the précieuses. The imitators hardly came into existence before the Fronde broke out in 1648, and they were certainly known after its close in 1652. The tone of affectation then became more general, much stronger, and showed itself to be extremely silly. There were then the "vraies précieuses" and the "fausses précieuses," and these two titles, dividing the classes, show that the second epoch had arrived and that the name had fallen into discredit.

In the novel by the abbé de Pure, already mentioned, there is a short passage that I must quote :—

"The précieuse is not the child of its father nor of its mother. She has neither one nor the other, any more than the sacrificer of the ancient law. Nor is she the work of sensitive and material nature. She is an extract of intelligence, the substance of reason. This intelligence, this reason, is the germ which produces her."

After this Bedlam biology no one will be surprised to hear that at one of the meetings of these exceptionally clever people

---

[1] *Œuvres de La Bruyère*, par M. G. Servois, i. 236, 237. (In the Collection des Grands Écrivains de la France.)
[2] *Ibid.* 238.

a discussion arose as to whether it was right to say "J'aime le melon." It was held that the word "aimer" would not so be used correctly, and that it was proper to say "J'estime le melon."

Enough has been said to show that there were précieuses of different kinds. They were all actuated by a love of sociability and good-humour, but they showed differences of manner which must have been recognised.

The *Précieuses Ridicules*, first acted on the 18th of November 1659, is in one act and in prose; and here in his first comedy of manners Molière characterised his personages very plainly by their speech. There is much that is extremely ludicrous. If a comic dramatist has to portray the exaggerated manners of a set of people, laughter is the only fair means by which he can accomplish it.

Madelon and Cathos, daughter and niece of Gorgibus, a burly, substantial bourgeois, have their heads filled with preciosity from reading sentimental novels, and they wish to appear in the world like people in a rank of life above their own. In turn they astound Gorgibus. Madelon gives a highly romantic picture of how a courtship should be conducted: ". . . But to come abruptly to the conjugal union, to make love only while you are signing the marriage contract, to begin the novel at the tail end, I say, father, that nothing can be more commercial than such a proceeding." Cathos is not behind her cousin in her opinions. She says, scornfully enough, that the two gentlemen presented to Madelon and herself as lovers "are altogether incongruous in gallantry. I will wager that they have never seen the Carte de Tendre, and that Billets Doux, Petits Soins, and Jolis Vers are unknown countries to them."[1] Then she finds fault with their

---

[1] I fear that a long note is necessary here. The Carte de Tendre is a map in Mlle. de Scudéry's second allegorical novel, *Clélie*. The idea of a map to this novel and to Bunyan's allegory, *The Pilgrim's Progress*, is the same. The Carte de Tendre shows that Jolis Vers, Billet Galant, and Billet Doux, are three villages that one has to pass to get from Nouvelle Amitié (a town on the river Inclination), to Tendre sur Estime (a town on the river Estime); and Petits Soins is a village on the other side of the river Inclination, through which one has to pass to get from Nouvelle Amitié to Tendre sur Reconnaissance (a town on the river Reconnaissance).—In a word, Cathos meant that her own and her cousin's suitor knew nothing of the fashionable gallantry of the time; and Molière meant also to poke his fun at the taste for allegorical novels then in vogue.

clothes: "To come on a love visit with an untrimmed leg, a hat deprived of its feathers, hair irregularly dressed, and a coat which suffers from a poverty of ribbons! . . . My stars, what lovers are these!" The main idea in the play is to show how Madelon and Cathos are thoroughly hoaxed by a valet named Mascarille, an eccentric and lordly fellow who writes verses and sets up for being a wit, and who before introducing himself to them has dubbed himself the Marquis de Mascarille. We are made to see in the early scenes that the two young women are discontented and peevish, but that when they hear that a marquis has come to call upon them they are moved to immoderate joy. The sham nobleman, too, tries to hector the men who have carried him in his chair; but he has to pay them when he finds that they mean to have their money and that they do not care for his quality.

The ladies receive the marquis very graciously. When he is seated he takes a small comb out of his pocket and combs his wig, then he adjusts his canons. The canons were lace ruffles worn below the knee; smartly dressed men wore them deep, but Mascarille outdoes the fashion with wild extravagance. He asks the ladies what they think of Paris, . . . whether they receive many visits, and who is the wit most constant in his attendance upon them.

" Madelon.

" As yet we are not known, but we are in the way of becoming so ; and we have a special friend, a lady, who has promised to bring here all the gentlemen who figure in the *Recueil des pièces choisies.*" [A collection of elegant extracts by different authors.]

" Cathos.

" And certain others whom we have heard spoken of as oracles in polite matters.

" Mascarille.

" I will do what you want better than anybody. They all come to see me, and I may say that I never get up without having half a dozen wits in my room."

The ladies are enchanted. Madelon's answer is too long to quote, but it shows admirably that she and her cousin want to be reckoned among those who know what is going on in society—to know who has composed this sonnet, who this madrigal, etc. " It is this that makes people think much of you, for if one is behindhand in these matters all the cleverness in the world is not worth a button."

Mascarille's self-glorification is charming :—

"For me, such as I am," he says, "I have some skill in these matters when I like to use it ; and you shall see two hundred songs, as many sonnets, four hundred epigrams, and more than a thousand madrigals, without counting enigmas and portraits, that I have spread about in the best ruelles in Paris." [1]

He delivers an impromptu which he had made at the house of a duchess, one of his friends :—

> " Oh oh ! je n'y prenois pas garde :
> Tandis que sans songer à mal je vous regarde,
> Votre œil en tapinois me dérobe mon cœur,
> Au voleur, au voleur, au voleur, au voleur."

Mascarille's criticism of his own verses is as delightful nonsense as the verses themselves. He explains the last line, and Madelon cries: "That shows the meaning of things, the real meaning, the meaning of the meaning." And when he has sung his impromptu, though " the brutality of the season has furiously outraged the delicacy of his voice," Cathos asks him : " Have you learnt music ? "—" I ? not at all."—" How can that be ? "—" People of quality know everything without learning it."

He offers to take the two ladies to the theatre and says :—

"But I must beg of you to applaud properly when we are there. For I have promised to push the play, and the author came to me again this morning to ask for my assistance. It is the custom here among us people of quality for authors to come to us to read their plays to induce us to think well of them and to bring them into reputation. And you cannot imagine that when we say anything the pit should dare to contradict us. For me, I am most exact, and when I have given my word to a poet I always cry out, ' That is good,' before the candles are lighted."

This is strong satire, though it ends with a bit of intended nonsense. A little later Mascarille says that he has written a play himself. Cathos asks him to which actors he means to give it. He replies :—

---

[1] The ruelle was a name then given to social gatherings. Ladies often received their friends in bed, the head of which was placed against the wall, and the space at each side where the visitors sat was called the ruelle. Réduit and ruelle were almost synonymous.

"A nice question! To the 'grands comédiens,' of course. (That is to the Hôtel de Bourgogne.) It is only they who are able to make the most of things. The others are ignoramuses who recite just as one talks. They do not know how to declaim their lines, nor to halt at the proper moment. How can we distinguish a fine verse if the actor does not pause, and if he does not tell you that there you should sing your bravos?"

The matter in this speech will be referred to at length later on, but it should be said here shortly that this was Molière's first attack against his rivals, the actors at the Hôtel de Bourgogne. No one can say how far it was directly provoked. It is certain, however, that Molière was pretending here to laugh at his own troop because they spoke their words simply, and it is equally certain that he was satirising the inflated declamation of the actors at the Hôtel de Bourgogne, and that they knew he was quizzing them. They felt his irony and they did not like it. A few years later there was war between the two troops. The actors of the Théâtre du Marais do not appear to have sided with either of the disputants.

Compared even with Oronte, the fop in the *Misanthrope*, Mascarille is most ludicrously over-dressed. He is not a little proud of his person, he knows his ground and he asks the ladies to admire his trimmings. Scented gloves were then fashionable, and he says: "Attachez un peu sur ces gants la réflexion de votre odorat." Madelon replies, "they smell terribly good"; and Cathos, "I have never inhaled a perfume of higher distinction." Then follows an amusing talk about clothes.

This scene[1] (sc. 9) is the chief scene in the comedy, but it is hardly fair that Mascarille should have all the fun to himself. Therefore the Vicomte Jodelet, a friend of his, and of as noble birth, is brought on the stage. I can only refer to this incident and say that Mascarille and Jodelet offer to take Madelon and Cathos outside Paris and give them a supper. This is impossible, so a dance is improvised and musicians are called in to play. In the middle of the amusement the masters of the

[1] It is unfortunate for the purpose of reference that in the various editions of Molière's comedies the scenes should not begin and end at the same place. As I have said in the preface, all the references made here to the *Œuvres de Molière* apply to the edition of his works published by Messrs. Hachette in the Collection des Grands Écrivains de la France, unless of course any other edition is specified.

two valets come in and find their servants dancing with the ladies, and they beat them for their impertinence. The sham marquis and the sham viscount are stripped of their clothes and made to stand bare in their shirt sleeves. Their condition is almost pitiable, though very ludicrous. Then Gorgibus appears and he roundly scolds his daughter and his niece. At last he vents his anger upon the occupations of the précieuses generally :—

"And you who are the cause of all their folly—silly nonsense, pernicious amusements of idle minds, romances, verses, songs, and sonnets—may the devil run away with you all."

There was a fortnight's interval between the first and the second performance of the play. If Baudeau de Somaize, not a man whose evidence was the safest, can be trusted, it would seem that the comedy had given offence, and that one of the society gallants had sufficient influence to get the play prohibited for a time.[1] If the play was prohibited there is nothing to show that Madame de Rambouillet was the cause of it. It was said, however, that she was hurt by Molière's satire, but that she had the good sense and good taste not to show her annoyance. The evidence on which this statement rests is not convincing. I should imagine rather that Madame de Rambouillet's good sense and good taste showed her that Molière's comedy was meant as a bit of fun, and that she was proud enough to think that her late salon—then a thing of the past—was not included in the picture. She would have told herself that the satire was directed against other salons where the attempt at distinction or notoriety was evident to anybody who had eyes to see. The tone of high breeding at the Hôtel de Rambouillet had led to pretentiousness and "shoddiness" elsewhere, and it was this that Molière wished to ridicule; and I believe him when he said in his preface to his play : "I should have liked to show that it nowhere exceeded the bounds of courteous and becoming satire, that the best things may be aped by sorry imitators who deserve to be laughed at; that these pitiful imitations of what is really excellent, have always offered matter for comedy. . . . So also the true précieuses would be to blame if they were offended because one makes fun of the ridiculous précieuses who imitate

[1] *Le Grand Dictionnaire des Précieuses, historique, etc.* See *Prédictions.*

them badly." Madelon and Cathos in Molière's comedy do not perceive that the sham marquis is at times very vulgar in his manners, nor that his wit, though excellent in its way, is sometimes like the bantering familiarity of a pushing young man who likes joking with a couple of pretty barmaids. Molière himself nowhere offends against good taste, and there is all the difference between showing vulgarity in a character and showing a character vulgarly. Molière here was playing with his personages in the vein of caricature, and there is too much true comedy in his caricature to prevent his play being a farce. Affectation of a more or less ridiculous kind had been a foible of the guests at the Hôtel de Rambouillet, but in later salons it had grown stronger; and it was this that Molière seized upon as suitable for his purpose. He made the most of it, and with fair caricature he showed that the pretence and the language of the précieuses were in truth a fit subject for comedy. He drew two young women of bourgeois rank, ignorant of the ways of people whose manners they would like to adopt, and he showed that their ambition to be known in society was so great that they were gulled by a lackey outrageously over-dressed who introduced himself to them as a person of high quality.

Did the caricature in the *Précieuses* give a truer picture of the different salons in vogue after the Fronde than of the late Hôtel de Rambouillet? On the whole I think it did, though nothing can be less absolute than the customary thoughts of men and women. As well as I can judge, the tone of the Hôtel de Rambouillet, the parent assembly, was simpler and better than in that of its children, who exaggerated its playful affectations and made a business of what had been introduced more or less often as an amusement. The tone of high breeding had given way to pretentiousness, and it was this that Molière wished to ridicule. Let those who know his plays think for a moment how much of his satire was directed against humbug of various kinds. Tartuffe's humbug was wicked, and he was hated; Philinte adopted gaily the conventional humbug of the world, he knew what that meant, but he knew nothing more; Monsieur Jourdain so humbugged himself that he was a laughing-stock.

When the *Précieuses* first appeared it followed Corneille's

Cinna, as an after-piece. For the first twelve months at the Petit Bourbon Molière adopted the practice that was then common of giving each day only one play in five acts; but in adding his own one-act comedy after the tragedy he was in reality going back to the old custom of giving a short light play after the set piece for the day.

On the stage Molière was his own Marquis de Mascarille in the *Précieuses*, and La Grange and Du Croisy played under their own names. Jodelet also gave his name to his part. The other rôles were probably distributed as follows : Gorgibus was acted by L'Espy, Madelon by Madeleine Béjart, Cathos by Mlle. de Brie, Marotte by Mlle. Ragueneau.[1]

There are three stories connected with the first performance of the *Précieuses*. I will give the best, and no one will be injured by believing it. An old man in the pit of the theatre was so delighted with the play that he cried aloud : "Bravo, Molière! That is good comedy." The two other stories appear to be more spurious. Public curiosity to see the second performance of the comedy, on the 2nd of December, must have been great, for on that day the price of entry into the parterre —the largest place in the theatre—was doubled. This was done in accordance with a custom of which more will be said in chapter ix. The success of the comedy was brilliant. It was acted thirty-three times as a new play; this for a play in one act was very remarkable. The average receipt taken at these thirty-three performances was more than double the average receipt of the 228 public performances at the Petit Bourbon theatre—from October 1658 to October 1660—even though the little comedy helped so largely to raise the general average.

The acting copyright in a play was then governed by custom. A play was held to belong to the theatre where it was first acted until it was printed. Any other troop might then act it if they pleased. On the whole the custom was fairly observed. But sometimes booksellers interfered : they fraudulently got a copy of the play, obtained the privilege to print it, which was then often given easily enough, and sold it without the writer's permission.[2] In the Notice to the *Précieuses Ridicules* Despois

---

[1] L. Moland, *Œuvres de Molière*, 2nd ed. Additions at the end of vol. xii.
[2] Taschereau, *Vie de Molière*, 5th ed. 53.

says: "It is more than probable that this is the first of Molière's comedies that was printed; it is quite certain that it is the first that was printed with his sanction." [1] But it was very nearly printed without his sanction. Jean Ribou, a bookseller, obtained a stolen copy of the play, and got surreptitiously on the 12th of January 1660 a privilege or leave to print it. This is the meaning of Molière's words in the preface to his comedy: "I have had the misfortune to see a stolen copy of my play in the hands of the booksellers, accompanied with a permission to print it, obtained without my knowledge. . . . I must either let my play be printed or have a lawsuit." He had his play printed at once. A new privilege was made out in favour of another bookseller, though Molière's name was not mentioned in it. This was dated 19th of January 1660, and on the 29th the printing was completed. Ribou's surreptitious privilege was annulled, and his intended theft prevented.[2] Molière's preface to his *Précieuses* should be read. With sound common sense and characteristic humour he mixed his seriousness and his ridicule together, but in reality he was very angry at the fraud so nearly practised upon him. The little play had been intended for the stage, and he was well satisfied with its success there; but "he had no wish to make it jump from the Théâtre du Bourbon to the Galerie du Palais"—where there were many booksellers' shops—thereby affording the two rival troops the opportunity, if they chose to use it, of performing his play in their theatres. He knew also that to complain of injustice was not the way to propitiate the world in his favour, and he was able to throw a tone of pleasantry into what he said, as though he enjoyed the satisfaction of being considered an author and of seeing himself in print for the first time.

It is not worth while to give a page to say how Somaise wrote two plays: *Les Véritables Précieuses*, and *Les Précieuses Ridicules*, "comédie représentée au Petit Bourbon. Nouvellement mises en vers." They were both impudent attempts to gain some success after the great popularity of Molière's comedy. The first at least of these two plays was probably acted at some minor theatre in Paris, and both of the plays reached a second

---

[1] *Œuvres de Molière*, ii. 41, 42; and i. 98-100.
[2] *Ibid.* ii. 42, 43; xi. 1, 2.

edition in print. And it would be useless to go into the question whether Molière's *Précieuses* had been acted in the provinces before he returned to Paris. Despois argued strongly against this idea,[1] and with every appearance of right on his side.

But it may be said shortly that Molière put on to his stage on the 7th of May 1660 a comedy by Gilbert called *La Vraie et la Fausse Précieuse*. Gilbert was an author of reputation. M. Victor Fournel reprinted one of his comedies in the second volume of his *Contemporains de Molière*, and in a short notice tried to say a good word for him; but if Gilbert was ever well thought of, his reputation died with him. He was paid 500 livres for his comedy acted by Molière's troop, but the play was never printed. Though it was acted only nine times, it had a good pecuniary success compared with other plays, except Molière's, that were put on the stage at the Petit Bourbon theatre.

Molière's next comedy, *Sganarelle ou le Cocu Imaginaire*, was first played at the Petit Bourbon theatre on the 28th of May 1660. The play is in verse, and as it has only one act, it was always performed after a longer piece. Its success was very good, though less brilliant than that of the *Précieuses*. While it was new it was given thirty-four times, it was played three times before the king; and during the author's lifetime it was acted in public oftener than any other comedy that he wrote.[2] Molière gave the name Sganarelle to half a dozen characters in his plays; it is believed that he invented the word. Etymologically, it means one who is undeceived to his own discomfort; and both the sound and the appearance of the first syllable indicate that the name was meant to have an ungracious signification. In nearly all cases the name represents a man who is a churl and a poltroon, one who is selfish, mean, and tyrannical. There is a typical likeness amongst them all. Sganarelle, the valet in *Don Juan*, is the best of his race, but he differs from the others in that he is a servant and must obey. He has not much chance of being a tyrant, and by his master's side he shines as a good man. Yet these six characters, bearing the same name and belonging as it were to one family, have all their own peculiarities. They are all recognisable one from the other.

[1] *Œuvres de Molière*, ii. 7-10.   [2] *Ibid.* i. 548; ii. 140-2.

The circumstances under which they appear are different; the men therefore speak and act differently. By so constantly bringing forward the same type under various guises, Molière shows how thoroughly he knew its nature. The character was not a noble one, but the dramatist made admirable use of it in bringing out the satire in his comedies.

In *Sganarelle* Molière was laughing at the ignoble jealousy of a man who fancied without cause that his wife was untrue to him. The intrigue of the story lies in the mistakes made both by Sganarelle and his wife, and in those made by the two young lovers. They all believe things to be other than they are. The amusement lies in the skilful manner the events are worked out, and in the way that Sganarelle shows his character. He is represented as a jealous husband, imputing thoughts to his wife which were groundless. No doubt the woman was a vixen, but he was such a self-satisfied, fretful poltroon, that if she occasionally " combed his hair," he richly deserved it.

In scene 17 Sganarelle delivers a long monologue. He knows that he ought to fight his enemy, but he excuses himself for his want of spirit. Despois points out that analogous situations bring about the same idea in different authors; [1] and he refers to a passage in Shakespeare's *Henry IV.* Part I. Act v. end of sc. 1, where Falstaff shows himself to be not more courageous than Sganarelle. Comparing these two passages as far as one can, I prefer Molière's, though his monologue here is long. Sganarelle shows by his speech that he has all the shilly-shally earnestness of a coward. He has only strength to be frankly cynical. His wife, though a shrew, is perfectly innocent of the imputed fault; but as he thinks she is untrue, he will proclaim her misconduct everywhere. He shows a mixture of sham bravery and real cowardice, and this with the humour and the aptness of language to the situation makes his speech very entertaining. There is no passage of any length in Molière's comedies which shows more of the old " esprit gaulois " than this speech. In thought it seems to belong to two or more generations before his day. But none of the writers in verse at the end of the 16th century had

---

[1] *Œuvres de Molière*, ii. 200 note. This note begins on p. 198, but I omit the first part of it where reference is made to a play of Scarron's.

Molière's largeness of style, and if they had possessed his sense of humour they would have expressed themselves with greater crudity. Those who wrote in prose showed a half vigorous manner, rich perhaps in their own vernacular, but their style was the language of the people, and was not literary except in a simple and uncultured form.

There is nothing in *Sganarelle* that should offend anybody. The play is not a high class comedy, though there are excellent points in it, and one may raise the objection that it does not involve an exalted moral. It would, however, be more just to say that the lesson given is so elementary that no man ought to need it. Unfortunately there are in the world men who are bullies and cowards, vain and proud of themselves, jealous, selfish, obnoxious creatures, hateful to all who know them. Such a one was Sganarelle in this comedy; and Shakespeare's Falstaff, though larger hearted and with more humour in himself, was not otherwise very different. Molière meant to show some of the ugly sides of human nature, and from his satire we see that such a husband will probably have a querulous wife. It was not the dramatist's wish to extol his Sganarelle, but to show what manner of man he was; and it is for us to see how he accomplished his task. Nobody respects him and nobody respects Falstaff, but many admire the way the two personages are drawn.

Speaking of the French play, M. Mesnard asks: "But where is the truth of the characters, and even the probability of the incidents?"[1] It may be answered that the dramatist took certain incidents which would lend themselves to ridicule and based his characters upon them. Both are ludicrous and they were worked out on ludicrous lines, but the characters are made to follow the natural ideas of the type of personages described; therefore in their place they are true. Truth in fiction does not necessarily exclude what is ludicrous, or even grotesqueness, for a character or an incident may be ridiculous without being absurd. Ridicule and absurdity in fable are not synonymous. Truth in humour may often seem to be irregular, but without it comedy descends to farce. Perhaps there is some farce in *Sganarelle*, but by his faithful rendering of a ridiculous character or grotesque situation, Molière showed

[1] *Notice biographique sur Molière*, 228.

his power of realisation, or if you like of idealisation, very strongly. Ludicrous comedy, therefore, when it is true to itself, stands upon a higher level than farce, however amusing.

Like other French writers, M. Moland does not doubt that the plot of *Sganarelle* came from Italy, but he says: "Nothing is more French than the spirit and the gaiety which animates the whole of the dialogue. This has all the piquant flavour, all the ironical vigour that may be seen in the contes and in the fabliaux. Those who know our ancient literature recognise in Molière's plays not only the broad touch of pleasantry, the free traditions of the satire of the middle ages, but also numerous reminiscences of old authors, of Noël du Fail, of Rabelais, of the *Quinze Joyes de Mariage*, of the *Cent Nouvelles Nouvelles*." [1]

In this comedy Molière played the part of Sganarelle; and du Parc, who with his wife had returned to the Petit Bourbon from the Marais at Easter, played the part of Gros René. Despois says that the attribution of the other rôles is uncertain.

The story of the printing of *Sganarelle* is curious, but it is long and only the outlines can be told here. On the 31st of May, three days after the comedy had first appeared, Molière obtained a privilege or leave to print his play, which also forbade any one else from doing so. He then thought he was safe. But one Neufvillenaine also got, fraudulently, on the 26th of July, a privilege to print the play; and on the 26th of August the comedy, with laudatory arguments written by him at the head of each scene, appeared in type. Neufvillenaine said that he had seen the play six or seven times and had written it all from memory. Most probably a stolen green-room copy had been given to him. Molière at once went to law. Ribou, the bookseller, was punished, but Neufvillenaine escaped punishment, or nothing is known of it. The version of the play given by him must have been pretty accurate, for Molière allowed his edition of twelve hundred and fifty copies to run its course, and the lines now read are those which were printed fraudulently. [2] I have not been able to tell all of

---

[1] *Œuvres de Molière*, by L. Moland, 2nd. ed. iii. 272.
[2] This story is told by Despois, *Œuvres de Molière*, ii. 147-159; and completed by M. Desfeuilles in vol. xi. pp. 3 and 4 of the same work. See also the prefatory notice to *Sganarelle ou Le Cocu Imaginaire* by M. Moland in his second edition of Molière, vol. iii.

Neufvillenaine's barefaced impudence. The fact that nothing more was heard of him might make one think that the whole affair was a hoax, even that Molière might have been an accomplice in it. But the legal documents published by M. Campardon prove that such an idea is impossible. Neufvillenaine was probably the invented name of some struggling author, and I am much inclined to suspect de Visé. This man will be heard of again.

Two months after the first appearance of Molière's *Sganarelle ou le Cocu Imaginaire*, one F. Doneau obtained leave to print a comedy called *La Cocue Imaginaire*. This play was merely an inversion of Molière's: the principal characters were transformed, and Doneau made a woman go through the same scenes of anxiety that Molière had shown in a man. His play does not appear to have been acted, but two editions of the printed copy were sold.[1]

In the month of October an incident happened which troubled the minds of the actors at the Petit Bourbon. They were suddenly turned out of their theatre, and it would seem unnecessarily for the reasons that were alleged. The idea of building the present colonnade or façade of the Louvre opposite the church of Saint Germain l'Auxerrois had been mooted, but the first stone was not laid until the autumn of 1665.[2] After chronicling the last performance at the theatre on the 10th of October, La Grange gives an account of the expulsion of the troop:—

"On Monday the 11th of October, M. de Ratabon, surveyor of the royal buildings, began to pull down the Petit Bourbon theatre without giving notice to the troop, who were much surprised to find their theatre taken from them. Complaint was made to the King, to whom M. de Ratabon said that the site of the theatre was necessary for the building of the Louvre, and that as the interior of the theatre had been planned for the royal ballets and belonged to his Majesty, he had not thought it necessary to consider the claims of the theatre while the work at the Louvre was being pressed forward. M. de Ratabon evidently wished to play the troop a nasty trick. But as the troop had the good fortune to please the King, his Majesty gratified them by allowing them the hall in the Palais Royal, Monsieur having asked for it to indemnify his actors for the wrong done to them; and the Sieur de Ratabon received a special order to

---

[1] *Œuvres de Molière*, ii. 137-9.
[2] Despois, *Le Théâtre Français sous Louis XIV.*, 29.

do the important repairs in the hall of the Palais Royal. There were three rotten, propped-up beams in the timber work, and half of the hall was uncovered and dilapidated. A few days afterwards the troop set men to work at the theatre and petitioned the King to let them remove from the Bourbon the boxes and other things necessary for their new home. . . . Besides all these bickerings [relating to decorations] our troop had to contend against another trouble. The actors at the Hôtel de Bourgogne and those at the Marais tried to separate us, each troop making overtures to entice some of us into their company. But every one in Molière's troop remained firm. All the actors, liked the Sieur de Molière, their leader, who besides his good qualities and singular ability has also a polite and engaging manner, which obliged them all to assure him that they would take their chance with him whatever offer was made to them and whatever advantage they might find elsewhere.

"Thereupon it was noised about in Paris that the troop remained united and that it was to be established at the Palais Royal, with the protection of the King and of Monsieur." [1]

For more than three months Molière and his comrades were without a theatre. They had been expelled from the Petit Bourbon with high-handed officialism on the 11th of October 1660, and they were not installed in the Palais Royal until the 20th of January following. But in the meanwhile they were not altogether idle. La Grange has chronicled that they went "en visite" eight times at private houses, and for these visits they received 2115 livres. They also played five times at the Louvre and once at Vincennes, for which the king gave them 3000 livres. But the demolitions at the Petit Bourbon and getting into the Palais Royal cost them 2115 livres.[2] There still remained to them the gratification of 3000 livres from the king, but they had to live for fourteen weeks and were without their customary employment.

An examination of La Grange's Register shows that all the real successes at the Petit Bourbon, with the partial exception of Gilbert's comedy, *La Vraie et La Fausse Précieuse*, came from Molière's two one-act plays. And it will be seen, too, afterwards at the Palais Royal that Molière's comedies were almost the only plays that were profitable to his troop. This was partly because neither Molière nor his comrades could act tragedy, or the public thought they could not do so. Something will be said about this in a later chapter. During the

<hr>

[1] *Registre de la Grange*, 25, 26.   [2] *Ibid.* 27, 28.

two years that Molière was at the Petit Bourbon the theatre was open 228 times, and the average daily receipt was 311 livres. Gilbert's new five-act comedy was acted nine times, and gave a daily average of 330 livres; but while they were new Molière's *Précieuses Ridicules*, acted 33 times, gave a daily average of 647 livres, and his *Sganarelle*, acted 34 times, an average of 461 livres. It may seem unfair to estimate the day's receipt as having been made by a one-act comedy; but a comparison of the daily receipts, when these two plays of Molière's were acted and when they were not, shows indisputably that it was the one-act comedy in both cases that attracted nine-tenths of the audience.

A play was considered new until its freshness had so far declined that it was withdrawn, perhaps temporarily, from the stage; or, if it had any fair success, until it was printed. Taking these, therefore, as the general dividing lines between new and old plays, La Grange shows that among the contemporary authors of old plays acted at the Petit Bourbon, Pierre Corneille was brought forward 26 times, Scarron 41, but Molière himself 59—the *Étourdi* was acted 27 times, and the *Dépit Amoureux* 32. *Sanche Panse*, a comedy by an unknown writer, and probably not then new, was acted 17 times; Gilbert's tragedy, *Endymion*, 11 times; and Thomas Corneille's comedy, *Don Bertrand de Cigarral*, 8 times. Desmarets, Tristan l'Hermite, and Boisrobert were acted 7 or 8 times each; Rotrou only 3 times. Old plays were naturally not so well liked as new ones, and when an old play was given alone, the receipts exceed the mean average of 311 livres only 8 times— Molière's *Étourdi* 3 times, his *Dépit Amoureux* 3 times, and two comedies of Scarron's each once.

On the whole it may be seen from the last quotation made from La Grange's Register that the actors were satisfied with the results of their first two years' work in Paris. In after years, at the Palais Royal, an actor's share in the theatre became more valuable. This was owing chiefly to the excellence of Molière's comedies, or to the way in which they were acted, though in a few cases the hostility which his plays provoked doubtless increased the number of spectators.

CHAPTER VIII

MOLIÈRE'S IDEAS OF COMEDY, ETC.—SHAKESPEARE AND MOLIÈRE

IF Molière had written only half a dozen comedies this chapter would not be necessary; but as he was a very fertile author some general remarks should be made about his ideas of comedy, as to how he put them into effect and what may be learned from his teaching. These ideas and the way he showed them formed part of Molière's nature, and they should be noticed by any one who wishes to understand his plays. A little forbearance, I hope, may be allowed to me for saying here some things that are said in more or less different ways in other parts of this book. Such repetition is almost unavoidable in trying to interpret the thoughts of a prolific comic dramatist with large sympathies; who, in spite of his sadness, was a man of clear and sound judgment, who knew the intricacies of human nature perhaps better than any of his countrymen, and who loved to ridicule its vagaries. It might seem that Molière's ideas of acting should be spoken of here, but it will be more convenient to consider the general style of acting among his contemporaries and the judgments passed upon himself as an actor before attempting on our part to say how he strove to personate the characters he had to represent.

Everybody has not the same ideas about comedy and everybody will not think of Molière's plays in the same way, for men's humours and their sympathies are often widely different. As a branch of the representation of human nature it is useless to speak about comedy in an absolute manner, and though I have expressed my own opinions, I trust it may not be thought I have wished to lay down the law or to propound canons of criticism where lines of thought are much involved. In dealing with comedy, questions become very complicated; few of them stand alone. We should endeavour to consider them together as forming a part of a great whole. I believe, however, that truth, with its many-sidedness, is a fundamental basis in all arts. It is extremely difficult to see into it, really get at it in all its aspects, many of which seem to be divergent, bring them together, co-ordinate them and conciliate them. A man would be bold if he thought he had done so much.

Comedy may be seen in various branches of art; but with regard to the drama, which should show how people of different natures are made to act and react upon one another, I take it that comedy means a mirthful dramatic representation of the humours of men, and that some exaggeration or caricature may be used to heighten the effect. Comic is an adjective applying to the picture, and means appertaining or belonging to comedy. Alceste in the *Misanthrope*, and the Marquis de Mascarille in the *Précieuses Ridicules* are both comic personages, because in different ways they show the attributes of comedy—the first with seriousness, though ridicule is cast upon him, the other with jesting caricature. When the *Tartuffe* was forbidden, Molière, in pleading his cause, began his first petition to the king: "The function of comedy is to correct men while it amuses them." Comedy should before all things amuse and be mirthful, it should appeal to the heart and to the head, it should be written with the intention of satirising men's bad or foolish qualities and their manners, and also of showing the good sides of their natures; and every comedy—apart from farce, which is the nonsense of comedy— should have a moral.

Molière did not offer his moral as a precept. He made it form part of the plot and of the characterisation in a play, but he so disguised it by satire or irony that the reader or spectator enjoys his lesson as though it were a thing of delight. Molière knew exceedingly well how to gild his pill. It was he who wrote, in the last scene of *Amphitryon* :—

"Le Seigneur Jupiter sait dorer la pilule."

He shows that it is distinctly not the office of the comic dramatist to preach to his audience. When most in earnest he wrote thoroughly in the vein of comedy, often mixing strong ridicule with his censure, and his lessons nearly always afford amusement, and are read with pleasure. He teaches that it is the office of comedy to show how men and women act and react upon one another in the play of life, and proclaim themselves to be what they are by their speech and by their deeds. Comedy concerns itself far more with men's likes and dislikes, with their fads or their caprices, than with their mental abilities. Man's nature is strangely interwoven; but, if we think of it, our humours and how we show them in their frequent contradictions—be they grave or gay, fickle or persevering, mean or honest, generous or selfish, courageous or timid—will be a tolerably sure guide, from the point of view of comedy, to our personal characteristics. A large part of Molière's comedy is seen in satire or irony against the world's humbug. Carlyle called this sham, and growled over it contemptuously. Molière showed wrong-doing more clearly and in a better spirit, and he made people laugh at their own weaknesses. The comic dramatist is fully within his province if he can by fair satire expose vices and foibles and thus exhibit their harm and their folly; and if it is given to him to make others feel disgust or dislike by his laughter, he may perhaps effect his object. When Molière had a strong moral purpose in view, he made true comedy the vehicle for teaching his lesson, and he showed his purpose with great comic force. When he condemned the cruelty or the selfishness of fathers or guardians, the heartlessness of women, hypocrisy, and what passed for atheism, and the dishonesty of doctors, his characterisation gives so much pleasure that no one feels his lesson to be wearisome; though there have been some who have missed its teaching because they have not understood the intended caricature and its ridicule. It was not in Molière's nature to wish to preach. He gave satirical and comic pictures of what he saw and heard, and he described with censure or with ridicule the results produced by bad or foolish actions. He loved pleasant raillery and the fun of good satire and irony, and his wish to ridicule was always governed by charitable intentions, and by a desire not to wound when chastisement was not deserved. He was never ill-natured, though, when he meant to punish, he knew how to use his whip. But mere punishment for its own sake of a bad man, say a Harpagon, is distasteful. It savours of coarseness—

> "It is excellent
> To have a giant's strength, but it is tyrannous
> To use it like a giant."

M

Molière did not forget that he was a comic dramatist, whose office it was to amuse by showing the comedy of life. Though satire was part of his function, he recollected that the public, who were his judges, would soon be listening to him; and that when chastisement was necessary, unless it were given fairly and in the spirit of good comedy, the censure would recoil upon his own head and do him more harm than good. No satirist ever knew better that he should be careful how he held his rod; no satirist was ever less of an over-zealous policeman either in thought or in deed.

Laughter of some sort in a comedy is essential, for a comedy that does not make one laugh or that has no mirth in it is like a dull beast not worth feeding. Mountebank wit is rarely comedy; setting that aside, therefore, and also pure farce showing little or no comedy, there are different notes in the laughter of comedy. They arise from the spirit of the play and from the tone of the words used. The natural effect of comedy should be to create merriment of some kind. It may be loud, even uproarious, or appeal softly to the more delicate sense of gentle humour. In all cases laughter should spring of its own accord, gladly, as though it enjoyed its own presence; there should be some sense of thoughtfulness behind it, and it is always happiest when it brings with it a feeling of rejoicing. The laughter of a comic dramatist should at least be sociable, so that many can join in it, everybody laughing together in the theatre at the same time and at the same thing. Inside the theatre emotional feelings are infectious. Every one does not think alike, but if the play really interests, a sentiment of gladness or of mirth spreads itself through the house; if the play be tiresome, a sensation of dulness is diffused in the same way. A sort of magnetic influence is at work, carrying with it delight or boredom, and the infection is caught. High and low comedy are terms sometimes heard as general distinguishing marks, but the distinctions have very frequently not been observed in practice. The so-called divisions have naturally been confounded. It is impossible to draw a line between the manners and humours of persons in gentle life and of those who are socially below them—between the quality and the people. Molière has shown humours in different ways, but he did not divide men into classes.

Though some of his plays belong to high comedy, there are many others which, so far as they can come under any designation, would perhaps be better known as popular comedy. The title is not precise, it is vague enough; but our humours or our fancies, instead of being precise, are generally complex or contradictory. All comedy should appeal to natural instincts, and its office is to delight as well as to amuse. The tone of the wit or humour shown, of the pleasure it gives and of the laughter it provokes, are good indications, as far as they go, to tell you how to think of the comedy you have seen or read. Is the humour displayed good or ill natured, is it clean or is it coarse? Is the laughter it causes only a giggle, or does it show a meaning of its own? Does the wit or the fun seem to come easily out of the subject, or is it forced and pretentious? Does the play raise your spirits and make you feel happier? Is the folly or the vice spoken of shown with complacence, or with rebuke and honest anger? Answers to these questions will not differentiate high from low or even popular comedy, and they will not tell whether the incidents and the personages have been well or ill described, but they should help to characterise a comedy seen on the stage.

If I understand Molière's teaching aright, his object was to show amusing comedy from a frank and wholesome point of view. In nearly all of his plays written after his return to Paris from the provinces, he took for his groundwork a subject that might be made to illustrate the thoughts of his countrymen; and though, as he treated it, his meaning was clear, his ridicule sometimes proved a stumbling-block, especially to men in authority. With the licence of fair caricature allowed to a comic dramatist he represented people's manners and actions as he saw them, laughing at what was ridiculous, satirising or condemning what was vicious, and extolling virtues as being noble—but he has done this latter more rarely, as though he thought the province of comedy was rather to reprove than to admire. He tried to show by comic examples that from evil or foolish conduct bad results would follow, and that the laughter coming from satire in comedy might possibly be beneficial. Beyond this he was not a reformer. He had no idea that it was the duty of a comic dramatist to speak with the tone of an enthusiast, or to endeavour to correct men's conduct by telling them what they ought to do. Such teaching belongs properly to the divine. Spiritual instruction was not Molière's function, and his comedies do not lead one to suppose that he thought of it. He wrote from an open and honest worldly point of view; and he thought that if by comedy he could expose the harm or the folly caused by greed, selfishness, injustice, dishonesty, over self-love, vanity or humbug, he might indicate the evils coming from these faults. It was not his office to do more, and he would not attempt it. Molière was warm-hearted, but he did not let his enthusiasm destroy his comedy. He did not forget that human nature is strong, that it works in its own way, and that it is often capricious and perverse. He wished earnestly to see many things otherwise ordered, but he did not suppose that he could do much to alter the world's ways. He could hardly have hoped in the *Tartuffe* to give a death-blow to hypocrisy and to the frauds of the directors of conscience, nor in *Don Juan* to crush pretended atheism. His audience in the pit might rejoice to see a daughter escape from the tyranny of her father, but churlish fathers because they had power over their children would continue to use it. Boileau tells us that Molière's satire did put down the nonsense talked by the précieuses; therefore his later comedy against the pretentiousness of the femmes savantes may have had some good effect. These affectations, however, were transient follies, they were social crazes of the time which gave pleasure and, ordinarily speaking, were not morally wrong. His satire against the doctors, a more important matter, was in the main justified, but there is no evidence to show that it appreciably diminished the number of quacks.

Molière's tendency to ridicule bad or foolish things and his condemnation of them went hand in hand; he gave the world his play while he himself was often moved to anger. It is remarkable that he should have combined the opposite qualities of earnestness and love of ridicule in such a strong degree. Ridicule with Molière was not intended merely to create laughter. It had in it a feeling of reverence, and he tried to make it serve a good purpose. If ridicule in serious matters is to command respect, it must be shown with reverence, and not in a scoffing spirit, and with this thought in our minds Pascal and Molière may be considered together. Those who say that Molière's ridicule was only clever jesting, or that it was misplaced, have, I think, not read it truly; they have not looked at his comedy closely enough, and seen the meaning of his satire beneath his laughter. The comedy in the *Tartuffe* and in *Don Juan* are two instances in point. La Bruyère wrote some twenty years after Molière, and what he says of the "directeurs" and of the "esprits forts" is a strong argument for thinking that the dramatist's pictures of the hypocrite and of the atheist were justified. Take two other instances. George Dandin's wife receives the addresses of a gallant very kindly; she lies impudently about them, and she insults her husband. Can it be urged seriously in palliation of her offence that her husband is an egregious ass? The satire against Harpagon is often very amusing, but it is grim. Surely Molière meant to show that the miser was so odious and tyrannical that even his children could not respect him, and that happiness in his household was impossible. If the comic writer knows how to teach, he may prove as able a moralist as the professor who hangs up his signboard. I have seen the words "Castigat ridendo mores"—he laughs at manners and chastises them—applied to Molière. I am told they are not classical. They express, however, very truly the moral purpose in his comedies. When he ridiculed those whom he would punish, honest laughter was in his thoughts, and he knew that people would not go to his theatre to see a dramatic performance of a homily, however well it was performed. Mere humbug, when it injures no one, is a less serious matter, and though Molière trounced Monsieur Jourdain for his extraordinarily silly vanity, he did it very kindly. Who does not join in Nicole's hearty laughter when she sees her master dressed up in his fine clothes? Molière's mockery of the marquises, and of their grand airs, is proverbial; and they liked it. Men of fashion used to go to his theatre to see his pictures of themselves, many a one boasting to his friends that he was the model of the personage exposed to view. They would not have done so if the pictures drawn had been ill-natured.

Teaching by laughter is not an easy thing to do. It comes sometimes half by chance, as in conversation, and then, perhaps, it is remembered. We all know of comedies written "with a purpose." The crux of their authors lies in teaching a lesson in a tone of comedy. It has been found difficult to draw by true and lively and interesting characterisation a picture of men's faults that shall .by the way they are shown create both hatred and mirth. Yet both may be felt in the *Tartuffe*, in *Don Juan*, in the *Avare*. It has been found difficult to mix together censure and raillery, condemnation and ridicule, so that the spectator or the reader may rejoice and laugh at both. Among comic dramatists I doubt if any one has succeeded in the attempt better than Molière.

Molière's sentiments were never ecstatic or Utopian. He did not give examples of transcendental virtues clothed in magniloquent language. He was not an idealist who loved to frame images of people whose conduct was abnormally high. Instead, his lessons are worthy of the simplicity of the nursery. Learn to think and speak honestly and avoid vain pretence, do as you would be done by, give honour where honour is due, seem to form the code of morality in his plays. In speaking of Montaigne, Sainte-Beuve lauds Molière as being more expansive, truer. He says finely: "Molière, c'est la morale des honnêtes gens." A few pages earlier the critic had explained what he meant by "la morale des honnêtes gens": "It is not virtue, but a mixture of good habits, good manners, kindly actions, depending usually on a disposition more or less generous, on a nature more or less well inclined."[1] . Molière shows this quality in some of his characters, though he generally mixes satire with it. The *Misanthrope*, one of his finest comedies, will afford a good instance. Philinte, who is cool-blooded, has "la morale des honnêtes gens" slightly; he has the outside of it, and his own words are ironical against him. Éliante has it more fully, and as hers is a warmer nature the irony against her is less strong. Alceste, whose temper is high, has this quality deeply implanted in his breast, and it remains there half-hidden; he would show it naturally, but from egotism and from passion he throws away the pleasant appearance of it, and his manners are a severe satire upon him. Célimène does not know what it means, except in a perverted sense. In other comedies Molière

[1] *Port-Royal*, 3rd ed. iii. 260; 271, 272.

drew three men in whom he wished to show its total absence : Tartuffe, Don Juan, and Harpagon.   It is easy to see their crimes, but the harm coming from these crimes should be noticed.

The hardness of life caused by injustice, by lying, and by self-interestedness, made Molière unhappy   There were moments when he became misanthropical, and that he knew to be wrong.

> "Je hais tous les hommes :
> Les uns parcequ'ils sont méchants et malfaisants,
> Et les autres pour être aux méchants complaisants,
> Et n'avoir pas pour eux ces haines vigoureuses
> Que doit donner le vice aux âmes vertueuses."

These lines, spoken by Alceste in the first scene of the *Misanthrope*, indicate a tendency of one side of Molière's mind, and they show how a sensitive and overflowing nature can be made angry by meanness and dishonesty.   I have often thought that Thackeray was like Molière in this.   Their hearts were high and generous, but frauds practised upon others for the sake of profit pained them and made them suffer.   Then they got angry, and were not afraid to show it, and their anger did not come from spite or injured vanity. Honesty of intention, when you can get at it, is the best test how far satire is well meant.   But honesty lies truly in one man's breast, in another's it may mean exposing wares for sale whether they are nasty or not.   Like Thackeray, Molière generally took an unhappy subject for his groundwork, and upon the idea that he chose he based his comedy, throwing into it his satire and his humour with earnestness and depth of purpose.   Like Thackeray, Molière saw that men who know the difference between the substance and the shadow often prefer the shadow because it is easier to follow, or because the act of following it gives a bright semblance in the eyes of others ; or, again, there are those who like bad ways best. There is some cynicism in both writers, but Thackeray showed his more unguardedly, more openly, and a good part of the world was angry with him because he spoke so plainly.   Both showed their censure and their subtle humour against faults and foibles, which every one should try to avoid ; but they did not use their satire quite in the same way.   Thackeray laughed at his readers and put them out of conceit with themselves, and that they did not like: some found their consciences awakened by pricks and uncomfortable qualms; others abused their monitor, gave the lie to their conscience, and told themselves boldly that they had done no wrong at all. Molière, on the other hand, laughed with his audience and made them laugh with him; everybody was thus laughing at himself, while he thought he was laughing at his neighbour. Consequently Molière's satire shows more fun, which we all enjoy, for his open laughter takes away from the sharpness of his sting. However strongly Thackeray and Molière may have exposed deceit and humbug, they did not forget what one man owes to another. They did not wear their hearts on their sleeves, but their innermost cry was for honester dealing and more sympathy among their fellow-creatures. If there be any who do not feel the compassionate qualities in Thackeray's and in Molière's nature, I think they have missed seeing a large part of their personality, and also much of what is highest and best in their work as they strove to use the faculties which had been given to them.

Sainte-Beuve speaks also of the great sadness of Molière's thoughts, and says that his nature was more unhappy even than that of Pascal.[1] Molière, however, was not an ascetic like Pascal, he did not punish himself for uncommitted faults; he was, metaphorically speaking, more round-headed, and though sceptical by nature was more free from pessimism. Molière had in him some pessimism; but it was kept under by his knowledge of the value of hard work both in himself and in others, by generous feelings, and by a belief in the slow improvement in the mental and moral condition of mankind, brought about by industry and by a sober and wise use of free thought. He was unselfish and loyal as a friend, hot-tempered perhaps and exacting in the performance of work, but always thinking more of the wants of those who were dependent upon him than of the trouble he gave himself, though his health was not strong and demanded that he should labour less and be free from the daily anxieties of his theatre. It was fortunate for him that his life was a very busy one. His love of honest satire and of pleasant raillery was a great blessing to him. Between his unhappy thoughts and his keen appreciation of

[1] *Port-Royal*, 3rd ed. iii. 275.

what was ludicrous, his strong common-sense kept his mind straight and free from ill-considered or warped ideas. And he turned his powers of clear comic characterisation to good account in describing so many of men's foibles and their more serious faults. He had the sense of proportion, and knew that if things were looked at beyond their proper sphere, wrong or one-sided ideas would follow. He had strong convictions and was persistent in them, but his mind was open and flexible enough to consider the opinions of others when they differed from his own. Like a wary advocate, he got up the case on the other side.

Yet Molière's sadness clung to him closely. It is not infectious, and he often tried to hide it; but it may be seen in his smiles, even in his laughter. A hasty reading of some of his plays may lead one to think that he loved to be joyous and merry and to brim over with fun, and he certainly had a keen appreciation of the delight that good-natured fun gives, liking to see other people enjoy it; but a careful study of his scenes will reveal a sorrowful mind often sick at heart as he thought of men's selfishness, their trickery, their greed, and their vanity. The effect of his comedies is neither gloomy nor depressing, and a man must be of a strange temperament if he is made unhappy by reading them. Nevertheless, in the *École des Maris*, the *École des Femmes*, the *Tartuffe*, *Don Juan*, the *Misanthrope*, the *Avare*, *George Dandin*—and especially in the two last-named plays—the subjects were chosen from unhappy causes, and the comedies reveal the workings of an uneasy mind made melancholy because of the wrongs men and women were doing daily to one another. There are everywhere Philintes who are callous to social evils, and there are Alcestes who roar aloud at them. Molière's strong sense of humour did much to hide his unhappiness, and he brought amusement so easily out of trifles that his fun seems to lie on the top of everything. As a comic dramatist it was his duty to endeavour to amuse, but his feelings were often moved to anger as he wrote, and his comedies were conceived with seriousness of purpose. He did not go out of his way to be melancholy, he did not like sadness. I imagine that he did not laugh much or easily, that he wished he could laugh more, and that he liked to see brightness and joyfulness in those round about him. I think that he looked for sympathy and for happiness, but he could not find them as often as he wished. It was this that made him sceptical and doubtful of the goodness of men's conduct until he saw it. He was not an idealist, for his nature was too practical, and he knew too much of the everyday knock-about and rough-and-tumble life in the world to allow him to contemplate Utopian bliss. Yet he would gladly have seen more fair dealing among men and greater concord. He looked for truth, for kindliness, for charitable feeling, and thought he found instead too much vanity and self-interest. If men's conduct one to the other were better than he believed it to be, Molière would have been less unhappy. That was the reason for his misanthropy, as far as it existed. His heart was high and willing to trust, but he wanted more charity from the world than it had got or was willing to show. His mind was not morbid, though when annoyed he could be morose. He showed his displeasure at many things which he condemned, but with a hearty and vigorous dislike that could hardly have come from a diseased mind, or from a man too much given to brooding about himself. He was very unlike Jean Jacques Rousseau, whose genius was spoiled by egotism, vanity, and selfishness; and, as well as I can see, these causes were at work in Rousseau when he wrote against the *Misanthrope* and against the *Avare*, and made his criticisms worse than worthless. Had Rousseau a knowledge of the meaning of comedy he would have written differently. Molière, with all his sadness, was obliged to live in the world and take his part in it; Rousseau lived more by himself and for himself, and with the faults above named his judgments on an author who tried to give pictures of the play of life are not likely to be of value. Molière saw unhappiness in men, and the causes which led to it, and he could not help thinking sadly; on the other hand, he loved good-humoured satire and raillery, and one may see that he laughed in his sleeve for worrying himself so closely about the troubles of other people.

In some of his plays Molière has one central character, and he grouped others around it, bringing in the by-play of his comedy; but he threw his satire or his irony chiefly on his most important personage, in order to show his salient features —as in *Sganarelle*, *Don Juan*, the *Médecin Malgré Lui*, the

Avare, Monsieur de Pourceaugnac, the *Bourgeois Gentilhomme,* and the *Malade Imaginaire.* Still, these are not one-character plays. In his other comedies the method was virtually the same, though the plan was enlarged and partly modified. Instead of a personage he sometimes took the subject of his comedy as his central idea, and worked up his characters and the incidents in his play to show objectively that he meant to satirise a general custom or general thoughts—as in the *Précieuses Ridicules* and the *Femmes Savantes,* the *École des Maris* and the *École des Femmes,* the *Mariage Forcé* and the *Amour Médecin,* the *Tartuffe,* the *Misanthrope.* But in these comedies the plan is not really different from that in the others. The interest is properly confined chiefly to one event, but the dramatist widened it by introducing more by-play, and by distributing his satire more generally. In point of fact, the groundwork of Molière's comedies, when examined, shows a broader foundation than may appear after a cursory reading. This is seen in the *Tartuffe,* in the *Misanthrope,* in the *Avare,* in the *Bourgeois Gentilhomme.* And in the *Femmes Savantes* the three learned ladies guide the course of the action; they are all ridiculed together, yet each of them is individually exposed to personal satire of a separate kind.

Molière always thought more of characterisation than of plot, as the words are usually understood. But plot and characterisation in comedy are closely mixed up together; for though the term characterisation is usually applied to individuals, it is shown in narrating the incidents, as well as in describing the personages. There are comedies of incident and comedies of manners. It is difficult to define either exactly, for there are involutions from one into the other. But in both it is essential that the humours in the play of life should be shown. And in the comedy of manners, with more or less of caricature, clear personal characterisation is a prominent feature. Molière thought a great deal of writing in a spirit of mirthful comedy, of making his incidents amusing, of the natural play of the scenes, and of making one scene follow easily from another; also of forming his characters broadly and with bold outlines, giving to each its own distinctive features, and keeping each personage true to his nature and to his part in the comedy. He thought mainly of his personages, and

contrived his incidents so that they should harmonise with the
characters he wished to portray. On the whole, his male
characters are the best remembered; but it is worth noticing
that in the *École des Femmes*, in the *Tartuffe*, in the *Misanthrope*,
and in *George Dandin*, though the chief male character is outwardly the most important personage, yet in all of these plays
there is a woman who really determines the events, and is the
pivot on whom the comedy hangs.

The comedy in a play lies, of course, in the characterisation,
and more in that of the personages than of the incidents.
Taking Molière's work all round, his power of personal
characterisation was intellectually his strongest point. In
portraying a character he recollected that though each feature
may be supposed to have its own place and play its own part,
there are frequent irregularities or inequalities in the composition, one trait often overlapping or contradicting another. He
looked at many things at once, considering the characterisation
as a whole, and especially in connection with the general comic
environment. He drew his personages clearly and firmly, and
he painted in strong colours. But in portraying men and
women he was careful to mark the lights and shades of their
features, to avoid hard and fast lines, yet by delicate and pointed
touches that define and illustrate, that give life and interest to
the characters, to show them to be active human beings with
wills and passions of their own. He used a plot to suit the
requirements of his own characterisation. He took, where he
could find it, the idea of a story that would lend itself to the
particular object of his satire, and to the characters by which he
meant to illustrate it; then, by bringing half a dozen or more
men and women together and making them converse and act
their parts with dramatic movement, and putting into his
scenes an air of fiction and natural humour to heighten the
effect, he wove a plot out of their joint concerns in a manner
that each of the personages should tell something of the tale,
and that each one should show the individuality of the others
as well as his own. This was to him the real plot in his
comedies. His nominal plot was often slender enough, and
while writing I do not think he cared very much as to the
final issue of events. Here he was now and then at fault, for
the dénouements are sometimes a weak point in his plays. But
he set all his mind to work to place upon the stage true

pictures of human beings with strong vitality; to show the distinctive features of each in a spirit of comedy, usually with some ridicule, elucidating at the same time either the action or the characterisation in the play ; and he tried to make his scenes animated and amusing. He looked upon comedy as an exhibition of the play of human life, exposing people's faults or their foibles with satire or with raillery, and showing in a mirthful manner how men and women act and react upon one another. With such ideas the characterisation of his personages would naturally be his chief object, and the plot in his play only of importance in so far as it would lend itself to the end he had in view. In a word, he wanted to show comedy, but he cared little about telling a story except as a means to that end. The outline of a good story was very well if he got it, but he thought infinitely more of the way in which his story was told. Are not the same features to be found in the best remembered plays by other comic dramatists ? Youthful or romantic taste that asks only to be excited or amused by the incidents in a story, may be pleasant enough, and in fiction of all kinds it cannot be disregarded; but there are more important things to be considered before giving to a comedy a large measure of praise. The main points, of course, are : does the comedy amuse, does it interest, does it make one feel happy ? It is of some consequence to feel that you like or hate this man or that woman, especially if you see the comedy acted; yet for any sort of criticism it is essential to understand the author's object, and what kind of characters he wished to create, to see how the personages are drawn, and to mark how the various characters and incidents are made to develop one another. That personal characterisation stands above plot, and takes a higher and a more lasting place, may be seen in the best plays that have been written by the world's greatest dramatists. It is impossible to separate things that are naturally linked together; yet, speaking generally, it is the human characterisation, and the way it is shown, much more than the subservient plot, that gives life to a comedy, and engages the attention of readers perhaps for many generations afterwards. Unless a comic dramatist creates a lively interest in his personages, what happens to them by way of good or ill fortune is not felt to be of much consequence.

It is by no means certain that the supposed personalities in

old plays were real. Those writers who have dwelt upon them
with the greatest pleasure have not always been the most
diligent in investigating the circumstances. There has been
more or less a foundation of fact, and this has been seized
upon with the idea of making a telling story, or of showing
the perspicacity of the critic. But in old comedies, say in
Molière's, even if the facts related were true, and that the
personalities were real, what we should think of is: how far
did the author show them with comic effect? The real interest
in the supposed pictures in the *Misanthrope* of the poet and
his wife is not how they quarrelled, nor even as a description
of what each of them was like, but how far do the imaginary
pictures show good comedy. I do not think that Molière
meant here to draw personal likenesses, nor that he troubled
himself much as to what people said about the resemblances.
Perhaps these have been spoken about more in our day than
they were in his, and that without such talk the comedy
would have been judged more justly. It has been generally
accepted that Molière gave a description of his wife in the
dialogue between Cléonte and Covielle in Act III. scene 9 of
the *Bourgeois Gentilhomme*, where the master and valet are
talking about Lucile, M. Jourdain's daughter. Here, again,
the dramatist was thinking of the play of his comedy, and he
cared little what people said about personal resemblances.
That is the way I look at the matter, though it implies a
certain cynicism. It might, however, be argued, on the other
hand, if facts and dates could be ascertained and made to
agree with the picture, that Molière wished to say that he
and his wife had become reconciled.

It is just as easy to say decisively that Molière intended
this or that personage to represent a certain man or woman,
as it would be difficult to maintain that in a given personage
he portrayed the features of a man or woman of whom he
knew nothing. He had first to think of the meaning of his
comedy, and adapt his characters to it; then he had to be
careful to show their features with suitable comic effect. And
though resemblances were found between his supposititious
personages and persons in daily life, I believe that he drew
the main characteristics of his men and women without intentional purpose of representing particular individuals, of

drawing their likenesses, and that he often had little conscious-
ness that he was doing so.   If his characterisation was good,
resemblances were inevitable.   The salient or distinguishing
features seen in his characters were, ordinarily speaking, of
his own invention.   In small matters he sometimes took
certain natural traits of people from actual life when they
would adapt themselves to the spirit and the play of his
comedy, and when he could show them in a comic manner
suitable to his personage.   But, as a rule, these were details,
valuable perhaps in their place, but not essential; for other
details of a similar kind might have been substituted for them
equally well.

Molière must have drawn his pictures from characteristics
of people planted and assimilated in his mind, for the power
of invention has not been wholly creative in the brain of any
man that has ever lived.   The best chance of an attempt at
the pure creation of anything would lie with the greatest
impostor.   Like a bee that gathers honey from many flowers,
Molière collected what were to him his facts from many sources.
Without special forethought, but instinctively, he stored in his
mind his intuitively acquired knowledge, and used it at need,
most likely half unconsciously, disentangling and joining the
contrasts and the likenesses in human nature, and welding
them all together, and fitting them to the scenes and to the
personages he wished to portray.   As other authors who have
been strong and exuberant in personal characterisation, Molière
had an inborn faculty of clear, swift, true, and sympathetic
observation and discernment; his memory, or perhaps rather
associations of ideas, helped him to recall half-forgotten
thoughts; and his imagination, or his fancy, aided by a
peculiarly graphic and natural comic style, fashioned images
of people and incidents out of what he had seen and heard,
may be the day before, or perhaps many years earlier.   An
author who has these faculties loves to be free in his work—
must, in fact, be free.   He cannot copy.   He knows that
modelling produces only wooden or unnatural figures.   Wherever there is a natural figure, there has been more or less of
creativeness behind it.

The middle or temperate characters in comedy, without
marked peculiarities for good or for ill, and offering small

ground for satire or irony, have always been difficult to portray so that they shall create an interest directly on their own account. They may be excellent models of characterisation of people of their own kind, but they do not usually show strong comic personalities. They may give good advice; and it is amusing to notice how happily and instinctively, as it were, Molière has contrived that their sage counsels can be of no avail. Clever people like to think that reason governs their daily actions; humours, however, which, after all, come more from the heart than the head, perhaps play a larger part in governing mankind when men are left to do as they please. This is certainly the case in a comedy, or the comedy had better not have been written. If men and women did not show so many instances of wrong-headedness, there would be fewer comedies, and it is not likely that many would give much pleasure. Moreover, a plain reproduction of an ordinary scene in daily life will rarely make a good scene in a comedy; it will want the excitement coming from natural exaggeration to give to the picture a show of comedy, and in its general characterisation it must have the freshness coming from originality to make it interesting. Goodness, folly, villainy, wisdom, are met with every day, and given merely as such in a comedy they will not attract; they want a setting to show them off. They must be heightened by imagination or fancy, and the picture should be enlivened by fun of some kind, even though there be a little exaggeration, if we are to take pleasure in it. One may be at first inclined to think that as Molière showed so much of men's feelings by means of ridicule, his mind was not prone to consider their more equable qualities; that as he depicted what was ludicrous in so many plays he could hardly be trusted to draw fairly men and women who had not some strongly marked eccentricity. This charge will not be made, I think, by those who know his comedies and what his laughter meant. A little thought will show that the dramatist who in his lighter plays contrived so cleverly to mix comedy and farce together, and with full purpose, knew also the use of fair caricature and its effects. I shall speak of Molière's caricature presently, but will say now that caricature without truth shows only absurdity, though possibly it may be funny; the writer who can give good caricature in comedy must at least have an idea of the value of truth in comedy. True formation of character implies, in the first place, strength of insight, of observation; and the more unusual or original is the character drawn, the more imagination or fancy—besides observation—is required to form that character on lines that are fairly true. When Molière put a middle or temperate character into the foreground of a comedy, he placed his personage beside another of an opposite nature, to show their different qualities and to bring the objects of his satire into fuller relief. On the whole he managed his middle characters well. Each has his own distinctive personality, one cannot be mistaken for another, they all show their different natures by the way they speak. The principal instances are Cléante and Elmire in the *Tartuffe*, Philinte and Éliante in the *Misanthrope*, Clitandre and Henriette in the *Femmes Savantes*. In any comedy of manners one or more of such personages should be put more or less prominently forward to endeavour to restrain a bad or foolish action, though Molière did not choose to make them successful in their efforts. The chief difficulty is to invest them with an interest belonging to themselves, and this can only be done by natural and delicate characterisation strongly shown.

Caricature is generally almost inseparable from the work of a humorist; for his aim is to paint, and, if he can, to show truth, by means of honest satire with mirth or laughter. And in the pride of laughter there is usually some exaggeration. This is especially the case with the comic dramatist. He cannot banish caricature from the stage before an audience who have come together to see and hear that they may be delighted and amused. He must use caricature and ridicule more or less to give full meaning to his ideas and colour to his picture. As he may not preach he tries to produce his effect by laughter. In most cases Molière's caricatures are fully justified as giving pictures of comedy. Take as examples: the admiration of the three ladies when Trissotin reads his verses to them, or Harpagon's meanness in his instructions about his supper-party, or M. Jourdain's crazy desire to be like a man of quality, or the chastisement of the ignorant routine of empiric doctors. If there had been no caricature at all in these instances the comic meaning would have been hidden and the

N

fun of a feeble kind. Good caricature of a person or thing is
like the person or thing intended to be described; it has its
truth, it does not allow disfiguration. Oddities or prominent
features may be accentuated, but unless a fair resemblance is
preserved caricature descends to farce. Ridicule in comedy
is not the same as absurdity. It is generally useless to speak
absolutely on matters connected with human nature, but it
would seem that caricature in comedy in its proper place and
not pushed beyond its fair limits may be quite natural. Both
the *Précieuses Ridicules* and the *Femmes Savantes* are comic
satires on the affectations of women. The affectations described were not quite the same in the two comedies, and the
people depicted did not hold the same position in society.
Both comedies contain caricature that is fitting in its own
place; but if the caricature in either of these plays were
transferred to the other, for which it was not intended and
where the circumstances are different, it would be untrue and
unnatural. The question of what is natural in comedy is very
complicated. Time and place, however, are two determining
factors. Conditions also vary so much that each case should
be judged separately, for what is natural in one instance may
not or will not be so in another.

Molière seized upon men's humours, and in his smaller
plays exaggerated them purposely more strongly than in his
serious comedies; but, speaking generally, by mixing his
lights and shades together, and, as I conceive, by not out-
stepping nature, he painted truly and showed how men's
humours tend very largely to make them what they are. He
did not try to draw men as they ought to be; his object was
to show them as they are and very often as they ought not to
be. He knew that different and often contradictory humours
exist in the same person, and he has shown men's natures by
blending their humours together. It would be a great mistake
to look upon Molière as a caricaturist, or to think that because
he had and enjoyed the power of making foolish persons
appear very ridiculous, his chief talent lay in showing people
whose heads were screwed on in a wrong way. He did wish
to bring forward what was unwise or laughable in their
manners or in their actions, and to say that by their too
strong belief in their own opinions their thoughts were often

one-sided or foolish. At the end of the first scene in the *École des Femmes* there is a charming bit of irony against Arnolphe, who is silly, when he says of his friend Chrysalde:—

> "Chose étrange de voir comme avec passion
> Un chacun est chaussé de son opinion."

They separate, each one thinking that the other is so impracticable that no one can reason with him. If there be caricature in this scene, it proves how closely comedy and caricature are allied together. Molière had the rare power of heightening or caricaturing the ordinary characteristics of men and women without altering their natures, and of showing his personages in the spirit of comedy in a natural way. Imaginativeness and realism are thus brought close together, and are made to work into one another.

In revealing men's designs Molière exposed their fads, it may be thought, too persistently, and too strongly, as no doubt he well knew, for absolute realism, but he had the view of stage representation always before his eyes. He saw with perfect clearness what men's fads are, and he knew how to make their crotchets appear ludicrous without altering the main features in the characters of his personages. He kept nature before him as his groundwork, using ridicule and laying stress upon it in order to show the lessons he wished to teach. In this respect Molière and Dickens were not unlike. The technical differences between the work of the dramatist and of the novelist do not prevent their ideas being the same ; each showed his own thoughts in his own way, at length or in a few pages. Both of these writers saw the humorous aspects in certain people and in the ludicrous situations which might arise from their singularities, and both writers made the most of their comic personages, and created laughter in order to show the purpose they had in view. Of the two the tone of Dickens's laughter is more cheerful, but its ring is often more forced and is, on the whole, less true. Good lessons may be taught by satire when it is rightly employed, and neither Molière nor Dickens abused their strong powers. As humorists they were both within their province in using caricature and ridicule as a means of unfolding the natures of the men and women they wished to portray, and by comedy true to itself they have created what our imagination leads us to believe are true pictures. So also in *Don Quixote*. There is much ridicule and purposely intended caricature in that novel; but no one in his senses will contend that the gallant-hearted knight and his foolish squire do not show pictures of true and excellent comedy.

Farce is the nonsense of comedy. It is a medley of absurd incidents and ideas stuffed into a play without natural sequence of thought or of characterisation, so as to make the personages pretend to be funny. If the acting is good the result may be a happy one. Amusing nonsense, almost apart from comedy, is seen in some of Molière's lighter plays, as in the *Médecin Malgré Lui, Monsieur de Pourceaugnac*, the *Fourberies de Scapin*. Yet when his light plays are examined, one cannot help remarking how cunningly he mixed comedy and farce together—as he also mixed his earnestness and his mockery—knowing well what he was doing, and that upon the whole comedy will be found to predominate, and farce will occupy a much smaller place, as in the *Précieuses Ridicules, Sganarelle ou le Cocu Imaginaire*, the *Mariage Forcé*, the *Amour Médecin, George Dandin*, the *Bourgeois Gentilhomme*, and the *Malade Imaginaire*. The working out of these plays belongs much more to comedy than to farce, because the characterisation of the incidents and of the personages is maintained with a natural sequence of ideas and is truthful of its kind. The caricature in these last-named plays does not destroy the comedy, because it characterises the personages and the incidents; in its way it is naturally shown. The incidents are well adapted to exhibit the personages introduced, and the satire or the ridicule seen in the characters is shown in a truthful manner, even though it be very ludicrous. Before Molière had completed the first half of his career in Paris Boileau wrote to him:—

> " Et ta plus burlesque parole
> Est souvent un docte sermon."

One of the peculiarities of Molière is that he seems to have done what is difficult very easily. He taught by laughter and by ridicule; and many of his good things in his lighter comedies are so true and so simple that they are often passed over almost carelessly. The lightness of manner and the facile happiness of touch with which he showed mirthful comedy in his personal characterisation in nearly all his plays are in truth remarkable. His power as a comic dramatist meant more than cleverness : it indicated high intellectual faculties, though there was generally a wish to hide them. He purposely avoided abstruse ideas, and before presenting his thoughts to his audience he ground them down in the mill of his brain, rejecting what he knew they did not want, and he tried to say what would interest them if he could make it serve his purpose. His originality is seen in his strong personal characterisation and his racy style, in the way that he drew true pictures of the comedy of life, and showed them in a fresh and lively manner, so that persons of fair intelligence should understand and take pleasure in his scenes; but he did not want to make a display of his abilities, and he had no sort of wish that men should speak of him as a wonderful fellow. A good comedy of manners demands, no doubt, a keen, bright, and clear intelligence, but in its representation the last thing a spectator wants to see is an exhibition of intellect; and this has been recognised instinctively by the ablest and best writers for the comic stage. Molière did not write poetical comedy. The comic characterisation, with more or less of satire and of ridicule, of men and women as they are seen in daily life was his study, and in telling how they thought and spoke to one another he showed the master's hand. He was certainly not superficial; his nature was too deep to allow him to do superficial work. What seems to some readers to take away from his greatness is that the simple truths in his plays, and chiefly in those in prose, the easy naturalness of his comedy generally, and his facile pen, make his thoughts appear sometimes to be elementary, because he showed them so readily or so lightly and so often in a vein of ridicule. I repeat, he did what is difficult apparently very easily.

It would seem that Molière accepted the dramatic laws of the unities because other playwrights of his time thought themselves bound by them, and that he worked freely under the narrow harness. He cut his coat according to his cloth and adapted himself to circumstances. The rules were that the duration of the action in a play should be limited to twenty-four hours—to this I think he always confined himself ; the scene was to be unchanged—that also he observed except in a few instances ; the main interest in a play should be centred in one idea or on one event—and this he followed, as it was a natural law common to every work of art, but he introduced by-play, and so widened the scope of action a good deal more than contemporary dramatists.   In his *Critique de l'École des Femmes* Molière alludes to the farrago of nonsense that was talked about the rules, and says : " If those plays which are regular are not liked, and those plays which are liked are not regular, it must follow necessarily that the rules have been badly made.   We may leave all this chicanery alone by which they [the critics] want to govern public taste.   The only thing to be noticed in a play is the effect it produces.   Let us enjoy honestly the things that delight us ; we need not look for arguments to destroy our pleasure."   The English and Spanish dramatists were not governed by laws of time or place. Their chief law was to please their audience ; to do this they exercised their imaginations as they liked, for they meant to be their own masters.   But French dramatists were ruled by officialism.   They allowed themselves to be crippled by the false reasoning of men who had set themselves up as their masters, and disobedient pupils were punished as naughty schoolboys for going out of bounds.   To a large extent Molière made the rules his own, but they must have hindered his range of thought.   His imagination was not lofty, nor was it strongly poetical.   When he spoke of such tragedies as he knew he did so in a tone of satire.   But his mind was clear and practical, he knew what he wanted and he rarely attempted what he could not achieve.   He was fettered by rules, but he moved easily in the prescribed circle.   His personages are full of comic dramatic vigour, and he has shown a large number of men and women of various characters who play their parts in comedy fairly and truly according to their natures.

English readers of Molière will find that, with a few exceptions, his love-scenes do not give them the pleasure they feel they have a right to expect from a popular dramatist.   In most of his comedies we are told that a certain man loves a certain woman, but a warm feeling of love on both sides is not

often seen. Before Molière's day there had been almost no
poetical comedy in France.   Though plays were written in
verse none showed much feeling of poetry.   The comedy in
the plays was artificial, prosaic, matter of fact, and inanimate.
The dramatic laws of the unities stifled what imagination the
playwrights possessed, and they added to the natural difficulties
of creating strong love-scenes.   An imaginative and romantic
writer might have done something to show a feeling of warm
love between two young people without offending too strongly
against the rules of the stage which limited the action of a
play to twenty-four hours and confined it to one place.   But
real love-scenes are very rarely found in old French comedies.
As a matter of fact they did not often take place in daily life.
Young men and girls were not allowed to see much of each
other in a sense of intimacy, and in most instances they were
made to marry as they were told by their parents.   Nevertheless, had the dramatists been able to portray real love-scenes
they would have done so ; had they been able to show natural
comedy they would have preferred it to dull plays in which
stateliness of manner and ceremonious observances held too
large a place.   No doubt that in plays, as in other things, there
are formalities to be observed ; but on the early French stage,
though love-making of some sort had to be introduced, the
dramatists did not get beyond a formal show of it, they
hardly tried to make the fiction appear as a reality.   It would
seem that they played with their love-making, which was an
easier matter, thinking much of decorum and deportment, and
that the audiences were satisfied if the play were well done
according to rule.

It is difficult to say why Molière, so humane and sympathetic in what he wrote, and who expressed the thoughts of
others so happily, should not have wished to describe oftener
one of the most natural sentiments in the human breast.
Various reasons may be alleged, but it is not easy to make
them appear to harmonise and work together.   In addition to
those already given, it may be that his mind was set in an
unhappy cast, and that whatever he felt as a young man, as he
grew older he became indifferent to love-tales, thinking that
he had no time for them ; that with a keen sense for ridicule
he took refuge from his melancholy in indulging in good-

humoured or well-intentioned satire; and he certainly appears to have thought more of the meaning of his satire than of making lovers say soft words to one another. Much of his satire where girls were concerned was directed against men in authority over them, who made them marry so that they, the guardians, might reap an advantage. Molière's mind was naturally sceptical. He doubted because he looked for something he could not find. He wished to trust, he wished to love, but often found himself disappointed in his hopes. Perhaps also he was difficult to please. Judging him by other authors, one is justified in saying that if he had possessed the power and the inclination to create strong love-scenes he would have done so oftener. He did show a feeling of poetry in some of his plays, but as a writer he was not poetical. And if the manner in which Molière portrayed women in his more important comedies may be taken as evidence, it would seem that he did not think of them very highly. On the whole he does not present them in a too favourable light. He has shown very few women of full, rich, and generous natures; he has shown others with indifferent qualities, not meaning them to be attractive or fascinating; while others he meant to be ludicrous or disagreeable. In the *École des Femmes* there is a good girl drawn brightly and in a charming manner, and in the *Tartuffe* there are three women who give pleasure; but in the *Misanthrope* and in the *Femmes Savantes* — perhaps the two most important instances—the good women, so to speak, attract our attention less than those who think chiefly of themselves or those who are foolish or malicious.

Molière was not romantic, nor was he imaginative in creating love-scenes. He felt the sense of love truly, but he did not idealise it in a manner that made him wish to write about it. His nature was too practical to allow him to draw pictures of dreamy scenes of love with their passions of joy or of despair. When he laughed at his Oronte for saying,

> "Belle Philis, on désespère,
> Alors qu'on espère toujours,"

his mind was following its natural bent; but he would not of his own accord have set himself down to write a scene showing warm love, and without other purpose, hoping that when it was finished he might find it satisfactory. He was warm hearted and knew what love is, but he was also clear sighted, and could look into his own lines and see if they showed the picture he meant them to represent.

Still, it would be untrue to say that Molière was unable to portray the passion of love so that others could see it and feel it for themselves. He has done so occasionally, though he always had some other end in view. He played with his love-scenes as other playwrights had done, but with different intentions. He subordinated his love-making to what he thought were the higher interests in his comedy, and he used it mainly as an instrument for his satire. He certainly thought more of interesting his audiences by his satire than of pleasing them by mere love-pictures. He wrote the *École des Femmes* to laugh at the folly and to condemn the selfishness of men like Arnolphe, who wish to marry girls who care nothing for them. As this was the chief purpose of the dramatist, we should follow the comedy in the play, and see why and how the satire is brought to bear against Arnolphe, and how in his real love for Agnès he struggles against his misfortunes. In the *Tartuffe* Orgon, as paterfamilias, can do what he pleases with his children; he does not wish to be unkind to his daughter, but he regards her as a means of attaching Tartuffe more closely to himself. Valère and Mariane do love each other, though they are not much brought together; what is chiefly interesting in their loves is the amusing manner in which Dorine reconciles them after they have quarrelled. In the *Avare* there is another Mariane; Harpagon tries to make love to her, and is rendered more odious on that account. The love-scenes of his children are in themselves not in the least engaging. The dramatist's meaning was a grim one. He wished that the interest in the play should be centred against the cruel father who had no sense of his fatherly duties, and he made use of the loves of his children as a means to that end. Molière's finest picture of love is shown in the *Misanthrope*. Alceste is very unhappy, largely through his own fault. He loves Célimène intensely; she, who has no love in her, plays with him, and he speaks to her according to his rugged and uncompromising nature. His love is bottomless and fearful in its reality ; but even there it was rather the man's wild conduct in his passion than the passion of love itself that the dramatist wished to portray.

In Molière's lighter comedies the girls are not in themselves interesting. They are hardly more than small pieces of the machinery necessary for the action or the satire in the play. They were meant to play their parts as puppets, as they did on the Italian stages and in the older French small comedies, and not much more was expected from them. They were made to appear to be in love with some man, though the interest that the reader feels for them is not in their love-story, but that they may escape from the tyranny of their fathers and that their fathers should be punished for their selfishness. A quotation from the *Amour Médecin* (Act I. sc. 4) will serve as a general instance. Lucinde is telling Lisette, her waiting-woman and confidante, how she loves *Clitandre*, though she has never spoken to him :—

" Perhaps it is not delicate for a girl to explain herself so freely ; but I must confess that if I were allowed to hope for anything, he would be the object of my wish. We have never had any conversation together, and in words he has never told me of his love ; but in every place that he has seen me his looks and his actions have spoken so tenderly, and the demand that he made for my hand seemed to me to be so like that of a well-bred man, that my heart could not remain insensible to his passion. And now you see to what a pitch the harshness of my father has brought all this affection."

Many of Molière's lighter plays were commanded for performance at court, and were often hurriedly written. As make-belief of love was necessary in a comedy, he gave it as such, and used it as an instrument for his satire. To his mind that was its most important feature. In the *Bourgeois Gentilhomme* Cléonte's love for Lucile is little more than a device for hoaxing M. Jourdain, it is given as part of a big joke ; and in the end M. Jourdain is completely bamboozled and is made supremely happy.

In my remarks on Molière's style I wish to speak of his manner of writing in giving clear pictures of comedy and in showing the thoughts of his personages, and to say how easily, as it seems, he chose his words to portray his scenes and his characters. His style is essentially that of a comic dramatist who wrote for the stage, and as such it should be considered. He wrote for listeners, but for readers he cared less. In prose and in verse he framed his language so that his men and women showed themselves by their manner of speech.   In almost every play that he wrote each one of his characters has his or her distinctive utterance peculiar to the speaker; they all speak so that one cannot be mistaken for another, the words of one would be out of place if put into the mouth of another.   He makes his personages talk in an easy and sometimes familiar way, changing more or less with the subject or the occasion, showing their varying moods, and agreeing with their condition in life.

In the language of a true comic dramatist peculiarities of construction will naturally be found ; and now and then Molière has phrases that are not easy for a foreigner to construe readily, though his general meaning is not obscure. He thought more of the effect his verses would have upon the stage than of literary embellishment ; his lines were meant to be spoken and heard, and when read the main object with which they were written should be remembered. He did not forget his possible readers, but he was intent upon giving his listeners a true picture. Besides being an actor and playing important parts, he had exercised during very nearly the whole of his career the chief management of a theatre ; and this double employment must have taught him the values of the sounds of words spoken before an audience.   It should be remembered that in plays in verse, owing to their greater frequency, theatre-goers in those days paid more attention to the rhythm of the lines than is the case now. We can see from Molière's comedies that his eye for verbal refinement was keen, but had he much indulged in a taste for literary varnish it might easily have taken away the effects he desired most to produce.   Those who know the meaning of his comedies will not be the first to find fault with his forms of expression.   He once said to some friends that he had not time enough to give to elaborateness of style.   I suspect this was only a natural subterfuge at the moment ; for had he been less fully occupied, or had he written fewer comedies, it may be doubted if his lines, with more labour spent upon them, would have been more perfect in saying happily what he wished them to say, whether he would have spoken with better effect or truer intention.   When his Marquis de

Mascarille was praising his own absurd impromptu he said : " Tout ce que je fais a l'air cavalier, cela ne sent point le pédant." This is good burlesque, and it is also, in its place, good comedy. And dropping the burlesque, the same ease of manner is seen in Molière's lines when he wrote his comedies in verse. They have a free air, they do not taste of the oil, they do not sound academical. Look at the *Étourdi*, his first play in verse : few would care now to read it a second time but for the charm of lively and graphic style. The same may be said of the *Fâcheux*, a comedy of quite a different kind. In the *Tartuffe*, in the *Misanthrope*, in the *Femmes Savantes*, the language adapts itself naturally to the spirit of the comedy. The first of these plays was written against religious lying and against those who were deceived by palpable imposture ; the second was against various forms of amour-propre, social lying and backbiting ; the third against softer kinds of social humbug ; and in each comedy the tone of the satire or of the irony corresponds with the humours of the characters described. Also in the three comedies each of the personages has his or her own distinctive voice, and this sometimes varies from one scene to another. As you read, the words fall upon your ears with different sounds from each of the speakers, distinguish their natures and show how their pulses were beating at the moment. All this marks the spirit of characterisation, and much of its value depends upon the distinctions being easily observed.

In their avertissement to the *Lexique de la langue de Molière*, MM. Arthur and Paul Desfeuilles, the authors of the *Lexique*, say admirably :—

"Molière kept something of the oratorical tone of his age. His sentences are so constructed that they carry to the furthermost part of the theatre ; they are very rhythmical, they are sonorous enough to be heard above the laughter of the pit, they are so full that if a word or two be missed the right meaning will still be gathered from them." [1]

The large number of Molière's plays, about two in each year from 1659 to 1673, in addition to his other work, is a proof

---

[1] *Œuvres de Molière*, vol. xii. p. b. I did not see this volume until some time after my own remarks had been written. The quotation helps to show that Molière's instinct told him that in addressing an audience he should write more for the ear than for the eye. But the quotation has not led me to alter anything of what I had written previously.

that he wrote quickly. And without facility in composition I doubt very much if he could have drawn his characters with so much vitality and ease of manner, if he could have shown so freely how their thoughts arose and have made them talk to each other in verse so naturally, and if he could have given to his scenes the spontaneous effects that comedy should produce. Supposing, as one must for the time, that men and women speak their thoughts in measured rhyming verse, Molière's lines come as near to the style of speech as any language should do when addressed to a public audience. They have an air of freshness which it would have been almost impossible to give if much time and labour had been spent in fashioning them. Molière, like other men, went through some form of apprenticeship as a writer, though not much is known of it. It is a mark of men of genius that they do their work better and more quickly than other people. Doubtless Molière had his difficulties, for in writing there are many conditions to be observed, and they have come blindly to no man. But Molière's difficulties were rather with thought and manner than with the technicalities of composition. He had to show comedy in a mirthful way and to portray his characters truly and with dramatic effects. As we read his plays it would seem that when he had formed an idea of a scene his pen, obedient to his will, put it at once on to paper and acted it there, his words coming to him readily and taking the form and colour of his thoughts. Perhaps his work was not done quite so easily as that; but it has that effect, and the efforts made are hidden very cunningly. We may at least be sure that he was more interested in giving a vivid picture of comedy than in polishing his verses. It was his nature to work quickly; had he not followed his instincts he would have done his work differently, and I believe less well. Let those who demand constant perfection of form in dramatic poetry compare Molière's lines with those of any other French dramatist, and see whose words or whose thoughts remain most easily in their memory.

French writers have sometimes complained of inelegancies and inaccuracies in Molière's language. It would not become me, a foreigner, to speak of them. Indeed, for the most part I have not noticed them. I will say, however, that I do not

think that they sprang from heedlessness, that rather they
were intentional; and that on the other hand his words show
abundant instances of the best forms of literary scholarship.
There are numberless examples in his plays of sentences which
could only have been penned by one who knew instinctively
the value of the shades and finesses of language. It was partly
by these subtle signs that Molière gave strength and truth to
his character-painting. His verses often show a delicate
texture not unlike the niceness of good lace-work. And in
many of these passages his faculty as a comic dramatist is
marked with manifest clearness. Seeing and feeling all this,
which only wants ordinary understanding, one learns that
academical precision may sometimes be out of place.

Both La Bruyère and Fénelon, almost Molière's contemporaries, criticised his language. La Bruyère said in a few
words: "Il n'a manqué à Molière que d'éviter le jargon et
d'écrire purement."[1] Fénelon said: "In thinking well he
often writes badly; he uses the most forced and the least
natural phrases. Terence says in four words and with the
most elegant simplicity what Molière says in a crowd of
metaphors which are not far from gibberish. I like his prose
much better than his verse. For instance, the *Avare* is less
badly written than his plays in verse. It is true that French
versification hampered him; it is also true that he succeeded
better in the *Amphitryon*, where he chose to write in irregular
verses. But generally, it appears to me that even in his prose
he does not talk simply enough to express every passion."[2]
These censures on Molière's language are, I believe, read now
in France with some surprise by those who consider the meaning of comedy. La Bruyère and Fénelon were large-minded
men; they were both masters of style, but of different kinds,
because they wrote with different ends in view. And I think
that if Molière had read their remarks he might (if he had cared
to do so) have gone a long way towards convincing them both
that they were wrong. The language of comedy has its own
purposes, its own uses. Its style should reflect its natural
qualities; it should have a vernacular, a raciness, of its own,

[1] *Les Caractères*, chapter "Des ouvrages de l'esprit," about the middle,
in a paragraph beginning "Il n'a manqué à Térence que d'être moins
froid."

[2] *Lettre sur les Occupations de l'Académie Française*, sect. 7.

and be bright with the thoughts, expressed in a comic manner, that the author wished to show in his personages. One of its distinctive marks is an openness of feeling and of understanding common to all. Even as one reads, these attributes are more essential to good comedy than elegance of diction, and on the stage a comedy without these attributes will hardly prove to be a good acting play.

Grammar is only a means to an end. No one can do without its lessons, yet there are times when its rules may be relaxed. Molière knew very well that he allowed himself some freedom of language, and that he here and there chose a familiar, and perhaps an ungrammatical, form of expression which other writers would have rejected. He was a comic dramatist who wrote for the stage, and he preferred a graphic phrase which really gave the thoughts of his personage at the spur of the moment to speech that was strictly regular shown in an exact and methodical manner. We may see this from his instruction, given in a tone of satire, to du Croisy, who was to play the part of the poet in the *Impromptu de Versailles*.[1] And in a discussion with some friends as to the first or second reading of a satirical verse—which was not his—Molière thought the first reading was the best. He said: "The first is the most natural, and you must sacrifice all regularity to get the right expression. Art ought to teach us how to overcome the rules of art."[2] These last words seem to be sententious as coming from Molière, but he certainly acted upon their meaning very largely—as only those can do safely who are masters of their art. In Shakespeare the same general ideas about style may be seen, though his plays show a higher elevation of thought than Molière's. The man who found fault with "This is the most unkindest cut of all" would be set down as a dolt. The poetical dramatist is in fact allowed a rather larger licence of language than the poet whose lines are not intended for stage representation. Shakespeare and Molière knew this, and they took the licence without thinking about it. Molière's style, like Shakespeare's, is so sympathetic, it has so many attributes of a large humanity, that one feels

[1] Scene 1, near the end.
[2] Louis Racine's *Mémoires* of his father, printed by M. Mesnard in the *Œuvres de Jean Racine*, 2nd ed. i. 234, 235.

that he was not a precisian in anything. His nature was not fastidious, he had not an over nice love for elegance of phrase; he might then have easily missed more important matters, and the strength of his character-painting would have suffered, and with it the various shades of colouring. Yet his insight was true, and he thought clearly, whether in ridicule or in seriousness, for his pictures show exactly the scenes he wished them to represent. He was always master of his language, and he made it his servant to do his bidding. This is one of the tests of a writer; without it he can hardly hope for strength, or accuracy, or persuasiveness. For firm portraiture the choice of words and the manner of using them are very important. Any dramatic character loosely described carries no weight; the picture is soon forgotten after the lines are read, or immediately after they are spoken on the stage unless the acting has been unusually good.

There are many English readers of French plays who do not like their perpetual rhyming lines. A more or less monotonous and jingling sound is produced, unless the structure of the verses is hidden under the greater importance of the meaning of the words. Even then, for the free expression of spoken thought, blank verse is more apt than verse in rhyme. But there is, I think, no instance of a French play in blank verse. In the 16th century a few plays were written in lines of ten syllables, and comedies in lines of eight syllables were fairly common in the first half of the 17th century. This measure had not quite died out in Molière's day, though he never used it. All of his plays in verse were in the long Alexandrine line of twelve syllables except *Amphitryon* and *Psyché*, in which last play Molière and Corneille were joint collaborators. These two plays were written in " vers libres " or " vers irréguliers," consisting sometimes of lines of eight syllables and sometimes of twelve. There the rhymes are less frequent than in the other metres, they do not follow each other successively ; and this measure, if difficult, seems perhaps to give to the poet who can use it a freer hand in the disposition of his words. Its greatest master was La Fontaine. He was more truly a poet than Molière, and verses in nearly all measures may be seen in his Fables, in his Tales, and in his other poems. La Fontaine also wrote plays, and there the most frequent measure is the line of twelve syllables. As a comic dramatist Molière was bound to write according to custom, but he held his pen so lightly that he made the rhymes and the rules of versification seem to fall into their places unnoticed. Nobody wants to see the trouble a poet has taken, and in a curious kind of way Molière reminds one of his own jesting words: "Les gens de qualité savent tout sans avoir jamais rien appris."

I have alluded mainly to Molière's plays in verse, for language can show a higher form of expression in verse than in prose, and poetry conveying the sense of passion—which poetry should always inspire—has charms for many readers which prose does not offer. Molière fashioned in a poetical form the plots and the characters in his plays, creating pictures of the comedy of life which will long be studied with pleasure, and he put them into excellent dramatic verse, but he had not the highest feelings of poetry. With strong and natural powers of characterisation, helped largely by the excellence and the charm of style, it may be thought that he exhibited his most native sentiments, his innermost ideas, more delicately and more seductively in verse than in prose. He must have had the desire to express himself in the form of language that poets used. When still a boy he translated much of Lucretius' poem partly into verse, showing that verse-making came easily to him even then; and the facile turn of the lines in his comedies, written later, may lead one to think that his inborn love of ridicule and of satire sprang from him more happily when he wrote in verse, and that in verse he gave the most delicate and most amusing pictures of his thoughts. Excellence in verse, when found, is often more attractive than in prose, perhaps because of its greater technical difficulties. But Molière made light of these entanglements; he walked over them as a spider does over his web, and his lines are so easy that they seem to have cost him no trouble. He knew at any rate how to hide the taste of the oil. I have often found myself dwelling with pleasure on Molière's aptitude for putting words together so as to produce a comic effect. Some Frenchman has said, " On ne fait pas de drames avec des mots." That may be the case with plays where the interest is confined chiefly to producing "powerful situations"; but true comedy is more dainty and wants a nicer handling. Good satire and good irony demand a skilful use of words, and it was partly by this means that Molière showed both strength and delicacy in his personal characterisation. His exquisite comic raillery is perhaps seen more amusingly in the *Femmes Savantes* than any other play that he has written. Yet if one compares half a dozen of his best comedies in verse with as many of those in prose, one hesitates before saying whether in prose or in verse he proved himself to be the greatest master of satire, of irony, of banter, and of pleasantry. I am not speaking now of Molière generally as a dramatist, but of his style and of the skilful use he made of language. Everybody likes to have an opinion of his own about an author he has read, and it seems to me that Molière's satire or his raillery is on the whole more delicately shown, or is given in a more refined way, in verse than in prose, and that in prose it is more open or more popular and will provoke the most laughter. Perhaps, too, in his prose plays Molière shows most fully his rare capacity for mixing together comedy and farce, realism and caricature, earnestness and mockery; and it is also in prose that one sees the strongest instances of his vis comica, or power of making an audience merry, by his direct and simple speech. On the other hand, there are two of his prose comedies that show his sadness the most strongly, the *Avare* and *George Dandin*. But in whatever he wrote, his humane and sympathetic manner was among his characteristics. If his style is really humane, it is tolerably certain that his thoughts were humane also. Without his strong humanity his cleverness and sense of humour would have taken a different turn, and his comedies would not have been so pleasant to read.

Among comic dramatists Molière ranks next, I think, to Shakespeare. It sounds strange to speak of Shakespeare as a comic dramatist, but had he written no other plays than his comedies the qualification would literally be just; and it is only with reference to comedy that I wish to bring him and Molière together for a moment, though hardly by way of parallel or comparison. Shakespeare put some comedy into almost all his plays, purposely mingling it with historical or

tragic incidents; but if one can consider his plays that are
called comedies apart from his other work, they are so different
from Molière's that any fair comparison or judging of one
beside the other is nearly impracticable. Not only is Shakespeare's level higher in general and in many particulars, but
complicated side issues constantly arise which show that their
intentions and their styles were much at variance. Lines of
thought that would be right when applied to one author
would soon lead us on to a wrong track if applied to the
other. This is remarkable in two dramatists who in their
pictures of comedy stand so high above others that they form
a class by themselves. They more fully than any others have
shown by their comic characterisation how largely our actions
result from our humours, how contradictory our humours often
are; and that, so far as can be distinguished, our hearts have
generally a greater share than our heads in forming our
characters and persuading us or compelling us to be what
we are. Shakespeare wrote more imaginatively, with higher
idealism, with more poetical feeling; Molière more playfully,
with greater satire or irony and a stronger vis comica—each
one drawing and painting his pictures truly, but with different
aims or ambitions. For each writer strove to please a people
who would not, when the plays were written, have enjoyed
the comedies which delighted the other. Nevertheless, perhaps in spite of their dissimilarities, certain points of likeness
that were not merely casual may be found between them;
and for this reason, in an English biography of Molière, I
may be allowed a word on the matter, even with the certainty before me of being often at fault. I have, however,
just mentioned some of Molière's characteristics, and I
have no wish to speak of Shakespeare's comedies in any
detail.

The mental temperament of the English dramatists in the
latter part of the reign of Elizabeth and under James I., and
that of the French dramatists a generation later, under
Louis XIII., during Mazarin's government, and in the early
part of the reign of Louis XIV., was very different. The objects
aimed at by the writers for the stage in each country show
that the theatre-loving people of each nation had quite different tastes. In England the dramatists were large-minded,

fresh and buoyant with their own thoughts; they were impatient of all control except that which they exercised upon themselves; they struggled with life hardly enough, but in what they wrote they showed that they had strong ideas of individual liberty; they were vigorous, hearty, and glorious in their own high spirits, and they poured forth their rich vein of poetical feeling in the free measure of blank verse. In France, on the other hand, there was less originality of thought; the spirit of imitation had been predominant in most cases since the renaissance of the drama about the middle of the 16th century—Corneille and Molière, however, were exceptions to the general practice of imitation; and the stiff but senseless laws of the unities, devised by the pedants with the intention of preventing extravagant ideas, crippled the imaginative powers of the writers, who as a class were not poetical; and long before Molière began to write, poets composed their verses in rhyming lines of twelve syllables, and they were bound to make masculine and feminine rhymes follow each other alternately. And the early French dramatists, following the Italian playwrights, were too often content, having found a type, to reproduce it with such variations that did not really alter the character, so that a personage once known remained more or less a stock figure until the end of the play. The presence or the absence of poetical feeling is a strong distinguishing feature in the comedy of each country at the periods already mentioned. In both the early English and early French comedies there is much that, were it produced now for the first time, would be thought excessively tedious, and the reader would often feel that his sympathies were not aroused, for poor plays were written in both countries; but there were very wide differences of design and of treatment distinguishing one set of comedies from the other. It is well known that in the last quarter of the 16th century and in the first quarter of the 17th, English dramatists took their plots freely from Spain, and nobody has thought worse of them for doing so. Our old playwrights, like Molière, took their good things where they found them and moulded them in their own way to their own uses. Whether they turned everything they touched into gold is not the point in question. But after the incidents in the story had been borrowed from

Spain or elsewhere, they set to work honestly and bravely to give a life and form of their own making to the events and characters in their plays. The drama, or the action in the poem, was drawn from their own imagination, and the poetical feeling was also theirs. They borrowed the skeleton, but the flesh on the bones, the blood in the veins, the action of the heart, were all of their own providing. They imitated and copied nobody, because the desire for imitation did not exist among them. There was no imitation in the sense of copying, because there was too much independence of thought. This reason alone gave to our dramatists a large number of characters —an element much wanting in the French drama because their writers had not acquired the power or the habit of thinking and working out a character for themselves. That independence of thought has much to do with the imaginative powers may be seen from the fact that when in the second half of the 17th century English dramatists, imitating those of France, composed plays in rhyme upon what they believed were regular models, they produced monstrosities or sterile abortions. We have had our period of imitation, and have small reason to be proud of its results.

Shakespeare and Molière thus lived in different mental atmospheres, and they wrote under different conditions. The plays that pleased one people would not have pleased the other; and though both writers spoke to their audiences much as their own feelings prompted them, Molière's hand was not completely free. The contrast between them is very wide, and is seen at once in their thoughts and in their manner of expressing them. Shakespeare wrote poetical comedy and he loved the glamour of romantic tales; Molière wrote comedies of manner and he loved wholesome satire and pleasant raillery; and both writers in their very different ways have given the best comedies the world has seen. Had they known each other, their opinions on the conduct of men in the affairs of life would have been fairly similar. Shakespeare was also a satirist and he enjoyed its fun, and Molière had the habit of examining men's thoughts and tracing their actions from them. But nature had given to Shakespeare higher ideals and greater powers wherewith to picture them. His knowledge of the human heart and human mind has not been equalled, and the greater richness of his intellect demanded a wider and a loftier sphere than is to be found in Molière.

The difference in their styles, in thought and in words, is the first thing that strikes a reader. Partly from causes just alluded to, Shakespeare's style is more imaginative, fuller, stronger, and more poetical than Molière's, but his language is not so easily understood. His words and phrases, there can be no doubt, have a peculiar richness and flavour of their own, they are particularly apt and well chosen and leave no trace of effort; but his lines appear sometimes to be overweighted with thick luxuriance of ideas, so that their meaning is more or less obscure or is not readily seen. Those who have learned their Shakespeare have learned to love his language because of its poetical imagery, its intensity, and the truth shown in it, its eloquence, its largeness of manner and full sweep of thought. Still, I take it, there has always been a period of self-tuition, which may have been difficult, even though the lesson has come gladly. But there are many English men and women who like to be thought fairly well educated, who have never accustomed themselves to Shakespeare's manner, and who do not know his plays. The difficulties of language hinder them. I confess I have felt more than once that Shakespeare's comedy would have been more enjoyable if his thoughts had been given in a simpler manner. His diction is sometimes confusing. He wrote after the fashion of the poets of his age, grandly, gloriously; but however truly he may have written, he has often long winded periods showing involved constructions that are not easily decipherable when read for the first time. I believe there are few persons who really understand a great play after a first reading; but I think also that after a first reading the meaning of Molière's lines comes home more readily to a young Frenchman of one or two and twenty than the meaning of Shakespeare's lines does to a young English lad of the same age. This is not from mental superiority in the young Frenchman, but because Molière's thoughts are more definite, less complex, and are given in less profusion, and that the construction of his sentences is easier than that of Shakespeare's. Molière was born six years after Shakespeare died, and the diction in French has altered less since Molière wrote than it has in

English since the time of Shakespeare. In prose greater differences may be seen in the manner of expression than in verse. Look at Milton's prose and that of Pascal, who died in 1662; or at Molière's prose and that in English comedies written between 1660 and 1673. French prose had then taken its present form, and cannot be considered old; the manner of expression in English prose has changed since that time, and we now think the style of authors in Charles II.'s reign old fashioned. The national characteristics of a country show themselves in language, and owing to many causes French prose at the beginning of the second half of the 17th century is more easily read now by one who has no acquaintance with old authors, than English prose of the same date.

Both Shakespeare and Molière were great humorists, with more or less of scepticism and of worldly cynicism. They saw men's meanness, their vanity, and their boastfulness with a feeling of sadness, yet both were generous and large-hearted. Neither probably were great laughers, though Shakespeare, one would say, must have had a very large capacity for enjoyment; and Molière had the greater power of giving fun and of making others laugh with him in his satire. The laughter that Shakespeare causes is louder and generally heartier; Molière's laughter is funnier, smaller in volume, and it shows a finer and often a sadder note. The lines in the comedies of both are full of mirth, but Molière laid more stress upon ridicule than Shakespeare. This is a form of satire well within the province of a comic dramatist, though much will depend on its object and the way it is shown. Molière's ridicule was generally reverential, it was used for a good purpose, and his satire was not ill-natured when it was most severe.) Shakespeare has shown, perhaps in every comedy, that his love of natural objects was intense. Molière very rarely mentions them; he did not conceive that it was part of his work in describing men and women to speak of earth, air, fire, and water. Few of his countrymen did so, either in his lifetime or for nearly a century after his death. Shakespeare's comedies, too, are rich in strong love-scenes; he took pleasure in dwelling upon them, in picturing them in all the sweetness and splendour that language can show, because he thought that the love and trust of a woman for a man is in itself a beautiful thing, and not merely an idea. He felt that it glorifies and rejoices the heart, that it heightens our morality and gives us a clearer perception that men and women are put into the world to help and comfort each other. Molière's heart was strong and high; he knew what love is, and occasionally he painted it truly; but he did not care about his love-scenes as Shakespeare did, he did not take the same sort of interest in them. He rarely idealised them, he used them chiefly as an instrument for his satire. It does not appear either that Molière had any real love of music; while Shakespeare had it very strongly. Shakespeare had in his heart a love for the "concord of sweet sounds"; this is seen in the flow of his verse and in his songs. Molière has very few songs, and the only one that anybody cares to remember is spoken by Alceste, and that, in spite of the rhyme, pleases rather by the sweetness of feeling than of sound :—

> " Si le Roi m'avoit donné
> Paris, sa grand' ville,
> Et qu'il me fallût quitter
> L'amour de ma mie,
> Je dirois au roi Henri :
> Reprenez votre Paris :
> J'aime mieux ma mie, au gué !
> J'aime mieux ma mie."

The meaning of these simple lines is that they were opposed to Oronte's pretentious and nonsensical sonnet. Molière's other songs he knew to be trumpery; he put them into his plays to be laughed at. Every English reader of Shakespeare recollects the pretty and mirthful lines :—

> " The man that hath no music in himself,
> Nor is not moved with concord of sweet sounds,
> Is fit for treasons, stratagems, and spoils ;
> The motions of his spirit are dull as night
> And his affections dark as Erebus :
> Let no such man be trusted."

Though Molière had not known by name one note of music from another, these words of Shakespeare's are no more applicable to him than to Handel or to Beethoven. Whatever likeness there may be between the comedies of Shakespeare and of Molière is to be sought in the excellence and the strength of their dramatisation, their characterisation and their mastery of racy language, though each worked with different aims in view. Shakespeare's plots are better and stronger than Molière's, yet, like Molière, he gave more thought to unfolding and exposing his characters and to the working out of his scenes than to the outward structure of his story. These points of likeness between them should be noticed.

Molière's humanity and his sympathies were unusually large, but Shakespeare's were larger still. His outlook and his range of thought was wider, his mind much more imaginative, more comprehensive. The scope of action in each of his comedies was greater, the idea worked out was more general, and he showed the natural attributes of men and women under more varied aspects — to some extent because his comedy stood on a broader basis than the laws of the French drama permitted Molière to use. Shakespeare, too, loved romance; Molière mostly avoided it. They both revealed men's purposes: Shakespeare with higher imaginative realism and poetical feeling, Molière on a smaller scale and with more definiteness, so that to many readers he is more easily understood. The style of thought in Shakespeare's men and women hardly proclaims their nationality; they spoke their feelings with the open voice of nature that calls every country its own. Molière's men and women also spoke openly and very naturally, but their tone of thought is generally French, and would have sounded more or less strange if heard outside France. As general instances: the comedy and the characterisation in the *Merchant of Venice* might be seen anywhere in Europe, but the *Femmes Savantes* is distinctly a French comedy laughing at the affectations of a fashion then running in Paris. On the other hand, the *Merry Wives of Windsor* is a peculiarly English comedy; but all the chief features described in the *Misanthrope* might be seen in any country where there is polished society, and the same may be said of the *Avare* wherever there is a miser who has to maintain a position in the world.

Bearing in mind the arbitrary laws which governed the drama in France, a partial comparison is perhaps possible in the way that Shakespeare and Molière characterised their personages; and as far as this goes it shows that Shakespeare gave wider play to his thoughts, and that Molière concentrated his ideas more closely on the subject immediately at hand.

Molière's practice in the greater number of his plays was to work up the incidents in his comedy in order to portray strongly the features in his chief characters, and he used his minor personages and his by-play with this end in view; whereas Shakespeare considered his personages more broadly and thought of them more individually. Shakespeare did not characterise men by their eccentricities so much as Molière did. As his power of ridicule was less keen he thought less of it, he did not use it so fully. His characterisation took a wider sweep, and he described men's moods more generally, mixing better their good qualities and their weaknesses, and letting each fall into their places in a more usual way. I do not wish in the least to contradict now what I said earlier in this chapter, for I believe that Molière had very great and very true powers of personal characterisation; but with the natural reflections that everybody makes while thinking of one author beside another, it is quite impossible not to feel that Shakespeare's strength in showing personal characterisation was the greatest. The two dramatists had different aims, one larger, one more definite than the other, and they wrote for audiences with different tastes. The reader who enjoys comedy will try to see how each writer described men's humours and what his laughter meant.

Though Molière was generally justified in the way he showed his caricature, Shakespeare used this means of ridicule more sparingly. Molière has shown men's faults, and he loved to portray their follies; instead of poetical or imaginative feeling we see a clear note of amusing and satirical comedy, and happily of a healthy kind. It would be a huge mistake to look upon Molière as a character-monger. His personages, if taken in connection with the incidents in his plays, do not show this; they are too true to nature; and there is real comedy in most of his plays that are acted and read because they show good, honest fun. And it is remarkable that after two hundred and fifty years his wit should have lost so little of its brightness. Molière wished that his light plays should make people laugh, but there is behind his merriment a deeper purpose which anybody may see if he will but open his eyes. I must repeat that Molière had a serious purpose in most of his comedies. His plays show that he was in earnest in trying to do good work, though he wrote with a light hand and used ridicule and broad and good-natured satire as his instruments. Some distinction, however, should be made between those plays that he wrote to be acted before the court and those that he wrote for the public theatre.

I am not meaning to compare him with Shakespeare, though I fear I have been led unavoidably more into comparison than I had intended. Real comparison is hardly possible, for Shakespeare's design was broader, his plane was higher, and his comedies were conceived and executed in a larger spirit than Molière wished or was able to adopt. Shakespeare's imagination, too, led him to heights of fancy which Molière would have admired, but which he would not have attempted to reach. The less liberal focus of events allowed on the French stage made concentrated action more necessary than was the case with us in England, or, at any rate, than was Shakespeare's custom, and Molière had to observe laws which to Shakespeare would have been intolerable. The thought—

"Let observation with extensive view
Survey mankind from China to Peru,"

was not Molière's wish, nor would he have been able to carry it out as Shakespeare has done ; but the idea expressed in the next two lines—

"Remark each anxious toil, each eager strife,
And watch the busy scenes of crowded life,"

Molière did show with very great dramatic clearness as regards what passed in his own country. And I feel sure that if Shakespeare had known Molière's comedies he would have been wonderfully struck with the accuracy of observation and of thought underlying his ridicule, with his strong dramatic characterisation and the excellence of his style ; he would also have enjoyed his irony and have laughed heartily at his fun.

Though the styles of their comedies were so dissimilar, Shakespeare and Molière, as dramatists, had some main ideas in common. One broad likeness between them was in the absence of formalism, and this is more singular in Molière than in Shakespeare, because routine had been more common on the French than on the English stage. In the first half of the 17th century French playwrights conceived their characters too much after a methodical pattern, they thought too much of the " genre noble " in comedy ; and Molière, as he discarded their upholstery and drew his personages naturally —that is as men and women would speak and act under the given conditions—broke away from routine more widely than Shakespeare had done. Also, both Shakespeare and Molière thought more of characterisation than of plot, and they thought infinitely more of the effects their words would have on the stage than of the literary beauties of their lines when printed. Their chief labour was to get their thoughts into the right shape, into the form of comedy proper at the moment. It would seem that their words came quickly, picturing their thoughts, acting their comedy on paper in the way their minds had conceived it. Each had in his inner mind an idea of the value of his own work. For it rarely happens in the competition of life that a man who is much stronger than others does not know that he can do more than his fellows. I believe they both had with quite modest thoughts an opinion of their own powers, and that they trusted in them, writing often to please themselves or to satisfy their own ideas of what was good or fitting in comedy. Their audience was their first care, but they each had their own aspirations which they wished to court—not for the sake of glory, not because they wished to say something fine, but because the natural ambition in man urged them in a conscientious spirit to seek after excellence as far as they were able to do so. They both considered very little the readers of their own day, and to those in a future generation neither gave more than a momentary thought. Few dramatists of the first rank have been so little desirous of posthumous fame.

They would both have rejected the theory of a literary drama, knowing well that an audience wants to be touched with what it sees and hears, and that literary graces, rightly never absent, hold a subsidiary place in the representation of a play. A comedy, whether in verse or in prose, is intended to be acted ; and as its words are to be spoken they should, with the necessary proprieties, have the flavour of speech. You may act comedy or tragedy ; you cannot act literature in the sense of giving on the stage a literary flavour or effect to spoken words. If you try to do so you are working in a wrong direction. In reading a comedy an idea of its representation should, if possible, be kept in view; but the literary and the dramatic effects are to some extent antagonistic to one another. Shakespeare and Molière, the greatest masters of comedy, have both shown in their verse and in their prose that they were careful to give to their words the effect of speech addressed by one living person to another; and as far as the literary flavour crossed the stage effect, it would almost seem that they wished to avoid it. In good comedy one looks for strong or natural feelings expressed in a sympathetic and easy way, but its literary style should be used to conceal itself. It ought to be there, like salt in a soup, but even as one reads a play it should not be much more noticeable. Take the six or twelve best comic dramatists: it will be seen that they thought much of their language, for it helps to characterise a play in all its parts, yet that they wished to hide its literary style rather than bring it forward, and that their plays became known and are remembered partly by this concealment—the dramatic effects taking the foremost place and outweighing all other needs. The value on the stage of the scenes in a comedy is tested by the dramatic very much more than by the literary merits; and even as one reads a printed comedy, if literary effort is too prominent it will usually damage the worth of the lines whether in verse or in prose. It has the appearance of an exercise in mental gymnastics. Comedies of the first class are very often examples of good literature; literary excellence forms part of their merits. But the style has come naturally from the orderly working of the author's brain. He has, no doubt, aimed at giving good literary expression to his thoughts; but he has instinctively made it subordinate to the comic effects in his play, even though appropriate language has had much to do with producing comic results. Goodness in a style in any branch of literature depends largely on the fitness to the matter in hand. Comedy and comic are words with large meanings; and the most imperative needs in a comedy are true comic thought and comic exhibition shown truly and in a natural, lively and mirthful manner. Without them there can be no real comic style, for style is the outcome of thought and is generated by it. Mere style or language has never yet made a good comedy, though it has often given invaluable assistance. Also, if the beauties of language in a play are so great that you like to learn three or four passages by heart and remember them,—unless you keep in mind the bearing of these passages to the rest of the play you will lose much of their dramatic effects, and might almost as well have learned Milton as Shakespeare, or La Fontaine as Molière.

The literary charms in Shakespeare's and in Molière's comedies come naturally from the subject in each play, characterise it and are one with it, and rarely, especially with Molière, obtrude themselves for their own sake. Shakespeare's fancy was so exuberantly poetical that his language takes all sorts of forms, for he delighted in framing images for the sake of their illustrative beauty. If Molière had possessed the poetic gifts which burn and must find an outlet, he would have shown them. The styles of both writers, however, varied with the subjects chosen and with the personages, and are peculiar to them. Differences may be seen in Shakespeare's manner in his comedies, and Molière's comedies in verse were written in different tones. As masters of the language of comedy in verse, Shakespeare and Molière stand as gods among men. Examine their thoughts and the apt way they are expressed in giving a clear picture of comedy and its personal characterisation, their words will be found to have a fuller meaning and to carry with them a stronger vitality than those of any other comic dramatist who wrote also in verse ; and the excellence of the passages that are most admired lies chiefly in manifesting the genius of comedy, in suiting the occasion and showing the character of the speaker. Take these passages out of their setting, and much of their value will be lost. This does not mean that the writers wished their plays to be examples of literature ; it does mean that they were both masters of their language, and that they made it very pliable to suit the needs of comedy. Instances may be seen where both Shakespeare and Molière found what may be called a collision between correctness of language and true comic expression. They have both shown that correctness or strict regularity of language must then for the moment go to the wall, and that ungrammatical words giving a true picture of comedy should prevail.

Molière wrote many comedies too in prose ; and the language in half a dozen of the best of these will bear comparison with that in any English plays also written in prose. His style for the purposes of comedy is not more old-fashioned than that of Congreve, hardly more so than that of Sheridan. These two Englishmen, between them, wrote about six comedies that are now generally known, and for the excellence of his language Molière is on a par with either of them. In some ways Congreve is more delicate in his delineations than Sheridan, though he has repelled many persons by his cold-blooded nastiness. But as you look at his and Sheridan's scenes, they do not fill your mind so intensely with dramatic personations of character, nor do they give you such a big idea of intellectual comic strength, or of the lessons that comic satire may teach, as do the pictures drawn by Molière. Style and language have certainly much to do with this.

No real likeness, however, can be maintained between Shakespeare's and Molière's comedies. Shakespeare's were full of poetry; Molière thought how he could best gain his purpose by wholesome and amusing satire. If a likeness exists between any of their characters, it is between Falstaff and the race of Sganarelles in showing in their different ways the meanness of men who are boastful, vain-glorious, cowardly, domineering and self-interested—and in another to be mentioned immediately. Admirable as is the character of Falstaff, it is often felt that much of Shakespeare's low or popular comedy in this character has lost its flavour for us now, and Molière's graphic portraiture of his Sganarelles is not the best part of his work. But Molière's fun is generally more really funny than Shakespeare's, and his droll scenes are more amusing; the vis comica in his plays creates laughter more easily than that shown by Shakespeare. For an example of the difference of design and treatment in their comedies, look at *As You Like It* and the *École des Maris* or the *École des Femmes*; at the *Merry Wives of Windsor* or the comedy in *Henry IV*. and the *Bourgeois Gentilhomme*; at the *Merchant of Venice* and the *Avare*. In these two last plays there is a likeness in the conduct of Shylock and Harpagon to their children, and in the absence of affection and respect that both fathers inspire. Harpagon has a son and a daughter, but he loves his money better than either; Shylock has only a daughter, but he prefers his ducats, and his revenge is sweeter to him than his gold.

Both plays present terrible pictures of how greed can take hold of a man, but it is shown in different ways. Shakespeare has given a poetic and ideal conception of flint-hearted brutishness; Molière in his picture of beastly avarice pours out his grim irony and his satire. What Shakespeare says of Shylock will apply to Harpagon :—

> " A stony adversary, an inhuman wretch
> Uncapable of pity, void and empty
> From any dram of mercy."

Molière's *Avare* has some excellent scenes in which his powers as a comic dramatist are manifest, but even if this play had been written in verse one might look in vain for such pictures of beautiful ideas as are to be found in the *Merchant of Venice*.

The frame of Molière's comedies was smaller than of Shakespeare's ; his plays were planned on a narrower scale, better suited to his more definite understanding and his less poetical nature. But inside his limits, which, when examined, will be found to be more than ordinarily wide, his characterisation was broad, easy, and bold, and his fancy was exuberant in healthy and amusing satirical portraiture. He was somewhat hampered by arbitrary rules, but as far as the rules allowed he drew his personages with perfect freedom and showed their humours with truth and clearness. I have said that Shakespeare possessed powers that were beyond Molière's reach : but for firm and distinct portraiture and dramatic formation of character ; for a knowledge of handling events and small incidents and making them agree with his characters and be suitable for representation on the stage ; for the expression of human sympathies ; for a great command of racy language peculiar to the speaker and to the occasion—giving through it all a clear picture of comedy—Molière, I think, comes nearer to Shakespeare than any other comic dramatist. While for his vis comica, or power of making an audience merry with dramatic effects ; for pleasant and laughable irony ; for healthy and humorous enjoyment to be found in his satire ; for the wonderful way in which he blended together his ridicule and his censure with comic effect and earnestness of purpose— I believe that among men who have written for the stage Molière stands unrivalled.

CHAPTER IX

It may be well to give again at the outset of this chapter the names of the three French acting companies in Paris while Molière was playing there from 1658 to 1673, and to say shortly how the Comédie Française was formed from them—though we are not to be concerned with that institution. It would be useless to mention the minor companies, for they were short-lived and but little recognised; nor is it necessary to speak of the Italian actors, for though while Molière was in Paris they shared the same theatre with him they had no other connection with his troop.

After permission had been given to Molière in October 1658 to play at the Petit Bourbon, there were three troops of actors in Paris:—

(1) L'Hôtel de Bourgogne, or "la troupe royale";
(2) Le Théâtre du Marais;
(3) La troupe de Molière, or "la troupe de Monsieur" until 1665 when it became "la troupe du Roi." In October 1660 Molière and his friends were made to leave the Petit Bourbon, and in January 1661 they began to play at the Palais Royal.

After Molière's death in 1673, four of the actors who had belonged to his troop went to the Hôtel de Bourgogne; the others allied themselves with the troop at the Marais; and the company thus formed left the old Marais theatre and went to play in a new theatre at the Hôtel Guénegaud, under the title of "la troupe du Roi." The Palais Royal theatre was given to Lulli for the Opera.[1] Then in 1680 the king thought that one theatre was sufficient; the actors at the Hôtel Guénegaud were united with those at the Hôtel de Bourgogne,

---

[1] *Registre de la Grange*, 145, 146; and La Grange's preface to the edition of Molière in 1682, given in the *Œuvres de Molière*, vol. i. p. xviii.

and the new company played at the Hôtel Guénegaud under
the title of "les Comédiens du Roi."[1] For very many
years afterwards there was only one French theatre regularly
established in Paris; but the number of actors was greater
than had ever been the case in one house before, and the
theatre was open every day, whereas the custom at each
theatre had been to play only three times a week. Because
of the king's edict in 1680 the Comédie Française is now
officially dated from that year, though I have seen no contemporary authority showing that the name was then in use.
The following diagram will show the descent of the different
theatres :—

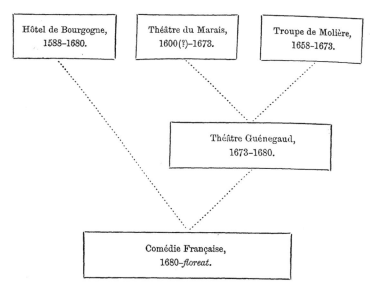

Thus it will be seen that the Comédie Française was formed
in part from the actors who had belonged to the Hôtel de
Bourgogne, while some had come from the Théâtre du Marais,
the others from the Palais Royal and had been taught by
Molière. La Grange's Register has been spoken of already;
but he wrote only of what took place in his troop. Less is
known of what went on at the other theatres, for no one

[1] Œuvres de Molière, i. p. xix; Despois, Le Théâtre Français sous
Louis XIV., 2.

there kept a record of events or of money matters. I think, however, it may be assumed that the Marais was the least prosperous of the three playhouses, and that the public took less interest in that theatre than in either of its rivals.

The first writer who gave general information about the customs of the French stage was Samuel Chappuzeau. His book, *Le Théâtre François*, was published at Lyons in 1674, and speaks therefore of the time that concerns us here. A reprint of it was published in Paris in 1875, with a preface and notes by M. Georges Monval, and my quotations from it refer to that edition. Chappuzeau divided his small volume into three books : the interest lies in the second half of the second book and in the third. His optimistic tone here and there provokes a smile, and one becomes tempted to think that the picture he painted was the bright side. Nevertheless, in the main he may be trusted. He was an inveterate play-goer; he had visited the theatres of other countries besides his own ; and he wrote comedies which were acted at the Hôtel de Bourgogne, at the Marais, and at the Palais Royal theatres.[1] His book, *Le Théâtre François*, was evidently written from actual observation, and shows that he knew what he was saying. The facts he has given concerning the usages of the Paris stage in the 17th century have been accepted by modern French writers who have studied the early dramatic history of their country, and many of his statements have been borne out by other pieces of evidence.

M. Victor Fournel says on page 101 of his little volume *Curiosités Théâtrales* :—

"In the 17th century the Hôtel de Bourgogne, the Marais, and the Palais Royal theatres, were real republics [each] with a president chosen by themselves. They were not private enterprises under the responsibility of a manager ; they were associations in which every one had equal rights, and each member shared the gains and losses as is now the case among the sociétaires of the Théâtre Français."

These words should be remembered, for they describe the keynote to the administration of the Paris theatres in the 17th century. The same customs governed them all, and were observed as nearly as possible by strolling companies

---

[1] Two of his comedies, with a biographical preface and notes, are given by M. Fournel in *Les Contemporains de Molière*, vols. i. and iii.

in the provinces. The principle of partnership was a very old one with French actors, and it formed the basis of their theory of government. Probably enough it arose among the ancient Confrères de la Passion, the first owners of the Hôtel de Bourgogne theatre, who were all artisans of Paris, and from them descended to the company of actors to whom they let the Hôtel de Bourgogne in 1588, forty years after they were forbidden to play the mysteries and when they found that they could not amuse the public by other performances. However that may be, we see in *La Comédie des Comédies* (Act I. sc. 1), a play by Gougenot acted in 1633, that when two actors had just become members of the troop one says to the other in a tone of raillery : " Tu ne sais pas que la condition comique ne connaît point de maîtrise ni de servitude ! " That points to a well-established custom, and forty years later Chappuzeau wrote :—

" There are no people in the world who love a monarchy more than actors, who find it more advantageous to them, and who show a stronger interest in its welfare ; but they cannot endure it among themselves. They will call no man master, and the idea of subjection would frighten them." [1]

" But if actors do not like living under a republic, they are very fond of a republican government among themselves. They will admit no superior, the name alone hurts them. They all wish to be equal, and they call each other comrades." [2]

The theatrical year always ended a week or ten days before Easter Sunday, and began a week or ten days after that day. During the interval, new actors were taken into a troop if they were wanted, and old actors who wished to leave one troop and enter another did so then. There were two exceptions to this custom at the Palais Royal : La Thorillière and Brécourt joined Molière's troop on the 9th of June 1662. They both came from the Théâtre du Marais.[3] As a rule the actors in Paris did not care to change their theatre without good cause. Each troop had its own esprit de corps and more or less its own traditions, and these things created a bond of unity among the members. At the Hôtel de Bourgogne their position was assured ; many of those at the Marais would perhaps have been glad to better their fortunes, and in fact four of Molière's

---

[1] *Le Théâtre François*, 97. [2] *Ibid.* 102.
[3] *Registre de la Grange*, 44.

actors came to him from that theatre; and at the Palais Royal
the receipts were good and the actors did not want to change.
As will be seen later, it is not surprising that during Molière's
lifetime no actor went to the Palais Royal from the Hôtel de
Bourgogne. But at Easter 1664 Brécourt left the Palais Royal
and went to the Hôtel de Bourgogne. He was replaced by
Hubert from the Marais. As each actor entered his troop at
Easter the payment of his "part" dated from that time and
was continued until the Easter following. Du Parc, one of the
actors at the Palais Royal, died on the 4th of November 1664,
and his "part" for the remainder of the theatrical year was
paid to his widow, Mlle. du Parc, until Easter 1665.

The socialism among the actors was not merely theoretical,
for the net profits from the theatre were divided into as many
shares as there were members in the troop. Chappuzeau
describes the way this was done:—

"When the play is finished and the public has left the theatre, the
actors every evening settle the day's account. They may all be
present, but the treasurer, the secretary, and the controller ought to
be there, as the money is brought to them by the clerk in the box-
office. . . . When the money has been counted the day's expenses
are divided, and sometimes in certain cases, either to pay off a debt
gradually or to make an advance, a sum decided upon is set aside.
Then whatever remains is divided at once, and everybody takes away
with him his share." [1]

There is nothing said here to lead one to suppose that only
those actors who played on any given day got their share of
the receipt in the evening. La Grange's pages, too, would
contradict such an idea, for he mentioned the sum due to each
actor as though the shares were equally divided among all the
members of the troop. But when a "gagiste," or hired person,
was employed he was paid so much for his day's work; he
did not form part of the troop. There can be no doubt that
the best actors at the Palais Royal gave the most constant
service; yet there is nothing to show that Molière, La Grange,
Mlle. de Brie, and Mlle. Molière, were better paid for their
work than de Brie, Geneviève Béjart, or Mlle. du Croisy, all
of whom might have been replaced by gagistes. From what

[1] *Le Théâtre François*, 113. It may be seen also in Act v. sc. 5 of
Corneille's *Illusion Comique*, acted in 1636, that the same custom was
observed then.

La Grange says about Mlle. du Croisy it would appear that her share was taken from her.[1] The number of shares in Molière's two theatres, from Easter 1659 to Easter 1673, varied from eleven to fifteen; the fewer actors there were gave, of course, to each greater profits.

It was not until the troop had been nine years at the Palais Royal that the plan of dividing the shares was introduced there. At Easter 1670, Beauval and his wife joined Molière's troop. Mlle. Beauval was a clever woman, and a whole share was given to her; but her husband, who was almost a fool, had but half a share, and from that large deductions were made.[2] The only other instance of a fraction of a share at the Palais Royal was that of Mlle. La Grange, who entered the troop in 1672. A few years later at the Théâtre Guénegaud, and later again at the Comédie Française, fractions of shares were common.

Louis XIV. gave to the Italian companies when they were in Paris a pension of 15,000 livres a year; to the Hôtel de Bourgogne 12,000 livres; to the Palais Royal 6000, dating from 1665, and in 1671 this was raised to 7000 livres. When Molière's troop arrived in Paris, Monsieur, the king's brother, promised 300 livres a year to each actor, but La Grange says that the payment was never made.[3] So far as is known the Théâtre du Marais got no royal pension, nor the troop at the Hôtel Guénegaud. It would seem that the pension to the Hôtel de Bourgogne was stopped temporarily in 1674;[4] but La Grange shows that in 1681 the Comédie Française received a pension, and that it was continued to them for some years.[5] An actor who had a share or fraction of a share in the receipts of his theatre, got the same proportion in the pension given by the king. There were also other sums of money, known as "gratifications," which Louis XIV. gave to Molière's troop; they will be spoken of later. What gratifications the king may have given to the other troops are not known.

Besides the pension given by the king, the actors established amongst themselves a system of retiring pensions. Chappuzeau says:—

[1] *Registre de la Grange*, 64, 72.   [2] *Ibid.* 111, 131.
[3] *Registre*, 3.
[4] Despois, *Le Théâtre Français sous Louis XIV.*, 101 note.
[5] *Registre*, 286.

"They will not suffer that there should be any poor among them, and they take pains to prevent any of their body from falling into want. When age or illness forces an actor to retire, his successor is bound to pay him during his lifetime a comfortable pension ; so that when a man of worth comes on to a theatre in Paris, he is assured of a good income of three or four thousand livres a year while he can work and of a sufficient sum to live upon when he retires. And at the Hôtel de Bourgogne, when an actor or actress dies the troop makes a present of a hundred pistoles [the pistole was worth eleven livres, or francs] to his or her nearest relation, thereby giving that relation in the loss sustained a more solid consolation than any compliments. It is noble of the king's players to behave in this way, so that those who have grown old in the service should have sufficient to maintain themselves honourably to the end of their days." [1]

This was the principle acted upon both for men and for women, and it would seem that it arose first at the Hôtel de Bourgogne. At Easter 1664, Brécourt, who had left the Palais Royal after he had been there two years, was admitted into the Hôtel de Bourgogne with a nominal whole share. Étiennette des Urlis, his wife, was also admitted at the same time, provisionally, into the troop, partaking of the same share as her husband : on the conditions that if she owed her admission to the retirement of an actress, she should pay to that actress a yearly pension of 1000 livres, or if her admission was gained by the death of any actress, she should pay the same sum every year to Mlle. de Villiers, who had retired from the company. Not long previously the actors at the Hôtel de Bourgogne had agreed to give Mlle. de Villiers a pension of 1000 livres, but in admitting Mlle. Brécourt, who was an indifferent actress, into their troop, they wished to relieve themselves from paying this pension. The agreement as to Brécourt and his wife was passed on the 17th of March 1664, and four days later the same company passed a resolution that when any actor or actress left the stage on account of old age or of illness, all those remaining in the troop should contribute towards a life pension for him or her of 1000 livres annually, each one paying in proportion to his receipts.[2] The only instance of an actor at the Palais Royal receiving a pension was Louis Béjart, who left the stage at Easter 1670, after eleven years' service in Paris. Taschereau quotes the

[1] *Le Théâtre François*, 95.
[2] Soulié, *Recherches sur Molière*, 205-210 ; Bonnassies, *La Comédie Française : Histoire Administrative*, 13, 14.

document conferring 1000 livres a year for life on Béjart,[1] and says that he retired from the stage in consequence of a wound he had received. Apparently the injury had been caused eighteen months or more previously, and in connection with the theatre. At the end of the year 1669-70 La Grange wrote : " Cette pension a été la première établie à l'exemple de celles qu'on donne aux acteurs de la troupe de l'Hôtel de Bourgogne."[2] After the break-up of the troop at the Palais Royal, consequent upon Molière's death in 1673, Béjart's pension was paid to him until he died in 1678 by the troop at the Hôtel Guénegaud.[3]

The following extract from page 143 of La Grange's Register shows that for the fourteen years Molière was acting in Paris, a share in the Petit Bourbon and Palais Royal theatres averaged, one year with another, 3690 livres :—

"Total of what I have received since I became an actor in Paris, from the 25th of April 1659 up to the death of M. de Molière on the 17th of February 1673, and the remainder of the said year " [that is up to the 21st of March following] :—

			Livres.	Sous.
1. To 12th March 1660,	.	.	2,995	10
2. To 1st April 1661, .	.	.	2,477	6
3. To 26th March 1662,	.	.	4,310	9
4. To 12th March 1663,	.	.	3,117	18
5. To 28th March 1664,	.	.	4,534	4
6. To 20th March 1665,	.	.	3,011	11
7. To 11th April 1666,	.	.	2,243	5
8. To 29th March 1667,	.	.	3,352	11
9. To 17th March 1668,	.	.	2,608	13
10. To 9th April 1669,	.	.	5,477	3
11. To 23rd March 1670,	.	.	4,034	11
12. To 17th March 1671,	.	.	4,689	
13. To 5th April 1672,	.	.	4,233	
14. To 21st March 1673,	.	.	4,585	13
			51,670	14 "

French writers have said that to estimate the spending value of money in Molière's time by money in our day we ought to multiply by five.[4] And Macaulay, whose first volume of his *History of England* was published in 1849, has

[1] *Vie de Molière*, 3rd. ed. preface, pp. ii, iii.
[2] *Registre*, 111.　　　　　[3] *Ibid.* 146.
[4] Soulié, *Recherches sur Molière*, 68 ; *Œuvres de Molière*, viii. 230, note 1 ; *Œuvres de Molière* by M. Louis Moland, 2nd ed. i. 94.

shown in his famous third chapter that in the reign of Charles II. agricultural labour in England was paid on the average four times less in nominal value than it was when he wrote. The question of ascertaining the comparative value of money now and two hundred and fifty years ago is very intricate. I accept, however, the French estimate; it differs little from that given by Macaulay. La Grange's income of 3690 livres, multiplied by five, would give now 18,450 francs, or £738 sterling.

It has been explained how the actors, who were the masters in their theatre, got their livelihood; we must now see how the writers of plays were paid for their work. Dramatic copyright, in Molière's day, was governed by unwritten laws, and on the whole the established customs were well maintained. It was commonly held that a play belonged to the troop of actors who first put it on the stage, and that when a new play had been brought out at one theatre no other troop should put it on their boards until it had been printed. If after the novelty had worn off the author chose to print his play, the acting copyright lapsed, and any other French troop might perform it if they pleased. If the author did not print his play, it was usually not worth printing.

In the early part of the 17th century a poet was sometimes in the pay of the actors, and was dependent on them. They ordered a play of him as they would have ordered a piece of work from a carpenter, and they paid him low carpenter's wages. But for them he would have had no existence; they made him feel his dependence and often treated him with indignity. Rotrou was at one time the poet of the troop at the Hôtel de Bourgogne, and there is a passage about him which may be noticed in a letter from Chapelain to Godeau, dated 30th of October 1632 :—

"Le Comte de Fiesque brought to me Rotrou and his Mecænas. I am sorry that a young man of such good parts should have accepted such shameful servitude; and it will not be my fault if we do not deliver him from it. He tells me that he has used your name besides that of his introducer in order to give himself some consideration in my eyes. Let me know if you will lend a hand in the assistance which he expects from me, for I am determined to do something for him." [1]

---

[1] *Lettres de Jean Chapelain*, edited by Tamizey de la Roque in the Collection des documents inédits sur l'histoire de France, vol. i. 6.

Chapelain's words may be taken without comment as explaining the situation in which Rotrou had placed himself. Pierre Corneille, Rotrou's senior by three years, was never poet to a troop. He lived at Rouen, and his plays were acted in Paris. There are two lines in his *Illusion Comique* (Act v. sc. 5) showing that play-writing had been profitable to him :—

"D'ailleurs, si par les biens on prise les personnes,
Le théâtre est un fief dont les rentes sont bonnes."

And from indications in his "Examens" of his own early comedies—though these examens were not written until a good many years after the comedies were printed—it would seem that Corneille was proud of the position he had won for himself. Until the middle of the century the actors used to give an author so much every day his play was performed, or they bought it from him outright for a stipulated sum, "prix fait." There is an often-told story to the effect that Tristan l'Hermite, in negotiating the sale of *Les Rivales* (1653), a comedy by Quinault, to the troop at the Hôtel de Bourgogne, proposed that the actors should give the author one-ninth of the receipts so long as the play was new, and that it should afterwards become their property. This suggestion was agreed to, and by degrees was established the system known as "les droits d'auteur," based on a ninth of the receipts of each performance of new plays in five acts.[1] But the plan of author's profits was not followed invariably, at least for some years. For his *Précieuses Ridicules* and a few subsequent plays Molière received presents of money; and La Grange shows that, at this period, the troop to which he belonged used to pay other authors in the same way. In 1667 and in 1670 Pierre Corneille was paid 2000 livres for each of his two tragedies, *Attila* and *Tite et Bérénice,* acted at the Palais Royal. And even later, on the 8th of March 1677, the troop at the Hôtel Guénegaud completed the payment of 200 louis d'or (2200 livres) for the *Festin de Pierre.* This was Molière's *Don Juan* put into verse by Thomas Corneille. As Molière's play had not been printed it belonged to his widow, and she

---

[1] Parfaict, *Histoire du Théâtre Français,* vii. 428-430. M. Bonnassies thinks that the anecdote told about a ninth of the receipt given to the author is "a pure invention, at least as regards the manner of determining the right." *Les Auteurs dramatiques et la Comédie Française au 17e et au 18e siècles,* end of note to p. 4.

received one half of the money and Thomas Corneille, for his version, got the other half.[1] It would seem, however, when Chappuzeau wrote, that the plan of buying plays "prix fait" was nearly abandoned, and that a new method was in vogue for giving an author profits on his play dependent upon its success. Chappuzeau says:—

"The most usual and the fairest way on both sides is to give the author two shares in every performance of his play up to a certain time. For instance, . . . if one performance makes 1660 livres profit, and the troop is composed of fourteen shares, the author will get 200 livres that evening for his two shares; the other 60 livres, more or less, are put aside for daily expenses, such as lighting and paying the servants of the theatre."[2]

This statement may not be clear to us now. Chappuzeau supposed that there were fourteen actors in a troop, each having a whole share; then while a play was considered new two more shares, called author's shares, were added to the fourteen, and their value was given to the author in the evening after the performance. So that if a net profit of 1660 livres were declared from any performance of a new play, the author's two shares from that performance were worth 200 livres, or $\frac{2}{16}$ of 1600 livres—the remaining 60 livres, more or less, were put aside, for expenses of the theatre. A play was considered new, and the author entitled to his two shares, only as long as the receipts continued to be satisfactory. In recording the first performance of the École des Femmes, on the 26th of December 1662, La Grange gave the total receipt as 1518 livres, and he added : " Partagé en 17 parts, deux pour l'auteur." There were then fifteen actors in the troop at the Palais Royal. That was the only time La Grange mentioned the author's shares. It may be imagined, therefore, that for all of his subsequent comedies Molière got as author his two shares in the receipt, but only so long as his plays were considered new on the stage.

I do not like to anticipate on a matter which will be spoken of later, but to prevent misconception it may be said shortly that, according to La Grange's Register, very few new plays made as much as 1600 livres, as an average, on the first few days. The exceptions were Molière's Don Juan, his Tartuffe,

[1] Registre de la Grange, 188 ; Œuvres de Molière, v. 50.
[2] Le Théâtre François, 67.

and a spectacular play *Circé*, by Thomas Corneille and de Visé, acted at the Théâtre Guénegaud in 1675, after Chappuzeau had written his book. There is no means of knowing what were the receipts at the Hôtel de Bourgogne nor at the Théâtre du Marais, but it is not likely that even at the Hôtel they were generally higher than at the Palais Royal.

It was the custom for an author to read his play aloud to the members of a troop, who were to judge if they would put it upon their stage. Between each act there was a pause, when the actors made their remarks upon what they had heard; and when the reading was finished they gave their decision :—

"The women," says Chappuzeau,[1] "out of modesty, leave to the men the judgment of plays and are rarely present at the reading, though it is within their right to be there. . . . Some of the most celebrated authors read admirably. . . . But there are others whose reading is pitiful, and who do their own work injustice."

Chappuzeau was usually quite impersonal in his remarks; but it is hardly doubtful that among the authors who read well he was thinking of Racine, and among the others of Corneille.

As regards the distribution of the parts in a new play, it may be remembered that one of the clauses in the "Contrat entre les Comédiens de l'Illustre Théâtre," in 1643, was that when a new play came before the troop, the author should have the undisputed right to distribute the parts as he pleased. These words seem to imply that such was the custom. It may be gathered from Chappuzeau that the same practice prevailed, at least in theory, thirty years later :—

"When the author knows the abilities of each of the actors . . . the troop are glad that he should have the trouble of distributing the parts, in which duty he takes counsel from one of the troop. But even then he is often worried, and it is difficult for him to please everybody."[2]

In a later chapter, Chappuzeau says that in this respect men are less troublesome than women :—

"There is not one woman among them who would not always like to appear young. . . . The poet has to be artful not to represent mothers at an age when they are no longer charming, and not to give them sons who show that they have passed their fortieth year."[3]

---

[1] *Le Théâtre François*, 66.　　　[2] *Ibid.* 71, 72.　　　[3] *Ibid.* 85.

The three days on which the theatres were open were Sunday, Tuesday, and Friday. Chappuzeau[1] gives the reasons why convenience had established this custom:—

"Monday is the great post day to Germany and to Italy, and for all parts of the kingdom which lie on the route; Wednesday and Saturday are business and market days, when the tradesman is more engaged than upon other days; and Thursday is kept as a holiday in many places, especially in academies[2] and colleges."

When Molière's troop began to play at the Petit Bourbon, they had to take the "jours extraordinaires," or the off-days; for the Italian company who were in possession of the theatre used to play there on the "jours ordinaires." At first Molière's troop often acted four days a week, until July 1659, when the Italians left Paris; after that date Molière opened his doors on the Sunday, Tuesday, and Friday, as was customary at the other two theatres. Chappuzeau adds: "The first performance of a new play is always given on a Friday, so as to prepare people to come in greater numbers on the Sunday following, after the praises have been given by the 'annonce' and by the 'affiche.'" At the Palais Royal new plays were generally brought out on a Friday, but not always. In a note to page 70 of Chappuzeau's volume, M. Monval has given a list, compiled from La Grange's Register, of the names of the plays first acted on Fridays and of those upon other days.

The "annonce," just mentioned by Chappuzeau, was a friendly communication from the management of the theatre to the audience, delivered from the stage. It is not easy to say when this custom arose, but it died out in the 17th century. A popular member of the troop was chosen as "orateur," and when the day's performance was concluded, or at the end of the principal piece, the orator came forward, thanked the audience for their attention, told them what play would be next acted; and when a new play was to be brought out he announced its performance for a future day. The following extract is taken from page 4 of a pamphlet by Édouard Thierry, *Quatre Mois au Théâtre de Molière* (*Novembre 1664– Mars 1665*):—

---

[1] *Le Théâtre François*, 70.
[2] Despois says that this word meant schools for gymnastic exercises for youths. *Œuvres de Molière*, iii. 395, note *b* to note 1.

"The annonce was one of the most delicate and important functions connected with the stage. The actor who spoke it, as he declared what would be the programme for the next day, learned in point of fact what were the wishes of those in the theatre. He was the interpreter between the actors and the public, and between the public and the actors. He said a good word for the play that had just been given, or for the play still in rehearsal. He said nice things of the play that had been well received, or he cleverly excused the deficiencies of the author who had been less fortunate. Every spectator had an undeniable right to ask him questions, and this privilege was sometimes pushed too far; but the orator of the troop was always bound to give an answer. He either evaded the question or he answered it plainly; but his word was taken to be that of his comrades, and once given they were bound by it. An old stage hand was therefore chosen for the post of orator, a man who knew from experience what he was talking about."

On the 18th of October 1671 and three following days, after *Psyché* had been played thirty-four times at the Palais Royal, the receipts rose suddenly to twice as much as they had been before the 18th of October. It may be imagined from this that the orator had announced that there would be a change in the programme on a certain date, and that those persons who had not seen the play wished to do so. . It had been customary to make these "annonces" at length, but people got tired of flowery speeches; then the orator spoke in a more businesslike way. At the end of his volume[1] Chappuzeau says :—

"The troop at the Palais Royal had for its first orator the illustrious Molière, who, six[2] years before his death, was very glad to be relieved of the office, and begged La Grange to take his place. La Grange always acquitted himself admirably in this respect until the break-up of the Palais Royal troop; and he continues to exercise the same function to the great satisfaction of the audience in the nouvelle troupe du roi."

Then follows a eulogy on La Grange's merits as actor, as orator, and as a capable and trustworthy man of business.

Chappuzeau confounds the "annonce" with the "affiche," and says that they were much alike.[3] The affiche, in the sense of a playbill, was composed by the orator of the troop. It was posted up at street corners, and was sometimes written

---

[1] *Le Théâtre François*, 165, 166.
[2] This word "six" should be *huit*, for La Grange wrote on the 14th of November 1664 : "J'ai commencé à annoncer pour Monsieur de Molière."
[3] *Le Théâtre François*, 139-141.

in verse. At first it stated that the poet of the troop had composed a new play, the title of which was given ;—about the year 1625 authors allowed their names to be used.[1] The two rhymed affiches by Scarron,[2] to which Despois alludes, were imaginary ; and so also was the affiche given in the first scene of Dorimon's play *La Comédie de la Comédie.*[3] The date of this play was 1661 or 1662. The affiches of the different theatres were distinguished by their colours, either of the paper or of the printing. Those of the Hôtel de Bourgogne were red, those of the Théâtre Guénegaud were green,[4] of the Opera yellow, of the Petit Bourbon and Palais Royal red and black.[5] These 17th century playbills are extremely scarce. In the *Moliériste* for July 1880 (vol. ii. 99) M. Nuitter published facsimiles of four—one belonging to the Hôtel de Bourgogne, two to the Marais, and one to the Petit Bourbon. They are much alike, the chief difference being that both of those of the Marais are printed in red letters, those of the other two theatres in black. Unfortunately the affiche that belonged to the Petit Bourbon was so mutilated that only half of it is left. M. Nuitter tried to reproduce it, guessing, in some measure, what might have been the words in the missing half. The heading seems to bear the title: " Les Comédiens de Monsieur, Frère Unique du Roy " ; and in the half of the bill that remains there is the word " Gorgibus." One of the farces attributed to Molière was called *Gorgibus dans le Sac* ; it was played once before the king at Vincennes, on 31st January 1661, and five times at the Palais Royal, from 4th February 1661 to 15th July 1664.[6] I will copy one of the affiches that came from the Théâtre du Marais. It begins by announcing that the troop were " Les Comediens Dv Roy Entretenvs par sa Maieste," which seems not to have been quite warrantable—and then goes on :—

" Comme les diuertissemens enjouez sont de saison nous croyons vous bien regaller en vous promettant pour Mardy iij iour de Fevrier,

[1] Despois, *Le Théâtre Français sous Louis XIV.,* 141 note 2.

[2] *Œuvres de Scarron,* ed. 1737, viii. 432, 433.

[3] Reprinted by M. Fournel in his *Petites Comédies Rares ou Curieuses du 17ᵉ siècle,* vol. i. M. Fournel had previously given the affiche in question in his *Curiosités Théâtrales,* p. 104.

[4] Chappuzeau, *Le Théâtre François,* 150.

[5] *Registre de la Grange,* 18, 45.   [6] *Œuvres de Molière,* i. 8.

la plaisante *Comedie* du *Iodelet Maistre* de Monsieur Scaron   Avec une *Danse* de *Scaramouche* qui ne peut manquer de vous plaire beaucoup

"A Vendredi sans faute les *Amours* du *Capitan Matamore* ou *L'Illusion Comiqve* de Monsieur de *Corneille* l'aisné

"En attendant les superbes machines de la *Conqveste* de la *Toison D'Or*

"C'est a l'Hostel du Marais Vieille rue du Temple, a deux heures "

This affiche appeared probably some time in the third quarter of the 17th century.

The music in the Paris theatres in the 17th century was of a simple kind.[1]   Chappuzeau wrote:—

"There are generally six musicians, and the most capable men are chosen.   Formerly they were placed either behind the stage, or in the wings, or in a recess between the stage and the parterre, as in a parquet.   Latterly they have been put into one of the boxes at the back, where they make much more noise than they would anywhere else.   It is well that they should know by heart the two last verses of the act, so that they may begin to play at once without waiting for some one to cry out *Ioüez!* which often happens." [2]

In those plays of Molière's which were called "Comédies-Ballets," such as *Les Fâcheux, Le Mariage Forcé,* and others, a ballet with music was given as an interlude between the acts, and at the end; and the Théâtre du Marais seems to have had a specialty for what were called "pièces à machines," which were probably accompanied by music of some kind.   But usually there was little music in the theatres at this period. When the Palais Royal theatre was given to Lulli after Molière's death for the Académie Royale de Musique, or the Opera, he obtained from the king an order limiting the number of singers in the theatres, properly called, to two, and of the musicians ("les violons") to six.[3]   This order, it seems, had to be renewed.

As a rule, tragedies were played in the winter months and comedy in summer.   "The great authors," says Chappuzeau,[4] " do not wish to have their plays acted except between All Saints Day and Easter, when the court is at the Louvre or at

---

[1] See the pamphlet by M. Jules Bonnassies, *La Musique à la Comédie Française.*

[2] *Le Théâtre François,* 146, 147.

[3] *Registre de la Grange,* 142, 169, 295.   Also M. Bonnassies' pamphlet just quoted, 14, 17, 20.

[4] *Le Théâtre François,* 69.

Saint Germain." But this custom was perhaps observed more strictly at the Hôtel de Bourgogne and at the Marais than at the Palais Royal, for Molière could not always bind himself to it absolutely. He conformed to the usage with all the tragedies played at his theatre except Racine's *La Thébaïde* (his first play), first acted 20th June 1664; but with many of his own comedies he was probably guided by circumstances. It may be said, however, that most of his own five-act plays were brought out in the winter months; and it is possible that if the *Misanthrope* had appeared in the winter instead of in June, the audiences might have been a little larger. The *Avare*, a play in prose, was first acted on a 9th of September, but one can hardly suppose that if it had been first played on a 9th of January its failure would have been virtually less.

The hour at which the theatres opened got later as the century advanced.[1] Under Louis XIII. performances began generally at three o'clock. Twelve was the customary hour for dinner, but as some of the better classes began to dine a little later they wished to go later to the theatre. In Molière's time performances were due to begin at four. But four o'clock meant if everybody was ready at that time. Grimarest has told how Molière insisted that the performance of the *Malade Imaginaire* on the 17th of February 1673 should begin at four precisely.[2] Alas! it was the last time that Molière ever went on the stage. In 1685 the actors made a law among themselves that those who were not ready to begin their parts at a quarter past five should be fined thirty sous.[3]

We have seen that in the 17th century in France tennis-courts were often converted more or less temporarily into theatres. Such was the case with Molière's two first theatres in Paris; and the Théâtre du Marais had been originally a tennis-court. The Hôtel de Bourgogne had been built as a theatre in the middle of the 16th century, but nothing has been said to show that its shape inside was not like that of a tennis-court. The Palais Royal theatre, where Molière played for twelve years, was the theatre in the Palais Cardinal

---

[1] Despois, *Le Théâtre Français sous Louis XIV.*, 144-46; V. Fournel, *Curiosités Théâtrales*, 109.

[2] *Vie de Molière*, 155.

[3] Bonnassies, *Comédie Française: Histoire Administrative*, 129 note 3 to preceding page.

which Richelieu had built for himself. The theatre stood in the right wing of the palace, close to the commencement of the present Rue de Valois, which begins at the Rue Saint Honoré, at one side of the Place du Palais Royal. And on the side of the building now known as the Conseil d'État, at the corner of the Rue de Valois, there is a marble tablet bearing the inscription :—" Ici s'élevait la salle de spectacle du Palais Cardinal, inaugurée en 1641, occupée par la troupe de Molière de 1661 à 1673, et par l'Académie Royale de Musique depuis 1673 jusqu'en 1763." Sauval, one of the chroniclers of the history of Paris, a contemporary of Molière though his book was not published until 1724, describes the theatre rather ambiguously, though he seems to say that it had undergone alteration. Inside, it was an oblong room with four walls at right angles. Sauval says that "it was not more than 9 fathoms (toises) wide, the space intended for the audience was 10 or 11 fathoms deep, and yet it contained as many as 4000 persons."[1] This is clearly impossible. There were two rows of boxes, one above the other, until Easter 1671, when a third or top row was added.[2] But the boxes on the side-walls were not rounded in front, and the occupants had to turn to the right or to the left to see the stage. Ladies who went to the play were seated there, and they enjoyed the comedy. A few seats for men, chiefly for the dandies, were placed on the stage. There was, of course, the parterre or the pit, and there was the amphitheatre. I think that the amphitheatre consisted of rows of raised seats behind the parterre and facing the stage. People there were far from the scene, but the places must have been considered good, for the price charged for them was relatively high. An extract from Hubert's Register for the year 1672-73, giving the prices of places in the theatre, which I quote in the next paragraph but one, shows that on one occasion there were 394 tickets taken for the parterre and only 60 for the amphitheatre; on another day there were 514 persons in the parterre. Hubert had been a member of the troop at the Palais Royal for some years, and must have known how the audience was placed. But a German professor, Herr Fritsche, who tried to throw light on Sauval's

[1] *Les Antiquités de Paris*, ii. 161, 162; iii. 47 (first pagination).
[2] *Registre de La Grange*, 123.

account of the interior of the Palais Royal theatre, estimated that the parterre might hold 300 persons and the amphitheatre 700.[1] I cannot but think that Herr Fritsche was mistaken. It is not likely that the parterre, the popular and the cheapest part of the house, should have been so much smaller than the amphitheatre. Sauval says that Richelieu's theatre was better than the others, in that the floor of the parterre sloped downwards towards the stage.

The prices of the different places at the Palais Royal were: the parterre or pit, where no one was seated, cost 15 sous (there were 20 sous in the livre or franc, as it is now called); the third row of boxes, 1 livre; the second row of boxes, or "loges hautes," 1 livre 10 sous; the amphitheatre, 3 livres; the first row of boxes and the seats on the stage (called "le théâtre"), 5 livres 10 sous.[2] In the 17th century "le théâtre" was held to mean that portion of the house devoted to the stage. The charges for all places in the theatre were high in comparison with those of our time, and sometimes the prices of most of the places were raised. This was called "jouer au double," or "à l'extraordinaire." The prices in the parterre, in the third and second row of boxes, were in fact doubled; they rose to 30 sous, 2 livres, and 3 livres respectively. A seat in the amphitheatre rose from 3 livres to 5 livres 10 sous. The first row of boxes and the seats on the stage remained unchanged at 5 livres 10 sous. Performances were given "au double" on one or more days when a new play by a known author was being acted and public curiosity was excited. But even with La Grange's Register before one, and comparing the receipts taken on the first five, ten, or twenty days on which any of Molière's comedies were performed, it would be very hazardous to try to determine when or for how long a play was acted "à l'extraordinaire" and the majority of the spectators were forced to pay double prices; and there must have

---

[1] *Le Moliériste* for June 1887 (vol. ix. 74, 75).
[2] Taschereau, *Vie de Molière*, 5th ed. preface, p. ix; Bonnassies, *Comédie Française: Histoire Administrative*, 237, 238; Despois, *Le Théâtre Français sous Louis XIV.*, 105-7.—In note to p. 106 of his book just quoted, Despois says that even in Molière's day the prices were charged in an arbitrary manner; but that Hubert's Register for 1672-73 proves that the places on the stage and in the best boxes were always 5 livres 10 sous. And see Despois' note to *Œuvres de Molière*, ii. 13, note 3.

been many persons who put off going to the theatre until the
ordinary charges were made. The only time during Molière's
lifetime that La Grange mentions this custom was on the
occasion of the second performance of the *Précieuses Ridicules*,
on the 2nd December 1659. Chappuzeau leads one to think
that it was quite possible that a play should be performed
twenty times "au double." He says, "If a play has a great
success, and is acted 'au double' twenty times consecutively,
the author is made rich and the actors also."[1] I cannot
contradict Chappuzeau, but I fancy that the hypothetical
event he mentions did not happen very often. It might have
happened with the *Tartuffe*; and La Grange shows that the
first seventeen performances, or thereabouts, of the *École des
Femmes*, of the *Critique de l'École des Femmes*, and of *Psyché*,
gave very high receipts.

When the Palais Royal theatre was quite full it might
perhaps have held 1000 persons.[2] At a performance of *Psyché*
"à l'ordinaire," which gave a receipt of 1316 livres, there were
944 persons present; and of these 514 were in the parterre.
From this perhaps it may be presumed that at the first
performance of the *Tartuffe* "au double," which gave 2860
livres—the highest receipt at the Palais Royal—not many
more persons were present than at the performance of *Psyché*
just mentioned. In the last-mentioned footnote Despois made
an extract from Hubert's Register for 1672-3 which I will
copy, as it shows how many persons were present at the first
performance of the *Malade Imaginaire*, given "au double,"
and how they were placed:—

	Livres.	Sous.
" Théâtre, 25 billets, ...	137	10
Loges, Cinq (5 loges entières) et 59 billets,	544	10
Amphithéâtre, 60 billets, ...	330	
Loges hautes, 81 billets, ...	343 [3]	
Loges de 3me rang, 23 billets, . . .	46	
Parterre à 30 sous, 394 billets, . . .	591	
	1992 "	

---

[1] *Le Théâtre François*, 68.
[2] Despois, *Le Théâtre Français sous Louis XIV.*, 363 note.
[3] I do not understand the figures in this line. The price of a seat in the
loges hautes "au double" was 3 livres, and 3 times 81 do not make 343.
La Grange also gives the total receipt at 1992 livres.

Despois reckoned that there were eight persons in each of the five loges, besides the 59 billets de loge; so that at this performance there were 682 persons present. The receipt was very high, but the theatre was by no means full. It is at all events clear that the parterre was the popular part of the house, and that when the parterre was full no other part of the house contained so much money. Molière knew the meaning of his words when he said that he trusted to the judgment of the parterre.

The seats on the stage were chiefly frequented by the exquisites who liked to show themselves. At a time when rich men of fashion wore expensive Venice point-lace, they naturally wished to display it. But they might have done so without annoying both the actors and the audience by their folly. Molière gives two instances of this: in the first scene of the *Fâcheux* (verse 13 *et seq.*), and in the fifth scene of the *Critique de l'École des Femmes*. As well as for men of fashion, there was a bench on the stage for poor authors, who entered gratuitously. Despois quotes a short passage [1] from Scarron's dedicatory epistle to Dame Guillemette, written in 1648: "The Hôtel de Bourgogne is filled with authors even on the stage, because, like the page-boys, they pay nothing." And Boursault, in giving an account of the first performance (at which he was present) of Racine's *Britannicus* in 1669, speaks distinctly of an authors' bench.[2] The seats upon the stage were not abolished in the Paris theatres until 1759.

With a hedge of spectators on each side movable scenery was impossible.[3] There was a sort of rough scene-painting, and if any kind of transformation was intended, the audience was willing to believe that it took place. In a tragedy represented in 1662 one of the personages exclaims, "A moi, soldats!" and instantly a sheet was let down on which was painted an army in battle array crossing a bridge.[4] In every country, stage scenery was then of the simplest kind; but it may be said that as the early French drama had been in a large measure borrowed indirectly from that of Greece and

---

[1] *Le Théâtre Français sous Louis XIV.*, 117, 118.
[2] *Œuvres de Racine*, in the Collection des Grands Écrivains de la France, ii. 226.
[3] On this matter a small book by M. Ludovic Celler may be consulted.
[4] Despois, *Le Théâtre Français sous Louis XIV.*, 127 note.

Rome, the laws of the unities which governed time and place helped to dispense French playwrights from the necessity of changing their scenes. The rude tableau once given sufficed usually for the performance of the whole play. In most of the comedies anterior to Molière the scenes were laid in a street or open place in some large town, generally near to the house where one or more of the principal personages lived; sometimes it was laid in the country, near a wood or forest. Had these stage arrangements been more complicated probably more would have been written about them; but it may be gathered that until the middle of the 17th century the actors were supposed generally to play their parts in the open air. The first of Molière's comedies in which the scene was laid in a house was the *Précieuses Ridicules*, but in many others of a later date it was laid in a "place publique," in Paris or some other town. Idle objections were made at the time against the *École des Femmes*, because the incidents described were narrated in a place where a passer-by could have heard what was said; but in putting the scene of his comedy "dans une place de ville" the dramatist was only following customary usage. For external details Molière cared very little. In those days plays were mounted with a simplicity of taste that ought to have charmed a Puritan. Despois has given[1] from a manuscript in the Bibliothèque Nationale indications of the mise en scène that was required for the tragedies of Corneille and of Racine and for most of the comedies of Molière, as they were played after 1680. For three-fourths of the tragedies we read: "le théâtre est un palais," or "un palais à volonté," with some few accessory details; and for Molière's comedies the directions given are hardly more complicated. In *Don Juan*, however, there was a change of scene between each act;[2] but in 1680 Molière's comedy in prose had been prohibited, and instead was performed a versified and altered edition of the play by Thomas Corneille. I will quote the indications for the mise en scène of Molière's three chief comedies in verse; the indications for his other plays are not very different, except in the case of the *Malade Imaginaire*, where instructions for the interludes are given:—

[1] *Le Théâtre Français sous Louis XIV.*, 410-15.
[2] *Œuvres de Molière*, v. 77 note 3.

"*Le Misanthrope.*—Le théâtre est une chambre.   Il faut six chaises, trois lettres, des bottes (?).

"*Le Tartuffe.*—Le théâtre est une chambre.   Il faut deux fauteuils, une table, un tapis dessus, deux flambeaux, une batte.

"*Les Femmes Savantes.*—Le théâtre est une chambre ; il faut deux livres (?) quatre chaises et du papier."

The actors at the Théâtre du Marais seem to have had a specialty for plays known as "pièces à machines"—plays with movable scenery.   The contrivances, however, must have been simple, and if the other two theatres did not adopt them the reason was that they did not wish to do so.   Curtains were employed for stage decorations, and the actors had to pass through them when they made their entrances and their exits.   The inside of the theatre was lighted by candles.   Some amelioration took place in this respect as time went on.   In the earlier pages of his Register La Grange speaks of some "chandeliers de cristal" bought by the troop ; they cost 138 livres and were paid for gradually.

It is curious to notice that some of the customs that were followed in the Paris theatres in Molière's day had been common in the London theatres when Shakespeare's and Jonson's comedies were first acted fifty or sixty years earlier. The necessities in each case were much the same, and they were met in the same way.

But if French actors in the 17th century did not spend much money on scenery or stage decorations, they made what amends they could to the public by dressing themselves splendidly.   It was not unusual in the first half of the century for a nobleman to give an actor a richly embroidered coat or other article of clothing.[1]   The gift was accepted gratefully, for each actor had to provide his own costumes.   In a chapter entitled "Grande dépense en habits," Chappuzeau says :—

"This article of expense to the actors is greater than one would imagine.   There are few new plays which do not cost them new clothing, and as gold and silver tinsel which tarnish very soon are not employed, a single 'habit à la romaine' will often mount to five hundred écus. [The écu was three livres.]   They would sooner be

---

[1] See Soulié, *Recherches sur Molière*, 34, 35 ; V. Fournel's edition of Scarron's *Roman Comique*, ii. 162 note ; and his *Contemporains de Molière*, iii. 83 note.   M. Marty Laveaux shows that the legend is at least doubtful which says that Richelieu gave Bellerose "un habit magnifique" to play Dorante in Corneille's *Menteur*. *Œuvres de P. Corneille*, iv. 126.

sparing in anything else to give satisfaction to the public, and there is more than one actor whose wardrobe is worth more than ten thousand livres. It is true that when they play a piece solely for the king's pleasure the Gentlemen of the Chamber are told to give to each actor a sum of a hundred écus, or of four hundred livres, for his apparel; and if it happens that one actor has to represent two or three personages he receives money due for two or three." [1]

La Grange, speaking only for himself, drew up a memorandum "of the moneys he had received for clothes worn in the plays that were written for court amusements." He shows that 2000 livres were given to him, but he added: "As what the king gave was not sufficient to meet the necessary expenses, the said clothes have cost me more than two other thousand livres out of my shares in the profits of the theatre." [2]

The "habit à la romaine" mentioned by Chappuzeau was worn in all tragedies taken from ancient history; it was the conventional term employed in contradistinction to the "habit à la française" worn in modern plays. Tragedies were also often played in court dress; this was handsome and therefore costly. Contemporary comedies were played in the costume of the period, and, as may be understood, the clothing of the men was more elaborate than that of the women. In the *Médecin Malgré Lui*, every one except Léandre, the lover, might have been dressed simply enough; but in the *Misanthrope* an expensive costume was absolutely necessary for all the actors. La Grange's wardrobe must have cost him a good deal, for all of his parts required that he should be nicely dressed. [3]

Disorders in the Paris theatres in the 17th and 18th centuries seem to have been frequent. [4] In 1635 pages and footmen were forbidden to go to the theatre wearing swords; and Scarron in his *Roman Comique* (1650) complains bitterly of the disturbances in the parterre. In Molière's time all the men belonging to the king's household arrogated to themselves the right of entering the theatre without payment. Molière

---

[1] *Le Théâtre François*, 111, 112.   [2] *Registre*, 144.
[3] There is not much satisfactory knowledge on this subject. M. Fournel has a chapter on theatrical costumes in his *Curiosités Théâtrales*, so has M. Bonnassies in his *Histoire Administrative de la Comédie Française*. I have seen an article by M. Émile Lamé in a review called *Le Présent* (No. 13) from which M. Fournel made short extracts, but this article refers only to tragedy.
[4] Chappuzeau, *Le Théâtre François*, 153-55; Grimarest, *Vie de Molière*, 70-75; Bonnassies, *La Comédie Française: Histoire Administrative*, 328-35; V. Fournel, *Les Contemporains de Molière*, iii. 196 note 1.

obtained from the king a suspension of these free entries. Then there was an uproar, in which the porter of the theatre was killed in defending himself against the king's musketeers. Men belonging to the king's household were great offenders, and pages and servants in livery were often the cause of disturbance.

The tax known as " le droit des pauvres " may be mentioned, though it was not formally established until a quarter of a century after Molière's death. We have seen that when Molière was strolling in the provinces his troop were taxed on several occasions for the benefit of the poor in the town where performances were given. In Paris the prices of all the places in the theatre were increased by a sixth in the year 1699.[1] This extra charge was supposed to go altogether to the poor, but probably some of it was spent in another way. There is no reason to distrust Chappuzeau when he says that the actors as a body were good to the poor;[2] but from the little La Grange has said on the matter it would seem that the charities were individual. The only considerable sum he mentioned as given by the troop was on the 26th of March 1662, when he wrote: "Donné au curé de la paroisse 100 livres pour les pauvres." La Thorillière, one of the troop at the Palais Royal, kept a register for the year 1663-64, and there, where the details of daily expenses are given with greater minuteness than by La Grange, it may be seen that various small sums of money were given away in charity. For the year they amounted to 114 livres 9 sous.

It would be interesting to know what was the feeling among ladies of good birth in Paris in the middle of the seventeenth century as to going to the theatre. We can understand that some thought it more or less derogatory to go there, and that others were not so fastidious. It is certain, at all events, that rich people used to bespeak the services of a troop of actors to play at their houses on a certain day. This was an aristocratic entertainment, and it was a pleasant way for those who could afford it to give amusement to their friends. There is little information as to visits made by the actors at the Hôtel de Bourgogne, or those at the Marais, but La Grange

[1] Despois, *Le Théâtre Français sous Louis XIV.*, 107 and 240-45; V. Fournel, *Curiosités Théâtrales*, 116.
[2] *Le Théâtre François*, 90.

shows that Molière's troop often went "en visite" to private houses during the first five or six years they were in Paris. After that time fewer visits are recorded, though five were made in February and March 1669, within the first month after the *Tartuffe* was allowed to appear. I have reckoned that from October 1658 to February 1673 Molière's troop were asked to play at private houses about sixty-five times. Commands sent by the king are not included in this number. The visit usually took place on a day when there was no public performance, and the actors always received a gratification. For all visits made by Molière and his comrades the gratification averaged about 400 livres. Chappuzeau has only a few lines about the visits made by the troops; he does say, however, that when a person of quality engages the services of a body of actors, carriages, etc., are put at their disposal.

"Orders are given that they shall be received very civilly. They are treated with kindness, and they always return in a happy mood, as everybody prides himself upon showing good feeling and liberality to the actors, who, on their part, spare no pains to give pleasure. They do not stop to inquire if they are put to much expense; and if they get presents from the court and from the town, if they receive money from the king and from the public, they do not deceive themselves. They regard it as a mark of honour, and all the actors and actresses vie with one another as to who shall have the most magnificent clothes." [1]

Chappuzeau also tells (pp. 106, 107) how the actors were treated when the king commanded their presence. They were furnished with carriages; and when they went to Saint Germain or to Chambord, or wherever the court was staying, lodgings were found for them, and each one had two écus a day, their servants in proportion, and certain articles of consumption were given. Then follow some effusive lines extolling the consideration of great noblemen who pleased the king by receiving the actors in a kindly manner.

While Molière's troop belonged to Monsieur, Louis XIV. gave them at different times presents of money, known as gratifications. In August 1665 the king signified his wish that the troop should belong to him, and he promised them 6000 livres a year pension.[2] Nothing was given then, and perhaps by some oversight no pension was paid to them

---

[1] *Le Théâtre François*, 110.   [2] *Registre de La Grange*, 76.

in the spring of 1666; but in February 1667 they received 12,000 livres—the promised pension for the two years, 1665-66 and 1666-67.[1] The reader will remember that the theatrical year began after the Easter holidays; it is necessary, therefore, to couple two years together. At Easter 1671 the royal pension was increased to 7000 livres, and so it remained until Molière's death. I will now put in a tabular form the gratifications and the pensions that Molière's troop received from the king. The figures in brackets refer to the pages in La Grange's Register, the source of authority.

SUMS OF MONEY GIVEN BY LOUIS XIV. TO MOLIÈRE'S TROOP.

Livres.

October	1660	(28),	3,000, ...	gratification.
May	1662	(43),	1,500, ...	,,
August	1662	(46),	14,000 (in three instalments), .	,,
October	1663	(59),	3,300, ...	,,
May	1664	(65),	4,000, ...	,,
August	1664	(66),	3,000, ...	,,
October	1664	(68),	3,000, ...	,,
February	1667	(86),	12,000 (for '65-66 and '66-67),	pension.
November	1667	(91),	6,000 (for '67-68), . . .	,,[2]
November	1668	(99),	3,000, ...	gratification.
April	1669	(103),	6,000 (for '68-69), . . .	pension.
February	1670	(109),	12,000, ...	gratification.[3]
March	1670	(110),	6,000 (for '69-70), . . .	pension.
March	1671	(119),	7,000 (for '70-71), . . .	,,
April	1672	(130),	7,000 (for '71-72), . . .	,,
March	1673	(141),	7.000 (for '72-73), . . .	,,
			97,800	

There were two other gratifications given not included in the above list, because La Grange did not state the total amount received. He spoke (Register, p. 116) of a visit to Chambord in October 1670, and (p. 129) of a visit to Saint Germain in February 1672. In both cases he said how much each member of the troop received, but he lumped together

[1] *Registre de La Grange*, 86.

[2] The pension was paid this year in November 1667, instead of at the end of the theatrical year at Easter 1668.

[3] M. Mesnard reckons this gratification of 12,000 livres as payment of two years' pension (*Notice biographique sur Molière*, 403 and note 2). But La Grange (p. 109) states that the 12,000 livres were given for two journeys, to Saint Germain and to Chambord. Also (p. 110) in March 1670 La Grange states that 6000 livres pension were paid for the past year; and (p. 119) in March 1671 that 7000 livres pension were paid for the past year. Moreover, the pension for these two years came to 13,000 livres, not 12,000.

the gratification and the money (two écus a day) given for "nourriture." I imagine from his accounts, which in these cases are not very clear, that for the first visit the troop received about 6000 livres as gratification, and for the second visit about 2400 livres—making together 8400 livres. These, added to the 97,800 livres, make a total of 106,200 livres which Molière's troop received in pensions and gratifications from Louis XIV.

But this money was given for services rendered, and I believe that the actors fairly earned it all. No doubt they had a full sense of the honour of receiving so often the king's command to play before them, and this honour certainly gave them a material support against their rivals during the first few years they were in Paris. Yet the annoyance of being called away from their work, often suddenly or for long periods, must have been considerable, and must also have entailed upon the actors individually expenses for smarter clothes. I reckon, on account of their journeys to court, that they were prevented from playing in their own theatre 196 times. Now, 106,200 divided by 196 gives almost 542; and it will be said presently that the average daily receipt at the Palais Royal was 511 livres. If these figures are correct, they show that the actors gave their sovereign a good return for his liberality.

It is unwise, however, to wish to put everything into a profit and loss account, and often it cannot be done. Molière's prefaces show that he worked very hard for the king's pleasure; but Louis XIV., in spite of his colossal egotism, knew that he was well served, and he proved himself a good friend to the poet at a time when other assistance would have been of no avail. For court festivities of different kinds Molière wrote twelve plays. All, or nearly all, of these were known as comédies-ballets, the subject of the play admitting a ballet to be introduced at the end of each act. Some of these comedies are admirable examples of his lighter humour, and there is no doubt that the king preferred the poet's amusing comedies to his more serious work. During Molière's lifetime *Sganarelle ou le Cocu Imaginaire* was played at court nine times, the *Misanthrope* not once.[1] The fact that Louis XIV.

[1] *Œuvres de Molière*, i. 557.

wished the actors of the Palais Royal to play so often before him gave them a moral protection which was undeniably valuable to them. Ten more places might not have been taken in the parterre if the king were known to have laughed at Monsieur Jourdain being hoaxed by the Grand Turk; but it is likely enough that the king's laughter would have sent fifty more persons into the best boxes, and would have made half of the gallants in the town rush to secure a place on the stage. In a note to his Register (pp. 45, 46), La Grange, after recording that the troop had been at Saint Germain from the 24th of June to the 11th of August 1662, says: "The Queen Mother sent for Floridor and Montfleury, actors at the Hôtel de Bourgogne, who solicited her to procure for them the advantage to serve the king, Molière's troop giving them great cause for jealousy." This expression of feeling was quite unusual with La Grange, for he very rarely alludes to prejudices or rivalries between the different troops.

CHAPTER X

DIFFERENT ASPECTS OF THE HÔTEL DE BOURGOGNE AND
PALAIS ROYAL THEATRES—MOLIÈRE AS AN ACTOR

THERE is, I think, sufficient evidence to show that the play-going public in Paris regarded Molière's theatre and the Hôtel de Bourgogne from different points of view. It would be too much to say that each theatre had its own followers, yet the best plays acted in each house gave entertainment of a different kind. Molière's troop excelled in comedy; the other troop—"les grands comédiens," as they were called—were thought to excel in tragedy. The Hôtel de Bourgogne had long been the privileged and official theatre, and in days when privileges were understood such distinctions were valuable. The actors there since the early part of the reign of Louis XIII. bore the title of "la troupe royale"; and not many years later, under Richelieu's government, they were allowed a yearly pension from the king. These were marks of honour on which they piqued themselves, and of which they thought they had reason to be proud. The actors at the Marais had no such distinctions; and, as has been said here already, were less fortunate than either of their rivals. Conservative minded people liked to keep up the traditions of the Hôtel, they gave their support to the theatre which for so many years had been the privileged playhouse; and when Molière and his friends came to Paris and made a third troop, the same feeling of conservatism operated against them, but with stronger force.

Many of those who went oftenest to the theatre regarded Molière's two first one-act comedies, the *Précieuses Ridicules* and *Sganarelle ou le Cocu Imaginaire,* as trifles—they called them farces—and they looked upon the new troop at the Petit Bourbon as interlopers who filled their pit by acting plays without serious intention or ennobling purpose. A

254

little later, during the first few years that Molière was at the Palais Royal, this feeling became stronger. There were many men who were accustomed to the old, dull style of plays, and thought they liked them best; others, who were not fastidious, welcomed Molière, because he strove to make the theatre a place of amusement where comedy might show her features. Those who prided themselves on their good taste were disagreeably astonished, for they thought him an intruder who wished to destroy their long-established ideas, and who was bent on leading the public in a wrong direction. It is curious to realise this condition of mind; it is difficult for us now to imagine that a quick-witted people should not enjoy a good and laughable comedy when they saw it well acted. But from one cause or another there were a fair number who did not do so. Jealousy was one reason, another was that men clung to custom because they were used to it; and so prejudice got the better of their understanding. As a new author, new actor, and chief manager of a new troop in Paris, Molière had many difficulties to overcome. During the performances of the *Fâcheux*, the *École des Femmes*, the *Critique de l'École des Femmes*, and the *Impromptu de Versailles*, his theatre was the rendezvous of the wags and idle men of fashion, who went to laugh at his pictures of their own conceits because they thought it was the proper sort of thing to do—

> "And coxcombs, alike in their failings alone,
> Adopting his portraits are pleased with their own."

They thought him a clever and impertinent fellow who had learned the knack of his trade, and though they were amused by his wit they considered his business a poor one, and they jeered at him because he did it very well.

The great dandies could go where they liked and do what they liked; they belonged to their own set. But men of acquired position were bound to be careful of their reputation. They thought they would be lowered in their friends' esteem if they were known to be admirers of Molière, and if they said openly that they preferred his theatre to the Hôtel de Bourgogne. They spoke condescendingly of the *Précieuses*; and though the *Cocu Imaginaire* was quite inoffensive, few judges, public professors, or doctors in good practice, would have declared that they admired the cleverness of the characterisation shown in the personage of Sganarelle. Serious plays were allowed to be a pastime for a gentleman, but not plays at which all the crowd was delighted to laugh. "Noblesse oblige," and to join in such laughter would be derogatory.

This was, I believe, the feeling during the first five or six years of Molière's career in Paris. The thoughts of those who, between 1658 and 1673, looked upon Molière as a clever buffoon were in a measure mitigated as they learned by degrees that so many of his drollest comedies were played and laughed at in the king's presence before they were put on the stage at the Palais Royal. By opening men's minds a little Molière did something to lessen their hostility. But even to the last his position as an actor who played the most ludicrous parts in his own comedies—the various Sganarelles, George Dandin, Monsieur de Pourceaugnac, Scapin—militated against his position as author of what were known to be the best comedies that had been written in France. The author of the *École des Femmes*, the *Misanthrope*, the *Tartuffe*, the *Femmes Savantes*, could not live down the obloquy that was heaped upon the actor who, of his own accord, made himself appear ridiculous for the amusement of the pit. *La Gazette*, the official journal of the time, sometimes mentioned plays that were played at court, and added the author's name if the actors engaged belonged to the Hôtel de Bourgogne, but it was apparently always hostile to Molière. Mention was made in its pages of the deaths of all the well-known writers of the time, but of Molière's it said nothing.[1] When a comedy of his was played before the court some sort of good word was thought necessary in speaking of the performance, but more often than not the title of the play was not given. Envy and ill-will were shown by the conductors of the official journal, because Molière's comedies drew the public away from the old and well-established theatre. The fact that the author was also funny on the stage made certain people look down upon him quite as much as his supposed attacks upon religion annoyed others. Molière knew all this, but he went on with his work to his life's end. It is easy to condemn ignorant superciliousness when it happened so long ago; but if a parallel case presented itself now

---

[1] Despois, *Le Théâtre Français sous Louis XIV.*, 307 note 1; see also pp. 275, 276.

would our thoughts be more charitable, more evenly generous? They might be more intelligent, for the spread of education has made men more appreciative of high merit. Audiences have become larger, consequently there would be more admirers. Yet many detractors would be found because the actor or the dramatist did not act or write according to their ideas of what was best in comedy. A few months before Molière's death, Boileau begged him to confine himself to writing, and to give up acting. "You are destroying your health," he said, "for the stage is wearing you out. Why do you not give it up?" "Ah!" answered Molière with a sigh, "it is a point of honour that forbids me." Boileau replied: "You smear a Sganarelle's moustache on your face, and come on the stage to get a drubbing with a stick; that is a nice point of honour for a philosopher like you!"[1] Yes, with Molière it was a point of honour that kept him to his work. In days gone by one of the reasons why he did not want to become secretary to the Prince de Conti was that he knew that his troop, who had long been with him, were dependent upon him for their subsistence. And about twelve hours before his death he made the same answer to his friends, who tried to induce him not to go on the stage that afternoon; but to no purpose. Molière had his ambition, and to shine as an actor was part of it. He felt that he had to play his Sganarelles as well as his Orgon, his Alceste and his Harpagon, and he thought more of the needs of those engaged in his theatre than of his own comfort. The outside world did not know his troubles, and his enemies wished only that their rival's power might be stopped.

Many more new plays were acted at the Hôtel de Bourgogne than at the Palais Royal. The comparatively long runs enjoyed by most of Molière's comedies dispensed him and his comrades in a measure from changing their programme so frequently as was the case at the rival theatre. Yet they would gladly have changed it oftener had moderately good plays with some show of life been offered to them. It will, however, be seen presently that both Molière and the other

[1] For Montchesnay's version of this story given in the *Bolœana*, see *Œuvres de Molière*, x. 414, 415; for Louis Racine's, virtually the same but shorter and better told, see *Œuvres de J. Racine*, 1st ed. i. 262, 263; 2nd ed. i. 270, 271.

members of his troop found out by experience that an old play that he had written filled their theatre better than a new play by another author. Possibly, too, Molière and his fellow-actors were difficult to please in judging of other men's work. But they all had a vote in the choice or rejection of a new play, they were all working together for their common welfare, and their object was to draw the public to their doors. From 1658 to 1673 Molière, as head manager, put on to his stage twenty-eight comedies of his own, and twenty-three new plays by other authors; at the Hôtel de Bourgogne during the same period, more than one hundred new plays were acted.[1] The repertory at the Hôtel was therefore larger and more varied. Most or all of Corneille's best tragedies after the *Cid* (1636) were first acted there, though that was before the time that concerns us now; and all of Racine's plays, dating from *Andromaque* (1667), the first that made his name famous, were also brought out there. It is impossible to suppose that Molière would not have welcomed plays by well-known writers had they been willing to entrust him and his comrades with their work. The feeling that his troop could not play tragedy will not altogether account for the difference in the number of new plays brought out at his theatre and at the Hôtel de Bourgogne, for among the twenty-three new plays, not written by Molière, produced at the Petit Bourbon and at the Palais Royal, there were eleven tragedies, eleven comedies, and one pastoral. And in all of these ventures there was but one moderate success at the Petit Bourbon—Gilbert's comedy, *La Vraie et la Fausse Précieuse*; and one substantial success at the Palais Royal—Corneille's tragedy, *Tite et Bérénice*. By a substantial success I mean a large number of performances as a new play, which, when taken together, would give an average money receipt well above the average daily receipt at the theatre. On a later page I shall show the correctness of this assertion. Of the eleven comedies five were by de Visé; and his plays, judging by the receipts taken, seem to have had no other merit

---

[1] Despois, *Le Théâtre Français sous Louis XIV.*, 8. On one point here I think Despois was mistaken. He says that from 1659 to 1673 at Molière's theatre hardly more than fifteen new plays were acted, other than those written by Molière himself. I have gone through La Grange's Register and have counted twenty-three.

than making a temporary change in the programme. With one exception, therefore, all the real successes gained at Molière's two theatres were in plays that he himself had written. At the Petit Bourbon old plays, not written by Molière, were acted very often; at the Palais Royal they became by degrees less common, and in the last years were rarely seen. During the twelve years that Molière was at the Palais Royal, there were four periods of more than twelve months each in which no new play, not written by him, was brought out at his theatre.[1] But though his comedies appeared again and again, when they were no longer new, La Grange has shown that during the fourteen years he was with Molière the income of each actor in the troop averaged, one year with another, 3690 livres—equal now to £738 sterling. La Grange's Register shows also that at least four-fifths of this sum was made from the production of Molière's comedies.

It is not known what were the number of performances of Corneille's and Racine's tragedies, nor the receipts they made; but it may at least be presumed that Molière's comedies produced on the whole larger sums than did the comedies at the Hôtel de Bourgogne, acted between 1659 and 1673. The best of these, as we should judge of them now, probably are Quinault's *La Mère Coquette*, Racine's *Les Plaideurs*—his only comedy — and Montfleury's *La Femme Juge et Partie*. These may still be read with pleasure; and there are others that may well have given amusement at the time, for they were intended as actualities, having reference to passing events and contemporary manners.[2] Rival jealousies had much to do with preventing authors from offering their plays to Molière. Also, to put the matter plainly, in the warfare that followed the *École des Femmes*, Molière set the men of fashion against him by telling them that they did not know a good play when they saw one, and he angered authors by telling them that they chose the worst possible way to determine whether a play

---

[1] From 21 May '61 to 3 Nov. '62; from 22 Dec. '62 to 18 Jan. '64; from 21 Feb. '66 to 4 March '67; from 15 Jan. '69 to 1 Aug. '70.

[2] M. V. Fournel has done a good deal to explain some of the comedies of this period in his three volumes, *Les Contemporains de Molière*, though for the most part the plays he included in his collection are not the best known. He omitted purposely comedies that had been often reprinted.

was good or bad. The pedants had been surprised at the success gained by his open way of looking at the comedy of life, which to them was a new thing; and they did not like being told that Aristotle and Horace had little to do with the matter, and that they themselves were dunderheads for thinking about them. Such was the gist of Molière's meaning, but he wrote with comic satire and expressed himself with becoming courtesy.[1]

Molière looked at society from a much larger and more liberal point of view, and he had a much truer knowledge of the world and its ways, than any other French dramatist in the 17th century. He wrote his light plays—what were then considered farces—because he knew that light plays when they are good are always enjoyed. Had he disdained popular comedy his name would be less loved in France than it is now, and I think also that as a comic dramatist he would be less highly esteemed. One of the good signs of his intellect is that he knew when and how to hide it. His smaller plays show that he possessed the uncommon but most necessary qualification for a comic dramatist—the power of making an audience merry and joyous with manly vigour; and this same quality was, during his lifetime, better appreciated by the homely understanding of those in the pit than by the patented culture of the critics. Fastidiousness is apt to be a bane in all kinds of criticism. It may not always be easy to know how to avoid it, but it will prevent good judgment as surely as dulness, or destroy it as surely as ill-nature.

Ever since the renaissance of the drama in the middle of the 16th century, tragedy had always been more highly esteemed in Paris than comedy, and when comedies became more frequent—dating from the early plays of Corneille, about 1630—they were generally of an exalted kind and showed little of the humours of men. Molière was in truth the father of comedy in France. He was the first French dramatist who introduced true and sprightly characterisation into written comedy. This was then a new thing, a new event; it was a departure from the well beaten track. But

---

[1] See the speech of Dorante in the *Critique de l'École des Femmes*, sc. 6, beginning: " Vous êtes de plaisantes gens avec vos règles " (*Œuvres de Molière*, iii. 357). But the whole scene should be read. In some editions this is given as scene 7.

many people still preferred the old, half-stately, inanimate pictures which to them had become classical. Those who liked to be considered good judges of a play thought much of decorum in comedies. They had seen no examples of faithful and comic portraiture, and did not know what it meant, but they insisted upon a show of outward good breeding in the personages before them. They liked the "genre noble" on the stage much in the same way that in everyday life they preferred good manners to rusticity. Their misfortune was that they thought good manners and laughter were not compatible. And when they first saw short comedies in prose that were really laughable without being vulgar, they could not disconnect them in their own minds from the coarse farces which had been so long in vogue, but which because of their vulgarity had almost disappeared from the large theatres. For some years past comedy and farce had been considered as things distinct, and in the middle of the 17th century farce was banished from the Hôtel de Bourgogne as being low. The "grands comédiens" piqued themselves upon maintaining the "genre noble" at their theatre. The troop at the Marais were obliged to be less proud, and they continued to play farce, probably of an improved kind.[1] But, in fact, comedy in an animate sense hardly came to life before Molière showed what it was and what might be learned from it. The critics who talked over a play they had just seen got their ideas of comedy from Aristotle and from Horace, and were exacting that what they thought were rules should be observed. Affectation of culture with regard to plays was quite the mode, but three-quarters of the public, who took the good things provided for them as they were meant, knew more about the matter than the most determined of the pedants.

Before Molière had been two years in Paris the troop at the Hôtel de Bourgogne perceived that the actors at the Petit Bourbon theatre were guided by fresh ideas, and that new principles in the art of elocution had been taught them. In his *Précieuses Ridicules* (sc. 9) Molière pretended to laugh at his own troop for reciting just as one talks, instead of speaking in a high-flown manner and claiming the plaudits of the audience when the verses were considered fine ; and four years

---

[1] V. Fournel, *Les Contemporains de Molière*, iii. pp. xvii, xviii.

later, in his *Impromptu de Versailles* (sc. 1), he expressed the same ideas at greater length. Though some of his satire may have told against himself because he spoke his words truly and with plainness of speech, what he wrote serves to show the difference of manner at the two theatres. This difference in the style of acting at the two theatres is a point that should be remembered. The frequent use of the word " déclamation," employed when speaking of the acting at the Hôtel de Bourgogne, helps also to show that the players there tried to adopt a grand manner becoming to the dignity of tragedy. "Déclamation" may have been a conventional term; still, had a simpler manner of utterance been common perhaps a simpler word would have been used. A grand manner is exceedingly impressive when it is carried out perfectly; otherwise the fall may be woful. Molière saw that his rivals were absurd, and he laughed at them; they were made to feel his ridicule, and they smarted under it. I say nothing about the players at the Théâtre du Marais, for in the hot dispute occasioned by the success of the *École des Femmes* (first performed 26th December 1662) the actors at the Marais, so far as can be judged now, were silent. They were known to be inferior to the two other troops, and it is not told how far they sided with either party in the quarrel.

Grimarest in his biography of Molière (1705) refers to the poet's satire against the acting of the troop at the Hôtel de Bourgogne :—

"He [Molière] had very good reason to attack them for their bad taste. They did not know any principles of their art, nor even that there were any. Their only idea of acting was in high-flown and turgid elocution ; all their parts were performed in the same way. They showed neither emotion nor passion, and yet Beauchâteau and Mondory were applauded because they ranted their lines in a pompous manner. Molière, who knew what acting should be, was annoyed to see it so badly done and that an ignorant public should applaud it. He endeavoured to teach his own troop to be natural ; and before his time, in comedy, and before Baron, whom he trained in serious parts, as I shall say later, the play of the actors was distressing to persons who had a sense of taste. Unfortunately we see now that the majority of actors do not study the principles of their art, and that they are already losing those that Molière had inculcated into his troop." [1]

---

[1] *Vie de Molière*, 30, 31.

It is not unlikely that Grimarest got most of his ideas of Molière's acting from Baron, who had been Molière's pupil, and to whom when a boy the poet had shown marks of affection. Baron was a proud and vain man, he was the greatest actor of tragedy in his time, and Grimarest's depreciatory remarks on the actors may have been Baron's thoughts rather than his.

At all events, it may be fairly gathered from Molière's satire against the actors at the Hôtel de Bourgogne, that a pompous and declamatory mode of recitation was in vogue at that theatre, and that he disapproved of it because it was ridiculous and false. If a vicious style of acting was common in tragedy, one cannot suppose that the same faults, with certain differences, were not also seen in comedy. Long speeches were frequent in all plays in verse, and there an actor, in his endeavour to maintain "le grand art," could show good elocution or mouth his lines abominably. Though Molière's performances in tragedy were generally thought to be poor, he had very good eyes to see, and his sense of what was fitting told him that his rivals, in their enthusiasm to show fine acting, passed the bounds of rational conduct. Nearly all the five-act plays at the Hôtel de Bourgogne were in verse, and the actors there tried to set off the force of the lines and to display their powers of elocution by loud and bombastic utterance. They had not learned to speak their speech trippingly on the tongue. Their manner was often terribly vehement. Several tragic accidents—bursting of veins, apoplexy dying from sword-cuts, and so forth—are reported to have happened to men who could not contain their ill-judged fury while they were personating the parts they had to perform.[1] Perhaps, if similar faults had not been common in England two generations earlier, Shakespeare would not have made Hamlet give his advice to the players.

Before speaking of Molière's acting it was necessary to say something about that at the Hôtel de Bourgogne, the oldest and principal theatre in Paris, and also of the public taste in acting when Molière came to Paris and for some years later. Thinking moderately, one may say that both Molière's troop and their rivals might have learned something one from the

[1] V. Fournel, *Curiosités Théâtrales*, chap. xiv.

other, had they been able to do so. It is certain that Molière's ideas of acting in tragedy were much opposed to those of his contemporaries. They liked the conventional bombast which the tragedies of the time demanded more or less; he was in favour of simple speech, and perhaps pressed his point too strongly. In tragedy he was generally thought to be a very indifferent actor, and judging by the few tragedies that were played at his theatre with the much larger number performed at the Hôtel de Bourgogne, it would seem that the common opinion was not altogether wrong. If Molière had been a good tragic actor some expression of opinion to that effect would have come down to us. Because he could act comedy well and bring the public to his theatre to see him personate his own characters, his rivals were not slow in jeering at him when he failed in another direction. If Molière's ideas as to acting in tragedy were sound, they did not find favour with his contemporaries, or he did not give them proper effect. The public, however, liked to see tragedy on the stage, and for some years Molière tried to satisfy the public taste. But the bent of his mind was too realistic for tragedy; his instincts ran in another way. He had long been the head of his own troop, many of his comrades were his old friends, they trusted him, and they submitted to be guided by his teaching. In comedy his lessons produced very good effect, but tragedy was never welcomed at his theatre.

Molière's performances in tragedy were condemned even more strongly than those of his fellow-actors; consequently the best known dramatists generally took their plays to the Hôtel de Bourgogne. Few of the comedies or of the tragedies acted there were good, but the tragedies were preferred both by the actors and the public because they gave more opportunity for inflated gesture, pompous declamation, and tearing poor passion to tatters. The public liked ranting, Molière did not, and it would seem from what he said that he would have very little of it at his theatre. If he tried to teach his comrades how to act in tragedy he was far from successful. In comedy he taught them excellently, though some years had to elapse before he could put many of his own plays on the stage. Like all other acting associations, Molière's troop had their weak points. They could not get good new plays from other authors, and when they put tragedy on to their stage the public thought they did not know how to act it. The troop at the Hôtel de Bourgogne were more fortunate in that their worst faults were glorified by those who saw them oftenest.

Very little direct contemporary evidence of Molière's acting has been preserved, and of what there is one half is hostile and the other laudatory. He was thought to be an admirable exponent of comedy, but to play tragedy abominably. These opinions appear to be extreme, but much may be said in their favour, and perhaps they are borne out by later judgments and by evidence of other kinds. The warm feeling between the actors in Molière's troop and those at the Hôtel de Bourgogne grew deeper in the year 1663 when all the playgoers in Paris were talking about the *École des Femmes* and Molière's two subsequent plays. Besides the actors at the Hôtel there were among their partisans authors and others who had a poor opinion of comedy and who looked upon tragedy as much the higher art. What passed for tragedy had always been the mainstay at the Hôtel, and when those interested in that theatre saw that Molière conceived and wrote comedy in a new and better style than they had known before, they tried to belittle it; and when they found that his acting in his own comedies was popular, they said that he was an excellent buffoon.

Most actors of repute at that time were called upon to play both in tragedy and comedy, and we are told that Molière wished to shine as an actor in the " genre noble." If this was the case, he was cured of his ambition slowly and against his will. During his stay at the Petit Bourbon his troop played tragedies much oftener than they did afterwards at the Palais Royal, and it is tolerably certain that when he put one of Corneille's tragedies on to his stage at either theatre he acted a principal part in the play. La Grange's Register shows that the receipts taken at the performances of these plays were low, and from this and other indications it may be gathered that Molière's acting in them was not considered good. In his Notice to *Don Garcie de Navarre*, Despois said: " It is not known if in tragic parts which he persisted in playing Molière was really worse than contemporary actors whom people were in the habit of applauding in the same parts, but it seems to be certain that he differed from them and that he wished to break away from routine."[1] But even if Molière's dislike to the accepted style of declamation were well founded, there might still have been fair grounds for objection against his acting in tragedy. It is difficult to believe that he could have been anything but a very indifferent tragic actor, for all the bent of his mind and of his sympathies was opposed to the somewhat exalted ideas and expressions that tragedy demands. In nearly all of his own comedies he took a principal part, and played it with success. It would seem that few have understood better the art of representing comedy on the stage; but he did not act tragedy to the satisfaction of men of his own age, and in all probability would not have done so to that of men in any other. He had a wish to play tragedy, and was deceived in his aspirations. Liston, we are told, had the same ambition ; and he also made a mistake.

Acting is seeming to be, but it wants large and often high qualifications. It certainly wants creative force and versatility. In comedy Molière seemed to be the character he wished to personate. He could personate the part he had to play in a supposed comic action so as to make the action appear lifelike and true to others. He simulated and created a pretended character so well that he awakened the ideal sensibilities of his audience, and made them see and feel the passions he strove to represent. In comedy, from a combination of various causes—sympathy, truthful observation, clear imagination or fancy, love of fun and keen sense of the ridiculous, love of good satire and knowledge of what it meant, and strong mimetic powers—he put on the right air of seeming; but in tragedy his appearance was against him, and his utterance made the matter worse. He could put on the mask of comedy and wear it as naturally as though it were his own face, keep his presence of mind—remain himself under it though he seemed to be another—while he showed comic features truly and gave true and clear expression to them in their many and various forms. But with tragedy the case was wholly different. As he had no sympathy with its counterfeits he did not understand their effects, could not get its note, could

[1] *Œuvres de Molière*, ii. 225 and 226.

not put on its mask and wear it naturally; and he could not have acted Rodrigue or Don Diègue in Corneille's *Cid* any more than Charles Mathews could have acted Othello.

We are now concerned with comedy, and there is the evidence of a frequently well-filled theatre to show that Molière's acting was highly thought of by those who saw it. He played in Paris for more than fourteen years, and unless he had been welcome to his audiences his comedies would not have been acted so often nor have made such large receipts. The characters he represented are varied and full of life, and if he could play them well, he would have been able to act well in other comedies if the parts gave possibilities of animate personification. Very shortly after his death it was said of him in the *Mercure Galant*,[1] probably by de Visé :—

"The ancients never had an actor equal to him whose loss we now lament; and Roscius, the famous actor in classic days, would have yielded to him the first place if he had lived in his time. And he [Molière] would have deserved it. He was an actor from head to foot. It seemed that he had several voices : everything spoke in him, for by a step, a smile, a wink of the eye, or by a nod of his head, he gave you more ideas than the greatest talker would have done in an hour."

A generation after the poet's death Grimarest wrote of his acting :—

"Though the composition of Molière's comedies was excellent, they were acted in such a delicate manner that even had they been indifferent they would have passed for being good. His troop was well formed, and he did not confide his characters to actors who did not know how to play them. He did not let them trust to chance, as is done now. He always took the most difficult part himself. He was not a born elocutionist like Baron. At first, even when he was in the provinces, many persons thought that he was a poor actor, perhaps because of a hiccough or convulsive movement in his throat which made his acting very disagreeable to those who did not know him. But if one observed the nicety with which he conceived a character and expressed its sentiments, one saw that he thoroughly understood the art of speaking. Habit had given him this hiccough. When he first went on the stage he found that he had a great flow of language which he could not control, and which made his acting unpleasant; then from the effort to speak his words clearly he contracted a hiccough which he never lost. But he concealed this fault by showing all the cleverness with which a part can be played. He did not fail in any intonation of voice or any gesture which could move a spectator. In his manner of speaking he left nothing to chance, as do those who, ignorant of the principles of elocution, are not certain of their play; he showed every detail of action that the meaning of the words conveyed. But if he came back to life now, he would not know his own words in the mouths of those who speak them." [1]

Grimarest was repeating here what he had heard, and in speaking of contemporary actors he wrote with some feeling against them. He was not born until 1659, and must have been a small boy when he saw Molière. And Baron, if he was his chief prompter, was only six years older. But Baron's father and mother were both actors, and he had been brought up, as it were, on the stage; he had performed certainly two parts at the Palais Royal theatre; he must have heard the members of the troop there talk of Molière's acting, and have remembered seeing him in many parts that he played.

Mlle. Poisson has long been credited with having written the account of Molière's acting in the *Mercure de France* in May 1740.[2] The authorship of that article has lately been disputed, but it will be better to speak of that a few pages later. This account of Molière's acting confirms in a measure what was said in the *Mercure Galant* and by Grimarest. It runs:—

"Nature had highly favoured his intelligence, but she did not give him those outward arts that are so necessary on the stage, especially in tragic parts. A hollow voice, hard intonations, a volubility of speech which made him precipitate his words, showed him in this respect to be much inferior to the actors at the Hôtel de Bourgogne. He knew all this, and confined himself to plays in which his faults were more easily pardoned. Even then, he had many difficulties to overcome, and his constant efforts to master the quickness of his speech, so adverse to clear articulation, brought on a hiccough which he kept until his death, and which he now and then turned to good advantage. To vary the inflexions of his voice he was the first who spoke in certain unusual tones which made people say he was a little affected, but they got accustomed to it. He not only gave great delight in parts like Mascarille, Sganarelle, Hali,[3] etc., but he excelled in characters in high comedy such as

---

[1] *Vie de Molière*, 111-13.
[2] Reprinted, *Œuvres de Molière*, iii. 383, par. 2.
[3] There seems to be a mistake here (*Œuvres de Molière*, vi. 224-26; 294). Hali is a character in the *Sicilien*, and the part was played by La Thorillière.

Arnolphe, Orgon, Harpagon. Then by truthful sentiments, by making his play clearly understood, and by all the cleverness of his art, he so fascinated his audience that they could not distinguish the personage represented from the actor who performed it. He always undertook the longest and most difficult parts, and he kept for himself the position of orator of the troop." [1]

There are few things that some people resent in one who often comes before the public more than a mannerism. Yet it is common in other arts besides acting, and not many persons who have practised their calling for a long time can divest themselves of it completely. That Molière had some mannerism is probable, but underneath it might be seen a broad intelligence and strong mimetic powers, real versatility and creative force. And it is better to notice and admire large gifts than to think of smaller matters and condemn faults which so few can avoid altogether. Outside effects have naturally much to do with the success or failure of what takes place on the stage, but the reason for and the meaning of those effects should be considered. The article in the *Mercure de France* says that Molière had a "hollow voice and hard intonations." These sounds, which cannot have been pleasant, came from his weak chest and delicate health. His hiccough, too, must have sounded disagreeably; it existed, no doubt, but how strongly one cannot say. And apparently most persons were willing to forgive him this fault because he could personate a supposed comic action so as to make it appear real, either with seriousness or to stir up laughter.

From the short accounts just given of his acting in comedy, an idea may perhaps be formed of what it was like by those who know his plays. Various conceptions will be formed; I will say how I look at the matter. It would seem natural to suppose that Molière wished to act comedy in the same spirit in which he wrote it, and that on the stage he gave full effect with satire or irony to the serious or to the ludicrous side of his personage, but without disfiguring the man's nature. His first care was to represent his personage broadly and boldly; then to show, in their place, by delicate and pointed touches, the minor traits in his character. One can imagine Molière acting Arnolphe, Orgon, Alceste, Harpagon, Chrysale, so as to

[1] That is, until the 14th of November 1664.

show what manner of men they were, and to paint also their picture in comedy. They all have their laughable sides, and there is in them all a purpose serious enough to satisfy the strictest ideas of legitimate but amusing comedy. To say that ridicule should be excluded from high-class comedy would be manifestly absurd. And in his lighter plays, a Marquis de Mascarille, a Sganarelle, a George Dandin, a Monsieur de Pourceaugnac, a Monsieur Jourdain, may be shown to be very ludicrous, very comical in the best sense of the word, without being farcical, if the actor understands his part and can play it properly. Doubtless farce may be seen in some of these characters; yet they all have a meaning of their own, they were conceived with serious intention, though more or less of ridicule is thrown upon them.

Taking the sense of what Préville—an actor in the 18th century, and one of whose best parts was Monsieur Jourdain—wrote in his *Mémoires*, M. Louis Moland says: "Certain parts, such as Harpagon in the *Avare* and Monsieur Jourdain in the *Bourgeois Gentilhomme*, and others, allow the actor to use a kind of exaggeration both in his manner of speaking and in his gestures; but to give the highest pleasure to the spectators he must be able to excite them so that they cannot scrutinise his play so calmly as they would in cold blood. They should, in fact, meet him half-way, so to say, in the acting of a part; and the greater or lesser degree of fun he makes them feel should be his thermometer to guide him in being reticent in his acting and in his manner of speaking." [1] Molière's hostile critics said that he exaggerated his parts on the stage; but beside their natural envy, which may be discounted and pardoned to some extent, they did not understand his own characters as well as he did, for they had not his close insight nor his fancy. And he knew better than they did how self-glorious men may grow or how mean they may become under certain conditions, and how ridiculous they will appear when their foibles are shown truly on the stage and in a laughable manner. As he was creating his personage on paper Molière knew in most cases that he would afterwards act it; he had in his mind a clear idea of the character to be represented, and he had also a healthy love of ridicule from

[1] *Œuvres de Molière*, 1st ed. vi. 252.

the mere fun that it gave. All this belongs fairly to comedy, and one can imagine that when Molière was acting his parts he tried to bring out their human weaknesses so as to provoke laughter. Grimarest says (p. 113) "that Molière was always successful in comedy, but that persons of delicate taste reproached him with grimacing too much." It may well be that their taste was more delicate than sound, and that they did not know how far ludicrous characterisation in comedy may extend without being farcical. Before Molière's time there were very few examples to teach them.

Tradition has said that the article quoted a page or two back from the *Mercure de France*, giving an account of Molière's acting, was written by du Croisy's daughter Angélique, who, after she married, was known as Mlle. Poisson.[1] She retired from the stage in 1694, and died in 1756 at the age of ninety-nine. Despois thought, too, that Mlle. Poisson was the author of this article when he printed it among some "Extraits des Mémoires publiés dans le *Mercure de France* par Madame Paul Poisson, née du Croisy, sur les principaux comédiens français."[2] But in a table of "Additions et Corrections" to this same edition of Molière (vol. xi. 290, 291), M. Arthur Desfeuilles seems to agree with M. Monval that the only part of these extracts from the *Mercure de France*, written by Mlle. Poisson, is the well-known portrait of Molière. The other and longer part of the extracts may have been written by one of her sons or by Boucher d'Argis. Here is the portrait :—

"Molière was neither too fat nor too thin ; his stature was large rather than small, his carriage was good, and he had a well-made leg. He walked thoughtfully, he had a very serious air, a big nose, a large mouth, thick lips, a brown complexion, and the different movements that he gave to them made him look extremely comical. As regards his character he was kind, desirous to please, and generous. He was very fond of speaking in public, and when he read his plays to the actors he liked them to bring their children, to draw his own impressions from their natural emotions."

Molière probably conformed to the general rule that an

---

[1] In the 17th century actresses were never called Madame. In strictness this title belonged only to women of noble birth, but it was commonly used by ladies in society.

[2] *Œuvres de Molière*, iii. 378-83.

author should read his play to the actors at the theatre where the play was to be given; and one can well believe that when Molière read his light comedies he liked his fellow-actors to bring their children so that he might draw his own impressions from what they thought of his reading of a play in which he was to take a principal part. We are told, too, that he read his comedies to his maid-servant, La Forêt, for the same purpose; and that once he tried to take her in by reading a play which was not his, but that she was not deceived.[1] Tales more or less similar are told of other men, and the most has been made of them. As a rule, persons of strong powers learn confidence in their own judgment, they are often jealous of interference and often obstinate against correction. In the case of a comedy to be acted, even of a light play, so much depends upon stage-craft that it is very doubtful if an experienced hand would have trusted to such a looking-glass. I can believe that Molière enjoyed seeing the delight of children, perhaps that of his maid-servant, at his drolleries, and that he learned something from their laughter; but hardly that he would have altered his comedy if the laughter did not come when he expected it.

[1] Taschereau, *Vie de Molière*, 3rd ed. 97, 98.

Iт is difficult to say how far any play acted at the Hôtel de Bourgogne or at the Théâtre du Marais may have been successful, for at neither of these two theatres was a record or register kept showing what was the business done. When an opinion about a new play was pronounced it was reported at second-hand; and unless the gossip of the world was more accurately spoken two hundred and fifty years ago than now there are many who would put no great reliance upon it. Yet the gossip of the world is a great element in making or marring the fortune of a new play. People like talking about a new piece they have just seen, and others like listening to them. In this way judgments are soon formed. It may not, however, be too paradoxical to say that in theatrical matters a critical opinion was of more consequence then than it would be now, for those who were qualified to speak had a better chance of being listened to than with us. More reverence was paid to authority. Men said what they thought about a new play at the afternoon meetings of friends when the wits were assembled, and judgments were passed from mouth to mouth as having been spoken by such a person. At a time when there was no daily press, hearsay evidence was the foundation of the greater part of the theatrical traditions that have come down to us; and though the tendency of this was generally optimistic, yet when various plays by different authors were discussed, it is on the whole not unlikely that a fair expression of contemporary thought was given. We must therefore take what evidence we have got about the fortune of a play acted at the Hôtel de Bourgogne or at the Théâtre du Marais, and esteem the author lucky who, unless his play was damned, was spoken of at all.

But the surest way of testing the success of a play brought out more than two hundred years ago is by the number of times it was acted and by its receipts. If a new play, in the reign of Louis XIV., was performed twenty times, it was more than ordinarily successful.[1] A play was considered new so long as it was acted on consecutive days or nearly so, or taking its turn with another piece. Most of Molière's comedies were acted more than twenty times while they were new, and there were a few plays by other authors acted very much oftener. *Timocrate*, a tragedy by Thomas Corneille, first acted at the Marais in 1656, was played 80 times; *Circé*, a spectacular tragedy, also by Thomas Corneille, was acted 75 times at the Théâtre Guénegaud in 1675; *La Devineresse*, a comedy by the same author and de Visé, was acted 47 times at the Guénegaud in 1679-80. Thus *Timocrate* "made the record" of the century, but *Circé* "came in a good second." At the Palais Royal only two plays, not written by Molière, were acted twenty times—Pierre Corneille's *Attila* and his *Tite et Bérénice*. In considering the receipts the matter becomes more complicated. The knowledge how much money each play brought to the actors is only of importance in helping to determine what was its success; in that way, comparing one play with another, it will afford valuable assistance. But the reader will remember that La Grange's Register is the only authority telling what receipts a play made, or, with a few exceptions, how often it was acted; and he wrote only of what took place at his theatre. It would be interesting if we could compare the fortunes of plays at the Hôtel de Bourgogne and at the Théâtre du Marais with those at the Palais Royal, but as this is not possible let us be thankful to La Grange for what he has done. His pages show that a new five-act play by Molière generally gave a receipt of 1000 livres more or less often, and so did many of his smaller plays; but, as we shall see directly, a day's receipt of 1000 livres was high. Perhaps I should not be far from the mark in assuming that when a new five-act play by Molière made 1000 livres two or three times, that might be taken as a sign that the play had a moderate success —as was the case with the *Misanthrope*; when it made 1000 livres half a dozen times, the success was a good one—as with the *Femmes Savantes*; and when it made 1000 livres nine times or more, the success was brilliant—in this class may be

---

[1] Despois, *Le Théâtre Français sous Louis XIV.*, 197 note 2.

counted the *École des Femmes, Don Juan,* the *Tartuffe,* the *Bourgeois Gentilhomme,* and *Psyché.* Of course there is nothing absolute in these assumptions, for the difference between a receipt of 900 and 1000 livres was not enormous, and the number of representations should also be considered. Of Molière's three-act comedies, the *Fâcheux* made over 1000 livres on five days, and the *Malade Imaginaire* on eleven; and of his one-act plays, the *Précieuses Ridicules* five times, and the *Critique de l'École des Femmes* eleven.

I make no apology for the figures given in the next few pages. My chief object has been to ascertain the comparative successes and failures of Molière's comedies while they were new; then to show shortly how often each one was performed from 1659 to 1870. By speaking of his comedies together, putting one beside the other, the reader, if he cares about the matter, will see more easily what were the fortunes of each play than if the figures were given in different chapters.

ANALYSIS OF THE YEARLY RECEIPTS TAKEN BY MOLIÈRE'S TROOP
AT THE PETIT BOURBON AND PALAIS ROYAL THEATRES.

Theatrical Year.	No. of perform-ances each year.	Receipts from public perform-ances.		Average receipt each day.		Value of one share as given by La Grange.[1]	
		Livres.	Sous.	Livres.	Sous.	Livres.	Sous.
Petit Bourbon { 1659-60	145	41,825		288	12	2995	10
{ 1660-61	118	41,397		350	12	2477	6
Palais Royal { 1661-62	125	69,082		552	15	4310	9
1662-63	103	47,243		458	12	3117	18
1663-64	128	72,946		569	18	4534	4
1664-65	95	48,763		513	6	3011	11
1665-66	112	38,891		347	5	2243	5
1666-67	92	43,701	5	475		3352	11
1667-68	90	36,262		402	19	2608	13
1668-69	124	59,895	5	483		5477	3
1669-70	89	36,869	5	414	5	4034	11
1670-71	115	61,932		529	11	4689	
1671-72	127	86,507		681	3	4233	
{ 1672-73	131	84,856	15	647	15	4585	13
	1594	770,170	10			51,670	14

I worked out the above table from La Grange's Register. It shows that *the average daily receipt taken by Molière's troop*

[1] *Registre de La Grange,* 143.

from Easter 1659 *to Easter* 1673 *was* 483 *livres.* The first
two years, or nearly so, at the Petit Bourbon were not so
successful as the remaining twelve at the Palais Royal; for *at
the Petit Bourbon the average daily receipt was* 311 *livres, and
at the Palais Royal it was* 511 *livres.*

Public performances only are counted in this analysis.
Twelve are omitted : there were nine days at the Palais Royal
for which La Grange gave no receipt; and one day at the Petit
Bourbon and two at the Palais Royal on which there was a
" four "—*i.e.* there were so few people in the theatre that the
orator of the troop came forward, and politely told those
present there would be no performance that day and that
their money would be returned to them at the box-office.
The average yearly number of performances was about 114.
The inequalities in this respect may be accounted for by the
absence of the troop at Versailles or other royal residences,
where they went at various times to play before the king, and
where they remained for a week, a fortnight, even a month or
longer; and also by the frequent " interruptions " mentioned
by La Grange, which lasted generally for a week or ten days
at a time. The causes of these interruptions cannot be now
determined. But in 1667-68, owing to the sudden prohibition
of the *Tartuffe*, the troop was prevented from playing from the
7th of August to the 25th of September.

The receipts varied considerably. On twenty days less than
100 livres were taken, and on ten days more than 2000. On
four of these happy days *Don Juan* was the play performed,
on the six others the *Tartuffe*. The first performance of the
Tartuffe, after the comedy was definitely allowed to appear,
on the 5th of February 1669, gave 2860 livres to the actors.
That is the highest receipt mentioned by La Grange in his
Register. Soon after Molière's death, the first nine performances of *Circé* at the Théâtre Guénegaud gave each day more
than 2000 livres ; and there were two performances of *Andromède*, an old play by Pierre Corneille, at the Comédie Française
in July 1682, both of which gave over 2000 livres. These are
the only instances of the receipt mounting to 2000 livres
recorded by La Grange, and he kept his register for six-and-
twenty years. New plays naturally attracted the largest
audiences, but some of Molière's comedies showed strong

exceptions. With *Sganarelle*, the *Médecin Malgré Lui*, and the *Bourgeois Gentilhomme*, the receipts from the first ten performances were not so high as those from the second ten; and with the *Fâcheux* the second ten performances made less money than the third ten. With an old play, especially if not written by Molière, the receipts might fall very low indeed. It is certain that Molière's comedies made much more money than the plays of any other author acted at the Palais Royal. Molière put on to his theatre Racine's two first tragedies, but these plays were by a young hand and were much inferior to Racine's later work. The second one, *Alexandre le Grand*, began very well. On three of the first four days the receipts exceeded 1000 livres. On the fifth and sixth days they fell below 500 livres. Then Racine withdrew his tragedy, thinking that it was badly acted. When Corneille's *Attila* was brought out at the Palais Royal in 1667 it fared indifferently; the first performance only made 1000 livres. Three years and a half later Molière bought from him another tragedy, *Tite et Bérénice*, and ran it alternately with his own *Bourgeois Gentilhomme*, which was then quite new. The two first performances of Corneille's tragedy gave higher receipts than did any of those of Molière's comedy; but at the end of three months the *Bourgeois Gentilhomme* had made over 1000 livres twelve times, and *Tité et Bérénice* only four times. The only other instance of a play, not written by Molière, acted at the Palais Royal, making 1000 livres at one performance—which indeed it did twice—is *La Bradamante Ridicule*, a comedy by an unknown author and not printed. It was acted eight times in January 1664. The Duc de Saint Aignan, first gentleman of the king's chamber, gave the play to the troop and told them to act it; he also gave the troop 1100 livres "pour la dépense des habits qui étaient extraordinaires."

In order to test the comparative successes and failures of Molière's comedies while they were new, I have compiled from La Grange's Register a table showing the number of performances of each play when new, the total receipts of each play, and the average daily receipt made by each play. The comedies are mentioned here in the order they were acted at the public theatre. But in some cases, dating from the year 1668, transpositions would have to be made if the performances of the plays at court were considered as the first performances of those plays. Thus, in 1668, the *Avare* was acted in public before *George Dandin*; but *George Dandin* had been performed at court before the *Avare* was seen in public. So also with the *Fourberies de Scapin* and *Psyché*, with the *Femmes Savantes* and the *Comtesse d'Escarbagnas*. The *Tartuffe*, too, is given here as belonging only to the year 1669; its single performance in August 1667 is not counted.

AVERAGE DAILY RECEIPTS OF MOLIÈRE'S COMEDIES WHEN NEW.

	No. of performances of each play when new.	Total receipts of each new play in livres.	Average daily receipt of each new play in livres.
Les Précieuses Ridicules (1659) . .	33	21,363	647
Sganarelle (1660)	34	15,699	461
Don Garcie de Navarre (1661) . .	7	2,884	412
L'École des Maris (1661) . .	32 [1]	17,991	562
Les Fâcheux (1661) . . .	38	29,247	769
L'École des Femmes (1662) . .	31	29,141	940
La Critique de l'École des Femmes (1663)	32	28,639	894
L'Impromptu de Versailles (1663) .	19	11,671	613
Le Mariage Forcé (1664) . .	12	8,727	727
La Princesse d'Élide (1664) . .	25	15,281	611
Don Juan (1665) . . .	15	20,034	1335
L'Amour Médecin (1665) . .	27	14,646	542
Le Misanthrope (1666) . .	21	12,543	597
Le Médecin Malgré Lui (1666) .	26	13,315	512
Le Sicilien (1667) . . .	17	3,041	178
Amphitryon (1668) . . .	29	19,731	680
L'Avare (1668)	9	4,326	480
George Dandin (1668) . .	13	6,126	471
Le Tartuffe (1669) . . .	43	43,554	1012
M. de Pourceaugnac (1669) .	20	13,464	673
Le Bourgeois Gentilhomme (1670) .	24	24,102	1004
Les Fourberies de Scapin (1671) .	18	7,519	417
Psyché (1671) . . .	38	32,962	867
Les Femmes Savantes (1672) .	19	16,537	870
La Comtesse d'Escarbagnas (1672) .	14	6,967	497
Le Malade Imaginaire (1673) .	13	17,214	1324

Molière wrote also two other comedies, *Mélicerte* and the *Amants Magnifiques*, which were acted before the court, but which he did not put on to his stage at the Palais Royal.

The above table will show that *Molière's comedies, when new,*

[1] Despois gave 38 performances to the *École des Maris* as a new play (*Œuvres de Molière*, ii. 334-36). I reckon that its last performance as a new play was on 11th September 1661.

taken one with another, gave a mean daily receipt of 693 *livres.*
But in comparing the fortunes of the plays, besides looking at
the receipts, the number of performances should also be considered. Taking these two tests together, they give on the
whole a fair idea of the success of the comedies at the time.
More than that should not be expected from them. Counting
the number of times each play was acted, *Don Juan* gave the
highest daily receipt. But the comedy was played only fifteen
times. M. Mesnard thinks that Molière was asked to withdraw his play on the grounds of religious scruples.[1] Second
highest among the daily average receipts was *Le Malade
Imaginaire.* It had only thirteen performances as a new
play. The success was cut short by its author's death a few
hours after the fourth representation, and by the fact that six
weeks later the troop at the Palais Royal theatre was broken
up, and most of its members united themselves with their
former rivals at the Théâtre du Marais. Of the other
comedies which ran their natural course on the stage, the
most successful were : the *Tartuffe,* the *Bourgeois Gentilhomme,*
the *École des Femmes,* the *Critique de l'École des Femmes,* the
Femmes Savantes, Psyché, the *Fâcheux,* the *Mariage Forcé.*
Each one of these plays while new gave a daily average
receipt of over 693 livres ; the average daily receipt of all the
others was below that sum.

As to the short plays, it does not seem fair on first thoughts
to make the day's receipt dependent on a three, and more
especially on a one-act comedy performed as an after-piece.
But knowing that plays attracted the public most while they
were new, also looking at the circumstances under which
some of these short plays appeared, and comparing the
average daily receipts taken during the fortnight or month
before and after the short plays were first acted with the receipts
produced during their representation, I am disposed on the
whole to think that when a new three or even a one-act
comedy was given, the day's receipt depended much more on
the new short play than on almost any longer old play acted
with it on the same day. This was strongly the case with the
Précieuses Ridicules, and nearly as much so with the *Critique
de l'École des Femmes*—both of them comedies in one act.

[1] *Notice biographique sur Molière,* 325.

Though the mean daily average of the *Précieuses* was below 693 livres and that of the *Critique* very much above it, I believe that the above table will give a fair idea of the comparative fortunes of Molière's different comedies while they were new.

More often than not Molière's five-act comedies gave the best pecuniary results, though *Don Garcie de Navarre,* the *Misanthrope,* and the *Avare* were exceptions. *Don Garcie* was condemned the first day it appeared; since Molière's death it has only once appeared on the stage, and then in an abbreviated form. La Grange's Register seems to prove that the welcome given to the *Misanthrope* was comparatively small; also that Grimarest was in error when he said that Molière wrote his *Médecin Malgré Lui* to assist the former play on the stage. The Register shows that the *Misanthrope* was played 21 times before the *Médecin Malgré Lui* appeared; then that comedy was acted 11 times before it was played on the same day with the *Misanthrope*; and the two comedies were acted together only 5 times.[1] The *Avare* was certainly a failure as regards popularity at the time. On the first day only the receipt was over 1000 livres. This is on the whole Molière's best comedy in prose, and its want of success as a new play is curious. And perhaps there may be some who know Molière's humour who will be surprised to hear that *George Dandin,* a three-act play in prose, met with a poor welcome. I find, speaking of his plays generally, that Molière's comedies in prose, when taken together, gave a little higher money average as new plays than those in verse. This is somewhat singular, because the taste of the time was much in favour of verse when plays were in five acts; but it shows how thoroughly popular Molière was as a dramatist. The number of scenes that he wrote in verse and in prose is about equal.

The reader will see that, in trying to form a comparative estimate of how Molière's plays were regarded by the public at the time, I am taking the evidence of the box-office of the theatre as the sole criterion. Trustworthy contemporary opinions would be worth having if we could get such evidence. Something of the sort, more or less true, may be found about many of Molière's comedies, though mostly of a scrappy kind

[1] *Registre de La Grange,* 81-83.

and quite useless for comparing the fortunes of his various plays. I prefer the safer testimony of La Grange's figures.

Let us now look for a moment at plays which Molière did not write :—

AVERAGE DAILY RECEIPTS OF NEW PLAYS, NOT WRITTEN BY MOLIÈRE, ACTED AT THE PETIT BOURBON AND PALAIS ROYAL THEATRES.

	No. of performances of each play when new.	Total receipts of each new play in livres.	Average daily receipt of each new play in livres.
Tite et Bérénice, ... by P. Corneille (Nov. 1670).	21	15,377	732
Le Grand benêt de fils aussi sot que son père, ... by Brécourt (Jan. 1664).	9	4,472	297
Attila, ... by P. Corneille (March 1667).	20	7,414	370
Tonnaxare, ... by Boyer (Nov. 1662).	15	5,499	366
La Vraie et la Fausse Précieuse, . by Gilbert (May 1660).	9	2,976	330
La Pastorale, ... by de Visé (Oct. 1667).	11	3,382	307
Cléopâtre, ... by La Thorillière (Dec. 1667).	11	3,329	302
Le Désespoir Extravagant, . . by Subligny (Aug. 1670).	12	3,419	285
La Thébaïde, ... by Racine—his first play— (June 1664).	14	3,811	271
La Mère Coquette,[1] . . . by de Visé (Oct. 1665).	14	3,663	261
Le Favori, ... by Mlle. des Jardins (April 1665).	13	3,200	246
La Critique d'Andromaque,[2] . . by Subligny (May 1669).	17	4,084	240

If we contrast the average daily receipts of new plays not written by Molière, but acted by his troop, with those made by his plays while they were new, we shall see at a glance how great was the difference. In the above table I have taken the twelve plays written by other authors that were acted oftenest at the Petit Bourbon and Palais Royal theatres; of those that

[1] Quinault also wrote a comedy called *La Mère Coquette*, acted at the Hôtel de Bourgogne.

[2] The first two or three performances of this play are not recorded by La Grange ; but in any case it is hardly possible that its average for nineteen or twenty performances exceeded 300 livres.

had less than nine performances nothing need be said. We have seen that all of Molière's twenty-six comedies, while new and taken one with another, gave a daily average receipt of 693 livres; whereas of plays that he did not write, but which were acted by his troop, the table just above shows that the twelve that were performed the oftenest at his two theatres gave, while new and taken one with another, a daily average receipt of 342 livres. Remembering, too, that the daily average receipt for all plays, both old and new, acted at the Palais Royal was 511 livres, it will be seen that Pierre Corneille's tragedy *Tite et Bérénice*, of which the average for its twenty-one performances was 732 livres, was the only play, not written by Molière, that had what I have described already as "a substantial success" at the Palais Royal theatre. Perhaps the same mark of good fortune should be allowed to Gilbert's comedy *La Vraie et la Fausse Précieuse* acted at the Petit Bourbon, where the mean daily receipt from all plays averaged 311 livres.

Now, as to the number of representations of each of Molière's plays from 1659 to 1870. At the end of the first volume of the edition of Molière to which I usually refer, Despois gave a "Tableau des représentations de Molière depuis Louis XIV. jusqu'en 1870." This table is divided into two parts: the performances in public and those given at court. I shall speak only of the first part. If the reader will look at pages 548 and 549 of Despois' volume, he may see how often each of Molière's plays was acted at his theatre during his lifetime; afterwards from 1673 to 1680 at the Théâtre Guénegaud; and at different later periods from 1680 to 1870 at the Théâtre Français. Two gaps have, however, been found in the registers of the Comédie Française: the first during the theatrical year 1739-40; the second, more important, during the years of the First Republic, from 1793 to 1799. I have added up Despois' figures, giving the number of performances of each play in public from 1659 to 1870, as this is the best ascertainable test of their comparative popularity on the stage.

Le Tartuffe .	.	.	.	.	.	.	.	1908
Le Médecin Malgré Lui		.	.	.	.	.	.	1652
L'École des Maris .	,	.	.	.	.	.	.	1291
L'Avare	.	.	.	.	.	.	.	1279

L'École des Femmes	1178
Le Misanthrope	1126
Les Femmes Savantes	1027
George Dandin	959
Le Malade Imaginaire	883
Amphitryon,	788
Les Fourberies de Scapin	715
Sganarelle ou le Cocu Imaginaire	680
Monsieur de Pourceaugnac	677
Le Dépit Amoureux	666
Le Mariage Forcé	662
Les Précieuses Ridicules	617
La Comtesse d'Escarbagnas	584
Le Bourgeois Gentilhomme	526
L'Étourdi	447
L'Amour Médecin	359
Les Fâcheux	334
Le Sicilien	218
Psyché	213
La Princesse d'Élide	95
La Critique de l'École des Femmes	92
Don Juan (Le Festin de Pierre) [1]	60
Les Amants Magnifiques	41
L'Impromptu de Versailles	22
Don Garcie de Navarre	9
Mélicerte	3

This list shows upon the whole that those comedies which are generally thought to be the best reading have been acted oftenest. If any English reader, fond of Molière, who has never seen him on the stage, is curious in the matter, let him put down on a slip of paper the twelve comedies he likes best, and see how many of the twelve are among those that have been performed the most frequently. There is one comedy, *Don Juan*, which ought to find a place on any such list, but which stands quite low among the representations. The performances of *Don Juan* were stopped a month or five weeks after the play first appeared, and Molière's comedy was not acted again until nearly two hundred years later. Then there were plays which were very popular when they were new, but which ceased to be so after the dramatist's death. The *Précieuses Ridicules* was a satire upon a form of affectation in

---

[1] A few years after Molière's death Thomas Corneille versified this play; and in that form it was always acted until the year 1847. These 60 performances refer to the representations of Molière's play since 1847.

vogue at the time, and which the laughter in the play did much to destroy ; the *Critique de l'École des Femmes* was a short play full of banter evoked by the criticisms, some silly, some hostile, that were passed upon the *École des Femmes* ; the *Fâcheux* was " une pièce à tiroirs "—a play made up of unconnected scenes—and therefore not likely to have a permanent interest as an acting comedy; *Psyché*, part of which only was written by Molière, was a " tragédie-ballet" which owed much of its good fortune to scenic display, but as theatrical scenery continued to improve and as people's ideas changed, the attractions of the play diminished ; and there was *Sganarelle ou le Cocu Imaginaire*, which was acted oftener than any other of Molière's plays during his lifetime, but after the poet had written comedies in a higher vein and when French short comedies became more numerous, people were tempted to lose sight of its dramatic qualities and to prefer plays that were less visibly borrowed from the Italian stages. There were, on the other hand, comedies that were not popular at first but which were afterwards more justly appreciated. As new plays the success of the *Misanthrope* was comparatively small, the failure of the *Avare* was great; and it seems strange that *George Dandin* should have met with so poor a welcome. The *École des Maris* and the *École des Femmes* have always been favourites. The *Femmes Savantes* is certainly one of the best acting plays of Molière's high-class comedies, yet in more than two hundred years it was performed nearly nine hundred times less than the *Tartuffe*. The preponderating success of the *Tartuffe* and of the *Médecin Malgré Lui*, judged by the number of representations, is remarkable.

The lists above given are only meant to show how the plays mentioned in them were regarded by the public. What they tell is interesting as far as it goes, but unfortunately little or nothing is known of the number of performances or of the receipts of the plays acted at the Hôtel de Bourgogne or at the Théâtre du Marais. Doubtless plays could be named showing that both of these theatres had their red-letter days, though the best of those at the Marais came before Molière was known. It is generally believed that while the three theatres were in rivalry the actors at the Marais prospered least ; but it would only be guesswork to try to determine if the general level of success at the Hôtel de Bourgogne was higher or lower than that at the Palais Royal, or which theatre had most constantly the largest audiences. Much more often than not the merits of a play will decide its good or ill fortune on the stage, though the talents of the actors have to be considered, and sometimes the public takes a freak. Absolutism of opinion in such a matter may easily be wrong, and we have seen that a few of Molière's best comedies were not warmly welcomed when they first appeared. Yet the lists help to show indirectly Molière's powers as a dramatist. And they show, too, that the best of those plays not written by him, but acted at the Palais Royal, were not on the whole performed more than half as often as his plays were, and that his plays gave receipts twice as large as those written by other authors, also acted at his theatre. For one who wrote so much and who was often compelled to write very hurriedly, his measure of contemporary popularity was great. And both from a reader's and from the stage point of view, the *Femmes Savantes*, and the *Malade Imaginaire* with its burlesque cérémonie at the end of the comedy, seem to prove that his later work gave no sign of failing powers.

CHAPTER XII

SOME description has been given of the inside of the Palais Royal theatre. La troupe de Monsieur began to play there on the 20th of January 1661, and on the 4th of February appeared Molière's heroic-comedy *Don Garcie de Navarre*. This play was a failure from the first, and from its first condemnation it has never recovered. Molière was ambitious there on a false track. Hitherto he had drawn amusing pictures showing human thoughts; but in *Don Garcie* he made an attempt at the "genre noble" for which he had no aptitude; he cast aside the comedy of life as his predecessors had ignored it, and instead of showing men's natural propensities he drew automata who were unfortunately gifted with the power of making speeches. The heroine alone shows some lifelike indications, but her lover, instead of engaging our attention, is preposterous. The other personages are nonentities; they talk, but one forgets what they have said as soon as the words are spoken.

The taste of theatre-goers was then more in favour of plays in verse than of plays in prose; they liked a show of grand sentiments and noble ideas; and Molière, more or less the child of his age when he wrote *Don Garcie*, wished to exhibit the same fine feelings that had actuated other dramatists. *Don Garcie* is described as a heroic-comedy; it bears a different aspect from every other play that Molière had written. In the first place, we miss in it much of his humanity, one of his strongest characteristics, and one of the causes which makes him so pleasant to read. This is stifled in the effort to be romantic and to appear glorious; and the comedy in the play is very indifferent, or it is wanting. Had Molière made a burlesque of the incidents in his play he might have succeeded better. His predecessors in their tragedies and tragi-comedies had tried to make their personages add a cubit to their stature by putting them metaphorically on to stilts, and in his heroic-comedy the poet showed partly the same ambition. The style of thought is high-flown, but the style of the language is generally simple. Hence there appears to be a sense of incongruity. This was probably felt rather than said at the time, and was perhaps one of the causes of the failure of the play. The verses throughout are superior to those in any play written previously, except perhaps those in some of Corneille's tragedies; but the excellence of versification will never redeem the want of vitality in a stage play. The spectator demands imperatively, above all other things, a lively interest in the personages before him and in their concerns, and he wants to have the incidents and the characters in the story shown to him in a dramatic way. However much his ear may be flattered by the smoothness of the lines, the spoken words will tell him before long whether they please by the action they express, or merely by their sound. This was doubtless the case even in Molière's day, when men listened to the rhythm of the lines more carefully than they do now. Subsidiary graces may be very pleasant, and no play in verse can delight in all respects without the charm of style, but during its representation purely literary merits are felt to have a very secondary value. And it may be doubted if even the higher quality of poetry, when found, can give, or ever did give, much lasting success to the acting of a play on the stage.

As a new play *Don Garcie de Navarre* was acted only seven times, and the receipts were not good. The poet obtained a privilege to print his comedy on the 31st of May 1660, but he never used it. The play was first printed nine years after his death. The success of Molière's earlier comedies had made him enemies. Authors became envious of him, and the members of the two rival troops tried to belittle his merriment; and when the new play, or the acting in the play, excited a spirit of censure they were delighted to foster it. Molière had quizzed the " grands comédiens " at the Hôtel de Bourgogne, so that when his *Don Garcie* fell flat they jumped on him. He met with a check, and they did not fail to make the most of it. In common with the public they laughed at

his acting, and his play was condemned without mercy. De
Visé wrote in his *Nouvelles Nouvelles* in 1663: "The failure of
his *Don Garcie* made me forget to speak to you of it in its
proper place; but it is enough to say that it was a serious play,
and that he [Molière] acted the chief part, to let you know that
it could not be very entertaining."[1]

Molière had built hopes on this play, and he did not like to
be disappointed in them. In November 1663 he again put
Don Garcie on the stage. It was played twice, before the first
two performances of his own one-act comedy *L'Impromptu de
Versailles*. This was a bold stroke on Molière's part. His own
acting in the part of Don Garcie had been severely criticised,
and in the first scene of his *Impromptu* he ridicules the turgid
declamation of the actors at the Hôtel de Bourgogne. But his
appeal from the first judgment of the public against his heroic-
comedy did not succeed. From the 6th of November 1663
until the year 1871 *Don Garcie de Navarre* never appeared on
the boards of the Comédie Française. On the 26th of February
1871 some scenes of it were given at a matinée; four actors
instead of eight then came on the stage.[2]

There is, however, a point of interest in the failure of this
play which seems to show that Molière afterwards recognised
its faults. Some years later he gave to the finest male
character he ever drew the same failing that he had tried to
depict in Don Garcie. But this man is haunted by a stupid
and unintelligible jealousy, and has no cause to be dissatisfied
with the loyalty of his mistress, whereas Alceste in the
Misanthrope, among other faults, shows strong jealousy for a
heartless coquette who can love nobody. In the first case
jealousy is shown to be despicably mean; in the second it is
so mixed up with other qualities, good and bad, and is shown
in such a noble manner, that it is not regarded as a crime, and
its weakness is forgiven. Molière must have had *Don Garcie*
in his mind when he was writing the *Misanthrope*, for Alceste
repeats the same sentiments, the same words, as were spoken
by Don Garcie.[3] Also, *Le Prince Jaloux* was added as a second
title to *Don Garcie*, and there is evidence to show that the poet

---

[1] Appendix to M. Mesnard's *Notice biographique sur Molière*, 466.
[2] L. Moland, *Œuvres de Molière*, 2nd ed. iii. 378.
[3] Conf. *Don Garcie de Navarre*, Act II. sc. 5, and Act IV. sc. 8, with the
Misanthrope, Act IV. sc. 3.

at one time intended to qualify his *Misanthrope* with a second title, *L'Atrabilaire Amoureux,* but he abandoned the idea. But the plan and the composition of the two plays are so very different that dry criticism alone would not show the progress of ideas in the author's mind during the five years' interval between the false and the real comedy. In the first case Molière forgot himself and ignored the nature of man in his attempt to write something fine; in the second the ideas expressed are true and are consistent with the comedy of human life.

The first five months that Molière and his friends were at the Palais Royal were not very successful. A week after *Don Garcie* was withdrawn a new tragedy by Gilbert, *Le Tyran d'Égypte,* was put on the stage, but it fared poorly. Before Easter 1661, however, the troop seem to have paid off the expenses of getting into their new theatre; and they also paid 550 livres to Molière for his *Don Garcie de Navarre.* As La Grange says nothing about any payment to Gilbert for his *Tyran d'Égypte,* it may be presumed that he got his two shares out of the receipts of the play.

After he had finished his accounts for the year 1660-61 La Grange wrote in his Register :—

" Before beginning again after Easter at the Palais Royal, Monsieur de Molière asked for two shares instead of one which he had. The troop allowed [them] to him, for himself or for his wife, in case he married. So that instead of there being twelve shares in the troop, which had been the case since April 1660, another share was added in 1661."

As Molière's marriage took place some ten weeks after his play *Les Fâcheux* had been running, I will mention the circumstance again at the end of this chapter.

Shortly after the Easter holidays the troop brought out a new comedy by Chappuzeau, whose name was mentioned so often in chap. ix., called *Le Riche Impertinent.* It was performed eight times with indifferent results. Chappuzeau was alive to what he thought was his interest, for he changed the title of his comedy into *Le Riche Mécontent,* and had it acted the year following at the Hôtel de Bourgogne.[1] Under that name it was printed (Paris, 1662), bearing on the title-page

[1] Preface to Chappuzeau's *Le Théâtre François,* ed. 1875, by M. G. Monval, p. ix.

the words " Représentée à l'Hôtel de Bourgogne," and the play
was dedicated to Mademoiselle—the daughter of the Duke of
Orleans, brother to Louis XIII. The comedy was again printed
with the title *Le Partisan Dupé* (Lyons, no date), and was
dedicated to the Princess of Anhalt.[1] The traffic in dedica-
tions in the 17th century is well known. M. Fournel, in his
two notices prefacing the plays of Chappuzeau,[2] shows that
the needy author was an adept at this kind of trickery, for he
practised it with at least four of his plays. The two versions
of each play were printed at different places ; in the case of
one play no town is mentioned on the title-page of the second
edition ; with the three other plays the first or the second
edition was printed either at Paris or at Lyons, but those of
Lyons show no date. I have read the two comedies given by
M. Fournel, *L'Académie des Femmes* and *La Dame d'Intrigue.*
The former repays one best, for there something may be
gathered of the ways of thinking at the time by people who
gave themselves the airs of persons of quality or of women of
learning. But the comedy in Chappuzeau's two plays did not
tempt me to have a more intimate acquaintance of his work
as a dramatist. He has, however, written one book, *Le Théâtre
François*, for which those who interest themselves in the
French stage in the 17th century ought to be grateful to him.

On the 24th of June 1661 Molière brought out the *École des
Maris.* This was felt to be his first high-class comedy, or at
least his first comedy that was seriously meant. In the first
two scenes we are reminded of the lines :—

> " Look here, upon this picture and on this,
>   The counterfeit presentment of two brothers."

The whole of the play is intended to show how differently
two brothers bring up girls confided to their care, and the
different effects of their teaching.

Molière took his main idea from the *Adelphi* of Terence, but
he substituted girls for young men and so altered much of the
groundwork of the comedy. His play was intended as a satire
on the harshness of parents or guardians who brought up their
girls as though they were animals who existed only for their
master's pleasure, instead of being human creatures with wills

---

[1] Parfaict, *Histoire du Théâtre Français*, ix. 91 note.
[2] *Les Contemporains de Molière*, i. 359, 360 ; iii. 207, 208.

and passions of their own. Mrs. Malaprop found it easy to say "preference and aversion don't become a young woman"; it was against the cruel enforcement of this sentiment that Molière wished to make his protest. Domestic tyranny was more common in his day than now, and the scenes which he drew were being enacted with certain differences in many households. The dramatist wished to show that harsh treatment is likely to produce bad results, and that in the married lives of the women so brought up both the women themselves and their husbands would probably suffer. Sganarelle is a despicable creature who believes only in himself; respect for him is impossible. He holds with all the conviction hereditary in a caste that liberty is a bad thing for young people, and like a tyrant he keeps Isabelle, his ward, a close prisoner. She is made miserable and takes her first opportunity to escape. Ariste, on the other hand, believes in the beneficial exercise of a healthy freedom; he loves his ward Léonor and is trustful; he allows her to enjoy herself, and says:—

"Il nous faut en riant instruire la jeunesse."

Consequently Léonor has been happy in her home and wishes to remain in it.

In an under-plot in the play there is some scheming borrowed from Boccaccio, given in an altered form and carried out more or less in the style of Italian comedy. The action is, however, dependent on the natures of the persons introduced, and the characterisation is well maintained to the end. And the kindly nature of one brother, and the vanity and the churlishness of the other, are both shown very graphically and with admirable comic irony. The dramatist treated the same subject in a different manner in the *École des Femmes*, where he showed more delicate characterisation, though the story there is not so well told.

In the *École des Maris* Molière played the part of Sganarelle, de l'Espy was Ariste, La Grange was Valère, Mlle. de Brie was Isabelle. Of the other parts there is some doubt, but in all probability Mlle. du Parc was Léonor, Madeleine Béjart was Lisette, du Parc was Ergaste, and de Brie the commissaire.[1]

[1] *Œuvres de Molière*, ii. 347.

In the middle of July the actors at the Palais Royal had a week of hard work. They were invited by Fouquet, the surintendant of finance, to play at his seat at Vaux.[1] Fouquet had invited there the Queen of England, Monsieur and Madame, the daughter of Charles I. The troop left Paris on Monday the 11th of July, and on Tuesday,[2] at Vaux, they played the *École des Maris*. The king was then at Fontainebleau, not far from Vaux, and on Wednesday they played before his Majesty the *École des Maris* and *Sganarelle*. The same evening they were called upon by Fouquet's wife to perform the same two comedies. On Thursday they were engaged by the Marquis de Richelieu, and acted the *École des Maris*. After this performance the troop travelled back to Paris at night, they got to the Palais Royal at noon on Friday, in time for their customary day's work there. When that day's receipt had been divided, division was made of the two gratifications they had received :

> " Part de l'argent de M. de Richelieu, 58 l. 10 s.
> Part de l'argent de M. le Surintendant, 115 l."

So that each member of the troop got 173 livres 10 sous.

The *École des Maris* was the first of Molière's comedies that he printed of his own free will. He says this himself in the dedication of his play addressed to Monsieur, the protector of the troop. The privilege was dated 9th July 1661, a fortnight after the play had appeared on the stage. It was granted to Jean Baptiste Pocquelin de Moliers [*sic*]; and in it are set forth the wrongs that had been done to the dramatist by surreptitious printing of his previous plays, and Ribou was mentioned by name as a delinquent. The printing was finished on the 20th of August.[3]

Molière's next play *Les Fâcheux* (the bores) is a disjointed comedy, and it is difficult to speak of it except in a disjointed way. Fouquet invited the king, the queen-mother, Monsieur and Madame, to a specially magnificent fête at Vaux on the 17th of August. Only a fortnight before he had engaged Molière to compose for the occasion a new play in which there

---

[1] *Registre* de La Grange, 34.
[2] Taschereau, *Vie de Molière*, 5th ed. 62.
[3] *Œuvres de Molière*, ii. 349, 350 ; xi. 6, 7.

should be dancing and music as interludes. The notice was a short one, but the poet, in spite of his daily work, had his comedy of three acts in verse ready at the appointed time. Pellisson, Fouquet's secretary, wrote a prologue; the ballets with their verses, the music and the decorations were entrusted to others. The affair was very urgent, and Fouquet, whose greed and dishonesty had made him colossally rich, wished to make a display of magnificence before the king. La Fontaine was present on the occasion, and in a letter to a friend, dated 22nd August 1661, gave some account of the splendour of the scene. We may best omit this and come to what he says of the play and its author :—

> " C'est un ouvrage de Molière.
> Cet écrivain par sa manière
> Charme à present toute la cour ;
> De la façon que son nom court,
> Il doit être par delà Rome :
> J'en suis ravi, car c'est mon homme.
> Te souvient-il bien qu'autrefois
> Nous avons conclu d'une voix
> Qu'il allait ramener en France
> Le bon goût et l'air de Térence ?
> Plaute n'est plus qu'un plat bouffon
> Et jamais il ne fit si bon
> Se trouver à la comédie ;
> Car ne pense pas qu'on y rie
> De maint trait jadis admiré,
> Et bon in illo tempore ;
> Nous avons changé de méthode ;
> Jodelet n'est plus à la mode,
> Et maintenant il ne faut pas
> Quitter la nature d'un pas."

La Fontaine's praise of Molière in these light verses is worth noticing. He had read the plays of earlier dramatists and knew what they were like, but when he came to Molière he tapped him on the shoulder and said, " C'est mon homme." Such comedy as had existed sufficed; people were content to laugh at Jodelet's buffooneries, but now that a better way had been shown, nature's pictures must be followed. The *Fâcheux* was evidently not the first of Molière's comedies that La Fontaine had seen or read, but unfortunately he did not say what he thought of any other.

There is no sort of story in the *Fâcheux*. Éraste is in love with Orphise and wants to see her, but is detained at every turn by his friends who bother him with their trivialities; others who do not know him accost him and talk nonsense. They present themselves one after another, each beset with some crazy idea, and torture the impatient lover so that he is continually thwarted in his attempt to speak to the woman he loves.. The *Fâcheux* is what is called "une comédie à tiroirs"; it is made up of detached scenes having no connection with one another. Molière's play was almost the first instance of this kind of comedy in France. In 1637 Desmarets showed in the *Visionnaires* a comedy that was made up of scenes nearly detached, but yet having a thread of a story running through the play connecting the scenes together. Desmarets' comedy had been very popular, and Molière had frequently put it upon his stage at the Petit Bourbon. What was thought to be the fun in the *Visionnaires* was that the exalted or visionary ideas, then supposed to be held by a good many people, were satirised with fair caricature. The play was so much enjoyed that for some years it was spoken of as "l'inimitable comédie"; and when Molière was much pressed for time he may perhaps have taken from Desmarets the idea of a play that would not demand complicated dramatic exposition. As to the workmanship, one reads Desmarets' comedy now with a sort of fossil interest, but Molière's play is still instinct with life. A dozen people are not brought together for the purpose of dramatising a story out of their joint concerns; a file of different personages, mostly men, and generally only one at a time, come before Éraste to worry him with their rubbish. But the talk is so lively and so natural that one is amused at the way each man shows his conceit and his self-sufficiency. The clearness of the portraiture is shown with a raciness of style that still makes the play very good reading. It is not dramatic in incident, it is so in the humorous personification of the different characters. The interest in the comedy lies there.

The *Fâcheux* was the first of the poet's comedies in which he laughed at the foppishness of the grandees who thought that they should be considered as a race apart and above other people. At a time when a line of demarcation was recognised between the nobles and the non-nobles, offices which conferred a title to nobility were bought often enough by rich men of very inferior condition.[1] Molière did not concern himself with the social problem how far it was well that a state should be aristocratic or democratic; he took the order of men as he found it, and drew his comedy from the prevailing manners of his time. It is the business of a comic dramatist to show the humours of men, not to discuss them, and it is impossible in reading Molière, who thought seriously about the meaning he wished his work to convey, not to be struck by the open and healthy tone in which he satirised the foibles of society. He disliked pretentiousness, but instead of crying out at its vulgarity he ridiculed it with the banter of good-natured irony, so that his audience should see the nonsense and laugh over it. That was his way of moralising upon the world's humbug. In the play that he wrote for Fouquet he exposed to ridicule before the royal party assembled at Vaux a number of importunate bores —fatuous noblemen who thought that the world was not big enough to hold them, and needy individuals who imagined that by a mark of royal favour their fortunes would instantly be made. No doubt there was flattery in the homage thus indirectly addressed to the king who was present. But the comedy was felt to be an actuality; for among the courtiers invited were some who saw and laughed at their own follies, while all saw similar weaknesses in other men shown in an impersonal way and with an air of good breeding and good humour. Sainte-Beuve was certainly right when he said: "Molière, c'est la morale des honnêtes gens." Unless a writer has this quality, if he cares for good reputation, he had better leave satire alone and laugh at that of others when it contains honest fun, or try to honour it when it shows honest anger.

There is a story taken from the *Ménagiana* (1st ed. 1693) to the effect that after the performance in Fouquet's garden, Louis XIV., pointing to the Marquis de Soyecourt, said to Molière: "Voilà un grand original que vous n'avez pas encore copié." M. de Soyecourt was very fond of the chase, and he was known to bore his friends with his hunting talk. After the king had spoken to Molière, the poet set to work to add a new scene to his play. It is probable that he received some assistance, for the description of the stag-hunt as related by

---

[1] See what La Bruyère says in his *Caractères*, in the chapter "Des biens de la fortune," and at the beginning of his chapter, "De quelques usages."

Dorante (Act II. sc. 6), though it is very spirited and shows all the hot-headed eagerness of an enthusiastic sportsman who likes talking about his favourite amusement, is so technical that not many readers would understand it thoroughly without explanatory notes. A few days after the fête at Vaux, the actors at the Palais Royal left Paris for Fontainebleau, where they played the new comedy twice before the king. Then Louis XIV. had the satisfaction of seeing represented "la scène du chasseur" which he had good-naturedly hinted to Molière.

The *Fâcheux* was the first of the many comédies-ballets that Molière wrote to be played before the king; and it is hardly to be doubted that the dramatist owed much of the favour or protection that he received from his sovereign to the success of his plays at the court fêtes. Louis XIV. as a young man liked to be amused, he liked things around him to be bright, and he liked the show and the music of the ballets. In the comédie-ballet the ballet was given as an accompaniment to the play. It was meant to be a humorous illustration designed so as to add a side lustre of gay splendour to some of the incidents in the comedy. In his Avertissement to the *Fâcheux* Molière says that the joint performance was "un mélange nouveau pour nos théâtres." The joint performance was highly applauded, and there were many who liked the ballet part best, as a child likes looking at pictures better than reading a book.

Grimarest could not have chosen a more inopportune moment than in speaking of this play to say that no one worked with greater difficulty than Molière.[1] If he had said that no one took more pains than Molière to make each of his personages say the right thing in the right way, he would have come nearer the mark. From his boyhood, Molière's mind was constantly busy in noticing how men thought, how they spoke, how they acted; he was, in fact, doing much of his work when his friends thought that he was enjoying himself—as when on Saturday afternoons he sat in barber Gély's arm-chair at Pézenas. Nature had given him the faculty for observing men closely wherever he saw them; otherwise he might have been content to have remained in his father's shop. It is mainly

[1] *Vie de Molière*, 26.

by sympathetic and accurate observation that most of the best work in the world is done, whether in literature or in science; imagination follows more or less hand in hand and builds upon the first foundation. Molière's instinctive habit of close observation, his wide sympathies and his rapid insight, gave him his power of quick production. Unless he had been a very fast worker he could not have written the *Fâcheux* in a fortnight; he could not in rather more than fourteen years have written twenty-six plays in prose and in verse (two others were not given at the Palais Royal, and there were also two poems), besides the constant work of chief manager at his theatre and his labour as an actor—taking nearly always himself the longest or most difficult parts in his comedies.

On the 4th of November the *Fâcheux* appeared on the stage at the Palais Royal, and with it the ballet that had charmed the royal party at Vaux. The new comedy was given uninterruptedly until the end of January 1662; then in the latter half of February there were six more performances, all of which were consecutive.

In the first five performances the chief male part, that of Éraste, was taken by La Grange; then he fell ill and du Croisy took his rôle. Soulié thought that Molière acted four or five parts in the comedy: "Lisandre the dancer, Alcandre the duellist, or Alcippe the gamester, and perhaps all three with some changes of costume; also Caritidès, the man who wants to correct the signboards, and Dorante the sportsman."[1] Despois quotes this passage, as though agreeing with it, but seems to doubt whether Molière played Alcandre.[2] The other men's parts are not known, but that of La Montagne, the valet, was probably played by du Parc. As to the women's parts guesses only can be made: Madeleine Béjart as Orphise, Mlle. du Parc as Orante, Mlle. de Brie as Climène.

Molière printed the *Fâcheux* in February 1662, and this was the only play he dedicated to the king. He begins as though in terms of bold familiarity: "Sire, I add a scene to the comedy, and a man who dedicates a book is always a bore." Then he graciously thanks his Majesty for his appro-

---

[1] *Recherches sur Molière*, 88; 276, 277.
[2] *Œuvres de Molière*, iii. 15 and note 2; iv. 230, continuation of note 5 from p. 229.

bation and for having told him how to add another bore to his play, and says that this scene was thought by everybody to be the best part of the work.

Some weeks after the Easter holidays in 1662, La Thorillière and Brécourt, two actors at the Marais, left their theatre and joined Molière's troop. It was said of La Thorillière that he was serious when he ought to be gay, and smiling when he ought to appear serious. Such a disposition was perhaps serviceable to him in the part of Philinte in the *Misanthrope*, and it may have relieved some of the lecturing of Cléante in the *Tartuffe*. Nevertheless, La Thorillière must have been a good actor. He was also the author of *Cléopatre*, a tragedy acted at the Palais Royal, but without much success and never printed. The eldest of his two daughters married Baron, the great tragedian; the other married Dancourt, well known as the author of light comedies after Molière's death. It would seem that Brécourt also had high capabilities as an actor. While at the Palais Royal his two chief rôles were Alain in the *École des Femmes* and Dorante in the *Critique*. He joined the Comédie Française in 1682. He was the author of several plays, two of which were reprinted by M. Fournel in the first volume of his *Contemporains de Molière*. One of Brécourt's comedies, *Le grand bênet de fils aussi sot que son père*, was acted at the Palais Royal on the 18th of January 1664, but it was not printed. A few weeks later, in a fit of temper, Brécourt left that theatre for the Hôtel de Bourgogne. The year after Molière's death he brought out at the Hôtel a little comedy, *L'Ombre de Molière*. As a play it is poor, but Brécourt seems to have been actuated by a desire to speak well of one who had once been his friend, and with whom he had quarrelled before he left the Palais Royal.

I come now to Molière's marriage. The full name of his future wife was Armande Grésinde Claire Élizabeth Béjart; and it may be accepted that she was born late in 1642 or early in 1643. Legal documents, to which I shall refer presently, state that she was the daughter of Joseph Béjart and of Marie Hervé, his wife. But her contemporaries believed without much questioning that she was the illegitimate daughter of Madeleine Béjart (therefore the grand-daughter of Joseph);

and if this opinion, which prevailed for nearly two hundred years after her birth, be correct, it is impossible to tell who was her father, though the Comte de Modène may be reasonably suspected. Because Molière's name is so popular much interest has been taken to try to show the parentage of his wife. On the whole, I cannot but think that Armande Béjart was the legitimate daughter of Joseph Béjart and Marie Hervé, though it must be admitted that there is ground for doubt on the matter. As the legal documents have not been proved to be untrue, it is safer to trust to them than to other statements which cannot be guaranteed or which may admit of explanation. I cannot shirk this subject, but must now go into details which I fear will be uninteresting to those not familiar with the circumstantial names and facts, or to those who, though they may admire Molière's comedies, do not care to bother themselves with the troublesome question of the parentage of his wife. If they wish to do so they will skip the remainder of this chapter.

It has been said already that Joseph Béjart, the father of the Béjarts who were to become Molière's comrades on the stage, died probably early in 1643; and that shortly after his death his widow, Marie Hervé, acting under the advice of her friends, renounced by deed in her own name and in those of her five children all claim to his succession because he died heavily indebted and his inheritance would be likely to prove more onerous than profitable. Marie Hervé's deed of renunciation was dated the 10th of March 1643. It is the earliest document (apart from registers of baptism) that tells who were her children, and that states, though only approximately, the date of the birth of Armande Béjart. Armande's baptismal certificate has not been found; but it is accepted, I believe by all, that she must have been the child described in the deed of renunciation as "une petite non baptisée." Soulié thought that Joseph Béjart died at the beginning of 1643,[1] and that as Armande was not mentioned in the deed as a posthumous child, she was born very shortly before his death.[2]

Towards the end of the third paragraph of an anonymous book, *La Fameuse Comédienne*[3] (of which I spoke in chap. v.

[1] *Recherches sur Molière*, 31.   [2] *Ibid.* 33.
[3] Ed. by M. Jules Bonnassies, pp. 6 and 7.

p. 109), it is said of Armande : " She passed her youngest years
in Languedoc with a lady of distinguished rank in the province. Molière, the head of the troop to which Madeleine
belonged, determined to go to Lyons; and her [Madeleine's]
child was taken away from the lady who, having become very
fond of her, was sorry to give her back to her mother to be
brought up amongst a company of strolling actors." This
statement refers probably to the year 1652 or 1653, and,
except in the question of Armande's maternity, it cannot be
contradicted.

In the performance of Corneille's *Andromède* at Lyons in
1653, the part of Éphyre, of only four lines, was given to a
Mlle. Menou ; and it is now believed that this was a pet name
given playfully to little Armande Béjart, then a child of ten
years old. Many French writers think that Molière took
charge of her education, and as evidence of this M. Mesnard
refers to passages in the *École des Maris* and in the *École des
Femmes*.[1] If we are to look to those plays for biographical
details, allowances must be made for the spirit of comedy in
which they are told. The idea, however, seems to be true
enough ; though Armande's upbringing was not of the best
kind. To teach nicely such a girl, the child of a strolling
company, whoever her mother may have been, was a difficult
matter. That Molière was really fond of her seems to be
undoubted. Very little is known of her, but it may be easily
imagined that her young, bright, and pretty face was often a
source of great joy to him, and also of much anxiety.
Chapelle alluded to her playfully and poetically in a letter
to Molière written in the spring of 1659 ; but though this
letter shows Molière's affection for Armande, then a fascinating girl of about sixteen, it hardly adds to our information
about her.

The next thing heard of Armande is her marriage with the
poet. Beffara, who found in 1821 the certificate of Molière's
baptism, found also in the same year the certificate of Molière's
marriage. This document caused great surprise, for it stated
that Armande Béjart was the daughter of the late Joseph
Béjart and of Marie Hervé, and that Madeleine Béjart was
her sister. The marriage ceremony took place in Paris in the

[1] *Notice biographique sur Molière*, 252.

church of Saint Germain l'Auxerrois, on Monday the 20th of February 1662, and was in all respects perfectly regular. Among the witnesses were Jean Poquelin, Molière's father; André Boudet, who had married Molière's sister; Marie Hervé, his mother-in-law; Louis Béjart and Madeleine Béjart, the brother and sister of Armande.[1] This evidence is in flat contradiction to the old tradition that Madeleine Béjart was the mother of Armande. Some men believed the certificate to be true, others did not. Forty years later it was supported by the marriage settlement between Molière and his future wife, dated 23rd of January 1662, nearly a month before the marriage ceremony, and published for the first time in 1863 by Soulié.[2] There it is stated that Armande Béjart, "âgée de vingt ans ou environ," was the daughter of Marie Hervé, widow of the late Joseph Béjart, and that Louis and Madeleine Béjart were her brother and sister. But though Molière's marriage settlement corroborated the certificate of his marriage ceremony in saying that Armande Béjart was Marie Hervé's daughter, everybody was not convinced that the old tradition was false. And there are reasons which make it appear difficult to conciliate the two contradictory opinions. I will try to state the essential facts as briefly as possible.

One objection against the belief that Marie Hervé was Armande's mother is her somewhat advanced age, say on the 1st of January 1643, about which time Armande was born. It is not, however, possible to be sure how old Marie Hervé then was. She was buried on the 9th of January 1670,[3] and the certificate of her burial states that she was eighty years old. If that be true, she was born in 1590, and in January 1643 she was fifty-three and unlikely to have borne a child at that age. But Madeleine Béjart's epitaph on her mother, composed not long afterwards, according to one reading, says that Marie Hervé was seventy-five when she died, according to another reading seventy-three.[4] If the first reading of the

---

[1] The certificate is given by Jal, *Dictionnaire*, 871 col. 1; and by M. Mesnard, *Notice biographique sur Molière*, 471.

[2] *Recherches sur Molière*, 57, 58; 203-5. Also given by M. Mesnard, *Notice biographique sur Molière*, 468.

[3] Jal, *Dictionnaire*, 184 col. 2. Jal printed here "iv janvier 1670" for "ix janvier," but he notified the small mistake among his list of errata.

[4] For this difference of opinion see *Le Moliériste* for May 1883 (vol. v. 51), and for October 1886 (vol. viii. 211).

epitaph be correct, Marie Hervé was forty-eight in January 1643; if the second is to be trusted, she was then forty-six. Now, Marie Hervé's burial certificate was signed by her son Louis Béjart, and by her son-in-law Léonard de Loménie (the first husband of Geneviève Béjart); but Madeleine Béjart is perhaps more likely to have known her mother's age than her brother Louis, twelve years her junior, and certainly more likely to have known it than her brother-in-law. According to the epitaph Marie Hervé was either forty-six or forty-eight at the time of Armande's birth, at the end of 1642 or early in 1643; and this agrees fairly well with Soulié, who says Marie Hervé was married in 1615 and was more than forty-five at the end of 1643.[1] Even at the age of forty-eight she is more likely to have become the mother of Armande than at the age of fifty-three. And I am more inclined to trust to either reading of the epitaph, in determining Marie Hervé's age, than to her burial certificate.[2]

Another objection to the belief that Marie Hervé was Armande Béjart's mother, is that in Armande's marriage settlement Marie Hervé promised to give Armande 10,000 livres; and in fact five months later Molière gave an acknowledgment that he had received 10,000 livres from Marie Hervé.[3] In March 1643 Marie Hervé had represented herself as a poor woman, and it is difficult to imagine how she could have had so much money of her own to give away in 1662. Her daughter Madeleine, however, is believed to have been rich, and if she gave 10,000 livres in her mother's name to Armande, that would not make Armande her child. I think it is safer to make that supposition—for no one can tell now what were the intimate relations between the persons concerned—than to deny the truth of the legal documents in

---

[1] *Recherches sur Molière*, 32. It will be seen that reference is made here to the end of the preceding paragraph.

[2] There were two other instances in Molière's family in which doubt is thrown on the validity of the burial certificates. Marie Cressé, Molière's mother, the parish register says, was buried on the 11th of May, but the lawyer's inventory taken after her death says that she died on the 15th of May. (See *ante*, chap. i. p. 52 note 1.) Both of these authorities cannot be right. And in the case of Molière's widow, afterwards Mlle. Guérin, the parish register says that she died " âgée de cinquante-cinq ans." Soulié held firmly that Mlle. Guérin must have been fifty-seven or fifty-eight at the time of her death (*Recherches sur Molière*, 105).

[3] Soulié, *Recherches sur Molière*, 204, 205.

stating that Armande Béjart was Marie Hervé's child, because Marie Hervé could not have given Armande so large a dowry. It has also been urged that when Geneviève Béjart married, in 1664, her marriage portion was only 4000 livres. Of this 500 livres was paid in money and 3500 livres was reckoned in "habits, linges et meubles."[1] But the husband of Geneviève was not in a position to expect that his wife should have such a large dowry as was the husband of Armande.

Because I did not wish to enter into too many details, I purposely refrained in speaking of Marie Hervé's deed of renunciation on the 10th of March 1643, from saying that she there described all her children as minors.[2] Twenty-five was then the age of majority, and Madeleine was certainly twenty-five; and her brother Joseph was probably older than she was. It is not easy to see why Marie Hervé was advised by her friends to make this false declaration. French writers have thought that if all her children were minors legal matters would be simplified and money saved, but they have not been able to prove any other effect. M. Mesnard condemns the false declaration, as it might have given rise to many frauds,[3] though he gives no instance of a fraud resulting from it. Because Marie Hervé made a false declaration as to the ages of her children it does not follow that the rest of the deed of renunciation was untrue. Those who believe that both the marriage settlement between Molière and Armande Béjart and the certificate of their marriage ceremony were founded more or less fraudulently upon Marie Hervé's deed of renunciation, should give stronger evidence for their belief in the frauds which they think are contained in those two documents, than the assertion that Armande was Madeleine's child.

M. Jules Loiseleur, who holds that Armande was Madeleine's child, says that if Marie Hervé made a false declaration as to the ages of her children she would not have scrupled to say that Armande was her child when she knew that she was not. M. Loiseleur thinks that Armande was Madeleine's child, but that the Comte de Modène was not her father. He begins by assuming, as far as I can see gratuitously, that at the end of

---

[1] Soulié, *Recherches sur Molière*, 213.   [2] *Ibid.* 31 ; 172.
[3] *Notice biographique sur Molière*, 254.

1642 or early in 1643 Madeleine was going to give birth to
a child, and from that assumption he declares that Marie
Hervé's deed of renunciation was a fraud as regards the
parentage of Armande,[1] and that other documents framed
upon it—doubtless Armande's marriage settlement and the
certificate of her marriage—when investigated will be found
to be untrue.[2] M. Loiseleur's theory is that Madeleine was
anxious not to lose her influence with her old lover the
Comte de Modène, and to conceal her maternity persuaded
her mother to declare herself the mother of her child. He
thinks that if Armande's baptismal certificate were found it
would be worthless, because it was based on Marie Hervé's
declaration on the 10th of March 1643, false in his opinion
in saying that Armande was her daughter; and that this and
subsequent frauds emanated from the deed of guardianship to
the children—in itself a fraud—which the deed of renunciation implied as having been signed.[3] But as the deed of
guardianship has not been found it is hardly fair to condemn
it as being false.

Besides the documents already mentioned, there are many
others in Soulié's volume which state that Madeleine and
Armande Béjart were sisters. To one of these I should like
to call attention. On the 9th of February 1672 Madeleine
Béjart made her will.[4] Her mind was sound, but she thought
that the hand of death was upon her; in fact she died a week
later, aged fifty-four years. Would she have very fervently
implored the mercy of her God and have prepared to die with
a lie upon her soul, saying that Armande was her sister, if
Armande had been her child? She was either right or
grievously wrong. Madeleine Béjart's life when she was
young had not been pure, but she was a keen and intelligent
woman of the world; and to think without proofs that on
her deathbed she refused to acknowledge her own child is to
pass a hard judgment on her.

It may not be amiss to ask, how did the tradition arise
which said that Armande was Madeleine's daughter? If it
was founded on solid fact nothing more can be said, but

---

[1] *Points obscurs de la Vie de Molière*, 239 ; 242.
[2] *Ibid.* 247.   [3] *Ibid.* 238.
[4] Soulié, *Recherches sur Molière*, 243.

most Frenchmen who have taken an interest in the matter hold now that Armande was Madeleine's sister. It would not be wonderful if the tradition were founded on spite, and accepted by some out of ill-will, and by others from natural thoughtlessness—caring no more about Armande's parentage than about that of the wife of their grocer. There can be no certainty in answer to the proposed question, but I will try to state fairly what appears to me a probable conjecture.

In a letter to a friend, written in November or December 1663, Racine, then quite a young man, said that he had been to court, that he had seen Molière there, and that Montfleury (an actor at the Hôtel de Bourgogne) had presented a petition to the king saying that Molière had married the daughter of a woman who had been his mistress. Racine's only remark was: "Mais Montfleury n'est pas écouté à la cour."[1] If Montfleury did present this petition, it is extremely unlikely that the other members of his troop did not know that he had done so. The actors at the Hôtel de Bourgogne were very bitter against Molière, because they found that his plays took the public away from their theatre, and because they believed that their plays were superior to those acted at the Palais Royal. We all know how spite can warp men's minds when interests of various kinds are concerned; it need not be surprising, therefore, if the actors at the Hôtel de Bourgogne tried to spread about a report intended to injure a rival who was doing his best, though fairly, to take the bread out of their mouths. Something has been said already about this hostility towards Molière, and we shall see in the next chapter how open war broke out between him and the men at the Hôtel de Bourgogne. Happily, however, we do not read that the name of Mlle. Molière—for she was then married—was dragged into this quarrel. Small attention seems to have been given to Montfleury's petition; for in the year after it was presented the Duc de Créqui, in the king's name, and the Maréchale du Plessis, in the name of the Duchess of Orleans, were sponsors to Molière's first-born child. If the report as to Armande's birth had no better foundation than

---

[1] *Œuvres de J. Racine*, by M. Paul Mesnard, in the "Collection des Grands Écrivains de la France," vol. vi. 506 ; also M. Mesnard's *Notice biographique sur Molière*, 265, 360.

U

Montfleury's petition and, more especially, the talk among the actors at the Hôtel de Bourgogne, I can understand very well that Molière did not choose to contradict the charge; and no contradiction of it by him is now known to have been made.

The accusation was taken up after the poet's death, and in the way of printed evidence the tradition that Armande was Madeleine's daughter rests now upon three heads. Firstly, what was said by the anonymous author of *La Fameuse Comédienne* [Mlle. Molière], a book printed in 1688, and in which one reads : "Elle est fille de la défunte Béjart," etc. ;[1] secondly, upon some words spoken by Boileau to Brossette in 1702 : "M. Despréaux [Boileau was often called Despréaux] m'a dit que Molière avait été amoureux premièrement de la comédienne Béjart dont il avait épousé la fille " ;[2] and thirdly, upon Grimarest's *Vie de Molière*, published in 1705, where the author takes for granted that Madeleine was Armande's mother.[3] Whatever truth there may be in the pages of *La Fameuse Comédienne*, it is a book cleverly written in some parts but composed in spite to throw scandal on Molière's widow, then another man's wife. A word from La Grange in his preface in 1682 might, perhaps, have prevented the above mentioned assertion; but if Molière had not denied the charge, La Grange, who was certainly not garrulous when his pen was in his hand, thought well to say nothing about it. His business in this preface was to speak of Molière and his plays, not of his wife, and he made no allusion to her name. In his Register, too, though he mentioned Molière's marriage and gave the name of his wife, he said nothing about her parentage; and that also was a book where, with very rare exceptions, he spoke only of the details of the theatre. As to Boileau, he was an upright man, and would not willingly have wronged the memory of one who had been his friend but his words have a strong air of everyday gossip. He was not one to inquire into the private affairs of other people, and he, like others, may have been misinformed. He was intimate with Racine, who, from his own fault, had ceased

[1] Edited by M. Jules Bonnassies, p. 6.
[2] *Correspondance entre Boileau et Brossette*, par A. Laverdet, 517 ; and P. Mesnard, *Notice biographique sur Molière*, 255.
[3] See pp. 35 and 36.

to be Molière's friend, and Racine may without ill-will have told him what he had heard from the actors at the Hôtel de Bourgogne, where nearly all of his plays were performed. And as to Grimarest, he had, as he says himself, been largely supplied with information by Baron, who, when he was a lad, had quarrelled with Mlle. Molière after he had tried to make love to her. Baron was one of those who seceded from the Palais Royal to the Hôtel de Bourgogne after Molière's death, and he may have told Grimarest what he had heard, as, perhaps, Boileau had told Brossette. Now, if it be a fair conjecture that these three authorities—the book *La Fameuse Comédienne*, Boileau and Grimarest—derived their information as to the parentage of Armande Béjart from one source, that is from the talk among the actors at the Hôtel de Bourgogne, the value of their testimony becomes weakened very considerably.

The whole of this matter is unpleasant. The alleged past relations between Molière and Madeleine Béjart have indeed not been proved, but it would be futile to deny them ; and the fact of his marriage with Armande, even supposing that she was the daughter of Marie Hervé, causes a disagreeable feeling. Molière loved little Armande when she was a child, and the charm grew upon him until he found it to be irresistible. The story of his life shows that he was a straight-thinking man, and his satire shows that he was guided by good sense and delicacy of taste ; but no one can think that, under similar circumstances, he would have approved of such a marriage between other persons.

CHAPTER XIII

THE *École des Femmes*, first acted on the 26th of December 1662, was the eighth play that Molière put on the stage. It would seem that, conscious of his own desires and aspirations, he had hitherto proceeded cautiously in his endeavours to show dramatically the humours of the persons he wished to describe. One of his early plays, however, *Don Garcie de Navarre*, was a failure; his heroic comedy was a poor attempt at a play of a bad kind. Otherwise, Molière appears to have kept his ambition well in hand, and to have recognised that the lesson he had to learn was not an easy one. A little later he wrote: " C'est une étrange entreprise que celle de faire rire les honnêtes gens." Making the crowd laugh was not sufficient. Molière did not disdain popular laughter, but he wished also to enliven and amuse the better educated part of his audience by showing them the faults and follies of their neighbours in a spirit of good comedy. He knew that the task was difficult, and, perhaps because it had not been accomplished in plays before his time, he spoke of it as " a strange undertaking."

More than a year elapsed after his arrival in Paris from the provinces before he brought out a new play of his own. And, modest in his ideas of his own powers, he thought he would be more likely to attain his object by writing short light plays before he felt his hand strong enough to fill a seriously meant five-act comedy in a manner satisfactory to himself and to his audience. Speaking broadly, Molière's early plays show a gradual improvement in the tone and spirit of comedy. It was felt in Paris that a comic dramatist had arisen with new and bright ideas, and that he showed them in a way that was more sparkling, truer, and with greater vitality than had been seen hitherto. Dramatists before his time, too, often looked upon the stage as a platform for mental exercises. Molière soon grasped the truth that if comedy does not amuse audiences will not be really interested in it, and that unless their feelings are stirred no other kind of eloquence will be effectual.

Despois began his Notice to the *École des Femmes*[1] by saying that this comedy " was not only Molière's greatest dramatic success in the whole course of his career, but that after its appearance rival actors and jealous authors began to write against him a series of pamphlets assailing his private character as well as his reputation as an author and as an actor." No comedy in France before the *École des Femmes* had excited so much interest. It was both loudly abused and loudly praised. Though it is far from being Molière's greatest play, it is in point of characterisation the best comedy that he had written up to that time. Before its appearance playgoers had not seen on the stage a picture of a bright, fresh-minded girl shown in an easy and natural way. This was to them a new thing and was the chief source of their delight. But there were many critics who immediately found fault with the construction of the comedy. The complaint was not quite ill-grounded, for the greater part of the story is told in narrative, much of the dialogue relates to what has happened, showing indirectly what has been done or said. The play was attacked by some because of its supposed impieties, and jeered at by others for what they thought were trivialities. If the comedy had not given pleasure to very many it would not have continued to fill the theatre for so long a time. It will be convenient to look at the idea shown in the comedy before speaking of the quarrel which arose from the success of the play.

The *École des Femmes* was the complement to the *École des Maris*, and might have been so called if the other play had not been written. In the first the dramatist showed that bringing up girls under lock and key was likely to defeat its object; in the second, that enforced ignorance will not prevent an intelligent girl from knowing her own mind, that like should mate with like, and that a man should not say to the woman he wants to marry—

"Du côté de la barbe est la toute puissance."

---

[1] *Œuvres de Molière*, iii. 107.

In both comedies, especially in the latter one, there is some satire on the selfishness of husbands; but the gist of the censure did not lie there. Molière wished in both comedies to put forward a plea for more humanity towards girls who were treated as chattels, having no property in themselves, but were owned by those who had authority over them, and made to marry—not that they might be happy, but that parents or guardians should reap an advantage.

The plot in the *École des Femmes* was taken from some stories in the middle ages that had long been popular, and also from a romance of Scarron's *La Précaution Inutile*.[1]

Arnolphe has taken charge of Agnès, no relation of his, since she was a baby; he is truly in love with her, but he is selfish, and though some have said that he is " un homme d'esprit," he has extremely silly ideas. Agnès is perhaps the favourite among Molière's young heroines. She is regarded as the type of the " ingénue " in French fiction—a simple-minded girl who believes what is said to her and thinks no harm of any one. Her disposition is bright, she is charmingly portrayed, and she has a coquetry of her own which is both piquant and amusing; but Arnolphe wished to bring her up so that she should learn nothing and know nothing—

> " Pour la faire idiote autant qu'il se pourroit."

Horace, a well-meaning, giddy youth, has fallen in love with her, and she is captivated by his addresses. Molière himself said that the keynote to his comedy was the thoughtless confidence with which Horace relates his adventures to Arnolphe, who was his rival, and the open way in which Agnès tells Arnolphe what has passed between herself and Horace, and yet that Arnolphe should not be able to prevent the catastrophe. Arnolphe is severe on the frailties of women, and talking to himself on their worthlessness, he says :—

> " et malgré tout cela,
> Dans le monde on fait tout pour ces animaux-là."

These words gave great offence to the précieuses. Because he does not believe in women's good intentions Arnolphe has determined that he will mould a wife for himself. He is

---

[1] *Œuvres de Molière*, iii. 115-17; xi. 126; also M. Louis Moland's *Œuvres de Molière*, 1st ed. ii. 389-93.

in love with the idea of marrying a fool, and he dreads the presence of a clever woman. In spite of the ridicule seen against him, there is a pathos, often shown with poetry, in his love for the girl he has fostered since she was a child, and whom he had cherished with the hope of making his own. His jealousy of Horace will be understood and forgiven, but his tyranny, his egotism, and his folly, all condemn him.

It is amusing to see how Arnolphe struggles hard under his ungovernable selfishness to keep his temper while he is being played upon by Horace quite innocently, and to notice how Agnès seconds her lover, not knowing in the least what he has done. Molière saw the comic side of the picture, and in planning his play he directed his thoughts to that purpose. Ridicule thus shown is a keen weapon, and taking the comedy as it was intended Molière did his work excellently well. In fiction it is generally safer criticism to accept an author's ideas as he meant them, to see what use he has made of them and how he worked them out, than to find fault with his story because it does not accord with our own tastes. Tastes alter. There are long speeches in the play which the audiences of two hundred and fifty years ago listened to gladly, but which would now be thought wearisome. It would now be thought strange that Horace and Agnès should not be brought together on the stage until the third scene of the fifth act; and we should certainly think now that Arnolphe sermonises Agnès at too great length in Act III. sc. 2. When he told her that if she did not obey his lessons she would go as one of the devil's own

" Bouillir dans les enfers à toute éternité,"

his lines caused some scandal on the score of impiety, and this was the first time that Molière was censured for profaning the doctrines of the Church. But Molière was not thinking of the doctrines of the Church. He wished to satirise an egoist who made himself ridiculous, and he threw all his earnestness into his satire. And one is tempted to think that, though Horace is not without good sentiments, if the dramatist had given him a finer nature instead of making him appear to be a heedless young beau, he would have enhanced the value of the character and have given to the lover a stronger interest on his own account. But it was the

Arnolphes of the world, as common as house-tops in every street, that Molière meant to censure. Such men were fathers, or uncles, or guardians, who wished to make their girls marry rich, elderly bachelors whom in many cases the girls hardly knew ; or they might be elderly bachelors who wanted to marry young girls who had no wish to have them for husbands. It was the self-interestedness of those in power that Molière strove to denounce, and he did not trouble himself much to sing the praises of his hero who was to rescue Agnès from her keeper. Agnès was not the simpleton that Arnolphe had tried to make her, and perhaps he had a lucky escape from what he dreaded most.

Even hostile critics said that the play was well acted. Molière was his own Arnolphe, Mlle. de Brie was Agnès, La Grange was Horace. The other actors had smaller parts. L'Espy is said to have been Chrysalde ; Brécourt and Mlle. Marotte (a gagiste in the troop) were Alain and Georgette, Arnolphe's two servants. Some of the scenes in which they appeared had a capital effect. It was after a performance of the *École des Femmes* that Louis XIV. said of Brécourt, " That man would make a stone laugh." De Brie is supposed to have been the notary who has an amusing scene with Arnolphe in the fourth act ; and perhaps Molière spoke what he thought of de Brie when Arnolphe says of the notary :—

" La peste soit fait l'homme et sa chienne de face."
(Devil take the man and his beastly mug.)

So far as is known, Mlle. de Brie was quite forty when she first played Agnès, and she kept the part for more than twenty years. At the end of the 17th century M. de Tralage wrote of her :—" A few years before she left the stage her comrades advised her to give up the part to Mlle. du Croisy " [du Croisy's daughter, Angélique, then Mlle. Poisson]. " When this actress came forward, the whole of the pit cried so loudly for Mlle. de Brie that she was fetched from her house and made to play the part without changing her dress. One may imagine the applause she received. She appeared as Agnès until she retired from the stage." [This was at Easter 1685.] " She played it even when she was sixty-five years old."[1]

[1] *Œuvres de Molière*, iii. 149.

Mlle. de Brie was a pretty, thin, graceful woman, and must have been very popular.

Molière could console himself for the hard things that were said against his play, from the fact that while it was new his theatre was better filled than it had ever been before. But the censure began at the first performance. It would seem that Boileau was then present. He was twenty-six years old and did not know Molière. He was delighted with the new comedy, and wrote at once a short poem which he sent to the dramatist as a complimentary new year's gift. As this poem has some pointed and graceful lines I will quote the 1st, 3rd, and 5th stanzas:—

STANCES À M. MOLIÈRE, SUR SA COMÉDIE DE L'ÉCOLE DES FEMMES QUE PLUSIEURS GENS FRONDAIENT

" En vain mille jaloux esprits,
Molière, osent avec mépris
Censurer ton plus bel ouvrage :
Sa charmante naïveté
S'en va pour jamais, d'âge en âge,
Divertir la postérité.

" Ta muse avec utilité
Dit plaisamment la vérité.
Chacun profite à ton école :
Tout en est beau, tout en est bon ;
Et ta plus burlesque parole
Est souvent un docte sermon.

" Laisse gronder tes envieux :
Ils ont beau crier en tous lieux
Qu'en vain tu charmes le vulgaire ;
Que tes vers n'ont rien de plaisant :
Si tu savais un peu moins plaire
Tu ne leur déplairais pas tant."

The first edition of the *École des Femmes* was printed on the 17th of March 1663. It bore a frontispiece showing Arnolphe sitting in a chair with a book in one hand and pointing to his forehead with the other. Agnès is standing in front of him. He is going to lecture her, and he says (at the beginning of Act III. sc. 2) :—

" Là, regardez-moi là durant cet entretien."

La Grange says in his Register that at Easter 1663 L'Espy

retired from the troop, thus reducing the number of shares from fifteen to fourteen.　Then he adds :—

"At the same time M. de Molière received a pension from the king as a bel esprit, and his name was inscribed on the state list for the sum of 1000 livres.　Thereupon he wrote an acknowledgment in verse to his Majesty."

Despois printed Molière's *Remercîment au Roi* immediately after the *École des Femmes*, thinking that La Grange was correct as to when the pension was first given; but M. Mesnard says that Molière's name was not put on the list of pensions until some six or seven months later.[1]　The small difference in date was of no consequence, and it was not in Molière's nature to trouble himself because the sum allowed to him was less than that granted to many others.　He must, however, have had a sense of pride that his work had been recognised and esteemed by the king and by those who had placed his name upon the list of gratifications awarded to men of letters. This was a mark of distinction, and Molière had good reason to feel honoured at having received it.　Looking back at a past time, it is curious to read :—

"Au sieur *Chapelain*, le plus grand poëte françois qui ait jamais été et du plus solide jugement . . . 3000 livres.

"Au sieur *Pierre Corneille*, premier poëte dramatique du monde . . . 2000 livres.

"Au sieur *Molière*, excellent poëte comique . . . 1000 livres."

Molière's *Remercîment au Roi*, printed some time in 1663, is a satirical picture showing how eager were noblemen to be admitted to the king's levee; and in a tone of banter the poet describes how a courtier who wishes to pay his respects should dress, how he should enter the chamber, and when he has reached the chair how he should make his compliment :—

> "Mais les grands princes n'aiment guères
> Que les compliments qui sont courts."

As soon as the courtier has opened his mouth the king will smile softly, knowing all that his subject has to say : with that the subject should rest satisfied.

For a sterner picture of the self-interest of noblemen who left no stone unturned to get themselves in place, one may

[1] *Œuvres de Molière*, iii. 284 ; *Notice biographique sur Molière*, 286.

look at the chapter "De la Cour" in La Bruyère's *Caractères ou les Mœurs de ce Siècle*. This book was first published in 1687, and it reached a ninth edition, very much enlarged, in 1695, the year of its author's death. In France La Bruyère is ranked high among the prose classics, but in England he is little known. Yet he is worth knowing both as a thinker and as an author; though it may seem to us now that he wrote in riddles, and his style is that of a mannerist. His *Caractères* is a good complement to Molière's comedies; it is a faithful chronicle of the feelings of men and women of the time. But it was intended for careful readers, not for the larger public who enjoyed the effects of stage representation. La Bruyère as well as Molière had opportunities of watching the carriage of men who pushed themselves at court. They were both of bourgeois birth, yet they satirised men and women of the world with so much good taste that they have always had the laughter on their side. Skill in writing will not alone account for this; their hearts were true and their minds were free from vulgarity.

The quarrel occasioned by the success of the *École des Femmes* was much talked about in Paris, and, from a biographical point of view, it is important. I dwell upon it because it throws light on Molière's character in showing how he thought and what he said when the storm was raised against him by the rival troop at the Hôtel de Bourgogne theatre; and it shows the brightness of one man's mind against the dulness of those of his opponents. In his *Critique de l'École des Femmes* and in his *Impromptu de Versailles*, Molière told honestly and in a spirit of comedy what were the matters in dispute; he put his adversaries' case so well that they could not contradict what he said, nor could they urge anything more on their own behalf. He had something to say that is still worth reading; and though some of their censures against the construction of the plot of the *École des Femmes* were valid they gave way to angry jealousy, they had little wit for attack or for self-defence, and what they wrote was certainly very poor comedy.

De Visé's name has been mentioned already. He was young, clever, industrious and pushing; he recognised Molière's great abilities, and when he saw that there was a

quarrel between the poet and his rivals, the troop at the
Hôtel de Bourgogne, he took their side because he thought
it would be most advantageous to him. He was perhaps the
first who began this battle with pen and ink, though tongues
had been at work some time before. About seven weeks after
the appearance of the *École des Femmes* he published a three-
volume novel, *Les Nouvelles Nouvelles*, and there he both
extolled and blamed Molière's play. It was most probably de
Visé who later wrote two comedies against Molière—*Zélinde*
and *La Vengeance des Marquis*—though as to the authorship
of these plays there has been some confusion. De Visé did
not put his name to his work, but it is hard to suppose that
his friends did not know what he had done; and Molière, if
his eyes were open, must have known it also. In 1665, when
all this quarrel had passed, Molière put one of de Visé's
comedies on the stage at the Palais Royal; and in 1666 de
Visé wrote a *Lettre sur le Misanthrope*, praising the comedy
very highly, though Molière knew nothing of the letter till it
was printed, and was not glad to see it. Later three or four
comedies appeared at the Palais Royal, written by this man
who had been the adversary of the head of the troop at that
theatre. De Visé wished to make his way in the world; and
at a time when ideas of honesty in literary matters were often
lax he might well have extolled Molière at one moment,
abused him afterwards, and later again have praised him, if
his inclinations or his interest ran that way. Molière knew
what it all meant, he was good-natured and forgiving towards
one who was struggling with the battle of life and who did
not really mean mischief; and it is not likely that the
dramatist bothered himself about what de Visé had written in
a novel against a play which the town had applauded very
loudly. In 1672 de Visé established *Le Mercure Galant*, a
poor periodical which was intended to give exalted social
news; and after Molière's death this paper brought him the
kind of notoriety that he wanted.[1]

Boursault was another of Molière's opponents. He had
already written two or three plays, and one of these, *Le
Médecin Volant*, was called by the same name as one of

[1] A short account of de Visé is given by M. Fournel in his *Contemporains
de Molière*, iii. 445-50.

Molière's early farces. Both authors drew their sketch from the same groundwork. As an adversary Boursault was hardly more formidable than de Visé, but he was more honestly ambitious, for he had the courage to write under his own name. He was pushed into the fray and made the mouthpiece of others, and it has been said that he was punished too severely. He was only twenty-five, but he need not have been such a simpleton. His vanity brought him more than he bargained for, and he did not meddle with Molière again. I should add that Boursault's head seems to have been more to blame in this matter than his heart. He is spoken of as a man who had the esteem of his contemporaries. Boileau once satirised his verses; Boursault forgave him and afterwards lent him money. Late in the century two of Boursault's comedies were successful on the stage.[1]

I will quote what de Visé said in his *Nouvelles Nouvelles* about the *École des Femmes*, as his opinions represented a fair section of contemporary thought.

"This comedy produced effects that were quite new. Everybody thought it was bad, and everybody rushed to see it. Ladies spoke ill of it, and they also went to see it. The play was successful but it did not please, and it pleased many who did not think it good. But to tell you my opinion, no plot was ever so badly managed, and I am ready to maintain that there is not a scene without numberless faults. Nevertheless, I am bound to confess, to be just to the author's merits, that this comedy is a monster with fine points, and that no one ever saw so many good and bad things put side by side. There are some so natural that it would seem they were nature's own work; there are passages which are inimitable, and which are so well expressed that I cannot find language strong or pointed enough to give you a true idea of them. . . . They are nature's portraits, which might pass for being original. It seems as if she were speaking herself. These passages occur not only when Agnès is on the stage, but they are to be found in every character. Never was a comedy better performed or with so much ability. Each actor knows how many steps he ought to take, and every wink of the eye is counted."[2]

From his preface to the *École des Femmes*, printed 17th March 1663, it may be seen that Molière had soon conceived the idea of answering his detractors by writing a little comedy. A certain abbé du Buisson, whom the poet alludes to in this

<hr>

[1] V. Fournel, *Les Contemporains de Molière*, i. 93-102.
[2] P. Mesnard, *Notice biographique sur Molière*, 467.

preface as " a person of quality whose wit is well known in the world, and who does me the honour to love me," pressed him to carry out his idea. The abbé even wrote such a comedy, or sketch of a comedy, himself, and showed it to Molière. But Molière dissuaded him from publishing it.[1] I have little doubt that Molière thought that if any play of his required a public answer, he himself ought to make it. For a while he was uncertain what to do; then his answer came.

The *École des Femmes* had been acted as a new play from Christmas 1662 up to the Easter holidays in 1663. Easter fell early in 1663, for the Palais Royal theatre was opened after the holidays on the 6th of April. On the 1st of June the *École des Femmes* was revived, and with it, as an afterpiece, Molière put on the stage the *Critique* upon his own play that had created so much stir. The *Critique de l'École des Femmes* is a one-act comedy in prose, in which the dramatist gives an amusing picture of the hard things that were said of his former play which he pretends to criticise. He shows here his own views of comedies and of the manner of writing them much more than in any other play that came from his pen. At the same time, it is well to notice his irony and to recollect that it was his humour to mix satire and earnestness together. His *Critique* must not be looked upon merely as a defence. Unless he had more than a defence to offer he had better have been silent; unless he could throw his shells into the enemies' tents and do some damage there, he was dooming himself to defeat. Molière thought far less of answering the objections made against his late play than of laughing at his opponents and showing that they were on a wrong tack. His enemies were to be found in various camps. There were the actors at the Hôtel de Bourgogne; authors who had written or who hoped to write for that theatre, and those men who set themselves up as good judges of a play and who liked the old style of comedy better than his; fine gentlemen and men of good position in the world who thought that their dignity would be compromised if they were known to take Molière's part; prudish women and those who were proud of the title of

---

[1] P. Mesnard, *Notice biographique sur Molière*, 468. What Molière says in his preface, printed 17th March 1663, seems to agree tolerably well on this point with what de Visé had written in his *Nouvelles Nouvelles*, printed 9th February in the same year.

"précieuse"; and many who said they were shocked at Arnolphe's sermon to Agnès and at the "maximes du mariage." I may say here that if Molière mentioned this objection he did not dwell upon it. To the nonsense of his critics who did not like "tarte à la crême," "les enfants par l'oreille," and "la scène du potage," he replied by nonsense of his own in which there is some fun; he showed what prudery was, and he answered the trivialities of the précieuses who were disgusted because he had made Arnolphe call women animals. The scene known as "la scène du potage" is short, and its fun will be understood by those who read it. But explanation of the words "tarte à la crême" and "les enfants par l'oreille" would be long, and no one would thank me for giving it.[1] In both cases a harmless jest was used to satirise Arnolphe's folly and to make him talk in a ridiculous manner. The expressions disgusted many who were delicate; they thought the words showed very bad taste. To talk in such a way in a farce might be allowed, for those who found their amusement in farces were not discriminating; but in a five-act comedy in verse it was deplorable. Molière, happily, was not so dainty.

All through his *Critique* Molière throws off his banter admirably. But he was in earnest when he said that comedies written according to rule were not likely to be better than those dictated by common-sense; he was also in earnest when he spoke of authors' jealousies and of their "trafficking for reputation." His allusion to the court should not be taken too literally. By that term he meant to include good society, of which the court was then the natural head. He meant, too, that joining in the society of one's fellows, taking one's part in it, and noticing the play of life seen there, gave better opportunities for judging a comedy than reading disquisitions on the drama. Molière, I take it, did not like to find himself blamed for not showing the dull-headedness that he had observed to be general in other comedies. The crowd saw that he was right, but those who ought to have known better abused him. His objects in the *Critique* were to uphold the

---

[1] For the first see Despois' note, *Œuvres de Molière*, iii. 165 note 4; and for the other an article by M. Martin-Dairvault in the *Moliériste* for March 1888 (vol. ix. 359).

judgment of the crowd and to satirise those who had found
fault with him wrongly.   He brings forward by degrees three
ladies and three gentlemen, and by the quickness of their
dispute he tells, as it seems with perfect fairness, what were
the objections raised against the *École des Femmes*.   The new
play may be enjoyed thoroughly without any knowledge of
the other, for it is managed with much pleasantry and dramatic
skill, and it shows all the babble that the excitement of a
quarrel produces.   The action lies in the rapid exchange of
opinions on a subject which a few months earlier had been
the gossip of every playgoer in Paris.   To that extent all
the personages show themselves for what they are; men and
women are talking about one thing, and they say very plainly
what they think.   As a picture of an animated conversational
scene the dramatisation in the little comedy is excellent.
The satire is frank and good-humoured, and this will usually
carry further and be better remembered than ill-natured wit,
however clever it may be.   There is some quasi-argument
towards the end of the comedy, and there Molière says what
he thinks of plays intended to be regular and of the kind of
satisfaction they gave to those who applauded them.   But the
preciseness and the doctrinaire opinions are all on one side,
for they certainly formed no part of Molière's creed; he speaks
of them in order to show that in a stage play they are entirely
out of place.

Much of the satire was directed against those persons,
authors and others, who considered short and amusing plays
as farces—good enough perhaps to satisfy the multitude—
but that men of taste demanded tragedy, or at least comedy
that showed nobility of style.   Lysidas, a jealous poet, is
made to say: "On voit une solitude effroyable aux grands
ouvrages, lorsque des sottises ont tout Paris."   It has been
said that these words were a hit at Pierre Corneille, whose
tragedies at this time were far less popular than his earlier
ones had been; his *Sophonisbe* had fallen nearly flat a few
months before at the Hôtel de Bourgogne.   If, however,
Molière meant anything personal in his satire, he was perhaps
thinking rather of Thomas Corneille and of a letter which he
had written a few years before to the abbé de Pure—the gist
of which had most probably been made known to Molière—

saying that though the troop at the Petit Bourbon could act a trifle like the *Précieuses Ridicules*, a serious play was beyond their power.[1] In any case, Molière could say with pardonable pride that his own plays, whether "sottises" or not, filled his theatre. In battling against ideas which for the most part he believed to be absurd, but which were prevalent among a large class of persons, Molière says that "comedy is perhaps more difficult to write than tragedy." We must remember here that he spoke only of such tragedy as he had seen, and that he wrote in a vein of satire.

"When you draw heroes you may do what you like. They are fancy portraits, in which no one looks for a resemblance. You have only to let your imagination soar at will, though it leaves aside what is true in its attempt to seize upon what is wonderful. But when you draw men you must draw them naturally. In these portraits there should be a likeness, and your picture is worthless unless you show the people of your own age." [2]

Besides pointing to the want of naturalness in the characterisation, this passage tells also that Molière felt that most of the tragedies of the time were dramatic poems rather than dramas. Whatever his appreciation of tragedy may have been, he knew that the interest in the plays should lie less in exciting incidents or in magniloquent speeches from "heroes" than in the truthful way in which the personages in the play show themselves when their strong or dark passions are aroused, and that it is in the conflict of passions between the personages that the drama in the story is seen. Among those who liked to be considered good judges of plays, tragedy was still more popular in Paris than comedy. These critics held that tragedy was more ennobling than comedy, they believed it was a higher art, and they sided with the Hôtel de Bourgogne against Molière because they considered that tragedy was acted best at the old theatre. They had a full right to think as they pleased, though their opinions were not always sound. Molière had not yet written any of his best plays, but he had already shown that comedy has a life and truth of her own, and that she should have a place beside her more ambitious and perhaps too self-satisfied sister. This

---

[1] P. Mesnard, *Notice biographique sur Molière*, 219, 220.
[2] *Critique de l'École des Femmes*, sc. 6. The quotation is taken from the middle of a speech by Dorante.

was a reform that Molière was gradually accomplishing, and it will be understood that the exponents of tragedy did not look upon his efforts with favourable eyes when they found that his lessons were easily learned and that his teaching was welcomed by an intelligent public.

At the end of the first scene in the *Impromptu de Versailles* Molière says that his wife had played the part of Élise in the *Critique*, Mlle. du Parc that of Climène, and Brécourt that of Dorante. For the other parts it is probable that du Croisy was Lysidas, and that Mlle. de Brie was Uranie. Some editors have assigned to La Grange the part of the Marquis, but Despois thought it was Molière himself who jeered at his own "tarte à la crême." It is believed that Mlle. Molière did not go on the stage before she played the part of Élise in the *Critique de l'École des Femmes*.

The first edition of the comedy was printed on the 7th of August 1663.

The *Critique de l'École des Femmes* was played thirty-two times as a new play, and for a one-act comedy its success was very great indeed. Strong partisan feeling had doubtless much to do with the rush of people to the doors of the Palais Royal, and as this went on Molière's rivals at the Hôtel de Bourgogne became furious. They could not sit still with folded hands and say nothing.

A still-born answer came in the shape of de Visé's *Zélinde, ou la Véritable Critique de l'École des Femmes et la Critique de la Critique*, a one-act comedy in prose, printed on the 4th of August but never acted, at least in public.[1] It is probable enough that de Visé had read his play to the actors at the Hôtel de Bourgogne, and that they declined it as too poor for representation. The purport of *Zélinde* is to show how Molière's

---

[1] It seems to be decided now that de Visé, not de Villiers, was the author of this play.—See *Œuvres de Molière*, iii. 112 note, where Despois corrects his former opinion in favour of de Villiers, given in vol. ii. 339 of the same work. In any case, Despois agreed with M. Fournel that *Les Nouvelles Nouvelles* (printed 9th February 1663), *Zélinde* (printed 4th August 1663), *La Vengeance des Marquis* (acted at the Hôtel de Bourgogne in November or December 1663), and the *Lettre sur les affaires du théâtre* (printed 7th December 1663) were all by the same author. Both M. Mesnard in his *Notice biographique sur Molière*, pp. 220, 277, 298, 300, and M. Desfeuilles in his *Notice bibliographique* to the *Œuvres de Molière*, vol. xi. pp. 120, 128, 130, concur with Despois in attributing these productions to de Visé. In some of them he may have received assistance from de Villiers.

enemies decried his two last comedies. We read that too much of the *École des Femmes* was told in narrative; but for the rest, the criticisms are idle and some of them are uttered in an exceedingly silly manner. Whatever industry or cleverness de Visé may have had, he could not write a tolerable acting comedy, and in his double capacity of playwright and critic he made a clumsy mess of what he had better have left alone. He was the first, I think, who made an anagram of Molière's name, and called him "Élomire." The following extract, taken from scene 8 in the comedy, will show how Molière was looked upon by many who went to see his plays. It may be said that noblemen were then common characters in comedies; Molière had laughed at their inanities, and he continued to do so. Zélinde is a learned woman; Oriane, a lady, is a nonentity; Aristide is a poet:—

" *Zélinde.*

"I have just had a happy thought. I should like to have him [Élomire] tossed in a blanket, and four marquises ought to hold the corners.

" *Aristide.*

"The marquises are too fond of him, and would perhaps put themselves in his place to be well laughed at all round. To make fun of their good friend is the last thing I shall do. I should be torn in pieces if I were to attempt it. There would be less danger in laughing at the marquises themselves. Those whom he takes off best do all they can to patronise him, for fear somebody else should not show their absurdities so well. They like to look at themselves in Élomire's clear mirror better than in their own, and they find the sharpness of his satire useful to them.

" *Oriane.*

"It is useful to those who profit by it, but not many do so, I think.

" *Zélinde.*

"They would be very sorry to profit by it. Élomire laughs at that air of quality which distinguishes them from the bourgeois, and they would not like to have their glory taken from them.

" *Oriane.*

"If so, why do they smile upon Élomire, and why do those whom he ridicules most embrace him when they meet?

" *Zélinde.*

"Because he makes them laugh at one another and call each other turlupin [punster] as they do at court since the *Critique* was acted.

"*Oriane.*

"That should be an encouragement for Monsieur Aristide to set to work.

"*Aristide.*

"Élomire's reputation is too well established, and I am not going to strengthen it; for the more people laugh at him the more he will succeed. . . . Why should I destroy my own reputation by attacking a man who, every turlupin in France vows, can never be equalled? And though they talk in that way without knowing how another may be able to write, one is bound to believe them because they are the persons most interested in it.

"*Zélinde.*

"Do you still hold to this idea? You should make the world laugh as he does, and you will succeed. They only take his side because he amuses them. Make your satire better, go with the taste of the age, and you will see if every one does not say you are as clever as Élomire.

"*Aristide.*

"But . . .

"*Zélinde.*

"What, but . . .

"*Aristide.*

"But fortune smiles upon him."

In his other writings de Visé had spoken of Molière's good luck; and here, in spite of himself, he was praising Molière while he wished to belittle his fun.

The actors at the Hôtel de Bourgogne had to wait some time before they could bring out an answer to Molière's *Critique.* About the middle of October (1663) appeared Boursault's comedy *Le Portrait du Peintre.* The peintre was of course Molière. Boursault pretended that Molière had meant to show him up as Lysidas in the *Critique.* It is not likely that Molière had any such intention. Boursault was one of the hostile critics to the *École des Femmes*; but there were many others. He had written three comedies, none of which could be classed as serious plays, and Molière's Lysidas was represented as a jealous author who is wedded to the tedious regularity of plays in which the laws were observed. Boursault, too, at this time was only twenty-five years old, but Lysidas gives one the idea of a man whose age was nearly fifty. He was a pedant who liked it to be known that he could read Greek and Latin, but Boursault could read neither. Molière's enemies had to look about for some one who could reply to his *Critique de l'École des Femmes*; they hit upon Boursault, and they flattered him into the belief that he was Lysidas. At the end of scene 7 in *Zélinde* Oriane asks : " Who is the Lysidas in the *Critique* ? " Aristide answers : " He is a great man, for he represents all the authors who write for the stage." I think this is the first hint given that Boursault was assisted in the composition of his play *Le Portrait du Peintre*. Molière said so very plainly in his *Impromptu de Versailles*. In one sense Boursault's play is better than de Visé's : it does not read so much like a string of monologues, and it had the advantage of being acted. Molière went to one of its first performances and took a seat on the stage where he could be plainly seen. He had satirised actors, authors, pedants, fashionable gentlemen and affected ladies ; now his turn was come to be laughed at if his adversaries had any show of wit in them. If they could amuse the audience with fair raillery, I believe that Molière would have enjoyed the pleasantry ; if there had been good fun he would have laughed at it. He knew what " chaff " was, and could take it as well as give it. But after the satire in his *Critique* there was too much sore feeling among the party at the Hôtel de Bourgogne to allow of friendly fencing.

One is naturally inclined to ask, How did this quarrel begin ? As far as printed evidence goes, it would seem that Molière first threw down the challenge. When in his *Précieuses Ridicules* he pretended to laugh at his own troop because they spoke their words simply, his rivals did not like his irony. The satire was meant for them, and they knew it. If there had been provocation for this satire the cause is not known now, though we may suppose that it came from emulation between the two companies. Personally, I am not inclined to think that Molière was much in the wrong ; but taking the world as we find it, I imagine that sharp words had been spoken by the actors at the Hôtel de Bourgogne when they saw that Molière and his troop were making great advances in the popular favour, and that he answered the sharpness by irony. As Molière's comedies drew the public to his theatre, jealousies became stronger ; his rivals tried to disparage his plays and looked for any handle that would serve for abuse. He answered them in his *Critique*, and had the

laughter of the town on his side. Boursault in sc. 4 of his play
alluded to what was known as the "le" in Act II. sc. 5 of the
École des Femmes, because it was said that the word "le" had
an improper signification. As far as I can see, there was
nothing in the play of the actors on the stage to warrant such
a charge. One is surprised now that so much spite should
have been shown about a piece of trumpery. The word "le"
either meant, only that Agnès did not want Arnolphe to know
that Horace had stolen the knot of ribbon or tie that he had
given her, or it had a wrong meaning; and Molière's adversaries construed it to his disadvantage. It is tolerably certain,
too, that those who affected to be scandalised were the most
pleased at what they attacked. A huge pother was made about
a trifle because people liked talking : the guilt lay there. When
men fight they must expect hard knocks. Molière in his
Critique had hit straight out from the shoulder, but he found
himself in front of an adversary who tried to wound him by
underhand thrusts. Also in sc. 4, Boursault makes one of his
personages affirm that he has seen a printed key to Molière's
Critique.[1] The key turns out to be the key of a door! He
called his comedy *Le Portrait du Peintre ou la Contre Critique
de l'École des Femmes*. He called Molière "notre singe," yet
he took his *Critique* to pieces and fashioned his own play upon
it in an inverse sense—as had been suggested in de Visé's
Zélinde. He tried to satirise people as Molière had done and
to satirise Molière at the same time ; he ends only by imitating him. The joke of the town amuses people for a time, but
when it is repeated with falsifying intent it becomes nauseous.
One writer said that when Molière went to see Boursault's
comedy he was disconcerted at what he heard about himself.
It is far more likely that he was annoyed at having to listen
to rubbish, and that he expressed impatience at the thin wit
shown. Poor Boursault ! He was young ; vanity had laid her
hand upon him, and he was led into a trap. He was made to
write the *Portrait du Peintre*, and he suffered in consequence.

Molière's next comedy, the *Impromptu de Versailles*—so
called because it was written quickly and was first acted at
Versailles—would probably not have been written but for
Boursault's *Portrait du Peintre*. Unfortunately the day of the

[1] See V. Fournel, *Les Contemporains de Molière*, i. 144 note 2.

first performance of either play cannot be determined. One would like to know which play—Molière's or Boursault's—was acted first, for there are circumstances connected with them both that have not been recorded. A German eye-witness wrote that he saw Boursault's "new" comedy at the Hôtel de Bourgogne on the 19th of October 1663. M. Mesnard supposes that was the first performance;[1] but does it follow necessarily? As the theatres were open only three times a week, the first performance may have taken place some days earlier.[2] The first performance of Molière's *Impromptu* was given before the king at Versailles, possibly on the 16th of October 1663, but more probably on the 18th or 19th.[3] It was, at all events, between the first and last of those dates. The play appeared for the first time in public on the 4th of November. Internal evidence seems to show that Boursault's comedy had the priority.[4] It is clear, however, that if the words now read in the *Impromptu* are the same as those spoken at the representation at Versailles, Molière must have known a good deal about Boursault's comedy, even though it had not been acted.

All the actors in the *Impromptu* play under their own names. The scene of the comedy is the stage of the theatre in the palace at Versailles.[5] The comedy opens by Molière, as head of his troop, calling his actors together for the rehearsal of a play which, we are to suppose, is to be acted before the king in an antechamber in the palace. There is, however, an illusion: the supposed performance before the king does not take place, and the pretended rehearsal is a counterfeit which the dramatist used as a means of showing his satire. Molière is terribly anxious as to the fate of the representation before the king, and all his troop annoy him further by declaring that they do not know their parts. Mlle. Béjart says to him: "You should have been better advised, and not have undertaken to do what you have promised in a week's time." Then

---

[1] *Notice biographique sur Molière*, 282, 283.

[2] *Œuvres de Molière*, iii. 132 ; xi. 128, 129.

[3] P. Mesnard, *Notice biographique sur Molière*, 283, 284; *Œuvres de Molière*, xi. 14, and note 1.

[4] V. Fournel, *Les Contemporains de Molière*, i. 99 ; 241 note 3; *Œuvres de Molière*, iii. 131, 132 ; 420 note 1.

[5] The scenic indication is so given in the *Œuvres de Molière*, iii. 386 ; and see note 1 to that page.

Molière answers: "How could I help myself, when a king gave me his orders?" Three times in this play Molière says that the king told him to write the comedy.[1] It seems strange now that Louis should have intervened in the quarrel between Molière and his rivals, and have told him to write a comedy against them. But the dramatist would not have three times alleged the king's order to write the play unless the order had in fact been given.

For our purposes here the satire in the *Impromptu* may be divided under two heads: Molière's ridicule of the inflated declamation at the Hôtel de Bourgogne, and his attack upon Boursault and those who had assisted him in the composition of *Le Portrait du Peintre*.

The actors at the Hôtel de Bourgogne had jeered at Molière for his performance in his own heroic-comedy *Don Garcie de Navarre*, and now Molière tried to turn the tables upon them. Most of his troop are with him on the stage, and in giving them the idea of a comedy he had thought of writing he supposes that he is a poet, proud of his own work, who brings his play to a company of actors just arrived from the provinces. At the supposed poet's request one of the Palais Royal actors recites, "in the most natural way possible," a line and a half from one of Corneille's tragedies. The would-be poet (Molière) is not at all satisfied at the elocution shown, and recites himself the same passage and various others, also from tragedies of Corneille, imitating with admiration different actors at the Hôtel de Bourgogne, in the pompous and inflated manner common at that theatre. After the imaginary poet had recited the first passage, the Palais Royal actor, who was doubtless expressing Molière's personal conviction, says: "But it seems to me that a king, alone with the captain of his guard, would speak in a more humane tone and would not rant like a maniac." The would-be poet (Molière) answers: "You do not know anything about it. You go and recite as you have done, and you will see if you hear a single bravo."

These two contrary opinions contain the gist of the matter, and Despois has a good note upon them. He says: "From this it is clear that there were not only two rival troops who

[1] "Deux fois dans la première scène (pp. 391-92 et p. 393), une fois dans la scène ii. (p. 406)," *Œuvres de Molière*, iii. 133 note 3.

tried to disparage each other, but two different systems of elocution—one trying to be natural and simple, the other not afraid of extravagance but looking on it as a sure means of producing effect." [1] Molière's banter in his *Précieuses Ridicules* against "les grands comédiens" was pleasantly covered, but the sting in it was felt. He said there that his own troop were "ignoramuses who recite just as one talks. They do not know how to declaim their lines, nor how to halt at the grand moment. How can one distinguish a fine verse if the actor does not pause and if he does not tell you that there you should sound your bravos?" In the *Impromptu* his satire touches the same points, but it is stronger. Molière's ideas of acting in tragedy were much at variance with those that prevailed among the actors at the Hôtel de Bourgogne. Theirs were in favour of bombastic utterance, his were for smooth and simple speech. I have said already that according to public opinion at the time tragedy was much better performed at the Hôtel de Bourgogne than at either of the other two Paris theatres. None of Molière's actors were welcomed in tragedy, and after they went from the Petit Bourbon to the Palais Royal tragedy was seen less and less often on their stage. In comedy Molière's acting was always popular, as his rivals found out to their cost, but in tragedy they thought him ridiculous. In the same parts he thought they were absurd. The public were the judges, and they decided against him.

It must be understood that in the *Impromptu de Versailles* Molière and his troop were playing imaginary parts. We are to believe that the dramatist is a poet giving his instructions to a company of actors newly arrived from the provinces for the play they are to perform before the king. The supposed poet's instructions to the different members of the troop are interesting, as they come from the real Molière in the form of satire; but I will give only what he says to du Croisy, who, it is believed, acted Lysidas in the *Critique* :—

"You represent the poet" [that is the poet in the play, not the author], "and you must identify yourself with the character. You should show that pedantic air which is observed in the best society, that sententious tone of voice and that precise pronunciation which emphasises every syllable and does not omit a single letter from the strictest mode of spelling."

[1] *Œuvres de Molière*, iii. 398 note 5.

The rehearsal is about to commence when it is interrupted by an unwelcome intruder. It does begin in scene 3 with Molière's satire against those who thought he had wished to represent them personally on the stage. At the commencement of scene 5 (according to Despois' edition), Mlle. de Brie, continuing the rehearsal, says :—

"Would you like, ladies, to hear some fine news ? Monsieur Lysidas says that a play has been written against Molière, and that the grands comédiens are going to act it.

" *Molière.*

"Yes ; somebody wanted to read it to me. It is written by one Br— Brou— Brossaut.

" *Du Croisy.*

"Sir, it is published under the name of Boursault ; but to tell you the secret, many persons have put their hand to this work, and great things are expected from it. As every author and every actor looks upon Molière as his greatest enemy, we have all set our heads together to put a spoke in his wheel. We all gave a touch to his portrait, but we were careful not to add our names. It would have been too fine a thing for him to sink before the world under the efforts of all Parnassus ; and to make his downfall more ignominious we have purposely chosen an author of no reputation.

" *Mlle. du Parc.*

"I confess I am delighted.

" *Molière.*

"Gad, so am I ! The railer will be paid back in his own coin. He will get something to make his fingers smart."

The five actresses in the troop show their satisfaction that Molière is to be well trounced for his impertinent remarks upon women.

" *Du Croisy.*

"This comedy, madam, should be well backed up, and the actors at the Hôtel . . .

" *Mlle. du Parc.*

"Make your mind easy ; they need fear nothing. I will warrant the success of their play, every line of it.

" *Mlle. Molière.*

"You are right, madam. Too many people have an interest in thinking well of it. Can you imagine that all those who think they have been satirised by Molière will not be ready to revenge themselves by clapping their hands at this play ?

.   .   .   .

" Molière.

"Gad! I am told they are going to crush both him and his comedies, and that actors and authors, from the cedar to the hyssop,[1] are devilishly bitter against him.

" Mlle. Molière.

"He will get what he deserves. Why does he write paltry comedies that all Paris goes to see, and in which he paints people so well that everybody recognises himself? Why does he not write plays like those of Monsieur Lysidas? He would not make an enemy, and all the authors would speak well of him. It is true that such plays do not always draw large audiences; but on the other hand they are always well written, nobody writes against them, and every one who sees them is dying of envy to think them good.

" Du Croisy.

"It is true that I have the advantage not to make enemies, and all my works are approved of by the savants.

" Mlle. Molière.

"You are right to be satisfied with yourself. That satisfaction is better worth having than all the public applause and all the money gained by Molière's comedies. What does it matter to you if people go to see your plays, so long as your fellow-authors think well of them?"

By the device of the imaginary rehearsal Molière made all the actors of his troop, who were his friends, repeat what his enemies were saying against him, and he made them say also what he thought of Boursault and his comedy. Later Mlle. Béjart interrupts the rehearsal—it is in fact now finished— and says to Molière, as author :—

"If I were you I would have taken a different line. Everybody looks for a strong answer from you, and from the way you were spoken of in this play [*Le Portrait du Peintre*] you have a right to say what you please against the actors, and you should not spare one of them.

" Molière.

"You madden me to hear you talk like that; it is the way with all you women. You want me to fly into a passion against them and break out into opprobrious language and abuse as they do. What should I gain by it, and how much would it annoy them? Did they not set about all this with a good will? And when they were hesitating whether they should play the *Portrait du Peintre,* fearing

---

[1] Molière probably meant from the highest to the lowest. Among authors the greatest was, no doubt, Pierre Corneille. *Œuvres de Molière,* iii. 420 note 3.

a retort, did not one of them say : 'Let him abuse us as much as he pleases so long as we make our money'? Does that show a mind very sensitive to reproach? How can I revenge myself upon them by doing what they want me to do?

" Mlle. de Brie.

" At the same time, they were very angry at three or four words you said about them in the *Critique* and in your *Précieuses.*

" Molière.

"Yes, those three or four words gave great offence, and they have good reason to quote them. But that is not it. The worst harm I have done them is that I have had the good fortune to please the public a little more than they like. All their behaviour since we came to Paris shows plainly where the shoe pinches them. But let them do what they will, all their attempts need not make me uneasy. They fall foul of my plays, so much the better ; and God save me from ever writing anything that could please them. It would be a bad look-out for me.

" Mlle. de Brie.

" It is not pleasant to see one's work reviled.

" Molière.

" Does that hurt me? Did not my comedy give me all that I expected from it, for it had the good fortune to be acceptable to the august personages whom I am particularly anxious to please. Have I not reason to be satisfied with its fate, and does not their condemnation come too late? Does this concern me now? And when a successful play is censured, does not the criticism censure those who approved of it rather than the skill of him who wrote it?

" Mlle. de Brie.

" I would have given something to this little gentleman, the author, who tries to write against people who are not thinking about him.

" Molière.

" You are talking nonsense. Monsieur Boursault would be a nice subject to bring before the court ! It would be making too much of him to ridicule him before an august assembly. He would ask for nothing better. He attacks me with a light heart so that he may make himself known, no matter in what kind of way. He is a man who has nothing to lose, and the actors only set him on at me to entice me into a foolish squabble, and by this means to prevent me from doing other work. And you are all simple enough to fall into the trap ! But now I say publicly, that I do not mean to answer any of their criticisms or counter criticisms. They may say all the harm they please of my plays ; I don't care a button. They may take them after we have done with them, they may turn them as one does a coat and put them on their stage, and make any profit they can out of the good things they may find and out of any good fortune I have had. I agree to this, for they have need of it, and I should be glad to help them to get a living provided they will be satisfied with what I can allow them with self-respect. Courtesy must have its limits, and there are things which do not amuse either spectators or him who is spoken about. I will gladly give them my work, my acting, my gestures, my words, the intonation of my voice, and my manner of speaking, to do what they like with them if these things can be of any advantage to them. I say nothing against all this, and I shall be delighted if it will amuse people. But in conceding so much they should do me the favour to let other things alone, and not touch on matters about which I am told they have attacked me in their comedies. I will civilly beg so much of the polite gentleman who interests himself in writing for them, and that is all the answer they will get from me."

To my mind these last four speeches of Molière's do not show much self-sufficiency, but they show undeniably that he was very angry. When he found that the actors at the Hôtel de Bourgogne, from motives of jealousy against himself, had instigated Boursault to write his play, each of them more or less giving him assistance, he did not scruple to say so and to show his anger before the royal audience at Versailles. He insinuated pretty plainly—what is as clear as daylight—that the *Portrait du Peintre* was taken so closely from his *Critique de l'École des Femmes* that it was like a coat that had been turned; and Boursault could not repel the charge. Moreover, from the latter part of Molière's last speech it would seem that there were lines in the *Portrait du Peintre* referring to his own private family affairs. If this be so, Boursault omitted the allusion when he printed his comedy.[1] Boursault may have pleased his friends by what he wrote against Molière, but one looks in vain now for any strength or wit in his comedy. Molière, with right on his side, was better armed, and he brought down his whip so that it should sting. To most of his satire no fair objection can be taken, and he was quite justified in what he said against the actors at the Hôtel de Bourgogne. But when he made du Croisy say of Boursault: "To make his downfall more ignominious we have purposely chosen an author of no reputation"; when he himself said of Boursault: "Monsieur Boursault would be a nice subject

---

[1] V. Fournel, *Les Contemporains de Molière*, i. 144, middle of note 2; P. Mesnard, *Notice biographique sur Molière*, 285.

to bring before the còurt! It would be making too much of
him to ridicule him before an august assembly. . . He is a
man who has nothing to lose ";—one feels surprised to see such
sarcasm coming from a writer who in his ridicule and in his
satire always took a high-bred tone which gave no offence and
which amused his audience pleasantly. Had Molière said to
Boursault in actual words : "Get away, you wind-bag, you are
a cheat," the open charge would have been less objectionable
than his cutting personal sarcasm. This is a feature very rare
with Molière ; but here, in his disgust at being treated unfairly,
it escaped him. Grimarest says somewhere : "Molière était
vif quand on l'attaquait," and here we have the clearest instance of it in all his comedies.

Perhaps because the *Impromptu de Versailles* was the issue
of a hot personal wrangle Molière did not print this comedy.
It was printed for the first time by La Grange in 1682.

Of the plays and other writings that followed Molière's
Impromptu de Versailles,[1] I will only mention one. Antoine
Montfleury, a son of Zacharie Montfleury, whose acting
Molière had ridiculed, wrote a comedy, *L'Impromptu de l'Hôtel
de Condé*, which was acted at the Hôtel de Bourgogne in
November or December 1663. He there satirised Molière's
acting in tragedy, and gave a picture of it which was probably
like enough in spite of its hostile caricature. The following
extract relates to comedy, and the praise awarded to Molière
in the form of censure shows the animosity against him. Alis,
a bookseller, offers to the Marquis plays by different authors.
The Marquis refuses Corneille ; he disdains Quinault, Boursault, Poisson, and Boyer :—

> "*Alis.*
> Dites-moi donc, Monsieur, afin que je vous vende,
> De qui vous les voulez.
>
> "*Le Marquis.*
> 　　　　　　　De qui ! Belle demande.
> De Molière, morbleu ! de Molière, de lui,
> De lui, de cet auteur burlesque d'aujourd'hui,
> De ce daubeur de mœurs, qui, sans aucun scrupule,
> Fait un portrait naïf de chaque ridicule ;
> De ce fléau des cocus, de ce bouffon du temps,
> De ce héros de farce acharné sur les gens,

---

[1] Their titles are given by M. Louis Moland, *Œuvres de Molière*, 1st ed.
vii. 470-72 ; see also the bibliography to the *Œuvres de Molière* (compiled
by M. Desfeuilles), xi. 129, 130.

Dont pour peindre les mœurs la veine est si savante
Qu'il paraît tout semblable à ceux qu'il représente.

. . . .

. . . . Il faut que tout cède au bouffon d'aujourd'hui ;
Sur mon âme à présent on ne rit que chez lui,
Car pour le sérieux à quoi l'Hôtel[1] s'applique
Il fait, quand on y va, qu'on ne rit qu'au comique.
Mais au Palais Royal, quand Molière est des deux,
On rit dans le comique et dans le sérieux." [2]

In the rest of the play the satire is in the same tone.
Nevertheless, Montfleury's comedy is the most readable of all
those written at this time against Molière.

It is impossible in reading the plays in this dispute not to
see that Molière's line of thought was higher, more manly and
more honest than that of his opponents. In the way of
argument his two plays show some comedy and some wit,
though in the last one there is some unpleasant temper; his
adversaries could only laugh at his acting in tragedy as he
had laughed at theirs, and the absolute flatness of their comedy,
relieved only by anger, shows that they were fighting a losing
battle. One other remark may be made. The asperity with
which Molière was pursued, because of the success of the
École des Femmes, was not unlike the angry fuss made by
Richelieu, nearly thirty years before, when Corneille's *Cid*
created an enthusiasm such as had never been seen before on
the French stage, and which was never surpassed in the 17th
century. Richelieu was annoyed at Corneille's great triumph,
and unwisely told the members of the French Academy to
write a criticism on the play. Against their better judgment
they had to do as they were bidden. In 1667 Boileau said in
his ninth Satire :—

" En vain contre le *Cid* un ministre se ligue ;
Tout Paris pour Chimène a les yeux de Rodrigue.
L'Académie en corps a beau le censurer,
Le public révolté s'obstine à l'admirer."

Rival authors were jealous of Corneille, and Richelieu took
their part; wiseacres abused Molière, and rival actors upheld
them : in both cases the public sided with the dramatists, and
still continue to do so.

[1] L'Hôtel de Bourgogne.
[2] Sc. 3.—M. Fournel has given this comedy in vol. i. 239-60 of his
Contemporains de Molière ; and his notes are worth reading, especially those
to sc. 4.

The *Mariage Forcé* was acted for the first time at the Louvre on the 29th of January 1664; it was given at the Palais Royal theatre on the 15th of February. This was the second of the comédies-ballets that Molière wrote to please the king and his royal guests; and before the performance the king declared his intention of taking a part in the ballet. Louis XIV. danced as an Egyptian in the second entrée. The short play was at first divided into three acts, and at the end of each there was music and dancing. Lulli composed the music; Beauchamps devised the ballet, and he may have written some of the airs.[1]

As Molière was told to write a play, to be acted before the court, he was bound to be amusing; but the seriousness of his nature made him try to show a purpose in his amusement. The *Mariage Forcé* is an instance which shows how well in his smaller plays Molière formed his lightly drawn characters, how he sketched their main features in broad outline, giving a few peculiar and distinctive touches to each; and the cunning way in which he mixed farce and comedy together, dovetailing one into the other with wonderful instinct. The play was written after a short notice, it was intended as a piece of drollery; and Molière did not fear to put before the king an example of the light comedy or farce—improved, no doubt, and free from coarseness—that had been common on the stage in France in his own boyish days. Some of his editors have shown that he was indebted to Rabelais, and it has been said here already that the Italian troops of actors in Paris had taught him that in light plays quick movement of thought and open and easy action should be prominent features. Two hundred and fifty and three hundred years ago, audiences in theatres were more amused than they are now with thin conceits drawn out at great length, or with verbal disputations showing puns or quibbles. There are instances of this in Shakespeare, and in Molière's shorter plays in prose there are examples of antiquated wit given with much verbiage. At the same time, a plea may be put forward for the farce in the *Mariage Forcé*, for underlying it there is the sense and meaning of laughable comedy; and the farce was intended to amuse an audience not disposed to be critical. The chief personages are Sganarelle, a stupid rich man, cowardly and selfish, but

---

[1] *Œuvres de Molière*, iv. 12 and note 2; 74 note 4.

otherwise without much harm in him; and Pancrace and Marphurius, two would-be philosophers. The play is chiefly remembered because of the scenes in which these three men appear. Molière wished to show the silliness of a well-to-do dunderhead, and the nonsense spoken by two pseudo-philosophers, so he brought them together and let them talk in their own way.

Pancrace, a follower of Aristotle, is beside himself with rage because an ignorant fellow, who did not know that form refers to bodies that have life and shape to bodies that have no life, spoke in public of the form of a hat instead of the shape of a hat! Sganarelle stands aghast with his eyes and his mouth open; his bewilderment at seeing a man, reputed for his learning, wild with fury because somebody had said the form of a hat instead of the shape of a hat, is really amusing. A good deal of the actor's art depends upon knowing how to listen. Whether Sganarelle or Pancrace is the bigger fool may be doubted, but each is full of his own thoughts, and the folly of one is used as a set-off against that of the other. Later, Marphurius, a disciple of Pyrrho, who doubts of everything, corrects Sganarelle for saying "I have come to see you" instead of "it seems that I have come to see you." Sganarelle had wished to ask Marphurius whether he would do well to marry; he is very patient, but can get nothing out of the philosopher except uncertainties. At last he takes a stick and gives him a good drubbing, and says: "Correct, if you please, this manner of talking. We ought to doubt of everything; and you should not say 'I have beaten you,' but 'it seems that I have beaten you.'"

In ridiculing Pancrace and Marphurius, Molière had no intention of bringing philosophical questions before his audience. That was not his province. But it was quite open to him to satirise pedants who wished to have the reputation of men of learning—men who when they had acquired some philosophical terms were proud of using them, though they did not know that philosophy is only a word to express the habit of thinking and acting wisely and well. Molière's object was to show that the science of his Pancrace and Marphurius lay in verbal disputes, and that they were ignorant of the aim or end of philosophy. Such men were more common then than now.

Y

The dramatist wanted to ridicule them, and to do so he allowed himself to take some bad instances of the effects of scholastic jargon. And his scenes are not so exaggerated as to be beyond a fair comic caricature of what such men were. Molière did not laugh at philosophy, but at the pretentiousness of those who wished to ape its teaching and who wanted to make a show of small knowledge while the better and larger part was lacking. A very large part of the meaning in Molière's comedies is satire against the world's humbug. Taking the *Mariage Forcé* in connection with his other plays and conciliating their meaning generally, it does not appear that he made light of learning or that he wished to belittle its professors. He knew too well what learning meant, and his mind was too reverential. When Pascal said, "Se moquer de la philosophie c'est vraiment philosopher," he meant that there was a vast deal more bad philosophy written and spoken in the world than good. Molière thought so too ; and in bringing before us in this little play a foolish disciple of Aristotle and another of Pyrrho he had no wish to pit one master or one creed against the other. He did want to show that each ignorant champion of his cause, by vaunting the little that he had learned, talks rubbish. It would have been beyond Molière's function as a comic dramatist to do more.[1]

I shall say nothing of the other personages in the comedy, though the way in which the forced marriage was accomplished is amusing. When the play first appeared in public it was given "avec le ballet et les ornements" which had been seen at court, but the daily expenses of the little comedy were so great that after twelve performances it was withdrawn. The play was not acted again until February 1668, when it was given with *Amphitryon*, as an after-piece ; but then "sans le ballet et ses ornements." A few days before its revival Molière printed his comedy, and the play which had been divided into three acts was reduced into one. The ballet was omitted and a little alteration was made in the text. Because of these alterations and of some changes in the members of the troop at the Palais Royal it would be tedious to mention the

---

[1] There is a good paper, *La Philosophie dans les comédies de Molière*, read by Paul Janet at the Institut de France. It was printed by the Institut; also in the *Revue Politique et Littéraire*, 26th October 1872 (2e série, 2e année, No. 17).

names of the actors who took the different parts in the *Mariage Forcé*. Molière, however, played the part of his own Sganarelle.

At Easter 1664 Brécourt, who had played so well the parts of Alain in the *École des Femmes* and of Dorante in the *Critique*, left his theatre and went to the Hôtel de Bourgogne. He was an excellent actor, but his nature was quarrelsome, and apparently he had a dispute with Molière. His place was filled by Hubert, who came from the Théâtre du Marais. The new recruit was a good actor; some of his rôles were those that should have been played by women, but he did not at first, as has been often thought, play the part of Madame Pernelle in the *Tartuffe*. In the autumn of this year the troop lost one of their oldest friends, du Parc, who had very likely joined Molière's company at Albi in 1647. Jal says that du Parc died on the 28th of October, and quotes some words from the register of a church in Paris showing that he was buried on the 29th.[1] But La Grange wrote: "Mardi 4 Novembre on ne joua point à cause de la mort de M. du Parc"; and he placed a diamond-shaped black lozenge in his diary as a mark of sorrow for the event.

In the early part of 1664 Molière was at work upon the *Tartuffe*, but he had to lay this aside for a while because he received an order from the king to write a play for another court rejoicing; and on the 8th of May *La Princesse d'Élide*, "comédie galante mêlée de musique et d'entrées de ballet," was performed for the first time at Versailles. The notice given to Molière was a short one, and he had not time nor inclination afterwards to finish his play as apparently he had at first intended. One act and one scene only are in verse, and what remains in prose of the five acts shows that he was much hurried in his work. This court fête was known as "Les Plaisirs de l'Ile Enchantée." It lasted nominally for three days, but the festivities were continued for four days longer—altogether from the 7th of May to the 13th. The four additional days were called "Les fêtes de Versailles." Molière's new play was mixed up with the general amusement and made part of it.[2] On the second day of the fête, the 8th of May, the *Princesse d'Élide* was performed;[3] on the fifth day,

---

[1] *Dictionnaire*, 936 col. 2.
[2] *Œuvres de Molière*, iv. 107. See the two last lines of the note on this page and the continuation of the note on p. 108.   [3] *Ibid.* iv. 127.

the 11th of May, the *Fâcheux*; on the sixth day, the 12th, the first three acts of the *Tartuffe*; and on the seventh, the *Mariage Forcé*.[1] So that the members of the troop at the Palais Royal theatre were called upon to take a large part in the work for the royal entertainment. La Grange records that they left Paris for Versailles on the last day in April and that they remained there until the 22nd of May.[2] They received from the king a gratification of 4000 livres. This was to be divided among the troop in equal shares; but Molière, as author of the new play, received an additional present of 2000 livres.[3]

For any meaning to be gathered from the *Princesse d'Élide* the comedy was intended to show very lightly how a beautiful princess disdained all her suitors, though of three princes there was one she was fond of; and how this prince, in his turn, though he loves his haughty charmer, announced that he was going to marry one of her cousins. The " genre noble " in comedy was turned into a kind of masquerade. With this idea, if Molière had been given more time, he might by his ridicule have shown some good fun; but the only amusing personage in the play is Moron, a sort of Sganarelle turned into a court jester. Most of the plays that Molière wrote for the court festivities are amusing or interesting in the satire shown, but the *Princesse d'Élide* does not appear to be one of them. Yet when it was put on the stage at the Palais Royal on the 9th of November following it was acted twenty-five times with good receipts. The music and dancing that accompanied the play were no doubt the reasons for its success. The list of the actors who played in the various parts is to be found in most good editions of Molière. This was taken from the livret of the comédie-ballet which was given to the spectators of the performance at Versailles.

The first edition of the *Princesse d'Élide* was printed with the official narrative of " Les Plaisirs de l'Ile Enchantée," in 1664, but without further date. Three other editions of the play, published in Molière's lifetime, were printed in the same way.[4]

---

[1] *Œuvres de Molière*, iv. 228-232.
[2] *Registre*, 65. A small mistake of La Grange's here should be noticed. He said that the *Princesse d'Élide* was performed on the 6th of May, but the date was the 8th (P. Mesnard, *Notice biographique sur Molière*, 305 note).
[3] Émile Campardon, *Nouvelles Pièces sur Molière*, 41.
[4] *Œuvres de Molière*, iv. 98; xi. 16, 17.

CHAPTER XIV

LE TARTUFFE

LE TARTUFFE aroused very strong animosities, and something should be said of the difficulties Molière had to undergo before Louis XIV. gave him permission to put his play on the stage. An explanation should also be given of the principal personage in the comedy, for though most of us know that Tartuffe was a hypocrite, he belonged to a class of men which we are not familiar with in England.

As was said at the end of the last chapter, the first three acts of the *Tartuffe* were played before the king at Versailles on the 12th of May 1664. On the 29th of November in the same year the whole play was performed for the first time at Raincy, near Paris, by the invitation of the Prince de Condé. The first time the play was acted in public was at the Palais Royal theatre on the 5th of August 1667 ; but the next day future performances of the comedy were forbidden. At last, the comedy was put on the stage at the Palais Royal on the 5th of February 1669, and it was played afterwards without further hindrance.[1] Thus, some editors of Molière have given the year 1669 as the date of the *Tartuffe*, others 1667, and M. Mesnard says that 1664 was its real date.[2]

For biographical purposes I have thought it best to consider the play as written in 1664, though the dramatist meant it for the public and it was not acted in public till 1667 ; then only one performance was given, and the ban against it was not taken off until 1669. In speaking of the *Tartuffe* as though it belonged to the year 1664, the author's ideas will be best understood. There are chronological objections to this course, and doubtless alterations were made in the comedy before it was finally given to the public, but I do not think these were of a radical kind. Molière had great tenacity of purpose, and

[1] *Œuvres de Molière*, iv. 270.   [2] *Ibid.* 272.

when he had once made up his mind about a thing he did not change his opinions easily. When Louis XIV. saw the first three acts of the *Tartuffe* at Versailles in May 1664, he refused to allow the play to be acted in public; nine months later, in February 1665, Molière brought out his *Don Juan* at the Palais Royal theatre. When Molière found that his picture of a hypocrite was forbidden, he set to work to give a picture of an atheist. The *Tartuffe* was written in verse, it belongs essentially to high comedy; *Don Juan*, its counterpart, was written in prose, and though the comedy in the latter play had a very serious meaning, it is funnier than in the other and shown in a more popular manner. *Don Juan*, too, is less open to misconstruction if it is considered as written after the *Tartuffe*.

The king's prohibition of the *Tartuffe* was probably given on the day or day but one after the performance of the first three acts of the comedy at Versailles.[1] The prohibition was printed some time later in the same year, in the official description of *Les Plaisirs de l'Ile Enchantée*—in the narrative of what took place on the 12th of May, the sixth day of the fêtes at Versailles :—

"In the evening was played before his Majesty a comedy called *Tartuffe*, which le sieur de Molière had written against hypocrites. But although the play was thought to be very entertaining, the king knew there was so much conformity between those whom a sincere devotion puts on the road to heaven and those whom a hollow show of good works does not prevent from committing bad actions, that his extreme delicacy in matters of religion would not allow this resemblance between vice and virtue, which might be taken one for the other; and although the good intentions of the author were not questioned, he [the king] nevertheless forbade the play to be given in public and deprived himself of this pleasure so that others might not be deceived who were less capable of good discernment."[2]

This is carefully chosen language, and M. Mesnard thinks that Molière may have had a hand in it, even though it was subjected afterwards to examination.[3] But the *Gazette*, a semi-official, semi-court newspaper, never friendly to Molière,

---

[1] *Œuvres de Molière*, iv. 280; L. Moland, *Œuvres de Molière*, 1st ed. iv. 384.
[2] The prohibition is given in many editions of Molière. M. Mesnard has given it in vol. iv. 231, 232; Taschereau, 5th ed. iii. 108; M. Moland, 1st ed. iii. 331.
[3] *Œuvres de Molière*, iv. 92 and note 1.

wrote of the performance of the *Tartuffe* at Versailles in a different tone; and in its number of the 17th of May 1664 said that Louis XIV., as eldest son of the Church, forbade the representation of " a stage play called *L'Hypocrite*, which his Majesty, fully enlightened in everything, considered to be absolutely injurious to religion and capable of producing very dangerous consequences." [1]

In his first petition to the king, Molière, alluding to the prohibition to play the comedy in public, says : " Your Majesty found no fault in this comedy." Now, I do not believe that in addressing the king Molière would have used these words unless he had thought they were true. And Boileau's opinion, as given by Brossette, seems to have been that Louis XIV. thought there was no great harm in the play. Brossette was not born till 1671; but in 1702, nine years before Boileau's death, he wrote some notes of what he had heard from Boileau —or Despréaux, as he was often called by his contemporaries. What Brossette says in these notes is worth reading :—

" . . . M. Despréaux spoke to me at length about Molière's *Tartuffe*. When Molière wrote his *Tartuffe*, he recited to the king the first three acts." [Brossette used here the word " récita," but there is little doubt that he alluded to the performance at Versailles.] " This pleased his Majesty, who spoke of it too highly not to irritate the party of dévots. M. de Péréfixe, Archbishop of Paris, put himself at their head and spoke to the king against this comedy. The king, pressed several times on the matter, said to Molière, that he must not irritate the dévots who were an implacable people, and therefore he could not be allowed to play his *Tartuffe* in public. . . ." [2]

Unless Molière knew that Louis had been personally favourable to his comedy he would not, on the 5th of February 1669, have addressed a third petition to his Majesty asking a favour for the son of a friend in a tone of gracious banter ; nor would he have told a piquant story at the end of his preface to the first edition of his comedy, printed in the following month :—

" A week after it [the *Tartuffe*] was forbidden a play called *Scaramouche Ermite* was acted at court, and the king as he left the theatre said to the great prince I have just alluded to [Condé] :

---

[1] *Œuvres de Molière*, iv. 232, end of note 2 ; Taschereau, *Vie de Molière*, 5th ed. 101.

[2] A. Laverdet, *Correspondance entre Boileau et Brossette*, 563, 564.

' I should like to know why people who are so greatly scandalised at Molière's comedy say nothing about *Scaramouche.*' The prince answered : 'The reason is that *Scaramouche* laughs at heaven and at religion, about which these gentlemen care nothing, and that Molière's comedy laughs at the men themselves, and that they will not tolerate.' "

Scaramouche Ermite, a small unprinted comedy, is said to have been licentious, but can we be sure that those who enjoyed its immorality were also those who were violent against the *Tartuffe* ? Nevertheless, the Prince de Condé expressed broadly the secret opinions of many who were hostile to Molière's comedy. There is reason to think that the king would have allowed Molière to bring out his play if, as head of the State, he had not been surrounded by men whom the poet, in addressing his Majesty, boldly called "les Tartuffes." This he did as early as August 1664 in his first petition, and again later in his second petition in August 1667. Louis in his own mind thought that Molière, as one who knew the world, would be able to form a pretty good opinion as to the honesty or dishonesty of religious guides; and the king, from what he had seen of Molière's comedies, was prepared to believe that the poet had not drawn an unjust picture. In a word, I imagine that Louis XIV. trusted more in Molière's judgment than in that of his counsellors. And from the tone of Molière's three petitions to the king, in which he was bold but never disrespectful, one is led to think that he knew what was passing in the king's mind. Molière felt that Louis, if he had been allowed to have his own way, would have sanctioned the performance of his comedy, but that the king had to listen to objections made against the play, and that he could not do quite as he liked.

While strong feeling was growing among the church party against the performance of the comedy, one Pierre Roullé, a doctor of the Sorbonne and a curé of St. Barthélemy, a church in Paris, wrote and published a pamphlet *Le Roi Glorieux au Monde.* After referring to the king's prohibition, he says :—

"A man, or rather a demon clothed in the flesh and dressed as a man, and the most notorious profaner and libertine the world has seen, has been so impious as to send forth from his diabolical brain a play now ready to be shown in public on the stage, scoffing at the whole Church. He jeers at its most sacred character and its most divine function . . . the leading and directing of souls and families by wise guides and holy conductors." [1]

The curé of St. Barthélemy, like many others, misjudged Molière's meaning and the purport of his comedy. He imagined that churchmen generally were vilified, and he wrote wildly as his inclinations prompted him. But he was right in understanding that the comedy was an attack on the spiritual directors of conscience. Of these men I shall say something later. M. Mesnard thinks that Roullé wrote his pamphlet at the end of July or in the first half of August 1664; [2] and that it was in the same month of August that Molière presented to the king his first petition in favour of his comedy. [3]

Molière, in this petition, after alluding to "all the studied grimaces of those outrageously good persons, all the underhand tricks of those false coiners of devotion, who wish to ensnare men by counterfeit zeal and sophistical charity," says that he intended to draw a thorough-paced hypocrite so that there should be no mistake about the man's evil designs. He tells the king "the Tartuffes have secretly been artful enough to find favour with your Majesty, and the models have caused the copy to be suppressed"; he says that his misfortune was softened by the manner in which the king had refused to allow the play to be acted, adding that his Majesty had the goodness to say that "he found no fault in the comedy." Molière alludes to a reading he had given of the *Tartuffe* before the papal legate and Roman bishops, and says that they had approved of his work. [4] And he speaks of Roullé's pamphlet as though he had read it, for he says in evident allusion to it: "My comedy, though it has not been seen, is diabolical, and my brains are diabolical. I am a demon clothed in the flesh dressed as a man, a libertine, an impious personage who deserves exemplary punishment. It is not enough that flames should publicly atone for my offence, for I should be let off too easily. The charitable zeal of this gallant man does not stop there; he will not allow that I may find mercy before God; he is determined that I must be damned, and there is an end of the matter."

---

[1] *Œuvres de Molière*, iv. 283; Taschereau, *Vie de Molière*, 5th ed. 161; Moland, *Œuvres de Molière*, 1st ed. iv. 388.
[2] *Œuvres de Molière*, iv. 285.   [3] *Ibid.* 385, 386, in the footnote.
[4] But see M. Mesnard's note here: *Œuvres de Molière*, iv. 388 note 6.

Louis XIV. may or may not have been a good judge as to whether the *Tartuffe* should be acted on the public stage, but it is clear from the tone of the petition that the poet believed that the king was personally favourable to him. In his pamphlet Roullé said that Louis had ordered Molière's comedy to be burned, but it is not likely that Louis gave such an order. It is more probable that the king said that the curé should be told to keep his temper cool. And there is some reason to think that at Molière's request Roullé's pamphlet was suppressed.[1] The curé of St. Barthélemy died in 1666, before the *Tartuffe* appeared on the stage in Paris.

Though performances of the *Tartuffe* were forbidden in public there were a few representations of the play before royal or semi-royal audiences.[2] Therefore, among the nobility, a good many must have seen Molière's comedy acted on a private stage. And the poet was permitted to read his play at some private houses. Boileau in his third satire, written in 1665, relates how a coxcomb, in inviting a friend to dine with him, promised a reading of the *Tartuffe*:—

" Et Molière avec Tartuffe y doit jouer son rôle."

It has been said that Molière gave several readings of his play; but very few have been recorded, and to those of which mention has been made no exact date can be fixed. M. Mesnard would put the reading at the house of Mlle. Ninon de Lenclos either a few days before the performance of the comedy at the Palais Royal in August 1667, or else early in 1669; but he says that Sainte-Beuve thought this reading was the first of all.[3]

At the single performance of the *Tartuffe* at the Palais Royal theatre on the 5th of August 1667, the comedy was played under the title of *L'Imposteur*, and Tartuffe himself was called Panulphe. La Grange recorded the single representation,[4] and called the play by the name its author had first given to it. The king was then with his army in Flanders, and in his absence M. de Lamoignon, the first president of the Parliament of Paris, which was the highest law court in France, forbade future performances of the play

---

[1] *Œuvres de Molière*, iv. 285, 286.   [2] *Ibid.* iv. 270, 293.
[3] *Ibid.* iv. 288, 289.   [4] *Registre*, 89.

until the king should order otherwise. After chronicling the representation of the comedy, La Grange added that on the 8th of the month he and La Thorillière (both members of the troop) went to Flanders to see the king on the matter of the prohibition. The king sent them word " that on his return he would have the play of the *Tartuffe* examined and that we should act it." The two emissaries took with them Molière's second petition to the king; and in the second paragraph of this petition there are passages that have been much noticed :—

" My comedy, Sire, has not been allowed to enjoy the advantages that your Majesty was willing to show to it. I gained nothing by bringing it out under the title of *L'Imposteur* and by disguising the personage in the dress of a man of the world. It was to no purpose that I gave him a small hat, long hair, a wide collar, a sword, and that lace was put all over his coat " [this refers of course to changes of costume on the stage] ; " that I softened the play in several places, and that I carefully cut out everything I thought might furnish a shadow of a pretext to the celebrated models of the character I wished to draw. All this availed nothing. . . . My comedy had no sooner appeared than it was struck as with a thunderbolt by a power that should command respect ; and all that I could do to save myself from the fury of the storm was to say that your Majesty had the goodness to allow me to have the play acted, and that I did not think it necessary to ask for this permission from others since it was only your Majesty who had forbidden it."

When Molière told the king in this petition that M. de Lamoignon's prohibition of his play scandalised all Paris, he chose to ignore the opinions of men in authority and of those who thought that authority must be right. He knew that officialism in Paris was all-powerful, but he felt with the people who frequently found it vexatious. In advocating his own cause he thought he was speaking truly ; he was endeavouring to persuade the king that the order against him was unjust, and he begged his Majesty to revoke it. Molière wrote his comedy to show that religious lying is the worst form of intellectual poisoning; and he believed that " the most scrupulous minded " and " persons of well-known righteousness " thought that he had done no wrong, and that they were " scandalised " at the animosity shown against the performance of his play.

Molière's word is the only authority which tells that the

king had the goodness to allow him to have the *Tartuffe* acted in public; but it has been supposed that the permission was given verbally before the king went to Flanders in the month of May, and that the leave was granted on the condition that changes were made in the comedy.[1] M. Mesnard thinks that the permission was not so complete as Molière imagined it to be. That may be so; yet I do not believe that in addressing the king Molière, who has never been accused of shiftiness, would have urged his Majesty's permission unless it had been granted. It may be asked why, if the king had said as early as the month of May (1677) that the *Tartuffe* might be acted, the representation of the comedy should have been delayed until August? In the spring of that year Molière was very ill, and in April there was a report that he was going to die.[2] Two months later he was able to reappear on the stage, but he was probably still weak, and the rehearsals of the comedy had to be completed before the play could be given to the public.

Nobody can tell what were the changes in the text of the play before the one public representation in August 1667. But at that representation Tartuffe's costume had been changed; and if it could be shown plainly what this had been at the three court performances prior to the single performance at the Palais Royal, more than idle curiosity would be satisfied. Molière, in his second petition to the king, said that he had "disguised his personage as a man of the world." It may be assumed, therefore, that Tartuffe was not represented as "a man of the world" before August 1667. There are various lines in the comedy, as we have it now, showing that Tartuffe, before Orgon relieved him from his distress— that is, before he appears on the stage—was very poorly clad; and his dress at the court performances may, likely enough, as M. Mesnard supposes,[3] have been not at all that of "a man of the world," but rather that of humble poverty, and it may also have indicated that he was connected with the Church in a humble capacity. I take this idea gladly, but I am inclined

---

[1] *Œuvres de Molière*, iv. 311, 312; x. 376-8; Taschereau, *Vie de Molière*, 3rd ed. 120, 121; 5th ed. 163; Louis Moland, *Œuvres de Molière*, 1st ed. iv. 391.

[2] *Œuvres de Molière*, iv. 311; L. Moland, *Œuvres de Molière*, 1st ed. vol. i. p. cci.

[3] *Œuvres de Molière*, iv. 325.

to think that the alteration in Tartuffe's costume was more nominal than real. There is no evidence to show that his dress was, at any performance, changed during the representation of the play. Before the representation on the 5th of August 1667 he bore signs of poverty; on that day, and afterwards, of affluence. But in spite of his sword, his small hat, his long hair, and his lace, those persons who knew how well-to-do men connected with the Church were dressed would not be altogether deceived by his costume. I do not think that from first to last Molière made any radical difference in the character of his personage. There are strong indications in the play that Tartuffe was meant to show a director of conscience, and it is not to be supposed that he was dressed in gaudy colours even though Molière had "disguised his personage as a man of the world." The idea that Tartuffe was ever meant to show a man in priest's orders may be set aside as impossible.

It must have gone across the grain with Molière to alter the title of his play and the name of its chief personage. The word "Tartuffe" had a significance in the public mind, and the dramatist could not have made the change willingly. Taschereau tells us that in those days men still said "truffer" for "tromper"; and he adds that in a book printed in Paris in 1505 a certain chapter was headed "Des Truffes ou Tartuffes." Etymologically, and in a popular sense, "un tartuffe" meant "un trompeur."[1] Molière, therefore, did not coin the word, he did better: he took an old French word with a well-accepted meaning. The word "Tartuffe" is sometimes printed with only one f. But, according to M. Mesnard, on the title-page and in the preface to the first edition of the play there are two f's; also in the second edition, which followed some seven weeks later, and which contains the author's three petitions to the king, the letter f is always doubled, as: "Tartuffe."

For the remainder of Boileau's account of M. de Lamoignon's interdiction of the *Tartuffe* I must refer the reader to the continuation of Brossette's notes,[2] from which a quotation was made a few pages back. We read in these notes that Molière

[1] *Vie de Molière*, 3rd ed. 126; 5th ed. 168; *Œuvres de Molière*, iv. 312 note 2; and M. Moland's *Œuvres de Molière*, 1st ed. iv. 383.
[2] A. Laverdet, *Correspondance entre Boileau et Brossette*, 564, 565.

went with Boileau to see the first president, who said to the dramatist:—

"With all the good will I have towards you I cannot allow you to play your comedy. I am persuaded that it is very good and very edifying, but it does not become comedians to instruct men on matters of Christian morals and on religion; the stage is not the place to preach the Gospel."

At the end of these notes Boileau is made to say that "all Molière's anger fell upon the Archbishop (de Péréfixe), whom he considered as the head of the faction of the dévots who were hostile to him." It may be guessed that this last opinion of Boileau's came from Molière himself.

At the performance of the *Tartuffe* on the 5th of August 1667 there was some one present who wrote a detailed account of the play as he saw it then. This account, in the form of a *Lettre sur la Comédie de l'Imposteur*, bears at the end the date of 20th of August 1667. It was printed in that year, though nobody knows where; and certainly once more, in 1668, before the interdiction was taken off the comedy. Nobody knows, too, who wrote this Letter. It has been attributed to Molière himself, but it is more generally thought that the style is not such as might have been expected from him. And it is exceedingly unlikely that Molière would have published an anonymous dissertation upon his own comedy. For myself, I am inclined to suspect de Visé to be the author, as I suspected him of having written the arguments to *Sganarelle ou le Cocu Imaginaire*. Unless I am mistaken, the arguments at the head of each scene of *Sganarelle, La Lettre sur la Comédie de l'Imposteur*, and *La Lettre sur la Comédie du Misanthrope*— this last was known to be by de Visé—bear a likeness in the lines of thought which shows that the three bits of criticism probably came from the same hand. It is known too that de Visé criticised the *École des Femmes* just after it appeared on the stage. It was not common in those days for a man to rush into print, saying what he thought of a new play and give the reasons for his opinions. De Visé had done so in at least two instances. However all this may be, the *Lettre sur la Comédie de l'Imposteur* gives an idea of the comedy when it was first acted at the Palais Royal theatre; and, if one chooses to take the trouble to make comparisons, it seems to show some at least of the alterations made in the text of the play between August 1667 and February 1669. Nothing material to the character of the play was changed. The most important alterations were in the first act; and in the last scene there Molière made an alteration in his text, or probably an addition to it.[1] It would seem very likely that he wished to refute the condemnation of his play by the Archbishop of Paris—this will be mentioned immediately; and that when he spoke, as plainly as words can speak, of the difference between real and sham devotion he made Cléante the mouthpiece of his own feelings.

M. de Lamoignon's prohibition gave Molière a severe blow, but a worse one was to follow. A few days after the dramatist had sent his second petition to the king there came an ecclesiastical mandate that seemed to crush his last hope of being allowed to bring out his play. On the 11th of August Hardouin de Péréfixe, Archbishop of Paris, published a decree setting forth that a comedy under the new name of *L'Imposteur* had been acted at one of the theatres in Paris—" a very dangerous comedy, and which is all the more likely to be prejudicial to religion because, under the pretext of condemning hypocrisy or false devotion, it tends to accuse indifferently of these faults all those who profess the most earnest piety, and thus it exposes them to the railleries and continual calumnies of libertines." [2] Whether well founded or not, this was the real cause for hostility against the play. It was not Tartuffe's villainy that was condemned; but his seeming righteousness was thought to be a satire on truly righteous people, and his seeming righteousness made dupes of good men and they were ridiculed because of their goodness. The Archbishop felt so strongly on the matter that he forbade any acting or reading of the comedy in his diocese either publicly or privately under pain of excommunication, and his mandate was to be read aloud in two churches in Paris. Such an order would carry weight, and by it Molière was condemned as having written an impious play in the eyes of persons who previously had thought no ill of him.

But was this censure just? The Archbishop thought that

---

[1] *Œuvres de Molière*, iv. 420 note 1.
[2] Taschereau, *Vie de Molière*, 3rd ed. 123; 5th ed. 165; *Œuvres de Molière*, iv. 322.

by his satire Molière was sneering at those who were in
earnest in their religious duties.   Surely we may say now
that this was a misconception of the comedy; surely we may
say now that the satire on Tartuffe was directed against frauds
conceived and carried out under the pretext of religion, and
that the satire or irony on Orgon and his mother was directed
against those who in religious matters were totally bereft of
common-sense.   If the impiety in the play consisted in showing
that a man in Tartuffe's position could be a hypocrite, then
lay criticism ridiculing false religious guides was stricken
dumb; if his hypocrisy existed, only rebuke in a scriptural
sense might be written against it.   Molière did not trust the
divines; he thought there were too many "Tartuffes" among
them.   He said in his second petition to the king: "the
Tartuffes have secretly been artful enough to find favour with
your Majesty, and the models have caused the copy to be
suppressed"; he believed that these men would work together
in order to maintain the influence of their order, and that
hypocrisy would be protected.   On the other hand, every one
should have seen that if libertines laughed at Orgon and
Madame Pernelle for their folly, so might others who were
not libertines; for there could have been no calumny in
laughing at those whose egregious nonsense was as patent
as daylight.   Molière ridiculed Orgon and his mother,
Madame Pernelle, for being inordinately credulous, for being
gulled by a palpable knave whom everybody else dis-
trusted.   Had there been no religious hypocrites, no too
simple-minded dupes, the comedy need not have been written.
Then there were those who thought it wrong to write a
comedy attacking the interests of religion and its ministers.
But Moliere did not attack religion, nor speak of it contemptuously.   His whole comedy told very plainly that
earnest piety should be respected; it never for a moment
cast a suspicion of ridicule on true religion, or true devotion;
the invective fell only on hypocrites, and laughter only on
those who from mental weakness were deceived by them.   Nor
was the comedy a satire on the teaching of the Church, or on
the righteous practices of its ministers.   There is nothing
in the play to show that Molière intended disrespect to the
ministration of holy services in conformity with the rules of

the Church; but he certainly wished to denounce those who carried on the ministration of false service that was meant to deceive others as being in conformity with the rules of the Church. The only member of the Church alluded to was the director; it was his hypocrisy in the abuse of his office that Molière satirised. The dramatist portrayed a vicious example of a director, because he thought that many of his class were fit subjects for condemnation, even on the stage. The incidents in the comedy are shown in Tartuffe's bad conduct, and in the effects his evil teaching had on those who foolishly allowed themselves to be gulled by it. Honest satire may surely speak on such a matter as this. And if one looks at the style and at the tone of the comedy and its characterisation, and sees what is meant by its satire or irony, it will not be possible to find irreverent mockery. What Molière did attack was the abuses that had grown from the interests of religion, abuses which dishonest men had fostered because they made their profit by them.

In the 11th *Lettre Provinciale*, Pascal wrote:—

"There is a great difference between laughing at religion and laughing at those who profane it by their extravagant opinions. It is wicked not to feel respect for the truths which the Spirit of God has revealed, and it is wickedness of another kind not to feel contempt for the falsehoods which the mind of man has opposed to them."

And later in the same Letter :—

"When there is need to employ a little raillery the spirit of piety demands that it be used against error only, and not against things that are holy ; whereas the spirit of buffoonery, impiety and heresy mocks at everything that is most sacred."

Whatever may be thought of these sayings of Pascal, Molière's comedy may be judged by them on the score of reverence. Pascal is not accused nowadays of being irreverent, and if Molière's words and their meaning are understood, it will be difficult to show a charge of irreverence against him. Pascal's anger was so much roused by the deceitful practices of the Jesuit fathers that he took the readiest means he could find to denounce them. He appealed to the reading public, and by his satire and his ridicule he did much to effect his purpose. Molière's means of addressing the world was the stage, where every one could go to hear and see what was said and done, and all could laugh together at his picture. He showed what was flagrantly dishonest; and because he wrote in a tone of pleasantry his satire has often been misunderstood, as it was condemned by those whom it attacked. In his 7th Provincial Letter Pascal had satirised the Jesuit doctrine of " directing the intention," and Molière in Act IV. sc. 5 of his comedy makes Tartuffe try to inculcate this belief into Orgon's wife;[1] also in his 9th Letter Pascal had ridiculed the doctrine of " mental restrictions," and Molière in Act V. sc. 1 of his comedy shows that Tartuffe had actually taught this creed to Orgon.[2]

As the *Lettres Provinciales*, which appeared at intervals between January 1656 and March 1657, were an event in the literary world, so was the *Tartuffe* an event in the annals of the stage. Like Pascal's Letters, Molière's comedy was an actuality. It spoke of matters that were of daily occurrence in well-to-do households, and was therefore likely to create strong interest. People thought very differently about it. The public, on the whole, enjoyed the comedy, and as far as they really thought about it perhaps they considered the satire well deserved. But men in authority decried it as being scurrilous. The play was regarded by the Church and by the Bench as an impious lampoon, holding up to scorn and ridicule devout people who were to be reprobated and laughed at by any one who wished to see them travestied. We who live now can see more clearly than those who were alive at the time that Molière's morality was sounder than that of his opponents. We can see now that he was bold enough to tell the world, with all earnestness and reverence, how a wicked man can scoff at religion and invoke heaven for his own bad ends. We can see now that Molière's intentions may have been misunderstood at the time, and that moderate-minded people regarded his play as dangerous. Yet Tartuffe's villainy is perfectly transparent. It is utterly impossible to confound him with a true-speaking or a God-fearing man. No ingenuity, no special pleading, can palliate his baseness. When he is first seen he talks with unctuous piety; and in a few minutes, in the same tone, he makes a

---

[1] *Œuvres de Molière*, iv. 496 and note 3.
[2] *Ibid.* iv. 504 and note 1.

strong declaration of love to the wife of his protector. When Molière spoke to the king about "the Tartuffes," he knew what he was saying. He knew that the type of man he had portrayed existed, and that there were such men belonging to the Church, or connected with it—a disgrace to themselves and a stigma on the profession they pretended to serve.

The province of comedy has always been to laugh at the follies and attack the vices of the age, and Molière felt himself justified in exposing to derision and contempt the double-facedness of some members of a class of men who were increasing in numbers, and whose influence was gaining strength in the households of good families. Molière knew that the charge he was making was very severe, and I cannot quite agree with those who hold that he bravely threw down his gauntlet into the arena as the champion reformer of a bad abuse. He was not a reformer by nature, nor was he an enthusiast. But his sensitive and sympathetic nature was pained to see men in places of grave responsibility gaining power, comfort, and pecuniary profit from their office, while they walked through the world with a lie continually in their faces and on their tongues. I interpret in the same way, though in a lesser degree, his attacks on the doctors; against "the Tartuffes" the accusation was terribly serious. In both cases his object was to teach by satire and by laughter. Whenever true comedy is shown, the tone and spirit of the mirth or laughter it creates will generally indicate the intentions of the writer.

I must now try to explain what Tartuffe was, and to what order of men he belonged. To do this something should be said about the "directeurs de conscience" and about the "dévots," and how each were considered in France about that time by men whose opinions should carry weight. Most English readers know that Tartuffe was a hypocrite, but it is not so generally known what his calling was, nor how self-seeking men of his class drew their profit from it. There have been hypocrites at every time and in every country, but the forms of society under which they have lived have not always been the same. Other people, other manners. The wiles of hypocrisy will vary according to the conditions favourable to their existence. Tartuffe is not a rascal of English growth, nor could he be transplanted easily on to our soil. We have had our hypocrites in fiction, drawn more or less from actual life, but our imaginative literature does not supply us with a Tartuffe. For us he must remain a foreigner. It is not the enormity of his offence that differentiates him from our native-born villains, but its kind. The circumstances under which we live, our customs and our habits of thought, do not leave an easy opening for his schemes. Our lives, morally speaking, may be no whit better than those of the French people; but that is not the question. Our form of Protestantism and our national sturdy independence of character almost debars the entrance of a Tartuffe into our households. But in France in the 17th century everything lay ready to his hands; the will only on his part was wanting. If a man in his position did not scruple to become a villain he could easily find scope for his talents.

Early in the 17th century the Catholic Church in France had regained much of its supremacy over the free-thinking tendency which the Wars of Religion had fostered in the century previous. The latter half of the 16th century in France has been likened to the 18th, inasmuch as the foremost men in each age were known for their incredulity, their love of free thought, and their habit of laughing at religious matters. Under Louis XIV. the people were usually more devout than the nobles. It would be too much to say that this was an age of faith, but many among the upper middle classes were actuated by a wish to believe. Many of those whose grandfathers had piqued themselves on unbelief and had enjoyed what they thought was the fun of irreverence tried to think religiously; they considered that forms of worship were necessary for them; and when the country was at rest from the Civil War of the Fronde (1648-1652) conformity to the rules of the Church was looked upon by the spiritually minded as needful for the salvation of their souls. Among these persons were many who were bent upon practising some visible marks of devotion, and if they were but honest to themselves they were certainly to be commended.[1]

Besides their confessor, persons who could afford it engaged the services of a director. He was known as the "directeur

---

[1] Ch. Révillout, *Études littéraires et morales sur le* 17ᵉ *siècle*. Deuxième partie, Louis XIV., Molière et Tartuffe, pp. 7-9.

de conscience," and was chosen as a guide to direct the conduct. The most distinguishing mark of the office of the director was in the social·and domestic nature of his functions. The confessor was always a man who had taken orders, and his duties were prescribed to him definitely by the Church; it was not necessary that the director should be in orders, though such was usually the case. There were lay directors connected with the Church, though not absolutely belonging to it. Sainte-Beuve says: " A director is different from a counsellor, he is more obliged to look closely into things and to give his opinions decisively."[1] On the next page Sainte-Beuve adds, speaking of Saint-Cyran in his quality of director of the solitaries at Port-Royal: " He never forgot to be upon his guard against the secret ambition which insensibly tends to wish to get the mastery over souls and take possession of them." This was certainly an important and a difficult matter. The office of the director was thus peculiar and special, and it held out strong temptations to men who were not possessed of more than an ordinary share of moral courage. When chosen, the director should be acquainted with the style of living of the family under his care, and with what went on in the household. He was to instruct the members of the family how to regulate their daily actions, he was allowed to offer his opinion on the most intimate family affairs. When a woman put herself under his guidance he was ever at her hand to guide her in all her projects, in all her difficulties; he was to prescribe her pleasures, and nothing could be done without his sanction. This sounds to us, in England, like tyrannical supervision, and we wonder how a sensible woman could submit to it. Very much would depend on the choice of a director and what manner of man he was. The lady made inquiries about him, and questioned him before engaging his services if he was rigid or lax in his precepts. If she had a director she would have one to her taste, and when she got tired of him it was open to her to dismiss him and take another. Bourdaloue spoke of the way in which people went from one director to another, and said they wished to be directed in the way they would like to go.[2] When we recollect how rare are the qualities of sound discernment and

[1] *Port-Royal*, 3rd ed. i. 355.   [2] *Œuvres* (Paris, 1826), xiv. 420, 421.

nice discretion, it is easy to imagine the errors into which a director might be led whose conscience and common sense did not tell him that the path between right and wrong where men and women are concerned is both intricate and slippery. Doubtless there were directors who performed their duties honourably and well, but that there were many others quite unfit for their position is undeniable. Priests, monks, spiritual and lay directors, were sought after by those who wished to ease their consciences by religious practices. If directors were wanted directors could be found when they knew that their services would be remunerated. Consequently there arose a set of men whom Molière called "dévots de place":—

> "Ces gens, qui par une âme à l'intérêt soumise,
> Font de dévotion métier et marchandise."

The demand for directors regulated the supply. In the latter part of the 17th century these men were in vogue, in the middle of the 18th they were not so much in request; but while the mode lasted many ladies of fashion thought their director was as necessary to them as their cook. Those who were less well off did not receive so much attention. But once in his position in the families of the well-to-do the director reigned supreme. He learned to direct consciences so well that women under his influence became tools in his hands. Boileau gave a portrait of a director in his tenth satire (v. 559 *et seq.*), published in 1693:—

> "Mais de tous les mortels, grâce aux dévotes âmes,
> Nul n'est si bien soigné qu'un directeur de femmes."

Just about the same time, La Bruyère, whose judgment may be trusted, wrote with mordant satire against the directors and against the women who allowed themselves to be governed by them. The two following quotations are taken from his *Caractères*, about the middle of the chapter "Des Femmes":—

"A woman is easy to govern if a man will give himself the trouble to do it. One man alone governs several. He educates their mind and their memory, he tells them what their religion should be, and he even undertakes to regulate their hearts. They do not approve nor disapprove, they offer neither praise nor censure, until they have watched his eyes and his face. They confide to him their joys and their griefs, their hopes and their jealousies, their hatreds and their loves. He makes them quarrel with and he reconciles them to their husbands, and he takes advantage of the intervals. He busies himself in their affairs, interests himself in their lawsuits and visits their judges.[1]   He gives them his own doctor, his trades- men and his workmen.   He takes upon himself to find their apart- ments, to furnish them, and he gives orders for their attendants. He is seen with them in their carriages in the streets of a town and on the promenades ; he is seated beside them in church and at the theatre.   He goes visiting with them, he accompanies them to the baths, to the watering-places, when they are travelling, and he has the best apartment at their country seat.   He grows old but his influence does not wane ; a little intelligence and much time wasted are sufficient to maintain it.   Children, heirs, daughter-in-law, niece, servants, are all dependent on his will.   At first he made himself respected, he ends by being dreaded.   This old and needful friend dies without a tear shed for him, and ten women over whom he had tyrannised gain their freedom by his death." [2]

Think also for a moment of the meaning in this short sentence :—

" I wish I might be allowed to cry with all my strength to those holy men who have been formerly hurt by women : ' Fly from women, do not direct them, leave the care of their salvation to others.' " [3]

That a churchman with honest purpose should undertake the care of souls La Bruyère believed to be right and good, but that a divine or a layman in accepting such functions should allow himself to become a petted darling of society was to him abominable.   He speaks of " the inexhaustible nursery garden of directors " ; and from the difficult nature of their duties, the faults into which the men were led, and the folly of the women who submitted themselves to their guidance, he seems to have thought that the directors did more harm than good, and that women at least would have been better without them.   Molière may have thought so too, but when he alluded to the directors of conscience he did not attack the office itself ; his satire was against the abuse that Tartuffe made of his position in the office.   La Bruyère wrote very strongly against the directors and against the " dévots,"

---

[1] It was the custom then for suitors to visit the judges of their case and offer them bribes.   Molière alludes to it in the first scene of his *Misan- thrope* ; so does Racine in Act I. sc. 1 of his comedy, *Les Plaideurs.*
[2] *Œuvres de La Bruyère*, par M. G. Servois (in the Collection des Grands Écrivains de la France), i. 184, 185.
[3] *Ibid.* i. 181, 182.

for at the time of his death in 1696 the number of men in both of these classes was greater than it had been a generation earlier.

Molière composed his comedy mainly against those who make a false profession of religion :—

> " Ces dévots de place,
> De qui la sacrilége et trompeuse grimace
> Abuse impunément et se joue à leur gré
> De ce qu'ont les mortels de plus saint et sacré."

The word "dévot" was then and for some years later generally used in an ironical sense. Among men and women who knew the ways of the world "un dévot" was recognised as the opposite of a devout man. When writers spoke of a dévot, unless the meaning of true devotion was gathered plainly from the context, it was nearly always synonymous with a hypocrite. There are several instances of this in the *Caractères* of La Bruyère. He says in the chapter "De la Mode ": "A dévot is one who under a king who is an atheist would be an atheist himself." [1] And in the chapter "Des Femmes," while speaking of the directors, there is a witty bit of satire: "It is too long odds against a husband for a woman to be both a coquette and a dévote; she should make her choice." [2] And Fléchier, the Bishop of Nîmes, who died in 1710, said :—

"There is a great difference between a good man and a dévot. The former has virtuous principles in his heart, he always seeks to acquire them, and in a quiet way he does many good actions; the latter aims only at the appearances of virtue, he does not like things which do not show, and if he can pass for a dévot he is happy." [3]

On page 279 of the same volume Fléchier says :—

"The first thing that a dévot or a dévote does is to look for a director who is not too severe and who will accommodate himself a little to his or her infirmities. A dévot thinks himself a public personage who deserves marks of respect that are not shown to others. He is very proud of the services he gives to the poor and to the Church, and he urges this belief on the director, who carefully makes use of him on every occasion. . . . It is with the dévot as with the wit: both are taken for what they are worth. But one cannot pass for a witty man or for an honest man without having a good measure of either quality. When a man wishes to be thought

---

[1] *Œuvres de La Bruyère*, par M. G. Servois (in the Collection des Grands Écrivains de la France), ii. 152.
[2] *Ibid.* i. 182.   [3] *Œuvres de Fléchier* (Nîmes, 1782), ix. 276.

a dévot he is at once known to be otherwise. . . . If I speak of the dévots in a way not to wish to increase their number, the fault does not lie in devotion but in the characters and in the minds of the false dévots."

What Fléchier wrote against the professional dévots bears out Molière in his delineation of the character of a hypocrite. Had Molière and Fléchier exchanged their views on the dévots and on hypocrisy, neither knowing to whom he was talking, they would probably have parted friends.

No one will suppose that Molière wrote his play from a directly spiritual point of view. As a comic dramatist that was not his function. He intended his comedy for men and women in Paris who lived ordinary lives and enjoyed ordinary pleasures in a rational way, and he gave a picture of a false religious guide whose daily conduct was contrary to every principle of morality. About religious guides who were honest men he said nothing. There are many bad sides to Tartuffe's character. Besides his hypocrisy we see in him selfishness, ingratitude, want of charity, fraudulent covetousness, gluttony, and lust. All these bad qualities are mixed together, exposing the whole character of the man and showing a personage of an exceptionally odious kind. Molière wished, no doubt, to provoke a laugh against those who allowed themselves to be duped by the hollow speciousness of men who professed to live saintly lives, and whose exterior proclaimed them to be what they were to any one who could look about him with open eyes; but his hot anger was shot against the false guides who deceived others for their own profit. Without making the dupes appear ridiculous he could not, in the spirit of comedy, have made the knave's villainy apparent. Though we may accept Tartuffe as a "dévot de profession," the play which bears his name shows with abundant clearness that he belonged to the particular class of men known as the directors of conscience. Dorine calls him a director in the second scene of the first act, when she is speaking of him and of Orgon to Cléante :—

> " C'est de tous ses secrets l'unique confident,
> Et de ses actions le directeur prudent."

In itself this is not conclusive, but throughout the first act of the play Tartuffe is often indirectly mentioned as a director.

And just after he has made his declaration of love to Elmire in Act III. sc. 3, he speaks some remarkable lines, in which the word "nous" is repeated three times and "notre" twice, thus showing that he belonged to a body of men who were supposed to act with a common object :—

> " Mais les gens comme nous brûlent d'un feu discret,
> Avec qui pour toujours on est sûr du secret :
> Le soin que nous prenons de notre renommée
> Répond de toutes choses à la personne aimée,
> Et c'est en nous qu'on trouve, acceptant notre cœur,
> De l'amour sans scandale et du plaisir sans peur."

It was not Molière's practice to model a personage for the stage on the character of any one individual, and he did not draw his hypocrite from any one of his contemporaries, though at the time the abbé Roquette, afterwards bishop of Autun, was very generally spoken of as the object of his satire. Two other names have been given as models of Tartuffe : the abbé de Pons and one Charpy, who later became a prior.[1] If there were two or three churchmen whose likeness to Tartuffe was remarked, there were presumably others who offered points of resemblance that were noticeable. It is in this way that characters in fiction are formed. An author has observed various traits in different persons. He assimilates these together with others of his own imagining, and so creates a character that makes a more or less lasting impression according to the way it is shown. There is a difference between drawing the portrait of a certain man or woman and describing a personage of a certain type, and in his character of Tartuffe Molière did not draw a picture of any one individual ; he conceived an ideal character of a particular stamp, and from that conception he framed his personage. There can be no doubt that the dramatist wished to show the wiles of some dishonest men connected with the Church, and worldly prudence did not deter him from inflicting a blow where he thought it was deserved.

It is not known with any certainty to what means Molière owed the king's permission to place the *Tartuffe* on the public stage. Bazin says[2] that there had been a long quarrel between some of the French clergy and the pontifical authority in

---

[1] *Œuvres de Molière*, iv. 303-308.
[2] *Notes historiques sur la vie de Molière*, 156, 157.

Rome, that this was terminated, at any rate for a while, by a papal brief dated 19th of January 1669, and that the reconciliation may have been favourable to Molière. In M. Mesnard's opinion this explanation is not unlikely.[1] Perhaps my readers may be more fortunate than I am in understanding it. Nothing, however, is known of any first-hand record showing the king's permission to play the *Tartuffe* in public. The earliest authority is that of La Grange and Vivot, the editors of the first complete edition of Molière's plays, published in 1682, who say: " La permission de représenter cette comédie en public sans interruption a été accordée le 5 Février 1669, et dès ce même jour la pièce fut représentée par la troupe du Roi.'[2] These words were written some thirteen years after the event they refer to, and though they do not mention the king's name there can be no doubt that it was his Majesty who had granted the permission. The leave to play the *Tartuffe* was given on the 5th of February 1669, and in the afternoon of that day the comedy appeared on the public stage and was played thenceforward without hindrance. At all the court performances of the play before 1669—the last of which was at Chantilly on the 20th of September 1668— and at the single performance at the Palais Royal on the 5th of August 1667, the principal parts were probably taken by the same actors, so that most of the work to be gone through in the way of rehearsals had been done when leave to act the comedy in public had been given. But it would seem that the appearance of the comedy caused surprise.[3] Some kind of notice to this effect must, one would say, have been given to the public—if it was only by advertisements at the corners of the streets—for the receipts taken at the first performance of the *Tartuffe* on the 5th of February 1669 were by far the highest ever known at the Palais Royal theatre.

Instead of speaking of the incidents in the play I shall say something by way of interpretation of its principal personages. From what has been told, an idea may be gathered of Tartuffe's position in Orgon's household; and unless this is kept in view much of the meaning of the comedy is lost. Orgon, the husband of Elmire and the father of Damis and

[1] *Œuvres de Molière*, iv. 332.　　[2] *Ibid.* iv. 270 ; 332.
[3] *Ibid.* iv. 333.

Mariane, was by nature a good man, affectionate to his wife and children, and loved and respected by them. Nothing is said about his religious creed, and he is not represented as being sanctimonious. Earlier in life he had served the State at the time of the Fronde, but he has since become infatuated with Tartuffe, and through weakness has grown besotted in his admiration for one who was unworthy of his trust. Those who find fault with Arnolphe in the *École des Femmes* as being too ridiculous will perhaps bring the same charge against Orgon in the *Tartuffe*. But. neither personage was meant to be an ordinary character. In both cases the dramatist wanted to show by ridicule how a man acting under strong emotion, unless he has a good foundation of common sense, may lose his reason and behave in a very foolish manner. Molière knew well what he was doing, and as a sort of half-apology for Orgon's folly he makes the sage Cléante speak some prosaic and rather didactic lines which, in a comedy showing clear characterisation, could only have come from a man of his stamp :—

> "Les hommes la plupart sont étrangement faits !
> Dans la juste nature on ne les voit jamais ;
> La raison a pour eux des bornes trop petites ;
> En chaque caractère ils passent des limites ;
> Et la plus noble chose ils la gâtent souvent
> Pour la vouloir outrer et passer trop avant."

Cléante is really a most estimable person, and we should all feel honoured at having such a man for our friend. He is loyal, upright, and not dull-minded, though unimaginative; and if there were many more like him the world might be a better place. We have, however, in judging men to take them as they are as well as what we may think they ought to be. Comedy, too, should be mirthful, it should not show the events of daily life just as they pass. The comic dramatist turns a Cléante to account, but if he can show humour and the lessons that honest satire may teach he will make more and better use of an Arnolphe or an Orgon.

For reasons of his own Molière chose that a man, not a woman, should be the victim of the schemes of his hypocrite. Perhaps he saw this was necessary to give a more comic effect to his play. If Orgon had kept his senses, and his wife had been cajoled and deceived, he would have turned Tartuffe out of his house. The play would then have been different, and no one can judge of Molière's work by what he did not write.

The comedy in the play is seen in various ways, but almost always tending either to proclaim Tartuffe's hypocrisy and unmask his villainy, or to show how he has duped others and to laugh at them for their folly. With the exception of a lovers' quarrel, drawn better and more amusingly than the well-known scene in the *Dépit Amoureux*, every incident in the play is made to bear upon Tartuffe's character. His personality pervades everything. He is not seen in the first two acts. The dramatist used them to define and establish the character of his hypocrite before presenting him to his audience. As soon as Tartuffe appears every one has an idea of what he is like; the man reveals his whole nature later. The scene is laid in Orgon's house in Paris, and the play opens by showing the annoyance the dishonest director has caused in Orgon's household. The family would be happy but for him. They used to live comfortably, enjoying the pleasures of life in a rational way; they have no vices and are not given to self-indulgence. But Tartuffe criticises their innocent amusements, all their daily actions, and makes his tyranny felt. In the first scene nearly all the personages except Tartuffe and Orgon are on the stage. Madame Pernelle, Orgon's mother, a querulous woman, has, like her son, been deceived by Tartuffe; and because all the other inmates of the house strongly distrust Tartuffe's pretended piety and hate him for his interference and his reprimands, she resents this dislike, and believing Tartuffe to be a good man she imitates his impertinence and tells them all what she thinks are home truths. Damis, Orgon's son, always hot-headed, answers his grandmother:—

> "Quoi? Je souffrirai, moi, qu'un cagot de critique
> Vienne usurper céans un pouvoir tyrannique,
> Et que nous ne puissions à rien nous divertir,
> Si ce beau Monsieur-là n'y daigne consentir?"

The word "céans" used here in the second line is found six times in the first act of the comedy. The word is now obsolete or little used, and meant inside this house. It was more precise in its meaning than *ici*; and considering the domestic nature of the director's functions it seems to have been specially applicable.

In his character of Elmire, Molière thought less of enlisting strong sympathies on her behalf than of portraying a good woman and a good wife, in no way coquettish, handsome or pretty and pleasing if you like, of a temperate disposition and with sound common sense, who would stand her ground against her intended seducer. Except for the very important scene in the fourth act where Elmire, acting on her husband's behalf, pretends to accept Tartuffe's declaration of love, hers is, I imagine, a rather ungracious part to have to play. Except in this scene she cannot assert herself, but rather should show discretion under disagreeable or unhappy circumstances. Tartuffe doubtless admired her, but there is nothing to show that she ever had a kind thought about him. She is used mainly as a means to make Tartuffe disclose himself and show what manner of man he is. And she must do this quietly rather than by force of will. There is almost no satire or irony in Elmire's nature, and ridicule cannot lay its hand upon her. She has a strong sense of amour propre, she is cool-minded but not cold-hearted. It should be remembered that she was Orgon's second wife, and was not the mother of Damis nor of Mariane; perhaps therefore the dramatist gave no familiar or home scene between either of these two and their step-mother.

Of Damis and Mariane little need be said here, nor of Mariane's lover Valère. But I must say a word about Dorine. Though nominally a subordinate character she is, at least on the stage, the brightest figure in the play, and her irony and her banter come as a pleasant relief by the side of Tartuffe's self-seeking and perpetual falsehood. In the list of the dramatis personæ Dorine is spoken of as the "suivante de Mariane," and in the comedy she appears in the position of a well-trusted upper servant. She is very outspoken and talks in a satirical and familiar manner, giving her opinion sometimes as a clever woman of the world, at other times as a dependant to whom very friendly liberties were allowed. The suivante, or waiting-woman, had been a common personage in old French comedy, always more or less inanimate; and in this play Molière transformed the character by putting life into it, and he showed his Dorine as an upper servant, perhaps of middle age, who mixed with her betters and who was permitted to say what she thought. She may, too, have been nurse to Orgon's children when they were young. Her sharp raillery is certainly amusing; and, in my opinion, the healthy tone of her satire against her master—see Act I. sc. 2 and Act II. sc. 2—is a strong sign that in his own mind the dramatist did not sneer or scoff at religious practices, and that he was very far from wishing that others should do so. Dorine's wholesome ridicule of nonsense and disgust at false-hood is as sure a sign that Molière did not mean irreverence in his comedy as all the wise words spoken by Cléante. There are not many marks of character which, taken alone, afford a truer test than laughter. Occasionally it lies with bad intention; then have as little to do with the laugher as you can.

The *Tartuffe* is certainly a serious comedy, condemning religious imposture very strongly, and yet showing both satire and ridicule. There are scenes of mirth in it, but only one, where Dorine reconciles Valère and Mariane after they have quarrelled, that creates hearty enjoyment. It has seemed to me more than once that on the stage this play is heavy, that it is more stiff from its seriousness or solemnity than comedy should be; and that in the representation the humour of comedy, especially in the personage of Tartuffe, is not seen so plainly as in reading Molière's own words. There are dramatic characters, more often found in tragedy than in comedy, written by a master-hand and giving all the fulness of meaning that language can portray, which hardly any actor can personate thoroughly. It is not so much that the reader trusts to his own imagination, or that during the representa-tion he likes his own fancy better than the simulated rendering of the part, as that the author had a bigger mind than the actor, and that the written words bring home a stronger picture of the personage intended than is within the power of an actor to show. Tartuffe is one of these personages, though he belongs to comedy and has the ridicule of comedy of a grim kind thrown upon him causing more disgust than amusement; but he has also a tragic element in his character in the feeling of horror that his evil influence inspires. I am

only giving my own impressions; others may judge better.
I think it has been said that no male character in French
comedy is so difficult to play well as Tartuffe; but the actor
who undertakes it will not give pleasure unless he animates
or enlivens the audience, and so interests them in his interpretation.   Molière's lines show that Tartuffe is a wretch both
proud and mean; his hypocrisy is so great that he is thoroughly
immoral and irreligious. He is bold and daring because he
can gain his objects best in that way; yet he fawns as a
parasite upon Orgon, he cringes before Elmire as he makes
love to her, and he is contemptuous to every one else. This
contradictory baseness is plainly in his character and is
exceedingly difficult to render on the stage in a spirit of
comedy; but I doubt if the traditions of the Comédie Française
do not make him appear to be more burdened with his own
meanness, with his abject pride, than Molière intended. He
is so solemn, too, that he rarely provokes a smile. He is not,
and cannot show himself to be, a frank villain until close
upon the end of the fourth act, and when he is seen afterwards in the last scene of the play he is again brave; but I
think that before he rises to bay against Orgon he might, in
spite of his dependence and snake-like conduct, act his part
with more assumed nobleness of manner, exhibit a little more
lightness and less appearance of servility towards his benefactor.   His general demeanour, as seen on the stage, shows
that he has the strength of a really bad man, but not that
he comes of a noble family of which we are told that he
boasted.

The dénouement to the *Tartuffe* has been blamed because
of the king's interference in the events of a comedy meant to
portray actual life. In a tale for children a romantic ending
is thought to be quite proper, but grown-up people, some
critics say, should not be asked to accept improbabilities.
Children are not altogether wrong in their liking for romance,
and their elders need not condemn it unnecessarily.   It
may be admitted that the action of the sovereign to rescue
Orgon and his family from Tartuffe's cruel clutches has the
appearance of a Deus ex machinâ; yet looking at the facts
of the case—the events in the comedy and the knowledge
that but for the king's interference the play would not have

been allowed to appear—it is difficult to see how the dé-nouement, or the unravelling of the knot, could have been solved in a better way. For the purposes of characterisation Molière made Orgon not only give his own property to Tar-tuffe, but also place in his hands a casket belonging to a third person. In the latter case the law might perhaps have inter-vened and restored to Orgon that which was not his own to give; but in the other, if the gift of his own property was valid, the law could not rightly annul it. No other power, therefore, remained but that of the king to render moral justice. Who is to define between moral and legal justice in the events of a stage play? It is moral justice, or, if you will, poetical or romantic justice, that the spectator in the theatre wants. He does not go there to reason; he judges of what he sees and hears by effects. If his sympathies are moved by the events or the characterisation in a play, emotional feelings will have their place. If he cannot rely upon his natural thoughts to determine the merits of a play, what he thinks is pure reason may easily lead him upon a false track. Intelligence rather than intellect is wanted in the matter, and the striving or searching after intellect has before now blunted the understanding of critics as to what should be the aim of comedy.

Considering all the abuse that had been heaped upon Molière and the animosity shown against his comedy, remem-bering the king's personal willingness to allow the *Tartuffe* to be acted, though he had at first forbidden its representation, and that it was the king who finally gave permission for the play to appear on the stage—considering all these circum-stances and recognising that the dramatist was writing for Parisians of his day, we may say that the long speech in the last scene of the comedy addressed to Orgon by the "exempt," or police officer, beginning:

> "Remettez-vous, Monsieur, d'une alarme si chaude.
> Nous vivons sous un prince ennemi de la fraude,"

contains a fair eulogy on Louis XIV. for his clearness of judgment and sense of justice. Molière's purpose here was not to flatter the king, but to proclaim publicly that he owed his sovereign a debt of gratitude.

M. Louis Moland,[1] M. Paul Mesnard,[2] and other writers, while fully believing in the originality of Molière's creation both of the *Tartuffe* as a comedy and of the character of its chief personage, have indicated some of the sources from which the dramatist drew his picture of a hypocrite. Molière certainly did not invent his Tartuffe solely out of his own brain, but he had ears to hear and eyes to see what was passing around him. Before he wrote his play his thoughts were full of the subject; he wanted to put a hypocrite on the stage and show the wiles and evil qualities of the man's nature. Molière was the author of the characterisation in the comedy, just as much as he was of the verses in which the play is written. He owed something in the way of groundwork to others before him, as has been the case with every writer of fiction; but from his own observation and imagination he formed the characters, planned the scenes, and worked out the execution of the comedy. He did not absolutely invent the story told in the play, but he dramatised in a poetic form what he had seen or heard, or may be read, and left the world to judge of his picture as it pleased.

Towards the end of his Notice to the *Tartuffe*, M. Mesnard, following the contemporary authority of Robinet's *Muse historique,* gave the names of the actors who played the different parts in the comedy in February 1669.[3] The order observed is that of the names of the personages at the head of the play:—Béjart as Madame Pernelle, Molière as Orgon, Mlle. Molière as Elmire, Hubert as Damis, Mlle. de Brie as Mariane, La Grange as Valère, La Thorillière as Cléante, du Croisy as Tartuffe, Mlle. Béjart as Dorine. Robinet did not say who played the minor parts of M. Loyal nor of l'Exempt; it has been thought likely that de Brie filled them both. In his *Notice biographique sur Molière,*[4] published eleven years later than the volume which contains the Notice to the *Tartuffe,* M. Mesnard expresses a doubt whether, when the first three acts of the comedy were performed at Versailles in 1664, Mlle. Molière then played the part of Elmire, on the ground that she was young and inexperienced; and he thinks

[1] *Œuvres de Molière,* 1st ed. iv. 369-76.
[2] *Œuvres de Molière,* iv. 348-55 ; x. 311.
[3] *Ibid.* iv. 334, 335. [4] *Ibid.* x. 313.

that at that time the rôle was more suitable to Mlle. du Parc. However that may be, Mlle. du Parc left the troop at the Palais Royal theatre at Easter 1667, and she died eighteen months later. In May 1664 Mlle. Molière was twenty-one years of age; but, it may be asked, if she played the part of Célimène in the *Misanthrope* in 1666, as appears to be certain, might she not have been entrusted with that of Elmire two years previously? For myself, I should say that Célimène's part is the more difficult of the two. I have seen both Madame Arnould Plessy and Madame Madeleine Brohan in the two parts, and I think that Célimène's requires higher imaginative and stronger imitative qualities from an actress, and should say that to be well rendered it demands more art and more consummate skill.

The first edition of the play, with the author's preface, was printed on the 23rd of March 1669, and on the title-page were the words: " *Le Tartvffe, ov L'Impostevr,* Comédie. Par I. B. P. de Molière," etc. The second edition, printed on the 6th of June following, besides the preface, contained the author's three petitions to the king, then published for the first time.[1] Molière parted with the rights of selling the printed copies of the *Tartuffe* to the bookseller, Jean Ribou, for 200 pistoles, or 2200 francs. Ribou pretended to think that he had given too much money for the play, but Taschereau says there is ground for not believing in the supposed regrets of Ribou for having given so high a price.[2]

For biographical reasons, already explained, I thought it well to speak of the *Tartuffe* before *Don Juan* ; but in doing so have had to depart from the chronological course of events.

Don Juan ou le Festin de Pierre was first seen at the Palais Royal theatre on the 15th of February 1665; no other previous performance of the comedy elsewhere has been recorded. It was acted fifteen times before Easter, but when the theatre re-opened after the three or four weeks' holiday it was withdrawn. Probably the authorities intervened, thinking that the play was an attack on religious ideas.[3] It was never put on the stage again at the Théâtre

---

[1] *Œuvres de Molière*, iv. 365, 366 ; xi. 33, 34.
[2] *Vie de Molière*, 5th ed. 191. [3] *Œuvres de Molière*, v. 38, 39 ; x. 325.

Français until the year 1847. Of Thomas Corneille's version of the *Festin de Pierre* I will say a word later. La Grange's Register shows that at all the performances of Molière's comedy, except the last, the receipts were high, and that on four days they exceeded 2000 livres. The *Tartuffe* was the only other play of Molière's that made so much money at one performance. La Grange thus disproves the assertions put forward in the 18th century that *Don Juan* had but a poor success because it was written in prose. There had long been a prejudice in France against seriously meant comedies in prose. It was thought that prose was not worthy of the occasion. Molière, as a man of the world and chief manager of a theatre, was not likely to go strongly against popular prejudices, but he did something to break them down; and *Don Juan* was the first of his comedies in more than one act that was written in prose.

The prime cause, probably, which led Molière to write his *Don Juan* was the refusal of Louis XIV. to allow the *Tartuffe* to be acted on the stage. In May 1664 this latter play had been forbidden. Doubtless the poet was much annoyed, for he believed he had drawn a fair picture. Like all earnest men he was intent on his work, and as he was not allowed to put his play satirising hypocrisy on the stage he determined to write a comedy satirising atheism. As his first play was in verse he thought that the second should be in prose and shown in a more popular manner. Pascal's niece, Marguerite Perier, said that when her uncle was on his deathbed he was asked if he was not sorry he had written the *Lettres Provinciales*, and he answered: "Instead of being sorry, if I had to write them now I would make them still stronger."[1] It is often thus that men of deep natures strive to vindicate their opinions in the face of hostile criticism; and Molière in his second play did not overshoot the mark by exaggeration. There may be still some persons who dislike the pictures he gave in these two comedies; and even some, intolerant against him, who think that he was largely imbued with irreligious ideas, and who say that the two plays were written in an anti-religious or

[1] *Pensées de Pascal*, par E. Havet, 2nd ed. vol. i. pp. cxi, cxii; Sainte-Beuve, *Port-Royal*, 3rd ed. iii. 142.

scoffing spirit, presenting opposite sides of mental depravity. Every one will judge as he pleases. My own impressions lead me to think that when a strong work of imagination has been given to the world its author has not drawn his picture from caprice—though warm feeling may have had something to do with it—and if it has elicited disapproval, that time has generally shown he was much more just and true in his conceptions than his adverse critics were willing to allow. Very likely Molière was anxious to produce his *Don Juan* as soon as possible, and comparing it with his other five-act plays it seems to show signs of hurried work. Many of the scenes are nearly as episodical as those in the *Fâcheux*; they characterise very clearly the chief personage, but they are not in a general sense linked together as those in the *Tartuffe* or those in the *Avare*. In this way *Don Juan* is not one of the best of Molière's comedies, though its principal character is certainly one of the strongest he ever drew. There is some reason for thinking that the dramatist was pressed by his fellow-actors to write a play in which Don Juan should be the hero. They may have suggested the subject to him as the groundwork for a comedy, or he may have first spoken about the matter to some of his friends in the troop; but in either case I do not believe he would have written the play unless he thought he could make the satire attaching to the principal personage serve his purpose.

The conception of a Don Juan was a very old one. If Molière's personage is still well known and the Don Juans seen on the stage during his lifetime are forgotten, that is because he was able to draw a firmer dramatic character than were his predecessors or contemporaries, and thus invest it with an air of greater reality. With Molière's comedy in view the following extract, taken from M. Moland's work,[1] is worth reading :—

" The first idea of the drama came from Spain. In the old Andalusian chronicles there was a legend, of uncertain date, which both in character and in construction was very like some of our own tales of the middle ages. A debauched nobleman, named Don Juan Tenorio, a descendant of one of the Twenty-Four of Seville, was said to have mortally· wounded the Venerable Commander of Ulloa after he had

---

[1] *Œuvres de Molière*, 1st ed. iii. 338, 339.

run away with his daughter. This illustrious seignior was buried in the church of the Franciscans, where his family had a chapel; and a tomb and a statue were erected to him there in his honour. At first the murderer, because of his high birth and family influence, braved the law and escaped the rigours of justice. Then there came a rumour that Don Juan had challenged the father of his victim, even in his tomb, and had railed at and insulted his statue; that the statue became inspired, and as the minister of justice it had hurled the impious man through the open earth into the flames of hell. Those who said that Don Juan was enticed into the church by the allurements of a love-meeting and slain there were not listened to, for whatever is marvellous obtains an easy mastery over the minds of men."

From this old legend a Spanish dramatist, Tirso de Molina (otherwise known as friar Gabriel Tellez), wrote a play early in the 17th century which he called *El Burlador de Sevilla y Combidado di Pietra*; and this was the father of at least five other plays, one Italian and four French, on the same subject which were acted in Paris in the third quarter of the 17th century. Of these the only one, except Molière's, that need concern us here was the first in date. An Italian imitation of Molina's play was made by Onofrio Giliberto under the title of *Il Convitato di Pietra*, and it was acted at Naples in 1652. Possibly it was printed there in that year, though both M. Mesnard and M. Desfeuilles say that no copy of it can be found.[1] Giliberto's imitation of Molina's play was put on the stage by an Italian troop at the Petit Bourbon theatre in Paris in 1657. As was customary with the actors of the commedia della bella arte, it was performed in a more or less impromptu way, and it is probable that some changes were made. M. Moland has, however, given an outline of the comedy as it was played at the Petit Bourbon theatre.[2] The subject then become popular on the stage in Paris, and it is curious that all of the four French plays in which Don Juan was the hero were written by actors. All of these French plays were in substance taken from Molina's play, or from Giliberto's, or from an Italian play by Andréa Cicognini called *Il Convitato di Pietra*, of uncertain date, but acted and printed before April 1664.[3] This latter play, though popular in Italy,

---

[1] *Œuvres de Molière*, v. 15; xi. 133.
[2] L. Moland, *Œuvres de Molière*, 1st ed. iii. 344-53; and the same author's *Molière et la Comédie Italienne*, 191-207.
[3] *Œuvres de Molière*, v. 21-24; xi. 133.

does not appear to have been acted in Paris, but Molière seems to have borrowed from it.[1] In three of the French plays, according to the printed editions, *Le Festin de Pierre* was the main title. But when Molière's play was printed for the first time in 1682 by La Grange and Vivot, it was called *Don Juan ou le Festin de Pierre*; though La Grange, in chronicling in his Register the daily performances of Molière's comedy in 1665, called it *Le Festin de Pierre*. As " le festin " means the feast, not the guest at the feast, M. Mesnard does well to point out that the words show an ellipse and were understood to mean " *Le festin de l'homme de pierre, de la statue.*"[2]

The conception of *Don Juan*, therefore, was not Molière's; but he made his principal character appear to be a real atheist, instead of a pretended atheist or giddy-headed libertine, as was the case with the Spanish and Italian authors. They thought principally of the incidents in their plays, he thought chiefly of the characterisation of his personage. Though in *Don Juan* Molière borrowed from Tirso de Molina, from Giliberto, from Cicognini, he was nevertheless working out his own thoughts with seriousness of purpose. " Un grand seigneur méchant homme est une terrible chose," is the keynote to his comedy. Tirso de Molina wrote a drama in verse, its character was mainly religious, its tone and style were noble, and his play contains few or no comic scenes. The Spanish Don Juan is not an atheist, though he is very wilful in his wickedness. He affects atheism in a dignified manner, and he rails at religion more from a love of raillery than from true disbelief. He always says there is time to repent, and at the end he asks for the services of a priest.[3] In Giliberto's play, from the sketch given of it by M. Moland, there seems to be an absence of any kind of religious thought. Such an idea would have been contrary to the feelings of an Italian audience. They wanted only to be interested and amused, and did not care for serious thought on the stage. In the way of amusement, of comedy, Molière always preferred Italian ideas to Spanish.

---

[1] For fuller information on the whole subject see M. Mesnard's Notice to *Don Juan* in the *Œuvres de Molière*, vol. v.; vol. xi. of the same work, pp. 133, 134; M. Moland's Notice to *Don Juan* in vol. iii. in his first edition of Molière's plays; M. Fournel's *Contemporains de Molière*, iii. 316, 318; and the same author's *Petites Comédies Rares et Curieuses du 17ᵉ Siècle*, i. 19, 20.

[2] *Œuvres de Molière*, v. 10, continuation of note 3 from p. 9.

[3] *Ibid.* v. 7.

There is excellent comedy in his *Don Juan*, some of which he may have borrowed from Italian sources, though the setting of it was his own; but the earnestness he showed was certainly not Italian, and it was deeper than Spanish seriousness. Molière did not mean to write a religious comedy, but he satirised some of the many aspects of immorality. He condemned irreligion, impiety, and want of all reverential thought; and because he used satire and jesting his words have sometimes been misconstrued. I have said before that he often mixed earnestness and ridicule together. His *Don Juan* was really a counterpart to his *Tartuffe*. The two plays should be considered together, the second in date complementing the first. Tartuffe pretended to live a holy life; Don Juan would deny the existence of all holiness, and when he denounces hypocrisy he does so in a scoffing and cynical manner. He thinks, or tries to think, that there is no right, no wrong, in the world; in the future no heaven, no hell; and as we see him he would believe in no God, in no devil, and is to all appearance an atheist. Here, as in the *Tartuffe*, Molière does not speak in a scriptural sense; but I gather from his comedy that he himself thought it doubtful if the thorough atheist is not an imaginary personage, and that when a man who believes himself to be an atheist is pressed hard on matters that touch his senses strongly, he is forced to admit the presence of a God who rules over him. At all events, Molière's *Don Juan* is a man who wishes to live as an atheist, though he is also a braggart. The character is very powerfully drawn; and except at one moment, when he shows personal courage, he is always represented as odious and despicable in his crimes.

It must be said that even good modern editions of Molière show some differences in the text of *Don Juan*. Words or lines are occasionally placed between brackets, or in inverted commas, or in footnotes; and though the sense runs clearly the interpolations or interruptions bother the reader. I will explain the matter shortly. Molière's *Don Juan* was printed for the first time, from the acting copy of the play, in the seventh volume of the first complete edition of the poet's works, published in Paris by La Grange and Vivot in eight volumes in 1682. As soon as vol. vii. was printed it was seized by the police. The authorities demanded that changes should be made in the text, that some pages, even some sheets, should be cancelled and reprinted with alterations. The newly printed pages or sheets were called " cartons." When the volume was " cartonné," or expurgated, according to order —that is, when certain pages and sheets had been cancelled and reprinted with the alterations demanded—its sale was allowed. Only three copies that were not " cartonnés " are known to exist now. They give the text that has been followed by M. Mesnard. But an edition of *Don Juan* was published at Amsterdam in 1683 which professed to be still more original. For after the first performance of the play, in 1665, the dramatist altered a few passages and made some excisions. His most notable alterations were in Act III. sc. 1, where allusion was made to the " moine bourru "; in Act III. sc. 2, known as " la scène du pauvre "; and in Sganarelle's monologue at the end of the play. And there is evidence to show that these corrections and additions in the Amsterdam edition of 1683, professing to restore Molière's words as they were spoken at the first performance of the comedy, were not apocryphal. A reprint of the Amsterdam edition was issued at Brussels in 1694, but this was virtually only a copy. Thus, as M. Moland says, there are three texts to *Don Juan* : the first printing of the Paris edition in 1682 ; the second printing of that edition in the same year, generally spoken of as the " édition cartonnée "; and the Amsterdam edition of 1683.[1] To the " édition cartonnée," or expurgated edition, I shall make no reference ; but I shall refer occasionally to the edition printed at Amsterdam.

The main features in Molière's comedy are in the character of Don Juan and in that of his valet Sganarelle, who is used as a foil to exhibit his master. The other personages, too, were designed with this end in view ; they were all intended to show in their various ways the wickedness of the licentious nobleman. And in what I have to say about the play I shall try to show Molière's meaning chiefly through the two prin-cipal characters. They nearly always appear on the stage together.

[1] M. Moland, *Œuvres de Molière*, 1st ed. iii. 361 ; vii. 497 ; Taschereau, *Œuvres de Molière*, ed. 1863, iii. 113 note ; P. Mesnard, *Œuvres de Molière*, v. 46, 47 ; 70, 71 ; and xi. 19, 20 ; 70, 71.

The Sganarelle in this play is unlike the Sganarelles in five other comedies of Molière's where the same name appears, except that all were meant to show ignorant men and more or less stupid. The nature of Sganarelle in *Don Juan* is better than that of his namesakes, and whatever intelligence he has got comes from his heart rather than from his head. He has an understanding of his own, but he shows it sometimes by buffoonery. He differs from the other Sganarelles in appearing as a serving-man, not as a master. His position is to obey, not to give orders. And perhaps for that reason he possesses some good qualities which he might not have had were he the ruler in his own house. He is partly like the valets in old French comedy, but he is not clever nor quick-witted as they were; instead he is dull-headed, at times he talks like a fool, and physically he is a coward. Apparently he has had some religious instruction and still believes in it; he is meant to show a man who has his own simple ideas of right and wrong and the insight that simple, uneducated honesty often gives. He knows his master to be a monster of iniquity whom he is bound to serve, for he cannot escape from him. To show his mental accomplishments Molière makes him at the outset of the comedy discourse on the virtues of snuff. He is talking to Gusman, the squire to Done Elvire, Don Juan's wife, and tells him that he fears she will be ill repaid for her trouble in running after her husband. Gusman asks if a man of Don Juan's rank could be so base as to insult the virtuous love of Done Elvire?

" Sganarelle.

" Oh, yes, his rank ! That is a good reason, and it is likely to prevent him !

" Gusman.

" But the holy ties of marriage hold him bound.

" Sganarelle.

" Eh, my poor Gusman, my friend, believe me, you do not know Don Juan. . . . Let me tell you, between ourselves, that you see in Don Juan, my master, the greatest scoundrel ever created, a fanatic, a devil, a dog, a Turk, a heretic, who believes neither in heaven, hell, nor goblin, who passes his life just as a brute beast. . . . You say he has married your mistress. . . . A marriage costs him nothing. . . . Noble, lady, townswoman, peasant, nobody is too hot or too cold for him ; and if I were to tell you the names of all the women he has married in different places, I shouldn't have done to-day. You are surprised, and change colour at what I am saying. I have only given you an outline of the man ; to finish the portrait a good many more touches are wanted. . . . I would sooner serve the devil than him. . . . But a great lord who lives a wicked life is a terrible person. I must be faithful to him in spite of myself. Fear alone makes me zealous on his behalf, conceals my sentiments, and often compels me to applaud what I hate from the bottom of my soul."

When Don Juan arrives he adds something himself to the picture Sganarelle has given of him. He boasts of his love for women. But his language is not that of a large or tender-hearted man who has a chivalrous feeling of regard or of affection for woman as a woman; it is not that of a man who likes honestly the soft companionship of a woman's society. Due allowance made for the rhetoric and tinsel that an audience in the theatre in the 17th century expected from a grandee when he was talking familiarly to his valet about his love-affairs, Don Juan's first long speech does not show the passion of love; it does show that of desire.

" *Sganarelle.*

" But, sir, with the leave that you have given me, may I be permitted to say that I am a little scandalised at the life you are leading ?

" *Don Juan.*

" What do you mean ? What sort of life do I lead ?

" *Sganarelle.*

" Very good. But, for instance, to see you get married once a month . . .

" *Don Juan.*

" Can anything be nicer ?

" *Sganarelle.*

" Yes, that is very nice and very amusing, and I should like it too if there was no harm in it. But, sir, to play in that way with a holy mystery, and . . .

" *Don Juan.*

" Let me be. That is an affair between heaven and myself, and we can settle it without your help.

" *Sganarelle.*

" Faith, sir, I have always heard it said that it is a bad sort of fun to laugh at heaven, and that libertines never come to a good end.

"*Don Juan.*

"Now then, master fool, you know that I have told you I don't like moralising.

"*Sganarelle.*

"But I am not speaking of you, God forbid. You know what you are doing, and if you believe in nothing you have your reasons. But there are certain little impertinent persons in the world who are libertines without knowing why, who are free-thinkers from vanity. And if I had such a master, I should say to him very plainly, looking at him in the face : 'Do you dare to laugh at heaven in that way, and are you not afraid to make fun as you do of the most holy things? Have you a right, little worm, little shrimp, that you are' (I am speaking to the master I just mentioned), 'have you a right to turn into ridicule that which all men revere? Do you think that because you are noble, because you have a fair wig nicely trimmed, feathers in your hat, a coat covered with gold lace and flame-coloured ribbons' (I am not speaking to you, but to the other master), 'do you think, I say, that you are a bigger man, that you may do what you like, and that no one shall dare tell you of your faults? Let me, your valet, tell you that heaven sooner or later punishes wicked men, and that a bad life leads to a bad death.' . . ."

Now such language is unusual in comedy, but it was used with serious purpose. It is manifest that the dramatist meant to show two personages of opposite natures, and he wished the contrast between them to be observed. It was of their natures that he was thinking chiefly. Molière did not wish to portray in Don Juan a man with religious doubts; as a comic dramatist, that was not his proper function. He chose him as a strong example, and meant to satirise men of high position in the world who lived bad lives, who affected atheism, or at least free-thinking, and who from their rank or their wealth set bad examples to others. He had already made Sganarelle say of his master: "Un grand seigneur méchant homme est une terrible chose." The scene of the play was laid in Sicily, but it was felt that the interest of the comedy lay among the French people and about what passed in their country. Like his fellows, Don Juan was a dandy, an exquisite; and his speech, though simple from the force of his character, shows that he had the grand manner of men of distinction; and Molière, in his comedy, took advantage of the familiarity that existed on the stage before his day between master and valet to make poor Sganarelle, who was certainly neither clever nor bright-witted, reproach his lord for his evil mode of living.

The personage of Done Elvire is a secondary one. Don Juan had but lately taken her out of a convent and married her; and when she upbraids him for deserting her a few weeks after their marriage, he will not deceive her by fine excuses, but he is callous to her sufferings, and he lies to her as only a wicked and blasphemous man can lie.

I pass over quickly the scenes in Act II. between Don Juan and the two pretty peasant girls, Charlotte and Mathurine. He sees them one after the other, makes love to each of them, and in succession promises to marry them both. There is a bit of good comedy in the way in which the two girls, rivals for the hand of the great lord, dispute before him which shall be his wife, and also in the amusing way in which the wretch satisfies them both. And I shall only just mention now the first part of the first scene in Act III. There is some droll by-play here against the doctors of medicine; but except that it shows Don Juan to be an unbeliever in medicine, as in everything else, the fun is purely episodical.

The latter part of this scene, however, should be given. Sganarelle says to his master:—

"I want to know what you really do believe. Is it possible that you have no belief in heaven?

Don Juan.

"Drop that.

Sganarelle.

"That means no. And in hell?

Don Juan.

"Eh!

Sganarelle.

"Just the same. And in the devil, if you please?

Don Juan.

"Yes, yes.

Sganarelle.

"As little. Don't you believe in another life?

Don Juan.

"Ah! Ah! Ah!

Sganarelle.

"Here is a man that I shall have trouble to convert. Tell me now (for one must believe in something), what it is that you do believe?

" Don Juan.

" What do I believe ?

" Sganarelle.

" Yes.

" Don Juan.

" I believe, Sganarelle, that two and two are four, and that four and four are eight.

" Sganarelle.

" That's a nice creed ! Your religion, it seems, consists in arithmetic."

The rest of Sganarelle's speech means that he, an ignorant man, who recognises that " one must believe in something," believes in the Creator and his works. At last he gets bewildered and says : —

" Oh, Lor' ! contradict me, if you please. I cannot dispute unless I am contradicted, and you let me go on talking so that you may laugh at me.

" Don Juan.

" I am waiting until you have finished your argument.

" Sganarelle.

" My argument is that there is something wonderful in man that all the learned people cannot explain. Is it not marvellous that I am here, and that there is something in my head that thinks of a hundred different things in a moment, and does with my body what it likes ? I want to clap my hands, raise my arms, look up to heaven, bow my head, move my feet, go from right to left, go forwards, backwards, turn . . . [*As he is turning he tumbles down.*]

" Don Juan.

" Good ! You have broken your nose with your argument.

" Sganarelle.

" Faith, I am a big fool to waste time in reasoning with you ! Believe what you like ; I don't care a button whether you are damned or not."

At the first performance of the comedy, according to the Amsterdam edition, when Sganarelle is questioning his master as to his beliefs, he asks him : " What do you believe about the ' moine bourru ' ? " Don Juan answers him : " Plague take the ass ! " And Sganarelle replies : " Now that is what I cannot stand. There is nothing more true than the moine bourru, and I would let myself be hanged for him."[1] The "moine bourru" is said to have been a phantom spirit who walked about at night and ill-treated the people out of doors. It was a popular superstition and had, or perhaps has still, much the same effect on the ignorant as the "bogey man" has with us upon young children. Some of Molière's enemies, blinded by bigoted passion to the spirit of comedy, were shocked at his impiety in claiming reverence for an imaginary being. They would not see that the dramatist, in a spirit of satire, made use of a very uneducated and simple-minded servant to convict his master, who believed only in arithmetic, of a total absence of any religious feeling. After the first performance of the comedy le moine bourru was not mentioned, and the lesson was lost.

I come now to the "scène du pauvre" in Act III. sc. 2. In some editions the pauvre is spoken of as Francisque. He meets Don Juan and Sganarelle in a forest, and asks the nobleman for a little charity :—

"I am a poor man, sir, living quite alone in this wood for ten years, and I shall not forget to pray heaven to give you all kinds of good things.

" *Don Juan.*

"Eh! pray that it will give you a coat, and don't trouble yourself about other people.

" *Sganarelle.*

"You don't know this gentleman, old man.[2] He only believes that two and two are four, and that four and four are eight.

" *Don Juan.*

" What is your occupation among these trees ?

" *Le Pauvre.*

" To pray to heaven all day for the prosperity of good people who give me something.

" *Don Juan.*

" Then you should be well off.

" *Le Pauvre.*

" Alas, sir ! I am in the greatest distress.

---

[1] *Œuvres de Molière*, v. 139 note 2.

[2] In the 17th century " bon homme " meant simply old man (Sainte-Beuve, *Port-Royal*, 3rd ed. ii. 537 note) ; and see the beginning of the second scene in the *Tartuffe*, where Cléante speaks of Madame Pernelle as " cette bonne femme," and Dorine's reply.

"*Don Juan.*

"You are jesting. A man who prays to heaven all day cannot fail to be in easy circumstances.

"*Le Pauvre.*

"I assure you, sir, that most often I have not a bit of bread to put between my teeth.

"*Don Juan.*

"I will give you a gold louis, and I give it to you for the love of humanity."

So runs the original edition, non-cartonnée, published in Paris in 1682, which has been followed by M. Mesnard. But there was a part of the dialogue in this scene spoken at the first performance of the play in 1665, omitted by La Grange and Vivot in 1682, which was not published until 1693 at Amsterdam. After the poor man declared that he had not often a bit of bread to put between his teeth, Don Juan offers him a gold louis if he will curse. The offer of the coin, under the same condition, is made and refused three times. Then Don Juan says to him : "There, that 's enough. I will give it to you for the love of humanity." [1]

Here again Molière made use of Sganarelle, who repeated his master's creed to the poor man, to tell the audience in the theatre that the gay young nobleman, the hero in the comedy, had no sort of religious faith or feeling. Don Juan further condemns himself by his sneer against the efficacy of prayer. And when he finds that the unfortunate fellow will not commit a sin for the sake of a gold piece, he says with bragging and bitter irony : "Va, va, je te le donne pour l'amour de l'humanité." Much has been written about these words. I have no doubt whatever that they were meant to show strong satire. It seems to me that Molière wanted his audience to understand that Don Juan, who was impious in everything, wished to say boastingly and blasphemously : "If God won't give you assistance, man will—I will do so for man's sake"; or almost, "If God won't help you, the devil will."

It must be remembered that besides being an atheist, Don Juan was thoroughly wicked. He knew that humanity was considered as a Christian virtue, therefore he railed at it. Of real

[1] *Œuvres de Molière*, v. 146 note ; see also Louis Moland, *Œuvres de Molière*, 1st ed. iii. 423, 424 ; and Taschereau, *Œuvres de Molière*, ed. 1863, iii. 162, 163.

humanity, or, in a familiar and concrete sense, a fellow-feeling for others, he thought nothing. But for the moment he was counterfeiting humanity, and in his gift he made the idea of humanity serve his purpose as a sneer against the charitable feeling towards others that God has put into men's hearts. A moment previous he had sneered against belief in God and trust in Him. It was thus that Molière by his satire showed the man's wickedness and his cruelty.[1]

Particular religious creeds have nothing to do with all this. Probably enough Molière cared little about them. Probably enough, too, he thought that they interfered in the minds of many men with morality in a large sense, about which he did care a great deal, and which he held was inseparable from all true religion of whatever creed. He has nowhere said what his own religious belief was, but I think it may be gathered from his plays generally that human charity had a large share in it. I do believe that he was actuated by the spirit of religion, apart from morality, and that he respected and revered religious-minded men, if they were but honest in their beliefs and if their acts were good and were truly done. What their beliefs were he thought was a less important matter. He thought more of conduct than of creed. Molière drew his character of a licentious atheist because he saw that such men were becoming too common among the well-to-do in his own country; he wished to satirise their shameless and barefaced wickedness because its immorality set bad examples and demoralised others. As a comic dramatist he was debarred from using severe argument; instead he chose ridicule as a means of causing horror and disgust. We can all enjoy the ridicule against Harpagon in the *Avare*, but that against Don

---

[1] I gather from M. Mesnard that the use of the word "humanité," as understood now, was rare among writers in France in the 17th century. (See *Œuvres de Molière*, v. 184, about the middle of the note.) But there is a good instance of it, hidden as it were, in a fragment of a comedy of Molière's that is little read—in *Mélicerte*, Act I. sc. 4, v. 179. There Lycarsis says that he has

"Pour les desirs d'autrui beaucoup d'humanité."

The word is used here lightly, but its meaning is plainly defined. And in the *Fourberies de Scapin*, Act I. sc. 3, there is another instance of the same kind, but a little stronger. Scapin has been begged by Octave and by Hyacinte to assist them in their love-affairs, and he answers: "Il faut se laisser vaincre et avoir de l'humanité." In other places Molière uses "humain" in the same sense; and it is certain that about "humanity," as we understand the word now, he thought a great deal.

Juan has not always been understood so well. There are such great difficulties in treating of holy and unholy things in a comedy meant for the stage that many people will say that such matters are best avoided; yet, as I read Molière's *Tartuffe* and his *Don Juan,* I do not think that the charge of irreverence can be fairly laid against him.

When Don Juan draws his sword and runs to the rescue of a man attacked by robbers, who turns out to be Don Carlos, one of his wife's brothers, he performs the only praiseworthy action that can be placed to his credit. Sganarelle, who is not courageous, runs away frightened.

It will be remembered that in the old Andalusian legend from which Tirso de Molina took his play, allusion was made to the Commander of Ulloa, whom Don Juan is said to have killed. In the Spanish play the Commander is first seen alive, then after a considerable interval his statue, supposed to be animated, appears on the stage. But the laws which governed the French drama would not allow a long interval between the acts. As all the incidents in a French play were supposed to have happened within twenty-four hours, Molière spoke in the second scene of his comedy of the death of the Commander whom his Don Juan had killed six months previously.

Don Juan and Sganarelle are still in the forest where they had met the poor man, and they see the Commander's sepulchre. The sepulchre opens, and a handsome mausoleum and a statue of the Commander are seen. Sganarelle is frightened at its lifelike appearance. Don Juan insists that his valet shall ask the statue if it will come to supper with him. When the statue bows its head Sganarelle is still more afraid.

"*Don Juan.*

"Come here, you knave, I will show you what a coward you are. Listen now. Will the Seigneur Commandeur come to supper with me? (*The Statue again bows its head.*)

"*Sganarelle.*

"I would not have had this happen otherwise for ten pistoles.[1] Well, sir?

"*Don Juan.*

"Now, then, let us go out.

---

[1] Molière's words here are: "Je ne voudrois pas en tenir dix pistoles." I give their meaning as understood by M. Mesnard. See *Œuvres de Molière,* v. 162 note 1.

"*Sganarelle.* (*Alone.*)

"That is one of my free-thinkers who believe in nothing."

The interview with Monsieur Dimanche, who tries to get money owing to him from Don Juan and from Sganarelle, is a deliciously amusing instance of light comedy, but the scene is almost purely episodical. Don Juan afterwards receives a visit from his father, Don Louis, who has come to reprimand him for his evil mode of living. Nearly at the end of the father's speech his son says to him : "If you were seated, sir, you would be able to talk better." And when the old man has gone the reprobate says of him : "Oh! die as soon as you can, it is the best thing you can do. Every one must have his day, and it maddens me to see fathers who live as long as their sons." Done Elvire appears once more to warn her husband of his bad life. She can be nothing more to him, but she speaks affectionately. Sganarelle is moved to tears, but Don Juan remains heartless ; and when his wife has left him he asks for his supper. Here Sganarelle shows a mixture of buffoonery and terror that must have strangely disconcerted those critics of dramatic propriety who thought that all the passions should be kept in their place. The statue, who had been invited, takes his place at the table. Don Juan is ever fearless, and accepts with full self-assurance a return invitation to supper given by the statue.

At the beginning of the fifth act Don Louis pays a last visit to his son. As a prelude to what follows, Don Juan feigns hypocrisy and gladdens the heart of his father, who goes away happy.

"*Sganarelle.*

"Oh, sir! how glad I am to see you converted. I have been waiting for that for a long time, and now, thanks be to heaven, my wishes are fulfilled.

"*Don Juan.*

"Plague take the fool !

"*Sganarelle.*

"What do you mean by fool ?

"*Don Juan.*

"Do you believe what I have just said, and do you think I was in earnest all the time ?

" Sganarelle.

" What ! It is not . . . You don't . . . You . . . Oh ! what a man ! What a man ! What a man !

" Don Juan.

" No, no, I am not at all changed ; my sentiments are just the same.

.　　.　　.　　.　　.　　.

" Sganarelle.

" What ! you believe in nothing, and you wish to set yourself up as a good man ('un homme de bien ').

" Don Juan.

" And why not ? There are many others like myself who take up the trade and who put on the same mask to deceive the world.

" Sganarelle.

" Oh ! what a man ! What a man !

" Don Juan.

" There is no harm in that now. Hypocrisy is a fashionable vice, and every fashionable vice passes for a virtue. The personage of a good man is the best that one can affect nowadays, and the profession of a hypocrite has wonderful advantages. The imposture of the art is always respected, and although it be discovered no one dares to say a word against it. All other human vices are open to censure, and everybody is free to attack them as he pleases. But hypocrisy is a privileged vice ; it closes everybody's mouth and quietly enjoys a sovereign impunity. By dint of shams a close society is made up from a party sect. If one of these persons is offended, all the others rise up in his defence ; and those who are known to be really honest, and those whom every one knows to be real believers, those, I say, are always the dupes. They fall openly into the traps laid by the hypocrites, and they blindly protect the imitators of their own actions. How many do you think I know who, by this device, have cleverly patched up the riots of their youth, who have made a shield of the mantle of religion, and under this honoured cloak have leave to be the wickedest men in the world ? You may know their intrigues and be sure of what these people are, they still maintain a high reputation ; and by bowing their heads, by venting deep sighs and rolling their eyes, they put a good appearance upon anything they do. I shall screen myself under this shelter, and there I shall conduct my own affairs safely. I shall not give up my pleasant habits, but I shall carefully hide myself and amuse myself secretly. If I am discovered I shall, without stirring, lay my interests before all the party, and they will defend me before and against everybody. In that way I can do what I like with impunity. I shall set myself up as a censor of other people's actions, judge harshly of every one, and only have a good opinion of myself. If I am offended I will never forgive, and will always quietly maintain an inplacable hatred. I shall be the avenger of the interests of heaven, and under this convenient pretext I will provoke my enemies, accuse them of impiety, exasperate them by those zealous, indiscreet persons who, not knowing what they are saying, will talk against them in public and cover them with reproaches, and from their own mouths will damn them openly. That is the way to take advantage of men's weaknesses, and he is wise who knows how to suit himself to the vices of the age."

Until now the character of Don Juan is not fully known; Molière reserved the deepest traits in his personage for the last act of his play. Therefore I have thought well to give this long speech in full. Hitherto Don Juan has been cruel and licentious, he has appeared as an atheist and a scoffer. We see now that the wicked grandee who had gloried in his crimes means to continue his bad life, and to add to his wickedness by screening himself under the mantle of religion. His speech may be divided into two parts. In the first the dramatist spoke against hypocrites and their conduct: he declared that hypocrisy was considered by many as a fashionable and a privileged vice; and, though he did not mention his play which was prohibited, he said, with some warmth, what he thought of the dévots who had combined together to prevent the *Tartuffe* from being acted. In the second part, beginning, "I shall screen myself," which is connected with the first, Don Juan spoke of himself, and declared with abominable cynicism how he meant to make hypocrisy serve his purpose. Here Molière had in his mind the class of persons whom in his first petition to the king, in August 1664, he had boldly called "les Tartuffes"; and he showed how a very evil-thinking and ill-conditioned man would attach himself to a clique of dévots in order to be protected by them, pretend to be honest but live in a slough of debauchery, play the hypocrite blasphemously by making himself the avenger of the interests of heaven, be harsh and uncharitable to others, and yet reap all the advantages of high opinion which the world is willing to give generously to those who do live a good and holy life. Molière did not suppose that all the Tartuffes were as bad as his Don Juan, but he showed how a Don Juan would take advantage of their protection for his own evil ends.

Sganarelle, more horrified than ever, cries:—

"Oh, heavens! What do I hear now? You only wanted to be a

hypocrite to give you the finishing-stroke, and this is the climax of abominations. What you have just said, sir, goes beyond everything, and I cannot help speaking. Do with me what you please; beat me, knock me down, kill me if you like, I must open my heart, and as a faithful servant say to you what I ought. Learn, sir, that if you go on taking the pitcher to the well it will break at last; and as that author, whom I do not know, says very finely: Man in this world is as the bird on the bough, the bough is attached to the tree, he who attaches himself to the tree follows good precepts [then come a dozen lines of like nonsense], necessity has no law, he who has no law lives like a brute beast, and consequently you will be damned for ever."

This is an instance of how Molière mixed his reproof and his ridicule together; and I must repeat that Molière meant his audience to see that the ignorant but honest-hearted fool, in spite of his buffoonery, was a much better man than the atheist grandee.

Don Carlos, one of Done Elvire's brothers, comes to demand satisfaction of Don Juan, or else that Don Juan should acknowledge his wife publicly. The villain feigns hypocrisy; he invokes heaven seven times, and says that both he and his wife have determined to retire from the world. Tartuffe, also, used to call upon heaven, but he did so as a hypocrite feigning piety; when Don Juan invokes heaven, he does so as an atheist feigning hypocrisy. Don Juan replies to Don Carlos:—

"You will do as you please. You know that I don't lack courage, and that at need I can use my sword. . . . But I tell you, for my part, that it is not I who mean to fight. Heaven forbids the thought. If you attack me we shall see what happens."

This was a bit of Jesuitical casuistry, borrowed directly, M. Mesnard says, from Pascal's *Lettres Provinciales.* If a man walks in a field and another attacks him, he may defend himself without doing wrong.[1] Sganarelle is astounded :—

"What devilish style, sir, do you take up now? That is far worse than the rest, and I liked you much better as you were before. I was always hoping for your salvation, but now I despair of it, and I think that heaven, which has borne with you so long, will not suffer this last horror.

"*Don Juan.*

"Stop now; heaven is not so exacting as you think, and if every time that men . . .

---

[1] *Œuvres de Molière,* v. 199 note 5.

"*Sganarelle.*

"Ah, sir! It is heaven that is speaking to you; it is a warning that it gives you.

"*Don Juan.*

"If heaven means to give me warning, it should speak a little more clearly if it wishes me to understand it."

A spectre now appears veiled as a woman.

"*The Spectre.*

"Don Juan has only a moment to avail himself of heaven's mercy, and if he does not repent now his destruction is certain.

"*Sganarelle.*

"Do you hear, sir?

"*Don Juan.*

"Who dares to utter these words? I think I know that voice.

"*Sganarelle.*

"Ah, sir! it is a spectre. I recognise its step.

"*Don Juan.*

"Spectre, phantom, or devil. I will see what it is." (*The spectre changes its form and represents Time with its scythe in its hand.*)

"*Sganarelle.*

"Oh, heavens! Do you see, sir, this change of figure?

"*Don Juan.*

"No, no, nothing can frighten me, and I will try with my sword whether it is a body or a spirit." (*As Don Juan is about to strike the spectre vanishes.*)

"*Sganarelle.*

"Ah, sir, submit before all these proofs and repent at once.

"*Don Juan.*

"No, no, it shall not be said, whatever happens, that I can repent. Now then, follow me."

The statue reappears and says :—

"Stay, Don Juan. You promised me yesterday to come to supper with me.

"*Don Juan.*

"Yes. Where must I go?

"*The Statue.*

"Give me your hand.

"*Don Juan.*

"Here it is.

"*The Statue.*

"Don Juan, the hardening into sin leads to a bad death, and the rejection of heaven's goodwill is followed by its chastisement.

"*Don Juan.*

"Oh, heavens! what do I feel? An invisible fire is burning me. I am quite spent and my whole body is afire. Ah!" (*Strong thunder and lightning descend upon Don Juan; the earth opens and swallows him up, and huge fires belch out from where he has fallen.*)

"*Sganarelle.*

"Now by his death every one is satisfied: angered heaven, laws transgressed, girls wronged, families dishonoured, parents outraged, women ruined, husbands driven to despair,—everybody is glad. I only am unfortunate, who after so many years of service have no other recompense than to see before my eyes my master's impiety punished by the most awful chastisement in the world."

According to the Amsterdam edition, this last speech of Sganarelle's began with a cry, "Ah, mes gages! mes gages!" and it ended with a similar cry after "unfortunate" ("malheureux"). These words were thought to be very scandalous, and after the first performance of the play they were omitted. Now, the exclamations can be looked at in a calmer spirit. Molière, I conceive, meant nothing more than to put into the mouth of his Sganarelle at the end of the comedy a characteristic but foolish cry that should have the appearance of buffoonery, and that would make the audience laugh at the nonsense. A servant who believed in the moine bourru, when he saw his master suddenly disappear for ever, would not unnaturally exclaim at the loss of his wages. Would not Sancho Panza have done the same? In the way of cowardice, ignorance, and self-interest, there is a certain comic family likeness between Sganarelle and Sancho Panza, though Don Quixote and Don Juan are hardly more unlike each other than a highly bred gentleman and an Australian savage.

It may be taken as certain that La Grange played the part of Don Juan and Molière that of Sganarelle; and in all probability Mlle. Molière represented Charlotte; Mlle. de Brie, Mathurine; Mlle. du Parc, Done Elvire; Béjart, Don Louis; and perhaps du Croisy, M. Dimanche.[1]

Something was said of the annoyances the poet had to bear before the *Tartuffe* was allowed to be put on the stage. After the appearance of *Don Juan* the same kind of religious zeal, partly well-intentioned, partly ill-natured, was manifested, though not to the same extent. When this play was a few

[1] *Œuvres de Molière*, v. 56, 57.

weeks old a pamphlet was published: *Observations sur une comédie de Molière, intitulée Le Festin de Pierre.* Par B. A. Sieur de Rochemont, avocat en Parlement. This writer vilified Molière; and then there followed a *Réponse aux Observations*, etc., and a *Lettre sur les Observations*, etc.—both endeavouring to defend the dramatist against the strictures in the first pamphlet.[1] In all three cases the author's anonymity has been preserved. What strikes one chiefly in reading these pamphlets now, is that none of their writers had any idea of what comedy is, and that they laboured with their arguments as a horse drags at his plough when pulling it through a heavy soil. And I do not think that reading their arguments will enable any soul alive to understand Molière's meaning one bit the better.

Apparently Molière paid less attention to the attacks made on his *Don Juan* than to those against the *Tartuffe*. His last written play was acted fifteen times, several thousands of people had seen it, and so far as he personally was concerned he was tolerably content; and it is not known that he made any complaint in writing when he was asked, or told, not to print his comedy. The privilege, or leave, to print it, was given on the 11th of March 1665, less than four weeks after it had appeared on the stage. This privilege was registered at the booksellers' syndicate on the 24th of May,[2] but the play was not printed until the year 1682.

It was perhaps owing to the popularity of the subject that Molière's *Don Juan* appeared in an altered form at the Théâtre Guénegaud in the year 1677. The poet had then been dead four years. The reader will remember that a few weeks after his death the troop of actors at the Palais Royal were joined to those at the Théâtre du Marais, and that when this fusion had taken place the new troop went to play at a theatre in the Rue Guénegaud under the title of "la troupe du Roi"—a title which the actors at the Palais Royal had borne since 1665. As Molière's *Don Juan* had not been printed, the dramatic copyright in the play belonged to his widow, and she must have given her consent that her late husband's comedy should be put into verse by Thomas Corneille, the younger brother of

---

[1] The three pamphlets have been printed by M. Mesnard, *Œuvres de Molière*, v. 217-55.   [2] *Ibid.* v. 39.

the more famous Pierre Corneille. The arrangement was profitable to her, for the troop to which she belonged gave 2200 livres for the new version of the play. Corneille and Mlle. Molière shared the money equally, and she gave the troop a receipt for the sum in his name and in her own.[1] Corneille altered Molière's comedy in some respects. He says : "I reserved to myself the right to soften certain passages which hurt those who were scrupulous. I followed his prose closely enough, except in the scenes in the third and fifth acts where I brought women on the stage." Thomas Corneille was an agreeable and a facile writer in verse, and though most Frenchmen naturally prefer Molière's prose because of its greater strength and because they are rightly proud of Molière's name, the altered version of his comedy has, considering all things, been thought to be good. When the new version of the play was put on the stage on the 12th of February 1677, it had at first a great success. There were six performances before Easter, giving an average of 1319 livres taken each day. After the Easter holidays, for some unexplained reasons, the fortune of the comedy suddenly changed : it was acted only seven times with an average daily receipt of 362 livres.[2] But it is much more strange that the rhymed version of *Don Juan* should always have been acted in Paris for some hundred and fifty years, and that Molière's comedy should not have been seen there until the anniversary of his birth in 1847. With reference to this revival there is an interesting article on *Le Don Juan de Molière* by Charles Magnin in the *Revue des deux Mondes* for the 15th of February 1847.

In August 1665 the actors at the Palais Royal, who had been known as "la troupe de Monsieur," received a new honour. They were called to Saint Germain, and the king told Molière that he wished that the troop should henceforward belong to him, and he asked this permission of Monsieur. The actors were promised a pension of 6000 livres, and they took the title of "la troupe du Roi au Palais Royal."[3] The "grands comédiens" at the Hôtel de Bourgogne were still "la troupe royale," and their pension was 12,000 livres, twice as much as that given to their younger rivals.

---

[1] *Œuvres de Molière*, v. 50, 51. [2] La Grange's Register, 188-91.
[3] *Ibid.* 76.

CHAPTER XV

MOLIÈRE's next new play, *L'Amour Médecin*, was first acted at Versailles before the king on the 14th or 15th of September 1665, and it was put on to the stage at the Palais Royal on the 22nd of the same month. This was another of the comédies-ballets that Molière wrote for a court amusement, and as a new play it was performed three times before the royal audiences at Versailles. The little comedy was then divided into three acts to allow music and dancing as interludes; though when it was given in public these accompaniments were omitted, probably because of the expense, and also probably enough the divisions between the acts were not maintained. When the author printed his play he wrote a short preface which he wished the reader to notice :—

"This is only a simple sketch, a small impromptu, which the king wished for an entertainment. It is the most hurried of all those his Majesty has ordered of me ; and when I say that it was suggested, written, learned, and acted in five days, I shall only say what is true. It is not necessary to warn you that there are many things that depend on the action. Everybody knows that comedies are only written to be acted ; and I do not advise people to read this one unless, while they are reading, they can imagine all the play of the scenes. What I will tell you is that it is to be wished that these sort of works could always be seen with the ornaments that accompany them in the king's palace. You would then see them in a more tolerable condition ; and the airs and the symphonies of the incomparable Monsieur Lulli, mingled with the beauty of the singing and the skill of the dancers, doubtless give them charms, and it is with the greatest difficulty in the world that they can do without them."

Since Easter the receipts at the Palais Royal had been unusually low ; and a new play, *La Coquette ou le Favori*, by Mlle. Desjardins, first given on the 24th of April, did not help to raise them. La Grange shows that in this year, 1665-66, each actor in the troop got less money for his share than in any other year either at the Petit Bourbon or at the Palais Royal theatre.[1] For a few days the *Amour Médecin* did very well, then by degrees the receipts fell off; but unless the fun in the comedy had amused the audiences, the play would not have been acted as an after-piece twenty-seven times.

In the *Mariage Forcé* Molière had ridiculed sham philosophers or pretended doctors of learning. In the *Amour Médecin* he ridiculed doctors who practised the art of medicine, because he thought that too many of them were empirics blindly following routine, that they were more ignorant of their art than they should have been, that through greed they pretended to be learned; and because he thought that their want of common sense, want of knowledge, and their pretence caused much trouble and often death unnecessarily to sick people under their care. In both of these plays he showed the caricature of comedy plainly enough, but not so far as to disfigure his personages, to alter their natures, or to turn the comedy in his plays into farce.

It may be fairly assumed from Molière's comedies that he had a poor opinion of the medical men of his day, and that he was distrustful of the power of medical skill in fighting against a bad illness. Had he been a doctor himself, he would have been sceptical, doubting of real improvement, but still trying to do something to effect it and hoping for gradual amelioration. As it was, he was incredulous. Two stories are told about him by Grimarest,[2] which are at least characteristic. The poet and one of his friends, a Dr. Mauvilain, were both dining at Versailles at the king's table, and Louis XIV. said to Molière: "Here is your physician; what does he do to you?" Molière answered: "Sire, we talk together, he gives me prescriptions; I do not take them, and I get well." The second story is that Molière said that a doctor was a man paid to chatter nonsense in the patient's bedroom until nature had cured him or the remedies had killed him.

One of Molière's early farces, *Le Médecin Volant*, written when he was strolling with his troop in the provinces, was a satire against the doctors of medicine. His next attack was in *Don Juan* (Act III. sc. 1). As this scene is purely episodical as regards the events in the play, I only alluded to it when

<hr>

[1] Register, 143.　　　　[2] *Vie de Molière,* 42, 43.

speaking of that comedy, but it will not be out of place if given here. Sganarelle dresses himself up as a doctor, and he prescribes to five or six peasants who have come to him for advice. He says afterwards to his master:—

"It would be a queer thing if those sick people get well and if they come to thank me.

"*Don Juan.*

"And why not? Why should you not have the same privileges as all the other doctors? They have no more to do than you have in curing their patients, and all their art is pure sham. All that they do is to take the credit when a case turns out well; and you as well as they may reap the advantage that comes from the good fortune of a sick person and see attributed to your remedies everything that may come from good luck and from the forces of nature.

"*Sganarelle.*

"What, sir! Do you think profanely about medicine also?

"*Don Juan.*

"It is one of the greatest errors among mankind.

"*Sganarelle.*

"What! Don't you believe in senna, in cassia, or in antimony?

"*Don Juan.*

"Why should I believe in them?

"*Sganarelle.*

"Your mind is villainously distrustful. You know that antimony is now making a great stir in the world. Its wonders have converted the most incredulous persons, and less than three weeks ago I saw it produce a marvellous effect.

"*Don Juan.*

"What was it?

"*Sganarelle.*

"For six days a man had been on the point of death; nobody knew what to prescribe, no remedy did any good. At last antimony was tried.

"*Don Juan.*

"He got well, then?

"*Sganarelle.*

"No, he died.

"*Don Juan.*

"The effect was marvellous indeed.

"*Sganarelle.*

"Of course it was. He had been dying for six days, and the antimony killed him at once. Could anything have done it better?"

The quarrel among the doctors in Paris in the 17th century about antimony, or, as Molière calls it, "le vin émétique," is related by Maurice Raynaud, himself a doctor of medicine, who published in 1862 a volume called *Les Médecins au temps de Molière*, of which a second edition appeared four years later. This book is temperate in tone, neither praising nor condemning Molière's satire strongly, but rather acknowledging that the dramatist's purpose was to show playfully some of the foibles of doctors; and the author is not very technical in the accounts he gives of the institutions and customs of the medical profession in France two hundred and fifty years ago. In every country men have their national idiosyncrasies; but probably the members of the Faculty in France at that time were not as doctors either more or less learned than in other countries, where equal opportunities for studying the science of medicine were given to aspiring practitioners.

In a paragraph in a preface to the *Tartuffe*, while stating that at different epochs comedy, medicine, philosophy, and religion have been turned to a bad account, Molière says: "Medicine is a profitable art, and everybody reveres it as one of the most excellent things that we have; nevertheless, there have been times when it has been made to appear hateful, and men have often made of it an art to poison each other." Molière, of course, wrote against the doctors in a tone of satire; but his sceptical mind told him that not enough was known about the science of medicine, and that more should not be expected from doctors than they could give. Had they been fairly honest, endeavouring to do the best with the knowledge they had got, he would have left them alone; it was their greed and their humbug that annoyed him. He thought that too many of them took advantage of the confiding innocence of their patients to fill their own pockets, that they hid their ignorance under a vain show of words intelligible only to themselves, and that in their ignorance they fell back upon what somebody had said or done before them, either making wrong attempts at cure or pre-

scribing severe remedies when they were not needed. Molière
certainly attacked the spirit of routine in the medical profession. He wished to see in doctors sane-minded men, who had
a faculty of insight and of common sense, who thought for
themselves intelligently, instead of a body of formalists who
were not even good working machines. He wished to open
the eyes of the public to the blind practices of those who
persisted in frequent bleeding and purging because others had
done it before them, whereas softer remedies and the experience gained by watching how nature, if left alone, would do
her work, were often what was most wanted. This or that
young man had passed his medical examinations, he said he
was a doctor, and he was taken at his word. He was not
necessarily a Thomas Diafoirus; but if in most cases he had
possessed a fair power of healing, and if he had not been pre-
sumptuous and ridiculous, I doubt if Molière's comedies against
the doctors would have been written.

And there were in France, as in every country, men of a
very low grade, more common then than now, really quite
ignorant practitioners, who deceived their patients wilfully,
and who thought every day how much money they could make
out of their credulity. One sees plainly enough that it was
not only the ignorance of the doctors that Molière attacked,
but their dishonesty and their pretence. He was an open-
minded man, and would have been one of the first to recognise
a pardonable want of knowledge in a difficult art, but when
he found that there were "tartuffes" in medicine, he threw his
ridicule upon them. It has been said already that tartuffe
was an old French word meaning an impostor; and when
Molière saw that medical tartuffes made lies part of their
stock-in-trade, he got angry and showed his wrath in that form
of satire that suited his purpose best. Every physician was
not a dishonest quack, as every spiritual director of conscience
was not a self-seeking hypocrite; but at that time, more than
now, there were in both professions inducements to trickery, if
a man chose to avail himself of them. People were more
confiding then than now, because the general level of intelligence was lower; they paid more respect to authority; and
perhaps, then more than now, they did what they were told
through fear of being found out if they were disobedient.

Perhaps it is hardly likely that Molière's raillery against the doctors so far made itself felt as to do much real good, at least in his day. Clever charlatans would not cry out that they were hurt; doctors in good position would belittle Molière's plays, call them farces, or say that he did not know what he was talking about; while the world generally would be credulous as before; and if people became distrustful of their doctors, they would in most cases have suffered from their want of belief.

Molière did not wish to "talk medicine" on the stage, though perhaps he might have made part of his audience think that he knew something about it. What he did want to do was to expose some bad faults of the doctors in a strong light, in the spirit of amusing comedy, and to make his audience laugh at his pictures of their presumption, their love of formality, their ignorance, and their greed. From Raynaud's volume it may be seen that there was then much in the personal appearance and manners of these men that made them ridiculous. Even in Paris many doctors going to see their patients used to ride upon a mule, they wore a long robe or gown, their hats were high and pointed ; and worse still, both in consultation and in the sick-room, they interlarded their speech with Latin, partly to hide their ignorance of what they should have said in their own language, and partly to impose on the unfortunate creatures under their charge. Before Molière's day writers had satirised the doctors, and both Taschereau and M. Moland, in speaking of the *Amour Médecin,* have given the following 17th century epigram as painting the physicians of the time :—

> " Affecter un air pédantesque,
> Cracher du Grec et du Latin,
> Longue perruque, habit grotesque,
> De la fourrure et du satin,
> Tout cela réuni fait presque
> Ce qu'on appelle un médecin."

All this might be fairly set forth in a satirical comedy that was intended mainly to amuse, and it may be said safely that without some caricature the satire would lose its salt and be wanting in strength. The question then arises : Is the caricature so great as to destroy the comedy in the play and turn the play into a farce ? In the play now under consideration,

I think on the whole it is not, and that the general character-isation is so fair that the notes or marks of laughable comedy are greatly predominant. It is difficult to define how far caricature in comedy can go without descending into farce; but every one will acknowledge that in high comedy it should be kept well in hand, while in comedy meant to be openly popular and to create laughter easily, greater latitude may be given to it. We should, at any rate, ask ourselves: Is the intended likeness fairly recognisable? Does the character-isation of the personages show them to be types of more or less ludicrous men and women, or is it so distorted that they appear to be only absurd figure-heads? It seems to me that these questions may be answered in Molière's favour. Even in those of his plays that come under the designation of high comedy, he wrote in a tone of playful satire. As a comic dramatist it was his aim to do so, and he succeeded most admirably in giving true pictures of the types of men and women he meant to represent, though he threw keen ridicule on their follies. None of the plays that he wrote against the doctors can be classed as high comedy—and it may be that there is some farce in the *Médecin Malgré Lui* and in *Monsieur de Pourceaugnac*; still I imagine that these plays also give true satirical pictures of the objects intended to be represented. Molière often meant what he said; he tried to think truly, though he conveyed his thoughts under the guise of raillery and ridicule. And as comedy, even in its highest flights, should be mirthful and give amusement, surely it is permissible in lighter plays to use caricature so long as the satire or ridicule shown does not descend into mere absurdity. In comedy, ridicule and absurdity are not synonymous. Fair caricature is the lawful province of a humorist—indeed he can hardly do his work well without it; and if in a ludicrous picture of a person or thing an easily recognisable likeness is shown of the object represented, the picture is more or less true, almost however great is the ridicule thrown upon it. The question of taste in satire underlies all this, but it may be judged apart. Some sin against taste because they wish to do so. If they have the power of raillery, the piquancy of their wit is telling, but their heads may score a triumph at the expense of their hearts.

The pleasantry in the *Amour Médecin* must have startled

those who saw the play when it was acted at Versailles. Molière appears to have ridiculed the personal and the professional eccentricities of the court physicians before the king and his guests, and to have amused the royal audience very thoroughly. In the *Fâcheux*, also first acted before the king, he had laughed at some of the foibles of the courtiers; but there the banter, though it was personal, for the most part touched the oddities of men who thought themselves above the condition of the bourgeois, and they were flattered at being noticed and rallied good-humouredly among their friends. The courtiers all knew each other, the public did not know them, and they enjoyed the fun among themselves, each one pleased to think that he had been chosen for distinction. But in the *Amour Médecin* the raillery was of a different kind, and though it was not ill-natured, it bore strongly against the professional duties of the doctors, and it was meant to show that in their daily practice they were both ridiculous and inept. Still I do not think that in his satire Molière went so far as to show coarseness or licentiousness. There is greater liberty of thought now than there was in his day, and on the whole men are more delicate in questions of good feeling and of manners. If artists and authors may be censured for work badly done, why not doctors? And, if discretion be used, why not churchmen? In those countries where free thought is allowed in the public press, political ministers are often ridiculed severely; yet the people there are better and more happily governed than in those countries where free thought is stifled. In Molière's day men did not like being laughed at any more than they do now; but the doctors knew their own failings well enough, they knew that they were fair game for chaff, they were accustomed to it and they made the best of it. Speaking of the court physicians, M. Mesnard says:—" It has been related, but without proof, that the king had himself indicated to Molière three great celebrities as subjects for merry-making."[1] And in 1802 Cailhava said: " It is very likely that before writing his play Molière communicated the subject of it to the king; otherwise would he have run the risk of displeasing his Majesty by putting his first four physicians on the stage and covering them with the finest but most cutting raillery?"[2] I

[1] *Notice biographique sur Molière*, 332.   [2] *Études sur Molière*, 132.

do not suppose that these statements are purely fictitious. It is not unlikely that Louis XIV. felt that he could trust in the good sense of Molière's satire, but that he had not the same belief in the skill of his own medical advisers.

There is some anecdote about the travesty of the court doctors in the *Amour Médecin*, and from this an idea may be gathered. Gui Patin, a member of the Faculty well known in his day for his satirical humour and his disputes among his colleagues, wrote to a friend on the 22nd of September 1665 :—

" A few days ago a comedy against the court doctors was acted at Versailles. They were made to appear ridiculous before the king, and he was highly amused. The first five doctors were singled out, and, in addition, our master, Élie Bréda, otherwise the Sieur des Fougerais, who is a great man of probity and very worthy of praise, if one believes what he would like to be thought of himself."

Three days later Patin wrote :—

" *L'Amour Malade* [*sic*] is now being played at the Hôtel de Bourgogne ; all Paris rushes to see the court doctors on the stage, and especially Esprit and Guénaut, with masks expressly made for the purpose. Des Fougerais has been added, etc. So every one is laughing at those people who kill others with impunity."

I take these details mainly from M. Mesnard's Notice to the *Amour Médecin*,[1] and he thinks that Patin spoke of Molière's comedy from hearsay ; and it is generally believed now that Patin was wrong as to the doctors appearing in masks. In this, however, a doubt is possible. Did Patin use the word " mask " in its primary sense as applying to the face only, or did he mean a general disguise that should be more or less apparent ? In any case, Molière's play was not called the *Amour Malade*, and it was not acted at the Hôtel de Bourgogne. Patin's first letter contained another small error: he spoke of six doctors in the comedy, but only five are named. Another writer, Cizeron-Rival, published a book in 1765, *Récréations Littéraires*, in which he spoke of Molière's comedy. He wrote from papers left by Brossette, who had got his information from Boileau. The passage relating to Molière in the *Récréations Littéraires* runs :—

" The comedy of the *Amour Médecin* is the first in which Molière

[1] *Œuvres de Molière*, v. 266-71. And see M. Moland's *Œuvres de Molière*, 1st ed. iii. 516, 517.

laughed at the doctors and at the art of medicine; and to make the pleasantry more agreeable to the king, before whom the play was acted at Versailles, he travestied the chief court physicians with masks made expressly for the purpose. These physicians were MM. des Fougerais, Esprit, Guénaud, and d'Aquin; and as Molière wished to disguise their names he asked M. Despréaux [Boileau] to give him some that would be suitable. He chose some names that were taken from the Greek, and which showed the character of each of these doctors. He gave to M. des Fougerais the name of *Desfonandrès*, which means *man-killer*; to M. Esprit, who stammered, that of *Bahis*, which means *yelping, barking*; *Macroton* was the name he gave to M. Guénaut because he spoke very slowly; and that of *Tomès*, which means a *bleeder*, to M. d'Aquin, who was very fond of blood-letting." [1]

Here Cizeron-Rival mentions masks in the same words that Patin had done. M. Mesnard thinks that Cizeron-Rival had merely copied Patin, whose letters had been published in 1692.

There still remains another doctor, M. Filerin. He appears only in the first scene of the third act; what he says shall be given later.

The object of the doctors' services must be mentioned. Sganarelle, not unlike his namesake in the *Mariage Forcé*, has a daughter Lucinde who is in love, and who feigns to be ill. Like her father she is obstinate; she will not say what is the matter with her. Lisette, her waiting-woman, divines the cause of her illness, and tells Sganarelle that his daughter wants a husband. She dins this into his ears with constant repetition: " C'est un mari qu'elle veut. . . . Un mari, un mari, un mari." Sganarelle says to himself:—

" It is wise sometimes not to seem to hear things that one understands only too plainly, and I did well to ward off the declaration of a wish that I do not mean to satisfy. Can anything be more tyrannical than this custom which fathers are bound to obey? Anything more impertinent and ridiculous than heaping up money one has worked hard to get, and bringing up a girl carefully and affectionately, to throw one and the other in the hands of a man for whom we don't care a button? No, no, the custom may go to the devil. I will keep my money and my daughter for myself."

Lisette has hit upon a plan for curing Lucinde. She rushes to Sganarelle and tells him that his daughter is dangerously ill and may not recover. The father, who, in spite of his

[1] Quoted by M. Mesnard, *Œuvres de Molière*, v. 270.

selfishness, does love his child, is horrified. He calls to his valet and tells him to go at once to fetch some doctors, and plenty of them. Lisette has not much faith in doctors, and she offers some pleasantry against them. As four physicians are about to appear she says to her master: "Now pay attention, you will be highly instructed; they will tell you in Latin that your daughter is ill." The character of Lisette is meant to show that she, a woman of the people, has her own rough common sense, and that she will speak energetically against what she believes to be absurdities.

The four doctors who have seen Lucinde are in no hurry to begin their consultation. Tomès relates the distances that his mule has taken him from one part of Paris to another, and des Fonandrès boasts of the excellence of his horse. Then there is a discussion (in Act II. sc. 3) between these two men which should be given here; for however ridiculous it may appear to us now, if as a picture it had not been a fair satire on the spirit of routine and formality then prevalent among the doctors, I do not think Molière would have shown it so pointedly in his comedy :—

" M. Tomès.

" But which side do you take in the quarrel between the two doctors Théophraste and Artémius? For it is a matter that divides all our body.

" M. des Fonandrès.

" I am for Artémius.

" M. Tomès.

" And so am I. It is not that his opinion, as we have seen, did not kill the patient, and that that of Théophraste was not certainly much better; but he was wrong under the circumstances, and he ought not to have held an opinion against that of his elder. What do you say?

" M. des Fonandrès.

" Of course. One should always observe the rules, whatever may happen.

" M. Tomès.

" For my part I am devilish strict, unless it be among friends; and three of our number were brought together the other day, with an outside doctor—'un médecin de dehors'[1]—for a consultation in

---

[1] " Un médecin de dehors was a doctor belonging to another Faculty than that of Paris. The doctors of Montpellier, for instance, were spoken of in that way."—Note by M. Moland, Œuvres de Molière, 1st ed. iii. 546.

which I settled the whole business, and I would not allow that any one should give an opinion unless things were done according to rule. The people of the house did what they could and the illness was pressing, but I would not give way and the patient died bravely during the dispute.

"M. des Fonandrès.

"You did quite right to teach people good manners and show them their ignorance.

"M. Tomès.

"A dead man is only a dead man and is a matter of no consequence, but a formality neglected does significant injury to the whole body of physicians."

Sganarelle comes in to the four doctors to say that his daughter is getting worse, and he asks them to say quickly what they mean to do. After some by-play, Tomès and des Fonandrès disagree in their opinions, and they wrangle. Tomès says: "If you do not instantly bleed your daughter she is a dead person," and he leaves the stage; des Fonandrès says: "If you do bleed her she will not be alive in a quarter of an hour," and he also goes out. Then the other two doctors give their opinions. Macroton talks very slowly, stopping between each word and halting between each syllable. Bahis speaks very quickly, but he stammers. They both agree in their remedies. Macroton says: "Your child may die, but you will have the consolation to know that it will be according to the rules"; Bahis says: "It is better to die according to the rules than to get well irregularly." Sganarelle thanks them both separately, drawling out his words when he speaks to Macroton, and stuttering hurriedly when he talks to Bahis. All this may be made very amusing on the stage, and we see that if there are lines of demarcation between light comedy and farce, they run into each other here very closely. The fact that the play was intended as a piece of ridiculous fun will not prevent it from giving a true picture in the spirit of comedy; and there may be some who say that even with the increase of medical learning human nature has not altered much.

At the beginning of the third act, M. Filerin, the fifth doctor, admonishes MM. Tomès and des Fonandrès for quarrelling among themselves and showing to the world the quackery of medical art :—

"For my part, I do not understand this bad policy of some of our people; and it must be admitted that all these bickerings have lately brought us into ill repute in a singular manner, and that if we are not careful we shall bring ruin upon ourselves. I do not speak for my own interest, for, thank God, I have settled my own affairs. Whether it blows, or rains, or hails, those who are dead are dead, and I have enough to live upon without thinking of those who are alive; but all these squabbles do not do medical men any good. Since Providence has been so kind to us for ages past as to make the world infatuated in our favour, we should not disabuse men with our senseless disputes, and we should take advantage of their innocence as gently as we can. . . . The greatest weakness in men is their love of life, and we avail ourselves of this by our pompous nonsense; and we know how to make the most of the veneration that the fear of death gives them for those in our profession. Let us therefore maintain for ourselves that degree of esteem which their weakness has given to us, and be united in our opinions towards our patients, so that we can attribute to ourselves the fortunate issues in an illness, and accuse nature of all the blunders we make in our art. . . ."

Lisette indulges in another sally against the doctors, and we do not see them again.

The hot disputes among the doctors themselves offered fair ground for satire. To that part of M. Filerin's speech, near the beginning, where he says "that all these bickerings have brought us into ill repute," M. Mesnard has a footnote which I will copy:—"This was doubtless an allusion to the violent quarrels about the circulation of the blood, the use of bleeding and of antimony among the members of the Faculty of Paris; and to the long battle between them and those belonging to other Faculties, especially against the doctors of the Faculty of Montpellier."[1] And commentators have pointed out that many of the ideas in M. Filerin's speech are found in Montaigne's *Essays*, Book ii. chap. 37. Molière, however, need not have gone back nearly a hundred years to learn from Montaigne what he saw for himself plainly enough.

Besides the satire against the doctors in the *Amour Médecin*, which was the main purpose of the comedy, there is some by-play against Sganarelle's selfishness, and his keeping resolutely to his own opinion in opposition to advice which he has solicited. Lucinde's father has the sort of cunning which comes from distrust. He says to his friends: "All these counsels are certainly admirable, but I find that they are

[1] *Œuvres de Molière*, v. 337 note 3.

rather interested; and I think you advise me very well for yourselves." To one who wants him to buy jewellery he says: "Vous êtes orfèvre, Monsieur Josse." The humour in these words has made them proverbial. It had long been common in light French comedies, that old men should be duped and made ridiculous. Molière's Sganarelles were mainly creatures of light comedy, but they were not pure caricatures. For fathers were very often selfish in the way they wanted to marry their daughters, and one object of these small plays was to punish them for their churlishness and their self-interestedness, and to make the audience laugh at their discomfiture. Molière here, as in his other light comedies, denounced their bad qualities and made them an object of derision, and his love-scenes were written to further that purpose. He knew very well that as love-scenes they were hollow, but he tried to make them amusing, and to show that there was an object in his satire. The last scenes in the *Amour Médecin* bear out the title given to the play. Clitandre, Lucinde's lover, dresses himself up as a doctor, and with the aid of Lisette hoaxes Sganarelle in a most extravagant manner. The old man is bamboozled in a fashion almost beyond belief. After the strong ridicule thrown upon the doctors, there would have been inconsistency in not showing in the later scenes the same spirit of jesting satire. The play should be considered in the way it was intended, and, as Molière says in his preface, the reader of the comedy would do well to try to imagine all the play of the scenes.

It is tolerably certain that Béjart played originally the part of des Fonandrès, but which actors took the other parts is not known, except that Molière was probably his own Sganarelle. La Grange may have been seen as Clitandre, and Mlle. Béjart as Lisette.

The printing of the first edition of the *Amour Médecin* was completed on the 15th of January 1666.

An unhappy incident must now be related. Racine, whose first tragedy, *La Thebaïde*, had been brought out at the Palais Royal theatre in June 1664, entrusted to Molière and his comrades his second tragedy, *Alexandre le Grand*. It was played by them altogether nine times, in December 1665. On the first four days the receipts were very good; on the fifth and sixth they were poor. Then it would seem that Racine submitted to be guided by his friends, who thought that the tragedy was badly acted at the Palais Royal;[1] and without saying a word to Molière or to his fellow-actors, Racine authorised the rival troop at the Hôtel de Bourgogne to perform his play. On the 18th of December it appeared simultaneously at the two theatres. After chronicling the performance for that day at the Palais Royal, La Grange wrote :—

"The same day the troop was surprised that the said play *Alexandre* was acted at the Hôtel de Bourgogne theatre. As Mr. Racine was one of the plotters in the affair, the troop thought that they were under no obligation to pay the author's shares to the said Mr. Racine, who behaved so shabbily as to have taken the play to the other actors and told them to perform it. The said author's shares were re-divided, and each actor got for his share 47 livres."

Racine received his two shares, as author of the play, for each of the first five performances of his tragedy, but not for the sixth. The troop at the Palais Royal acted his play three times more; it was not seen afterwards at that theatre. Racine must have known at the time that he was doing wrong. He must have known, too, of the old custom prevailing at the different theatres, that when one troop had put a play on to their stage no other troop should act it until the play had been printed.[2] This custom had had the force of law for many years, and though Racine was an offender against it the actors at the Hôtel de Bourgogne sinned perhaps more deeply than he did. We may be sorry now that Racine should have allowed his natural petulance to get the better of his judgment. Apart from the theatre he and Molière had been friends, and connected with the theatre Molière had behaved well to him; and though Racine was young—he was, in fact, close upon his twenty-seventh birthday—he was old enough to have known that his conduct was not loyal. The incident prevented a friendship which one would now like to think might have been maintained between two of the keenest minds of the time. Most likely Racine would before long have given his tragedies to the

[1] Taschereau, *Vie de Molière*, 3rd ed. 99-101 ; P. Mesnard, *Notice biographique sur Molière*, 364-67.
[2] P. Mesnard, *Notice biographique sur Molière*, 367.

troop at the Hôtel de Bourgogne, as they were thought to play tragedy best; but if the unfortunate breach between him and Molière had not happened, his single comedy, *Les Plaideurs*, would in all probability have been seen and applauded at the Palais Royal. That theatre was the natural home of comedy, and Racine must have known that comedy was acted best there. There are two tales, more or less true, dating after this rupture, to the effect that each poet expressed a generous judgment, differing from the opinion of the town, about comedies that the other had written—Racine defending the *Misanthrope*, and Molière ridiculing those who had found fault with the *Plaideurs*.[1] Even if the stories were true, the good opinion that each dramatist had of the other's work did not bring the two men closer together. How far their quarrel extended into their private lives is not known, but it was probably deepened a few years later by other incidents which will be related in their place.

We have now to consider a comedy of a very different kind from the last. The *Misanthrope* was acted for the first time at the Palais Royal theatre on the 4th of June 1666; there is no record of the play being performed at court until some years after its author's death.

From a large point of view the *Misanthrope* is generally thought to be the finest of Molière's comedies. Other plays of his have a stronger plot, or are more openly amusing, or may have a better acting effect—certainly three important elements in the making of a good play. None of his comedies, however, show a deeper insight into the human heart, or a wider, firmer, and more natural characterisation of the different personages. There is in this play an ideal picture of comedy which will remain true until human nature changes. Some Frenchmen hold the *Tartuffe* to be the greatest of Molière's plays. The plot there is stronger than in the *Misanthrope*, and the hypocrite is drawn with rare firmness of touch and dramatic skill. But though there will always be false religious guides, the personage of Tartuffe has not the same influence now that he had formerly, and there is much in

---

[1] Taschereau, *Vie de Molière*, 3rd ed. p. 100; P. Mesnard, *Notice biographique sur Molière*, 369, 370.

his character that will not be readily understood in every country. On the other hand, the type of man shown in Alceste will always exist everywhere. With all his faults Alceste's character is noble and touching ; he may create anger, he never creates disgust. Tartuffe is a coarse-minded wretch; Alceste is of much finer clay. In his strength you see generous and delicate instincts; the strength of the other proceeds only from villainy. The pictures, too, of amour-propre, of self-love or self-conceit, portrayed in the *Misanthrope*, are not peculiar to any country or any people. They may be found most strongly wherever society is hollow, or artful, or specious, and the meaning of the comedy should be seen by any fairly sensitive or fairly well educated man or woman who can read its lines. There are no exciting incidents in the play ; the interest lies in what is said rather than in what is done. The conduct or the action of the comedy consists in showing the thoughts and manners of the people concerned, and when the types of the different personages are understood, the dramatic characterisation becomes at once apparent. Perhaps in no comedy of manners aiming at clear and distinct portraiture has the characterisation of men's humours been more strongly shown. It may be objected that no one of the personages commands a full sympathy. Many readers have had the same sort of feeling about Thackeray's *Vanity Fair*; yet that is believed to be one of the finest novels in the English language.

Several of Molière's editors have pointed out that in describing some of the features of jealousy the poet repeated in Act IV. scenes 2 and 3 of the *Misanthrope* a good many lines from his luckless heroic-comedy *Don Garcie de Navarre*, which had been acted only a few times five years earlier, and which was not printed until after his death. Under these circumstances the repetition of verses or of the same lines of thought is of very small consequence. *Le Prince Jaloux* was added as a second title to *Don Garcie de Navarre*, and there is clear evidence to show that Molière at one time intended to qualify his *Misanthrope* with a second title, *L'Atrabilaire Amoureux*;[1] but he abandoned the idea. It may be noticed, however, that there is a partial likeness

[1] *Œuvres de Molière*, v. 384 and note 2.

between the abortive attempt to show Don Garcie to be a real personage, and the truthful picture given of Alceste in the later play, though as comedies *Don Garcie de Navarre* and the *Misanthrope* are very widely different. In the interval between them more than five years had elapsed. In that time Molière had written many comedies; he had seen the world; he had learned from his own failure that heroic-comedy, once popular in France, was at best a bastard kind of play with much rhodomontade, and that he was unfitted to write one that would satisfy even an uncritical audience. Nevertheless, I believe that the main ideas seen in the personage of Alceste had long been floating in Molière's brain, that he had worried and amused himself about them, and that allowing for the ridicule of comic characterisation, which means a great deal, some of them almost formed part of his nature. Then in the middle of his career, still constant in a measure to his first thoughts, he gave effect to them in true comedy, altering them, adding to them, and colouring them, as he found necessary for the characterisation of his personage.

The scene of the *Misanthrope* is laid in the best society in Paris; and the dramatist placed his hero, Alceste the misanthrope, among men and women who, with one exception, care for others only as they touch themselves, and are flatterers or are disloyal to those they call their friends. They cannot understand Alceste's generosity and noble-heartedness, and they exasperate him, laugh at him, and make him show much egotism, contradictoriness, and ill-humour. Their raillery is justified, but it is not this that annoys him, for he is so proud that he can hear it unmoved; it is their insincerity that enrages and embitters him. His extravagance often provokes a smile, even laughter, and thus the ridicule of comedy is fairly thrown upon him; and by his faults the dramatist shows faults of other kinds in people who have not his high moral sense, his delicate instincts, nor his steadfast honesty.

As a matter of fact, comedy has its own characters and its own language to portray them, and much of its office is to give mirth or merriment of some kind. As a comic dramatist it was Molière's aim to show comic ideals of certain types of men and women by means of imaginary incidents; he offered these ideals to his audience as personations of human beings with their good points and their failings, and he tried to dramatise their thoughts and their actions so that they should illustrate the humours of life and show the mirth of comedy. He thought the function of comedy was to reprove by satire, and he dwelt more strongly on men's foibles than on their virtues, and by satire he endeavoured to show their faults and the foolish sides of their humours. All the characters in the *Misanthrope* are creatures of comedy; they are ideal personifications dramatised with a view to showing them on the stage in a spirit of comedy. And although we cannot, and need not, put aside the feeling that we like one character better than another; yet I take it that so far as they are concerned we should try to see what type of personage each one was meant to represent, how far the ideal has been carried out, what is his or her part in the play, with what purpose they were brought together, how they all act upon one another, in opposition or in concord, and if in the combined action they give a true and mirthful picture of the humours of life with dramatic effect. No one of them was meant to stand alone; each was meant to be seen with the others, so that their different and generally opposite natures might be plainly distinguished.

The two chief characters in this comedy are the misanthrope, Alceste, and Célimène, a young imperious woman of the world, who is also a coquette. By the side of Alceste the poet placed Philinte, an affable man of society, who wishes to be everybody's friend; and by the side of Célimène he portrayed in Éliante an even-minded girl, not unlike Philinte, though her nature is higher than his. The other characters are Oronte, a silly sonnetteer, Alceste's rival for the hand of Célimène; Arsinoé, an ill-natured prude; and two foolish marquises, Acaste and Clitandre. By looking at the principal scenes in the comedy we shall see how the minor personages were intended to accentuate the features of the misanthrope and of the coquette. And I cannot help thinking that there is a likeness of idea between the position of Éliante by the side of Célimène and that of Amelia by the side of Becky Sharp. They were all meant to be considered from the point of view of Vanity Fair. Célimène and Becky were creatures of Vanity

Fair, its atmosphere was the breath of their lives, and they had prominent places in it. Éliante and Amelia had no heart for the fair, they did not belong to it though they were seen there, and had friends in it whose sentiments they did not share—consequently they were thrown more or less into the background. If the cleverness of cunning has its attractions, those who show their conduct in a better way deserve also their meed of praise.

The first scene in the play is well known for a long discussion between Alceste and Philinte, and as their characters have been variously interpreted, I should like to say how I understand them. Which of the two was morally most right or wrong may easily lead us on a false track. It is only indirectly that this question concerns us. We have to look at the comedy in the play from a comic point of view. Molière meant to give a picture of two men whose humours are diametrically opposite. He showed Alceste's over-rough energy against the deceits of the world with strong satire, and he painted Philinte's nerveless complacency with subtle irony. If we contrast the way the dramatist has thrown his satire on the misanthrope, and his irony on the man who wishes to be the friend of everybody, that will, I think, give a fair idea of the comedy in the characters of the two personages, and will tell how each had his different views of the conduct of life. Molière meant the ethical problem to be kept in the background, but he attached much importance to the way he showed it. He had his own philosophy, but as a dramatist his object was to exhibit the manners of others.

It is dangerous to compare a character in comedy with one in tragedy, for apart from the incidents related, the spirit of comedy and of tragedy are very different. Still, Alceste is like Coriolanus in his obstinate determination to maintain his pride and do what he believes is right in spite of what others may say. What Shakespeare makes Menenius say of Coriolanus (Act III. sc. 1) will apply to Alceste :—

> " His nature is too noble for the world :
> He would not flatter Neptune for his trident,
> Or Jove for 's power to thunder. His heart 's his mouth :
> What his breast forges, that his tongue must vent ;
> And, being angry, does forget that ever
> He heard the name of death."

And those who know Alceste will feel that he, as well as Coriolanus, might have said of himself (v. 3) :—

> "I 'll never
> Be such a gosling to obey instinct, but stand,
> As if a man were author of himself
> And knew no other kin."

It may be doubted if the word "misanthrope" describes Alceste exactly, though it would be hard to find a more fitting epithet. The term "misanthrope" may be applied to men of different natures. Swift, Byron, Jean Jacques Rousseau, were misanthropes, unlike one another; and not one of them offers a close resemblance to Molière's imaginary personage. There is, however, a strong likeness between him and Thomas Carlyle in their perverseness, in their contradictoriness; and, in spite of their high qualities, in their not being able to prevent themselves from thinking about themselves with persistent obstinacy. Like other men, Alceste's character cannot be defined by a single qualification. He has solid virtues and great social faults. He so tortures himself with absurdly exaggerated ideas of honesty that from his excessive fineness of feeling and strong passions he becomes ill-mannered and egotistical, and makes himself unbearable and ridiculous. The prime cause of his unhappiness is that he cannot get away from himself and his own thoughts. And his melancholy is greatly increased by his bottomless love for a woman who has no love in her. All this has so excited him that he is mentally ill. Like Hamlet, his brain is suffering. He wants nothing for himself except the love of a woman who can love nobody; and it is his nature to be kind and courteous, but his masterful temper overcomes his gentler instincts, and leads him into trouble at every step. Hence is seen the comedy in his character and the satire and the ridicule thrown upon him. In spite of his rough temper he speaks with a true tenderness and nobility of feeling that go straight to the heart. His high qualities plead eloquently in his favour; they show that he hates dishonesty and despises meanness, and that he longs for a better and larger humanity among his fellow-creatures. Molière nowhere jeers at him, but laughs at him compassionately, loving him really, though regretting his intemperance. Alceste is an ideal personage drawn with absolute realism, and I do not know of one male character that stands more boldly and more firmly on his feet in all the plays that comedy can show.

Philinte is, or would be, a friend to Alceste, and is his antithesis in almost every respect save in that of good birth. His chief features, as seen in the comedy, are those of a man who takes his colour from his friends and from surrounding circumstances. He relies much upon tact. Tact generally implies politeness, but with Philinte it comes more from good policy than from innate good feeling. He has worldly prudence, and he always maintains a show of nice manners; but he has also a varnished selfishness and an insensibility as to what happens to others. Cynicism need not be rough and brutal; it may be quiet and plausibly polite. So it is with Philinte. He does not bark or bite; he is neither satirical nor ill-natured. He is not dishonest in deed, but it does not annoy him to see fraud in others. He cannot change the ways of the world, and he looks upon them with easy indifference. It is not that he is tolerant of men's opinions and their doings; he is listless or callous. Philinte's placid cynicism, deep in his nature, is opposed to the turbulent cynicism of Alceste. There is a strong contrast between the disdain and the distrust in each. These are points of difference in the two personages that should be noticed. The dramatist has shown with the emphasis of comedy opposite types of men that will always exist. Every right-feeling person has at times something of Alceste's anger when he sees calm acquiescence in wrong-doing; and most of us, in whatever society we live, have in various degrees something of the moral obliquity of Philinte. Of the two the latter character is the most common, but as the type has many variations, it is well, in reading the comedy, to think of him only as he is described by Molière. Philinte has his good points. He would soothe Alceste in his passion, his counsels are generally admirable; but a toy terrier might as well try to lure a bloodhound off the scent of his quarry.

It was with the intention of portraying the workings of the mind of his misanthrope and of an affable man of the world, and of showing how such men would talk and act together, that Molière planned the first scene of this comedy. He has nowhere given a finer exposition of male characterisation. The wilful egotism of the one, full of virile passions, and the pliancy of the other, disliking and half afraid to think for himself, are brought into very full relief.   Philinte asks Alceste the cause of his angry temper, and is willing to be his friend. . . . Alceste interrupts him characteristically :—

> " Moi, votre ami ?   Rayez cela de vos papiers."

Alceste is furious with Philinte because he has rapturously embraced and expressed great willingness to serve a man whose name he does not know, and for speaking of him indifferently the moment his back was turned :—

> " Puisque vous y donnez dans ces vices du temps,
> Morbleu ! vous n'êtes pas pour être de mes gens ;
> Je refuse d'un cœur la vaste complaisance
> Qui ne fait de mérite aucune différence ;
> Je veux qu'on me distingue ; et pour le trancher net,
> L'ami du genre humain n'est point du tout mon fait."

His turbulent humour creates a smile, but his misanthropy is less amusing.   He is made very angry at the way men live together, each one trying to make a profit out of his neighbour. Philinte laughs at him, and says :—

> " Le monde par vos soins ne se changera pas ;
> Et puisque la franchise a pour vous tant d'appas,
> Je vous dirai tout franc que cette maladie,
> Partout où vous allez, donne la comédie,
> Et qu'un si grand courroux contre les mœurs du temps
> Vous tourne en ridicule auprès de bien des gens."

Alceste replies :—

> " Tant mieux, morbleu ! tant mieux, c'est ce que je demande ;
> Ce m'est un fort bon signe et ma joie en est grande :
> Tous les hommes me sont à tel point odieux,
> Que je serais fâché d'être sage à leurs yeux."

Instead of combating Alceste's opinions Philinte draws him out and asks if he will spare no one in his hatred. Alceste then lets his anger have full play, and his answer is one of the finest passages to be found in Molière's comedies :—

> " Non, elle est générale, et je hais tous les hommes ;
> Les uns parce qu'ils sont méchants et malfaisants,
> Et les autres pour être aux méchants complaisants,
> Et n'avoir pas pour eux ces haines vigoureuses
> Que doit donner le vice aux âmes vertueuses."

These and the following are wonderful lines, in which there is much nicety of language, and which, in spite of the violence shown, especially at the end of the speech, I can never read afresh without a feeling of the great reality expressed in the words and of compassion for the unhappy man who uttered them. His temper is very high; how far it is misguided will be judged according to personal tastes. There is no one so likely to put himself out of court among his fellows as the man who says he hates everybody and wants to hide himself; his friends will not listen to him, and those who are not his friends jeer at him. Yet the honesty of Alceste's thoughts compels admiration, and it is only from a generous and noble nature that one can expect to find such an outburst. He is very fierce against a thorough villain who has an action at law against him. Everybody knows this adversary to be a cringing, pushing, unscrupulous knave (a "pied-plat"); yet he has by his dirty practices wriggled his way into society, . . . and if by interest a place is given away he will gain it against the most upright man. It is not from jealousy that Alceste is bitter against the rogue's success, for he would spurn the wretch as an unclean thing, but it hurts him that clever meanness and dishonest cunning have prospered, and that people should give a welcome to a villain who they know should be shunned.

> " Têtebleu ! ce me sont de mortelles blessures,
> De voir qu'avec le vice on garde des mesures ;
> Et parfois il me prend des mouvements soudains
> De fuir dans un désert l'approche des humains."

Philinte's reply charms for a moment by the softness of its tone after the violence used by Alceste. He is, as always, moderate, and much of what he says is fair common sense ; yet his words show that the questions of right and wrong do not touch him. He accepts good and evil as he finds them, without thinking of their causes and not caring to know their effects. While things go well with him he is apparently an optimist; but he has no convictions, no strong desires. He wishes lazily to let the world go its own way and take care of itself. When you are really angry and believe that you have just cause for wrath, your temper is not improved if your friend says to you :—

> " La parfaite raison fuit toute extrémité,
> Et veut que l'on soit sage avec sobriété."

Philinte's last words in this speech are :—

> "Et je crois qu'à la cour, de même qu'à la ville,
> Mon phlegme est philosophe autant que votre bile."

Alceste shows his stiff-necked honesty in the way he refuses to bow to the common custom of soliciting the judge who is to try a suit brought against him. Morally he is right, but as the judges were often determined in their sentences by bribes,[1] Philinte—though he recognises that Alceste's case is undeniably just—urges his friend to make a stand against the canvassing on the other side. Come what may, Alceste will not stoop to what he conceives to be baseness :—

> "Je voudrois, m'en coûtât-il grand'chose,
> Pour la beauté du fait avoir perdu ma cause."

> "*Philinte.*
> "On se riroit de vous, Alceste, tout de bon,
> Si l'on vous entendoit parler de la façon.

> "*Alceste.*
> "Tant pis pour qui riroit."

I can only refer now to the last part of this scene where Alceste speaks of his love for Célimène in a manner that leaves no doubt of the strength of his passion.

But I will speak of the amusing "scène du sonnet" which follows. Alceste's different conditions of mind are shown here admirably. At first he tells Oronte politely that he has no wish to be made a judge of his sonnet, but when forced to give his opinion he shows that the verses are the veriest rubbish; then the two men quarrel. Unless it were well acted this scene would be insufferable on the stage. I have seen it played very gracefully and very amusingly at the Comédie Française, showing, necessarily with some caricature in Oronte and in Philinte, the nice elegance of the best form of dandyism in Molière's day. The dramatist was laughing at the self-sufficiency of a coxcomb who wished an over-honest man to advise him whether he should publish his verses, and in describing the scene he was bound to do so with the ridicule of comedy. Imagine an attempt to show the ridicule of

---

[1] See M. Mesnard's note here, *Œuvres de Molière*, v. 454 note 2 ; also the long speech by Dandin, the judge, in Racine's comedy, *Les Plaideurs*, Act I. sc. 4.

comedy in such a scene on the stage with no emphasis or no
caricature. The thing would manifestly be a failure. In
painting Alceste's disgust Molière had in his mind an idea of
the annoyance that Boileau, or a man of his stamp, would feel
while an author whom he did not know insisted on reading to
him his bad verses. Apparently Boileau acknowledged the
truth of the picture as applied to himself, and it would
seem that he was proud of it.[1] He thought very highly
of Molière's comedies, especially of the *Misanthrope*, and
with generous sentiments and some self-esteem he did not
suppose that Molière, who had been his friend, would have
laughed at him publicly on the stage in a way that was
at all offensive. Molière's business was in the first place
to think of his comedy, and Alceste is a dramatised picture
of a man who abhors all kinds of flummery. Boileau also
hated false taste in literature. Under similar circumstances
he would, probably enough, like Alceste, have denounced a
bad sonnet and shown that it was silly trumpery; though I
doubt if he would have brought forward the old song, " Si le
Roi m'avoit donné," as an instance of simple but heartfelt
poetry, and I doubt also if he would have allowed his anger
to rise as Alceste did in his quarrel with Oronte.

This quarrel has put Alceste into a thoroughly bad temper.
He had meant to declare his love to Célimène, but instead he
tells her roughly in his high pride that everything between
them must be broken off, for he cannot endure the thought
that she should be always surrounded by so many admirers.
The coquette answers him :—

> " C'est ce qui doit rasseoir votre âme effarouchée,
> Puisque ma complaisance est sur tous épanchée,
> Et vous auriez plus lieu de vous en offenser,
> Si vous me la voyiez sur un seul ramasser."

And when she tells him that he has the happiness of knowing
that he is loved, he asks : " Who can assure me that you do
not say as much to the others ? " Célimène knows her lover's
peculiarities, but she cannot let such a speech pass unnoticed.
Then follows a passage in which Alceste proclaims his passion
in language too energetic to please the ear of his imperious
mistress.

[1] *Œuvres de Molière*, ii. 228, continuation of note 2 from p. 227 ; and
vol. v. 390-92.

Célimène, though nominally not the most important, is the most central figure in the *Misanthrope*; she is the pivot on whom the action in the play depends. She is a young widow, only twenty years of age, but as cunning as a serpent. Her manner of talking is hard and contemptuous; she uses words and phrases which show a strong nature, but none that show softness or tenderness; and she is one of those women who do not like other women. She has told Alceste that she loves him; she allows another suitor for her hand, and she plays with two noble admirers. She cannot break with any of them, for the love of power and flattery are what come nearest to her heart; next is her love of slander. She is a woman of the world, who thinks only of herself and of what she can give to society by her presence and her wit. The scene of the comedy is laid in her house, and as its mistress she expects that homage shall be paid to her. What makes Célimène interesting is the manner in which her character is shown. There is excellent comedy in the clever way in which, in her disputes with Alceste, though she is much to blame, she makes him proclaim his faults and contrives to throw the wrong on his side and to maintain her command over him. The scenes in which she has her part are portrayed very vividly, and they seem to be given in a fresh light as though they were enacted here for the first time.

Éliante is on the whole the most sympathetic personage in the comedy, and some readers may think they would like to see more of her. She is intended as a contrast to her cousin Célimène, by whom she is thrown into the background. Like Philinte, she is a middle or temperate character, but her nature is higher than his. Some satire is directed upon the want of warmth of feeling in them both, and the dramatist makes it evident that their even-mindedness is little heeded when opposed by faults in persons of more vigorous dispositions. Éliante admires Alceste for his honesty of purpose, though she smiles at his excesses. In a quiet way she is as truthful as he is, and she does not flatter. She shows her calm common sense frankly and pleasantly, reminding one of La Rochefoucauld's saying, " C'est une espèce de coquetterie que de faire remarquer qu'on n'en fait jamais." In this way even Éliante shows her self-love.

In the backbiting scene in the second act Alceste, Célimène, Philinte, Éliante, the two silly marquises, Acaste and Clitandre, are present. Like all of Molière's marquises, these two show their supercilious fatuity. They ask Célimène what she thinks of certain of their friends, and she, not mincing her words, roundly abuses them all. The scene passes in her drawing-room, and as hostess she has the best right to speak. There is a somewhat similar scene in the *School for Scandal*, and as regards the one scene in each comedy Sheridan's, though less strong, appears to have an advantage. He makes the invective come from several persons, whereas Molière throws almost all the responsibility of slandering her neighbours upon Célimène. He must have had his own reasons for not making Arsinoé, an ill-natured prude, whom we shall see presently, take part in the conversation. Hearing this flow of abuse of their friends has been as gall to Alceste. He had placed himself as far from the others as possible, but he suddenly breaks his silence :—

"Allons, ferme, poussez, mes bons amis de cour."

He charges them all with traducing people into whose arms they would rush with signs of affection and oaths of friendship. Clitandre replies : "Are you speaking to us? If you are displeased at what has been said, it is upon Madame that your reproaches must fall." Alceste will defend his mistress at all costs, and he feels himself insulted at being spoken to by an empty-headed fop. "No, by heaven ! It is to you I speak. It is because of your complacent smiles that she throws her calumny upon others. Her satire is provoked by your base flattery. She would take less pleasure in jeering if she saw that no one applauded her wit." True or not, this speech was unnecessarily rude ; and Alceste injures himself in the eyes of everybody by his love of finding fault and by his contradictoriness.

As Cléante is the sage in the *Tartuffe*, so is Éliante, in a gentler manner, the soft voice in the *Misanthrope* ; and it is amusing to notice how completely Molière instinctively shows that all their evenness of temper and their attempts at pacification are of no avail against natures that are stronger than their own. In putting into the mouth of Éliante an imitation of some twenty lines of Lucretius (probably taken from the translation he had made when he was a lad), the dramatist gave the keynote of the character he wished to portray. Her speech (Act II. sc. 4) begins :—

> " L'amour pour l'ordinaire est peu fait à ces lois,
> Et l'on voit les amants vanter toujours leur choix."

Éliante meant perhaps to make an attempt at reconciliation ; but Molière also wished to show that the passion of love may arise without reason, and that, though singular, there was nothing unnatural in the love of a misanthrope for a coquette. The speech of Éliante seems also to be a sort of answer to four lines of Corneille's on the nature of love in Act I. sc. 5 of his tragedy *Rodogune* :—

> " Il est des nœuds secrets, il est des sympathies,
> Dont par le doux rapport des âmes assorties
> S'attachent l'une à l'autre et se laissent piquer
> Par ces je ne sais quoi qu'on ne peut expliquer." [1]

These lines were first spoken in 1644, and they were well remembered in Paris. When Molière wrote his *Misanthrope*, some twenty years later, he did not mean to contradict Corneille, but he thought that love might spring from other causes, and he wished to say so. And again, later in the comedy, when Éliante is talking to Philinte about Alceste's love for Célimène, she says to him :—

> " L'amour dans les cœurs
> N'est pas toujours produit par un rapport d'humeurs ;
> Et toutes ces raisons de douces sympathies
> Dans cette exemple-ci se trouvent démenties."

A guard of the court of marshals appears to demand Alceste's presence. They had heard of the quarrel between him and Oronte about the sonnet, and it was their office to prevent duelling and to effect a reconciliation between the adversaries. They therefore required Alceste to go before them. He seems to think that he is to be asked to say that the verses he had condemned are good, and that he will never do. " Ruat cœlum fiat justitia," should be his motto. Philinte, however, persuades him to obey the marshals' order. To that he consents,

---

[1] M. Mesnard, *Œuvres de Molière*, v. 516 note, quotes other passages from two of Corneille's comedies to the same effect.

but he will not go back on his judgment about the sonnet. He says :—

> "Hors qu'un commandement exprès du Roi me vienne
> De trouver bons les vers dont on se met en peine,
> Je soutiendrai toujours, morbleu ! qu'ils sont mauvais,
> Et qu'un homme est pendable après les avoir faits."

The two marquises laugh at this sally, and Alceste causes more amusement when he cries aloud :—

> "Par la sangbleu ! Messieurs, je ne croyais pas être
> Si plaisant que je suis."

Here we see a ludicrous side of the unhappy condition of the misanthrope, and as Molière was acting the part of his own Alceste he showed the bitter smile of cynicism coming from scornful anger as he pronounced these last words. More than thirty years later Boileau remembered Molière's play at the end of this scene, and having a talent for mimicry he amused his friends one day by reciting the short passage as Molière had done.[1]

Célimène had just given a very unflattering portrait of Arsinoé, the prude, when she receives a visit from her. Arsinoé has come from "heartfelt friendship" to remind Célimène of her faults, and to tell her how the world is saying hard things of her. Naturally the young widow, in her turn, cannot be behindhand in showing to her friend similar offices of good nature ; and to excuse her own faults Célimène says with strong satire :—

> "Madame, on peut, je crois, louer et blâmer tout,
> Et chacun a raison suivant l'âge ou le goût.
> Il est une saison pour la galanterie ;
> Il en est une aussi propre à la pruderie.
> On peut, par politique, en prendre le parti,
> Quand de nos jeunes ans l'éclat est amorti :
> Cela sert à couvrir de fâcheuses disgrâces.
> Je ne dis pas qu'un jour je ne suive vos traces :
> L'âge amènera tout, et ce n'est pas le temps,
> Madame, comme on sait, d'être prude à vingt ans."

I well recollect the terrible irony that Madame Arnould-Plessy put into these words on one occasion (about the year 1880) when she was acting the part of the young coquette. It seemed to me so great that I felt pity for the actress who was playing with her, and I wished that the poet himself could

---

[1] M. Mesnard, *Œuvres de Molière*, v. 494 note 2.

have heard his words spoken by so perfect an elocutionist.
The ladies' battle in this scene is wonderfully graphic.   If
Molière were writing it now he would not give so many long
speeches; at the same time, shorter ones would not bring
before us more clearly the action of the two women trying to
wound each other by all the malice that polite invective can
show.   One is glad to take Célimène's part and sympathise
with her for a moment.   She was not the first assailant, and at
the end the advantage lies certainly on her side.

There is a scene between Philinte and Éliante in which we
see the accommodating spirit of them both.   The poet satirises
their want of warm affections, and he probably meant this
scene as a prelude to the next.

Arsinoé had poisoned Alceste's mind against Célimène; and
while Philinte and Éliante are still together Alceste, wild with
passion, rushes to Éliante and tells her that he holds in his
pocket a letter that Célimène has written to Oronte.   Alceste's
rage here so far masters him that he suddenly makes an offer of
love to Éliante, which she laughs at delicately, and her sensible
answer does not improve his position.   It is to be presumed
that Molière wished to portray his misanthrope's furious anger
and jealousy with the satire of comedy.   For this two distinct different efforts are needed.   When describing strong
feeling in other plays, I think he has nearly always thrown
the satire of comedy on his personages, and so invested them
with comic interest.   But here, as far as Alceste is concerned,
I doubt if he has been successful in either effort—both when
Alceste makes his offer to Éliante and in the first forty lines
of the next scene when he is alone with Célimène.   In speaking of *Don Garcie de Navarre*, I tried to say that Molière
intended to give a picture of a man so infuriated by unwarrantable jealousy that he is hardly accountable for his speech, that
the poet attempted a flight of thought beyond his strength
and for which he was not fitted.   And it would seem that in
part of the fourth act of the *Misanthrope* Molière was making
another attempt, under altered circumstances, to carry out an
idea which had unfortunately beset him five years earlier.
The failure is not so great in the second as in the first play,
for Alceste is not absurd as was Don Garcie.   Nevertheless
much of what he says to Éliante, and to Célimène at the

beginning of his interview with her, falls flat and is in-
effective; his words do not carry with them the strength of
persuasion. They do tell heavily what he felt, but they do
not make others feel with him; and the situation is not shown
in an amusing manner.

But the remainder and the longer part of the scene between
Alceste and Célimène (Act IV. sc. 3) is full of the highest
comic interest. The misanthrope manages to think less about
himself and to throw aside his savage humour; he shows
instead a real and loving affection. He is still very unhappy,
and with a letter in his hand he charges Célimène with having
written to Oronte. There is some fencing, and she tries to
make him believe that the letter was written to a woman.
With a mixture of satire and contempt, which Célimène
rebuffs, Alceste offers to read her letter to prove that the words
could not have been intended for a woman's eye. Célimène
will not allow her letter to be read; he may think about it as
he pleases. He answers :—

> " De grâce, montrez-moi, je serai satisfait,
> Qu'on peut pour une femme expliquer ce billet."

But she is driven to confess :—

> " Non, il est pour Oronte, et je veux qu'on le croie ;
> Je reçois tous ses soins avec beaucoup de joie ;
> J'admire ce qu'il dit, j'estime ce qu'il est,
> Et je tombe d'accord de tout ce qu'il vous plaît.
> Faites, prenez parti, que rien ne vous arrête,
> Et ne me rompez pas davantage la tête."

Célimène's attitude here is very wonderful. She is beaten
down on all sides; all means of argument are cut off from her,
and she is left without a weapon to defend herself. Then,
desperate as a beast at bay, she turns round upon her adversary
with strong mock disdain, which he believes to be real anger,
and, tiger-like, she tears him so as to leave him helpless. And
the quick rattle of her words gives an appearance of truth to
what she says. She has disabled her lover by exciting his
jealousy, and has gained her point. Alceste, who has hitherto
held his head high in all his disputes, is now brought upon
his knees before the woman he loves. He says to himself :—

> " Quoi ? d'un juste courroux je suis ému contre elle,
> C'est moi qui me viens plaindre, et c'est moi qu'on querelle !
> On pousse ma douleur et mes soupçons à bout,
> On me laisse tout croire, on fait gloire de tout."

He knows her falseness, but he cannot rid himself of his love, and he despises himself for his weakness. He prays her to disarm the suspicion she has cast upon herself :—

> " Défendez-vous au moins d'un crime qui m'accable,
> Et cessez d'affecter d'être envers moi coupable ;
> Rendez-moi s'il se peut ce billet innocent :
> A vous prêter les mains ma tendresse consent ;
> Efforcez-vous ici de paroître fidèle,
> Et je m'efforcerai, moi, de vous croire telle."

There is pathos in what Alceste says, and Célimène laughs at it as she had laughed at his wildness when he upbraided her so fiercely. She says :—

> " Allez, vous êtes fou dans vos transports jaloux,
> Et ne méritez pas l'amour qu'on a pour vous.
> Je voudrois bien savoir qui pourroit me contraindre
> A descendre pour vous aux bassesses de feindre,
> Et pourquoi, si mon cœur penchoit d'autre côté,
> Je ne le dirois pas avec sincérité.
>
> . . . .
>
> Allez, de tels soupçons méritent ma colère,
> Et vous ne valez pas que l'on vous considère :
> Je suis sotte, et veux mal à ma simplicité
> De conserver encor pour vous quelque bonté ;
> Je devrois autre part attacher mon estime,
> Et vous faire un sujet de plainte légitime."

Alceste again tells her she is false, and again shows his weakness for her. She replies :—

> " Non, vous ne m'aimez pas comme il faut que l'on aime."

Her artifice is excellent, but there is no sign of love in it. She is so self-centred and has such a clear hardness of disposition, such a dazzling false honesty, that she can love no one. She knows what she is doing, and she plays her game very cleverly. Her object is to gain a triumph over her opponent by making him show his love for her, and then to take full advantage of his weakness.

I have said elsewhere, that in depicting Alceste's love for Célimène it was rather the man's conduct in his passion than the passion of love itself that the dramatist was anxious to portray. Alceste again displays his egotism in a peculiar manner. He says to Célimène, speaking of his love :—

> " Et dans l'ardeur qu'il a de se montrer à tous
> Il va jusqu'à former des souhaits contre vous."

He wishes that no one cared for her, that she was wretched,

poor, and of low birth, so that he, by making a noble sacrifice, might repair the injustice of fortune and through his deep love should have both the joy and the glory of claiming her for his own. This speech must of course be read in the light of comedy. Molière wished to accentuate Alceste's passion, and then not to jeer at him but to show in the vein of comedy the excesses of an overflowing heart. He showed also in Célimène the behaviour of a woman without heart, and therefore without generosity. Her reply, which she does not finish, is equally characteristic of her :—

> " C'est me vouloir du bien d'une étrange manière !
> Me préserve le Ciel que vous ayez matière . . ."

Besides his strong love, Alceste has in him a feeling of poetry, but the distinctive feature of the scene is the address of Célimène in her quarrel with Alceste. He knows her to be guilty; yet she forces him to beg of her to vindicate herself, and she answers his almost childishly affectionate prayer with cutting raillery. She leads him to make new protestations of love while she stands cold and firm, giving no explanation of her conduct but enjoying the pleasure of conquering him and of scoring a victory. It is the triumph of a coquette, who does not know what truth means ; but she has won the battle.

It was open to Molière to draw a noble but intemperate character, for such men exist; it is for us in reading his play to see how the virtues and the faults of his hero are mixed together, and how in the general environment and in the play of the scenes they serve to make a picture of comedy.

At the beginning of the fifth act Alceste is crying over the wicked injustice done to him. Through the perjury of his adversary he has lost his lawsuit, but he will not appeal against the judge's sentence. He has his grievance, and he means to enjoy it :—

> " Ce sont vingt mille francs qu'il m'en pourra coûter ;
> Mais pour vingt mille francs j'aurai droit de pester
> Contre l'iniquité de la nature humaine
> Et de nourrir pour elle une immortelle haine."

Philinte looks upon his friend's misfortune very placidly. He says to him :—

> " . . . Si de probité tout étoit revêtu,
> Si tous les cœurs étoient francs, justes et dociles,
> La plupart de nos vertus nous seroient inutiles."

He is a man without much feeling for others; but if he were tortured with sciatica, or had his house robbed, he would find that "life gave him means of exercising his philosophy" more fully than he had imagined.

Oronte, the sonnetteer, is a suitor for the young widow's hand. He entreats her to accept him and to banish his rival, or at least to say whom she means to favour. Alceste had hidden himself in a "dark corner"; he suddenly rises up from it, and he too calls upon Célimène to make her choice and decide between them. She naturally tries to defend herself. But her proud position of queen of her own society is not fated to last much longer. Letters that she had written to Acaste and to Clitandre, saying to each spiteful things of the other, are read aloud. All the men present come in for their share of her ridicule, except Philinte. Such a woman would think that he was not worthy of it. Indeed, in the whole of the comedy Célimène addresses only six words directly to Philinte. Acaste, Clitandre, and Oronte leave her, declaring their wish to see her no more. Arsinoé comments in her own way on what has happened, and pretends to pity Alceste, who did not deserve such treatment. Come what may, Alceste will not suffer Arsinoé to reproach his mistress. He says : "Let me, madam, I beg of you, settle my own interests in this matter, and do not give yourself unnecessary trouble. I do not wish that you should take up my quarrel, for I am not in a mood to be thankful for so much zeal." And he adds, with unjustifiable rudeness: "Nor is it of you that I should think if I sought to make another choice." The prude is stung to the quick. I will give only three lines of her reply :—

> " Hé ! croyez-vous, Monsieur, qu'on ait cette pensée ?
>
> .   .   .   .
>
> Le rebut de Madame est une marchandise
> Dont on auroit grand tort d'être si fort éprise."

Arsinoé finds that she is not welcomed, and she is not seen again.

Alceste would speak to Célimène, when she interrupts him with a confession of her faults. Her words seem to bear an air of truth, but he cannot believe them. For this woman he would make any sacrifice, but he has no faith in what she says. He knows that he is very infirm of purpose. Turning to Éliante and Philinte, but speaking of Célimène, he shows his humanity with its strength and its weakness :—

> " Vous voyez ce que peut une indigne tendresse,
> Et je vous fais tous deux témoins de ma foiblesse.
> Mais à vous dire vrai, ce n'est pas encor tout,
> Et vous allez me voir la pousser jusqu'au bout,
> Montrer que c'est à tort que sages on nous nomme,
> Et que dans tous les cœurs il est toujours de l'homme."

Alceste will forgive Célimène everything if she will accede to his last prayer to follow him into his desert where he has resolved to live away from mankind. She may thus repair her wrongs, and he can become fond of her once more. Célimène scoffs at the idea of going to bury herself in a desert. " La solitude effraye une âme de vingt ans," she says; and she adds : " If the gift of my hand would satisfy your wishes . . . and marriage . . ." Alceste suddenly stops her :—

> " Non : mon cœur à présent vous déteste,
> Et ce refus lui seul fait plus que tout le reste.
> Puisque vous n'êtes point, en des liens si doux,
> Pour trouver tout en moi, comme moi tout en vous,
> Allez, je vous refuse, et ce sensible outrage
> De vos indignes fers pour jamais me dégage."

Célimène cannot reply to Alceste's last words to her. She disappears, shorn of repute, lonely and unwept. She has perhaps deserved her fate, but it is fearful. Terror and pity make themselves felt, because the picture is painted in true colours. It is one that we can all understand and believe to have happened. The conditions which Alceste had placed upon Célimène were exacting, and no woman of her disposition would consent to them; but his will is the stronger of the two, and at the last he means to be the master. He obstinately maintains his amour propre to the end; he could not do otherwise. The more strongly he feels, the more will his failings and also his high and noble qualities make themselves seen. He pays a well-deserved compliment to Éliante, to whom in a fit of wild passion he had made an offer of love, and learns from her that she and Philinte are betrothed. He says to them both :—

> " Puissiez-vous, pour goûter de vrais contentements,
> L'un pour l'autre à jamais garder ces sentiments !

Trahi de toutes parts, accablé d'injustices,
Je vais sortir d'un gouffre où triomphent les vices,
Et chercher sur la terre un endroit écarté
Où d'être homme d'honneur on ait la liberté."

The dénouement to the comedy, as far as it relates to its two principal personages, is brusque, but Alceste was following his nature. He seems to have awakened suddenly out of a trance, and to have seen all at once that the woman whom he had loved so deeply and so unwisely had no love in her, but that her vanity and her ambition had led her to play with him, caring nothing whether he suffered or not. With these thoughts in our minds we may remember how Thackeray described Henry Esmond's love for his cousin Beatrix, and her conduct to him. · Beatrix had some softness in her heart, though not much; Célimène had none, and she knew it. The thoughts of both authors in dealing with the subject of the spider and the fly offer many points of similarity.

If there be any who have not a large sympathy both with and for Alceste, who have not felt with him in his anger and for him in his sorrow, I think that they have missed much of the comedy in the play and also of Molière's personality; that they do not see how the poet, in the *Misanthrope*, has shown some of the highest qualities of his sensitive nature. In 1840 Alfred de Musset wrote a short poem, *Une Soirée Perdue*; and after saying that he went one evening to see the *Misanthrope* at the Théâtre Français and found the house but half full (for in those days it was not the mode to admire Molière), he exclaimed :—

" O notre maître à tous ! si ta tombe est fermée,
Laisse-moi, dans ta cendre un instant ranimée,
Trouver un étincelle, et je vais t'imiter !
J'en aurai fait assez si je puis le tenter.
Apprends-moi de quel ton, dans ta bouche hardie,
Parlait la vérité, ta seule passion,
Et pour me faire entendre, à défaut du génie,
J'en aurai le courage et l'indignation ! "

It has often been said that in drawing Alceste and Célimène Molière portrayed some characteristics of himself and of his wife. This idea is commonly accepted, and it is impossible to refute it. But it may be pushed too far. From the comedy we see that the dramatist meant to characterise a very irrational type of man; and in order to show how contra-

dictory men's humours often are he made his wildly honest
and too sensitive Alceste, already melancholy from the deceits
of the world, fall very ardently in love with a heartless woman
who does not know what love is, and whose aims in life are to
appear in society, to fascinate, and to rule. Then he brought
them together as half affianced, and showed how incompatible
are their tempers. They have two faults in common, with
certain differences: a desire to command and an excessive
amour propre. Alceste would hide his self-love or self-conceit, but he is so proud that he cannot do so; while Célimène
is so vain that she makes no secret of hers, she even parades
it. Alceste decries men because he thinks they are liars,
Célimène abuses people because she thinks them silly. And,
as might be expected, their common failings do not tend to
reconcile them. Now, it is beside the point to consider
whether Molière was thinking of himself and his wife as he
drew his two characters. The question to be determined is
rather: Do the personages of Alceste and Célimène show
dramatically the attributes of good comedy? Very possibly
there was a likeness between the so-called models and the copies,
but there is only an idle curiosity in trying to see how far the
poet was describing his own domestic troubles when he wrote
his play. His lines may be read now everywhere, but what
happened in his own household, even if that were also known,
does not in the least alter the value of his scenes. It may well
be that because he showed the humours of comedy so plainly
many persons have been deceived, and that because the
imaginary picture is so graphic they have supposed it was
more or less a copy of what they have been told, and in some
cases half wished to believe, really took place. It is, however, very easy to perceive in certain lines an autobiographical
tendency. Towards the end of the first scene Philinte asks
Alceste how he can suffer Célimène's coquettish humour and
her backbiting, whether they cease to be faults in such a
charming woman, if he does not see them or if he excuses
them. Alceste answers in a speech beginning—

> " Non, l'amour que je sens pour cette jeune veuve
> Ne ferme point mes yeux aux défauts qu'on lui treuve." [1]

and ending by—

[1] *Treuve* for *trouve* was used occasionally by authors before Molière's day.

"Sa grâce est la plus forte, et sans doute ma flamme
De ces vices du temps pourra purger son âme."

Is there a man alive who has never felt the meaning of the words " sa grâce est la plus forte"? Here they are said in an unfortunate or unhappy sense, but when said happily, what a delight there is in them, and how joyfully true they will always remain! I am glad, however, to be able to say that there is no fair reason to suppose that Mlle. Molière had the backbiting propensities that were characteristic of Célimène.

If there is in some of the scenes in the *Misanthrope* a likeness to the disputes that took place between Molière and his wife, I believe that the dramatist showed it unconsciously far more than with determined purpose. He cared little whether he showed it or not. With such knowledge, or misknowledge, as we have got about Mlle. Molière—her fits of caprice, her coquetry, her love of display, her ambitions, her disdain, and her want of affection for her husband—it would be useless to say that she and Célimène were not more or less alike ; and it may be thought strange that the poet should have portrayed such a character on the stage. Molière did not allow his self-consciousness to interfere with the design of his comedy, and he did not trouble himself as to what the world said about the resemblances. The greater number of people who saw his play when it was new did not care about them. Why should we, therefore, trouble ourselves impertinently about them ? Their truth, or want of truth, will not make the comedy in the play better or worse. I can understand that as Molière was at work depicting the character of Célimène, he should have said to himself more than once : "That is like Armande"—such was his wife's name—and in the next breath : "Well, if the cap fits her she must wear it." But I think also that Célimène was not the personage that interested him most. It was to describe an Alceste and give a picture of his different humours that made Molière write the *Misanthrope*. That such an idea had long been in his thoughts may be seen from his previous abortive portrait of Don Garcie de Navarre. He recognised that Don Garcie did not show his wild passion in a spirit of true comedy, that the character was false ; and when he drew his Alceste he chose as his principal female personage in the new comedy a woman of a very different nature from the heroine of his tragi-comedy written five years earlier. The idea of Célimène's cap fitting Armande does not mean that a personal likeness was intended. Molière did not mean to think of his wife; he was not, in fact, thinking more of her as Célimène than he was of himself as Alceste. He did not intend to draw either her portrait or his own. But he had in his own mind the types of men and women he wished to describe; he, the creator, was whirled along passively by the strength of his own work; he had his ideas of comedy, to show people's faults by means of satire, and he felt bound to carry them out to the best of his ability.

Molière's sadness clung to him closely; but, as I read his character, he was not a misanthrope. He did not hate men nor like to think of them badly. On the contrary, his large sympathies with his fellow-creatures made him look into the causes of their troubles. He wanted to see among them more fair give and take, more confidence, less self-seeking. Mere pretence he could laugh at; a précieuse or a femme savante he thought was a disagreeable woman, and a man who constantly tried to show himself to be bigger than he was he thought was a bore, or that he made himself ridiculous. But in neither case was any great harm done. When, however, Molière found that unjust troubles were put upon the younger by their elders; that men were hard with those under them; that those who had influence over others were dishonest in their dealings—then he got angry. Distrust and disdain, which he did not like, were forced upon him; he brooded over the wrongs done to those who could not help themselves, and he became cynical and unhappy. That, I take it, was in a large measure the cause of Molière's melancholy, and so far he was in some lines of characterisation like his own Alceste. As a comic dramatist, however, he was bound to emphasise Alceste's features and show him to be a comic personage, that is a personage whose humours are emphasised and satirised by the fair ridicule of comedy. But I do not think that Molière was a misanthrope, in a fair acceptation of the word; and his human sympathies were too strong to allow him to have, in a marked way, the disdain of others felt by the cynic. He had some cynicism, it is true, but less than he showed in Alceste, or of a different kind in Philinte.

As to the actors who played originally in the *Misanthrope*, M. Mesnard has copied the list given by Aimé-Martin, and a more accurate list cannot be made now. Aimé-Martin distributed the parts as follows:—Molière as Alceste, La Thorillière as Philinte, du Croisy as Oronte, Mlle. Molière as Célimène, Mlle. de Brie as Éliante, Mlle. du Parc as Arsinoé, La Grange as Acaste, de Brie as un garde de la maréchaussée, Béjart as Dubois. Perhaps Hubert was Clitandre.[1] It has been accepted as certain that Mlle. Molière was Célimène in the comedy and that her husband was Alceste. About this latter part something may be said. In his Notice to *Don Garcie de Navarre*[2] Despois wrote: "If there is a strong stage tradition ... it is that which upholds the excellence of Molière's acting in the part of Alceste in the *Misanthrope*. Now, the part of Don Garcie is in a measure reproduced in that of Alceste. Can it be supposed that if Molière had been so weak in the first he should have shown himself so excellent in the second?" The seeming contradiction will be understood by any one who may have followed me in what I said about Molière's heroic-comedy *Don Garcie de Navarre*, about the different ideas of acting at the Hôtel de Bourgogne and the Palais Royal theatres, about Molière's quarrel with his rivals, and about his own acting generally. Also, Don Garcie was a false personage, and no interpretation of it by any one could have given much pleasure; Alceste's character was truly conceived, and the actor who performs it stands on firm ground. Molière, too, must have learned something in the art of acting in the interval of five years between the two plays; and when he played in the *Misanthrope* he was better known to the public than at the time of his earlier play. And one may easily imagine that Molière would have shown with clear, strong, and delicate cynicism his misanthrope's pride when the ridicule of comedy was cast upon him, and also have shown admirably the turbulence of an unhappy passionate man when his Alceste was railing at the faults of the world, or when he was being cheated by his mistress. In all this Alceste was a true personage, and Molière, unhappily for himself, understood the characteristics only too plainly.

It was on the 4th of June 1666 that the *Misanthrope* first

---

[1] *Œuvres de Molière*, v. 394 *et seq.*   [2] *Ibid.* ii. 227.

appeared on the stage. Leave was given to print the comedy on the 24th of that month, but the printing was not completed until the 24th of December following, and the first edition of the play bears the date 1667 on the title-page. The text of the comedy was preceded by a *Lettre écrite sur la comédie du Misanthrope*, by Jean Donneau de Visé. Of him I have spoken already. He wrote four or five comedies which were played at the Palais Royal theatre, but none of them appear to have had much success. De Visé seems to have been clever, except as a writer of plays, though he was not very scrupulous when he was trying to make his way in the world. His Letter on the *Misanthrope* may still be read; it contains some good criticism, showing that he understood the meaning of the comedy. According to Grimarest,[1] Molière knew nothing about the Letter until he was disagreeably surprised by seeing it printed at the head of his play. Brossette, repeating what he had heard from Boileau, says that de Visé obtained official leave to print his Letter, and meant to do so without Molière's permission, and that when Molière heard what his critic had done, he consented to the Letter being published rather than have a lawsuit.[2] Molière at any rate was annoyed at de Visé's officious interference, and I can quite believe Grimarest when he adds that the poet made his critic understand that he should not have attempted to defend his play. It has been said or hinted that de Visé repeated in his Letter some of Molière's ideas on his comedy ; but there is no evidence to lead one to suppose that Molière, consciously, had anything to do with the criticism contained in the Letter. And except its author's audacious self-advertisement, what purpose could have been gained by writing anything about a play that had been acted twenty-one times, and had been withdrawn from the stage nearly four months previously ? La Grange's Register shows that the comedy was only moderately successful on the stage; but it shows also that Grimarest cannot be trusted when he says that Molière wrote the *Médecin Malgré Lui*, his next comedy, to assist his *Misanthrope*. The dates of representation of both of these comedies, when they were new, prove conclusively that Grimarest was in error when he made this assertion.

[1] *Vie de Molière*, 99, 100.   [2] *Œuvres de Molière*, v. 369, 370.

After what has been said lately of the relations between Molière and his wife, this is perhaps the best place to speak of the interview between Molière and Chapelle at Auteuil. In August 1667 Molière was in possession of an apartment he had rented at Auteuil, then outside Paris. The inventory taken after his death states that in the autumn of 1672 he had paid 200 livres for half a year's rent for the apartment; also 10 écus for another room in the same house. There were probably four rooms in all, and a garden, or at least a right to walk and sit in the garden. It has been supposed that Mlle. Molière did not live at Auteuil with her husband, that he went there partly to be away from her, and also to free himself to some extent from the daily worries connected with his theatre inside Paris. Molière's old school friend Chapelle, however, was a co-tenant with him in the house at Auteuil.[1] Chapelle was undoubtedly a clever man ; unhappily he could fix his thoughts only on his love of society and his bottle. Molière had an affection for him, but he reproached him for his overfondness for wine and for making enemies by a bon mot. According to Grimarest,[2] Molière said to Baron : " Chapelle is my friend, but his unfortunate love of wine destroys all the pleasure of his friendship. I cannot confide anything to him without fear of exposing myself to everybody." The story now to be related is found for the first time in *La Fameuse Comédienne*,[3] of which I spoke in chapter v.; but this anonymous book is far from being a trustworthy authority. No one can say with any certainty what was the origin of the story. Édouard Fournier thought it was founded on a fragment of a letter written by Chapelle to the author of the *Fameuse Comédienne*, giving an account of what took place between him and Molière, and this surmise has been thought to be not improbable.[4] The tale has been often repeated, more or less. Sainte-Beuve gave it at length in his very excellent article on Molière in his *Portraits Littéraires*, and spoke of it as fair material for biography. The tale runs :—

" He [Molière] was thinking to himself one day in his garden at

[1] Soulié, *Recherches sur Molière*, 289 ; P. Mesnard, *Notice biographique sur Molière*, 379, 380.

[2] *Vie de Molière*, 93, 120, 121.   [3] Ed. by Jules Bonnassies, 16-21.

[4] Ed. Fournier, *Le Roman de Molière*, 20 ; and the same author's volume, *La Valise de Molière*, pp. xxxii, xxxiii.

Auteuil, when one of his friends, Chapelle, happened to be in the garden at the same time. Chapelle spoke to him and found him more uneasy in his mind than usual. He asked him several times what was troubling him. Molière felt ashamed at not being able to make a better stand against a very common misfortune, and tried to avoid the question ; but as his heart was full of his love he opened it to his friend, and told him that the manner in which he was obliged to live with his wife was the cause of his unhappiness.

"Chapelle, who thought himself above that kind of thing, rallied him, that he, who had painted so well the foibles of other men, should find himself in a condition which he had so often reproved ; and told him that no weakness was more foolish than love for a woman who did not show affection in return.

"For my part, he [Chapelle] said, I confess that if I was unfortunate enough to find myself in such a plight, and if I had good reason to believe that the woman I loved showed her favours to others, I should have so much contempt for her, that it would cure me for ever of my passion. And you have a satisfaction that you would not have if she were your mistress. Revenge usually takes the place of love in the heart of a man who has been insulted, and you can recompense yourself for the sorrow that your wife has caused you. You can place her in confinement. That would be a sure way of setting your mind at rest.

"Molière, who had listened to his friend calmly enough, interrupted him to ask if he had ever been in love.

"Yes, Chapelle answered, I have been in love as a man with common sense should be, but I should not have worried myself so much about a thing which my feeling of honour told me I ought to do, and I blush for you to see you so undecided.

"Molière replied, I see clearly that you have never loved any woman, and that you have taken the image of love for love itself. I will not speak of the numberless instances which would prove the strength of this passion, but I will tell you truly how hopeless my condition is, to show you how little one is master of oneself, when love has gained the upper hand and when it uses its power. In answer to your argument of the perfect knowledge you say I have of men's hearts by the pictures that I give to the public, I allow that I have done my best to learn their weaknesses ; but if reason has taught me that one may escape the danger, experience has shown me only too plainly that it is impossible to avoid it. I see proofs of this every day in myself. Nature gave me an affectionate disposition, and as all the efforts I have made have not conquered my instincts, I have tried to make myself happy, that is to say as happy as a man can be who has a sensitive heart. I felt that there were very few women who were worth loving truly ; that interest, ambition, and vanity were at the bottom of all their schemes. I endeavoured to choose a woman whose innocence of heart should form my happiness. I took my wife, so to say, from the cradle. I brought her up with every mark of affection, and this has given rise to the rumours which you have heard. I believed that I could, by teaching, implant in her sentiments that time would not destroy, and I used every effort to that end. As she was very young when I married her, I did not see the bad sides of her character, and I thought myself a little less unfortunate than most husbands. Marriage did not cool my ardour; but I found as time went on so much indifference, that I began to perceive that all my precautions had been useless, and that her feelings for me were quite other than those which I had hoped for. I reproached myself on a matter of delicacy which seemed to me to be ridiculous in a husband, and I attributed to her natural disposition what was really a want of affection for myself. I was only too plainly convinced of my mistake, and the extravagant passion which she showed soon afterwards for the Comte de Guiche made too much noise to allow me to continue in this state of seeming tranquillity. When I first heard of it I tried every means in my power to conquer my own feelings, knowing that I could not change hers. I set all my mind to work to gain my purpose; I thought of everything that might help to give me comfort. I considered her as a woman who had once possessed the single virtue of innocence, but who had lost it when she became unfaithful. For some time I resolved to live with her as a well-bred man does who knows that his wife is false, though it may be said that her bad conduct should not injure his reputation. But I discovered to my sorrow that a woman who is not really beautiful, and who owes whatever intelligence she has to the education that I gave her, very quickly upset all my reasoning. Whenever she came beside me I forgot my resolutions, and the first words that she spoke in her own defence convinced me so fully that my suspicions were ill-founded, that I asked her pardon for being so credulous. My kindness did not change her conduct. I have therefore determined to live with her as though she were not my wife. But if you knew what I suffer you would pity me. My love for her is so strong that I find myself taking her part; and when I reflect how impossible it is for me to conquer my feelings, I tell myself at the same time that perhaps she has the same difficulty in overcoming her coquetry, and I think more of sympathising with her than of blaming her. You will tell me that I must be a poet to love anybody in that manner. I think that there is only one kind of love, and that men who have never had these compassionate feelings have never loved truly. I think of her in connection with everything that happens. She fills my heart so entirely, that when she is not with me my thoughts are always with her. Whenever I see her I feel an indescribable affection and tenderness that deprives me of my senses. I have no eyes for her faults; I only know that I love her. Is not this the last stage of madness? And do you wonder, if I have still any power of reason, that it should only tell me of my weakness, but leave me helpless to overcome it?'

There is another account, given by Grimarest,[1] of an inter-

[1] *Vie de Molière*, pp. 79-81.

view between Molière and his friend Rohault, a natural philosopher, according to which the poet spoke of the unhappy relations between himself and his wife. There are points of similarity in the two accounts as to Mlle. Molière's indifference to her husband; the main difference between them is that the author of the *Fameuse Comédienne* says that she was unfaithful to him; in what Grimarest says, she is reported as being true but cold-hearted. Both descriptions were written after the date of the *Misanthrope*; both were probably more or less made up, though in both there is an air of truth which it is difficult to dispel.

Molière, like many other large-hearted and large-minded men, had more than one side to his nature. He was both affectionate and melancholy. It would seem from his plays, even considering the spirit of comedy in which they were written, that he had not a high opinion of women generally; and it may be gathered also that this want of a good opinion of women helped to make him unhappy. It may be accepted, at all events, that he was fascinated by Armande Béjart when she was a child, and that her charms grew upon him. When he was just turned forty he married her, she being then seventeen or eighteen, hoping and half believing that with his strong love for her he could mould her, and that she would adapt herself to his ways. In both of these expectations he was disappointed. She naturally had her own thoughts, her own aspirations, and they differed from his. Unfortunately she was less yielding than he was. It is safest to concur in the general impression that Molière's married life was not a happy one, and that he did not find in his wife the sweet disposition he had fondly anticipated. He was a man who looked for kindliness, for sympathy, but she had none to give him. His thoughts did not agree with hers; neither could make a close companion or friend of the other, and it would have been better for them both if he had been able to resist her fascinations. It may be true that in spite of himself Molière always continued to be fond of his wife, and that he reproached himself for speaking to her harshly. We read that for a time they were separated, but that through the mediation of friends they came together again a few years before the husband's death.

CHAPTER XVI

MOLIÈRE'S *Médecin Malgré Lui* was first acted at the Palais
Royal theatre on the 6th of August 1666, four days after the
Misanthrope had been withdrawn from the stage as a new
play. After the seriousness of the five-act comedy in verse,
which had been played twenty-one times, and at its later
performances with low receipts, the poet, as manager of his
theatre and leader of the troop for which he virtually had to
provide, wished to give the public a lighter form of entertainment. When the *Médecin Malgré Lui* had been acted eleven
times, the *Misanthrope* was again brought forward, and these
two plays were given together on five consecutive days.[1]
Grimarest's statement that Molière had written the *Médecin
Malgré Lui* to assist the *Misanthrope* should therefore be
dismissed.

Very few dramatists have been so successful as Molière in
both high, and in what may, perhaps, best be called popular
comedy. The link between them is in the desire and the
capability to show naturally and in an open comic manner
somewhat different sides of human nature. In the 17th century
society in France, more than was the case in England, was
divided roughly into two classes—the quality and the people.
And Molière, as he revealed in high comedy the thoughts and
the manners of the better educated, and in popular comedy
those in a lower or less cultivated rank of life, did not in
his own mind divide men into classes, either mentally or
morally. The wish with him to look upon all men as belonging to the large human family, was father to the thought. He
was no theorist. If what are now understood as socialistic
principles had then been known in France, he would have
been averse to them; but in marking in his own way, in a

[1] La Grange's Register, pp. 82, 83.

comic manner, the different ideas he saw around him, it may be seen that his thoughts were often with the people, that he recognised their hopes and their fears as well as those of their loftier brethren, and that he would gladly have seen more communication between them. Louis Racine, in his *Mémoires* of his father, tells a piquant anecdote, dating in all probability from after Molière's death, about Boileau's admiration for Molière:—" He always looked upon Molière as unique in his genius; and one day when the king asked him who was the most uncommon ('le plus rare') of the great writers who had honoured France during his reign, he named Molière. 'I did not think so,' the king answered, 'but you know more about the matter than I do.'"[1]

There is some excellent farce in the *Médecin Malgré Lui*, and the satire against the doctors is the most farcical part of the play. But allowing that the incidents told are meant chiefly to arouse laughter, the individual characterisation of the various personages is very well shown; and when different traits in human characterisation are painted truly in a farcical manner, then farce rises nearly to the level of comedy. One of Molière's rare qualities is that he knits comedy and farce so well and so closely together. The *Médecin Malgré Lui* has always been popular on the stage. Up to the year 1870 it had been acted at the Comédie Française oftener than any other play of Molière's except the *Tartuffe*.[2]

I need not repeat what was said early in the last chapter as to how Molière regarded the medical doctors of his day. The fun in the *Médecin Malgré Lui* is readily seen, but to give it at second-hand is not an easy matter. It is fine and delicate; you enjoy the freshness of its wit, but you cannot analyse it beyond feeling that it is shown with all the "go" of comedy and that the enthusiasm it creates is infectious. The play is hardly more than an amusing sketch composed in a popular manner, and two of the personages speak the language of the people. In all probability it was transformed from a farce known as *Le Fagotier* or *Le Fagoteux*, which Molière himself had written in earlier days and which had been acted a few times at the Palais Royal theatre. Some verbal in-

[1] *Œuvres de J. Racine*, by Paul Mesnard, vol. i. 1st ed. p. 263; 2nd. ed. p. 271.
[2] *Ante*, chap. xi. p. 282.

stances of what is now looked upon as coarseness are noticeable. They strike one because Molière, even in his popular
comedies, wrote very little indeed that any sensible man or
woman would wish to see bowdlerised.

This is the last of Molière's comedies in which a Sganarelle
appears. The dramatist made frequent use of this character
and has shown him under various aspects. He is hard, or
contemptible, or vicious, or foolish, or cowardly, or boastful, or
self-interested; and in exposing the same type of personage
under various guises Molière showed how well he knew his
thoughts. One would have liked to have seen a different
name given to poor Sganarelle in *Don Juan*, for though
cowardly he hardly answers to his family name, and by the
side of his master he shines as a good man. The Sganarelle in
the present comedy is by occupation a wood-cutter, by nature
a selfish curmudgeon, and by habit a tippler. He has a wife
who is a shrew. They quarrel, and he beats her, and it
is owing to her revenge that he is made a doctor against his
will.

I shall refer to only one small incident in the *Médecin
Malgré Lui*. It is in Act II. sc. 4, and in the well-known
words: "Nous avons changé tout cela." Sganarelle, the sham
doctor, has been talking furious nonsense to Géronte, the
father of his patient :—

" *Géronte.*

"I have no doubt your reasoning is most excellent. There is only
one thing that puzzles me : the side [in the human body] of the
liver and of the heart. It seems to me that you place them wrongly,
that the heart is on the left side and the liver on the right.

" *Sganarelle.*

"Yes, formerly it was so ; but we have changed all that, and now
we construct medical science upon quite a new plan.

" *Géronte.*

"I did not know that ; pray forgive my ignorance.

" *Sganarelle.*

"It is of no consequence ; you are not obliged to be as clever as
we are."

It is ungracious to say so, but the source of the fun here was
not originally Molière's. After the words in the text, "Nous

avons changé tout cela," M. Mesnard gives in a footnote[1] an extract from *La Gazette* (the official newspaper in Paris) of the 17th of December 1650 :—

"And because you ought to be not less informed of the wonderful changes that take place in the human body as well as in that of the States, it was discovered here this week, in a dissection made in public by a doctor of medicine of this Faculty of a body of a man who had been executed, that the liver which contains the spleen was on the left side, and the spleen on the right side where the liver should be, the heart inclining to the right side, and the majority of the organs placed otherwise than is ordinarily the case."

This discovery caused some laughter at the time, and sixteen years later Molière gave it a setting of his own when he satirised his quack doctor. In reading the poet's light plays we pass over his good things almost carelessly; they amuse, and we take them easily as they were intended. The truth of the comedy in his ludicrous characters depends largely on the way it is shown.

It is certain that Molière played the part of Sganarelle in the *Médecin Malgré Lui,* and his wife that of Lucinde, the young lady who feigns to be ill. La Grange was probably the lover, Léandre; and du Croisy, Géronte. M. Mesnard thinks that Mlle. de Brie was Martine, Sganarelle's wife.[2]

The comedy was printed at the end of 1666; the title-page bears the date 1667.[3]

On the 1st of December 1666 the troop at the Palais Royal were commanded by the king to go to Saint Germain. They remained there until the 20th of February 1667, and took part in a long fête known as *Le Ballet des Muses.*[4] For this fête Molière wrote two acts of a comedy in verse, *Mélicerte,* "comédie-pastorale-héroïque." The two acts were played in an entrée of the ballet; and the king having expressed his satisfaction with them, Molière did not finish the play.[5] He never completed it. The two acts were not put upon the stage at the Palais Royal theatre, and they were not printed until the year 1682. There are some pretty verses in the comedy, if it can be so called, at the beginning of the

---

[1] *Œuvres de Molière*, vi. 88 note 3.
[2] *Ibid.* vi. 22, 23.
[3] *Ibid.* vi. 30, 31.
[4] La Grange's Register, 85, 86.
[5] *Œuvres de Molière*, vi. 185.

fifth scene of the first act, where Myrtil, a young boy, is talking to a bird that he means as a present for his heroine Mélicerte ; and again later when he gives her the bird at the beginning of the third scene of the second act.

Molière made another sketch for the *Ballet des Muses* under the title of *La Pastorale Comique.* Only a fragment of it has been preserved, and this is so slight that it is hardly worth noticing. It seems to have replaced *Mélicerte* in the third entrée of the ballet. In his Register La Grange spoke of *La Pastorale Comique* as *Coridon,* because the part he took in it was that of Coridon, a young shepherd.

Later, and in the last week of the royal fête, on the 14th of February 1667,[1] another small play of Molière's was performed. This was *Le Sicilien ou L'Amour Peintre.* It was in one act and in prose, but there was music and dancing between the scenes. Given as part of a revelry or masquerade, the *Sicilien* is a pretty little comedy. It shows in a jesting way the lesson that its author had wished to teach more seriously in his former play, the *École des Maris* : that keeping young women jealously under lock and key is not the way to make them either loving or trustful to those in authority over them. Perhaps because Molière was seriously ill in the spring of this year the *Sicilien* was not put on the stage at the Palais Royal until the 10th of June.[2] For a few weeks it was given as an after-piece, following other plays ; but judging now by the receipts, it does not seem to have much attracted the public. The names of the actors who took the various parts are given by M. Mesnard ;[3] the title-page of the comedy bears the date 1668.

After the very short mention made by La Grange on page 86 of his Register of the journey of the troop to Saint Germain, he says that the king gave them 12,000 livres as pension for two years. In August 1665 the king had promised the troop a pension of 6000 livres, but at Easter 1666, the end of the financial year at the theatre, no payment had been made ; so that in February 1667 the pension for two years was given in one payment.[4]

On the 4th of March in this year, when the veteran Pierre

---

[1] *Œuvres de Molière*, vi. 205. [2] *Ibid.* vi. 209, 210.
[3] *Ibid.* vi. 294.
[4] Conf. La Grange's Register, p. 76 and p. 86.

Corneille was sixty years old, the troop at the Palais Royal bought from him his tragedy *Attila*, and gave him 2000 livres for it, "prix fait"—ready money. This was the first time that Molière bought a play from his older rival, a dramatist whom he must have admired in bygone days. The tragedy was acted twenty times, but the receipts show that the pecuniary success of the play was far from satisfactory.

When speaking of the *Tartuffe* I mentioned the single performance of that comedy on the 5th of August 1667, and related how future performances of the play were forbidden.

At Easter 1667, the end of the theatrical year, La Grange says in a note: "Mlle. du Parc a quitté la troupe et a passé à l'Hôtel de Bourgogne, où elle a joué Andromaque de M. Racine." Perhaps Mlle. du Parc thought that she was following her own interest in going to the rival theatre. She had first joined Molière's troop at Lyons after her marriage in February 1653, and she remained in it till Easter 1659. Then she and her husband went to the Théâtre du Marais for twelve months, but at the following Easter they rejoined their old comrades. It has been thought that bickering among the actresses of the troop at the Palais Royal was the cause of the temporary secession. Du Parc died in October 1664, and his share in the profits of the theatre were given to his widow until the following Easter. Two years and a half later Mlle. du Parc went, as we have just seen, to the Hôtel de Bourgogne to play an important, though not the principal, part in Racine's tragedy *Andromaque*, which was then new. If the year 1633 can be taken as the date of her birth, she was still a young woman. It is not unlikely that after Mlle. Molière had joined the troop at the Palais Royal, Mlle. du Parc found that her services were not so much needed. But her desertion from her old friends has been attributed to persuasion from Racine. And this last supposition is strengthened by the knowledge that Racine had behaved badly to the actors at the Palais Royal when he suddenly withdrew from them his *Alexandre le Grand* in December 1665; and also by the fact that in May 1668 Molière put on to his stage a parody on Racine's last play in the form of a comedy, *La Folle Querelle ou la Critique d'Andromaque*, by one Subligny. This comedy was acted a fair number of times, but apparently did not create much interest.[1] The parody, however, probably prevented any future friendly intercourse between the two poets. Mlle. du Parc did not remain long at the Hôtel de Bourgogne, for she died in December 1668.

We have seen already that in the spring of the year 1667 Molière was very seriously ill; and M. Moland says that in the latter part of that year he did not appear on the stage.[2] Indeed for seven weeks his theatre was closed in the absence of two of the best actors, La Grange and Thorillière, who had gone to Flanders to present to the king the poet's second petition on the matter of the prohibition of the *Tartuffe*. And after their return the plays that were acted at the Palais Royal theatre did not absolutely need the presence of the leader of the troop. He was the author of only one of them—*La Pastorale Comique*, the little sketch that he had written for the last royal fête at Saint Germain, and in which his small part might easily have been taken by another actor. And when the troop went to Versailles for a few days in November 1667, among the plays acted there the *Pastorale Comique* was the only one that could have been written by Molière. But early in January 1668 La Grange records three performances of *Les Médecins*, by which title he often used to designate the *Amour Médecin*, as five doctors are brought forward in the comedy; and in that play Molière, ever constant to the daily work of his life, doubtless reappeared in his part of Sganarelle.

On the 13th of January 1668 Molière's *Amphitryon* was first acted at the Palais Royal theatre. This was a mythological comedy, borrowed from the *Amphitruo* of Plautus and from an old French comedy by Rotrou called *Les deux Sosies*, acted at the Théâtre du Marais in 1636, which had also been taken from Plautus. Molière did not care whether he borrowed much from Plautus and from Rotrou or not; he wanted to show the humours of a mythological comedy in a playful manner. His *Amphitryon* is thoroughly French in treatment and in the way the wit is shown. It is written

---

[1] See La Grange's Register, 96.—M. V. Fournel has printed *La Critique d'Andromaque* in vol. iii. of his *Contemporains de Molière* ; and he and other French writers have said that La Grange did not state when it was first acted, and that he omitted to record its first performances—one to four in number.

[2] L. Moland, *Œuvres de Molière*, 1st ed. vol. i. p. 201.

with originality of style, not in the conventional Alexandrine verse of twelve syllables; but in " vers libres," where the lines are of various lengths, and where the rhymes do not follow each other consecutively. It is the only one of Molière's comedies, except *Psyché*, written later in collaboration with Pierre Corneille, in which he adopted this measure.

After it had been played twice in public there was a performance of *Amphitryon* before the court at the Tuileries on the 16th of January, and two months later, when the troop at the Palais Royal went to Versailles, *Amphitryon* was one of the plays then acted before the king.[1]

I do not see the strong flattery of Louis XIV. that apparently some French writers have found in the verses of this comedy. Sosie's lament on the ungrateful labour of men who work for princes, in the first scene of the play, certainly cannot have had the appearance of flattery. It seems to me that satire is more evident in the comedy, not of a personal kind against the king, but against current habits of thought. Flattery in a bad sense was not in Molière's nature; his disposition was too sceptical, too unhappy, and too honest to allow him to use it. But the ridicule coming from good satire was always congenial to him. He thought a great deal of comic irony, but it is next to impossible to suppose that he meant his lines in this comedy to have a literal signification. When, for instance, Jupiter is made to take upon himself a human form and is disguised as Amphitryon so that he may supplant him in the couch of his wife Alcmène, one cannot really believe that the poet meant to satirise the immoralities of Louis XIV. in the lines :—

> " Un partage avec Jupiter
> N'a rien qui déshonore."

No one can suppose that Molière meant here to insult his sovereign. M. Mesnard has shown from dates that the lines cannot contain an allusion to the love-makings of Louis XIV. and Madame de Montespan ; and that Rotrou, who had borrowed from Plautus as well as Molière, but who wrote fifty years earlier, might also have been accused on the same charge.[2] But there is a simpler and a stronger argument

---

[1] *Œuvres de Molière*, vi. 323-25 ; also x. 383, and note 1.
[2] *Ibid.* vi. 316, etc.

than that of dates. It is not likely that within a few months after Molière had presented his petition to the king to be allowed to put the *Tartuffe* on the stage, he should have rebuked his Majesty in an insolent manner. And there is no evidence to show that the king imagined that an indirect insult was intended. Molière loved the fun coming from amusing, piquant, and not ill-natured satire; and he made his mythological comedy, which he took largely from Plautus and from Rotrou, the vehicle for satirical allusions against general habits of thought. To say that he looked upon Louis XIV. as a divinity above the reach of allusion, and that the satire in his play was meant only for the courtiers, would be absurd. It would be more just to say that the playfulness of his wit and the sparkling cynicism in his banter were enjoyed by the king, who was both good-natured and sensible enough to take the fun as it was meant; and that the courtiers laughed among themselves at certain lines which had a general application in their tartness.

In the prologue to the comedy we read:—

> "Lorsque dans un haut rang on a l'heur[1] de paroître,
> Tout ce qu'on fait est toujours bel et bon,
> Et suivant ce qu'on peut être
> Les choses changent de nom."

M. Mesnard quotes these lines and says admirably:— " L'ironie ne manquait pas de clarté. Si quelqu'un la juge d'un méprisable flatteur il n'entend pas le français. On l'entendait certainement mieux à Versailles."[2] Another reason for thinking that Louis XIV. did not feel that Molière had been disrespectful to him is that this comedy was played at court eight times between 1680 and 1700, and five times between 1700 and 1715.[3]

Amphitryon shows certain defects in Molière's mind. He did not feel strongly the beauties of poetry, consequently he had not the power of language to show them strongly. In satirical or ironical comedy he has been surpassed by no one, and he wrote in excellent dramatic verse, but he could not reach the higher flights of imaginative poetry. To take the play we are now considering—which was meant as

---

[1] *Heur* is, of course, the equivalent here of *bonheur*.
[2] *Notice biographique sur Molière*, 384, 385.
    Œuvres de Molière, vi. 325.

a mythological comedy—in the scenes between Jupiter and Alcmène, in those between Amphitryon and Alcmène, and in the scene where Amphitryon delivers a long monologue showing his bewilderment, one looks for poetical imagination and poetical expression, and the reader is disappointed when he finds instead cleverly turned verses which do not really interest him because they do not arouse his sympathies.

The best drawn character in the comedy is that of Sosie, Amphitryon's servant; and the chief amusement in the play is in the comedy of errors when Mercure is disguised as Sosie and when Jupiter is disguised as Amphitryon. Some of the scenes seem to be fresh and bright, and as we read them they are full of wit. There are verses in *Amphitryon* so frequently quoted that they have become commonplaces. A few instances may be given :—

> " J'aime mieux un vice commode
> Qu'une fatigante vertu."

And :

> " Le véritable Amphitryon
> Est l'Amphitryon où l'on dîne."

And :

> " Le Seigneur Jupiter sait dorer la pilule."

And in daily life we often find there is good counsel in the words :

> " Sur telles affaires, toujours
> Le meilleur est de ne rien dire."

There is a tradition that Molière played the part of Sosie in *Amphitryon*, but for the other rôles there is much uncertainty, and contradictory guesses have been made.[1]

Molière dedicated this comedy to the Prince de Condé; the printing of the play was completed on the 5th of March 1688.[2]

It matters little whether the *Avare* or *George Dandin* be first spoken of here. M. Mesnard in his edition of Molière has printed *George Dandin* first because that comedy was performed at court before the other comedy was seen on any stage. It may be better, however, in a biography of Molière, to take the two plays in the order of their appearance in public.

[1] *Œuvres de Molière*, vi. 327-30.　　　　[2] *Ibid.* vi. 351.

There are no connecting ideas between them, and it is tolerably certain that the *Avare* was written first. Other instances of similar inversion—if it can be so called—will be found among Molière's later comedies. In all cases the inversion is of no consequence.

La Grange says in his Register that the *Avare* was played for the first time on the 9th of September 1668 at the Palais Royal theatre. No authority can prevail on such a point against that of La Grange. He was an actor in Molière's troop; he, as orateur in the troop, had to announce to the public in the theatre each time a new play was to be given, and he noted daily in his diary the names of the plays in which he and his fellow-actors took their parts. But Grimarest says that the *Avare* was first played in January 1668, and Voltaire in the year 1667. Both add that when first given the play was a failure because it was written in prose, but that at its revival some months later the public judged the comedy more soundly and that it was successful.[1] The reader may remember that in chapter xi. the figures in La Grange's Register were used to tell what were the fortunes of Molière's comedies while they were new. La Grange was a first-hand authority, and on such a subject the only one really trustworthy. And his pages prove beyond dispute that the *Avare*, one of the chief of Molière's comedies in prose, met with very poor success when it first appeared. It was acted only nine times, and judging by the receipts it attracted comparatively few spectators. And later, during its author's lifetime, the receipts taken for its performances were seldom good. On the other hand, it seems to have been very popular in after years. Despois has shown that from 1659 to 1870 only three plays of Molière's were acted at the Comédie Française oftener than the *Avare*.[2]

It is well known that in Molière's day playgoers preferred that seriously meant comedies in five acts should be in verse. In spite of the success of *Don Juan*, a five-act comedy in prose, it is quite possible that the fact that the *Avare* was also in prose may have contributed to its failure. But had

[1] *Œuvres de Molière*, vii. 3, 4 ; 47. M. Mesnard's references to Grimarest's *Vie de Molière* apply to the first edition, published in 1705. In the modern edition, printed in 1875, see pp. 58 and 104.

[2] *Œuvres de Molière*, i. 548, 549.

Molière written it in verse he would have planned the scenes differently, and the laughter against Harpagon would have been shown in a less popular manner. The comedy would then have been other than it is. The noble duke referred to by Grimarest was perhaps only expressing general opinion rather energetically and in a ludicrous way when he objected to the *Avare* because it was written in prose. " What is the meaning of this ? " exclaimed M. le duc de ——. " Is Molière daft, and does he take us for simpletons to make us sit through five acts of prose ? Did anybody ever see such nonsense ? Is it possible that anybody can like prose ? " Voltaire said later that when the public appreciated the merits of the *Avare* " they understood that very good comedies might be written in prose, and that it was perhaps more difficult to succeed in this common style, in which the author relies only upon his intelligence, than in verse; for in verse the rhymes, the cadence, and the rhythm lend ornaments to simple ideas which cannot be given easily in prose with a graceful appearance." This remark of Voltaire's is of greater importance than his error about the date of the play. The desire to give a graceful appearance and graceful sound to words in a comedy in the 17th century did much to hinder the spirit of comedy in plays. Molière showed clearly that comedies may very well be written in prose, and he made it evident that a comedy is best written in the form of language that its author can handle the most easily with comic effect.

As a comedy the *Avare* presents two ideas which should be considered together. It may be thought that the dramatist meant to give a comic picture of a miser and of his griping niggardliness; or that he wished to show the unhappy condition of a son and a daughter, the children of a father who had very little affection for them and no sense of his fatherly duties. Perhaps the latter view was strongest in the author's mind as the basis of his comedy, and hence his choice of avarice as the crime best suited to illustrate his thoughts. In any case the two ideas fit into one another, they work together and they cannot be considered separately. We have seen already in the *École des Maris* and in the *École des Femmes* how girls who had lost both father and mother were brought up badly, through great selfishness in both cases, and with great brutality in one instance and egregious folly in the other; and here in a later play the dramatist was reverting to the same idea, and he made extreme stinginess the vice of the parent who was the sole guardian of his two grown-up children. As the father showed his son and daughter no affection, inspired them with no respect, it is impossible that they could have felt real love for him or have had a warm sense of filial duties. Molière took his *Avare* from the *Aulularia* of Plautus; he had been reading Plautus before he wrote his *Amphitryon*, and a few months later he turned again to the Latin author for assistance.

Of all Molière's characters few are better known than the miser Harpagon. He and Tartuffe may stand beside one another. The conduct of Harpagon, however, is shown in a more amusing way. Still, the comedy in the *Avare* is grim, and there is a note of sadness in the picture of dislike and distrust felt by the son and daughter for their sordid father and in the hatred of him among all his dependants.

When Harpagon first comes on to the stage with La Flèche, his son's valet, he says to him :—

"Get out of this at once, and don't answer me. Pack yourself out of my house, arrant thief and true jail-bird, as you are."

La Flèche, who is a good fellow enough, says to himself :—

"I've never seen anything so wicked as this cursed old man, and I think, under correction, that the devil is in him."

The old man is on the point of dismissing the servant brutally; instead, he stops him and begins the following dialogue :—

"Stay : aren't you taking anything away?"—"What could I take from you?"—"Come here and let me see. Show me your hands."— "There they are"—"The others."—"The others?"—"Yes."— "There they are."

We have seen that the first words spoken by Harpagon give an instance of his surly and suspicious nature; and his demand, just made, to La Flèche to show him his "other hands" after the valet had shown the only two he has got, has been blamed by some critics, needlessly, I think, on the score of exaggeration. A mistake has been made in trying to judge a bit of jeering satire by the light of dry reason. Looked at in that way the demand is nonsensical; but as comedy tries to show men by their humours and to condemn or laugh at their faults or their foibles, Harpagon's demand describes and paints his crabbedness and distrust, and is therefore quite fair as a mark of human characterisation. In all plays, as more or less in all art, there is some exaggeration or heightening of the effect; and comedy should be looked at from the point of view of stage representation. Before finding fault here with Molière for caricature it would be well to consider the bad qualities of the man he was endeavouring to describe, and to recollect that these must be shown with humour.

Harpagon then points to La Flèche's hauts-de-chausses, or breeches, and the dialogue goes on :—

" *Harpagon.*

"Haven't you put anything in there ?

" *La Flèche.*

"See for yourself.

" *Harpagon.*

"Those large hauts-de-chausses are made to conceal stolen property, and I wish that somebody was hanged for wearing them.

La Flèche (aside).

"Oh ! A man like that just deserves to get what he is afraid of, and I should take a delight in robbing him."

As La Flèche said these last words he did not know that Harpagon had hidden 10,000 écus in a box in his garden, and that he was nervously anxious about his treasure. There is more quarrelling between these two, and when Harpagon is left alone at the end of the scene, he says to himself: "There is a rogue of a valet who bothers me a good deal. I don't like the sight of the lame dog." Béjart, Molière's brother-in-law, who played the part of La Flèche, was lame, and the dramatist was here indulging in a little bit of good-humoured drollery at his expense. And Béjart is said to have been a favourite actor with those who went into the parterre of the theatre.

To judge the miser properly he should be seen with his children. He wishes to marry his daughter Élise to Anselme, who is twice her age or more but who is willing to take her without any dowry. Élise is outwardly respectful to her father, but she is mutinous. Valère, her lover and her father's steward—"domestique"[1]—appears in the middle of their dispute, and for the purpose of the comedy in the play he pretends to take Harpagon's side in their difference. Here occurs the frequent repetition of the words "sans dot," used by Harpagon. Valère, who means to be true to Élise, but is working on the weak side of the miser, says, at the last mention of "sans dot": "That determines everything. Nobody can go against the argument of *sans dot.*" And later: "When a man offers to take a girl sans dot, further inquiries should not be made. Everything is included in that; and *sans dot* takes the place of beauty, youth, birth, wisdom, and honesty." Harpagon's son, Cléante, was extravagant, but this was his worst fault. He is in love with Mariane, who is very poor; and to assist her and her mother he is driven to borrow money at ruinous interest. And when he and his father find themselves face to face, one as the borrower, the other as the usurer, there is a quarrel between them. The father abuses his son for prodigality, the son condemns his father for enriching himself in an infamous manner. The idea of such a scene in a comedy is a good one, but it was not in the first instance Molière's. He may have taken it either from Boisrobert's comedy, *La Belle Plaideuse*, acted fourteen years earlier, or from a similar incident that had actually happened in Paris before Boisrobert wrote his play.[2]

The *Avare* affords an instance of how Molière made use of the minor characters in his comedies, and how he worked up the incidents in his plays, in order to bring the main features of his chief personages into full relief. Harpagon feels no sorrow that his son Cléante was trying to borrow money; he has no sense of shame that he, as a father, was discovered in trying to exact usury from his own son. He is a skin-flint who thinks only of how he can grind others to scrape money

---

[1] The word "domestique" occurs frequently in the social history of France in the 17th century. It meant in the first instance, attached to the household of a master. There was nothing menial in the office. Young men of good family often made their apprenticeship in the world as domestique in the house of some person of consequence, and older men of ability were often so employed as steward or as secretary. Valère's position was therefore quite consistent with that of a gentleman. (*Œuvres de Molière*, vi. 33 note 3 ; vii. 56 note 1.)

[2] *Œuvres de Molière*, vii. 96 ; 102.

together, and how to save it. When he meets Frosine, described as "a woman of intrigue," he is eager to know how she has prospered in furthering his suit with Mariane, whom he says he loves and hopes to marry. Father and son are therefore rivals for the hand of the same young lady. Frosine is an unpleasant creature; not much is seen of her, but she must just be mentioned. She hopes for some pecuniary assistance from Harpagon, and flatters him absurdly. She might as well pour oil on the sand to stay the raging of the sea. The miser, who is anxious to get his daughter married "sans dot," is equally anxious that his intended bride should bring him money. He thinks that her mother "should exert herself a little, make an effort, part with some of her property, for such an occasion. For no man marries a girl unless she brings him something." And he is ill-satisfied when he hears that Mariane's dowry, though large, consists only in her economical habits.

But for his niggardliness Harpagon would have a good position in the world. He keeps a steward, at least four servants, horses and a carriage; and he feels himself obliged to give a supper-party in his house in honour of Anselme, at which he hopes that Mariane may be present. The amusing scene (Act III. sc. 1) in which he gives his instructions to his servants for his party is one of the best in the comedy. He speaks to them all and chooses that Maître Jacques, his coachman and cook, shall take his orders last. This man appears dressed as a coachman, but when told he is to be spoken to as cook he quickly changes his clothes. It would seem from many early editions of Molière that the enumeration of the various dishes to be put on the table was left to the actor who played the part of Maître Jacques. In the edition of 1682, published by La Grange, who, one can hardly think, added to the text words that its author did not give, the list is ridiculously long.[1] Maître Jacques knew his master's proclivities, and, with the fair caricature of comedy, was playing upon them. No wonder, therefore, that Harpagon should scream: "Devil take it all! That is enough to feed a

---

[1] *Œuvres de Molière*, vii. 127 note 4; see also *Œuvres de Molière*, by L. S. Auger, vii. 87 and note 1; Louis Moland, *Œuvres de Molière*, 2nd ed. ix. 243 and note.

whole town." The cook, however, had not yet finished, and before he had done Harpagon puts his hand over his mouth and cries: "You wretch! you want to eat up all my property." But Valère, Harpagon's steward, will not allow profligate expenditure. He says, "Il faut manger pour vivre, et non pas vivre pour manger." The miser takes heart at this good counsel, and thinks he is repeating the ancient adage when he cries joyfully: "Il faut vivre pour manger, et non pas manger pour vi ..." As might be expected, Harpagon starves his horses, and Maître Jacques, who when addressed as coachman again changes his clothes, is glad to hear at last that he is not to drive the poor beasts to the fair. "All the better," he says; "I would sooner they die under anybody else's hands than under mine."

Mariane is very unhappy when told by Frosine that she must marry Harpagon, and when she first sees him she is nearly sick with disgust. She respects Cléante and is willing to give herself to him, but she does not know that he is Harpagon's son. The scenes in which Mariane has her part betray, to our thinking, a weak point in the play. She is said to be a good and charming girl, but not much is really known about her. The interest felt in her is passive; it is that she may not be bound to Harpagon. Also on behalf of Élise, the miser's daughter, the interest felt is rather compassionate than active. They are both good girls, but they would create more sympathy if they had been portrayed more fully, and if the good sides of their characters had been shown at greater length. In this, as in other comedies, Molière's purpose seems to have been to show the tyranny of parents or elderly people who exercised authority viciously over their juniors, and he thought more of his satire against their harsh conduct than of dwelling upon the brighter sides of younger natures. He showed these qualities more fully in the *École des Maris* and the *École des Femmes*; but while recognising that his purpose in the *Avare* was thoroughly sane and good, and that he exhibited it very strongly, one cannot help feeling that there is a want of lively and pleasurable interest in the two girls naturally looked for in a comedy. Molière felt with them keenly enough, and he wrote his comedy very largely on their behalf. But as in the *École des Femmes*, where he thought less of bringing the lovers

together than of pointing to the folly and the selfishness of
Arnolphe, so here, in the *Avare,* he thought less of the love-
scenes between the young people than of exhibiting in all its
force the bad qualities of the father of a family. And he
believed he would best show his meaning in satire against
the beastly avarice and the selfishness of the old curmudgeon.
His grim hatred of Harpagon is unquestionable, though with
it he often creates laughter. A miser who saw the *Avare* on
the stage said of it: "One may learn a good deal from
Molière's play; it gives some excellent lessons in economy."

There is a scene between Harpagon and his son Cléante,
rivals for Mariane, concerning her, in which there is a display
of cunning against cunning; and the father, as having authority,
gets the best of the dispute. Maître Jacques intervenes and
pretends to calm them both; but this leads to a further and
very violent quarrel. What they say to each other at the end
of it must be quoted. The father cries:—

"I forbid you to see me again."—"All the better," the son
answers.—"I'll drive you out of the house."—"Drive away."—"I
renounce you for my son."—"So be it."—"I disinherit you."—"Anything you like."—"And I give you my malediction."—"I'll have
nothing to do with your gifts."

Ethical criticisms on this quarrel between the father and
the son, I believe, are for the most part out of place. Molière's
concern as a comic dramatist was not to tell people what they
ought to do, but to show what their conduct was, what their
manners were, in a spirit of comedy. In that way he might,
perhaps, teach a lesson indirectly, by his satire. The use of
satire in comedy is not merely to amuse. Part of its higher
purpose may be seen here when we recollect that if the miser
had not brought up his son with criminal harshness and
neglect his son would at least have answered him respectfully.

When Harpagon finds that his box with 10,000 écus in it
has been stolen, he is beside himself with anger and with fury.
But his passion is that of a man whose mind is crazed at the
loss of gain over which he had gloated with stupid and hideous
selfishness as the pile grew larger. He feels his pain acutely,
and he cries over it like a child. His grief has unmanned him,
and he vents it in spluttering rage. Perhaps this is a true

insight into the miser's heart. His greed for money has mastered his nature; for money he has sacrificed reputation in the world, loss of friends, the esteem of his servants, and the love and respect of his children. His long monologue, which should be read as it was spoken, was not meant to have a pleasant effect. It was meant, I think, to show weakness. It gives no indication of the force of will in a villain who has become what he is partly by strength of character. Under great misfortune, Tartuffe and Don Juan would have spoken differently. The monologue shows the howling and the snivelling of a wretch temporarily distracted by the loss of hoarded treasure. It is very difficult to say if his wild condition has been painted too strongly.

Later, Harpagon accuses his steward, Valère, of the theft, and there is a dispute between them in which, for comic purposes, Molière uses words ambiguously. The equivoque consists in Harpagon's passion for his money, and in Valère's love for Élise, the old man's daughter; and it is aided by the fact that "elle" may apply to Élise or to the cassette, the stolen money-box. Hence has come the proverbial expression, "les beaux yeux de la cassette."

The dénouement to the *Avare* is somewhat romantic, and it is not the best part of the play. Anselme appears, and it is discovered that he is the father of Valère and of Mariane. Valère had nothing to do with Harpagon's money-box; La Flèche, who had a grudge against the old man, had taken it. But it is intact. The miser is so rejoiced to get back all his treasure, that he consents to do what is asked of him, so long as he gives no money. In the course of the comedy he spoke about the gallows; many men in the 18th century, when the *Avare* was popular, would have gone gladly to see him hanging there.

The want of success of the *Avare* as a new play is certainly curious, and the more so if we accept Robinet's evidence that everybody at the time thought the comedy was well acted.[1] Perhaps the grimness and the sordidness of the principal character in the play may have made people who like to see brightness in a comedy decline to go to see what was mean and repulsive. This reason is more likely to have operated

[1] *Œuvres de Molière*, vii. 7.

against a new play than against one that had been on the stage for many years, and in which the characterisation of its chief personage had long been recognised as a masterpiece. When you know that a man has such an aversion to the word "give" that he cannot bring himself to say "I give you good day," but only "I lend you a good day,"[1] you may smile at his currishness, but at first sight his appearance is disagreeable.

Molière acted the part of Harpagon; and though the article in the *Mercure de France*, in the year 1740, quoted in a previous chapter, was founded on tradition, there is no reason to doubt its truth when it said that this was one of the rôles in high comedy that the poet played excellently on the stage. It has been assumed that because of his lameness Béjart played the part of La Flèche. There is no certainty as to the names of the actors who performed the other parts. Aimé-Martin made out a supposed list, which M. Mesnard has reprinted, but he gives another distribution of the rôles in some cases as more probable.[2]

The *Avare* was printed in February 1669, rather more than five months after it was first seen on the stage; and M. Mesnard has given a curious little bit of contemporary evidence showing that this comedy, and *George Dandin*, Molière's next play in the order of public representation, were, when printed, each sold for a franc and a half.[3]

George Dandin was acted for the first time at a fête given by the king at Versailles in the middle of July 1668.[4] The comedy has three acts, and at the end of each there was singing and dancing. The words of the songs were written by Molière, and the music was composed by Lulli. In the appendix to the comedy M. Mesnard has reprinted two contemporary official accounts of the royal fête at Versailles. On the 2nd of November following, the troop at the Palais Royal were ordered to go to Saint Germain, and there they played the same comedy three times before the court.[5]

A week later, on the 9th of November, *George Dandin* was

---

[1] Act II. sc. 4.   Scene between La Flèche and Frosine.
[2] *Œuvres de Molière*, vii. 37.
[3] *Ibid.* vii. 45 and note.
[4] *Ibid.* vi. 473.   [5] Register, 99.

acted for the first time in public; but La Grange generally called the play by its second title, *Le Mari Confondu.*[1] In chronicling the first public appearance of every other play by Molière, La Grange added a marginal note in his Register, saying: "Pièce Nouvelle de M. de Molière," but with this comedy he did not do so; though when the play was first seen at Versailles he gave as a marginal note: "*George Dandin* première fois."[2]

In writing a play to be performed before the king and his guests at Versailles, Molière had to think of some subject that would lend itself easily to amusement. He fell back upon an old farce that he had written in years gone by and which had been acted by his troop in the provinces. He transformed his own *La Jalousie du Barbouillé* into *George Dandin ou Le Mari Confondu,* and perhaps he took something from Boccaccio.[3] It seems strange that the success of the new comedy at the Palais Royal theatre was not more marked; as a matter of fact the play fared indifferently. Probably enough the singing and dancing, given at the end of each of the acts when the play was performed before the court, were omitted at the public representations.[4]

I find myself in disagreement with some French critics who have spoken more or less severely on the moral aspect of *George Dandin.* The satire in the comedy has a double meaning. It is, firstly, to laugh at George Dandin, a rich peasant and a singularly stupid man, for having married a woman of noble birth; and secondly, a more serious matter, to show the pain a woman can give her husband by her contempt for him, by her flagrant coquetry, and by her constant falsehood. Angélique, Dandin's wife, may be young and pretty, she may have certain outward fascinations; if she has other good qualities they are not seen, and she is not painted so as to create sympathy. *George Dandin* does not pretend to be high comedy in any of its scenes; its second title shows that it was meant to provoke laughter. Still, the play is not a farce, for though the incidents and the characterisation are ludicrous they are not absurd, and the events follow each

[1] Register, 99. [2] *Ibid.* 97.
[3] See M. Mesnard's Notice to *George Dandin* in the *Œuvres de Molière,* vol. vi.
[4] *Œuvres de Molière,* xi. 30.

other with a natural sequence of ideas. The comedy creates most merriment on the stage, but when read one notices more easily that it has its sorrowful side. To my mind, the *Avare* and *George Dandin* show stronger signs of sadness of heart on the part of the author than any plays that Molière wrote. It is amusing in the latter comedy to see the clever way in which the wife outwits her husband who is a dunderhead, but it is also painful because she deceives him with bad intentions. As regards the moral in the play, the crux lies there.

Both *Don Juan* and *George Dandin* afford strong instances of Molière's practice of mixing together censure and jesting, earnestness and laughter. Few writers have shown his great capacity for uniting these opposite characteristics and making each of them work into the other. His nature was deep and thoughtful, it was quite sincere ; and as he threw his mockery at George Dandin and his invective at Angélique he told plainly that though he wrote his comedy in a light manner its subject was very serious, and that it had engaged much of his thoughts. As becomes a comic dramatist, he showed his purpose through satire, but because his fun and his earnestness were so closely dovetailed, his meaning has been sometimes misunderstood. As to the charge of adultery, even in project, brought by some writers against Angélique, I think it is critically a mistake to say anything about it. She does meet her gallant clandestinely, but as to the more serious charge I doubt very much if it entered Molière's head. The first words spoken by one of the chief personages in any of Molière's comedies may often be taken as an indication of the character he wished to portray ; and in Angélique's first speech [1]—too long to be quoted now—she shows under the veil of irony what sort of woman she is and how her rôle in the comedy should be considered. It should be remembered that she is speaking before her father and her mother, and that her husband, who has brought a grave accusation against her, is also present. Translate her words literally and she seems to be a paragon of virtue ; take them for what they are worth, and you see the machinations of a shameless coquette. *George Dandin* was meant to show in the style of amusing comedy the barefaced wantonness of a married woman, how she lied to her

[1] Act I. sc. 6 in M. Mesnard's edition.

husband, jeered at him and abused him; and also to show in a ludicrous manner the egregious stupidity of the husband in the blundering way he tried to stop his wife's misconduct. You may laugh at George Dandin as much as you please, and say that he should not have been such an ass; and if Molière, who was not a purist, had been at your side he would have agreed. But if your thoughts went no further he might have been disappointed. In the double satire, surely the condemnation of the wife has a stronger meaning than the ridicule of the husband. Which is the most criminal, her falseness or his ineptitude?

The funniest part of the comedy is in the scenes between George Dandin and his wife's father and mother, Monsieur and Madame de Sotenville, and especially in their first interview. Le baron de Sotenville is described as a " gentilhomme campagnard " — a gentleman with country manners. He boasts of his long descent from an illustrious family; and his wife is equally haughty on account of her noble ancestry. They are both ridiculous examples of persons extremely proud of their blue blood; and the way they receive their son-in-law, the rich peasant, and listen to his complaints against their daughter, is shown with much drollery. So far the fun is pleasant, and you laugh merrily enough at George Dandin when he is driven to make excuses before M. and Mme. de Sotenville to Clitandre, the gallant, because he said that Clitandre had made love to his wife. Dandin's impotency to prove the truth of his complaint before his noble connections, who have cowed him, is shown in such an amusing manner that hearty laughter is irresistible. His monologue at the beginning of the play tells that he knows he has made a fool of himself in marrying into a noble family; and you recognise the truth of what he says to himself at the end of the first act: " Tu l'as voulu, George Dandin, tu l'as voulu." He has brought his punishment on his own head, and he must bear it.

But later the tone of the fun changes, when Dandin finds more and more certainly that his wife has been keeping company with Clitandre. Everybody and everything conspires against the baffled husband to show him to be in error, when in reality the wrong is not on his side. He twice brings his father-in-law and mother-in-law to witness the presence together of his wife and her gallant, but his wife by her address and her falsehood always manages to throw the blame upon him and to escape scot-free from the charge laid against her. Aided by her suivante, she insults her husband while, in apparently equivocal language, of which, however, the meaning is perfectly clear, she makes love to Clitandre, her father and mother standing by and applauding her virtue. They all jeer at the unfortunate husband, and he is so thoroughly trounced that he is made to feel and look like a beaten dog. Poor Dandin's worst fault is that he is a fool. The acme of his misery is seen in the last act. He is shamefully maltreated, reviled and made an object of derision in order to show what sort of creature is his wife. His last words are : " I give in now, for there is no help for it. When a man has married a bad woman, as I have done, the best thing he can do is to throw himself into the water, head foremost." In all of this there is certainly pathos.

To my mind this comedy was written with a strong feeling of sadness at the cruel mockery of the baffled husband, which all the laughter against him cannot efface. Compare the tone of the *Médecin Malgré Lui* with that of *George Dandin*. The former is bright and gay with sparkling wit; the humour seen in the latter exhibits anxiety and sorrow. Both plays are admirable acting comedies. Both the sham physician and the rich peasant create great amusement on the stage, but as you read, the laughter that each comedy provokes strikes different chords and arouses different feelings. In one respect *George Dandin* is a counterpart of the *Misanthrope*. There the dramatist showed in high comedy how a clever, heartless woman, by her cunning, caused great pain to a man to whom she was half-affianced ; in the other play he showed the same thought in a more popular manner, but as the target for the woman's reproaches was her husband, the poisoned arrows penetrated more deeply.

It would seem, too, that there are other comedies of Molière's which were written to complement the idea seen in a former play or to present it in another light. The plot and the personages are different, and the subject matter, also more or less different, is treated from another point of view, larger or smaller, as the case may be; and if the first play was written in verse the second was in prose, and generally in a more popular style, or vice-versâ. Large-hearted and large-minded men reveal themselves in various ways, and if we wish to understand how Molière expressed his thoughts in these comedies, we should read the plays together and conciliate their meaning. For example: the *Femmes Savantes* after the *Précieuses Ridicules*; *Don Juan* after the *Tartuffe*—in these two comedies the subject matter is changed from one extreme to another, the personage of Don Juan is in some respects the opposite to that of Tartuffe; the *Avare* after the *École des Maris* and the *École des Femmes*; and, as to the point already referred to, *George Dandin* after the *Misanthrope*.

Molière played the part of George Dandin, his wife that of Angélique, and La Thorillière that of Lubin. Aimé-Martin's surmises as to the distribution of the other rôles are probably accurate: du Croisy as M. de Sotenville, Hubert as Mme. de Sotenville, La Grange as Clitandre, Mlle. de Brie as Claudine.[1]

The original edition of *George Dandin* bears the date 1669.[2]

[1] *Œuvres de Molière*, vi. 496-98.
[2] *Ibid.* 502, 503.

CHAPTER XVII

A MONTH after the last performance of *George Dandin* as a
new play the king gave Molière permission to put the *Tartuffe* on to the stage at the Palais Royal theatre. Of that
comedy I spoke in a previous chapter, and said that as the
five acts of the play had been written and were acted before
the Prince de Condé in November 1664, it would be well for
biographical reasons to consider the comedy as written in
that year. When the ban was finally taken off the *Tartuffe*,
and when the comedy was allowed to appear in public, in the
year 1669, it was played forty-three times—the performances
lasting from the 5th of February to the 25th of June following.

The troop at the Palais Royal went to Saint Germain twice
in the month of August 1669; and on the 17th of September
they were ordered to go to Chambord, another royal residence,
where they stayed until the 20th of October. In chronicling
this visit La Grange says on page 107 of his Register: " On
y a joué, entre plusieurs comédies, le Pourceaugnac pour la
première fois." *Monsieur de Pourceaugnac* was written purposely for the entertainment of the king and his guests, and
was first played at Chambord. According to two contemporary accounts the first representation took place on the
6th of October 1669; but twenty-three years later La Grange
and Vivot, in the preface to the edition of Molière published
in 1682, lead one to suppose that it was acted for the first
time in the month of September. The discrepancy in the
dates may be accounted for by accepting a fair supposition
thrown out by M. Mesnard: that the play was written
hurriedly at Chambord in the month of September.[1] La

[1] *Œuvres de Molière*, vii. 211-13.

Grange had gone to Chambord with his comrades ; and if Molière did not write his comedy until he got to Chambord, La Grange knew such to be the fact, though after twenty-three years he had forgotten the date of the first representation of the play. There is no doubt that this comedy was first acted in public on the 15th of November following.

Monsieur de Pourceaugnac was clearly intended as a piece of wild buffoonery. The play is full of practical jokes against a rich gentleman of Limoges, whose intelligence is " of the thickest kind that is made." He has come to Paris with a full idea of his own importance, equipped most absurdly, but, as he thinks, like a courtier in a country dress, in order to marry a girl about whom he knows nothing and whose father he has never seen. The unlucky provincial has his good points, but these do not prevent him from being trounced with all the ridicule of farce in every possible manner. The mockery seems to be cruel in spite of the open laughter it creates, and the dramatist has been accused of personal motives of revenge. Anecdotes to this effect are not wanting. It has been said that Molière wished to retaliate upon the people of Limoges because they had, twelve or more years previously, hissed his acting in a tragedy ; but it is not known that Molière and his troop had ever gone to Limoges. It is said, too, that not long before the date of the comedy a gentilhomme limousin had a quarrel on the stage with the actors at the Palais Royal theatre, and that in consequence Molière made a gentilhomme limousin bear the brunt of his satire. We read also that the play was directed against a newly made marquis who was in Paris at the time. But newly made nobles were then common in France. Many of them had gained their titles to nobility because they were clever, unscrupulous, and wealthy. M. de Pourceaugnac was hardly like them. He was certainly not clever, and though his name does not sound refined he had more idea of showing consideration to others than had many of the newly fledged nobles. Though he has come to Paris imagining that because he is rich and because he is a person of importance in Limoges he can marry a Parisian girl as he would buy a house, he is a man with some delicacy of feeling. His chief characteristic is that he is a simpleton. His foible is that he wants to be thought distinguished; and he does distinguish himself effectually by his folly and by his credulity. The inhabitants of the Limousin were not thought then to be the most wide-awake people in France. Molière had been among them and knew what they were like. And one may easily imagine that with his strong love of ridicule he should have pitched upon a silly gentleman from Limoges as the object of his raillery when he wanted to amuse the king and the royal party at Chambord. M. de Pourceaugnac is kindly by nature, he has no bad faults, and in reading his luckless adventures on his arrival in Paris you feel a compassion for him. You almost pity him in his misfortunes, though you cannot help laughing at the preposterous way he is treated. Trick after trick is played upon him, until the poor man does not know whether he is standing on his head or his heels. The doctors of medicine also come in for their share in the satire. You enjoy the ridicule in the play, in spite of its wildness and its buffoonery; and you feel unconsciously that the style is so well adapted to the incidents and to the personages that the farce seems to be shown in a manner almost worthy of comedy. There are, however, two scenes (Act II. scs. 7 and 8) written in strong patois which is difficult for a foreigner to understand; some editors of Molière have translated them into French. Taschereau [1] reports a saying of Diderot's: "Si l'on croit qu'il y a beaucoup plus d'hommes capables de faire *Pourceaugnac* que le *Misanthrope,* on se trompe."

In Act II. sc. 10 of the comedy Molière made use of very technical legal terms known only to professional lawyers, and French writers have been surprised that he should have employed them with strict accuracy.[2] The fact may perhaps afford a kind of evidence that the poet had not forgotten his own reading of law-books more than twenty-five years previously. It is more probable, however, that he did not depend altogether upon his own recollections. We have seen in Act II. sc. 2 of the *Fâcheux* that Molière had been able to assimilate to his own use, after some assistance given, the highly technical terms used in his long description of a stag-hunt; therefore it need not be surprising, if some assistance were again given,

---

[1] *Vie de Molière,* 3rd ed. 149.
[2] *Œuvres de Molière,* vii. 314 note 1; 315 note 1.

that he should have been able to assimilate equally well a few lines of the technical language of lawyers. However that may be, in the first scene of the comedy M. de Pourceaugnac is spoken of as an "avocat de Limoges." And in the third scene of the first act he says boastingly that he had read law. But in Act II. sc. 10 he wishes to be thought a fine gentleman and not a lawyer; and though he then quotes fluently and accurately the technical terms of penal jurisprudence, he denies that he has learned the practice of the courts, and says that he "recollected the words from reading them in novels." If that were the case, his intelligence must have developed suddenly to a marvellous extent.

In spite of the farce in *Monsieur de Pourceaugnac*, the absurdities in the play are shown in the spirit of laughable comedy. But it may be well to repeat here a few words of Molière's "Avis au lecteur" when he printed his *Amour Médecin*. "It is not necessary to warn you that there are things that depend upon the action. Everybody knows that comedies are only written to be acted; and I do not advise people to read this one unless, while they are reading, they can imagine all the play of the scenes." The dancing at the end of each act of *Monsieur de Pourceaugnac*, and the songs which had been set to music by Lulli,[1] must have added to the pleasure of the entertainment. When the comedy was put on the stage at the Palais Royal it was heartily welcomed. It was played twenty times, on the whole with good receipts; and except at the first performance, when the *Sicilien* was given on the same day, the new comedy was always played alone.

I have said nothing of the various personages in this comedy, but will give here, as I have done generally with Molière's other comedies, the names of the actors who played their parts in it for the first time. Molière himself took the rôle of M. de Pourceaugnac. For the other parts the distribution made by Aimé-Martin is the most accurate that can be depended upon now:—Béjart as Oronte, Mlle. Molière as Julie, La Grange as Éraste, Madeleine Béjart as Nérine, Hubert as Lucette, du Croisy as Sbrigani.[2] This last is, after the title rôle, the most important part in the play.

The original edition of *Monsieur de Pourceaugnac* bears the

[1] *Œuvres de Molière*, xi. 35.   [2] *Ibid.* vii. 228.

date 1670; the printing of the comedy was completed on the 3rd of March in that year.[1]

From a comic point of view there is little to be said about Molière's next play, *Les Amants Magnifiques*. It formed the chief attraction of a fête known as "Le Divertissement Royal," given by Louis XIV. at Saint Germain during the carnival of 1670. Molière wrote for this fête a semi-mythological comedy in five acts in prose, in which there is some small satire on judicial astrology. But the principal features of the entertainment were in the interludes between the acts in which there was music, dancing, and a display of bright and pretty costumes. The play was seen for the first time at Saint Germain on the 4th of February 1670, and four more performances were given at court in the course of the next few weeks.[2] But as the comedy in the play was very slight, and as its representation in public with the costumes worn in the interludes would have entailed considerable expense, Molière never put this play on to the stage at the Palais Royal. It was not printed until after his death, in 1682. It was, however, given in public in the year 1688 at the theatre known afterwards as the Comédie Française—for many years the only regular theatre in Paris. Before the death of Louis XIV. in 1715, it had been acted there altogether forty-one times, though whether with or without the interludes is not known.[3]

At Easter 1670 there were some changes in the troop at the Palais Royal theatre that were of importance to the actors there. Béjart retired from the stage. He was still just under forty years of age, and he had given eleven years' service in Paris; as his retirement was due to a wound he had received in the performance of his daily duties, his comrades granted him a pension of 1000 livres a year. Béjart then left the troop. In chronicling the fact, La Grange says: "This pension was the first one created [at the Palais Royal theatre] following the practice of pensions given to actors at the Hôtel de Bourgogne."[4] Baron's name has been mentioned already.

[1] *Œuvres de Molière*, vii. 231 ; xi. 35.
[2] *Ibid.* vii. 360.   [3] *Ibid.* i. 548 ; vii. 374.
[4] Register, 111. For the system of retiring pensions, see *ante*, chap. ix. pp. 230-31.

At Easter 1670 he was with a strolling company of actors in Burgundy, but a lettre de cachet was sent to him ordering his presence in Paris. Michel Baron was born in October 1653, so that at the time which concerns us now he was only sixteen years old. His father and mother had been actors, and he had been brought up, so to say, on the stage. Molière had seen him when he was a small boy acting in a troop composed of children, and perceived at once that the lad had strong histrionic talents. The poet was kind to him, took him into his own house to live with him, and gave him lessons in the art of acting. Young Baron had taken the part of Myrtil in Molière's pastoral comedy *Mélicerte*, acted at Saint Germain in December 1666, and Mlle. Molière played the title rôle in the comedy. On some occasion in connection with the play, whether because the boy was impertinent to Mlle. Molière, or from haughtiness on her part, or from both reasons, she gave him a box on the ear. Young Baron's pride and anger were roused; he ran away from his benefactor and re-entered the small and poor troop in which he had been when Molière first saw him. There he remained for some three years or more until the same kindly hand again delivered him. The lad seems to have recognised that he had been foolish, for he spoke of his former protector with marks of gratitude; and when he received a lettre de cachet ordering him to go to Paris, he got at the same time an affectionate letter from Molière, who went to meet him on his arrival. Though Baron was very young, he became at Easter 1670 a member of the troop at the Palais Royal theatre, and one share in its concerns was allotted to him. He died in 1729, but had retired from the stage some years previously. He is said to have been a great actor, especially in tragedy. He was the author of several comedies, of which the best known is *L'Homme à Bonnes Fortunes*. In writing this play he probably drew a good deal from his own experiences among women.

There were two other accessions to the Palais Royal theatre at Easter 1670. La Grange says that two months after Molière had sent for Baron he sent for Beauval and his wife, both of whom had been in the same provincial company with Baron. Mlle. Beauval was a very intelligent actress, and to her was given a whole share in the profits of the theatre in

Paris; but her husband, who was little better than a ninny, got only half a share. Out of his half share, for the first two years, Beauval had to pay half of the pension allowed to Béjart, and three livres each day the theatre was open to Châteauneuf, a hired servant hitherto paid by the troop; while for the last year he was at the Palais Royal he had to pay the whole of Béjart's pension.[1] It has been said that Mlle. Beauval was haughty and imperious, far from pretty, and that she married her husband because he was a fool. The following story seems to show, however, that Beauval had a sort of unreasoning sense seen sometimes in a very simple-minded person. In the *Malade Imaginaire* he took the part of Thomas Diafoirus, a newly fledged doctor of medicine and a greenhorn. Molière was one day directing the rehearsal of his comedy, and he found fault generally with the acting of the members of the troop. Mlle. Beauval answered her teacher with some warmth: " You are scolding us all round, but you do not say a word to my husband." Molière replied: " I should be very sorry to do so, for I should spoil his play. Nature has given him much better lessons than I can do for the part he has to perform."

At the king's command the troop at the Palais Royal left Paris on the 3rd of November 1670 for Chambord, where the court then was, and they stayed there until the 28th of the month. On the 14th they acted the *Bourgeois Gentilhomme* for the first time. Before they left Chambord three more performances of the comedy were demanded: on the 16th, the 20th, and the 21st.[2] Some days later the actors were called to Saint Germain, and there three more performances of the same comedy were given before the court: on the 9th, the 11th, and the 13th of November.[3] La Grange's Register says that the play appeared for the first time in public at the Palais Royal theatre on the 23rd of November in the same year.

We have seen that during Molière's lifetime his best comedies, as ordinarily understood, were performed at court much less often than his light plays that were written chiefly to cause laughter or to give an occasion for spectacular dis-

---

[1] La Grange's Register, 111, 113.   [2] *Œuvres de Molière*, viii. 1-6.
[3] L. Moland, *Œuvres de Molière*, 2nd ed. x. 241.

play. Molière worked very hard to please Louis XIV., and the *Bourgeois Gentilhomme* was another of the comédies-ballets written to order for the amusement of the king and the royal guests. In all of these plays the poet devised a light comedy that would lend itself to a show of gaiety in the interludes between the acts, and to a splendour in the costumes of the personages who took their parts in the interludes. He accepted the splendour as a necessary part of the entertainment, but amusement coming from the mirth of comedy was more natural to him; and in most of the plays that he wrote at the royal command he strove to make his satire serve some purpose. The *Bourgeois Gentilhomme* should be taken as it was meant, as a very ludicrous comedy composed for a court festivity. The follies of M. Jourdain are shown with strong caricature; yet the characterisation in the caricature in the first four acts of the comedy is so lifelike that the picture appears to be true in spite of its exaggerations. If that be the case, the imaginary portrait is not farcical. But it should be remembered that the character of M. Jourdain, as seen in the first four acts of the comedy, was meant to lead up to and fit in with the grotesque extravaganza which follows. The interludes between the acts were meant as complementary humorous illustrations of what had taken place in the comedy, and as spectacular shows they were no doubt pretty and graceful. Lulli composed the airs for the songs, and his music was much admired. The grotesque extravaganza at the end of the fourth act was really the kernel of the *Bourgeois Gentilhomme*, and I cannot speak of it out of its place; but as far as the comedy in the play is concerned, the idea in drawing the character of M. Jourdain was to ridicule in a preposterous manner the crazes of a childish and most ignorant man, haunted by self-love and by egregious vanity, who wished to imitate the habits of people in a rank of life above his own. Such foibles were not new in Molière's day, and he did not suppose that he could cure them any more than he could prevent thunderstorms. It was, however, open to him to portray in the spirit of laughable comedy the vagaries of a man whose ambition led him to dress himself in peacock's feathers. If that be frivolity, it is also a fair subject for comic satire. Everything depends on the execution. The plot in the play is so slight that no one takes thought of it. What interests is the comic manner in which the satire is shown.

It is to be remarked that the raillery against M. Jourdain is nowhere ill-natured. He is laughed at by his masters, mocked by his servant and bamboozled by others; but the ridicule against him is not unkind. The strongest sarcasm he has to bear is from his wife, and it must be admitted that she has ground for complaint. She is wronged, though not seriously, and if she did not get angry or showed no temper she would be an abettor in his faults. Pretentiousness is one of the marks of vulgarity. And we all feel, with as little unkindness as possible, that with his crazy ambitions M. Jourdain could not help being a vulgar man, and that he showed his vulgarity most strongly when he should have least desired to do so. But his pretentiousness is so ludicrous and is exhibited in such a frank and childish way that instead of causing disgust it creates hearty laughter. We take it as we find it and really enjoy the comedy seen. Though his speech was meant to betray an ignorance of good breeding, it would be a mistake to criticise it closely. The dramatist thought of the fun in his play, and he wished to show the satire in his comedy in a healthy and amusing manner. M. Jourdain is not a bad-thinking or a nasty-minded man; nobody really dislikes him. Molière speaks no evil of him, calls him by no hard names; he shows his foolish crazes in a strong light, so that everybody may be amused at them. As regards silly vanities that injured nobody, that was the way in this and other comedies, that Molière chose to moralise over them. No other course was fairly open to him. The comic dramatist may laugh at nonsense so that others shall see its folly, he may show bad faults through the satire of comedy so that others shall regret them or condemn them; but he must not preach to his audience. To give a comic exhibition is his function, and any lesson that he wishes to teach must be by comic presentation. Without some lesson, without some moral shown, no comedy will attain a high rank; but the teaching should be done by laughter. And genial laughter that raises one's spirits and makes one rejoice is more likely to be effectual on the stage and to be better remembered than wit that pleases only by its cleverness or by its pungency. A critic in his arm-chair, or many a young man talking to his friends, thinks he likes wit that sparkles and that titillates his brain by brilliant dashes. But the audience in a theatre are emotional in another and more natural way; they look rather to have their affections aroused, either by love or by hatred, and to have their sympathies gratified by what they see and hear.

Monsieur Jourdain is certainly forty years old; yet he has engaged the services of a music-master, a dancing-master, a fencing-master, and of a teacher of philosophy. "Visions of nobility and of gallantry" have got into his head, and he wishes to appear like a person of quality. When first seen, his music and his dancing-masters are with him. He is gorgeously clothed, and he wears a new-fashioned dressing-gown called an "Indienne." This was an expensive piece of luxury, and no child was ever prouder of a new frock than M. Jourdain is of his Indienne. He has taken it off; but when a song is being sung he puts it on again, then takes it off, and again puts it on—"in order to hear better." Though he has a daughter of a marriageable age his visions of nobility and of gallantry make him think he has fallen in love with a certain marchioness, Dorimène; and he wishes to be taught how to make a bow to her. His dancing-master says: "If you desire to present yourself very respectfully, you should first make a bow backwards, then walk towards her, making three bows, and the last one should be as low as her knees."

M. Jourdain's music-master and his dancing-master had both extolled their arts as being useful to the government of mankind. They had done so quietly and with moderation. But the fencing-master is an authoritative person. He is very noisy as he gives his instructions to M. Jourdain how to hold himself when the foil is in his hand.

"*Maître d'Armes.*

"I have told you already that the whole secret of fencing consists in two things: to hit and not to be hit. And as I showed you the other day by demonstrative reasoning, it is impossible that you should be hit if you know how to parry your enemy's sword from the line of your body; and this depends only on a slight inward or outward movement of the wrist.

"*M. Jourdain.*

"So that a man, though he have no courage, is sure to kill his adversary and not to be killed by him.

" Maître d'Armes.

" Of course. Did you not see the demonstration ?

" M. Jourdain.

" Yes.

" Maître d'Armes.

" And it is in this that one perceives the consideration that should be shown in a State to us professors, and how vastly superior is the science of arms to all other useless sciences, like dancing, music, etc."

Such arrogance cannot be borne by the other two teachers. At first the three masters wrangle together, then they come to blows. While the scrimmage is going on the master of philosophy arrives. He tries to calm them, but is soon drawn into the quarrel. Then all the four professors get to fisticuffs and call each other by the ugliest names they can find. M. Jourdain for one moment is wise. He says : " Fight now as much as you like. I can't prevent it, and I am not going to have my clothes torn in trying to separate you."

Of all the lessons given to M. Jourdain by his numerous masters, that by the master of philosophy is the most amusing. The middle-aged pupil is ridiculously ignorant, but the childish way in which he shows his ignorance is remarkable. He can understand that there are five vowels; and when he is told how they are pronounced he is in ecstasy at the beautiful learning displayed. But he is angry with himself at not having studied all this before, and very angry with his father and mother for not having taught him. He wants to write a letter to a person of great quality, and is astonished when he hears that his letter must be in verse or in prose. And he is more astonished at hearing that when he says to his servant: " Nicole, bring me my slippers and my nightcap," he is talking prose. He exclaims : " By George ! For more than forty years I have been talking prose without knowing it." As to the letter, he wishes to say : " Belle Marquise, vos beaux yeux me font mourir d'amour." He will have no other words than these, but he desires to put them in a very gallant manner. So his master inverts them nonsensically in five different ways. All of these inversions are purposely ridiculous, but M. Jourdain did not know the sense from the nonsense. When he is told that what he said at first was the best form of expression, he cries : " I have never studied, but I said that the first go off!" Those of us who are old enough to remember the absurdities of Lord Dundreary and how we laughed and laughed at Sothern's acting in the part may have an idea of Molière counterfeiting his own M. Jourdain.

After his lesson M. Jourdain is waited upon by a tailor and his assistant. They bring him a coat which the chief pronounces to be a masterpiece. M. Jourdain is disconcerted for a moment because he discovers that the flowers on the coat are set with the stalks upwards. Even were this a workman's blunder, he is appeased when the tailor tells him that all persons of quality have the flowers on their coats placed in that way. As he is going to put on his coat, the tailor stops him :—

"Stay, you must not do it like that. I have brought my men to dress you with the accompaniment of music. These sort of coats are put on ceremoniously. Now then, men, come in. Put on Monsieur's coat in the way that you do with persons of quality."

["Four tailor's workmen appear ; two strip M. Jourdain of the haut-de-chausses that he had worn during his lessons, and two others take off his shirt (camisole). Then they all put on his new coat, and he walks about between them to show it off, and to let them see that it fits well. During this performance a full orchestra is playing."]

There follows another bit of drollery in which the nonsense rises higher and higher. M. Jourdain is asked to give the workmen something to drink, and he is addressed as "Mon Gentilhomme." The title tickles his vanity, and he gives money; then he is thanked as "Monseigneur"; he is more delighted, and he gives more money; then he is thanked as "Votre Grandeur." He can hardly hold himself. He exclaims :—

"'Votre Grandeur!' Oh ! oh ! oh ! Wait, don't go away. To me, 'Votre Grandeur !' My word, if he goes up to Altesse he'll get the whole of my purse.'"

At the end of the second act there is an interlude in which the four tailor's workmen dance about in a sportive manner to show their joy at the handsome liberalities of the rich bourgeois.

The scene of the comedy is laid in Paris; and when M. Jourdain is next seen he tells two lackeys to follow him as he walks through the town to show his coat, adding that they must walk close behind him so that people can see they belong to him. Before he goes out, Nicole, the family servant, comes to him; and when she sees her master she bursts out into incontrollable laughter. It is his get-up, and especially his new coat, that moves her hilarity. "Hi, hi, hi. Comme vous voilà bâti! Hi, hi, hi." Perhaps others have felt with me that Nicole's laughter here is very infectious. She says little, indeed she can hardly speak; but her few words, joined to her master's astonishment and his annoyance at finding himself an object of ridicule, produce a singularly comical effect. When she finds that she cannot stop herself she says: "Well, sir, beat me if you like, but let me laugh my fill. That will do me more good." And off she goes again. But when M. Jourdain tells her that she is to get the house ready for company her laughter stops instantly. She does not like her master's company, and tells him so plainly.

When Madame Jourdain sees her husband she shows her surprise at his folly by anger and disgust. She rallies him, and Nicole joins in the banter against her master. M. Jourdain tries to turn the raillery against himself by showing his wife that she does not know that she is talking prose—she, poor woman, being as ignorant of prose and verse as her husband had been—and by telling Nicole how to pronounce the letter U. He then tries to instruct Nicole in the art of fencing by "demonstrative reasoning"; but when she has given him several thrusts he is indignant because she has not followed the rules.

Madame Jourdain is a plain-thinking woman, and she speaks her mind freely. "Visions of nobility and of gallantry" have no meaning for her, and she condemns her husband for his infatuation for the count—Dorante.

"*Madame Jourdain.*

"Yes, he shows you kindness and caresses you, but he borrows your money.

"*M. Jourdain.*

"Well, is it not an honour for me to lend money to a man of that rank? And can I do less for a lord who calls me his dearest friend?"

Madame Jourdain does not like the count; she knows him better than he knows her. As soon as she perceives him she says : " He is coming again, perhaps for another loan. I feel that I have dined when I see him." In other words, " I hate the sight of him." Dorante, or the count, is exceedingly amused at M. Jourdain's appearance.

" Dorante.

" That coat gives you a most splendid air, and we have few young men at court better dressed than you.

" M. Jourdain.

" He ! he !

" Madame Jourdain (aside).

" He scratches him where he itches.

" Dorante.

" Turn round a bit. Prodigiously smart, indeed !

" Madame Jourdain (aside).

" Yes ; as big a fool behind as in front."

Dorante is very plausibly polite in his manners ; he would pay his respects to Madame Jourdain, but she will not accept his soft words. Of course he has come to borrow more money. Childish and ignorant as M. Jourdain is, he enumerates seven instances of his lending money to Dorante, and he tells the amount lent on each occasion.

" M. Jourdain.

" Total sum, 15,800 livres.

" Dorante.

" The total sum is accurate : 15,800 livres. And add to that the two hundred pistoles [2200 l.] that you are going to lend me now ; that will make exactly 18,000 francs, which I will pay you on the first opportunity."

The nincompoop goes out to fetch the two hundred pistoles, and Dorante is left with Madame Jourdain. He tries his courtier-like manners on her, and she answers him as he deserves.

The reader may recollect that Molière had introduced lovers' quarrels into two of his earlier comedies, the *Dépit Amoureux* and the *Tartuffe*. In the *Bourgeois Gentilhomme* he reverted to the same idea. But the lovers' tiff in the last play is not so interesting as the scene preceding it, in which there is a supposed portrait of the poet's wife—in Act III. and sc. 9 in

M. Mesnard's edition.[1] The portrait is found in a dialogue between Cléonte, a personage in the comedy, and his valet Covielle. Cléonte is in love with Lucile, M. Jourdain's daughter, and though he has quarrelled with his mistress, he gives a description of her charms such as could have been traced only by a lover's hand. Nevertheless, French writers on Molière have generally accepted the idea that in the description of Lucile the poet was drawing a likeness, perhaps with some of the licence allowed in comedy, of his own wife, whom he always continued to love in spite of her failings. The portrait begins at the end of a speech by Covielle :—

" In the first place, her eyes are small.

" *Cléonte.*

" That is true, her eyes are small ; but they are full of fire, and they are the most brilliant, the most piercing, eyes in the world, the most touching that ever were seen.

" *Covielle.*

" Her mouth is large.

" *Cléonte.*

" Yes, but there are charms in it that one does not see in other mouths. When you look at it you are filled with longing. No other mouth was ever so inviting, so winsome.

" *Covielle.*

" She is not very tall.

" *Cléonte.*

" No, but her form is easy and very graceful.

" *Covielle.*

" She affects a want of animation in her speech and in her actions.

" *Cléonte.*

" That is true, but with it she shows a grace of her own ; and her engaging manners have an indefinable charm in the way they creep into one's heart.

" *Covielle.*

" As to her wit . . .

" *Cléonte.*

" Oh ! she has that, Covielle, of the finest and most delicate kind.

---

[1] *Œuvres de Molière*, viii. 130-32. Also viii. 26 note 2 ; and after this note see vol. xi. 308 (last paragraph) and 309 with references.

" *Covielle.*

" Her conversation . . .

" *Cléonte.*

" Her conversation is charming.

" *Covielle.*

" She is always serious.

" *Cléonte.*

" Must you have full-blown gaiety, joyfulness that is always brimming over ?   And can there be anything more insufferable than those women who laugh at every word that is spoken ?

" *Covielle.*

" At any rate, no one can be more capricious than she is.

" *Cléonte.*

" Yes, she is capricious, I allow, but everything becomes a beauty ; one tolerates everything from a beauty.

" *Covielle.*

" If that is to be the way of it, I think that you will always be in love with her."

The quarrel between Cléonte and Lucile is given in the next scene ; and, in the *Bourgeois Gentilhomme*, as in the *Dépit Amoureux*, because the master and mistress choose to fall out, their servants, Covielle and Nicole, think they will have their wrangle also.   I need only give the last words spoken by each of the male personages, after peace has been made :—

" *Cléonte.*

" Ah Lucile ! with one word from your mouth you know how to pacify my heart.   How easily we allow ourselves to be persuaded by those whom we love !

" *Covielle.*

" How quickly one is wheedled by those devilish animals ! "

Madame Jourdain is glad to welcome Cléonte as a future son-in-law, but when the young man makes his demand formally to Lucile's father, M. Jourdain replies : " Sir, before giving you an answer, I must beg of you to tell me if you are a gentilhomme."   Cléonte refuses to give himself the title of gentilhomme because he does not think he has a right to bear it. M. Jourdain replies: "Shake hands, sir; my daughter is not for you." This is an amusing trait, showing how M. Jourdain was governed by his infatuation. His wife rebukes him, and he replies hotly: "Those are just the sentiments of a small mind, to wish to remain always among the people. Don't answer me now. My daughter shall be a marchioness iu spite of everybody, and if you make me angry she shall be a duchess."

Hitherto the follies of M. Jourdain have been ludicrous, but he was more at fault in what he meant as love for Dorimène. No doubt he was in earnest in what he said to her, but one looks upon this piece of infatuation less as a fault than as a craze because the lady was a marchioness. If she thought of him at all it was only with amusement. The satire against Dorante was more serious. Though a count and a courtier, he was thoroughly dishonest. He is a type of a rogue who goes through the world smiling. He makes Dorimène believe that the diamond M. Jourdain had sent her was a present to her from himself; and he takes advantage of M. Jourdain's foible for Dorimène to allow her to think that the supper given to her by M. Jourdain, and in his house, was given by him (Dorante). M. Jourdain was a fool and may be laughed at, though his wife had cause for other feelings than laughter when she comes into her own dining-room, and finds that while she had been sent to dine with her sister her husband was entertaining another lady most sumptuously. For she did not believe one word of Dorante's excuses. But if M. Jourdain was a fool, Dorante was a knave. The courtier borrows the rich tradesman's money, makes dishonest use of his over-credulity for his own profit, and jeers at him because he has very bourgeois manners. Dorante's knavery is shown lightly, for in a play where the essence of the comedy lies in the laughter coming from the satire of ridicule it would have been scarcely possible to condemn trickeries except by laughter. This Molière knew how to do excellently, and he showed the knave and the fool side by side. The *Bourgeois Gentilhomme* was written to order, to be played before the king and his court, and few authors would have had Molière's courage in thus attacking a courtier who, in the play, boasts of his near approach to the king's person.

In Molière's previous comédies-ballets the dancing, with the costumes of the personages and the music, had been subservient to the comedy in the plays, though made to harmonise with it; whereas in the *Bourgeois Gentilhomme* the comedy was planned to harmonise with the spectacular exhibition seen in the interlude at the end of the fourth act, and known as "La Cérémonie Turque." It is well to bear this last fact in mind, in view of the characterisation of the principal personage in the comedy. For it was the idea of the masquerade that gave rise to the conception of M. Jourdain; and Molière had to create a personage that would fall in with the masquerade of the Turkish ceremony. The vain bourgeois knew nothing about his coming honours until they were pressed upon him.

In relating here shortly how the Turkish ceremony came to be planned I am naturally altogether under obligations to French writers on Molière. In December 1669 the chevalier Laurent d'Arvieux, who had long lived in the East, was called to Saint Germain to give the king a description of his travels and of Turkish manners. He says in his *Mémoires* that "the king and Madame de la Vallière laughed moderately at his account, but that the laughter of Monsieur (the king's brother) might have been heard two hundred yards away." From his description arose the conception of the *Bourgeois Gentilhomme*. Louis XIV. asked Molière to write a play in which a Turkish ceremony, shown in a burlesque manner, should appear in the interludes. The chevalier d'Arvieux, and Lulli, who had written the music for most of Molière's earlier comédies - ballets, were called upon to give the dramatist their assistance. M. Mesnard quotes from the chevalier's *Mémoires*:—

"His Majesty commanded me to co-operate with MM. Molière and de Lulli in composing a stage play which should show something of Turkish dress and of Turkish manners. I therefore went to the village of Auteuil, where M. de Molière had a very pretty house, and there we set to work at the play known in the Œuvres de Molière under the title of *Le Bourgeois Gentilhomme*, who becomes a Turk in order to marry the daughter of the Grand Seigneur. I was to be responsible for the Turkish dresses and for the description of Turkish manners. When the play was finished it was shown to the king, who was pleased with it, and I remained eight days with Baraillon, a master tailor, giving instructions about Turkish clothes and turbans. Everything was taken off to Chambord; the play was performed in the month of September, and it amused the king and the whole of the court." [1]

D'Arvieux's memory deceived him when he said that M. Jourdain became a Turk in order to marry the daughter of the Grand Seigneur; it was the son of the Grand Turk who married M. Jourdain's daughter. Baraillon was the tailor employed habitually by the actors at the Palais Royal theatre.

M. Jourdain is left alone, unhappy, after his wife had disturbed his small supper-party. He is startled by the appearance of Covielle (Cléonte's valet) disguised as a traveller, who tells him that he had known him as a child, and that he had been intimate with his father, who was a very well-bred gentleman.

" *M. Jourdain.*

"What do you say?

" *Covielle.*

"I say that he was a very well-bred gentleman.

" *M. Jourdain.*

"My father?

" *Covielle.*

"Yes.

. . . .

" *M. Jourdain.*

"There are foolish people who tell me that he was a merchant.

" *Covielle.*

"He a merchant! That is pure slander. He never was one. All that he did was to be very obliging and show kind services to others. And as he was an excellent judge of stuffs, he went everywhere to choose them, had them sent to his house, and gave them to his friends in exchange for money."

M. Jourdain's vanity and his childishness have been shown, and here he was flattered in his tenderest point. Covielle goes on to say that he has been a great traveller and that he has to announce grand news.

" *Covielle.*

"You know that the son of the Grand Turk is here. . . . And what is honourable for you is that he is in love with your daughter.

---

[1] *Œuvres de Molière*, viii. 11, 12; L. Moland, *Œuvres de Molière*, 2nd ed. x. 237.

"*M. Jourdain.*

"The son of the Grand Turk?

"*Covielle.*

"Yes; and he wants to be your son-in-law.

"*M. Jourdain.*

"The son of the Grand Turk my son-in-law!

"*Covielle.*

"The son of the Grand Turk your son-in-law. When I went to see him . . . he said to me: '*Acciam croc soler ouch alla moustaph gidelum amanahem varahini oussere carbulath*'; in other words: 'Haven't you seen a pretty young girl, the daughter of Monsieur Jourdain, gentilhomme parisien?'

"*M. Jourdain.*

"The son of the Grand Turk said that of me?

"*Covielle.*

"Yes. When I told him that I knew you intimately and that I had seen your daughter, he said to me, '*marababa sahem*,' or 'Ah! how deeply I am in love with her.'

"*M. Jourdain.*

"'*Marababa sahem*' means 'Ah! how deeply I am in love with her'? . . . Faith, you do well to tell me so. For I should never have thought that '*marababa sahem*' means 'Ah! how deeply I am in love with her.' What a fine language Turkish is!

.   .   .   .

"*Covielle.*

"Well, to finish my embassy, he desires your daughter in marriage; and that he may have a father-in-law worthy of himself he means to make you *Mamamouchi*, which is a certain great dignity in his country.

"*M. Jourdain.*

"*Mamamouchi?*

"*Covielle.*

"Yes, *Mamamouchi*; or in our language Paladin. . . . There is nothing higher than that in the world, and you will be on an equality with the greatest lords of the earth."

This nonsense is so good that no one is surprised that M. Jourdain should take it for sense. His enchantment has begun and he is in fairyland. Cléonte (Covielle's master) appears dressed as a Turk followed by three pages bearing his long train; and he and Covielle begin to talk pretended Turkish. Except a few words everything they say is pure gibberish.[1]

" Covielle.

" *Ossa binamen sadoc babally oracaf ouram.*

" Cléonte.

" *Bel-men.*

" Covielle.

"He says you must go with him immediately to prepare for the ceremony, so that you may see your daughter and conclude the marriage.

" M. Jourdain.

"So many things in two words?

" Covielle.

"Yes, the Turkish language is like that; it says much in a few words. Go with him wherever he wishes."

We come now to the Turkish ceremony, which takes place in the interlude between the fourth and the fifth act. As the play was devised with a view to showing the Turkish ceremony in a burlesque manner, and as it would be difficult to summarise the description satisfactorily, I give it as printed by M. Mesnard from the original edition of the play. After Molière's death La Grange published in 1682 a longer version of the ceremony; and M. Mesnard has printed this other reading also, believing that it was either written by Molière or accepted by him, and may be taken as authentic [2]:—

"The Mufty, four Dervishes, six Turks dancing, six Turks playing, and others playing on instruments in a Turkish fashion, are the actors in this ceremony.

"The Mufty invokes Mahomet with the twelve Turks and the four Dervishes; then the Bourgeois is brought before him dressed as a Turk, without turban and without sabre, and the Mufty sings these words to him :—

" Se ti sabir,[3]
Ti respondir ;

---

[1] *Œuvres de Molière*, viii. 171 note 2.

[2] *Ibid.* viii. 183, first par. ; xi. 37.

[3] In a note after this line on p. 185, M. Mesnard quotes the opinion of a modern traveller who says that this patois of Molière's is like the language still spoken by the people on the Mediterranean between Algiers and Marseilles. It is a mixture of Arab, Turkish, Maltese, French, Italian, and Spanish—a kind of pigeon French.

> *Se non sabir,*
> *Tazir, tazir.*
> *Mi star Mufti :*
> *Ti, qui star ti ?*
> *Non intendir,*
> *Tazir, tazir.*[1]

"In the same language the Mufty asks the Turks who are assisting of what religion is the Bourgeois, and they assure him he is Mahometan. The Mufty invokes Mahomet in lingua franca, and sings the following words :—

> " *Mahametta per Giourdina*
> *Mi pregar sera é mattina :*
> *Voler far un Paladina*
> *Dé Giourdina, dé Giourdina.*
> *Dar turbanta, é dar scarcina,*
> *Con galera é brigantina,*
> *Per deffender Palestina.*[2]
> *Mahametta,* etc.

"The Mufty asks the Turks if the Bourgeois will be firm in the Mahometan religion, and he sings these words :—

> "*Star bon Turca Giourdina ?*[3]

> "THE TURKS.

> "*Hi valla.*[4]

"THE MUFTY dances, and sings these words :—

> "*Hu la ba ba la chou ba la ba ba la da.*[5]

The Turks answer in the same words. The Mufty proposes to give the turban to the Bourgeois, and sings the following words :—

> "*Ti non star furba ?*

> "THE TURKS.

> "*No, no, no.*

---

[1] I give English translations of Molière's patois taken from M. Mesnard's literal French translation of the lines.—"If you know, you answer ; if you do not know, be silent, be silent. I am Mufty : you, who are you? You do not understand : be silent, be silent."

[2] "Mahomet, for Jourdain, I will pray night and morning. Will make a Paladin of Jourdain, of Jourdain. Give turban and give scimitar, with galley and brigantine, to defend Palestine."

[3] "Be a good Turk, Jourdain?"

[4] "Yes, certainly"; literally, "I affirm it by God."

[5] M. Mesnard thinks that this line of twelve syllables was meant only as nonsense. But Auger (who published a valuable critical edition of Molière in 1819) thought that by altering the syllables a little three real Turkish words could be seen : *Allah, baba, hou*; which mean "God, my father, Him (God)."—*Œuvres de Molière,* viii. 181 note 3. Auger's idea seems to be prodigiously ingenious.

"THE MUFTY.

"*Non star furfanta?*

"THE TURKS.

"*No, no, no.*

"THE MUFTY.

"*Donar turbanta, donar turbanta.*[1]

The Turks repeat all that the Mufty has said when giving the turban to the Bourgeois. The Mufty and the Dervishes put on their turbans used at the ceremony, and the Koran is given to the Mufty, who makes a second invocation, in which he is joined by all the assisting Turks. After the invocation he gives the Bourgeois the sword, and sings these words :—

"THE MUFTY.

"*Ti star nobile, é non star fabbola.*
"*Pigliar schiabbola.*[2]

"The Turks repeat the same lines, each holding his sabre in his hand ; and six of them dance round about the Bourgeois and pretend to hit him with the backs of their sabres.

"The Mufty orders the Turks to beat the Bourgeois, and he sings the following words :—

"*Dara, Dara,*
"*Bastonnara, bastonnara.*[3]

"The Turks repeat the same lines, and beat him with sticks to a musical accompaniment.

"After he has been beaten the Mufty sings to him :—

"*Non tener honta :*
"*Questa sta ultima affronta.*[4]

The Turks repeat the same lines.

"The Mufty begins another invocation, and retires after the ceremony, with all the Turks dancing and singing with many instruments after the Turkish fashion."

It is to be remembered that this Turkish ceremony was intended as a burlesque ; and seen with all the glitter of gold and the brightness of the new and handsome costumes, it must have been a pretty sight. As the play was composed and undertaken at the king's desire, his Majesty defrayed the expenses ; or perhaps it would be more just to say that they

[1] "You will not be a thief?—No, no, no.—Not a knave?—No, no, no.—Give turban, Give turban."
[2] "You are noble, and (that) is not a fable.   Take a sabre."
[3] "Give, give, beat, beat."
[4] "Do not be ashamed ; this is the last affront."

fell upon the taxpayers of the country. Taken together with an uncertain sum of money allowed to the actors at the Hôtel de Bourgogne theatre, who were summoned to Versailles in the following month, the total charges amounted to 49,404 livres. Of this large sum, it would seem that much the greatest part was due to the performances of the *Bourgeois Gentilhomme*. M. Moland has given a detailed account of this expenditure.[1] In a footnote at the end he estimates that the king had altogether not less than ten dramatic performances, and that as each performance cost, one with another, a little less than 5000 livres, "the voluptuary expenses were controlled with some strictness." I have said on a former page that, according to French writers, if we wish to get now the equivalent of the spending value of money in Molière's day we should multiply by five.

Though M. Jourdain has been bamboozled and beaten he is completely happy, for he believes that he is a great lord and that his daughter is going to marry the son of the Grand Turk. His wife, however, cannot understand what has taken place. He is so triumphant in his new honours that, instead of telling her how he has received them, he can only say that he has been made *Mamamouchi* and repeat the words he has heard.

" *M. Jourdain.*

" Hou la ba ba la chou ba la ba ba la da.

" *Madame Jourdain.*

" Oh, deary me ! My husband has gone mad.

" *M. Jourdain.*

" Silence, impertinent woman ; bear proper respect to Monsieur le *Mamamouchi.*"

When Cléonte arrives, dressed as a Turk, M. Jourdain horrifies his daughter, Lucile, by telling her that she sees before her her future husband. Lucile shows disobedience, but when she recognises her lover she instantly becomes touched with her filial duties. Madame Jourdain is also horrified at hearing that the son of the Grand Turk is to be her son-in-law, and it is difficult to persuade her to see the advantages of such a marriage.

[1] L. Moland, *Œuvres de Molière*, 2nd ed. x. 417-26.

" Covielle (aside to her).

"For the last hour, madame, we have been making signs to you. Don't you see that all this is only to complete your husband's visionary ideas ; that we have disguised ourselves in order to laugh at him, and that Cléonte is the son of the Grand Turk ?

. . . .

" Madame Jourdain.

"Oh ! if that is it, I agree. . . . I consent to the marriage.

" M. Jourdain.

"Now, everybody has come to his senses. (Then to his wife.) You wouldn't listen to me. I knew well enough that he would show you what it is to be the son of the Grand Turk.

" Madame Jourdain.

"He has shown me perfectly, and I am satisfied. Let us send for a lawyer."

The last words in the comedy are spoken by Covielle. Alluding to M. Jourdain, he says: "If a man can be madder than he is, I will go and tell it in Rome."

The fact that the *Bourgeois Gentilhomme* was played so often at court is a proof that the performances gave great pleasure. Doubtless the Turkish ceremony, the music, and the spectacular exhibition were among the reasons for its good fortune. But Grimarest, a generation later, wrote : "No play was ever so badly welcomed, and no play of Molière's gave him so much uneasiness. At supper the king said no word to him about it, and all the courtiers abused it." Grimarest's account of the reception of the play is in itself a little bit of comedy.[1] As Louis XIV. made no remark about the play after its first performance, said nothing to show whether he liked it or not, the courtiers imagined that their master did not think well of it. Thereupon a noble duke expressed his sentiments to his friends : "Molière must take us for simpletons if he thinks he can amuse us by such rubbish. What does he mean by *Ha la ba, ba la chou* ? The poor fellow is talking nonsense, he is worn out. If no other author takes his place he will descend into Italian farce." According to Grimarest, when Molière saw how his play was pulled to pieces by the courtiers he shut himself up in his room for five days, because the

[1] *Vie de Molière,* 141-43.

comedy he had written under the king's orders and with special desire to please his Majesty had been a failure. After the second performance [Grimarest had evidently not been told how often the play had been acted] the king lifted the cloud. He said to Molière : "I did not speak to you about your play after its first performance because I thought I had been deceived by the way it was acted; but indeed, Molière, you have never amused me more, and your comedy is excellent." On hearing this the courtiers looked at one another disconcerted. But they chose to get out of the difficulty in the easiest way. One of the poet's former hostile critics said of him : " That man is inimitable; he has a vis comica in everything that he does that is never seen in the ancient writers." Taschereau, who relates all this from Grimarest, adds himself : " Et voilà les bons amis de cour." [1]

Hitherto the public performances of Molière's comedies when they were new had succeeded each other regularly; but La Grange's Register shows that after the *Bourgeois Gentilhomme* had been acted twice the troop at the Palais Royal theatre put on to their stage *Tite et Bérénice,* a new tragedy by Pierre Corneille. Corneille's tragedy was acted three times before Molière's comedy again appeared, then there were three consecutive performances of Molière's comedy; and the two plays were so given—three consecutive performances of the tragedy and three consecutive performances of the comedy following each other alternately—until the end of the theatrical year at Easter 1671. I have said already that *Tite et Bérénice* was the only new play, not written by Molière, that had a substantial success at the Palais Royal theatre. This success was, however, eclipsed by that of the *Bourgeois Gentilhomme.* Corneille's tragedy was acted twenty-one times and gave an average daily receipt of 732 livres ; Molière's comedy was acted twenty-four times and gave an average daily receipt of 1004 livres.

The *Bourgeois Gentilhomme* was given to the public in Paris just as it had been played at Chambord and at Saint Germain.[2] If the courtiers had been delighted chiefly with the spectacle, we may suppose that the townsfolk were charmed in the

[1] Taschereau, *Vie de Molière,* 3rd ed. 158, 159 ; *Œuvres de Molière,* viii. 6, 7.

[2] *Œuvres de Molière,* viii. 19.

same way. In any case, this play appears, from a pecuniary point of view, to have been one of the most successful that Molière put on to his stage.

The names of most of the actors who played originally in the *Bourgeois Gentilhomme* are known. Molière was naturally his own M. Jourdain, his wife appeared as Lucile, Hubert, who often acted women's parts, as Madame Jourdain, Mlle. Beauval as Nicole, du Croisy as the maître de Philosophie; and in all probability La Grange as Cléonte, La Thorillière as Dorante, Mlle. de Brie as Dorimène, and her husband as the maître d'armes. The rôles of Covielle, and of the music-master and of the dancing-master, appear not to have been assigned. In the Cérémonie Turque, Lulli, the musician, appeared as Le Mufti when the play was acted before the court; M. Mesnard says that he did not go on to the stage in Paris.[1]

The printing of the first edition of the *Bourgeois Gentil-homme* was completed on the 18th of March 1671.[2]

Les Fourberies de Scapin, first acted on the 24th of May 1671, was the next play of Molière's seen at the Palais Royal theatre. From the point of view of comedy this is one of the weakest of Molière's plays that he put upon his stage. It may give amusement when well acted, but it shows little real comedy. It was borrowed partly from the *Phormio* of Terence, "with some reminiscences of Plautus"; Paul Lacroix thought it was a transformation of an old play, *Joguenet ou les Vieillards Dupés*, written by Molière some time between 1640 and 1655; one of its scenes was probably taken from an old farce called *Gorgibus dans le Sac*, which may have been written by Molière when he was in the provinces; and another scene, of which a word will be said later, was or was not taken from *Le Pédant Joué*, a play by Cyrano de Bergerac, written probably in the year 1645, but not printed until 1654.[3]

As we read the *Fourberies de Scapin* now we are reminded of Molière's first two comedies, the *Étourdi* and the *Dépit Amoureux*, where the incidents were directly borrowed from the Italian stage; we are carried back to the old comedy of

---

[1] *Œuvres de Molière*, viii. 24, 25.   [2] *Ibid.* viii. 36, 37; xi. 36-38.
[3] *Ibid.* viii. 387-98, in the Notice to the *Fourberies de Scapin* by M. Paul Mesnard; and vol. xi. 167.

intrigue in which the burden of the play lay chiefly in cheating. A man who can cheat cleverly doubtless shows ingenuity, and Scapin is a clever rascal. But though comedy of a certain kind is seen in the way he bamboozles two fathers out of their money for the benefit of their sons, he is not so well known as Mascarille, the honest rogue in the *Étourdi*, who seems to be alive now after two hundred and fifty years.

It would, I think, be unwise and ungenerous to Molière to reproach him for having fallen back from good comedy, even from ludicrous caricature which had a true comic meaning, to a farce intending to show how a cunning thief can lie and steal and make people laugh at his boldness. An author who writes much cannot be always at high-water mark. Molière was bound to fill his theatre, and La Grange's Register proves that only he could do so; he was obliged to think of his fellow-actors, who were dependent upon his exertions that they might live. The wonder is that he provided for them so well. One cannot say definitely when he wrote *Les Fourberies de Scapin*, but it may be supposed that he was at work upon it when the freshness of the *Bourgeois Gentilhomme* as a new play had diminished. And his mind at that time must have been full of *Psyché*—to be spoken of presently—a play that he was writing in collaboration with Pierre Corneille, and of the necessary preparations before it could be put on the stage.

Boileau had a very high opinion of Molière's work, and thought that his comedy generally gave excellent lessons. In speaking of comedy in his *Art Poétique*, Canto III. v. 393-400, Boileau wrote :—

> " Étudiez la cour et connaissez la ville :
> L'une et l'autre est toujours en modèles fertile.
> C'est par là que Molière, illustrant ses écrits,
> Peut-être de son art eût remporté le prix,
> Si, moins ami du peuple en ses doctes peintures,
> Il n'eût point fait souvent grimacer ses figures,
> Quitté pour le bouffon l'agréable et le fin,
> Et sans honte à Térence allié Tabarin.[1]
> Dans ce sac ridicule où Scapin s'enveloppe
> Je ne reconnais plus l'auteur du *Misanthrope*."

The pronoun *se* (of course abbreviated) in the penultimate verse has given rise to discussion; for Scapin does not go into

[1] Tabarin was the name of a clownish actor and juggler who, many years earlier, used to play before the crowd on the Pont Neuf and in the Place Dauphine. His jests and his quibbles were long remembered.

the sack himself, he puts Géronte into it. Boileau probably wished to convey the idea in a figurative sense of a personage exhibiting nonsensical buffoonery ; and when he published a carefully prepared edition of his works thirty years later the verse remained unaltered. Unless his lines are read too literally, they do not mean that in the play he was condemning Molière had brought a Tabarin on the stage—which in fact was not the case—but rather that Molière had fallen from good comedy to tabarinesque farce. Such censure was perhaps excessive. Boileau was pained that Molière, in making use of a comedy by Terence, should have written a play that exhibited, as he thought, mountebank triviality. The critic, occasionally too severe in his interpretations, was disgusted ; and when he spoke in the same breath of the comedy in the *Fourberies de Scapin* and of the comedy in the *Misanthrope*, by way of contrast, it is difficult not to feel that his teaching was at fault. I partly share his opinion in thinking poorly of the *Fourberies de Scapin*, because of the want of good comic characterisation in the play; but I imagine, taking the general sense of his lines quoted above, that he was writing of comedy too academically when he composed his *Art Poétique*. From the lofty height on which he was engaged perhaps he did not consider sufficiently the effects of comedy, and how they should be shown on the stage before an audience who do not, and should not, look at a play from an academical point of view. Then what are we to understand by Boileau's words " grimacer ses figures " ? Molière certainly often made his personages appear ridiculous, but he did not alter their natures. With few exceptions they are not absurd, for they showed a comic meaning of their own as they provoked laughter. There is generally a signification in Molière's laughter ; it is rarely an empty giggle. Molière was by nature a " friend of the people " ; so also was Shakespeare. If they had not been friends of the people as well as of the quality much of their comic force had not been born. Without familiarity with the ways of thinking of those who are highly placed in the world, or of those who belong to a lower social rank, there can be no real comedy. You may get fine sentiments, good advice, cleverness, even wit, shown in neatly turned verses or in plain prose ; but unless there has been sympathy with the humours of the persons portrayed, true comedy will not be seen. Imagination not based on sympathy will give hollow results.

In most of Molière's light comedies, even in those that are thought to be the most ridiculous, a fair idea can be formed of the principal personages and of what they are like. This is hardly the case with the *Fourberies de Scapin*; one thinks there of the machinery employed and how it is used, but little of the personal characterisation. A contrast between this play and the *Étourdi*, also a comedy of intrigue, will show the difference. *Scapin* was, nevertheless, acted eighteen times as a new play, and with three exceptions alone; and since Molière's death it has been generally considered to be a good acting comedy.

Cyrano de Bergerac's comedy, *Le Pédant Joué*, is remembered because Molière in his *Fourberies de Scapin* is said to have borrowed two scenes from it. In both plays a scheming valet persuades an old man that his son has been taken a prisoner on board a Turkish galley. The exclamation in Molière's comedy, " Que diable allait-il faire dans cette galère ? " is nearly the same as in Cyrano's, but from the setting it is more dramatically comic. The idea of the galley scene in Molière's comedy may have been taken from Bergerac or from an Italian play acted before either author was born. When they were lads Molière and Cyrano had read philosophy together under Gassendi, both were bright and clever, and Molière is said to have been fond of his friend in spite of his impudence and his lawless conduct. In those days there was more or less close companionship between them; and, according to Grimarest, when Molière was reproached that he had borrowed his fun in *Scapin* from Bergerac's play, he answered : " Je reprends mon bien où je le trouve ? " [1]

There is contemporary evidence to show that Molière played the part of Scapin, La Thorillière of Sylvestre, and Mlle. Beauval that of Zerbinette.[2]

The printing of the *Fourberies de Scapin* was completed on the 18th of August 1671.[3]

[1] *Vie de Molière*, 8.
[2] *Œuvres de Molière*, viii. 400, 401.   [3] *Ibid*. viii. 405 ; xi. 39.

We come now to *Psyché*, a play to be found among the works both of Pierre Corneille and of Molière. In the best days of the drama in England plays were very often written by more than one author, but in France this practice was the exception rather than the rule. *Psyché* is the only play in which, apart from the composition of a ballet, Molière shared the authorship with anybody. During the three or four years before its production Molière had worked very hard to provide dramatic entertainment for his sovereign, and at the end of 1670 he was told to compose " une pièce à grand spectacle " for the carnival festivities in 1671—just as an upholsterer might be told to furnish a palace handsomely on the spur of the moment. The time given to the poet was short, as was usually the case when he received royal orders. He therefore sought assistance. He chose as his chief collaborator Pierre Corneille, then sixty-four years of age ; and with some small help from others the two great dramatists wrote between them *Psyché*, a play in five acts and in verse, qualified as a " tragédie-ballet," which was first performed at the Tuileries Palace, probably on the 17th of January 1671.[1] It was put upon the stage at the Palais Royal theatre six months later, on the 24th of July.

In the original edition of *Psyché* there is, as a sort of preface, a notice from the bookseller to the reader, probably from Molière's pen, explaining the different shares in the authorship of the tragedy-ballet. Molière devised all the plans for the composition of the play, thinking more of the beauty of the spectacle than of exactness. He wrote the greater part of the prologue—the first fifty-six verses of it were probably by Quinault [2]—he wrote the whole of the first act, and the first scene in the second and in the third acts. But the versification of the greater part of the play devolved upon Corneille, and fifteen days were allowed to him for his work. There still remained the verses in the interludes and the music. All of the former were by Quinault, except the first, " la plainte

---

[1] *Œuvres de Pierre Corneille*, in the Collection des Grands Écrivains de la France, by M. Marty Laveaux, vii. 283 ; *Œuvres de Molière*, viii. 248 ; *Œuvres de Molière* by M. L. Moland, 2nd ed. xi. 13.

[2] *Œuvres de Molière*, viii. 274 note 2 ; and M. Moland's 2nd ed. of the *Œuvres de Molière*, xi. 26 note 2.

Italienne "; this was by Lulli. Lulli also composed all the music for the play.

Even now guesses can only be made why the legend of Cupid and Psyché was selected for the pièce à grand spectacle to amuse the king and his guests. If the choice of the subject was suggested by either of the authors of the play, it may be that it came from him who undertook the planning of the incidents and the arrangement of the scenes. A *Ballet Royal de Psyché* had been danced at court in 1656, and La Fontaine in 1669 had published a novel, *Les Amours de Psyché et de Cupidon*. Either or both of these events may have had some influence on the choice of a subject selected for the carnival festivities in 1671. But another reason has been alleged which seems to be rather more circumstantial, in spite of its grotesqueness. In the garde-meuble belonging to his Majesty there was a piece of scene-painting representing hell, and it was thought to be a pity that this should be left there lying idle any longer. M. Mesnard indulges in a little fair raillery at the idea of two men of genius being brought to work together in order to utilise a bit of painted canvas. The subject of the picture painted on the canvas would hardly accord with the style of thought seen usually in Molière's comedies. But the dramatist had lately, in *Monsieur de Pourceaugnac* and in the *Bourgeois Gentilhomme*, exhibited human foibles with strong caricature ; perhaps therefore he was glad in his next court play to turn his mind in another direction and take for his subject a semi-mythological fable and describe it in irregular verses, as he had done in *Amphitryon*, also borrowed in part from mythology.

Much trouble was taken to make the mise-en-scène of *Psyché* appear glorious. An idea of what it was like may be formed from the livret or programme of the interludes in the play. The splendour of scenic display was doubtless the chief source of delight to very many of the spectators both at the court and in the town. The stage effects of those days would appear simple to us now ; but Molière learned, not for the first time, when he brought out *Psyché* at the Palais Royal theatre and gave it to the public as nearly as possible with the same brilliancy as it had been seen by the courtiers at the

Tuileries, that a handsome spectacular show will make people spend their money to see it.

Just before the Easter holidays in 1671 the troop at the Palais Royal determined to have the inside of their theatre renovated. La Grange records what was done.[1] The total cost came to close upon 2000 livres, and the Italian actors in Paris who used to play in the Palais Royal theatre on the off-days of the week—" les jours extraordinaires "—shared the expense with Molière's troop. La Grange goes on to say that, on the 15th of April, the troop, after deliberation, determined to put *Psyché* on to their stage. This proved a costly matter, for the preparatory expenses rose to 4359 livres.[2] On the 24th of July the mythological tragedy-ballet was played for the first time in public. La Grange writes that the daily expenses rose to 351 livres; "and that while the play was running, Mons. Beauchamps received 1100 livres as recompense for having planned the ballets and for managing the music, not including the 11 livres that the troop gave him every day for beating the measure to the music, and for directing the ballets." Whatever *Psyché* may have cost to put on the stage, it was pecuniarily very successful. As a new play it was performed thirty-eight times—a number not exceeded by any other comedy of Molière's except the *Tartuffe*. And it had two revivals in Molière's lifetime. During the first it was acted thirteen times, during the second thirty-one times.

In planning the composition of *Psyché* Molière's chief desire was to give the old legend a semblance of dramatic form; he wished to interest his audience in the fate of the beautiful young girl and of her handsome lover. Nine-tenths of the courtiers who saw the play knew nothing about gods and goddesses, but they would be pleased if their senses were charmed agreeably. Perhaps that is the best way to look at the play now. Those who have read the allegory of Cupid and Venus in Apuleius will not receive additional pleasure from Corneille's and Molière's lines on that account. The verses will probably please more as a lyric than as a drama. *Psyché* is a play to be read, book in hand. When the imagination is left alone it can soar at will, and fancy can picture to itself a dramatic action which on the stage

[1] *Registre*, 122, 123.   [2] *Ibid.* 124.

may unfortunately not appear to be so evident. There is a note of comedy in the two first scenes, in the way that Molière makes Psyché's two sisters show their jealousy because she is sought after by suitors while they are left unnoticed. Elsewhere, too, Molière is gently amusing. But the subject of the play would not allow of frank, comic raillery; hearty, open laughter would have been thought out of place. And in Corneille's verses there is often a note of poetry in the scenes. Psyché has bravely submitted to her fate that for a husband she should have a foul serpent spreading his venom everywhere. But when Cupid (l'Amour) appears before her, saying he is the serpent, her fears are disarmed. She thinks he is a god.

> " Qu'un monstre tel que vous inspire peu de crainte ! "

She does not know what is the fire that is in her. Formerly she had respect, sympathy, compassion, but now :—

> " Je ne sais ce que c'est, mais je sais qu'il me charme,
> Que je n'en conçois point d'alarme ;
> Plus j'ai les yeux sur vous, plus je m'en sens charmer :
> Tout ce que j'ai senti n'agissoit point de même,
> Et je dirois que je vous aime,
> Seigneur, si je savois ce que c'est d'aimer."

These lines might have been spoken by Agnès in the *École des Femmes*. Psyché's couplet concludes :—

> " Par quel ordre du Ciel, que je ne puis comprendre,
> Vous dis-je plus que je ne doi,
> Moi de qui la pudeur devroit du moins attendre
> Que vous m'expliquassiez le trouble où je vous voi ?
> Vous soupirez, Seigneur, ainsi que je soupire ;
> Vos sens comme les miens paroissent interdits ;
> C'est à moi de m'en taire, à vous de me le dire.
> Et cependant c'est moi qui vous le dis." [1]

Among other pieces of scandal, the author of the *Fameuse Comédienne* wrote that the appearance of *Psyché* was the cause for the renewal of a liaison between Baron and Mlle. Molière. But this anonymous writer is the only authority for the story. The tale gives rise to a dispute which might go on for ever, because there is so little evidence either way that can be accepted as true. As a young boy Baron had quarrelled with Mlle. Molière, and had left Paris in a huff in consequence;

[1] Act III. sc. 3.

some three years later he is supposed to be making love to her. When *Psyché* appeared at the Tuileries Palace in the carnival of 1671, Baron was seventeen and a few months old; Mlle. Molière's twenty-eighth birthday fell about that time. There was therefore a wide difference in their ages. It may be almost admitted that both were haughty, vain, and absolutely selfish. Still, with it all, one should hesitate before attaching importance to a tale from the pen of an anonymous and scurrilous gossipmonger.

There is a healthier kind of interest in learning that Baron's great reputation as an actor began with his rôle of Cupid (l'Amour) in *Psyché*. In 1667, when he was very young, he had played the part of Myrtil in Molière's *Mélicerte*; and later, at the end of 1670, he appeared as Domitian in Corneille's *Tite et Bérénice*. But his acting in these two last-named parts was not well remembered; his personation of Cupid remained long in the minds or in the hearts of those who saw it. It was, however, in tragedy that Baron excelled chiefly. He was one of the four actors who, six weeks after Molière's death, left the Palais Royal theatre and joined the rival troop at the Hôtel de Bourgogne. It is probable that there he found a better scope for his talents than he would have found at the Palais Royal, had Molière lived and continued to direct that theatre.

The names of the actors who appeared in the various rôles in *Psyché* when the play was new may be found in M. Mesnard's edition of the *Œuvres de Molière*, viii. 367; and in M. Marty Laveaux's edition of the *Œuvres de P. Corneille*, vii. 290.

On the 31st of December 1670 leave was given to Molière to print *Psyché*, but the printing of the play was not completed until the 6th of October 1671. Molière's was the only author's name seen on the title-page. During Corneille's lifetime *Psyché* was never printed among his works.

CHAPTER XVIII

LES FEMMES SAVANTES—LA COMTESSE D'ESCARBAGNAS—
LE MALADE IMAGINAIRE—POÉSIES DIVERSES

In the *Femmes Savantes*, acted for the first time on the 11th of
March 1672 at the Palais Royal theatre, the gist of the satire
is not very different at bottom from that in the *Précieuses
Ridicules*, the first play that Molière wrote after his return
to Paris from the provinces. In the earlier comedy the
dramatist laughed at the manners of women whose heads
were so much turned by romantic and pretentious ideas that
they acquired a love of preciosity, or over-niceness, over-
refinement of thought; and consequently their affectations
became ridiculous. In the two middle quarters of the 17th
century, people in good society in Paris used to meet on
certain days of the week at each other's houses, and there
ladies were glad to hear from gentlemen expressions of
Platonic love and friendship shown with gallantry and
courteous respect. Playful satire was given and taken in
good part and was enjoyed. For some years these and similar
amusements went on gaily; the compliments and the small
railleries were understood in the spirit of pleasantry; they
were laughed at, and nobody was the worse for them. There
was doubtless an affectation with it all, but heartiness, sociability, and intelligent frivolity were the leading characteristics.

As might be expected, the affectations increased; the playfulness of intention remained, but an intellectual flavour was
demanded with it. Then ladies contrived to invent a diction
or language of their own, so romantic, so far-fetched, or so
high-flown, that it became a jargon, and few except themselves
could understand its technicalities; they liked it to be known
that they stood well with the authors of the day; they indulged in verse-making in various forms—enigmas, ballads,
madrigals, sonnets, impromptus—and some held what were

called "académies," or "bureaux de bel esprit." Naturally enough these ladies, in their attempts to be distinguished from others who did not belong to their set, rather overshot the mark by their absurdities; at the same time they amused themselves and enjoyed their follies in their own way. All this Molière showed with strong caricature that had also many of the features of good comedy.

Nearly a year before his death the poet showed his satire a second time against the same kind of foibles, but in a rather different manner. The *Précieuses Ridicules* is in one act and in prose, the *Femmes Savantes* is in five acts and in verse. It was proper that a comedy in five acts and in verse should be couched in a somewhat higher style than a one-act comedy in prose. And the personages in the later written comedy belong to a better rank of society than do those in the earlier one. The manners of the femmes savantes, though disagreeably haughty, give an air of better breeding than the open good-nature of the précieuses ridicules. Philaminte, Bélise, and Armande mistook the nonsense in Trissotin's verses for beauties, but they would have seen the vulgarities of the Marquis de Mascarille, though they might have been willing to overlook them. There are other differences between the two comedies. In the longer one the satire takes a wider form. The three ladies are ridiculed together for their love of a display of preciosity and of learning, but each one has to bear in addition other satire personal to herself. The caricature here is not so strong as in the shorter play; and in one instance where it may seem to be very absurd there was in reality no caricature, no exaggeration, but merely a simple reproduction.

In the first part of chapter vii. I tried to give shortly an idea of some of the drawing-room amusements of people in Paris in the middle of the 17th century, and I mentioned the names of a good many ladies and gentlemen who are known to have been guests at the Hôtel de Rambouillet. There were also, a few years later, other houses in Paris where people used to meet to see each other and talk over what was uppermost in their minds, and that of Mlle. de Scudéry is the best known; but none of these receptions enjoyed the same prestige as those in Madame de Rambouillet's salon bleu in the Rue

Saint-Thomas du Louvre. Cousin says that this lady opened her house to her friends between the years 1617 and 1620. Her receptions, broken off perhaps only temporarily in 1645, because of the death of her son, may have lasted until the outbreak of the Civil War in Paris known as La Fronde, in 1648. From different reasons, it is hardly likely that they continued longer. They lasted, therefore, for thirty years. It seems to be admitted that in the later years of the Hôtel de Rambouillet affectation among the guests grew stronger, that intellectual amusements, which had been taken up as playthings, as pleasant frivolities, became more or less a serious occupation. In 1652, after the Fronde, the number of afternoon parties in Paris increased. Preciosity, which arose among Madame de Rambouillet's friends during the last ten or twelve years of their meetings, grew to be the fashion. It was imitated, and the usual results of imitation followed : it was shown more extravagantly and with less good taste. People used to talk then of the " vraies précieuses " and of the " fausses précieuses," and of the former as being of older date. The later type had certainly been in existence for some years when Molière showed what they were like under the names of Cathos and Madelon. Had all these societies with their vagaries not come into vogue, Molière need not have given his *Précieuses Ridicules* in 1659, nor his *Femmes Savantes* in 1672.

Molière's power of teaching by laughter was one of his characteristics, and perhaps in no play has he shown from first to last more or better comic raillery than in the *Femmes Savantes*. Sometimes it is tempered with irony, sometimes it is so strong that it should rather be called satire, and in one well-known scene there is angry invective ; but throughout the comedy generally raillery and banter are the prevailing notes. The plot in the play is slight, but one thinks little about it ; one thinks of the comedy shown. What engages the attention is the comic manner in which the humours or the caprices of the personages are truly portrayed. These oddities are seen with the fair caricature belonging to comedy, and they are described in a racy comic style that shows both delicacy of touch and strength of instinct. In speaking of a great man who has laboured much, it is generally unwise to pronounce affirmatively that this or that is his best piece of work, for in the various efforts he has made excellences of different kinds will be found. Nevertheless, perhaps, I should not be far wrong if I were to say that the *Femmes Savantes* is the best acting play among Molière's high-class comedies, nor if I were to add, that in the way of amusement, no play of his affords better reading.

The first lines in the comedy are full of raillery. They are spoken by Armande to her younger sister Henriette :—

> " Quoi ? le beau nom de fille est un titre, ma sœur,
> Dont vous voulez quitter la charmante douceur,
> Et de vous marier vous osez faire fête ?
> Ce vulgaire dessein peut vous monter en tête ? "

Armande had refused to give herself to Clitandre; after an interval he became smitten with the softer charms of Henriette, and she has accepted his love. The two sisters are very unlike, and they show their different characters by their speech. Armande is jealous and angry, she is a précieuse, and she has her mother's love of pedantry. Henriette is a girl we should all like to know; she is pleasant, and has quite wit enough to take her own part against her strong-minded sister. When she expresses her delight at the hope that one day she may be united to Clitandre, her sister answers her :—

> "Mon Dieu ! que votre esprit est d'un étage bas !
> Que vous jouez au monde un petit personnage
> Que de vous claquemurer aux choses du ménage,
> Et de n'entrevoir point de plaisirs plus touchants
> Qu'un idole d'époux et des marmots d'enfants !
> Laissez aux gens grossiers, aux personnes vulgaires,
> Les bas amusements de ces sortes d'affaires.
>   .   .   .   .   .   .
> Loin d'être aux lois d'un homme en esclave asservie,
> Mariez-vous, ma sœur, à la philosophie,
> Qui nous monte au-dessus de tout le genre humain,
> Et donne à la raison l'empire souverain,
> Soumettant à ses lois la partie animale
> Dont l'appétit grossier aux bêtes nous ravale."

Henriette is willing to acknowledge her own inferiority, but she must use the faculties that have been given to her. She replies to her sister :—

> " Ne troublons point du Ciel les justes règlements,
> Et de nos deux instincts suivons les mouvements :
> Habitez par l'essor d'un grand et beau génie,
> Les hautes régions de la philosophie,

> Tandis que mon esprit, se tenant ici-bas,
> Goûtera de l'hymen les terrestres appas.
> Ainsi, dans nos desseins l'une à l'autre contraire,
> Nous saurons toutes deux imiter notre mère :
> Vous, du côté de l'âme et des nobles désirs,
> Moi, du côté des sens et des grossiers plaisirs ;
> Vous, aux productions d'esprit et de lumière,
> Moi, dans celles, ma sœur, qui sont de la matière."

And in her next speech :—

> "De grâce, souffrez-moi, par un peu de bonté,
> Des bassesses à qui vous devez la clarté ;
> Et ne supprimez point, voulant qu'on vous seconde,
> Quelque petit savant qui veut venir au monde."

The elevated raillery in the whole of the first scene is undeniable, and it shows how naturally Molière expressed his thoughts in a comic manner.

The author of the *Fameuse Comédienne* wrote, in 1678, that when Molière was at Lyons (say in 1653) he was in love with Mlle. du Parc, but that she rejected his addresses, and that he consoled himself with Mlle. de Brie. The statement may be true or not. Many French writers have adopted it more or less, and have asserted that when the dramatist made Clitandre transfer his affections from Armande to Henriette in the *Femmes Savantes*, he was alluding to his own former position at Lyons between two actresses in his troop. Even were this assertion true, it would not alter the comedy in the play for better or worse. Speaking generally, one may say that unless some fault against taste or conduct can be shown, it is of little consequence what was the source of the incidents dramatised, nor when, or where, or how they took place. What a reader or a playgoer demands is that the comedy in a play should be well and amusingly given and shown with pleasant comic vitality.

There is no love-scene worthy of the name between Clitandre and Henriette, but their engagement has proceeded from mutual respect or admiration. The consent of Henriette's father Chrysale, or of her mother Philaminte, has not, however, been obtained. Clitandre would go to Chrysale. But Henriette knows her father to be weak of purpose, and tells her lover that it is more important to gain the goodwill of her mother; for it is she who governs; she lays down the law and means that it shall be obeyed. Clitandre's answer is rather blunt, but there are in it some often quoted lines which suit the satire in the comedy admirably. He declares that pretentiously learned women are not to his taste; and then he goes on :—

> " Je consens qu'une femme ait des clartés de tout ;
> Mais je ne lui veux point la passion choquante
> De se rendre savante afin d'être savante ;
> Et j'aime que souvent, aux questions qu'on fait,
> Elle sache ignorer les choses qu'elle sait ;
> De son étude enfin je veux qu'elle se cache,
> Et qu'elle ait du savoir sans vouloir qu'on le sache.
> Sans citer les auteurs, sans dire de grand mots,
> Et clouer de l'esprit à ses moindres propos."

All this had been said more at length by Mlle. de Scudéry in her novel, *Le Grand Cyrus*, written at intervals twenty years or more before the date of the *Femmes Savantes*. Both Mlle. de Scudéry and Molière meant : let a woman learn and know what she likes and be well instructed, but let her be careful not to show her knowledge where it is not wanted. It is worth noting that the term " femmes savantes " was used by Mlle. de Scudéry. She drew a distinction between a well-informed woman and a femme savante, and spoke of the latter as though she did not like her : " Ce n'est pas que celle qu'on n'appellera point savante ne puisse savoir autant et plus de choses que celles à qui on donnera ce terrible nom, mais c'est qu'elle se sait mieux servir de son esprit, et qu'elle sait cacher adroitement ce que l'autre montre mal à propos." [1] Both Mlle. de Scudéry and Molière thought that a well-informed or a well-instructed woman might, happily, be a very different person from a femme savante. Mlle. de Scudéry's novels seem to show her to be an apostle of affectation, but in reality she was playing with the spirit of the time. She lived with others, and she drew her fun out of them in a lady-like manner.

One other thing may be noticed. In this as in other comedies, if Molière gives, as it often seems likely, his own personal opinions, he does so in a manner perfectly consistent with the play of the comedy he was writing. Like Mlle. de Scudéry, he was far from admiring the femmes savantes, or, as he calls them, " femmes docteurs." But throughout his plays

---

[1] See the long extract from *Le Grand Cyrus*, quoted by Victor Cousin nearly at the end of chapter xii. of his *Société Française au XVIIᵉ Siècle* (vol. ii. pp. 180-82, ed. 1858). Also *Œuvres de Molière*, ix. 72 note 3.

generally his own feelings are never thrust forward. They are never shown to be personal to himself or to anybody else. He presents his satire openly and in a true comic spirit. He makes no exhortation, expounds no thesis. In the play we are now to consider he shows fairly what are the attributes of the femmes savantes, how they make themselves ridiculous and often disagreeable. Henriette, though a young girl, appears to be well educated, but her mind is very different from that of her mother or of her aunt, and she is in every way opposed to her elder sister.

Clitandre goes on to tell Henriette that much as he respects her mother he cannot agree with her in her praises of the man she takes to be a great wit.

> "Son Monsieur Trissotin me chagrine, m'assomme,
> Et j'enrage de voir qu'elle estime un tel homme ;
> Qu'elle nous mette au rang des grands et beaux esprits
> Un benêt dont partout on siffle les écrits,
> Un pédant dont on voit la plume libérale
> D'officieux [1] papiers fournir toute la halle."

It would be useless to pretend that in the personage of Trissotin Molière did not mean to draw a comic picture of the abbé Cotin, who was then alive, and to ridicule his foolishness. But Cotin was one of a class, he was typical of others; and if he was chosen as the scapegoat, it is very likely that he deserved punishment the most. Two days before the *Femmes Savantes* appeared on the stage, Madame de Sévigné, in a letter to her daughter, spoke of the comedy by the name of *Trissotin*, and it is so chronicled in La Grange's Register on and after its twelfth performance. In the *Ménagiana*, first published in 1693, it is said : "Molière at first took off Cotin under the name of Tricotin ; then, with greater piquancy, under the pretext of a better disguise, he changed it afterwards into *Trissotin*, or *trois fois sot*." [2]

There have often been poor wits, honoured by some and belittled by others, whose names are known to posterity only because their nonsense and their more or less false position in society have brought down upon them well-deserved ridicule from contemporary authors who saw through their hollowness.

---

[1] M. Mesnard has a note here : "*Officieux*, doing a service, goes well with *libérale*. The papers do a service to the vendors in the market, for they serve to wrap around the articles that are purchased."—*Œuvres de Molière*, ix. 73 note 3.   [2] *Ibid*. ix. 9.

The abbé Cotin was a poor wit who, in an age when preciosity
was fashionable, gained for himself a position of consequence
among ladies who belonged to the best families in France, and
who thought his verses were ravishingly beautiful. He was
considered as one of the oracles, and because he had a facility
for writing he was placed above others who could not compose
rubbish so easily. Cotin was a man, he went to afternoon
parties and talked to the ladies there, and his church prefer-
ments did not prevent him from writing trashy à la mode
verses which were now and then in doubtful taste. Though
there was no freshness of thought in what he wrote and
published, perhaps when he was talking he showed to better
advantage. Even then, he must have guarded himself against
his natural self-sufficiency. If he would talk and say nothing
quietly, there were people who would listen to him. In days
gone by he had been one of the guests at the Hôtel de
Rambouillet, and later he was received kindly at other houses
which were not open to every one who wished for admittance.
One of these was the Luxembourg Palace, where an apartment
was given to Mademoiselle, the daughter of Gaston, Duke of
Orleans, brother to Louis XIII. At the Luxembourg Cotin
became a favourite. He did his best to please the ladies who
went there when Mademoiselle had her receptions, and he
worked harder at his madrigals and his enigmas than at his
sermons. Thus the abbé Cotin became a petted darling of
society. He was made much of and was spoilt, until Molière
gave him a blow from which he never recovered. As a con-
versationalist perhaps Cotin enjoyed at the Luxembourg the
same sort of reputation, in a lesser degree, that was allowed
to Voiture at the Hôtel de Rambouillet. Voiture could talk
easily, which is one of the first necessities for pleasant conversation, and it may be that Cotin was partially endowed with
the same gift. As to writing, Voiture's letters do not give one
the idea of a man of much brightness, and his printed portrait
looks like that of a ninny. Cotin knew how to put words
together on paper, though he said little in them; and when
he wrote on serious subjects it is to be hoped his inanities were
not so glaring as in his drawing-room verses. When he was
a young man he showed stupidly that he had learned Latin,
and he was made a member of the French Academy.

His vanity gave him a good opinion of himself and of his powers of preaching. Boileau naturally disliked his flummery, and wrote in his third Satire, published in 1663, that Cotin preached to empty benches. Molière and Boileau would dislike Cotin on the same grounds. They thought him a trifler and a windbag. And because they both waged war against false taste and bantered those who took pleasure in listening to nonsense, Cotin, on his side, naturally considered them as his enemy. He wrote a satire against Boileau, and Molière was not spared in the attack. And Cotin, with Ménage, we are told, had tried to persuade the Duc de Montausier that Molière meant to satirise him in the personage of Alceste in the *Misanthrope*. However this may be, the day after the *Femmes Savantes* appeared on the stage, a laudatory short account was given of the comedy in a new weekly periodical called *Le Mercure Galant* [1] :—

"Bien des gens font des applications de cette comédie ; et une querelle de l'auteur il y a environ huit ans avec un homme de lettres, qu'on prétend être représenté par Monsieur Trissotin, a donné lieu à ce qui s'en est publié. Mais Monsieur de Molière s'est suffisamment justifié de cela par une harangue qu'il fit au public deux jours avant la première représentation de sa pièce. Et puis ce prétendu original de cette agréable comédie ne doit pas s'en mettre en peine s'il est aussi sage et aussi habile homme que l'on dit, et cela ne servira qu'à faire éclater davantage son mérite en faisant naître l'envie de le connoître, de lire ses écrits, et d'aller à des sermons."

Cotin is pointed at here clearly as the original of Trissotin. The harangue mentioned in the *Mercure Galant* was the "annonce" customarily spoken by the orateur of the troop to the audience in the theatre. It would be interesting to know what Molière said in announcing the coming performances of his new comedy. He had good reason to be angry with Cotin, for the abbé had twice written against him and had tried to conceal the authorship of his attacks as far as he was able. One would say now that Molière might have left such an adversary alone, and have disregarded his lampoons. Molière had to bear harder contumely than any taunts Cotin could inflict. But he disliked the man's pedantry, his self-sufficiency, and his meanness. Cotin did not think much for himself ; he borrowed where he could from Latin authors, and from any

[1] Vol. i. pp. 64, 65.

modern writer whose lines might be of service to him. And he displayed his vanity in a curious manner. Before the date of the *Femmes Savantes* he wrote of himself:—"My cypher is composed of two C's"—alluding to the two initial letters of his name (Charles Cotin)—"and these, in a mysterious sense, indicate the circle of the globe which my works may be said to fill." Whether the dramatist knew of this hyperbolical foolery or not, he satirised very aptly the man who could publish it.

> " . . . mais Monsieur Trissotin
> M'inspire au fond de l'âme un dominant chagrin.
> La constante hauteur de sa présomption,
> Cette intrépidité de bonne opinion," etc.[1]

There are those who will say that Molière's satire against Cotin was cruel; others will say that Cotin deserved what he got, because he was such an arrant fool. But was Molière unjust in his treatment of one who in his semi-public life exposed himself to open raillery? Had Cotin not been a vainglorious humbug, Molière would have left him alone; Cotin lived by foppishness, and Molière bantered him for his inane verses, as Alceste had rebuked Oronte:—

> "Quel besoin si pressant avez-vous de rimer?
> Et qui, diantre, vous pousse à vous faire imprimer?"

But after Alceste's criticism Oronte did not publish his sonnet.

In Act III. sc. 2 Molière makes Trissotin read aloud before the three femmes savantes a poem of his composition: *Sonnet à la Princesse Uranie sur sa fièvre*. Unless this sonnet had been ridiculous it need not have been given in the comedy; it was, in fact, a textual reproduction of a poem entitled *Sonnet à Mlle. de Longueville, à présent duchesse de Nemours, sur sa fièvre*, written by Cotin and published for the first time in the first edition of his *Œuvres Galantes*, in 1663. Later in the same scene, Molière makes Trissotin read aloud an epigram that he had composed; and this also was taken textually from Cotin's *Œuvres Galantes*. The title only is changed a little.[2]

Molière's satire here was straightforward. He showed Cotin's imbecility by quoting his own words. Authors in the

---

[1] *Femmes Savantes*, Act I. sc. 3.
[2] *Œuvres de Molière*, ix. 11, 124 and 130; also M. Louis Moland's *Œuvres de Molière*, 2nd ed. xi. 421 and 426.

17th century often spoke of their fellow-authors whom they wished to disparage in terms that would now be thought beyond the bounds of fair reproof. We have nowadays our abusive criticism, and it is sometimes calumnious; that of two hundred years ago was expressed in a more downright manner. Perhaps the sledgehammer fashion is the least injurious. The works of Boileau and of La Bruyère were reprinted during their lifetime oftener than those of any of their contemporaries in their own country—if an exception may be made in the *Lettres Provinciales* of Pascal, who died in 1662—because of the hard-hitting in the personalities and of the curiosity of readers to see what writers whose names were respected said of men whom they wished to ridicule or denounce. The personalities shown by Boileau refer only to what an author had written and published; those alluded to by La Bruyère, to which exception might be taken, refer very largely to men who were well known and whose daily conduct, more or less public, was either ridiculous or worse. La Bruyère may seem to us now to be more open to blame than Boileau, yet those who know his written portraits in his *Caractères* will not be disposed to find fault with him for bad taste or for ill nature. Neither of these authors has been condemned by posterity, and I do not see that Molière in his strong satire against the abbé Cotin was more to blame than they were. He was much more amusing, and if that was a crime it was heightened by his having a greater number of listeners and spectators than either Boileau or La Bruyère had of readers.

Cotin had gained the reputation of a bel esprit, and Molière gave two samples of his wit. They were both flowery trash. In previous comedies the dramatist had satirised the kind of society verses that were then common, and each time he showed nonsense of different kinds. Mascarille's impromptu in the *Précieuses Ridicules* is so frankly droll in its absurdity that it causes joyous laughter; Oronte's sonnet in the *Misanthrope* is absurd because in many of the lines the words, when fairly construed, bear no meaning; Cotin's sonnet and his epigram in the *Femmes Savantes* disgust, for besides being silly they are full of embellishments out of place shown with the self-conceit of a pedant. In the *Précieuses* and in the *Femmes Savantes* we find a man reading trash to admiring ladies; but Cotin was stupid and had neither the imagination nor the wit of the Marquis de Mascarille. The sham marquis, as we know, is acting his part, and though his manners are not refined, he counterfeits with admirable caricature the character he is playing and is most amusing. Cotin was never other than himself; he had no cleverness in him, nor even the sense of judgment often found in a dull man. Verses like all those just mentioned were read aloud in many salons in Paris during Molière's lifetime, and in bantering their authors the dramatist was bound to laugh at those who expressed their delight as they listened to the reading. In the comedy that now concerns us the scene passes in the house of Chrysale, a well-to-do bourgeois. Whatever may be his foibles, he is free from affectations and from pedantry. But his wife Philaminte, his sister Bélise, and his eldest daughter Armande, wish to have æsthetic ideas above those of plain-thinking people. They want to be distinguished, and they intend to create a school or following of their own. Molière called them femmes savantes; he meant them to be also précieuses ridicules. Apparently they are honest in their glorification of Trissotin; at all events they show most amusingly that they are crack-brained in their ecstasies over his inflated balderdash, which they think is clever wit prettily expressed.

Of course there is exaggeration in the way the ladies show how they are enraptured. Unless they had extolled Trissotin's nonsense extravagantly, believing it to be poetry sparkling with beautiful images, there would have been little satire against them. Without some caricature the comic significa-tion of the scene would have been lost; without some heightening effect the representation of the scene would fall flat on the stage. I have already spoken of Molière's use of caricature. In most cases he did not push it beyond fair limits; with few exceptions he did not allow the comedy in his plays to degenerate into farce. I do not see how a comic dramatist can show open humour, in the characterisation either of the incidents in his play or of his personages, without a mixture of caricature. For good caricature has a truth, a delicacy and a strength of its own, which does not disfigure or materially alter. Its humour heightens or accentuates personal features or events, making them ludicrous, but without showing them to be absurd or without giving an unfair picture of the person or thing intended to be represented.

The three ladies have exalted ideas of making themselves known in the world. Philaminte is determined that women shall be no longer considered as inferior creatures; she thinks that they as well as men may learn the truths of science, of nature, and of art. Trissotin's position is to flatter the ladies; he knows as much about science as they do, but he must interest himself in their occupations.

" *Trissotin.*

" Je m'attache pour l'ordre au péripatétisme.

" *Philaminte.*

" Pour les abstractions, j'aime le platonisme.

" *Amande.*

" Épicure me plaît, et ses dogmes sont forts.

" *Bélise.*

" Je m'accommode assez pour moi des petits corps ;
Mais le vide à souffrir me semble difficile,
Et je goûte bien mieux la matière subtile.

" *Trissotin.*

" Descartes pour l'aimant donne fort dans mon sens.

" *Armande.*

" J'aime ses tourbillons.

" *Philaminte.*

" Moi, ses mondes tombants."

Then, when Armande says she hoped that their society would soon be formed, and that she, with her mother and her aunt, would gain renown by some discovery, the dialogue goes on:—

" *Trissotin.*

" On en attend beaucoup de vos vives clartés,
Et pour vous la nature a peu d'obscurités.

" *Philaminte.*

" Pour moi, sans me flatter, j'en ai déjà fait une,
Et j'ai vu clairement des hommes dans la lune.

" *Bélise.*

" Je n'ai point encor vu d'hommes, comme je croi ;
Mais j'ai vu des clochers tout comme je vous voi.

" *Armande.*

" Nous approfondirons, ainsi que la physique,
Grammaire, histoire, vers, morale et politique."

Here again the satire is given with caricature. It was

directed against certain ladies who displayed fussy pedantry in things they could not understand. Molière had said in the third scene of his comedy that it was right that women should be well informed, but that they should use modesty in the way they showed their knowledge. In his satire against vain displays of learning he gave examples of women who talked of science when they did not know what it meant, and he laughed at them for their foolishness—as he had laughed at his two sham philosophers in the *Mariage Forcé*; and in literary matters, which were less abstruse, he ridiculed their pretensions and hollow ideas. After the French Academy had been founded in 1635, a good number of its first members thought it was their duty to make reforms in the language of their country; they determined to publish treatises or disquisitions laying down grammatical and other laws for writers to follow, and they were to be the sole judges of the value of their own enactments. One member disliked the word *car*, and he proposed that it should be abolished. The learned ladies in the comedy before us were trying to emulate the aspirations of the early members of the French Academy, and the dramatist laughed at them for their folly, as the Academy had been laughed at many years before his comedy was written.[1] But Molière meant more than mere laughter. His mockery of the femmes savantes was in one respect like his banter against Climène, the précieuse and the prude in his *Critique de l'École des Femmes* and against the affectations of all women of her stamp. Molière disliked the whole class heartily, and he thought a pretentious woman was a more disagreeable person than a pretentious man. From the man there may be escape, but the woman who sickens with her affectations urges them with painful obstinacy. Climène in the *Critique* was disgusted at imaginary indecencies where no indecency was intended and where none existed; and Philaminte's greatest hope is that when she and her friends shall have established their academy they may effect—

> ". . . le retranchement de ces syllabes sales,
> Qui dans les plus beaux mots produisent des scandales,
>
> Ces sources d'un amas d'équivoques infâmes,
> Dont on vient faire insulte à la pudeur des femmes."

---

[1] See *Œuvres de Molière*, ix. 138 notes 1 and 2, by M. Mesnard.

The next few lines must be given:—

> "*Trissotin.*
>
> "Voilà certainement d'admirables projets !
>
> "*Bélise.*
>
> "Vous verrez nos statuts quand ils seront tous faits.
>
> "*Trissotin.*
>
> "Ils ne sauroient manquer d'être tous beaux et sages.
>
> "*Armande.*
>
> "Nous serons par nos lois les juges des ouvrages ;
> Par nos lois, prose et vers tout nous sera soumis ;
> Nul n'aura de l'esprit hors nous et nos amis."

The wit in this last line has made the words proverbial. Henriette, against her will, had been present while Trissotin was reading his verses, and she is present in the next scene (III. 3), when his friend Vadius makes his appearance. Trissotin introduces him to the ladies, and is anxious to recommend him properly :—

> "*Trissotin.*
>
> "Il a des vieux auteurs la pleine intelligence,
> Et sait du grec, Madame, autant qu'homme de France.
>
> "*Philaminte (to Bélise).*
>
> "Du grec, ô Ciel ! du grec ! Il sait du grec, ma sœur !
>
> "*Bélise (to Armande).*
>
> "Ah, ma nièce, du grec !
>
> "*Armande.*
>
> "Du grec, quelle douceur !
>
> "*Philaminte.*
>
> "Quoi ? Monsieur sait du grec ? Ah ! permettez, de grâce,
> Que pour l'amour du grec, Monsieur, on vous embrasse.
> (Vadius kisses them all except Henriette, who refuses.)
>
> "*Henriette.*
>
> "Excusez-moi, Monsieur, je n'entends pas le grec."

After a speech by Vadius, in which he says that it is a common fault with authors to annoy people by reading aloud their own compositions in society, and become

> "De leurs vers fatigants lecteurs infatigables,"

he and Trissotin extol each other's productions with most friendly generosity :—

" *Trissotin.*
"Vos vers ont des beautés que n'ont point tous les autres.

" *Vadius.*
"Les Grâces et les Vénus règnent tous dans les vôtres.

" *Trissotin.*
"Vous avez le tour libre, et le beau choix des mots.

" *Vadius.*
"On voit partout chez vous l'*ithos* et le *pathos*.[1]

" *Trissotin.*
"Nous avons vu de vous des églogues d'un style
Qui passe en doux attraits Théocrite et Virgile."

And so the mutual admiration goes on, until Vadius falls foul of a sonnet that he did not know Trissotin had written. At first the two men disagree, then they quarrel, and finally they pour upon each other all the vituperative words and phrases they can find :—

" *Trissotin.*
"Vous donnez sottement vos qualités aux autres.

" *Vadius.*
"Fort impertinemment vous me jetez les vôtres.

" *Trissotin.*
"Allez, petit grimaud, barbouilleur de papier.

" *Vadius.*
"Allez, rimeur de balle, opprobre du métier.

" *Trissotin.*
"Allez, fripier d'écrits, impudent plagiaire.

" *Vadius.*
"Allez, cuistre . . .

" *Philaminte.*
"Eh ! Messieurs, que prétendez-vous faire ?

" *Trissotin.*
"Va, va restituer tous les honteux larcins
Que réclament sur toi les Grecs et les Latins.

---

[1] In his compliment, Vadius meant to say, that Trissotin's writings showed pictures both of manners and of passions.

" *Vadius.*

" Va, va-t'en faire amende honorable au Parnasse
D'avoir fait à tes vers estropier Horace.

" *Trissotin.*

" Souviens-toi de ton livre et de son peu de bruit.

" *Vadius.*

" Et toi, de ton libraire à l'hôpital réduit.'

" *Trissotin.*

" Ma gloire est établie ; en vain tu la déchires.

" *Vadius.*

" Oui, oui, je te renvoie à l'auteur des *Satires.*"

Each disputant tries to palliate the rebuke he had received
from Boileau, the author of the *Satires*, and tries also to
heighten the force of the invective that Boileau had cast upon
his adversary. Boileau's mockery of Cotin had been constant,
and Cotin knew perfectly that Molière's personage of Trissotin
was meant to apply to him. It has always been believed that
in the personage of Vadius, Molière meant to characterise
Ménage, though that writer, perhaps from motives of policy,
denied that the dramatist had any such intention ; Ménage also
declared that the characteristics shown were not his. Boileau
had rallied Ménage in his second Satire, but soon afterwards
substituted another writer's name ; the only other instance was
in his fourth Satire where, in dealing some heavy blows to
Chapelain, the author of the terrible poem *La Pucelle,* he
quizzed at the same time Ménage and his scribbling friends.

Our concern is with the comedy in the play that was acted
on the stage ; but literary gossip or anecdotes are so closely
connected with a general view of the *Femmes Savantes,* that
something should be said of the two men who undoubtedly
served more or less as the models of Trissotin and of Vadius.

Ménage was intellectually a bigger man than Cotin, though
perhaps more of a pedant. He was a type of a savant who
could not turn his learning to any purpose useful to himself
or to others. He is said to have been spiteful and sharp-
tongued. His plagiarisms, which were well known, were due
in a great part to his very retentive memory and to his lack of
imagination. Still, Ménage showed that he had thoughts of
his own in his *Requête des Dictionnaires,* a squib in doggerel

verse on the labours of the early members of the French Academy. It would be too much to say that the poem was good, though there was truth and a little wit in the lines; but the satire provoked the anger of the forty immortals, and consequently Ménage's name was never added to their number. Ménage and Cotin had been friends, but they fell out; and Cotin alludes to their quarrel in a short poem of his, now scarce, called *La Ménagerie*, published in 1666. Had Ménage, like Cotin, shown himself to be a ladies' man; had he even been able to compose light frivolities that were meant to give pleasure and to amuse, his poem against the indolence and the incapacity of the Academicians might have been forgiven. Instead, he made enemies by his caustic tongue; he gave offence to ladies as well as to gentlemen. His satirical poem against the Academy was not in itself ill-natured, but it contained truths which were not forgotten because their author showed personal ill-nature in other ways.

The most effective scenes on the stage in the *Femmes Savantes* are those where Trissotin and Vadius make their appearance in the third act. In looking at the comedy in the play it matters little to have passed over for the moment Philaminte's husband Chrysale, and Bélise his chimerical sister. Bélise is a woman of very uncertain age; those who are charitable might say she was forty. Molière makes her think that every man who has seen her is smitten with her charms. Clitandre wishes her to give him some assistance in his love-affair with Henriette; but at the mention of the words "amant" and "sincère flamme" she takes fire and pretends to think that Clitandre had applied them to her. He assures her four times that he had not thought of her in that way, but still she rides her hobby. Clitandre is obliged at length to say openly:—

"Je veux être pendu si je vous aime . . ."

Commentators have pointed out that the dramatist borrowed the character of Bélise from that of Hespérie in *Les Vision-naires*, by Desmarets, acted at the Hôtel de Bourgogne in 1637. When it was new the *Visionnaires* was very highly praised, it was spoken of as "l'inimitable comédie"; and some years later Molière often put it on to his own stage at the Petit Bourbon, before his troop left that theatre for the Palais Royal. Very likely Molière saw that under Desmarets' caricature there was the spirit of comedy, not shown lightly perhaps nor with much vitality, but still with purposed intention and sensible effect. It may be also that the whimsical ideas of Hespérie in the *Visionnaires* made Molière think that similar ideas would be suitable to a middle-aged femme savante, and that they would assist in ridiculing her before an audience. In writing his comedies Molière thought very much of their representation; and to a woman in Bélise's position he was bound to give force of character. Philaminte and Armande have each their individual peculiarities, and they are both sufficiently disagreeable; Bélise is ludicrous or even grotesque, but she is a woman whose oddities are naturally shown. The laughter that she provokes is pleasant, almost joyous; the laughter felt against her sister-in-law and her niece has a sneer in it, and one enjoys its vindictiveness. It would be unfair to think of comparing Desmarets' work with Molière's; the probability is that the audiences in the theatre received as much pleasure in 1637 from the *Visionnaires* as those of a generation later did from the *Femmes Savantes*.

Chrysale, in Molière's comedy, is one of those men who do not stand by himself; he is his wife's husband. Philaminte is domineering in everything; she is determined to send away Martine, a good servant girl respected by her master, not because the girl has broken anything, nor even stolen, but because she has, her mistress says:—

> " Après trente leçons insulté mon oreille
> Par l'impropriété d'un mot sauvage et bas,
> Qu'en termes décisifs condamne Vaugelas."

Vaugelas was an excellent commentator on the language of his country.[1] His main standpoint was that good usage should be the guide for correct writing and correct speaking; and in his *Remarques sur la langue française*, published in 1647, he was less dictatorial than some other writers who had neither his knowledge nor his good sense. Though Molière mentions him several times in the *Femmes Savantes*, the satire in the comedy does not fall upon him; it is directed against the ignorance of pedantry. Martine knew how to cook her

[1] See Sainte-Beuve's first article on Vaugelas in the *Nouveaux Lundis*, vi. 340.

dinners well, which was what her master wanted; and Chrysale spoke from his heart when he said to his wife :—

> " Je vis de bonne soupe, et non de beau langage,
> Vaugelas n'apprend point à faire un potage ;
> Et Malherbe et Balzac, si savants en beaux mots,
> En cuisine peut-être auroient été des sots."

Chrysale has been lectured until he cannot stand it any longer. He is afraid to speak directly to his wife; he addresses himself to his sister, though they had both maintained the same arguments against him :—

> " Le moindre solécisme en parlant vous irrite ;
> Mais vous en faites, vous, d'étranges en conduite," etc.

His long speech, towards the end of the second act, is well known; it affords an instance of admirable comic raillery. Chrysale goes on to discharge his bile. He is angry with the ladies of his household because, instead of attending to their domestic duties, they are eternally thinking of books and of science. And he looks back upon the olden days when women were modest in their aspirations. But—

> " Les femmes d'à présent sont bien loin de ces mœurs :
> Elles veulent écrire et devenir auteurs.
> Nulle science n'est pour elles trop profonde,
> Et céans beaucoup plus qu'en aucun lieu du monde :
> Les secrets les plus hauts s'y laissent concevoir,
> Et l'on sait tout chez moi, hors ce qu'il faut savoir.
>
> .   .   .   .   .   .
>
> Mes gens à la science aspirent pour vous plaire,
> Et tous ne font rien moins que ce qu'ils ont à faire ;
> Raisonner est l'emploi de toute ma maison,
> Et le raisonnement en bannit la raison.
>
> .   .   .   .   .   .
>
> Je n'aime point céans tous vos gens à latin,
> Et principalement ce Monsieur Trissotin :
> C'est lui qui dans des vers vous a tympanisés ;
> Tous les propos qu'il tient sont des billevesées [1] ;
> On cherche ce qu'il dit après qu'il a parlé,
> Et je lui crois, pour moi, le timbre un peu fêlé."

There is some irony against Chrysale, who is fond of his creature comforts. His invective is partly caused because those who should have looked after his dinner were intent

---

[1] By *billevesées*, Molière meant here what we should now, less elegantly, call " Tommy-rot."

upon some theory or upon a volume of verses. And he speaks feelingly when he bewails the loss of his servant who was to be sent away because she had not learned to talk like Vaugelas. His wife and sister are nearly scarified at what they have heard.

> "*Philaminte.*
>
> "Quelle bassesse, ô Ciel, et d'âme et de langage !
>
> "*Bélise.*
>
> "Est-il de petits corps un plus lourd assemblage !
> Un esprit composé d'atomes plus bourgeois !
> Et de ce même sang se peut-il que je sois ?
> Je me veux mal de mort d'être de votre race,
> Et de confusion j'abandonne la place."

When Chrysale gives his brother, Ariste, to understand that he had not dared to speak to his wife in favour of Henriette's marriage with Clitandre, Ariste rallies him on his want of courage. Chrysale's answer is very near his heart :—

> "Mon Dieu ! vous en parlez, mon frère, bien à l'aise,
> Et vous ne savez pas comme le bruit me pèse.
> J'aime fort le repos, la paix et la douceur,
> Et ma femme est terrible avecque son humeur.
>
> .   .   .   .   .   .
>
> Elle me fait trembler dès qu'elle prend son ton ;
> Je ne sais où me mettre, et c'est un vrai dragon ;
> Et cependant, avec toute sa diablerie,
> Il faut que je l'appelle 'mon cœur' et 'ma mie.'"

We may see, therefore, that Philaminte means to give Henriette to her hero Trissotin. Armande compliments her sister upon her future husband; then both she and her mother abuse Clitandre most uncharitably. He hears how he is being unfairly treated, and asks what he has done to deserve such punishment. A wrangle between him and Armande follows. She says that she was his first choice ; he retorts that she had declined his offers. She who had told her sister that philosophy should be her husband now reproaches her former admirer with vulgar desires :—

> "Vous ne sauriez pour moi tenir votre pensée
> Du commerce des sens nette et débarrassée ?
> Et vous ne goûtez point, dans ses plus doux appas,
> Cette union des cœurs où les corps n'entrent pas ?
> Vous ne pouvez m'aimer que d'une amour grossière ?
> Qu' avec tout l'attirail des nœuds de la matière ?"

Clitandre answers her :—

> " Pour moi, par un malheur, je m'aperçois, Madame,
>   Que j'ai, ne vous déplaise, un corps tout comme une âme :
>   Je sens qu'il y tient trop, pour le laisser à part ;
>   De ces détachements je ne connois point l'art :
>   Le Ciel m'a dénié cette philosophie,
>   Et mon âme et mon corps marchent de compagnie."

Armande is beaten in the dispute. The manner in which she tries to recapture her former admirer is amusing :—

> " Hé bien, Monsieur, hé bien, puisque sans m'écouter,
>   Vos sentiments brutaux veulent se contenter," etc.

But Clitandre tells her that it is too late, for another has taken her place.

During the discussion Trissotin makes his appearance. He and Clitandre know that they are rivals for the hand of Henriette, and there is a lively duel between the man of the world and the pedant. This quarrel is not waged so fiercely as that between Trissotin and Vadius. It is too long to quote at length, but a few lines may be given :—

> " *Trissotin.*
>
> " J'ai cru jusques ici que c'étoit l'ignorance
>   Qui faisoit les grands sots, et non pas la science.
>
> " *Clitandre.*
>
> " Vous avez cru fort mal, et je vous suis garant
>   Qu'un sot savant est sot plus qu'un sot ignorant."

After a few more passages, Philaminte intervenes to stop their thinly veiled personal allusions. Clitandre answers her :—

> " Eh, mon Dieu ! tout cela n'a rien dont il s'offense :
>   Il entend raillerie autant qu'homme de France."

Clitandre did not mean that Trissotin's love of good raillery was keen, but that he had to put up with sharper blows than he would be likely to get in that instance. With the two ladies present, who are his friends, Trissotin cannot remain prudently silent when he is beaten. He sneers at Clitandre because he is familiar with what goes on at court, and adds :—

> " La cour, comme l'on sait, ne tient pas pour l'esprit."

Clitandre is not a man to boast of his relations with the court ; he is also not a man to say nothing when he hears the court abused by an imbecile. It has been thought that in Clitandre's answer Molière was giving expression to his own sentiments. It is clear, at all events, as M. Mesnard points out in a footnote,[1] that the dramatist was repeating here, in other words, what he had said in his *Critique de l'École des Femmes*. He now makes Clitandre say :—

> "Permettez-moi, Monsieur Trissotin, de vous dire,
> Avec tout le respect que votre nom m'inspire,
> Que vous feriez fort bien, vos confrères et vous,
> De parler de la cour d'un ton un peu plus doux.
>
> Qu'elle a du sens commun pour se connoître à tout ;
> Que chez elle on se peut former quelque bon goût ;
> Et que l'esprit du monde y vaut, sans flatterie,
> Tout le savoir obscur de la pédanterie."

On a former page I made a small quotation from the authors of the *Lexique* belonging to the *Œuvres de Molière*, to the effect that Molière kept something of the oratorical tone of his age, that his sentences are very rhythmical, and are so full and sonorous that if some small matter were not understood, his meaning would still be easily gathered in any part of the theatre. The words spoken by Clitandre in the *Femmes Savantes* afford an example of this. Perhaps this rôle is one that is understood better after it has been seen well acted on the stage. On first thoughts the character of Clitandre may appear commonplace. It is far otherwise. He is a man of the world, of good birth and frank address. He is very outspoken, and is not wanting in self-assurance. And he hates with all his blood the fawning disposition of Trissotin, his pretentious but inane rubbish written in quantities sufficient to paper the walls of a score of houses, his affected admiration of men simply because they have learned Greek and Latin, and his useless pedantry which he exhibits with all the vanity of a peacock and with all the ineptitude of a blockhead. Molière's open style proclaims this distinctly. Clitandre's robust self-assurance is very different from Trissotin's self-conceit. Clitandre hardly loses his temper; he shows his anger against his rival with honest-hearted enthusiasm. Trissotin smirks and flatters in order to maintain his miserable credit with three women, each more foolish than himself.

[1] *Œuvres de Molière*, ix. 173.

It has been explained that a good part of the satire against Trissotin was understood by contemporaries to apply to the abbé Cotin, who was then alive; and more than once in this book I have said that Molière was never ill-natured in his satire. There are some who, when they read how Cotin was treated in the *Femmes Savantes,* will not agree with this last statement. Molière's ridicule against M. Jourdain was jovial and kindly, that against Cotin was almost ruthless; it was like the felling of a tree, and in fact it morally killed the poor abbé. Does that show ill-nature? Against a Tartuffe, or a Don Juan, or a Harpagon, few will complain how severe were the blows. Cotin, it is true, was not criminal as they were; but if he was in effect a pompous nincompoop who enjoyed semi-publicly a silly life by means of pretentious false wit, I doubt very much if it was not a good and a wise thing to knock him on the head, morally, and thus slay him.

Readers who have been patient enough to get as far as this in my book will have made up their minds if Molière's satire against humbug was generally justified. In this particular case it must be remembered that Trissotin was not playing a part like the Marquis de Mascarille in the *Précieuses*; he was not quizzing others so that he might laugh at their folly. He tried to show humour or wit and elegance of style; instead he wrote nonsense because he could do no better. And he read his rubbish aloud in fashionable drawing-rooms, accepted the praises that were showered upon it, prided himself on the good opinions of his listeners, and published his verses, thinking them worthy of being read and enjoyed. If, as there is fair reason to believe, Trissotin was really like Cotin in all this, Molière's satire on the abbé was justified. For Cotin led a semi-public life, and anybody would think of it as he pleased. But there were attacks on Trissotin's personality which may seem now to be unfair when directed against a man then alive. Trissotin's manner was pretentious; under a humble guise he was puffed with self-conceit. Was Molière therefore warranted in proclaiming to all Paris these faults in Cotin, because he showed them in society? Did Molière here exceed the limits of fair comic satire when he thus took off Cotin on the stage? The question can hardly be answered by a direct Yes or No. Yet, if it be not allowed to try to kill hollow pretence by ridicule, the fault will grow and become intolerable. Taking Molière's satire against the abbé Cotin as we find it, comparing it with other personal satire at the time, I believe that on the whole it was healthy, not ill-intentioned, and that the culprit deserved it.

Henriette is of course married before the termination of the comedy, but the arrangements for her marriage do not go off smoothly. The difficulty is not so much to find a husband for her, as to say who shall be the favoured suitor. When the notary arrives to draw up the contract Henriette's father says he wishes for Clitandre, her mother for Trissotin. The man of law is bewildered, and exclaims :—

> " Deux époux !
> C'est trop pour la coutume."

Neither Chrysale nor Philaminte will give way in their choice of a son-in-law, so Martine, the condemned cook, intervenes in the argument and altogether on the side of Clitandre. She does not like Trissotin ; and she thinks that women have no right to dictate to their husbands :—

> " La poule ne doit point chanter devant le coq."

Martine continues to talk with the sound common sense, bluntly expressed, that Molière was so fond of putting into the mouths of the women of the people. The dramatist's object here was, of course, to contrast Martine's ignorance and mother wit with the preciosity and the pedantry of the femmes savantes. We are told that Martine was in fact Molière's domestic servant, and that she played her part in the comedy under her own name. Also that the dramatist used to read his plays to this woman in order to learn from her laughter or from her frowns whether his intended fun was good or not, whether or not his comedy was really amusing. Doubtless there is romance in the tradition; but we may take it that Molière liked Martine's ideas better than those of her three mistresses.

Molière had to find a dénouement to his play, and the dénouement to the *Femmes Savantes* is hardly a good one. To the exposition of his characters he gave all his thoughts ; and the comic ridicule attaching to his personages is worked out charmingly and in a most amusing manner. Nobody likes either Philaminte or Armande, but everybody likes to see how they are made to talk and express their foolish thoughts. The ridicule, too, thrown upon Bélise is delightful because of its perfectly natural caricature. But when the climax of the incidents related arrived and Molière had to unravel his own knot, he cut it by a contrivance that was commonplace and not amusing.

The list of the names of the actors who originally played the various parts in this comedy is believed to be fairly accurate. Molière played the part of Chrysale; Baron, Ariste; La Grange, Clitandre; La Thorillière, Trissotin; du Croisy, Vadius; Hubert, who had previously taken women's parts, was Philaminte; Mlle. Villeaubrun (Geneviève Béjart), Bélise; Mlle. de Brie, Armande; Mlle. Molière, Henriette; and Martine, probably Martine La Forêt, was the Martine in the comedy. About this last rôle there seems to be more uncertainty than about any of the others. M. Mesnard is sceptical of the romantic and traditionary legend; and he suggests, with very fair reason, that this part was played by Mlle. Beauval.[1]

The printing of the *Femmes Savantes* was completed on the 10th December 1672, just ten months after the play was first acted on the stage.[2]

There are a good many often quoted lines, now more or less proverbial, that are to be found in the *Femmes Savantes*. Considering the people who speak them, or those to whom they were addressed, they are not more than fairly satirical; and they show, what most moderately attentive readers of Molière have already seen for themselves, that he did not try to invent witty lines for the sake of saying something smart. He was a rare craftsman in the easy way he used his words to show the mirth of comedy, and he loved the fun of satire when it arose and showed itself naturally; but he disliked the idea of thinking of witty sayings in order to produce an effect. Both Pascal and La Bruyère, two of the best thinkers that France has produced, wrote: "Faiseur de bons mots, mauvais caractère." I took a few instances of well-known quotations, characteristic of Molière, from his *Amphitryon*; these from the *Femmes Savantes* serve the same purpose. Perhaps their chief merit is that they are all suitable in their place.

"Mariez-vous, ma sœur, à la philosophie."   I. 1 ; v. 44.

---

[1] *Œuvres de Molière*, ix. 47-52.   [2] *Ibid.* ix. 53, 54 ; xi. 45.

"Cette intrépidité de bonne opinion." I. 3 ; v. 254.

"Raisonner est l'emploi de toute ma maison,
  Et le raisonnement en bannit la raison." II. 7 ; v. 597, 598.

"Nul n'aura de l'esprit hors nous et nos amis." III. 2 ; v. 924.

"Excusez-moi, Monsieur, je n'entends pas le grec."
  III. 3 ; v. 947.

"De leurs vers fatigants lecteurs infatigables." III. 3 ; v. 958.

"On voit partout chez vous l'ithos et le pathos." III. 3 ; v. 972.

"Vous donnez sottement vos qualités aux autres."
  III. 3 ; v. 1013.

"Un sot savant est plus sot qu'un sot ignorant."
  IV. 3 ; v. 1296.

It would seem that *La Comtesse d'Escarbagnas* was the last of the comédies-ballets that Molière wrote for the royal pleasure. In November 1671 Monsieur married for the second time, and Louis XIV. wished to give a complimentary fête to his brother and to his new sister-in-law, the Princess Palatine, Charlotte Elizabeth of Bavaria, in honour of their marriage. To lend a grace to the event Molière was told to compose a play which should admit of music and dancing, and to select for the interludes the most admired portions of the ballets that had been previously danced at court. On the 2nd of December 1671 the new comedy was performed for the first time at Saint Germain. The play was written to show off the interludes, and these were taken from former plays written by Molière. The *Comtesse d'Escarbagnas* has only one act, and it is clear that both the author and the king's guests thought more of the magnificence of the spectacle than of the comedy in the play. The troop at the Palais Royal theatre had been called away from Paris to Saint Germain on the 27th of November; they remained there until the 7th of December. In the meanwhile at Saint Germain there was a constant round of festivities.[1]

La Comtesse d'Escarbagnas was first acted at the Palais Royal theatre on the 8th of July 1672. The scene of the play is laid at Angoulême. The little comedy is no more than a light sketch showing how an ignorant-minded and ill-tempered woman, countess though she be, has, after a visit of three months to Paris, become opinionated in her ideas about persons

[1] *Œuvres de Molière*, vol. viii., Notice to the *Comtesse d'Escarbagnas*, by M. Paul Mesnard ; and M. Louis Moland's *Œuvres de Molière*, 2d. ed. vol. xi., Notice to the same play.

of quality, and how she scolds her provincial servants because they are raw and clumsy. The Comtesse d'Escarbagnas might almost be the sister of Monsieur de Pourceaugnac. She is as great a simpleton as he is, though in a different way, and her natural instincts are not so good. If both were put together into society the gentleman would make fewer enemies than the lady. Country people were more behind-hand in their manners, compared with Parisians, two hundred and fifty years ago than they are now ; but Molière knew the type of woman he was sketching, what were her vanities, her heavy stupidities, and how she could not prevent her fits of ill-humour. Two hundred and fifty years hence such a creature will be much the same.

La Grange shows that the *Comtesse d'Escarbagnas* was acted at the Palais Royal fourteen times, and that each day it was followed by a performance of the *Mariage Forcé*.[1] But the pomp and the spectacle of the ballet, which had been the principal features in the play at Saint Germain, were found to be too costly to be given in public as an accompaniment to a very light comedy.[2] This was the only play written by Molière in which he took no part on the stage. The names of the original actors are given by M. Mesnard.[3] The play was never printed until nine years after its author's death.

The last of Molière's comedies, *Le Malade Imaginaire*, was acted for the first time on the 10th of February 1673, at the Palais Royal theatre. We are told that the author intended this comedy to be played before the court during the festivities of the carnival in 1673,[4] though not that he had received the king's command to write the play. MM. Mesnard and Moland both seem to think that the dramatist determined to have his play acted in public at the Palais Royal theatre, and not at court, because of a quarrel between himself and Lulli. The latter, it will be remembered, had composed the music for many of the comédies-ballets written by Molière. The reason of their quarrel was that Lulli, in his desire to establish an opera-house in Paris, had obtained a privilege or monopoly

[1] *Registre*, 133, 134. [2] *Œuvres de Molière*, viii. 539. [3] *Ibid.* viii. 546. [4] *Œuvres de Molière*, ix. 210 ; x. 428 ; L. Moland, *Œuvres de Molière*, 2d. ed. xii. 14.

for an *Académie royale de musique*, forbidding dancing in all other theatres in Paris, and limiting the number of singers to six, and of musical instruments to twelve. Molière may have been right to quarrel with Lulli. This man had gained his monopoly, which was generally very unpopular; but by some mark of favour, not specified, all the restrictions set forth in the privilege were not put in force when the *Malade Imaginaire* appeared on the stage at the Palais Royal theatre. Still, no proof has been given to show that Molière was asked to write this play for performance at court; and even supposing that he had been so asked, no word has been said telling how he could have withdrawn his play from the court programme without royal sanction. I am inclined to agree with Auger, who says in his edition of Molière's plays, published in 1819 (vol. ix. p. 477), that it seems that the poet did not receive any command from the king to write this play. It is clear, however, that the *Malade Imaginaire*, styled "comédie mêlée de musique et de danses," was planned, like Molière's other comédies-ballets, with the idea of giving music and dancing as interludes between the acts. It is well to bear this in mind, for though many readers pass over the interludes they should remember that the comedy was planned largely on their behalf. The music for this play, as for the *Comtesse d'Escarbagnas*, was composed by Charpentier.

Molière's last comedy contains perhaps his most severe attack on the doctors of medicine. As he had ridiculed them in at least four of his previous comedies, it cannot be thought that he meant no more than playfulness or light banter. Putting aside the *Médecin Volant*, one of his farces, written when he was in the provinces, his first attack on the medical Faculty was in *Don Juan*, acted in February 1665. Because this short piece of strong satire was purely episodical as regards the events in the play, I only alluded to it when speaking of that comedy, but I quoted it at length in what I had to say about the *Amour Médecin*, acted six months after *Don Juan* had been withdrawn from the stage. It is indisputable that Molière meant much of what he said against the doctors of medicine; but he wrote in a vein of comedy, and he covered his censure with strong ridicule. This was his constant practice. Because of his easy laughter his meaning has often been unheeded; because of his grotesqueness his earnestness has sometimes been rejected derisively. In other matters he used reproof in the same way. His object was to make people laugh at foolish habits, and to show by amusing satire, that should be reverent, how the evil conduct of men one to another was hurtful to all and morally wrong. If there were any who would learn a lesson from his comedy, they might do so. Molière was no doctrinaire, but he thought that many of the physicians in his day took money out of people's pockets by feigning knowledge they did not possess, that nearly all of them were too much given to following routine, and that they used the knowledge they had in a pompous and absurd manner; and of the value of the skill employed by well-intentioned practitioners he was sceptical in more or less of a good sense.

An idea of the comedy in the *Malade Imaginaire* will be gathered by looking at the personages in the play. We see an empty-headed doctor of medicine, Monsieur Diafoirus; his son Thomas, also a doctor, but newly fledged, and both a pedant and an ignoramus; Monsieur Purgon, whose name speaks for itself, the medical attendant of the malade imaginaire; Argan, a semi-imbecile, a selfish, angry do-nothing, besotted with the idea that he is ill, and that unless he swallows every month as much physic as would float a small boat, he will get rapidly worse; Béline, his second wife, a creature more greedy of gain and more heartless than Frosine in the *Avare*; Angélique, Argan's daughter, who does love her father; Béralde, who, because he is Argan's brother, sermonises him and tries to bring him to reason; and Toinette, a domestic servant who rallies her master on his hypochondriacal foolery, as Lisette in the *Amour Médecin* had rallied her master on his faith in quacks, and as Dorine in the *Tartuffe* had also rallied her master on his belief in imposture of a more serious kind. For the form of the thing, Angélique has a lover, Cléante; and there is a pretty scene between Argan and his second daughter, Louison, a child of six or eight years.

The plots in Molière's comedies are not the strongest part of his work. The *Misanthrope* and the *Femmes Savantes*, usually considered as among his best plays, seem to have almost no plot. But if there be any man who does not enjoy the comic characterisation in either of those two plays—also in the *Critique de l'École des Femmes,* in *George Dandin,* and in the *Bourgeois Gentilhomme*—it would not be intolerant to say of him that he does not understand Molière. It is very easy to see that Molière was far more interested in showing the play of life by good-humoured comic satire, and by true comic characterisation of his personages, than he was in contriving an elaborate plot and in unravelling it so as to create or produce wonder or delight. Love of true comedy was in his nature, as singing is in that of a blackbird, and he wished to portray his characters and the events in his plays with all the natural comic humour he could throw into them. In his last, as in nearly all of his previous comedies, his personages are interesting because they have a vitality of their own ; and one sees from the open and easy way they talk that they give an amusing and lifelike character to the incidents they help to beget and to accomplish. About the events themselves in his plays Molière did not care much except as a means of showing the natures of his personages.

At the outset of the *Malade Imaginaire* Argan is adding up the items in his apothecary's bill for the last month. As the bill is long, and as Argan is garrulous, he is made to begin on the 24th day of the month. From the 24th to the 28th inclusive, he enumerates the various prescriptions supplied by his apothecary, M. Fleurant, and he regulates the various charges as he thinks fit. It was customary at that time to reduce apothecaries' bills by one-half ; and according to two recent editors of Molière, it would seem that the dramatist was exaggerating very little the accusations he brought against M. Fleurant and others in his trade.[1] The total amount of the bill comes to 63 livres, 4 sous, 6 deniers.

"So that," Argan says to himself, " I have taken this month one, two . . . seven, eight doses of physic ; and one, two . . . eleven, twelve clysters. Last month it was twelve doses of physic and twenty clysters. I don't wonder that I am not so well this month as I was last month."

Argan shows one good feature in his character. He recognises that his daughter Angélique is following natural instincts

[1] *Œuvres de Molière,* ix. 284 note 1 ; L. Moland, *Œuvres de Molière,* 2nd ed. xii. 40, continuation of note 4 from p. 39.

iu being glad when she is told that a proposal has been made for her hand. But she and her father are thinking of different suitors. She is harping upon Cléante, he insists upon Thomas Diafoirus. The invalid wishes to have a doctor in his house, and this young man will have money. Toinette begins her raillery and makes her master very angry. His wife comes to him and cossets him with the affection that comes from the thoughts of his money-bags.

It has been shown [1] that a comedy by Brécourt, *Le grand benêt de fils aussi sot que son père*, had some sort of success at the Palais Royal theatre in January 1664. Not much is known about the play, as it was never printed ; but the title seems to have tickled Molière, for in it both Monsieur Diafoirus and his son are aptly characterised. A " benêt " is a greenhorn, a nincompoop, and when this father and son make a formal call upon Argan for the purpose of asking for the hand of his daughter Angélique, Thomas Diafoirus is described as " a great greenhorn fresh from the schools, who does everything clumsily and at the wrong time."

" M. Diafoirus.

". . . Now then, Thomas, come forward. Make your compliments.

" Thomas Diafoirus.

" Should I not begin with the father ?

" M. Diafoirus.

" Yes.

" Thomas Diafoirus (to Argan).

" Sir, I come to greet respectfully, to acknowledge, to love and to revere in you a second father ; but a second father to whom I must say that I am more bounden than to the first. The first generated me, but you have chosen me. He received me from necessity, but you have accepted me by grace. What I receive from him is a work of his body, but what I receive from you is a work of your good will ; and so much as the spiritual faculties are above the corporeal faculties, so much the more do I owe to you, and so much the more do I esteem precious that future filiation for which I tender now by anticipation my most humble and respectful homage.

" Toinette.

" Long live the colleges which made such a clever man !

[1] *Ante*, p. 281.

"*Thomas Diafoirus (to M. Diafoirus).*

" Was that well done, father?

"*M. Diafoirus.*

" *Optime.*

"*Argan (to Angélique).*

" Now then, make your curtsy to Monsieur.

"*Thomas Diafoirus (to M. Diafoirus).*

" Shall I kiss?[1]

"*M. Diafoirus.*

" Yes, yes.

"*Thomas Diafoirus (to Angélique).*

" Madame, it is with justice that heaven has allowed to you the name of belle mère,[2] for since . . .

"*Argan (to Thomas Diafoirus).*

" That is not my wife ; you are talking to my daughter."

M. Diafoirus tells his son to make his compliment to the young lady. The imbecile rolls it out of his mouth as he would pull string out of a bag :—

"*Thomas Diafoirus.*

" Mademoiselle, neither more nor less than the statue of Memnon uttered a harmonious sound when it was lighted by the rays of the sun, so do I just in the same way feel myself animated by a soft inspiration at the apparition of the sun of your beauties. And as the naturalists remark that the flower called heliotrope always turns towards this day-star, so will my heart henceforward always turn towards the resplendent stars of your adorable eyes, as it would towards its only pole. Suffer then, Mademoiselle, that to-day I lay on the altar of your charms the offering of this heart which lives for and aspires to no other glory than to be, through all its life, Mademoiselle, your most humble, most obedient, and most faithful servant and husband.

"*Toinette.*

" See what it is to have studied ! One learns how to make pretty speeches.

"*Argan (to Cléante).*

" Well ! what do you say to that ?

---

[1] The ridicule of the situation here is obvious ; but in a note, *Œuvres de Molière,* ix. 350 note 4, M. Mesnard explains that this old custom was not extinct in France at the time of the *Malade Imaginaire.*

[2] The French word " belle mère " must be repeated here. Thomas Diafoirus was probably going to make a pun upon " belle " for the sake of a compliment.

"*Cléante.*

" That Monsieur does wonders, and that if he be as good a physician as he is a good orator, it will be a pleasure to be one of his patients."

M. Diafoirus' praise of his son need not be given at length. He says that if his boy was slow to learn at first he flowered late, and that now his child rejoices his heart; for the lad is firm in his belief of the ancients, and he would never understand or listen to the modern imaginary discoveries about the circulation of the blood and such like rubbish.

When Thomas Diafoirus is next seen he begins his compliment to Béline, Argan's wife. Happily, however, he is interrupted in the middle of his period and his fine ideas vanish. He is rather pleased that his courtship of Angélique should take place in public, and he goes through with it as might be expected. Later he shows his learning and his intelligence when Argan asks him to diagnose his case. At the end of scene 6, in M. Mesnard's edition, M. Diafoirus intervenes :—

"*M. Diafoirus.*

" . . . He [M. Purgon, Argan's own doctor] tells you to eat a good deal of roast meat ?

"*Argan.*

" No, only boiled meat.

"*M. Diafoirus.*

" Well, yes ; roast, boiled, all the same. He prescribes for you very wisely, and you could not be in better hands.

"*Argun.*

" Sir, how many grains of salt should one put into an egg ?

"*M. Diafoirus.*

" Six, eight, ten—even numbers ; as in medicine, we go by uneven numbers."

This reads now like pure nonsense; it was not, however, Molière's invention, for doctors of medicine in his day or earlier used to reason in that way.[1] And a short speech made by Argan earlier in the comedy, and which highly amused Madame de Sévigné, may also be mentioned here : " M. Purgon told me to walk in my room in the morning, twelve times forwards and

[1] *Œuvres de Molière,* ix. 377 and note 1.

twelve times backwards, but he did not say whether it was to be along the room or across it."

The *Malade Imaginaire* has but three acts, and in Act III. sc. 3 there is a long and well-known discussion between Argan and his brother Béralde about the value of the art of medicine and of the power of doctors to stay or cure disease. Argan is of course strong in his belief of the need of medical advice; Béralde, on the other hand, is as firm that the so-called skill of doctors is worthless. And Béralde urges his argument, not with scepticism or doubt as to the power of healing given to or acquired by doctors, but disbelieving altogether that doctors have such power. As to Molière's own opinion about all this, judging from his character generally, I should be inclined to say that it was mainly sceptical, but that it hardly went so far as disbelieving altogether or denying. He could not believe, he doubted; and probably enough he hoped that as time went on more accurate knowledge about medicine would be obtained. His satire against the dishonest greed of doctors is another question. It is easy to have decided ideas as to whether, in this scene between the two brothers, Molière meant or did not mean to express his own opinions on the matter under dispute. The more absolute our ideas are, perhaps the more likely are they to be wrong. But I think we may be tolerably certain that Molière meant in the first place that his scene should be looked at in the light of comedy. There are abundant instances in his plays showing how admirably he gave comic pictures of arguments which, in less skilful hands, might have been hardly more than disquisitions with much talk and but little comedy. It is of small consequence whether Molière expressed his own opinions in these disputes or not. His desire was to give the opinions of others, and he felt it to be of great consequence in telling the dispute that the mirth of comedy should be shown. Molière wrote so frequently against the doctors of medicine, and always in a tone of satire, that it is difficult to suppose that he did not believe much of what he put into the mouth of Béralde, though perhaps he himself would not have gone so far. And it is difficult also not to feel that there were personal reasons, caused by his own bad health, affecting him when he wrote

[1] *Œuvres de Molière*, ix. 339 and note 5.

his *Malade Imaginaire.* We are now a bit behind the scenes, and are tempted to think, without sentimentalism, that Molière had an idea that his end was not far off, and that he wished in perhaps his last comedy against the doctors to treat the medical tartuffes, more clever in hiding their own ineptitude and their imbecility than in anything else, as they deserved. It is clear that the dramatist intended that Argan should make himself ridiculous ; but it may be asked did he not also mean to throw counter-satire on Béralde ?

The likeness, strong enough, noticed by M. Mesnard,[1] between some words spoken by Béralde and words spoken by Don Juan, which I quoted in what I had to say on the *Amour Médecin,* seems to point that way. A good part of the discussion between the two brothers should be given :—

" *Argan.*

" Let us argue the matter. You have no belief in medicine ?

" *Béralde.*

" No, and I do not see what good I should get by believing in it.

" *Argan.*

" What ! you dismiss as untrue a thing universally established, and which for centuries past has been revered ?

" *Béralde.*

" Instead of believing it to be true, I think, between ourselves, that it is one of the greatest follies of mankind ; and, in looking at things wisely, I say that there is no more idle mummery, nothing more ridiculous, than one man bothering himself by trying to cure another.

" *Argan.*

" Why cannot you think that one man may cure another ?

" *Béralde.*

" Because the active forces of our body are mysteries of which men, so far, have been able to tell nothing, and that nature has put such thick veils over our eyes that we are still in the dark.

" *Argan.*

" Doctors, therefore, according to you, know nothing at all ?

---

[1] *Œuvres de Molière,* ix. 396 note 1.

" Béralde.

" Yes, they do. Most of them are excellent humanists, they know how to talk fine Latin, they can call all maladies by Greek names, define them and distinguish them ; but as for healing, they know nothing about it.

" Argan.

" But you must admit that doctors know more about the matter than other people ?

" Béralde.

" They know what I have told you, which does not go far in the art of curing ; and all the excellence of their skill consists in pompous gibberish, in specious babble, which gives you words for reasons and promises for effects.

" Argan.

" But still, there are people as wise and as clever as you are ; and we see that in case of illness they do ask the advice of doctors.

" Béralde.

" That is a sign of human weakness, and not of the truth of their art.

.   .   .   .

" Argan.

" . . . What should one do, then, when one is ill ?

" Béralde.

" Nothing.

" Argan.

" Nothing ?

" Béralde.

" Nothing, except lie quiet. Nature, if left alone, pulls herself out of the hole into which she has fallen. It is our uneasiness, our restlessness, that destroys everything, and nearly every man dies of the remedies given to him, not of his illness.

.   .   .   .

" Argan.

" Ho ! Ho ! It seems that you are a great doctor, and I wish we had here one of those gentlemen to stop your jaw and take your talk down a peg.

" Béralde.

" I am not trying to fight against the doctor's art ; everybody may think about it as he pleases at his own risks. I am only talking between ourselves ; and to make you open your eyes and to make you laugh at all this, I should like to take you to see one of Molière's comedies.[1]

" *Argan.*

" Your Molière is an ignorant fellow with his comedies, and I consider him most impertinent to make fun of honest people like doctors.

" *Béralde.*

" It is not the doctors he makes fun of, but the nonsense of medicine.[2]

" *Argan.*

" What business has he to think about finding fault with medical practices? He is a big fool, an impertinent ass, to laugh at consultations and prescriptions, to censure the whole body of medical men, and to put on to his stage such venerable persons as these gentlemen !

" *Béralde.*

" Whom should he put there but men of different callings? You may see there any day kings and princes, and they have as good blood in their veins as the doctors.

" *Argan.*

" S'death ! But no ; in the devil's name, if I was a doctor I would pay him back in his own coin. I'd let him have it for his impudence. If he were ill, I'd let him die without help. He might talk and howl as he liked. I would not give him the smallest cupping and not one clyster. I'd say to him : ' Die, die ; that will teach you another time how to laugh at the Faculty.'

" *Béralde.*

" You are very angry with him.

" *Argan.*

" Yes, he's a loon, and if all the doctors were wise they would do as I say.

" *Béralde.*

" He will be wiser than your doctors, for he won't ask for their help.

" *Argan.*

" So much the worse for him if he goes without it.

---

[1] In the 17th century French dramatists used occasionally to allude to themselves in a tone of playfulness or of satire. Molière did so three or four times before this instance.

[2] See *Œuvres de Molière*, ix. 401 note 4. Here, as in annotating some passage in the *Amour Médecin*, M. Mesnard points to a likeness of thought between Montaigne and Molière.

" Béralde.

" He has reasons of his own for not wanting it. He maintains that only strong and robust people, those who have a good constitution, can fight against both the remedies and the malady ; but for himself, he has only just strength enough to bear up against his illness."

From the point of view of lecturing and of credulous belief shown in comedy this scene in the *Malade Imaginaire* between Béralde and Argan offers a certain likeness to the last scene in the first act of the *Tartuffe*, where Cléante endeavours to show Orgon how he has been deceived by imposture. The characters of Cléante and of Béralde are virtually the same, the same kind of acting would personate them both ; between Orgon and Argan there seems to be a greater difference, but it is only in the direction of their semi-imbecility.

It would be wrong to say nothing of Argan's medical adviser, M. Purgon. This learned pundit had sent M. Fleurant, the apothecary, with a clyster very specially prepared for Argan's use. But Béralde, in his wisdom, had persuaded his brother to leave drugs alone for one day. The apothecary thereupon goes to his chief and reports how the clyster had been neglected and scorned. M. Purgon enters furious against his patient for his contempt and for his misconduct. He says that Argan's action is a heinous insult against the science of medicine and a crime of high treason against the Faculty, that all intercourse between Argan and him must cease ; and then M. Purgon tears in pieces a deed of gift in favour of his nephew, Thomas Diafoirus, which was to have been given to his nephew at the time of his marriage with Argan's daughter, Angélique. But that is not all. Because the invalid had declared himself rebellious against the prescriptions, M. Purgon threatens him with half a dozen frightful diseases, each one worse than the last, and with death at the end as a final extinguisher. Even the buffoonery of the doctors against the unfortunate M. de Pourceaugnac was not more grotesque than the end of this scene in the *Malade Imaginaire*.

The poor fool believes what has been said to him, and feels that he is being punished for his fault. But he is ready to listen to the advice of another doctor. Toinette has told

Béralde that she has prepared a scheme, and she appears dressed as a doctor of medicine aged ninety years.

" Toinette (to Argan).

"Give me your pulse. Now then, beat properly. I'll make you move as you ought. Ho! That pulse is insolent; I see that you don't know me yet. Who is your doctor?

" Argan.

"M. Purgon.

" Toinette.

"That man is not on my books among the great doctors. What does he say is the matter with you?

" Argan.

"He says it's the liver, others say it's the spleen.

" Toinette.

"They are all ignorant creatures. It's your lung that is ill."

After every word that Argan speaks, giving as he thinks a sign of illness, his new doctor ejaculates, "The lung, the lung!" after every article of food Argan says he has been told to eat, his new doctor ejaculates, "Ignorant fellow!" And he prescribes a regimen of food that might be suitable for young men on a knapsack expedition.

Again the simpleton believes what is said to him, but he does not like being told that he must have one arm cut off, because it deprives the other of its natural subsistence; nor is he happy when told that he must have one eye taken out for the same reason. Perhaps the meaning of these scenes, where Toinette is disguised as a doctor, is to show once more how inordinately credulous and stupid were many people who put themselves under the care of ignorant practitioners and let themselves be guided by worthless advice.

What more there is to be said about the comedy in the *Malade Imaginaire* is soon told. Argan consents to feign that he has died in his chair. When Béline, his wife, is told of her husband's death, she exclaims: "Heaven be praised!" She congratulates herself on being freed from a man whose habits are disgusting, and she thinks only of clutching the money he has left in his house. She is going out to get the keys, when he cries out to stop her. Angélique, Argan's daughter, has to go through the same trial of affection. The result is very different; and when she implores her father, if he will not let her marry Cléante, that she should not be forced to marry another, he consents to their marriage on the condition that Cléante will prepare himself to be a doctor. The young man naturally consents gladly enough.

Then as a preparation for the third and last interlude, Béralde says to his brother:—

"An idea has just struck me. Become a doctor yourself. It will be more convenient, and you will have in yourself all that you want."

After some persuasion Argan consents to be made a doctor, and his admission into the Faculty forms the subject of the burlesque scene, complementary to the *Malade Imaginaire*, known as *La Cérémonie*. This is a satirical picture, written in amusing Macaronic Latin, of the manner in which young men in Molière's day were received as bachelors into the medical Faculty. A very small knowledge of Latin and of French words will enable anyone to see its meaning and to enjoy its humour.

As might be expected, there is some satire against the course of instruction given to the young men during their term of pupilage. The first question the bachelor is asked is: "Why does opium induce sleep?" He answers: "Because it has a dormitive quality." The chorus of the Faculty replies:—

"Bene, bene, bene, bene respondere,
Dignus, dignus est intrare
In nostro docto corpore,
Bene, bene respondere."

Then the bachelor is asked what remedy he would apply in half a dozen different cases of illness. To all the questions he makes the same answer:—

"Clysterium donare,
Postea seignare,
Ensuita purgare."

He is asked to swear to keep the written statutes of the Faculty with sense and good judgment; he complies, of course. Then, that in all consultations he will be of the same opinion as his elder, whether his advice be good or bad; and to that he swears. Also that he will never use any remedy but those prescribed by the learned Faculty, even though the patient were to die of his malady. The president then confers the doctor's cap upon the bachelor, and endows him with various medical powers; the last mentioned is that of killing everybody with impunity. The bachelor has to return thanks for the honour done him. He says :—

> "Grandes doctores doctrinæ
> De la rhubarbe et du séné,
> Ce seroit sans douta à moi chosa folla,
> Inepta et ridicula,
> Si j'alloibam m'engageare
> Vobis louangeas donare,
> Et entreprenoibam adjoutare
> Des lumieras au soleillo,
> Et des etoilas au cielo,
> Des ondas à l'Oceano,
> Et des rosas au printanno.
> Agreate qu' avec uno moto,
> Pro toto remercimento,
> Rendam gratiam corpori tam docto.
> Vobis, vobis debeo
> Bien plus qu' à naturæ et qu' à patri meo :
> Natura et pater meus
> Hominem me habent factum ;
> Mais vos me, ce qui est bien plus,
> Avetis factum medicum,
> Honor, favor, et gratia
> Qui, in hoc corde que voilà,
> Imprimant ressentimenta
> Qui dureront in secula."

Then the chorus sings :—

> "Vivat, vivat, vivat, vivat, cent fois vivat
> Novus doctor, qui tam bene parlat !
> Mille, mille annis et manget et bibet,
> Et seignet et tuat."

As Molière died almost on the stage, this is perhaps the place to record the circumstances of his death. Many strong men have wished to die in harness, in the midst of their labours. Molière certainly did so ; and this fact lends an additional lustre to the halo of glory which we should all be glad to see spread around the last hours of one whose work has ever been, and will always be, admired and respected by open-minded and generous-thinking men and women. Grimarest says :—

"The day on which the *Malade Imaginaire* was to be acted for the third time" [Grimarest should have said the *fourth* time] "Molière's chest annoyed him more than usual. He sent for his wife, and said to her in Baron's presence: 'So long as pain and pleasure have been equally mixed in my life, I have thought myself happy; but now I am worn out with trouble, and have no minute of enjoyment or of rest. I see clearly that I must give up the game. I cannot hold out against the pain and worry, which do not give me a moment's peace.' Then thinking to himself, he added: 'How much a man suffers before he dies!' Mlle. Molière and Baron were greatly touched at Molière's speech, which they did not expect from him, however great his suffering might be. They implored him, with tears in their eyes, not to play that day, but to take a little rest. He said to them: 'What can I do? There are fifty poor workpeople who live on their day's pay; what would they do if there were no performance? I should reproach myself if I were to keep their bread from them for one day, being actually able to give it to them.' He sent for the actors and told them that as he was worse than usual he would not play that day, unless everything were ready at four o'clock punctually. 'Otherwise,' he said to them, 'I shall not be there and you may give back the money.' The candles were lighted, and the curtain was drawn exactly at four o'clock. Molière went through his part with difficulty, and half of the audience perceived that in pronouncing the word *Juro* in the *Cérémonie* a convulsion came upon him. When he saw that this was remarked he made an effort, and by a forced smile he hid what had happened." [1]

When he had chronicled the fourth performance of the *Malade Imaginaire*, La Grange wrote in his Register:—

"This same day, after the play was over, about ten o'clock in the evening, M. de Molière died in his house in the Rue de Richelieu, having acted the part of the said Malade Imaginaire, very much troubled by a cold and inflammation of the lungs, which caused him to cough a great deal, so that in the strong efforts he made to spit he burst a vein in his body and did not live half an hour or three-quarters of an hour after the said vein had burst. His body is buried at Saint Joseph's chapel of ease belonging to the parish of Saint Eustache."

Nine years later La Grange wrote in the preface to the first complete edition of Molière's plays, of which he was one of the editors:—

"On the 17th day of February [1673], the day of the fourth performance of the *Malade Imaginaire*, he [Molière] was so much troubled by the inflammation in his chest that he had difficulty in acting his part. He got through it, though he suffered much, and

---

[1] *Vie de Molière*, pp. 284-87, ed. 1705.

the audience saw easily that his performance was far from what he wished it to be. Immediately the play was over he went home, and no sooner had he got into bed than the cough which troubled him perpetually became very violent. The efforts he made were so great that he burst a vein in his lungs. Finding himself in that condition, he turned all his thoughts to heaven. A moment later he became speechless, and in half an hour he was suffocated by the quantity of blood that came up through his mouth." [1]

Two sisters of charity, to whom Molière had given hospitality, were with him at his death. The curé of Saint Eustache refused to bury Molière. Thereupon his widow addressed a petition to the Archbishop of Paris, Harlay de Champvalon, setting forth that the deceased had asked for a priest to receive from him the last sacrament, that he had sent his valet and a woman servant to two priests belonging to the church of Saint Eustache, that they had refused to obey the call of the dying man; that then Molière's brother-in-law, Jean Aubry, went to fetch another priest from the same church, but that he arrived too late. The petition goes on to say that as the deceased had asked for the services of a priest before his death, that as he had died as a good Christian, and had received the sacrament at the previous Easter, grace might be accorded that he should be buried in the church of Saint Eustache. Finally the demand was granted, and probably owing to the king's interference, but with restrictions. Ecclesiastical burial was allowed in the cemetery of the parish, but on the condition that there should be no display, there should be only two priests, it should not take place in the day-time, and there should be no solemn service for the dead man said in the parish of Saint Eustache or elsewhere. The funeral was postponed until the 21st of February, at about nine o'clock in the evening. It is comforting to think that the wicked severity of the archbishop's order was not carried out. From a letter, apparently anonymous, addressed to " Monsieur Boyvin, prêtre, docteur en théologie," an account may be read of the ceremony showing that it was conducted with all proper reverence, and in a manner very different from the wishes of the archbishop. Harlay de Champvalon was far from being a good man; but Bossuet, whom everybody should respect, showed himself in another way equally intolerant.

[1] *Œuvres de Molière*, i. pp. 17, 18.

Twenty years after Molière's death the prelate wrote: "Posterity will know the end of this poet and actor who, while he was playing his *Malade Imaginaire* or his *Médecin par force*, received the last attack of the malady from which he died a few hours later, and went from the laughter of the stage, where he uttered almost his last sigh, to the tribunal of Him who said: ' Woe unto you that laugh now! for ye shall mourn and weep.' "[1] Had these words come from a lay writer of ordinary intelligence, they would not have been noticed; but coming as they did from a prelate and from one of the greatest minds that France has produced, their foolishness and their uncharitableness are astonishing.

Both M. Mesnard[2] and M. Moland[3] have written at length about the obsequies of Molière. It is said that in 1792 what were thought to be Molière's remains were, with those of La Fontaine, dug up from the cemetery of Saint Joseph, but what was done with them is not told; that in 1799 they were placed by Alexandre Lenoir in a mausoleum in the Musée des Monuments Français, and that in 1817 they were transported to Père La Chaise. But M. Mesnard thinks that these mausoleums were cenotaphs.[4] In 1875 the two mausoleums were restored. Among the different epitaphs written on Molière, that by his friend and admirer La Fontaine has been thought by Frenchmen to be the best:—

> "Sous ce tombeau gisent Plaute et Térence,
> Et cependant le seul Molière y gît.
> Leurs trois talents ne formoient qu'un esprit,
> Dont le bel art réjouissoit la France.
> Ils sont partis ! et j'ai peu d'espérance
> De les revoir. Malgré tous nos efforts,
> Pour un longtemps, selon toute apparence,
> Térence et Plaute et Molière sont morts."

Among great French writers who have not been members of the French Academy, Molière is the chief. Yet if we think for a moment what was his position as an actor who delighted the crowd in the pit of his theatre with his performances of ridiculous characters; when we think of him as the author of the *Tartuffe* which had brought down upon him the censure

---

[1] Quoted by M. Mesnard, *Œuvres de Molière*, x. 432.
[2] *Ibid.* x. 430-48.　　　　　[3] *Œuvres de Molière*, 2nd ed. i. 307-35.
[4] *Œuvres de Molière*, x. 447.

of nearly all churchmen and of many men who by their abilities had risen in the world, as the author of *George Dandin* where it was believed he had extolled the shameless effrontery of an impudent woman in order to jeer at the misfortunes she caused to her husband; when we recollect that the poet, about whose verses many of the Academicians cared nothing and whose wit they derided, was the leader of a troop of actors and lived much in their society; when we recollect also how many churchmen there were among the actual members of the Academy in Molière's day, and the unwillingness that men have very commonly and everywhere shown to admit into their choice society another of very opposite opinions to their own;—when we think of all this for a moment, we shall feel that the surprise would indeed have been great if Molière had been allowed to sit as one of the forty immortals. A little more than a hundred years after the poet's death the members of the Academy wished to grant him a posthumous honour. In the room where they held their sittings a bust of Molière was placed, and on it was engraved the following inscription :—

"Rien ne manque à sa gloire, il manquait à la nôtre."

At the end of vol. ix. of the *Œuvres de Molière* M. Mesnard has printed some *Poésies Diverses*, never intended to be spoken on the stage, that Molière wrote or may be fairly supposed to have written. The chief is a poem, entitled *La Gloire du Val de Grâce*, addressed by Molière in 1669 to the painter Mignard on his fresco in the dome of the church Le Val de Grâce in Paris, on the south side of the river. To this poem M. Mesnard has prefixed a substantial Notice. Apart from the province of comedy Molière's verses do not give much pleasure. The lines may be regular and correct, but they have little of the charm that true poetry inspires. There are, however, some lines in *La Gloire du Val de Grâce* which have an interest outside the mere skill of verse-making or of painting. One characteristic of Molière's work, which everybody must have noticed, is that it shows a free hand. When he had got his thoughts into the shape suitable for his purpose at the moment, the rest came to him fairly easily. The labour of composition which has hampered so many authors did not, we may imagine, give him great trouble. He evidently wished to see the effect of freshness in all work. When the house was built he did not like to see marks left by the scaffolding. And regularity or correctness was to him a smaller matter than true naturalness. These thoughts made him allude in his poem to the difference between frescoes and oil-painting. He preferred the fresco with its "brusques fiertés," which must be seized quickly to picture the passing thought and which cannot be erased, to the slower work which may be retouched and manipulated at pleasure. The following lines give some conception of Molière's ideas about the effect his and other work should produce:—

> "La fresque, dont la grâce, à l'autre préférée,
> Se conserve un éclat d'éternelle durée,
> Mais dont la promptitude et les brusques fiertés
> Veulent un grand génie à toucher ses beautés !
> De l'autre, qu'on connoît, la traitable méthode
> Aux foiblesses d'un peintre aisément s'accommode ;
> La paresse de l'huile, allant avec lenteur,
> Du plus tardif génie attend la pesanteur :
> Elle sait secourir, par le temps qu'elle donne,
> Les faux pas que peut faire un pinceau qui tâtonne ;
> Et sur cette peinture on peut, pour faire mieux,
> Revenir, quand on veut, avec de nouveaux yeux.
> Cette commodité de retoucher l'ouvrage
> Aux peintres chancelants est un grand avantage ;
> Et ce qu'on ne fait pas en vingt fois qu'on reprend,
> On le peut faire en trente, on le peut faire en cent.
> Mais la fresque est pressante, et veut, sans complaisance,
> Qu'un peintre s'accommode à son impatience,
> La traite à sa manière, et d'un travail soudain
> Saisisse le moment qu'elle donne à sa main :
> La sévère rigueur de ce moment qui passe
> Aux erreurs d'un pinceau ne fait aucune grâce ;
> Avec elle il n'est point de retour à tenter,
> Et tout au premier coup se doit exécuter ;
> Elle veut un esprit où se rencontre unie
> La pleine connoissance avec le grand génie,
> Secouru d'une main propre à le seconder
> Et maîtresse de l'art jusqu'à le gourmander,
> Une main prompte à suivre un beau feu qui la guide,
> Et dont comme un éclair, la justesse rapide
> Répand dans ses fonds, à grands traits non tâtés,
> De ses expressions les touchantes beautés."

What is chiefly noticeable here is that Molière liked to see large-mindedness, originality, and a show of ease and of quickness in all good work. Sainte-Beuve, in rallying Vauvenargues because he preferred La Bruyère as a painter of men's actions to Molière, says of him: "Vous êtes peintre à l'huile, M. de Vauvenargues."

By far the best, in my opinion, of Molière's poems, is the *Remercîment au Roi,* written in 1663, which was noticed in a previous chapter. There is there distinctly a comic interest, and the author shows his satire playfully and pleasantly. But Molière's ambition did not make him attempt to write pretty verses. The spirit of poetry was not sufficiently strong in him, and his hands were already so full with writing of another kind that he had small wish to manufacture tender lines which he knew beforehand would be worth very little. It is not likely that those printed by M. Mesnard are either widely read or admired. I must say here for the last time that the purpose of Molière's work was to portray the humours of men and women and their characterisation by amusing and satirical comedy, laughing at their foibles and condemning their faults. He certainly had keen imagination; and it led him to show with comic effect what people are like as they go through their parts in the play of life, and how for good and for ill they act and react upon one another. He would not preach, but he strove to teach honest lessons by playful and not ill-natured satire. His thoughts were bent towards mirthful comedy, and his style or manner of writing naturally followed his thoughts and took its colour from them. But though Molière often showed poetical feeling in his verses, he had not the higher or deeper feelings of poetry, nor had he the power of strong poetical expression. If an author has a high and rare faculty largely developed, it is better to see what use he has made of that force than to belittle his intellectual capabilities because he has not another faculty in a more or less opposite direction. When it has been proved that Shakespeare and Bacon were but one man, then it will be time for a new and a logical method of interpreting human thoughts to arise.

CHAPTER XIX

WE have finished considering Molière's comedies, but there are still a few biographical matters to be mentioned which could not have been spoken about earlier without awkward interruption in the narrative.

If facts could only be adduced, an extremely interesting chapter might be written about Molière and his friends. But unless imagination is to run riot, the facts are wanting which would enable me to deal here much more than has been hinted at already with the social side of Molière's character. Taken fairly and kept in its place, a good deal may be said in favour of the saying—I think an Irish one—" There never was a good story yet without a lie in it." But what is a lie ? If all fiction is a lie because the tale told is not as true as cold logic, the world must be in a bad state. The man who can deck a purely fictitious tale with real and fitting attributes gives a true life to it, for he shows that his imagination was sound and that it did not lie to him there. My reader will have seen already that I have not got that imagination. I have tried to say what were Molière's ideas about the actual work of his life ; but I have no wish at the end of a book that is already long, to enter into æsthetic-speculative, or speculative-æsthetic, literary theories on work that did not concern him directly.

Molière, doubtless, had his friends, but it is not certain that he had the time or always the inclination to enjoy much of their society. La Fontaine in his novel, *Les Amours de Psyché et de Cupidon*, published in 1669, described the meetings of four companions whom he called Poliphile, Ariste, Gélaste, and Acante ; and it has been said that in his tale the author told how he and Molière and Racine and Boileau met together and discussed all things in loving friendship. On this romantic idea castles in the air have been built, but the structures were so slight that no one could live in them. We read that Ariste was meant to be Boileau. Sceptical commentators who doubted that any actual meaning was to be found in La Fontaine's fable have admitted so much. But later criticism has muddled the other imaginary names with the real ones, and now nobody knows quite who was who, except that the proud title of Ariste has always been given to Boileau. Even then, nothing can be gathered from the conversation related that describes the thoughts of any one of the friends. There is a short discussion among them as to the differences between tragedy and comedy, but the opinions are given in a purely formal manner; they show nothing characteristic of the speakers, and not much that is characteristic of either tragedy or comedy. The probability may be that when La Fontaine began his story he had some half romantic idea which he did not carry out, and that names have been prefixed to his personages mainly for the pleasure of doing so. This has certainly been the case with regard to some novels written both in England and in France within the last sixty or seventy years. In December 1665 Racine and Molière had quarrelled. It is not likely that they became friends after that date, and there is nothing to show that before that date they and La Fontaine and Boileau used to meet, even now and then, with set purpose to enjoy each other's society and to listen while each in turn was propounding his opinions.

The following anecdote is amusing, and is not perhaps so wild as it may appear to be. When the dramatist was living at Auteuil, some of his friends, Boileau, Chapelle, Lulli, and two others, went one day to see him. Molière was far from well, and he begged Chapelle to do the honours of his house. Chapelle acted the host so well that before the party broke up not one of them knew clearly what he was saying. But instead of being merry they talked rank pessimism. They all said that the best thing that could have happened to any one was not to have been born; as it was, the best thing was to die. And they agreed, with a singular unanimity of opinion, to go down at once to the Seine, which was close by, and drown themselves. Their noise disturbed Molière, and when he heard of their determination he exclaimed: "How now, gentlemen! what have I done that you should carry out such a grand idea

without telling me about it?" Chapelle was forced to admit
that Molière had not been fairly treated. Then addressing
him directly he said: "But come along now with us and
drown yourself."—"Wait a moment," the poet objected. "This
is not a thing to be done clumsily. It will be the last action
in our lives, and it requires care. If we drown ourselves at
this time of day, people will talk nastily of us—say perhaps
that we were tipsy. The thing should be done properly so
that we may get some glory from it. Let us go to-morrow
morning about eight or nine o'clock, and when everybody is
afoot we will drown ourselves in the river."—"Yes, that's what
we'll do," Chapelle answered. "We can drown ourselves
to-morrow morning. In the meanwhile, let us go back and
finish our wine." When the next day came they found that
life still had its charms.[1] On one or two occasions in his plays
Molière seemed to think that people did not commit suicide
so often as they talked about doing it.

Though the French dramatists in the seventeenth century
did not join together in writing their plays, as the English
dramatists had done two or three generations earlier, few of
them probably declined all offers of verbal assistance from their
friends. The man who gave most assistance to Molière was,
of course, Boileau. He was "Le législateur du Parnasse," and
at times acted the critic among his friends. He gave Molière
Greek-sounding names for the doctors in the *Amour Médecin*;
and we are told that he gave him the idea of the scene between
Trissotin and Vadius in the *Femmes Savantes*; also of the
Latin ceremony at the end of the *Malade Imaginaire*. Boileau
thus showed that he had a sense of humour. And in the first
scene of the *Femmes Savantes* he suggested an alteration
which, with the exception of one word, Molière allowed.[2]

The main thoughts of Boileau and of Molière were much
alike on many subjects, but the two men expressed themselves
differently. Their satire against affectation and pretence was
shown in different ways. When affectations and pretence meant
no more than idle vanities that did no one any harm, Molière
generally laughed at them. Boileau tried to make his satire
laughable, but it was not given to him to do so. His honesty

---

[1] Taschereau, *Vie de Molière*, 3rd ed. 93, 94.
[2] *Œuvres de Molière*, ix. 63 note 3.

of purpose is to be respected, his comic seriousness is sometimes amusing, but light raillery that should carry weight was beyond his power. There are four verses in Act I. sc. ii. of the *Misanthrope*, spoken by Alceste when he is showing Oronte that his sonnet is worthless, which, in the thought that inspired them, might have come straight from Boileau or from Pascal as well as from Molière. All three disliked false taste in literature, and all three in their different ways would have said :—

> " Ce style figuré, dont on fait vanité,
> Sont du bon caractère et de la vérité ;
> Ce n'est que jeu de mots, qu'affectation pure,
> Et ce n'est point ainsi que parle la nature."

We have seen how Molière laughed at false literary tastes. Pascal's laughter was tersely expressed, as when he said that people call a king " an august monarch "; when he wrote " la vraie éloquence se moque de l'éloquence," and again : " se moquer de la philosophie c'est vraiment philosopher." But Boileau's anger got the better of him, and he felt inclined to roar. There was a mania in France in the second quarter of the seventeenth century and a little later for burlesque and trivial writing. This Boileau hated, and he showed his disgust at it in the first canto of his *Art Poétique*.

> " Cette contagion infecta les provinces,
> Du clerc et du bourgeois passa jusques aux princes ;
> Le plus mauvais plaisant eut ses approbateurs ;
> Et jusqu'à d'Assouci, tout trouva des lecteurs."

Boileau was probably right, and the way he expressed himself in the last quoted line seems to have given amusement to the man he wanted to censure.

At one time, at least, Louis XIV. was a good friend to Molière, for without the protection afforded by the sovereign to the poet it is doubtful whether the *Tartuffe* would have appeared on the stage during its author's lifetime. Molière recognised his Majesty's mark of favour and his sense of justice; and he proclaimed his gratitude loudly in the speech spoken by l'exempt, or police officer, nearly at the end of the comedy. Condé also was on the poet's side against the bigots who wished to crush the immortal picture of hypocrisy and concurrent vices. Taschereau speaks of Condé's esteem for Molière, and tells the following story, which, if true, was more witty than polite. The prince was so much upset by the news of Molière's death, that when an abbé presented to him an epitaph for the poet, Condé replied: " I wish he was alive to make yours."[1] Neither Louis XIV. nor his courtiers geneially had much real knowledge of Molière's power. As an actor, he amused them. They considered him an excellent mimic who could imitate admirably on the stage the ridiculous qualities of a man who was everywhere a laughing-stock. But for Molière as author they knew and cared little. A proof of this may be seen from a comparison of the number of times his more serious comedies and his comédies-ballets were played at court during his lifetime.[2] Molière tickled the vanity of the noblemen when he drew their portraits in the *Fâcheux*; but as to the comedies he wrote later, not many of the courtiers paid him the compliment to try to understand their meaning. The humour or the wit was appreciated by the men in the parterre of the theatre; it was too frank, too open, for the great dandies, and they jeered at it. This fatuous superciliousness annoyed Molière, and he gave pictures of two brainless noblemen, Acaste and Clitandre, in the *Misanthrope*. They are seen chiefly in the first scene of the third act, and in the fourth scene of the fifth act.

To come now to things more definite. There may be a natural curiosity, not altogether idle, to know how much money Molière earned in Paris from 1658 to 1673. But could the amount be stated accurately, it would not tell much unless its value could be compared with other values; and all that is a large matter. Of the various classes of writers in France in the seventeenth century, the dramatists were the best paid. A few of them might have lived more or less well, while their plays were new, upon what they got from the theatres; but even Boileau and La Bruyère, who wrote no plays, and whose works were reprinted oftener than those of any other author, would have starved unless they had other sources of income than from the sale of their books. As it happened, they both declined to receive what was owing to them in that way. Though the amounts paid to Molière for his many plays are known approximately, they cannot be compared with the sums

---

[1] Taschereau, *Vie de Molière*, 3rd ed. 97.
[2] *Œuvres de Molière*, i. 557, col. 1.

received by either of the two Corneilles, nor with those received by Racine, for these are not known at all.

There is in the *Magasin Pittoresque* for September 1860 (pp. 278-280) an article by Regnier on the *État de la Fortune de Molière*. As sociétaire of the Comédie Française Regnier had access to its archives. He estimated that for the representation of his comedies Molière got, as author, 49,500 livres. Other estimates, a little larger or smaller, may be formed; because, in taking the plays separately, every one will not agree as to the amount received from each. Regnier's reckoning is, nevertheless, I imagine, tolerably accurate. As to the sale of the plays when printed, little is known, but probably it was not large. A popular play, while new, has rarely found a comparatively large number of readers. Molière, too, did not think much about the reading public; his anxiety was to please those who went to his theatre to see and to hear. Like Shakespeare, he wrote for his audience, not for the few who read at home; and the thoughts of neither author went so far ahead as to trouble him with the attentive opinions of posterity. The amount that Molière received as an actor can be stated, for La Grange, on p. 143 of his Register, reckoned that he had received 51,670 livres as his share at the Palais Royal theatre during the fourteen years he played in Paris; and Molière's earnings as an actor were of course the same as those of La Grange. Regnier, in estimating Molière's earnings as an actor, counted his wife's share as belonging to her husband. I think that is hardly kind; because, for money fairly earned in this world, everybody should have his own purse. Molière was not a curmudgeon, to grab his wife's dues; and Mlle. Molière, we may feel tolerably sure, knew very well how to keep what she had got. If she spent no more than what she had gained lawfully from the theatre, her husband had so far no reason to be dissatisfied with her. We have seen already that in 1663 Molière received a pension of 1000 livres from the king as "homme de lettres"; therefore after ten years that mounted to 10,000 livres. And as tapissier valet de chambre du Roi, Regnier reckoned that at the time of his death Molière received 4337 livres. Regnier's total estimate is that since La Grange began to keep his Register at Easter 1659 Molière made 152,021 livres, 19 sous. If we multiply this sum by five, as French writers would do to get the equivalent in spending money in our day, Molière made altogether £30,404 sterling.

For the details in the inventory taken after Molière's death, telling the different articles of property that belonged to him and to his wife, and their debts, I must refer to Soulié's volume.[1] Soulié estimates that according to the values given in this inventory for linen, furniture, clothes, books, silver, ready-money, etc., Molière left behind him 18,000 livres worth of goods of various kinds, and that the total value of his estate should be put down at 40,000 livres—or 200,000 francs at the present day, and, if one considers depreciation, that this sum might be 300,000 francs.[2] Among Molière's books there were some Greek and Latin classics; and some French authors, of whom Montaigne, Balzac, and Pierre Corneille are the best known. But it seems strange that there was no Rabelais; for in largeness of view in their outlook upon human nature, and upon the way that men show themselves to be what they are, there was much likeness between Rabelais and Molière, and probably also much sympathy. And it is curious that among Molière's books, though there were some two hundred and forty volumes of French, Spanish, and Italian comedies, no copy of his own plays was mentioned in his inventory. Soulié says that altogether Molière had about three hundred volumes in Paris and about forty at Auteuil.[3] What Molière read it would be as impossible to tell as to say what the weather was like as he drove from Auteuil to the Palais Royal theatre. Some men as busily employed as he was have been voracious readers. Byron is an instance. Judging generally, and from the titles of the books owned by Molière, I should not fancy that Molière was a great reader; though other persons may very well think differently. One does find among the effects mentioned in his inventory descriptions of about twenty of the costumes worn by him in the different parts he played in his comedies. These descriptions are given collectively by M. Moland,[4] and to some people they may be interesting. I did not speak of them in saying which part Molière had acted in this or that comedy, for to

---

[1] *Recherches sur Molière*, 81-97 ; 262-92.   [2] *Ibid.* 97.
[3] *Ibid.* 93.   [4] *Molière, sa vie et ses ouvrages*, 310, 311.

have done so would have been tedious, and many of the French terms describing the costumes are untranslatable.

Mlle. Molière remained a widow for four years after her husband's death. On the 29th of May 1677 she signed a contract of marriage between Isaac François Guérin and herself, and two days later the marriage ceremony was performed.[1] Guérin had been an actor at the Theâtre du Marais; and after Molière's death, when the actors at that theatre joined themselves with those who had belonged to the Palais Royal, Guérin was one of the new troop who went to play at the Hôtel Guénegaud;[2] and seven years later he became a member of the only regular company of actors in Paris,[3] a company which was known afterwards as the Comédie Française. In this last list of actors' names, given by La Grange, the name of Mlle. Molière may also be seen.

Molière had three children, two boys and a girl. The girl only survived him. Their surname has generally been given as Poquelin. His eldest boy, Louis, born on the 19th of January 1664, was baptized on the 18th or on the 28th of the following month.[4] The duc de Créqui, in the king's name, was his godfather, and la maréchale du Plessis, in the name of the duchesse d'Orléans, was his godmother. M. Mesnard thinks that this royal honour was accorded to Molière because he was a valet de chambre du roi, not because of his writings. But little Louis died on the 10th of November in the year of his birth.[5] And Molière lost his other boy less than a month after his birth. Pierre Jean-Baptiste Armand, born on the 15th of September 1672, was christened on the 1st of October following.[6] On page 136 of his Register, La Grange, while chronicling the theatrical representations for that month of October, says in a marginal note: "Mardy 11, néant, à cause de la mort du petit Molière."

Molière's second child, Esprit Madeleine, was christened on the 4th of August 1665.[7] Her father took her to live with

[1] Soulié, *Recherches sur Molière*, 100.
[2] *Registre de la Grange*, 146.   [3] *Ibid.* 238.
[4] Jal, *Dictionnaire*, p. 875, col. 1, says on the 18th; M. Mesnard, *Notice biographique sur Molière*, 472 (Document IX.), says the 28th.
[5] Jal, *Dictionnaire*, p. 875, col. 1.
[6] *Ibid.* p. 875, col. 1; P. Mesnard, *Notice biographique sur Molière*, 357, 423.
[7] *Œuvres de Molière*, x. 474, Document XII.

him in his apartment at Auteuil, and when he died she was not eight years old. Little is known about her in her young days except that she once showed her wit in a piquant manner. About the year 1680 or 1681 Chapelle, with whom she was perhaps pretty intimate, asked her how old she was. She answered: "Fifteen and a half; but don't say anything about that to my mother."[1] Her late father could hardly have imagined a more graphic reply. There is a romantic story to the effect that when she was twenty years of age she eloped with Claude de Rachel de Montalant, but that as he could not obtain her mother's consent to their marriage the two lovers had to wait for her death. Mlle. Molière— for La Grange calls her by the name of her first husband, though she was in fact Mlle. Guérin—lived until the year 1700,[2] and her daughter did not marry M. de Montalant until five years later. The bridegroom was a widower of sixty years of age, or close upon it, and the bride had just passed her fortieth birthday.[3] He was a man of good family, but was poor. The marriage settlement between him and his future wife shows some curious clauses, for which I must refer to Soulié's volume. And there is much else, also to be found in Soulié's volume, referring to money matters consequent upon Molière's death, which not many readers would thank me to give here. A few circumstances, however, may be told very shortly.

When de Montalant married Mlle. Poquelin his income appears to have been stated at 500 livres a year, but adding up the few figures I cannot make them amount to more than 440 livres a year.[4] Madeleine Poquelin was more richly endowed, for she inherited money from her father, from her aunt Madeleine Béjart, and from her mother; and her fortune amounted to nearly 66,000 livres.[5] She died in 1723; her husband in 1738. There was no issue from their marriage.

The dates of the deaths of the Béjarts, Molière's oldest comrades on the stage, may be mentioned. Joseph, known until his death as Béjart aîné, died in 1659; Louis, known until his elder brother's death as Béjart cadet, died in 1678;

---

[1] Œuvres de Molière, x. 457.
[2] Soulié, Recherches sur Molière, 105.
[3] Ibid. 107.
[4] Ibid. 108-9 ; 331.
[5] Ibid. 109 ; 337.

Madeleine, their eldest sister, died unmarried in 1672; Geneviève, who had married twice, died in 1675; and Armande, who became Molière's wife, in 1700.

According to the inventory taken after his death in February 1669, Jean Poquelin, Molière's father, died worth only 937 livres, and Soulié remarks that this sum was much less than the 2200 livres that Poquelin had contributed to his marriage settlement with Marie Cressé in 1621.[1] The probability is that his life was not a happy one. Widowed for the second time when he was just over forty years of age, he lived thirty-three years longer and saw his business, which had once been prosperous, slowly lessening. What comfort he may have got from his children is not known, but there can be little doubt that the fact that his eldest son chose the stage as his profession gave him great pain. And perhaps it would not be wrong to suppose that his sorrow clung to him. If you can get to the bottom of a man's money dealings, large and small, and see with what spirit he parts with his money—generally an impossible task—you will learn much of his character. The world takes what knowledge it has got in this matter and estimates accordingly. And this test has not been favourable to Jean Poquelin. Perhaps he has been wrongly judged upon what is known of his money transactions with his children.[2] Soulié says that Voltaire's assertion that Jean Poquelin was an old-clothes merchant seems, from his inventory, to be nearly justified, at least during the last years of his life. He did not die a poor man, and though his disposition may have been morose, we should be wrong to look for his qualities in the character of Harpagon. Indeed, the fact that Molière drew the character of Harpagon may be taken fairly as a sign that Jean Poquelin was not a miser. Molière's sense of honourable feeling would have prevented him from wishing to portray the features of his father in such a character.

In this account of Molière's life and of his comedy there are, I fear, things omitted that should have been said; on the other hand, there are some details which might perhaps have been eliminated. But every one should try to tell his story in his own way, and while doing so work with his own brains.

[1] *Recherches sur Molière*, 66.　　[2] *Ibid.* 50-53; 63-68.

As Molière wrote many comedies, perhaps there are some persons who would like to have an idea as to which of his plays they should read. I cannot pretend to any royal road to such knowledge; and as Molière did not divide men into classes, perhaps no one should make that attempt with his plays. Possibly an English reader will choose at first the comedies in prose as more easy to understand. Molière wrote twenty-eight comedies of different lengths, and the amount of his prose and of his verse is pretty equally balanced. Of the comedies in prose shown in his lighter manner, the *Précieuses Ridicules*, the *Amour Médecin*, the *Médecin Malgré Lui*, *George Dandin* and the *Bourgeois Gentilhomme* are well known to be amusing; while his humour is shown in a more serious way in the *Critique de l'École des Femmes*, in *Don Juan* and in the *Avare*. Among the plays in verse the *Tartuffe*, the *Misanthrope*, the *Femmes Savantes*, stand in the first rank; below them, but each with its own characteristics, are the *Étourdi*, the *Fâcheux*, the *École des Femmes, Amphitryon*. These indications are only meant to be taken generally. After speaking of *George Dandin*, I said that Molière made some of his comedies complementary to others that he had written previously, and that in such cases it would be well to read the later written comedy after the first and then try to conciliate their meaning. That plan will tell how he made use of his thoughts in different ways. In prose and in verse Molière showed his purpose by laughter —more openly and in a more popular manner in prose; more delicately, with irony as well as with satire, in verse Thus in the *Tartuffe*, Dorine rallies her master thoroughly, but with refinement of language; in *Don Juan*, the satire strikes like the blow from a club. So also in the two plays against the affectations of women. The wit in the *Précieuses Ridicules* is rough, familiar, jovial; in the *Femmes Savantes* both silly and stupid pedantry are exposed with elegance and grace of manner, and in the disputes we enjoy the tartness shown by the combatants. In the *Misanthrope*, Célimène speaks like a hard woman of the world who had been bred up in an artificial school of cold politeness; in *George Dandin*, Angélique is a woman of the same stamp though of a worse nature, and we see in her the same thoughts pushed farther and shown with open effrontery and barefaced shamelessness. There is sadness in the satire in *George Dandin*, but at the same time the comedy in the play is most amusing.

One word in conclusion. I have often thought that those who wish to learn to read French would do well to take Molière as their instructor. If they have a liking for comedy he will interest them, and that is a great point gained. When young people are trying to educate themselves they are far more likely to do so with the aid of a book they enjoy than if they force themselves to read one that gives them little pleasure. Molière's irregularities of construction are those natural to comedy, and they are not so faulty as to count much against the large reasons which have always made him popular with those who know his plays; and the very few instances of what may now be called coarseness cannot be fairly urged with common sense or without uncharitableness. I think that as a teacher of language Molière would educate an intelligent young man or girl better and more thoroughly than an author who sat down to write with didactic intentions. Which would interest the most, which would confer, educationally, the greatest benefit—the *Avare* or *Télémaque*? Molière's mind was always clear and his views of life were remarkably broad and sound, and he was so human in his thoughts that except in some matters of form most of his scenes might have been written yesterday. If that be so, people two hundred and fifty years hence will think of them nearly as we do now. Frenchmen are rightly proud of their favourite author, and we English who enjoy his comedies feel that their cause for pride is both just and true.

INDEX

A

ABSURDITY and ridicule in fable and in comedy are not synonymous, 170 ; 194 ; 401.

ACADEMY, French (The), Origin of, 151. Ridicule thrown upon its early members, 514. The femmes savantes wished to imitate their labours, 514. Ménage wrote a squib against the Academicians, 517, 518. Why Molière was not a member of the Academy, 545, 546.

ACTING, Molière's ideas of, different from those at the Hôtel de Bourgogne, 261-265.

ACTORS' shares, how divided, 229, 230.

"AFFICHE" (The), 238-240.

"AFFICHE (Une) de Comédiens en, 1662," 122, 123.

AGEN, Molière played at, 104.

AIMÉ-MARTIN, gave for the first time the names of the original actors in Molière's plays, 140.

ALBI, Molière played at, 101.

ALEXANDRINE metre used by Molière in nearly all of his plays in verse, 208.

"ALLER à la comédie" meant going to the play, 96.

Amants Magnifiques (Les), comedy by Molière ; not acted at the Palais Royal theatre, 470.

Amour Médecin (L'), comedy by Molière, 395-408. The satire against the doctors in this comedy was not coarse, 402 ; names of all the original actors in the play not known, 408. Its success on the stage, 278 ; 283.

Amphitryon, comedy by Molière, 447-450. Written in "vers libres," 447, 448. Molière did not mean to flatter or to insult the king, 448, 449. The play shows that Molière had not a high sense of the feeling of poetry, 449, 450. Proverbial quotations from this comedy, 450. Uncertainty as to the original actors in, 450. Its success on the stage, 278 ; 283.

ANALYSIS of yearly receipts taken by Molière's troop, 275, 276.

Andromède, tragedy by P. Corneille, played by Molière's troop at Lyons, 110, 111.

"ANIMAUX," term of banter against actors used by Molière, 100 ; and against women, 310.

"ANNONCE" (The), 237, 238.

ARCHBISHOP of Paris (The), condemns the *Tartuffe*, and was his censure just ? 351-353.

ARISTOTLE and Horace ; wrong consideration given to them by the authors of plays, 260-261.

ARVIEUX, Laurent d', assists Molière with the Turkish ceremony in the *Bourgeois Gentilhomme*, 483, 484.

ASPECTS, Different, of, the Hôtel de Bourgogne and Palais Royal theatres, 254-265.

ASSOUCI, d', met Molière at Lyons, 116, 117. Satirised by Boileau, 552.

ATHEIST, Molière wished to draw a picture of an, 342 ; 372. He made his Don Juan appear to be an atheist, 375, 376 ; but perhaps the poet did not believe in absolute atheism, 376.

AUTEUIL, Molière rented an apartment at, 437. Interview between Chapelle and Molière at Auteuil, 437-440. Anecdote about Molière and his friends drowning themselves at Auteuil, 550, 551.

AUTHORITY, Compulsory obedience to, hampered the early French comic writers, 37, 38.

AUTHORS' bench on the stage, 245.

AUTHORS of plays, how they were paid, 233-235.

AUTHORS read their plays to the troop, 236.

AUTHORS' shares, 235.

AUTOGRAPH receipts by Molière, 105, 106 ; 117.

Avare (L'), comedy by Molière, 450-460. Wrong dates given to the first appearance of the play, 451. At first a failure on the stage, later very popular, 278, 282 ; 451.

Printed by T. and A. CONSTABLE, Printers to His Majesty
at the Edinburgh University Press

Printed in Great Britain by
Amazon.co.uk, Ltd.,
Marston Gate.